The Global Emerging Market

D0084183

Despite the growing importance of the global emerging market (GEM) for the world's business, economies, and politics, it has received a relatively scant amount of academic attention in business and economics courses. This textbook is the first to focus on the GEM and its strategic and economic characteristics.

The Global Emerging Market: Strategic Management and Economics describes the fundamental economic base and trends of the global marketplace (GMP) as well as business and management development for the conditions of emerging-market countries (EMCs). Focusing on the formation of a strategic mindset and the decision-making process, it explains how to analyze the basic economic factors and the global order, especially in times of crisis. This text also explains how to classify countries related to this new market of tremendous opportunities. Furthermore, the book includes recommendations on how to develop entry and exit strategies for the GEM, work in it, and create efficient management systems.

Features include:

- Extensive tables, charts, and graphs illustrating the strategic considerations of the GMP and the GEM
- End-of-chapter study questions
- Practical examples based on the author's involvement in the development of the GEM, from both sides of the international transactions

This academic book is the ideal guide for current business leaders and students on how to make strategic, symmetric, and asymmetric time-sensitive decisions related to the GEM.

Dr Vladimir Kvint is Professor of Management Systems at LaSalle University (PA), Chair of the Department of Financial Strategy of the Moscow State University's Moscow School of Economics, and member of the Bretton Woods Committee. He also has extensive experience working in the US, Europe, and EMCs, as an executive and advisor for businesses and government leaders.

The Global Emerging Market

Strategic Management and Economics

Vladimir Kvint

to the Connelly Library of the La Salle University,
Prof. V. Kvint

Routledge
Taylor & Francis Group

NEW YORK AND LONDON

2023 may 1.

First published 2009
by Routledge
270 Madison Ave, New York, NY 10016

Simultaneously published in the UK
by Routledge
2 Park Square, Milton Park, Abingdon, Oxon OX14 4RN

Routledge is an imprint of the Taylor & Francis Group, an informa business

© 2009 Taylor & Francis

Typeset in Garamond by
RefineCatch Limited, Bungay, Suffolk
Printed and bound in the United States of America on acid-free paper by
Edwards Brothers, Inc.

Library of Congress Cataloging in Publication Data
Kvint, V. L. (Vladimir L'vovich)
The global emerging market : strategic management and economics / Vladimir Kvint.
p. cm.
Includes bibliographical references and index.
1. Developing countries–Economic policy.   2. Developing countries–Foreign
economic relations.   3. International business enterprises–Developing countries.
4. Globalization–Economic aspects.   5. Strategic planning.   I. Title.
HC59.7.K885 2009
382–dc22
2008032797

ISBN10: 0–415–98839–X (hbk)
ISBN10: 0–415–98840–3 (pbk)
ISBN10: 0–203–88291–1 (ebk)

ISBN13: 978–0–415–98839–1 (hbk)
ISBN13: 978–0–415–98840–7 (pbk)
ISBN13: 978–0–203–88291–7 (ebk)

To my friends . . .

Remembering, not withstanding, that the true worth of a man is to be measured by the objects he pursues.[1]

(Marcus Aurelius Antoninus Augustus,
Stoic philosopher and Roman Emperor, 121–180)

Brief Contents

Extended Table of Contents   ix
List of Illustrations   xiv
About the Author   xx
Acknowledgments   xxii
Keynote Definitions   xxv
List of Abbreviations   xxvii
Introduction: A Path to Strategy   xxix

1   A Strategic Evaluation of the Global Marketplace   1

2   The Global Emerging Market   75

3   Ten Modern Global Political, Economic, and Technological Trends   111

4   Strategic Country Classification of the Global Marketplace   160

5   The Emerging Global Business Order   211

6   Global Economic Strategy   258

7   Strategic Management Systems   311

8   Investment Strategy for the Global Emerging Market   346

Notes   412
Bibliography for Reading on Strategy and Economics of the Global Emerging Market   440
Specialized Periodicals on the Global Emerging Market and Business Strategy   443
Index   445

Extended Table of Contents

Lists of Illustrations   xiv
About the Author   xx
Acknowledgments   xxii
Keynote Definitions   xxv
List of Abbreviations   xxvii
Introduction: A Path to Strategy   xxix

1   **A Strategic Evaluation of the Global Marketplace**   1

Keynote Definition 1
Genesis of the Global Marketplace 1
The World Economy and the Global Marketplace 5
   Defining the Global Marketplace 6
   Economic Integration in the Global Marketplace 8
Strategic Evaluation of the World Economy and the Global Marketplace 10
   Strategic Evaluations of the Basic Economic Factors of the World Economy 18
Study Questions 73

2   **The Global Emerging Market**   75

Keynote Definitions 75
Preconditions for the Birth of the Global Emerging Market 76
   Historical Precedents of the Creation of Emerging Economies 76
   Economic and Philosophical Inevitability of the Failure of Dictatorships and
      Command Economies 76
   The Global Emerging Market 78
Major Characteristics of an Emerging-market Country 82
Classification of Emerging-market Countries 84
The Genesis of the Global Emerging Market 88
   Growing Input of the Global Emerging Market in the World Economy 88
   The Business Perspective 89
   Emerging-market Countries' Regional Integration into the Global Marketplace 93
The Current Role of the Global Emerging Market in the World 100
   Technological Achievements in the Global Emerging Market 104
National Agendas and Benefits to Society of Emerging-market Countries 104
   Role of the Middle Class in Economic Maturation of Emerging-market Countries 108

The Future of the Global Emerging Market in the Global Marketplace 109
Study Questions 110

3   **Ten Modern Global Political, Economic, and Technological Trends**   111

Globalization and Democratization as Objective Trends 111
System of the Ten Global Trends 113
The Roots of the Global Trend of Political Disintegration 114
Regionalization as a Global Trend 118
The Trend of Regional Economic Integration 121
The Trend of Privatization 124
   Mass Privatization 127
   Cash Privatization 127
   The Role of Initial Public Offerings in Privatization 130
The Trend of Internationalization 131
   Strategic Reasons to Do Business Internationally 131
   Deficit of Investment as a Consequence of Internationalization 139
The Economic Impact of the Global Trend of Terrorism and Extremism 139
   The Roots of Terrorism and Extremism 139
   Defining Terrorism 142
   Responses to Terrorism and Extremism 143
   The Impact of Terrorism on the Global Marketplace 144
   Terrorism and the Global Emerging Market 148
Technological Trends 149
Study Questions 157

4   **Strategic Country Classification of the Global Marketplace**   160

The Strategic Necessity for Country Classification Systems 160
The Flawed Country Classifictions of Major Multilateral Institutions 161
   The World Bank Group Approach 162
   The International Monetary Fund Approach 165
   The World Trade Organization Approach 171
   The United Nations Approach 171
   Observations of Multilateral Institutions' Country Classification Systems 175
   Alternatives to the Classifications Systems of Multilateral Institutions 175
The Strategic Approach to Country Classification 177
   Indexation of Countries by Industrial Structure 178
   Indexation of National Economies' Technological Maturity 183
   Evaluation of National Environmental Protection 184
   A Synthesized Rating of National Technological, Economic, and Social Advancement 185
The Strategic Comprehensive Country Classification System 188
   Observations of the Superpower Category 193
   Observations of the Technologically Advanced Economies Category 194
   Observations of the Wealthy Nations Category 195
   Observations of the Emerging-market Countries Category 196
      Observations of the Economies in Bloom Category 196

Observations of the Emerging-market Democracies Category 197
Observations of the Oligarchic Emerging Markets Category 198
Observations of the Emerging-market Dictatorships Category 200
Observations of the Pre-emerging Markets Category 201
Observations of the Developing Countries Category 202
Observations of the Underdeveloped Countries Category 203
Evaluation of International Business Infrastructure 205
Classification Glossary 209
Study Questions 209

5   **The Emerging Global Business Order**   211

Keynote Definitions 211
Genesis of the Global Order 211
Bretton Woods Institutions of the Global Order 215
Dynamics of the Global Order 218
The Global Business Order in the Dynamics of the Global Order 219
The Evolution of the Global Order 224
The Revolution of the Global Order 225
Objective and Subjective Factors Influencing the Global Business Order 229
The Factor of Global Trends 230
The Global Optimum 231
Triggering Events of the Formation of the Emerging Global Business Order 235
The Changing Roles of Multilateral Institutions in the Global Marketplace 239
New Authorities of the Global Business Order 244
G8 and its Likely Enlargement 245
The Bretton Woods Committee 246
World Economic Forum 247
The Council on Foreign Relations 249
The Trilateral Commission 250
The Institutionalization of the Global Business Order 251
Major Characteristics of the Emerging Global Business Order 252
Study Questions 256

6   **Global Economic Strategy**   258

Keynote Definitions 258
The Strategic Mindset 258
Two Approaches of Strategic Thinking 260
Stages of the Strategic Thought Process 262
Characteristics of the Strategic Mindset 262
The Three Axes of Strategic Thought 264
The Professional Strategist 265
The Strategist's 15 Rules 266
Rule 1: Strategists Can Never Rely on Common Sense Alone 267
Rule 2: The Majority is Very Often Strategically Wrong 267
Rule 3: Strategically, the Present is Already the Past 268

Rule 4: The Strategist Must Learn from History 269

Rule 5: Nothing Lasts Forever 270

Rule 6: Inertia is the Strategist's Greatest Adversary 271

Rule 7: Strategists Should Not Fall into Predictable Patterns 272

Rule 8: A Successful Strategy Cannot be Dishonest 272

Rule 9: Strategists Must Make Systems Out of Chaos 273

Rule 10: An Asymmetric Strategic Response Is More Efficient than a Symmetric One 274

Rule 11: The Strategist Must Always be an Optimist 275

Rule 12: Always Overestimate the Competitor 276

Rule 13: Innovation Can Provide Huge Strategic Advantages 276

Rule 14: The Strategist Should Optimize Limited Resources, Using Time as the Determining Factor 277

Rule 15: Strategists Must Figure Out What their Clients Need, not What their Clients Want 277

System of Strategy 279

Hierarchy of Strategy 279

Correlation between Strategy, Tactic, and Policy 279

Development of Strategy 280

Stages of Strategy Development 280

Selection of Strategic Scenario, Tactic, and Policy 290

Strategic Factors and Limitations for Businesses Entering Emerging Markets 290

Strategy of Subordinate Units 295

Strategy Implementation 296

Time-sensitive Resource Analysis 296

Corporate Entry Strategy 301

Tactic 303

Cultural and Religious Environment of Strategy Development and Implementation 304

Culture as a Strategic Risk Factor 306

Exit Strategy 307

Study Questions 309

7   **Strategic Management Systems**   311

Concept of a Strategic Management System 311

Major Elements of a Strategic Management System 312

Strategic Leadership 312

Organizational Structure 316

Executives, Managers, and Staff 318

Strategic Decision-making Process 321

Managerial Tools, Aids, and Strategic Information Technology 325

Functions of Strategic Management Systems 327

Strategic Planning and the Strategic Plan 327

Strategic Motivation 328

Strategic Monitoring and Control: Evaluating Strategy and Strategists 330

International Joint Ventures as a Strategic Organizational Vehicle of
Globalization 332
Economic Genesis of the International Joint Venture 333
*The Letter of Intent or Memorandum of Understanding for International Joint Venture
Establishment 336*
International Joint Ventures' Market-entry Strategy 338
Key Factors to Consider When Making an International Joint Venture 338
Management Systems of International Joint Ventures 340
Study Questions 344

8   **Investment Strategy for the Global Emerging Market**   346

Keynote Definitions 346
Reasons for Cross-Border Investment 346
Economic Nature of Foreign Direct Investment 346
Rationale of Investment in the Global Emerging Market 349
Gauging Foreign Investment Risk in Emerging Markets 354
Systematic Risk in the Global Emerging Market 355
Unsystematic Risk of Investment 380
International Business Infrastructure in Emerging-market Countries 383
Technological Risk of Foreign Direct Investment 398
Foreign Direct Investment from the Global Emerging Market to Developed
Countries 404
Study Questions 410

Notes   412
Bibliography for Reading on Strategy and Economics of the Global Emerging Market   440
Specialized Periodicals on the Global Emerging Market and Business Strategy   443
Index   445

Illustrations

Maps

1.1 Energy Production in the GMP, 2005   28

Figures

1.1   GWP (Billions of 1990 International $), 1500–1950   2
1.2   Trade as a Percentage of GWP, 1960–2004   3
1.3   GWP (Millions of $), 1960–2006   3
1.4   Dynamics of GWP during its Internationalization   4
1.5   Development of GWP during the Formation of the GMP
      (Trillions of $)   10
1.6   GWP PPP during the Period of the Formation of the GEM
      (Trillions of Current $)   13
1.7   GWP per Capita (Current $)   13
1.8   Revised GWP Growth by New PPP Methodology   15
1.9   Industrial Structure of GWP   16
1.10 System of Basic Economic Factors   18
1.11 Oil Consumption per Unit of Output (Kilograms per Unit of
      Real GDP PPP), 1974–2004   25
1.12 Estimates of Proven Oil Reserves by World Region as a
      Percentage of World Total, 2008   26
1.13 Estimated Proven Reserves of Natural Gas by World Region as a
      Percentage of World Total, 2008   27
1.14 Estimated Recoverable Coal Reserves by World Region as a
      Percentage of World Total, 2008   27
1.15 Changes in Fuel Shares of Total Primary Energy Supply (TPES),
      1973–2005   29
1.16 Sources of World Electricity Generation, 2005   30
1.17 Changes in Regional Shares of Nuclear Production, 1973–2005   31
1.18 Changes in Regional Shares of Total Final Energy Consumption,
      1973–2005   33
1.19 Change in World Energy-related Carbon Dioxide Emissions by
      World Region and Country, 1973–2005   40
1.20 World, GEM, United States, and EU Unemployment Rates   55
1.21 Foreign Currency Reserves in Convertible Currencies (Millions
      of $), January 2008   60
1.22 Foreign Currency Reserves as a Share of Global Total, 2007   60

1.23	Bank Assets as a Share of the Global Total, 2006	62
1.24	Stock Market Capitalization of the GMP, 2006	63
1.25	Capitalization Growth Rates of Major Economies, 2007	63
1.26	Total Capital Inflows to Emerging and Developed Countries (Billions of $), 1994–2006	66
1.27	Disparities in Use of Patents and Various Technologies, 2004	73
2.1	EMC Classification by Socioeconomic Maturity	85
2.2	Unemployment in the US, EU, GEM, and the GMP	97
2.3	Size of Diaspora as a Percentage of Origin Country Population	98
2.4	Top EMC Recipients of Remittances (Millions of $), 2006	99
2.5	Top EMC Recipients of Remittances (Percentage of GDP), 2006	99
2.6	Input of GEM in Global GDP (Exchange Rate, Trillions of $)	103
2.7	Comparison of the Rate of Growth of the World Economy with the Dynamics of Economic Development of the GEM, US, and Russia	103
3.1	Number of New International Firms in the GMP, 1989–2000	135
3.2	Market Capitalization of International Firms as a Percentage of Total Market Capitalization, 1989–2000	136
3.3	Number of Multinational Corporations from EMCs, Developed, and Developing Countries (Thousands), 1992–2006	138
3.4	Transnationality Index for Host Economies, 2004	141
3.5	Non-resident Patent Filings as a Percentage of Total Filings by Office	142
3.6	Asset Forfeiture by US Government Agencies ($), 2002–2005	144
3.7	Mobile Phone Penetration by Country Categorization, 2002–2006	150
3.8	Mobile Subscribers by Country Categorization, 2002–2006	153
3.9	Internet Penetration by Country Categorization, 2002–2006	154
3.10	Resident Patent Filings per $1 Billion of GDP (PPP)	156
5.1	The Global Optimum in the Global Business Order	232
6.1	Stages of the Strategic Thought Process	262
6.2	The Strategic Position between the Past and the Future	269
6.3	System of Strategy	280
6.4	Stages of Development of Business Strategy: Scanning and Forecasting External and Internal Environments	283
6.5	Strategy Formation	289
6.6	Selection of Strategic Scenario, Tactic, and Policy	290
6.7	Strategy Implementation	297
6.8	Schedule of Strategy Development, Implementation, and Strategic Investment Recovery	299
6.9	Schedule of Intensification of Strategic Investment with Accelerated Period of Strategy Implementation by 0.6 Years	300
7.1	Concept of a Strategic Management System	312
7.2	Growth Rate of FDI, GWP, and Foreign Trade	332
7.3	Reasons for Failure of IJVs, 1988–1992	334
7.4	Reasons for Failure of IJVs, 1993	336
7.5	Reasons for Failure of IJVs, 1998	337
8.1	Top EMC Recipients of FDI (Millions of $), 2006	352
8.2	FDI Inflows by Category of Country (Millions of $), 2006	354
8.3	Emerging-market Risk System	360
8.4	EMC Systematic Risk Evaluation	360
8.5	Greenfield FDI Projects by EMC Recipients, 2006	362

8.6	Greenfield FDI Projects by EMC Investors, 2006	363
8.7	Changing Dynamics of the Kuznets Curve Under the Influence of Corruption in the GEM	375
8.8	Percentage of Respondents Who Have Paid a Bribe to the Police, 2006	376
8.9	Estimated US Trade Loss Due to Copyright Piracy (Millions of $), 2006	378
8.10	M2 Growth Rate in BRIC, 2001–2007	384
8.11	CPI in Russia, the US, EU, and the World, Percentage Increase from 2000–2006	386
8.12	Internet Users in the GEM, Total and Penetration (Ordered by Total), 2007	403
8.13	Acquisitions of US Targets by Emerging-market Investors (Country Percentage Share), 2006	407
8.14	Acquisitions of US Targets by Emerging-market Investors (Country Percentage Share), 2007	407
8.15	Acquisitions of US Targets by Emerging-market Investors (Country Percentage Share), 2008	408
8.16	FDI Outflow by Category of Country (Millions of $), 1991–2006	409

Tables

1.1	GDP (Exchange Rate) of the Ten Largest Economies ($), 2006	11
1.2	GDP per Capita (International $), 2006	11
1.3	The Role of the GEM and Developed Countries in the GMP	11
1.4	GDP PPP (Billions of $), 2006	12
1.5	Largest National Territories	19
1.6	Countries with Largest Total Renewable Water Resources (10^9 m^3/yr), 2007	21
1.7	Countries with the Largest Total Renewable Water Resources per capita, 2007 (m^3/inhab/yr)	22
1.8	Countries with the Lowest Total Renewable Water Resources per Capita, 2007 (m^3/inhab/yr)	23
1.9	Countries with the Highest Total Renewable Water Dependency Ratio, 2007	24
1.10	Countries with a Total Renewable Water Dependency Ratio of Less than 1 Percent, 2007	25
1.11	Energy Reserves by Region as a Percentage of World Total, 2008	26
1.12	Production of Hydro Electricity, as a Percentage of World Total, 2005	30
1.13	Production of Electricity from Nuclear Energy, 2007	32
1.14	Thirty Countries with the Lowest National Energy Intensity (Use of Energy per One Unit of GDP), 2005	34
1.15	Thirty Countries with the Highest National Energy Intensity (Use of Energy per One Unit of GDP), 2005	35
1.16	Energy Intensity (Use of Energy per One Unit of GDP) of Major Economies of the GMP, 2005	36
1.17	Energy Intensity (Use of Energy per One Unit of GDP) by Region (BTU per 2,000 $), 2005	36

1.18   Thirty Countries with the Lowest Energy Consumption per
        Capita, 2005   37
1.19   Thirty Countries with the Highest Energy Consumption per
        Capita, 2005   38
1.20   Energy Consumption per Capita (Millions of BTU) by Region,
        1990–2005   38
1.21   World Aluminum Production (Thousands of Metric Tons),
        2006   41
1.22   World Copper Mine Production and Reserves (Ordered by
        Production) (Thousands of Metric Tons), 2006   41
1.23   World Nickel Mine Production and Reserves (Ordered by
        Production) (Metric Tons), 2006   42
1.24   World Cobalt Production and Reserves (Ordered by Production)
        (Metric Tons), 2006   43
1.25   World Platinum-group Metals Production and Reserves
        (Ordered by Reserves) (Kilograms)   44
1.26   World Gold Production and Reserves (Metric Tons), 2006   45
1.27   Top 25 Countries in Terms of Forest Area (Square Kilometers)   47
1.28   Paper and Paperboard Production (Tons), 2006   48
1.29   Ten Largest Countries in Terms of Population, 2007   49
1.30   Fastest-growing National Populations, 2006   49
1.31   Most Rapidly Declining National Populations, 2006   50
1.32   Countries with Largest Percentage of National Population Age
        65 and Above, 2006   51
1.33   Countries with Largest Percentage of National Population Age
        15 and Below, 2006   51
1.34   Countries with the Lowest Life Expectancies, 2007   52
1.35   Countries with the Highest Literacy Rates, 2006   53
1.36   Countries with the Lowest Literacy Rates, 2006   53
1.37   Countries with Highest Level of Educational Attainment
        (Ordered by Graduates as a Percentage of Population), 2005   53
1.38   Countries with the Most Unequal Distribution of Wealth—
        Gini Index, 2007   54
1.39   Countries with the Most Equitable Distribution of Wealth—
        Gini Index, 2007   55
1.40   Working Hours by Country (Average Annual Hours Worked per
        Employee), 1995 and 2006   56
1.41   HDI Ranking, 2006   57
1.42   Global Gold Reserves Special Drawing Right   60
1.43   Major Net Exporters and Importers of Capital (Percentage of
        World Totals), 2006   64
1.44   US and GEM Capital Inflows (Billions of $), 1996–2006   65
1.45   North American Light Vehicle Production, December 2007   67
1.46   Western European Passenger-car Assembly, December 2007 (Estimated)   67
1.47   Central and Eastern Europe plus Kazakhstan, Russia, and
        Turkey Passenger-car Assembly, December 2007   68
1.48   The Knowledge Economy Index, 2007   70
1.49   R&D Performed Abroad by Majority-owned Foreign Affiliates of
        US Multilateral Corporations (Millions of $)   72
2.1   EMC Classifications According to Professional Publications   86

2.2	Global and Central and Eastern Europe/CIS Growth Outlook, 2005–2008	88
2.3	EMCs by GDP in PPP (Billions of $), 2006	90
2.4	EMCs by Size of Territory	94
2.5	Largest Countries in terms of GDP PPP (Billions of $), 2006	101
2.6	EMCs by Population, 2007	105
2.7	FDI Inflows to EMCs, 2006	106
3.1	Mass Privatization Programs in Central and Eastern Europe and the CIS	128
3.2	The Role of BRIC IPOs in the GMP	130
3.3	GEM Multinational Corporations from the List of the World's Top 100 Non-financial Multinational Corporations Ranked by Foreign Assets (Millions of $), 2005	137
3.4	GEM Multinational Corporations from the List of the Top 50 Multinational Financial Corporations Ranked by the Geographical Spread Index, 2005	138
3.5	Changes in Value of Exports in Selected OECD Countries	146
3.6	Changes in Value of Imports in Selected OECD Countries	147
3.7	Trends in Mobile Phone Penetration by World Region and Country Categorization, 2002–2006	151
3.8	Trends in Internet Penetration by Region and Country Categorization, 2002–2006	152
4.1	Dynamics of WBG GNI per Capita Brackets ($)	163
4.2	Sample of Fluctuating Classification of the WBG	164
4.3	Classification by World Economic Outlook Groups and their Shares in Aggregate GDP, Exports Goods and Services, and Population (Percentage of Total for Group or World), 2006	167
4.4	Subgroups of the IMF Classification "Advanced Economies"	168
4.5	Other EMCs and Developing Countries by Region, Net External Position, and HIPCs, according to the IMF's 2007 World Economic Outlook	169
4.6	Services Value Added as a Percentage of GDP, 2005	179
4.7	Percentage Share of Modern-tech Sectors in Total Manufacturing Value Added, 2005	182
4.8	Integrated Indicators and their Weights	185
4.9	Synthesized Country Rating of Technological, Economic, and Social Advancement (Kvint's Country Rating)	187
4.10	Kvint's Integrated Country Ratings, 2008	189
4.11	World Bank's List of the 10 Wealthiest Countries, 2000	195
4.12	World Bank's List of the 10 Poorest Countries in the World	204
4.13	Index of International Business Infrastructure	206
5.1	Top Ten Multinational Corporations Ranked by the Number of Host Countries and the Geographical Spread Index, 2005	236
5.2	Top Multinational Corporations from EMCs from the List of the Top 100 Multinational Corporations Ranked by the Number of Host Countries and the Geographical Spread Index, 2005	237
5.3	World Bank Lending (Comparison of China to Selected Underdeveloped and Developing Countries) ($), 2007	243
8.1	Employment in US Foreign Affiliates and US Outward FDI Stock, by Sector, 2003	348

8.2   Employment Related to Inward FDI, Most Recent Year
       (Thousands of Employees)   350
8.3   FDI Inflows as a Percentage of GDP, 2006   353
8.4   The World Bank "Ease of Doing Business Rank," 2008   358
8.5   Number of Greenfield FDI Projects by Sector/Industry, 2002–2006   361

Plates

Colour plates are located between pages 24–25

1.1   Global Distribution of Freshwater Resources
2.1   Worldwide Distribution of Remittances, Continents, Regions,
       and Country ($), 2006

About the Author

Vladimir Kvint (photo by V. Ivanov)

Economist and strategist Dr Vladimir Kvint was the first professor in Europe and the United States to teach a course on the global emerging market. He is currently the president of the International Academy of Emerging Markets (New York), a professor of management systems at LaSalle University's School of Business (Pennsylvania), and the chair of the Department of Financial Strategy of the Moscow State University's Moscow School of Economics. Dr Kvint is a US Fulbright Scholar, a member of the Bretton Woods Committee (Washington, DC), the Business Council for International Understanding (BCIU) (New York), and a lifetime foreign member of the Russian Academy of Sciences.

Prior to this activity he was a professor at American University's Kogod School of Business, Fordham University's Graduate School of Business (for 14 years), New York University's Stern School of Business, Babson College (Massachusetts), and Vienna Economic University (Austria). Dr Kvint is an honorary doctor and honorary professor of several universities.

In addition to his academic experience, Dr Kvint has worked as an executive and advisor for businesses and governmental leaders in Albania, Austria, Brazil, Bulgaria, China, Kazakhstan, Russia, Switzerland, Taiwan, Ukraine, the United States, and Uruguay as well as for the UN. He served as the director of emerging markets at Arthur Andersen (New York) until 1998; at the time, Arthur Andersen was the largest professional auditing and consulting firm in the world. Dr Kvint has received national and academic awards from several countries.

He has published many books and articles on economics, strategy, management, and the political economy of emerging markets. He has been a contributor to CNN, *Forbes*, the *Harvard Business Review*, Bloomberg, and the *New York Times*. In 2004, Fordham University Press published the second extended edition of a compendium of his works, *The Global Emerging Market in Transition: Articles, Forecasts and Studies 1973–2003*. Currently, he is an advisor to the governments of several EMCs. For more information on Dr Kvint please see www.vkvint.com.

Acknowledgments

This book is a culmination of 45 years of my professional life, from above the Arctic Circle in Siberia to lecture halls and executive offices in New York. Experience in business combined with my academic endeavors has given me a few ideas about that part of the world that I called the global emerging market (GEM). The goal of this monograph is to share my experience and ideas with readers.

I was indeed born and raised in Siberia, though it would be an exaggeration to say that I was born in a bear's den. It would also be hyperbole to claim that in Norilsk, where my business career began, there are 365 days without sunlight. In fact, the 24-hour polar night lasts only about two months. Nevertheless, I still meet some people who think that bears roam the streets of Siberian cities. The story of my life is an illustration of the many misconceptions that people from different parts of the world have about each other and how, with an open mind, these cultural misconceptions can turn into great friendships. For me, it is possible to see emerging-market countries (EMCs) and developed countries as one and the same in that both are the land of my friends, without whom I would have neither my optimism nor achievements, and nor would I be the person I am today.

No matter where life has taken me, my friends have always remained. When I went from the industrial heart of Siberia, the city of Krasnoyarsk, to the Siberian think-tank community Akademgorodok, I met wonderful friends, Alexander Granberg and Veleriy Makarov, two great economists with whom I later had the honor of working in Moscow. When I left Siberia for Moscow, I did not lose my childhood friend Vladimir Voschinin. And many years later, when I escaped the Soviet Union, a country that no longer exists, I never lost my friends there. I felt their support in my new life in Austria, and later in the US. Even during the several years when I did not travel back to my motherland, I maintained my friendships there. Not many people can say that decades after their first job, they are still friends with their first boss, but I have been lucky enough to maintain my friendship with Boris Kazakov, the chief economist of the Norilsk Mining Metallurgical Concern, with whom I speak almost every day. I also benefit from friendships with my current colleagues, such as Alexander Nekipelov, Sergey Shakin, and Murad Alimuradov from the Moscow School of Economics; Joseph Ugras and Praf Joklekar from La Salle University; and James Orr from the Bretton Woods Committee. I have to mention a new colleague of mine, whom I also consider a friend, my editor from Routledge, Nancy Hale. Without her enthusiasm, I would not have radically changed my schedule and dedicated an entire year to writing.

This book would not have been completed on time, in its present form, without the assistance of a young and talented individual, Thomas Kaufman. His intellect made him someone whose company I enjoyed throughout the process.

To write any book, but especially one as long as this one, requires the ability to work long hours and maintain focus. I would certainly not have been able to do so without the atmosphere created by my loving wife Dina, who was nearby, supportive, and caring. It is very special to have a wife who is a true friend.

The advice of my friends has always been important for me. My friends Ken Deghetto, Praf Joklekar, Art Rosenbloom, and Sir Fraser Morrison all took time out of their busy schedules to offer me feedback that substantially improved the early drafts of the manuscript. I am most grateful to my beloved daughter Liza, who, like all children, is often too busy when it comes to her parents, but was still willing to provide me with her insightful advice. Some of my friends started out as my students. Among them are Nikolas Kralev of the US and Bulgaria, Magomed Gamzatov and his family, as well as Zeydulah and Misha Uzbekov of Daghestan, and Jacqueline Gallus of the US, who was one of the first to review drafts of the manuscript. I also very much appreciate the input of Kate Crane, who was one of the final readers of the text.

For me, the United States is not only a country of freedom and the American dream, which I have enjoyed, but also one of new friends. I came to this country with two children. I barely spoke English, and had practically no money or connections. In America I met wonderful people—Ron and Vicki Weiner, Ann and Ken Bialkin, Arthur Rosenbloom and Evelyn Kenvin, David duPonte, Arthur and Kathryn Taylor, and Norman Resnicow—all of whom were my guides and supporters from the very beginning. But the first person who met me at JFK airport was Peter Tichansky, who is still a good friend of mine. One day in 1992, I got a call from a great economist, Charlie Cicchetti from Los Angeles, who would give me the pleasure of working under his leadership at Arthur Andersen Economic Consulting, where I gained a wealth of knowledge and experience. At Andersen Worldwide, I met a wonderful mentor and friend, J. Donald Hanson, from London. Ten years ago I left Arthur Andersen, but these friends are still with me.

During my life in New York, I did not spend time just with Americans. I was lucky enough to enjoy the company of my Russian friends who worked for some time in the US. It is always special when I have the opportunity to spend time with Slava Fetisov—hockey superstar, three-time Stanley Cup winner, and Olympian—who is not only an incredible athlete but also a great individual who played an important role in the destruction of the Iron Curtain. Although my dear friend, the great Russian advocate Gasan Mirzoev, no longer lives in New York, we have not grown any further apart. During my time as a consultant for the United Nations (UN), it was always a pleasure to meet with the Moldavian ambassador Ion Botnaru and economist Alexei Tikhomirov.

Throughout my life, I have benefited from great friends like these, people who offered me their support and counsel. I will always be grateful for the hospitality and friendship I enjoyed in Vienna, Austria, from Karl Schwarzenberg, Elisabeth Thausing, and Ernie Laudon. Having friends throughout the world has been wonderful, but staying in contact with everyone can be a challenge. However, despite less than constant contact, I have remained extremely close to Hazel Rose from London, whose care and warmth rival even that of my mother, Lydia, and my brother, Pavel, who were the best friends I have ever had. Some friends are my former or current clients, such as the very talented entrepreneur Alex Shnaider of Canada, Andrey Igoshin of Russia, and Shugeri Miraki of Japan.

My years at Fordham University gave me great experience as a professor as well as wonderful friends: Sharon Smith, Bob Wharton, and Joyce Orsini. When I worked at American University in Washington, DC, I was very lucky to have the opportunity to discuss global issues with a good friend of mine, Yuri Ushakov, at that time the Russian ambassador to the United States.

Finally, I have to mention several other good friends, whom I value as individuals of high quality. Working in EMCs, I became friends with Georgi Tasev in Bulgaria; Nicolas Barleta in Panama; Arben Malaj, Dritan Chilaj, and Ludmila Shkurti in Albania; and Elena and

Igor Podolev in Ukraine. I must also mention economists Valeriy Chichkanov, Sergey Kovalev, Vladimir Okrepilov, Yevgeny Ardemasov, as well as Yevgeny Velikhov, an outstanding physicist and person who destroyed many artificial barriers between Russia and the US. His input in people's diplomacy is invaluable. I cannot forget Vladimir Shamakhov, the great journalist Viktor Loshak, and Prince Nikita Lobanov, a great art aficionado from the UK and Russia.

The problem with acknowledgments is that there are so many friends who deserve to be thanked. However, I have to admit that there is no such thing as too many friends. The bigger problem is when someone does not have enough. This is why I consider myself lucky, and if I have any success, I have to share all of it with my friends, old and young, those with whom I have maintained a relationship for many years, and those whom I have not yet met.

If anyone continues to read this book, at least until the introduction, they will find that the first magazine in the US to publish my thoughts was *Forbes*. Almost 20 years later, I still write for this magazine and had the pleasure and honor to share thoughts and travel with the editor in chief, Steve Forbes, in several EMCs such as Romania, Ukraine, Bulgaria, Albania, and the Slovak Republic. Seeing his take on emerging markets was important for me in order to understand the Western point of view on the part of the world where I come from.

When I began this book, Thomas and I organized years of my research, notes, and reading materials into several filing cabinets. The book is finished, but a dozen or so of these filing cabinets remain untouched. I anticipate that these will be the basis for at least a couple of continuations of this book, with more of a practical focus on regional and industrial issues of the GEM. Exactly what unfolds will depend on the feedback from this book's readers.

Great friends, like a great strategy, always have minor problems; nevertheless, we accept them because of their virtues. This is not my first book, but it is the first one that I dedicate solely to my friends, even those who are not mentioned here.

Vladimir Kvint
July 15, 2008
New York City

Keynote Definitions

The global order   The global order is a political and economic system of cooperation that emerges organically or as a result of the influence of multilateral institutions, superpowers, and other nations, though not necessarily by cooperative means. The global order provides customary procedures, allowing the avoidance of conflict while promoting stability and sustainable development by offering countries, regional blocs, and corporations a means to negotiate disputes amongst themselves and to develop mutually beneficial solutions to global challenges.

The global business order   The global business order is a subsystem of the global order that provides a relatively stable framework for cooperation between businesses with global, regional, and national institutions, allowing the evolutionary development of the GMP. It is a set of customs by which corporations compete and cooperate with other businesses in the GMP, exploiting opportunities offered by it without violating human rights, national interests, or regional and global standards.

The global marketplace   The global marketplace (GMP) is a system of economic relationships between consumers, companies, governments, and multilateral institutions from around the world that allows real-time cooperation and competition regardless of location.

Emerging-market country   An emerging-market country (EMC) is a society transitioning from a dictatorship to a free-market-oriented economy, with increasing economic freedom, gradual integration within the GMP and with other members of the GEM, an expanding middle class, improving standards of living, social stability and tolerance, as well as an increase in cooperation with multilateral institutions.

Global emerging market   The global emerging market (GEM) is a new economic and political phenomenon of the GMP, encompassing EMCs and their regional blocs, which, despite varying geopolitical characteristics, are united by comparable levels of risk and developing free-market infrastructure. These factors of the GEM unify vectors of development of EMCs toward economic freedom and global integration, attracting international economic and business cooperation and competition.

Strategy   Strategy is a system of finding, formulating, and developing a doctrine that will ensure long-term success if followed faithfully. It is the result of a systematic analysis of the environment and existing forecasts for future circumstances based on a strategic mindset, deep knowledge, and intuition. The final product of the analysis will be a formal strategy that consists of a new *forecast*, *mission statement*, *vision*, and long-term *objectives and goals* with a particular scenario to be implemented via the *strategic plan* with a strategic system to monitor its implementation. Strategy is a guideline to selected objectives in the future through chaos and the unknown.

Strategist   The strategist is a disciplined and optimistic professional with a strategic mindset and a vision of the future, armed with a forecasting and strategic methodology to utilize deep knowledge of the entity, the economic environment, and a firm grasp of global trends, with the ability to set objectives and goals accordingly.

Economic nature of foreign direct investment   The roots of the economic nature of foreign direct investment (FDI) are in competitive opportunities abroad (which do not exist domestically), work power of the appropriate quality, capital availability, effective management systems and organizational forms, know-how and technology, all of which leads to a high level of return under a manageable level of risk according to comprehensive feasibility study and strategy.

Risk of FDI   Risk of FDI is an innate characteristic of cross-border business related to the threat of predictable or unpredictable negative changes of the external environment or of a company's internal resources, with manageable and unmanageable consequences leading to potential losses.

Abbreviations

AAI	Arthur Andersen International
ADIA	Abu Dhabi Investment Authority
ADR	American depository receipts
AIG	American International Group
APEC	Asia-Pacific Economic Cooperation
ASEAN	Association of Southeast Asian Nations
ATF	Bureau of Alcohol, Tobacco, Firearms and Explosives
BCIU	Business Council for International Understanding
BIS	Bank of International Settlements
BISIP	Bank of International Settlements Investment Pool
BOP	bottom of pyramid
BRIC	Brazil, Russia, India, and China
BTU	British Thermal Unit
CAFTA	Central American Free Trade Agreement
CARICOM	Caribbean Community
CBP	Customs and Border Protection Agency
CEO	chief executive officer
CIS	Commonwealth of Independent States
COMESA	Common Market for Eastern and Southern Africa
COO	chief operating officer
COSO	Committee of Sponsoring Organizations
CPI	consumer price index
C-TPAT	Customs-Trade Partnership against Terrorism
ECOWAS	Economic Community of West African States
EMC	emerging-market country
EMTA	Emerging Markets Traders Association
EU	European Union
FATF	Financial Action Task Force
FDI	foreign direct investment
G8	Group of Eight
GDP	gross domestic product
GDR	global depository receipts
GE	General Electric
GECF	Gas Exporting Countries Forum
GEM	global emerging market
GMP	global marketplace
GNI	gross national income
GNP	gross national product
GUAM	Georgia, Ukraine, Azerbaijan, and Moldova
GWP	gross world product

HDI	Human Development Index
HIPC	heavily indebted poor country
IAEA	International Atomic Energy Agency
IBRD	International Bank for Reconstruction and Development
ICC	International Chamber of Commerce
ICE	Immigration and Customs Enforcement Agency
IDA	International Development Association
IDR	international depository receipts
IFC	International Finance Corporation
IJV	international joint venture
IMD	International Institute for Management Development
IMF	International Monetary Fund
IPO	initial public offering
IRS	Internal Revenue Service
IT	information technology
LOI	letter of intent
MBA	masters in business administration
MIGA	Multilateral Investment Guarantee Agency
MSCI	Morgan Stanley Capital International
MU	memorandum of understanding
NAFTA	North American Free Trade Agreement
NASDAQ	National Association of Securities Dealers Automated Quotations
NATO	North Atlantic Treaty Organization
NGO	non-governmental organization
NYSE	New York Stock Exchange
OAA	Osaka Action Agenda
OECD	Organization for Economic Cooperation and Development
OPEC	Organization of the Petroleum Exporting Countries
OPIC	Overseas Private Investment Corporation
OTCBB	Over The Counter Bulletin Board
OTSW	opportunities, threats, strengths, and weaknesses
P-EMC	pre-emerging-market country
PERT	Program Evaluation and Review Technique
PPP	purchasing power parity
R&D	research and development
RBC	Royal Bank of Canada
S&P	Standard and Poor's
SAFTA	South Asia Free Trade Agreement
SAR	special administrative region
SDR	special drawing right
SPDC	Shell Petroleum Development Corp.
SWOT	strengths, weaknesses, opportunities, and threats
TCO	Tengizchevroil
TPES	Total Primary Energy Supply
UNCTAD	United Nations Conference on Trade and Development
UNIDO	United Nations Industrial Development Organization
USSS	United States Secret Service
USTR	Office of the United States Trade Representative
WBG	World Bank Group
WTO	World Trade Organization

Introduction: A Path to Strategy

Unlike the majority of books on strategy, this analytical monograph finds its roots in the permafrost above the Arctic Circle in Siberia, where I began my career in business. As a metal worker, underground mining electrician, and later a mining electrical engineer, my mind returned again and again to the same question: why do workers with radically different levels of productivity, integrity, and initiative receive the same remuneration? Later, when I became the deputy head of a large company, my superiors consistently discouraged me from creating substantial differences in remuneration for employees by distinguishing between those who worked hard and showed initiative, and those who simply counted down the minutes until day's end. My career began 20 years after Stalin's brutal dictatorship and 10 years after Nikita Khrushchev's "thaw," a period when Stalin's cult of personality had largely deteriorated and Soviet leaders were regularly visiting capitalist countries for the first time. One of the greatest benefits of this relatively less brutal period in Soviet history was the availability of several books on economics and management, translated from English, German, and Japanese: Dr Paul Samuelson's *Foundations of Economic Analysis*, Dr Jay Wright Forrester's *Industrial Dynamics*, and Dr John H. Hutchinson's *Management Strategy and Tactics*. These books, together with publications of a few Soviet economists such as Nobel laureates Wassily Leontief and Leonid Kantorovich, as well as Dr Leonid Abalkin and Dr Abel Aganbegyan, were the most important influences on my early academic career. My only other teacher was young economic-mathematician Anatoliy Alexeev, who built in my mind a mathematical bridge between economics and technology. Despite the Soviet Union's backward economic system, its economic research capabilities were quite strong. In fact, Russia produced three Nobel laureates in economics. With the aid of these books, the insight gained from the experience of my surrounding social and business life, and the preparation of my first PhD dissertation, I began to analyze the successes and failures of centralized economic systems. By the 1970s I identified what seemed to be the fundamental flaw of any dictatorship: oppressive systems inevitably produce goods of lower quality than those of free countries. The Soviet dictatorship had an established system of planning and (often savage) control but lacked a means of positive motivation—one of the most important functions of any management system. This caused the production of inferior goods, wide-scale environmental pollution, lower productivity, and the subsequent poverty found in all totalitarian regimes.

Shortly after reaching this conclusion, I was invited to work at the Russian Academy of Sciences, the premier Russian think-tank established by Peter the Great in the eighteenth century. For a number of reasons—chief among them, the secretive voting system used by its members—the Academy remained essentially the only free institution in the Soviet Union. At the Academy I began to calculate when—not if—the Soviet empire would disappear. Analyzing the trends of the unofficial—i.e. undoctored—economic statistics, collected primarily during economic expeditions, I tried to figure out how long the Soviet

Union could survive. This was impossible to do without analyzing the world economy and the international political environment. At the beginning of the 1980s, when Prime Minister Margaret Thatcher and President Ronald Reagan, two ardent anti-communist leaders, came to power, they increased pressure on the Soviet dictatorship, primarily by exponentially increasing military expenses. It was clear to me that the regime's centralized economy could no longer bear the military expenses needed to maintain the strategic balance with the Western world that was so important to Soviet leaders. In 1982 the future became clear to me. Chancellor Helmut Kohl had come to power with the goal of unifying Germany, and at the same time, Poland, the Soviet Union's biggest satellite, was beginning to experience intense tension from an internal democratic movement. I predicted that "by 1992, there will be no country called the Soviet Union," which was the exact phrase later published in my *New York Times* op-ed piece.[1] For roughly two years prior to the publication of this piece, I tried to publish an article with the following blunt title: "Russia Should Quit the Soviet Union." I sent a draft of the article to several publications; all of them either thought it was a joke or something for the distant future, or they could not even conceptualize the difference between the Soviet Union and Russia—terms generally used as synonyms in the West at that time. The publication of this article was further hindered by the fact that I was forbidden to travel outside the Soviet Union to the free capitalist world.

Eventually, with great difficulty, I was able to skirt this issue. In December 1988 I found myself in Vienna, thanks to great friends such as Karl zu Schwarzenberg, at that time president of the International Helsinki Federation for Human Rights. He and I discussed the history and future of our world. We both made a lot of predictions, but neither of us could have anticipated that he would one day become a citizen of the free, non-communist country of the Czech Republic—a state that did not yet exist—and eventually become a senator and minister of foreign affairs. For strategists it is often easier to predict the future of countries than of their own lives.

Later, during my first trip to the United States, in 1989, I met with three great visionaries and journalists, a pretty rare combination—Malcolm Forbes, editor in chief; Jim Michaels, editor; and Lawrence Minard, managing editor, all of *Forbes*. They understood my perspective, and on February 5, 1990, my article—and my title, "Russia Should Quit the Soviet Union"—appeared as a cover story in *Forbes*.[2] At that time it was called a "revolutionary proposal." When introducing new ideas, strategists are usually at odds with the current consensus; the overwhelming majority denounces them as wrong and unrealistic. When the new ideas do indeed become reality, it is natural for people to forget their initial skepticism. Strategists should anticipate selective memories of the majority.

When the Soviet Union did disappear, Jim Michaels wrote in the sideline of *Forbes*: "When few thought the Soviet empire could ever break up, Vladimir Kvint predicted and advocated the withdrawal of the Russian Republic from the USSR . . . Kvint's article in *Forbes* on events in the Soviet Union have been close to prophetic."

The above story is meant to illustrate two points: first, it is quite difficult for strategists to come to the right forecasts and prepare their strategic scenarios; second, strategists must be prepared to fight for and stick to their positions, even in the face of general opposition. Only time can prove if a strategy is correct. I made this conclusion after three decades of experience not only as a professor but also as an executive and advisor to companies and governments from two worlds: developed countries and emerging-market countries (EMCs). Once a strategy is proven correct, do not look for applause from people—look for new strategies. The right strategy can be based on great intuition, but it can never work without deep knowledge of the issues at hand.

The logic and the structure of this book unfolded based on my personal and professional experience in the development of the strategies for companies and several EMCs. It took

35 years of professional experience related to countries of new opportunities and 25 concurrent years of professorship on strategy and economics to produce this book. When I first began to teach these topics, the terms "emerging market" and "global emerging market" did not exist. By the end of the first decade of the twenty-first century, they have become phenomena of tremendous influence, attracting not only about 40 percent of global foreign direct investment (FDI), but also and most important, the interest of millions of young business leaders and entrepreneurs. This does not even include the billions of people inside EMCs looking for fruitful cooperation with the developed world to accelerate their path to prosperity.

The Gap in the Global Marketplace and the Need for this Book

The world economy of the twenty-first century is completely different from what it was 25 years before the dawn of the new millennium. While this is not surprising, the changes have been unprecedented in scope. In 1985 the international economy primarily comprised 23 developed countries. The remaining 141 developing and least developed nations barely participated in international business. Since that time, from these developing countries, 83 EMCs have appeared, all building market economies with high levels of economic freedom. Millions of business professionals from developed economies are drawn to work with and within this new land of opportunity. EMCs are found in North, Central, and South America, Pacific and Central Eurasia, the Indian subcontinent, Central, Eastern, and Southern Europe, and Northern and Southern Africa. It is impossible to overestimate the scale and importance of the GEM. As of 2009, this market accounts for nearly 69 percent of the global population, about 48 percent of the Earth's surface and roughly 45 percent of gross world product (GWP). EMCs are also a beacon for the remaining 90 developing and underdeveloped countries that are attempting to build market-oriented economies.

The continued expansion of economic freedom and the reduction of poverty in EMCs, developing, and underdeveloped countries have created a need to stringently prepare and train business leaders, strategists, economists, politicians, and governmental professionals to become involved with the GEM. As the growth rate of new jobs in EMCs is about three times that of developed countries, and 100 percent of outsourcing goes to the GEM, the current generation of young professionals from the developed world is increasingly looking to emerging markets for employment opportunities. For any school of business, economics, government and public service, law, and international studies in the developed world, *The Global Emerging Market: Strategic Management and Economics* will provide a comparative advantage to teach executives, strategists, young professionals, and other students how to successfully develop and implement strategy and management systems in EMCs.

The format and context of this analytical monograph is different from that of most business, strategy, and economics research and textbooks. The goal is not only to provide a strategic understanding of the developing global order and the role of the GEM, but also to forecast the dynamics and future of both. *The Global Emerging Market: Strategic Management and Economics* emphasizes my studies and forecasts of the future global order. The underlying intention is to prepare students, as well as strategists, economists, executives, and other readers, for the business reality that they will face in their careers, as well as to give them the tools to make their own projections, rather than relying on the extrapolations of the past and the opinions of others.

This book explores the social, political, economic, and technological values of global business as it transitions from the legacy of the twentieth century to the future of the twenty-first. In order to do so, it examines two new economic phenomena of tremendous historical significance that appeared on the cusp of the new millennium: the global market-place (GMP) and the GEM.

By reading this book, students, as well as strategists, business executives, and national leaders, will be able to:

- Develop a strategic mindset in order to analyze country-specific information in the context of the GMP and regional environment.
- Create mission statements, visions, objectives, and goals of a strategy, specifically for business with or within the GEM.
- Make practical decisions on how to conduct business and investment processes in EMCs.
- Understand the social responsibilities of firms from developed countries forming strategy, making investments, and doing business in EMCs.

This textbook is the first to focus on the GEM and its strategy and economics. Despite the growing importance of this market for the business, economics, and politics of the world, it has received a relatively scant amount of academic attention in the business and economic syllabi of educational institutions. In spite of much student enthusiasm, this is the first analytical textbook to offer a guideline for courses on this subject. *The Global Emerging Market: Strategic Management and Economics* describes the fundamental economic base and strategic principles of management specifically adapted to the conditions of the GEM. Furthermore, it offers insights on how to develop investment strategies for the GEM, work in EMCs, create international joint ventures (IJVs), and conduct successful mergers and acquisitions with or within this dynamic part of the world.

Curriculum Applications

This book covers issues related to the following courses: management strategies in emerging markets, the global marketplace, fundamentals of international business, macroeconomics, export/import management, comparative management systems, global business policy, manager in international economy, financial strategy, international politics and international economic relations, international law, among others.

The primary audience of this book is comprised of graduate and advanced undergraduate students in business and economics, researchers, strategists, executives and professionals of international business and economics, and governmental officials. This textbook is essential for schools of continuing education in which senior managers, professionals, and executives obtain knowledge about this market of new business opportunities.

1 A Strategic Evaluation of the Global Marketplace

A human being is part of a whole, called by us the "Universe," a part limited in time and space. He experiences himself, his thoughts and feelings, as something separated from the rest—a kind of optical delusion of his consciousness. This delusion is a kind of prison for us, restricting us to our personal desires and to affection for a few persons nearest us. Our task must be to free ourselves from this prison by widening our circles of compassion to embrace all living creatures and the whole of nature in its beauty.[1]

(Albert Einstein, 1879–1955)

The whole world and every human being in it is everybody's business.[2]

(William Saroyan, American author, 1908–1981)

Keynote Definition

The global marketplace: The global marketplace (GMP) is a system of economic relationships between consumers, companies, governments, and multilateral institutions from around the world that allows real-time cooperation and competition regardless of location.

Genesis of the Global Marketplace

The foundation for the GMP in the twenty-first century was laid by the formation and interaction of national economies, a process that began more than 2,000 years ago. Through this interaction, international economic integration gradually reached a level of intensity that created a true *world economy*. Key stages of world history are typically characterized by major economic developments. In the fourth century BC, Alexander the Great established the initial economic connections between Europe, the Middle East, and Asia. Significant economic ties within and between Europe and North Africa were later created by ancient Rome. This area of the world, 2,500 years ago, known as the "ecumene," was practically the entire known world of Romans and Greeks. A thousand years later, by developing economic activity in Central Asia, Genghis Khan and after him Tamerlane linked the economies of Eastern and Southern Europe with those of China and the Indian subcontinent. In the fifteenth century, Christopher Columbus indelibly linked the economies of Europe and the Americas. One hundred years later, Ivan the Terrible extended economic activity to Siberia, a territory larger than Europe or China. This was one of the largest economic expansions of the world economy in terms of the territory involved, second only to the discoveries of Columbus. Peter the Great, the first Emperor of Russia, established stable economic relations between Europe and Russia. Napoleon increased the intensity of the economic integration of European nations with each other and with Russia. The Monroe Doctrine, the 1823 declaration by the US president of the same name, created a base for regional economic cooperation of the nations of the Americas and was later used by US President Theodore

Roosevelt to improve regional economic stability. World War I and World War II provided the impetus for the reallocation of production facilities, and new territories became active and permanently involved in international business. The Bretton Woods Conference in 1944 created the base for the establishment of a new *global order*. This order rejuvenated international economic cooperation, which had been ruined by World War II and wartime economics, which caused the leading countries of the world to neglect civilian and social programs. At the time the entire world was divided into fighting camps; protectionism was a far less damaging issue to international economic cooperation than the impact of war itself. The global order created at the Bretton Woods Conference significantly increased and improved the world economy. This is clearly illustrated by the dynamics of gross world product (GWP) (see Figure 1.1).

Not even the barriers to international economic activity created by the Cold War were enough to stop the boost to the world economy provided by the new global order designed at the Bretton Woods Conference. In his famous Fulton Speech of 1946, Winston Churchill, the prime minister of Great Britain and Northern Ireland, referred to these barriers to international cooperation as the "Iron Curtain." This historic speech is generally viewed as the symbolic recognition of the Cold War, which had existed for only a few months at that time. Although the Iron Curtain did not entirely halt the birth of the GMP, it did significantly slow the development of international economic and business cooperation. Figure 1.2 clearly illustrates that the role of international trade in global output more than doubled after the most frigid years of the Cold War in the 1960s, allowing the GMP to become truly operational at the turn of the twenty-first century.

After World War II, the conversion of military technologies to civilian purposes brought revolutionary technological advances. This, together with relative global stability, the improvement of national economic systems in the developed world, and the beginning of the internationalization of business, caused an immediate boost in the rate of growth of world output and greatly benefited the world economy (see Figure 1.3).

During the last 20 years of the twentieth century and the first decade of the twenty-first, the global business world has gone though dramatic changes. In addition to developed and developing countries, a new economic phenomenon, *emerging-market countries* (EMCs), has appeared and become a significant force in the world economy. This new category of countries—EMCs—is characterized by an orientation toward economic freedom and

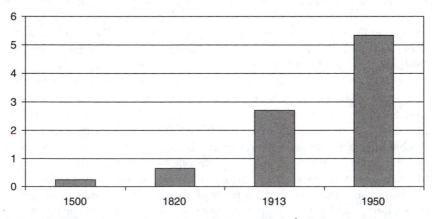

Figure 1.1 GWP (Billions of 1990 International $), 1500–1950.[3]

Note: In this text GWP and global gross domestic product (GDP) are synonymous, as both indicators are a summary of the annual national GDP of all countries that annually report their GDP.

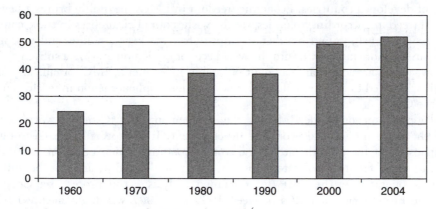

Figure 1.2 Trade as a Percentage of GWP, 1960–2004.[4]

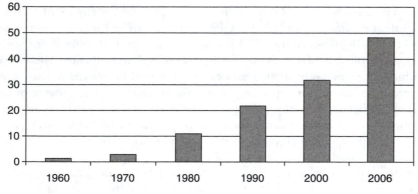

Figure 1.3 GWP (Millions of $*), 1960–2006.[5]

Note: * All figures in dollars throughout this book relate to US $ unless otherwise mentioned.

market-based economic reforms as well as by a legacy of political, social, and economic problems from their recent history as *developing countries*. In order for EMCs to reach their full economic and political maturity, these problems have to be addressed. EMCs have become partners and even competitors with developed countries. They are found in North, Central, and South America, Pacific Asia, the Indian subcontinent, Central, Eastern, and Southern Europe, in Central Eurasia in the territory of the former Soviet Union, and North-ern, Central, and Southern Africa. Simultaneously, EMCs have become partners and beacons for *underdeveloped* and developing countries that are attempting to build market-oriented economies and establish economic freedom. While they are not homogeneous, EMCs share many important social, political, economic, and technological characteristics and have established significant economic ties with one another. Furthermore, the futures they seek— free-market economies and prosperity—unite them. EMCs are part of a very important new economic phenomenon—the *global emerging market* (GEM).

The GEM is a new term that reflects a new economic, and to a certain extent, political phenomenon (see Chapter 2). The GEM has become a significant economic force as a result of the extension of the territory of global economic cooperation, i.e. the GMP. The forma-tion of the GMP dramatically expanded the territory and population that participates in international economic cooperation. Opportunities found in the GEM attract entrepreneurs, business leaders, governmental officials, and even blue-collar workers to invest their money and time and in doing so bring countries of the GEM closer to the level of economic maturity of developed countries. Economic freedom in EMCs inevitably brings a new level of political freedom, according to or despite the wishes of political elites in these countries. Most EMCs are transitioning from dictatorships to free-market economies and are continuously becoming more integrated into the world economy, demonstrating a substantial level of stability, which attracts a large amount of foreign investment. EMCs organically formed the GEM, which led to the birth of a major new economic phenomenon in world economic history, the GMP.

The new phenomenon of the GMP and the involvement of EMCs in the world economy changed the pattern of global economic development. It is especially clear through the rapid expansion of the growth rate of the world economy, which began after the 1980s as a result of the failure of dictatorships, the birth of the GEM, and the beginning of the practical operation of the GMP (for a detailed analysis of this process, see Chapter 2). The average growth rate of EMCs between 1999 and 2007 was 6.5 percent. The average growth rate of developed countries was 2.75 percent during the same period (see Figure 1.4).[6]

In order to understand the GMP, one must first understand the environment from which it arose. While it is difficult to assign the GEM an exact date of birth, it is obvious that the existence of the GMP (of which the GEM is a part) became possible only after the end of the Cold War, when the fall of the Berlin Wall symbolized and signaled the end of other barriers, which for many years divided national and regional businesses in the international arena and prevented them from operating on a unified territory. The collapse of the Soviet Union and other dictatorships throughout the world ushered in a period of unprecedented peace and prosperity, which initiated the rapid development of the unified GMP. While there were local and regional conflicts in many parts of the world, they were not on the global scale of the world wars or even the Cold War.

The number of people enjoying at least the basic conditions of democracy and economic freedom is unprecedented in the history of civilization, despite the remaining communist one-party system in China and Vietnam as well as the existence of various forms of dictatorships in several other countries. Never before have individual freedoms and quality of life been valued highly by so many political and economic national and multilateral structures. The general acceptance of democratic values, technological advancements (especially in communication), and international economic integration has created an unprecedented level of global consciousness regarding human rights, cultural and religious tolerance, environmental protection, and other "quality of life" issues. This is at once both a cause and result of a new wave of increased political cooperation, economic integration, and the widespread dispersion of technological advancements, creating a virtuous cycle, leading to

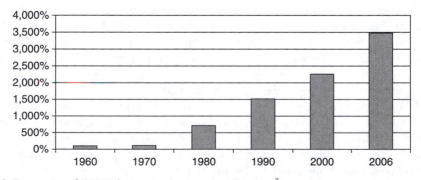

Figure 1.4 Dynamics of GWP during its Internationalization.[7]

Note: 1960 as 100 percent.

extraordinary improvements in the standard of living of most of the global population, despite the sad fact that the majority of the world's people still live in poverty. For the first time, the majority of nations share an orientation toward the achievement of prosperity for their people and global cooperation. These processes lead to the formation of not only the GMP but also its very important subsystem, the *global workplace*, in which companies cooperate in development and production of goods and services. The products of this cooperation are marketed, advertised, distributed, and sold in the GMP. Increasing standards of living across the globe are largely a result of these integration processes. All of this is an incredible achievement of human civilization that cannot be overemphasized. Of course the world is far from perfect, and substantial segments of the world population do not enjoy these accomplishments. Extending prosperity to these segments is one of the most formidable challenges facing contemporary civilization; attempts to solve these challenges are leading to the creation of a new global order.

The World Economy and the Global Marketplace

Although they share some mutual characteristics, the GMP and the world economy are two distinct economic phenomena and terms. The world economy consists of the sum of human economic activity. Ever since humans began hunting and gathering and domesticating plants and animals, the world economy has existed. At that point in human history, of course, most of the planet's surface was uninhabited or covered in permafrost or water. Although it was clearly far from global, a primitive world economy existed. For centuries, several nations and regions demonstrated economic growth and failure in the Middle East, North Africa, the Americas, Southeast Asia, Central Eurasia, and Europe. In the fourteenth century, human economic activity became increasingly sophisticated, especially in Europe under the influence of the Renaissance. However, the world economy was still not global, as European civilization was largely ignorant to the existence of American, African, Far Eastern, and Australian civilizations and vice versa. The world economy began to globalize toward the end of the eighteenth century as major geographic discoveries started influencing everyday business life. However, the world economy consisted of several distinct domestic economies that were essentially isolated from one another. The necessities that economic interests and technological advancement generated were not yet in place to integrate these economies. Political conflict and war throughout the twentieth century further hindered economic integration and the creation of a unified marketplace that included most of the world. The end of the Cold War and failures of most dictatorships throughout the world, the widespread utilization of new technological achievements in transportation and telecommunication, and the increasing liberalization of international trade and other cross-border economic relations led to continuous cooperation of almost all countries in the world economy. All of these drastic changes led to the moment when the critical mass of international economic cooperation brought the business world to a new level of tight economic integration—the GMP and its subsystem, the global workplace. At that moment civilization had become so unified in economic terms that some authors described the world economy as the global economy due to the fact that the world economy has many unique characteristics that, alone, any single nation does not. This is, for example, the opinion of Professor Horst Siebert, of Johns Hopkins University, who presents the world economy as a single entity under the influence of globalization, the increasing role of multilateral institutions and regional integration. Despite these trends, he also underlines conflicts between states related to the development of the world order. The key issues that have affected the world trade system since the turn of the millennium are thus very much to the fore.[8] However, Professor Siebert's opinion actually describes some characteristics of the world economy's segmentation. The world economy still consists of national economies at extremely different levels of maturity. This point can be illustrated by a comparison of the economy of the United States to that of Afghanistan. Some countries are still economically self-isolated, as Myanmar is from Canada or any European nation. In technological terms many national economies cannot be described by characteristics of the so-called global economy. In some countries, such as Bangladesh, the majority of people have never made a telephone call. Even within individual countries, especially those with large territories and/ or populations, there is a great deal of disparity in terms of economic and technological development. In India, despite sophisticated information technology (IT) in many cities, as of 2007 less than 10 percent of households in rural areas have telephone access. In Eastern Europe and the poorest areas of some of the former Soviet Republics, electricity is still not available in every village. In sub-Saharan Africa, only 8 percent of people in rural areas have access to electricity.[9] The world economy is still in the process of strengthening integration, and is not truly global. More than that, the differences in the development of national economies are still increasing, not decreasing. The process of economic development of the world economy has been

> uneven in space as well as time. The rise in life expectation and income has been most rapid in Western Europe, North America, Australasia and Japan. By 1820, this group had forged ahead to an income level twice that in the rest of the world. By 1998, this gap was 7:1. Between the United States (the present world leader) and Africa (the poorest region) the gap is now 20:1. This gap is still widening.[10]

However, in terms of the global integration of companies from different countries, it is a reality. Despite a lack of global economic harmonization, businesses, even from countries as self-isolated as Myanmar or Belarus, cooperate with international companies. The cooperation of individual businesses from *all* national economies initiated the creation of the GMP. The potential creation of the global economy is a different story. A truly global economy would require the complete economic integration of national economies, which will not happen for a long time. This is why there are two related but distinct phenomena—the world economy and the GMP. The GMP is part of the world economy, where businesses from around the world cooperate, compete, and merge with each other. One day this will lead to the formation of the global economy.

Defining the Global Marketplace

Companies have conducted international activity for hundreds of years. The first economic transactions of a global scale occurred in the sixteenth century, when companies from Europe, Asia, America, and even Australia occasionally conducted intercontinental transactions. However, the GMP began to take form only when technological advancements in telecommunications and IT allowed the practically instant transmission of business information, regardless of distance. This occurred when the necessity for the physical delivery of paper confirming business transactions no longer existed, and telegraph, fax, and, eventually, the Internet could immediately confirm transactions.

The first and most symbolically important instantaneous international business transaction occurred on March 30, 1867, in the intercontinental marketplace, the precursor of the global marketplace. On this date, US Secretary of State William Seward sent a cable to the president, Andrew Johnson, from St Petersburg, Russia. The cable announced the US purchase of Alaska from Russia for $7.2 million. Immediate transfer of information was possible only because of the completion of the transatlantic telegraph cable, which occurred less than a year earlier on July 18, 1866. This established the technological conditions necessary for the formation of the intercontinental marketplace. The technological conditions necessary for the GMP emerged 36 years later, when in 1902 a telegraph connection was established across the Pacific Ocean. The world was unified by people's ability to send and receive practically instant information regarding any transaction to and from all major business centers of the world.

The emergence of the GMP can be described through an understanding of its various stages of development. Although international trade transactions first occurred centuries before the implementation of overseas telegraph lines, it was the ability to get instant information about business transactions and to make instant payments that provided the technological conditions necessary for the birth of the GMP.

The first basic conditions for *global* trade were established at least by 1522 when Ferdinand Magellan completed his voyage around the world. The widespread practice of international economic and business transactions between governments, businesses, and with individual customers on a regular basis, and the establishment of long-term agreements regarding these transactions was the next stage of the GMP's development. The final stage took place when economic liberalization advanced to the point where transportation between countries and continents became part of the production process. When raw materials, energy resources, components, parts, and all other types of supplies, regardless of their place of origin, were delivered on schedule anywhere in the world to be enriched, assembled, and sold, the GMP reached its current stage of maturity. This created the global supply chain, which is an essential aspect of the GMP. Distance and time are no longer significant barriers to international supply chains, production, sales, and marketing. However, it is very important to note that there is one crucial element needed in order for the GMP to function—economic freedom. Without economic freedom, consumers and producers would be incapable of taking advantage of technological conditions. Prior to the end of the twentieth century and the collapse of most dictatorships, such was the case. Most consumers and producers were incapable of exploiting technological advances, which greatly inhibited the development of the GMP. *The GMP is a child of technological advancement and economic freedom.*

The key historical events that allowed the GMP to become operational were the internationalization of the Chinese economy (initiated by Deng Xiaoping in 1976), the fall of the Berlin Wall in 1989, and the opening of India to international business in the mid-1990s. The development of international regional economic and trade blocs at the end of the twentieth century and the establishment of the World Trade Organization (WTO) in December 1994 significantly aided the formation of the GMP. The constant improvement of international communications and IT continues to expand the GMP's reach, while the continuing development of the GMP is increasing global supply-chain efficiency and vice versa. The GMP is a venue without borders, owned by no one. It is open 24 hours a day, year round, to anyone who would like to participate in international business as a producer, salesperson, or buyer and has access to the necessary technology, funds, and economic freedom. The GMP is the major engine of the world economy of the twenty-first century and can be defined as follows: *The GMP is a system of economic relationships between consumers, companies, governments, and multilateral institutions from around the world that allows real-time cooperation and competition regardless of location.*

It is difficult to give an exact date of birth for the GMP. Nonetheless, its existence is indisputable. It became operational on the border of the twentieth and twenty-first centuries. Further development of the GMP will be the result of new technological achievements and the continued liberalization of national and international laws and under-law regulations. These processes will improve general standards of living by facilitating tighter business cooperation, improving the efficiency of the world economy, global business, and all participants of the GMP.

Economic Integration in the Global Marketplace

Local, regional, and even national markets have all been integrated within the GMP. This has created new challenges not only for national governments, multilateral institutions, and multinational corporations but also even for small companies operating in local or regional markets. Small companies have had to drastically reassess their strategies, in terms of sources of raw materials, scale of production, price setting, marketing, advertising, etc. Even when a company operates exclusively in a local market, it must be strategically prepared for global competition. In the GMP, individual entrepreneurs, companies of all sizes, governments, and multilateral institutions cooperate and compete for the utilization of basic economic factors. Through these processes these various players must efficiently achieve the appropriate balance between global supply and demand and further global economic integration.

In addition to the above-mentioned processes, the creation of the global financial system has significantly increased the level of global integration. Financial transactions can be made from the most remote parts of the world via the Internet. Vendors can buy, sell, and deliver products to and from consumers and producers around the world, cheaper and faster than ever before. Experts from around the world, once separated by distance and national borders, can collaborate, further accelerating technological progress and innovations. Peter Mandelson, former commissioner for external trade of the European Union (EU), emphasized the significance of the process of global economic integration in his Alcuin lecture in February 2008:

> In 1990 two in 10 people on this planet lived in societies that were significantly integrated into a global economy . . . Today about nine in 10 do. That is more than three billion people and probably one billion workers entering the global economy—pretty much creating the modern global economy—in less than two decades. This is the single most important change you need to grasp to understand the modern world. We are living in the wake of an openness boom.[11]

The development of the *knowledge-based economy* (discussed later in this chapter) is a direct result of such collaboration and could not exist without the GMP. Distance-learning programs and virtual universities allow students in South African deserts, Siberian taiga, and Brazilian jungles to participate in classrooms of the best universities of the world without leaving their native area. Constant cross-cultural exchange in the GMP is both a factor and product of global integration. The scale of the impact of the GMP on humanity is unprecedented. People and companies, once divided by time, space, and national borders, have deeper economic and business connections than next-door neighbors of a typical village two centuries ago.

In the few remaining dictatorships, it is almost impossible to keep entrepreneurs, companies, and economies totally isolated from the GMP. Information no longer recognizes national borders. Practically all vertical industries and regional economies collaborate under one global economic system. Under the Iranian dictatorship, for example, Iranian companies experience two types of barriers—those created by their own government and those created by international sanctions against the Iranian regime. Nonetheless, even Iranian companies conduct some international transactions. Despite the desire of the military junta of Myanmar to be self-isolated, it cannot avoid international collaboration. In order to control its population, the junta imports military equipment. By doing so it has begun to pull back its iron curtain and collaborate with the GMP, as military helicopters imported from India contained technology and components produced in six European countries.[12] The Chinese Communist Party may be able to maintain political restrictions, but unlike in Iran, Chinese companies, as well as the Chinese economy and financial system, actively participate within the GMP.

The business community of the GMP is more inclusive than ever before. It is no longer a club of the elite entrepreneurs and companies of rich nations. Companies and individuals can access the GMP regardless of their size, wealth, or country of origin. The equalizing effects of the GMP cannot be overemphasized. Prior to its existence, there was not a single billionaire outside of the developed world. As of August 2007, the richest man in the world is Carlos Slim,[13] who amassed his fortune in Mexico, an EMC. Slim is a product of globalization himself, as the descendant of an émigré from Lebanon. Prior to 1987, the Soviet Union, which covered one-fifth of the Earth's surface, did not receive a single dollar of foreign investment, nor did it have a single domestic millionaire. Twenty years later, in Moscow alone there are more billionaires than in New York City. It is, however, important to point out that individual entrepreneurs and small companies do not participate in the GMP in the same way as multinational corporations. Multinational corporations have always been involved in international business, unlike individuals and small business, which have traditionally focused on domestic markets or even futilely attempted to isolate themselves from the GMP.

The GMP provides an arena for foreign and domestic producers of goods and services to compete for consumers' purchasing power throughout the world. Increased efficiency, lower prices, and a constant search for innovation are a direct result of global competition. This is obviously very beneficial to consumers. However, one should not make the mistake of romanticizing economic liberalization. While the GMP could not function without it, national governments still play a crucial role in the GMP. Governments, especially in EMCs, enforce law and order, the standards of cross-border trade and investment, the protection of property and intellectual rights, as well as the maintenance of crucial infrastructure. Without governmental regulation there would be complete anarchy, which would make it impossible for the GMP to function. Yet no government controls the GMP itself, and nor can any national government be forced upon it. Not even the most influential multilateral institutions, whether the WTO, the World Bank, or the International Monetary Fund (IMF), have the authority or ability to manage the GMP. However, they do have the right to regulate the activity of individual companies and national governments. Global institutions are given this right by the national governments of their member countries, which in turn are authorized by their citizens and companies through the democratic process (although, in some countries the process is still only semi-democratic or not democratic at all). Nonetheless, international laws allow national governments to approve or disapprove decisions of multilateral institutions if the country is a member of the institution. Voluntary cooperation and competition resulted in the GMP. Governments and regional managerial bodies initiate and provide a dialectic response to global economic liberalization. They aim to protect domestic and regional markets and producers from unfair competition and unsafe products from abroad and create easy entry conditions into foreign markers for their exports. A proper balance between government intervention and economic liberalization allows consumers around the world to enjoy a more efficient, prosperous, and safe life as a result of the GMP. However, conditions in the GMP as a whole are far from uniform—the opportunities for rich and poor countries vary substantially. The GMP is not only a network of goods and services but also, most important, a system of economic relationships between consumers, companies, and governments that produce and exchange goods, services, and knowledge through a multitude of channels.

For centuries, international business was much less valuable than domestic business. But today it is very difficult to find a business that is exclusively domestic. The GMP is far from the mere sum of global national economic activity, however. After all, the GMP exists even in neutral territories that do not belong to a country, such as international waters.

Many individuals and companies that never intended to engage in international business are active participants in the GMP. In a small corner grocery store in Manhattan there are products from an average of 40 different countries, which are sold to customers who have come to New York from around the world. Even when entrepreneurs or companies try to isolate themselves from the GMP or are ignorant of its existence, in reality, it is impossible to operate without interacting (through cooperating or competing) with players of the GMP. But most companies and individuals purposefully increased their global business because it is more efficient and profitable. The GMP provides unprecedented access to the benefits of international trade. However, with such deep cooperation, the implications of political, economic, and financial events are more widespread than at any point in human history.

It would be naive to argue that international business and the GMP have had only a positive impact on humankind. Some of the most daunting challenges facing contemporary civilization, such as global terrorism, the global trade of illicit goods (especially drugs), illegal immigration on a global scale, large-scale ecological destruction, etc., would not exist without the GMP. The resolution of these challenges will require collaboration between private companies, governments, and multilateral institutions. The GMP is a global ocean of business, where, with the ripple effect of any crisis, both positive and negative actions and decisions reaches all shores. As a result, there is a need for new regulation and crisis management for all participants.

Technological advancement, increasing economic liberalization, and cross-cultural exchange are the driving forces behind the maturation of the GMP. Although there are important cultural aspects to the GMP, the dominant forces are economic and business-related.

Strategic Evaluation of the World Economy and the Global Marketplace

The formation and operation of the GMP gave a boost to world economic development, increasing the sustainability and rate of growth of the world economy. Figure 1.5 demonstrates the growth of the GWP in absolute numbers in terms of exchange rate since 1990.

Prior to the birth of the GMP, when international business activity was limited to North America, Western Europe, Japan, and Australia, comparisons of GDP provided an accurate picture of the relative strength of different national economies (see Table 1.1). Comparing

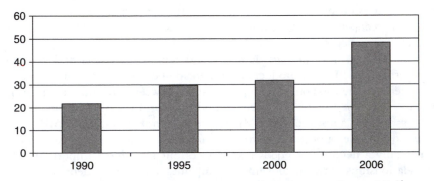

Figure 1.5 Development of GWP during the Formation of the GMP (Trillions of $).[14]

Table 1.1 GDP (Exchange Rate) of the Ten Largest Economies ($), 2006[15]

Rank	Country	GDP (Trillions of $)
1	United States	13.201
2	Japan	4.34
3	Germany	2.906
4	**China**	2.668
5	United Kingdom	2.345
6	France	2.23
7	Italy	1.844
8	Canada	1.251
9	**Spain**	1.223
10	**Brazil**	1.067

Note: In all tables of this book, EMCs will appear in bold.

Table 1.2 GDP per Capita (International $), 2006[16]

Rank	Country	GDP per Capita (International $), 2006
1	Luxembourg	69,246
2	United States	44,155
3	Norway	43,579
4	**Ireland**	41,925
5	Iceland	38,885
6	**Hong Kong**	38,065
7	Switzerland	37,919
8	Denmark	36,354
9	Netherlands	36,219
10	Austria	35,560

Table 1.3 The Role of the GEM and Developed Countries in the GMP[17]

Total GDP of the GEM (Billions $)	$29,908	Total GDP of Developed Countries (Billions $)	$30,356
GEM GDP as a % of GWP	45.44%	Total GDP of Developed Countries as a % of GWP	46.02%
Developed Countries and EMCs GDP as a % of GWP	91.64%	Total GDP of Developing Countries as a % of GWP	8.44%

GDP per capita (GDP divided by national population) was a simple and practical way to evaluate the efficiency of different economies, their stages of development, and the standards of living of their populations relative to other countries. This indicator is still a relatively efficient means of comparing the economic power of different countries (see Table 1.2). With time the majority of the world's largest economies will be EMCs.

Among the traditional participants of international business (developed countries), there were well-established ratios between respective currency values, economic and industrial structures, consumption, and standards of living. This situation totally changed when the GMP became operational. As of 2008 the GEM accounts for roughly half of the GWP (see Table 1.3).

The economic and industrial structure and standards of living in EMCs are diverse and substantially different from those of developed countries. In the developed world, when GDP per capita increases, it means that GDP growth has outpaced population growth. This indicates an overall improvement in standards of living. However, in all EMCs the cost of living varies among regions and strata of society to the extent that national GDP per capita growth does not necessarily indicate a general improvement in average standard of living. In the GEM extreme wealth and extreme poverty occur within a single national economy. In fact, the city with the highest cost of living is not New York, Zurich, or London, but one from the GEM—Moscow. Furthermore, it is difficult to compare the economic quality of life of people in countries with limitedly convertible or inconvertible currencies with that of people in developed countries who have freely convertible currencies in their pockets. Such comparisons are of great importance when a company is developing its strategy to enter or expand its activity in the GMP.

As cultural, economic, business, and financial ties strengthened between the developed world and the GEM, the practical needs of strategists led to the use of more sophisticated economic indicators, such as the purchasing power parity (PPP) methodology. Although the Swedish economist Gustav Cassel developed this concept in 1920, its application to GDP and GDP per capita was widely implemented and studied as a result of the expansion of international business and the formation of the GMP. PPPs are currency conversion rates that both convert to a common currency and equalize the purchasing power of different currencies. In other words, they eliminate the differences in price levels between countries in the process of conversion. This makes it much easier for strategists, executives, investors, etc., to compare the economies of different countries. Table 1.4 lists the 10 largest economies in the world in terms of PPP. The GDP of the GEM as a whole in terms of PPP has already surpassed the US GDP. It is important to note that the GEM does not include the input of developing and underdeveloped countries.

Table 1.4 differs substantially from Table 1.1, which lists the top 10 national GDPs in terms of exchange rate. In terms of GDP PPP, China is the second biggest economy in the world; its economy is more than twice the size of Japan's. But make the same comparison in terms of exchange rate and the picture is substantially different. China is not only far behind Japan but it is also behind Germany (though it has quietly surpassed two European economic giants, Great Britain and France). Because the aim of PPP is to adjust the exchange rate to equalize the price of the same products in different countries, it tremendously increases GDP figures of countries with lower-priced goods. This is why, with the increasing role of the GEM in the world economy, the GWP rate of growth will accelerate (see Figure 1.6).

GDP PPP per capita is an even more integrated economic indicator. First, it provides a better understanding of the efficiency of national economies. And it is more effective to use this indicator to compare economies than an evaluation of GDP in terms of exchange rate.

Table 1.4 GDP PPP (Billions of $), 2006[18]

Rank	Economy	GDP PPP (Billions $), 2006
	World	66,823
	GEM	32,784
1	United States	13,202
2	**China**	10,048
3	**India**	4,247
4	Japan	4,131
5	Germany	2,616
6	United Kingdom	2,111
7	France	2,039
8	Italy	1,795
9	**Brazil**	1,708
10	**Russian Federation**	1,704

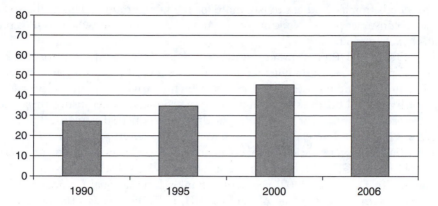

Figure 1.6 GWP PPP during the Period of the Formation of the GEM (Trillions of Current $).[19]

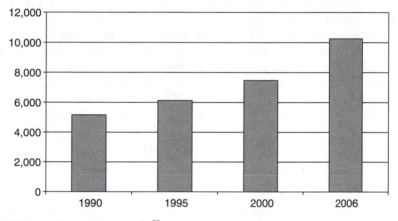

Figure 1.7 GWP per Capita (Current $).[20]

Different dynamics of dollar and national currency values and their differing purchasing power can distort the actual efficiency of national economies. Regardless, the GWP per capita has also risen steadily and rapidly since 1990, during the formation and operation of the GMP (see Figure 1.7).

An evaluation of GDP in terms of exchange rate reflects the strengths of a particular country's currency relative to the world banking currency—the US dollar. However, it does not represent the purchasing power of currency for the general population of a given country. The exchange rate is heavily influenced by the global money market. If the currency of an economy is strong, international financial speculators will invest in this currency.

A number of factors can influence the strength of national currencies. Significant foreign-currency reserves attract international financial speculators, which changes the ratio of that country's currency to the dollar. A large foreign-trade surplus and a high volume of international trade also increase the ratio of the domestic currency to the dollar. Contrary to popular opinion, the consumer purchasing power tends to decrease as national currency strengthens. The stronger a currency, the more expensive a nation's exports become, making them less competitive internationally. This causes an increase in imports for the country with the strong currency, which results in an increase in the cost of first-necessity goods and food. The more people buy imported goods, the more they have to pay when their currency gets stronger, relative to the dollar and other foreign currencies. For regular consumers, a stronger domestic currency results in more expensive goods, also because the company importing goods from abroad has to pay more for the same product. This will also factor in to the rise in consumer prices. None of these issues are accounted for when GDP is presented in terms of exchange rate.

While GDP and GDP per capita in terms of PPP are very useful indicators for academic and practical purposes, they do not take into account several factors, such as varying rates of inflation in different industries and goods, which can have a profound impact on the standard of living and business environment of an economy. When using these indicators for any purpose, it is important to consider the different industrial structure and production costs across economies. Two countries may have the same GDP per capita in terms of PPP but substantially different ratios of investment, employee remuneration, or energy con-sumption per unit of GDP. Variations in these factors create substantially different business environments. In December 2007, the World Bank's International Comparison Program, in cooperation with the Statistical Office of the EU, EUROSTAT, and the Organization for Economic Cooperation and Development (OECD), released a report on comparative price data. This report established a new estimation of PPPs for 146 national economies based on economic data from 2005. Previous purchasing power estimations were based on data as much as 30 years old. During this period, individual and governmental consumption has significantly changed, especially in EMCs, due to improvements in standards of living and the decreasing role of governments due to the privatization processes. In order to reflect these changes, the new estimation surveyed prices for approximately 1,000 products and services in emerging and developing economies. The reevaluation of PPP has tremendously changed the relative size of many national economies. For some countries, such as China, this was the first collection of accurate information, since previous estimates were done during the time of totalitarian regimes or the early stages of free-market development. The survey and its updated data decreased estimations of China's GDP PPP by 40 percent and found that

> China still ranks as the world's second largest economy with around 10 percent of world production and India is the fifth largest with over 4 percent of the world total. Overall, the 2005 benchmark results show that the size of the world economy measured in PPP terms is smaller than previously estimated. The Asian and African economies (exclud-ing high-income and oil-exporting economies) are one-third and one-fifth smaller, respectively. However, Asia still accounts for over 20 percent of the world's output.[21]

Prior to the expansion of the GMP, far fewer countries participated in international business. In order to more accurately reflect the scale of the GMP, the survey collected data and estimated the PPP of individuals and governments in 39 countries for which these estimates had never been made.[22] The IMF also revised its estimates of global economic growth in PPP by an average of half a percentage point each year from 2002 to 2007: "For example, the IMF's estimate for global growth in 2007 has been revised down to 4.7 percent from 5.2 percent in the October 2007 *World Economic Outlook*"[23] (see Figure 1.8).

Aggregate data, such as GDP or GDP per capita, can be analyzed using several methods. One approach is to analyze *the industrial structure of GDP or GWP*. The industrial structure of GWP has gone through many changes over the past 65 years. Following World War II, the leading economies of the world were still undergoing the process of industrialization. Most GDP in the majority of countries came from agriculture, followed by industry and services. A country's economy was considered very modern if more GDP came from the industrial sector than the agricultural sector. By the late 1970s and early 1980s, the world's most modern economies had entered the post-industrial stage of development, and the service sector accounted for the largest percentage of national GDP. In addition to the obvious economic importance of this achievement, there are important social implications, as "a

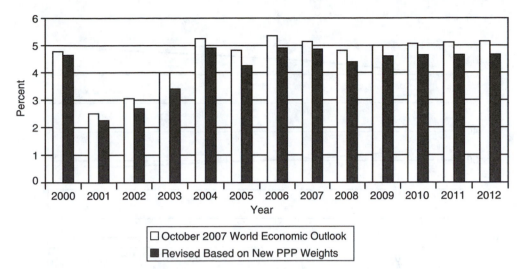

Figure 1.8 Revised GWP Growth by New PPP Methodology.[24]

Source: IMF Research Department.

post-industrial society, being primarily a technical society, awards place less on the basis of inheritance or property (though these can command wealth or cultural advantage) than on education and skill."[25]

In the twenty-first century, all developed countries are post-industrial and service-based economies. Some countries have already entered a new stage—*the knowledge-based economy* (or knowledge economy). This transition occurs when a substantial part of national GDP comes from the science, technology, and education sectors. A few EMCs, such as Hungary, the Czech Republic, Israel, Slovenia, Taiwan, and South Korea, have also reached this stage of development and can be considered knowledge economies. As a whole EMCs are a diverse group, and most are far less advanced. Some, in fact, are still agricultural economies— Ghana, Guatemala, and India—whereby agriculture accounts for 37.66, 22.70, and 17.55 percent of GDP, respectively.[26] However, many have transitioned to industrial economies (China, Brazil, and Morocco), whereby industry accounts for 47.00, 30.90, and 28.90 percent of GDP, respectively. Others have progressed to the post-industrial stage of development, such as Croatia, Uruguay, Ukraine, and Indonesia; the service sector accounts for 62.33, 61.28, 56.66, and 46.34 percent of GDP, respectively, and the role of this sector is growing rapidly. This is commendable progress for newly independent and newly market-oriented countries.

Globally, the role of the agricultural sector (the bottom line in Figure 1.9) is declining. In the first decade of the twenty-first century it accounts for less than 3.5 percent of GWP. The role of industry (the middle line in Figure 1.9) in GWP is also declining, despite the rapid industrial development in many GEM countries. Services (the top line in Figure 1.9) are definitely the only sector of the GMP besides the knowledge-based economy (which is still insignificant in terms of its percentage) whose role in GWP is increasing.

The structure of the GWP shown in Figure 1.9 is reflected by the changing dynamics of energy consumption. Since 1980 the percentage of energy consumed by the service sector in all emerging-market and developed countries has steadily increased. In developed countries, the service sector's energy consumption is already greater than that of the industrial sector. In many EMCs, this is still not the case. For example, in Russia in 2006, the industrial sector accounted for more than 50 percent of total final energy consumption, while the

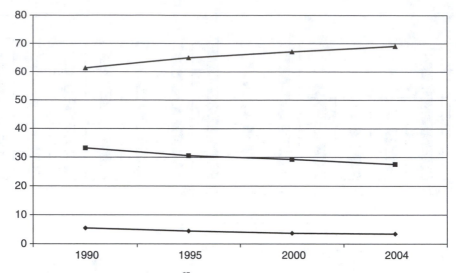

Figure 1.9 Industrial Structure of GWP.[27]

service sector, including transportation, consumed less than 40 percent. For the global business community, it is very important to understand that the rate of growth of available energy resources from 2000–2006 will not increase during the next 10 years by more than 2 percent annually. This means that energy strategies will have to focus on more efficient consumption.

Another important method of understanding an economy's efficiency is an analysis of energy consumption per unit of GDP. This can also be used to analyze the standards of living of people in different economies (further discussed later in this chapter). An evaluation of income by industry yields a totally different perspective on GDP or GWP. But in this case, variations in cost of products and production will have a substantial impact on the conclusions. A widely accepted way of evaluating GDP is to analyze public and private consumption. GDP is the sum of consumption, investment (business expenditures on capital), and net foreign trade (if the balance of foreign trade is positive, then GDP will increase by the net excess of exports over imports). Different ratios of these aspects of GDP have important strategic implications for a national economy.

GDP is not the only indicator of the total production of an economy; gross national product (GNP) can be a useful indicator. GNP summarizes the economic activity of a country's citizens regardless of whether they work abroad or domestically. GDP accounts only for economic activity within national borders. Gross national income (GNI) is yet another indicator, but as they are relatively similar, it is not necessary to analyze both GNP and GNI.

Unfortunately, no matter how thoroughly strategists and economists analyze GDP/GNP figures, the numbers never completely illustrate the economic and business environment of an EMC. This is because the informal sector accounts for as much as 25 to 50 percent of GDP in some EMCs.[28] Such economic activity is obviously not included in official statistics. In order to get an accurate understanding of an economy's size and efficiency, it is crucial to acknowledge the significance of unreported economic activity. In every single country, substantial parts of the economy, such as all black-market operations, as well as gray-market operations (legal but unregistered activity, i.e. companies that seek to avoid taxes), are left out of official statistics. During the initial transition from dictatorships and command economies to free-market-oriented economies, private business matured at a faster pace than the improvement of a legal system. A free-market economy emerged ahead of an appropriate legal structure, and many companies that would be perfectly legitimate in developed countries were considered illegal in EMCs because of lingering regulations and restrictions from dictatorships and command economies. The legal system eventually evolves the appropriate structure for a free-market economy, but because many of these companies do not report their activity for several years, their leaders worry that if they do start reporting, they will face prosecution for past infractions. As a result, the economic activity of these companies is obviously not included in official statistics. Governments of EMCs should conduct economic and financial amnesty, with the goal of legitimizing these businesses and their payrolls. Bringing these companies and employees into the mainstream economy is more important than the additional tax revenue that an amnesty program will eventually generate. Of course, the informal economy is also significant in developed countries. For example, according to the US Department of Health and Human Services, the estimated retail value of the annual marijuana crop in the US is $36 billion.[29]

The following issues are typical causes of miscalculations and misinterpretations of economic data and should be taken into consideration during a strategic analysis:

- In order to avoid and minimize taxes, companies often sell their products substantially below market value to subsidiaries that are officially registered in offshore zones with lower or non-existent tax rates.
- There are several intermediaries that would buy the product as cheaply as possible, and after several iterations, the government loses track of companies' real output. The solution is simply to register intermediaries or implement a regulation to decrease them. This problem also occurs with delivery systems, as they are a separate line of GDP and are usually underreported by statistics. Here, the solution is to register all players in the delivery system.
- In order to avoid and minimize taxes, entrepreneurs create large conglomerates from several formerly independent companies and report only the final product, not including all of the products that were used during the production process. For example, a mining conglomerate could consist of one company that extracts the raw materials, another that enriches these raw materials, a metallurgical company that produces the final metal product, and one that delivers the final product.

An analysis of GDP and GWP can also be done through the use of the achievements of Russian-born and educated American economist Wassily Leontief. Dr Leontief developed the matrix input-output economic analysis, which breaks down an economy by region and industry. Typically, this method can be used to understand the connections and relationships between different industries in the world, national, or regional economy and illustrate what part of the product of one industry is consumed as a raw material or component by another industry. For this work, Leontief received the Nobel Prize in economics in 1973. His method can also be used for an interregional-interindustrial analysis. Dr Leontief used this approach when he worked for the United Nations (UN) in the 1970s and for the development of his global forecast for the year 2000.

> "The United Nations had been pressing for an international development strategy for the 1970s ... In particular, the organization wished this strategy to aim at reducing the disparities between rich and poor countries and to take account of the new consciousness of the limited capacity of the earth. The interesting progress of modeling these relevant topics moved the United Nations to launch a study dealing with environmental issues raised by world development and looking for 'possible

alternative policies to promote development while at the same time preserving and improving the environment' . . . To embark on such a study, the United Nations required a solid methodological basis. Wassily Leontief, who had already analyzed the relations between the economy and the environment (Leontief, 1970[30]) . . . was, therefore, the United Nations' first choice . . . The model was built around a hypothetical case of two regions (developed and less developed countries), three commodities (the product of the extraction industry, other production, and pollution abatement), two components of final demand (domestic and trade), and two components of value added (labor and capital returns). Its theoretical formulation included both a quantity model and a dual price model, relying on the basic input-output relations."[31]

Strategic Evaluations of the Basic Economic Factors of the World Economy

After an analysis of the most integrated and aggregated economic indicators such as GWP, GDP, GDP PPP, GNP, and their per capita equivalents, the next step is a strategic analysis of the basic economic factors. The basic economic factors of a country or the GMP play an extremely important role in the decision-making process of a company considering expansion of its international business activity.

The economic and technological development of the world economy and the formation of the GMP have even changed the structure of basic economic factors. In addition to the traditional basic economic factors such as natural resources, labor, and capital, opportunities created by the GMP and modern technological innovations make it necessary to analyze other factors, such as existing production facilities, industrial infrastructure, and science and technology. The five modern basic economic factors shown in Figure 1.10 are key stages of a strategic analysis.

An analysis of these factors should be conducted on global, national, and regional levels, as well as for vertical industries and even individual companies. When this analysis is focused on the company level, the basic economic factors take a different form, but their economic nature does not change. For example, the natural resources for a company can take the form of raw materials, parts, or even assembled components (such as an engine for a car

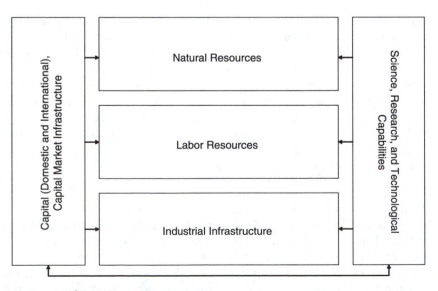

Figure 1.10 System of Basic Economic Factors.

or plane). Industrial infrastructure on a company level can be understood as corporate hardware, software, network technology, etc.

The following section presents the global allocation of the basic economic factors and their distribution in the processes of production and consumption in the GMP. Two important points should be conveyed. First, the formation of the GMP makes resources from around the world available to any country or company; and second, the role of the GEM is steadily increasing in terms of production and use of the basic economic factors.

Natural Resources (Including Land) of the Global Marketplace

THE FACTOR OF TERRITORY IN THE GLOBAL MARKETPLACE

Territory (land) is the most important natural resource. The role of this factor and its scale and location is heavily influenced by different dynamics of labor resources and capital and is constantly changing due to technological innovation. Nonetheless, there is no more strategically important factor than territory, especially in terms of national economic interests. For business concerns, the scale of territory is less important, though the size or location of a country's territory is always part of national pride. The regional allocation of resources and businesses, the allocation of construction sites of a new development of a company, and the geopolitical location of a country of current or potential business activity are always crucial elements of a strategic analysis. The scale of a nation's territory is almost always correlated to the potential agricultural capacity of the country. From this perspective, the percentage of arable land is a major characteristic of territory. For centuries the quality of soil predetermined the prosperity of a nation. However, the green revolution, which occurred during the twentieth century, reduced the importance of soil quality. But there are new factors. By the year 2050, the global population will double, and territories with high-quality soil will decrease by 60 percent, forcing strategists to reevaluate the role of soil as a natural resource. According to a study by Professor Bo R. Döös, chairman of Global Environmental Management, by 2030

> the loss of cropland is likely to be between 30 and 60 million hectares; the reserve land utilized will be about 100–200 million hectares; and the reserve land still in use by that time will be about 50–100 million hectares.[32]

Out of the ten largest countries in the world in terms of territory, six are from the GEM (see Table 1.5). This is one of many indications of its strategic importance.

Table 1.5 Largest National Territories[33]

Rank	Country	(Square Kilometers)
1	Russia	17,075,200
2	Canada	9,984,670
3	United States	9,631,418
4	China	9,596,960
5	Brazil	8,511,965
6	Australia	7,686,850
7	India	3,287,590
8	Argentina	2,766,890
9	Kazakhstan	2,717,300
10	Sudan	2,505,910

The formation of the GMP has had very important strategic implications regarding the allocation of natural resources. Prior to the GMP's existence, the location of global natural resources were understood as a summary of natural resources that belonged to particular nations. In the GMP, the location of most natural resources is much less significant. They are no longer understood solely as resources available to a certain country, but as resources available to any company in the world. And access to them is no longer determined by national identity. The only restrictions are legal regulations, environmental requirements, and the cost of production and transportation. This is important to keep in mind when analyzing the global distribution of natural resources.

THE FACTOR OF FRESHWATER IN THE GLOBAL MARKETPLACE

Access to freshwater resources has always been a major issue for particular regions and countries. However, in the twenty-first century humanity will experience a serious shortage of freshwater on a global scale. This is unprecedented in the history of modern civilization. Rapid population growth and improvements in standards of living in emerging-market, developing, and underdeveloped countries will result in a surge in demand for freshwater resources in absolute and per capita terms, especially in China, India, countries of the Maghreb, and the majority of African states, among others. It is possible that technological innovations will satisfy this growing demand via more efficient distribution systems and desalination techniques. This problem is not limited to emerging and developing countries. The majority of developed countries will have to deal with freshwater-supply issues for much of the twenty-first century, with the possible exception of Australia, Canada, and a few European nations such as Norway, Switzerland, and Austria. In 2008, in response to several years of drought conditions, two of the largest desalination plants in Europe were installed, with the capacity to produce between 200,000 and 240,000 cubic meters of water a day.[34] Despite increasing numbers of water-desalination projects throughout the world, barring significant technological progress, freshwater shortages will continue on a regional level and eventually on a global one. Unfortunately, control of and access to freshwater resources may be the cause of intense local and regional wars in the near future. As Plate 1.1 indicates, freshwater resources are distributed very unequally throughout the world. The availability of freshwater resources will have important implications for the intensity and location of business activity in the GMP of the twenty-first century.

As indicated by Table 1.6, most of the countries with the largest freshwater resources are EMCs (eight of the top fifteen). The US and Canada are the only two developed countries among the world leaders in terms of freshwater resources. A nation's freshwater resources should also be understood in terms of exploitability. A country's exploitable water resources are determined by

> the economic and environmental feasibility of storing floodwater behind dams or extracting groundwater, the physical possibility of catching water which naturally flows out to the sea, the minimum flow requirements for navigation, environmental services, aquatic life, etc. Methods to assess exploitable water resources vary from country to country depending on the country's situation.[35]

This indicator has very important implications for a country's economic development. For example, while China has recently been one of the fastest-growing economies and is currently considered (in terms of PPP) the second largest economy in the world, it is ranked 88th in the world in terms of exploitable water resources. This will be a major hindrance to China's continued development. Furthermore, the uneven territorial distribution of China's

Table 1.6 Countries with Largest Total Renewable Water Resources (10^9 m³/yr), 2007[36]

Rank	Country	Total Renewable Water Resources
1	**Brazil**	8,233
2	**Russian Federation**	4,507
3	Canada	2,902
4	**Indonesia**	2,838
5	**Colombia**	2,132
6	United States	2,071
7	**Peru**	1,913
8	**India**	1,897
9	Democratic Republic of the Congo	1,283
10	Venezuela	1,233
11	Bangladesh	1,211
12	Myanmar	1,046
13	**Chile**	922
14	**Vietnam**	891
15	Congo	832

freshwater resources will limit the development of certain regions. This will be an issue for the Northwest Territories. There is already a scarcity of freshwater in this region (usually less than 1,000 cubic meters of water per capita is considered to be a scarcity of freshwater resources. Such situations exist mostly in sub-Saharan Africa and in some areas of the Middle East). By 2030 China will have roughly 1,760 cubic meters of water per capita. Although this is not technically considered a scarcity of freshwater resources, it will substantially hinder both economic growth and social cohesion.

Scarcity of freshwater resources will lead to the development of a new economic practice: the mass cross-border trade of freshwater resources on a global scale. Exporting freshwater resources will be a very profitable undertaking for countries with excess resources, such as those listed in Table 1.7. However, in addition to analyzing freshwater resources per capita, it is very important to analyze freshwater resources in terms of domestic regional economic development and the industrial structure of a national economy. The consumption of freshwater resources by industrial and agricultural sectors is usually a more significant factor than freshwater consumption by individuals.

The countries from Table 1.8 will likely receive exports of freshwater from countries with surpluses of this resource. The oil-rich countries listed in Table 1.8, such as Kuwait, United Arab Emirates, Qatar, Saudi Arabia, Libya, and Bahrain, as well as the relatively rich countries such as Singapore and Israel, will be able to import large volumes of freshwater. However, some countries from Table 1.8, such as Maldives, Yemen, Burundi, Cape Verde, and Rwanda, will likely be in desperate need of international aid in order to provide an adequate supply of freshwater to meet the minimum health needs of their citizens. Meeting the demand of industry for freshwater in these countries will be extremely difficult.

An analysis of the freshwater dependency ratio of a country also has important strategic implications for future economic development and even political independence. This indicator reflects the amount of freshwater resources that originate from abroad. This is not an indication of the amount of imported freshwater, but rather a result of the geographical location of the source of a country's rivers. A high freshwater dependency ratio complicates bilateral relations with neighboring countries that control the source of another country's freshwater resources. The country that controls the source of a neighbor's freshwater can seriously threaten that neighbor's welfare by diverting freshwater for its own non-vital industrial purposes or by creating an artificial reservoir. In order to avoid conflicts over

Table 1.7 Countries with the Largest Total Renewable Water Resources per Capita, 2007 (m³/inhab/yr)[37]

Rank	Country	Total Renewable Water Resources Per Capita
1	Greenland	10,578,947
2	French Guiana	716,578
3	Iceland	578,231
4	**Guyana**	313,802
5	Suriname	276,018
6	Congo	212,191
7	Papua New Guinea	134,419
8	**Gabon**	119,273
9	Canada	90,767
10	Solomon Islands	88,690
11	Norway	83,589
12	New Zealand	83,164
13	Belize	69,756
14	**Peru**	68,400
15	**Bolivia**	68,126
16	Liberia	64,391
17	Chile	56,966
18	Laos	56,362
19	Paraguay	54,545
20	Equatorial Guinea	49,904
21	**Colombia**	46,754
22	Venezuela	46,290
23	**Panama**	45,743
24	**Brazil**	45,039
25	**Uruguay**	40,139

this issue, some countries that share freshwater resources have already signed bilateral and multilateral agreements. The Nile Basin Initiative is one of the best examples of such an agreement. While the Nile is traditionally associated with Egypt, its waters pass through the territories of Uganda, Sudan, the Democratic Republic of Congo, Ethiopia, Eritrea, Zaire, Kenya, Tanzanian, Rwanda, and Burundi. The White Nile, which originates from Lake Victoria (shared by Tanzania, Uganda, and Kenya) and the Blue Nile, which originates from Lake Tana in Ethiopia, converge to form *the* Nile. However, the ultimate source of the Nile is the Ruvyironza River in Burundi. In order to avoid potential conflicts and to assure the steady supply of freshwater to the 300 million people who depend on the Nile, all of the above-mentioned countries (with the exception of Eritrea) signed the Nile Basin Initiative in 1999. The vision of this Initiative is "to achieve sustainable socioeconomic development through the equitable utilization of, and benefit from, the common Nile Basin water resources."[38] Later, in June 2001, the International Consortium for Cooperation on the Nile was established to improve economic development and fight poverty in this area, in cooperation with other multilateral organizations. The ability of these countries to come to a consensus regarding the use of the Nile as a source of freshwater is heartening. Nevertheless, it is also an illustration of the complexities of managing internationally shared water resources. Countries with the highest dependency ratios are shown in Table 1.9.

It is also important to realize that a low dependency ratio does not mean that a country has an adequate supply of freshwater. It only signifies that all freshwater resources, be they extremely limited or vast, originate within national borders. Nations such as Cape Verde and Singapore have low dependency ratios as well as low freshwater resources. Table 1.10

Table 1.8 Countries with the Lowest Total Renewable Water Resources per Capita, 2007 (m³/inhab/yr)[39]

Rank	Country	Total Renewable Water Resources per Capita
1	Andorra	0
2	Kuwait	7.49
3	**United Arab Emirates**	48.29
4	**Bahamas**	62.31
5	**Qatar**	84.39
6	Maldives	88.76
7	Saudi Arabia	93.65
8	Libya	104.02
9	**Malta**	125.94
10	**Singapore**	137.24
11	**Jordan**	153.04
12	**Bahrain**	153.85
13	Yemen	190.88
14	**Israel**	249.81
15	**Barbados**	294.12
16	Oman	326.16
17	Djibouti	416.09
18	**Algeria**	435.56
19	**Tunisia**	454.09
20	Burundi	491.87
21	**Saint Kitts and Nevis**	571.43
22	Rwanda	604.16
23	Cape Verde	622.41
24	Antigua and Barbuda	702.7
25	**Egypt**	778.6

consists mostly of small island nations, which for obvious reasons do not have rivers that originate in foreign countries. It is important for strategists to consider several indicators regarding freshwater to get a complete and accurate understanding of the situation.

THE FACTOR OF ENERGY IN THE GLOBAL MARKETPLACE

The rate of development of any civilization is determined and at the same time can be characterized by its production and use of energy. The majority of technological achievements are incorporated into energy production, delivery, distribution, and consumption. Intensive use of energy per unit of production or per capita of an economy is usually a good indicator of its maturity. Energy intensity accumulates in any economic and industrial product, and even in the intellectual results of a society's development. The energy intensity of an economy can be understood via energy consumption per capita or per unit of GDP.

In developed countries, energy consumption per unit of GDP is decreasing, as is indicated in Figure 1.11, although it refers only to oil consumption. Developed countries have begun to implement energy-saving technologies, causing the overall downward trend in energy intensity. For future reference, primary energy consumption is typically evaluated in British Thermal Units (BTU).

Despite substantial improvements in energy efficiency in the developed world, global energy consumption increased by 33.2 percent from 347.424 quadrillion BTU in 1990, to 462.798 quadrillion BTU in 2005.[40] This is largely a result of the rapid development of the GEM economies. Unlike in the developed world, energy consumption as a percentage

Table 1.9 Countries with the Highest Total Renewable Water Dependency Ratio, 2007[41]

Rank	Country	Dependency Ratio (%)
1	Kuwait	100
2	Turkmenistan	97.09
3	Egypt	96.91
4	Bahrain	96.55
5	Mauritania	96.49
6	Hungary	94.23
7	Moldova	91.42
8	Bangladesh	91.33
9	Niger	89.6
10	Netherlands	87.91
11	Syria	80.26
12	Romania	80.04
13	Botswana	79.86
14	Serbia and Montenegro	78.9
15	Uzbekistan	77.37
16	Sudan	76.92
17	Pakistan	76.47
18	Slovakia	74.85
19	Cambodia	74.68
20	Congo	73.32
21	Azerbaijan	73.2
22	Paraguay	72.02
23	Luxembourg	67.74
24	Argentina	66.09
25	Namibia	65.66

of GDP is increasing in much of the GEM, as a result of the use of oil, gas, and coal and their price dynamics.

The energy intensity of a national economy and the global distribution of production facilities are largely determined by the allocation of major natural energy resources such as coal, oil, natural gas, and geothermal energy (see Table 1.11). Despite the fact that the GMP makes energy resources more widely available than ever before, national policies and legal systems can prevent foreign or even domestic companies from exploring and/or extracting natural resources. For example, the United States has not developed its largest oil and coal reserves due to environmental issues and the strategy of energy preservation for the future. The national strategy of a country may not allow companies, especially foreign ones, to directly utilize natural resources or invest in certain projects.

It is important to note that when a company sells raw materials or semi-products, its national government gets much less from foreign trade revenue than it would have from the sale of final products abroad. This was the cause of the negative foreign trade balance in the United States, until 1888.[42] Many EMCs have found themselves in similar situations in the late twentieth and early twenty-first centuries.

Figure 1.12 demonstrates the overwhelming role of Middle Eastern oil reserves. As a result, Middle Eastern countries often try to use oil not only as a source of economic strength but also as a bargaining chip in political negotiations. At the same time, it is important to realize that actual oil reserves may be distributed differently than indicated by Figure 1.12. There is a basis to estimate that the overwhelming majority of oil fields are still undiscovered. Some have been discovered but are still not measured by certain geological

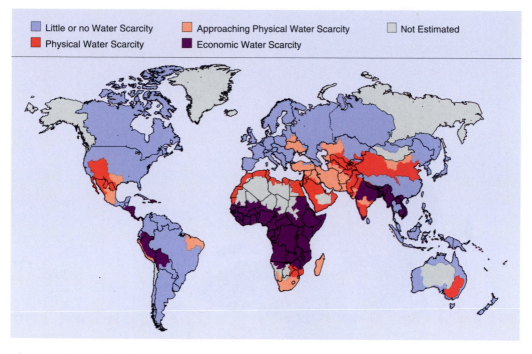

Plate 1.1 Global Distribution of Freshwater Resources.*

Source: © International Water Management Institute, 2007.

Notes:

Little or No Water Scarcity. Abundant water resources relative to use, with less than 25 percent of water from rivers withdrawn for human purposes.

Physical Water Scarcity (water resources development is approaching or has exceeded sustainable limits). More than 75 percent of river flows are withdrawn for agriculture, industry, and domestic purposes (accounting for recycling of return flows). This definition—relating water availability to water demand—implies that dry areas are not necessarily water scarce.

Approaching Physical Water Scarcity. More than 60 percent of river flows are withdrawn. These basins will experience physical water scarcity in the near future.

Economic Water Scarcity (human, institutional, and financial capital limit access to water even though water in nature is available locally to meet human demands). Water resources are abundant relative to water use, with less than 25 percent of water from rivers withdrawn for human purposes, but malnutrition exists.

* Molden, David, Frenken, Karen, Barker, Randolph, de Fraiture, Charlotte, Mati, Bancy, Svendsen, Mark, Sadoff, Claudia, and Finlayson, C. Mark. (2007). Trends in Water and Agricultural Development. In Molden, David (ed.). *Water for Food, Water for Life: The Comprehensive Assessment of Water Management in Agriculture.* London: Earthscan and the International Water Management Institute. p. 63. Retrieved December 27 2007 from http://www.iwmi.cgiar.org/assessment/Water%20for%20Food%20Water%20for%20Life/Chapters/Chapter%202%20Trends.pdf.

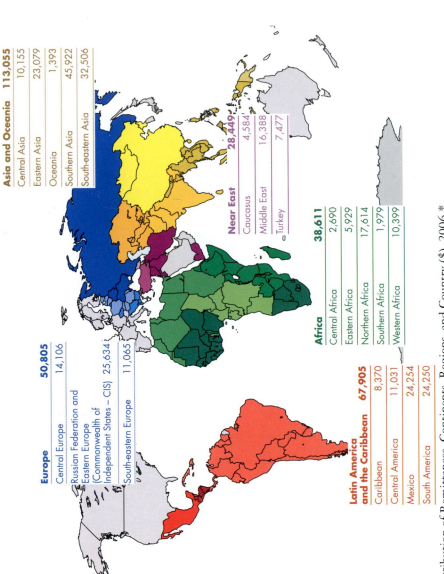

Europe 50,805

Central Europe	14,106
Russian Federation and Eastern Europe (Commonwealth of Independent States – CIS)	25,634
South-eastern Europe	11,065

Latin America and the Caribbean 67,905

Caribbean	8,370
Central America	11,031
Mexico	24,254
South America	24,250

Africa 38,611

Central Africa	2,690
Eastern Africa	5,929
Northern Africa	17,614
Southern Africa	1,979
Western Africa	10,399

Near East 28,449

Caucasus	4,584
Middle East	16,388
Turkey	7,477

Asia and Oceania 113,055

Central Asia	10,155
Eastern Asia	23,079
Oceania	1,393
Southern Asia	45,922
South-eastern Asia	32,506

Plate 2.1 Worldwide Distribution of Remittances, Continents, Regions, and Country ($), 2006.*

* International Fund for Agricultural Development. (2007). Sending Money Home: Worldwide Remittance Flows to Developing Countries. Retrieved November, 19, 2007 from http://www.ifad.org/events/remittances/maps/index.htm.

Table 1.10 Countries with a Total Renewable Water Dependency Ratio of Less than 1 Percent, 2007[43]

Rank	Country
1	Andorra
2	Bahamas
3	**Saint Kitts and Nevis**
4	Maldives
5	**Malta**
6	Antigua and Barbuda
7	Barbados
8	**United Arab Emirates**
9	Cape Verde
10	Djibouti
11	Libya
12	**Singapore**
13	**Cyprus**
14	Oman
15	Comoros
16	Sao Tome and Principe
17	Mauritius
18	Saudi Arabia
19	Lesotho
20	Burundi
21	**Trinidad and Tobago**
22	Yemen
23	Reunion
24	Rwanda
25	Denmark
26	Puerto Rico
27	Brunei Darussalam
28	**Jamaica**
29	**Burkina Faso**
30	**Czech Republic**

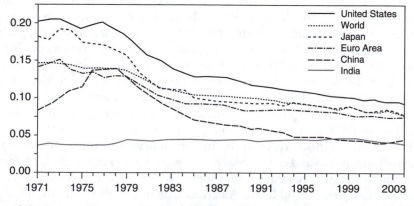

Figure 1.11 Oil Consumption per Unit of Output (Kilograms per Unit of Real GDP PPP), 1974–2004.[44]

Table 1.11 Energy Reserves by Region as a Percentage of World Total, 2008[45]

Region	Estimate of Proven Reserves		
	Oil (as a % of World Total)	Natural Gas (as a % of World Total)	Recoverable Coal (as a % of World Total)
North America	16.19%	4.48%	27.70%
Central and South America	7.80%	3.89%	2.20%
Europe	1.20%	2.92%	6.59%
Eurasia	7.51%	32.59%	25.11%
Middle East	56.11%	41.50%	0.05%
Africa	8.66%	7.84%	5.56%
Asia and Oceania	2.53%	6.78%	32.80%

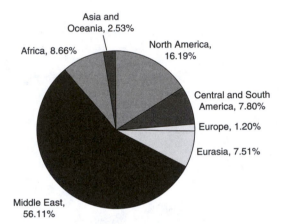

Figure 1.12 Estimates of Proven Oil Reserves by World Region as a Percentage of World Total, 2008.[46]

Note: In the category of Eurasia, Russia accounts for the overwhelming majority of reserves.

categories and are not proven; proven reserves "are estimated quantities that analysis of geologic and engineering data demonstrates with reasonable certainty are recoverable under existing economic and operating conditions."[47] This is the case in Russia, for example, whose role is underestimated in Figure 1.12, due to a lack of investment in geological studies over the past 20 years. The existence of oil reserves is not enough to draw a conclusion about the ability of a country to exploit these resources. Oil fields may be located in economically undeveloped regions that require large investments in industrial and social infrastructure in order to exploit fields. In some cases, the required investment makes exploitation of an oil field economically inefficient. At the beginning of the twenty-first century, unexplored oil fields typically lie in very remote or geographically isolated (by desert, permafrost, etc.) areas. For this reason, it is possible to predict that oil reserves in the Arctic zone of Russia (which accounts for more than 45 percent of Russian territory), are larger than those in Central and South America. Due to this fact, Russian oil reserves are likely much larger than currently estimated. This will change the ratio of potential oil production capacities of these world regions.

As indicated in Figure 1.13, the largest share of proven reserves of natural gas belongs to Russia—the most significant part of the "Eurasia" category. Despite huge domestic consumption of this resource, Russia is a major supplier to the EU and other European countries. Like Middle Eastern countries, Russia attempts to exploit its natural gas in

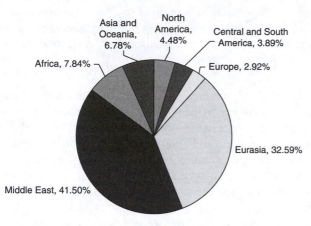

Figure 1.13 Estimated Proven Reserves of Natural Gas by World Region as a Percentage of World Total, 2008.[48]

Note: In the category of Eurasia, Russia accounts for the overwhelming majority of reserves.

bilateral and multilateral political relationships. For different countries, Russia establishes and changes prices per cubic meter of natural gas. The same practice is used by natural gas-rich Turkmenistan. The world's leading producer of natural gas is the Russian state-controlled monopoly Gazprom. With a market value of about $300 billion, Russia is the leading producer of natural gas in the GEM, and the fourth-leading producer in the GMP. The high profitability of this company encouraged more than $100 billion of foreign direct investment (FDI) in Russia from 1993 to 2008. During 2007, Gazprom began to buy gas-distributing companies abroad in order to control the entire technological process, from gas extraction to its distribution in Europe.

At the end of the twentieth century, under the influence of stricter ecological requirements, the role of coal as a source of energy was declining. However, new technological achievements renewed coal as an important source of energy. Because of modern technology of the twenty-first century, there is a new trend: small coal fields and those with a low quantity of coal in ore are considered economically exploitable. The US, as a major consumer of mineral energy resources, has the largest recoverable coal reserves in the world, a major source of energy security for the US (see Figure 1.14).

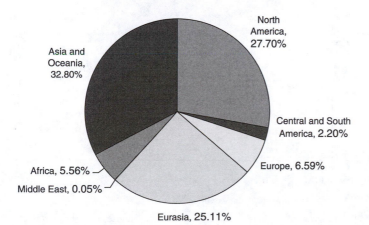

Figure 1.14 Estimated Recoverable Coal Reserves by World Region as a Percentage of World Total, 2008.[49]

Developing an understanding of the geopolitical allocation of traditional energy resources in the GMP is only the first step in a strategic analysis of the availability of energy resources for a particular company. It is also important to analyze the allocation of alternative energy resources such as biological, wind, tidal, etc.

Energy Production in the Global Marketplace   A strategic analysis of the allocation of energy resources is quite different from an analysis of energy production. Despite political and legal barriers, it is not uncommon for primary energy resources to be exported to different countries and continents for further enrichment and final production. Iran is the perfect example of this scenario. Despite the fact that this country is the no. 4 producer in the world of crude oil (5.5 percent of total world production as of 2007) and the no. 3 exporter of it, Iran produced less than 50 percent of its domestic consumption of gasoline. As a result, Iran "imported over 192,000 bbl/d of gasoline . . . costing $5 billion."[50] Countries with large primary energy resources are typically not the biggest producers of *final* energy products and are almost never the biggest consumers of energy (see Map 1.1).

Figure 1.15 shows the major sources of fuel in the world economy in 1973 and 2005. Since 1973 there have been no major changes in the relative production of different sources of fuel. Oil is still the leading fuel produced, though its role has declined by 11 percent. The other major change occurred in nuclear fuel. Its share increased from less than 1 percent to 6.3 percent. The tremendous rise in the production of natural gas in Russia, Turkmenistan, and Iran is the cause of the 4.7 percent increase in the role of natural gas in the fuel energy balance. Clearly, there have been no revolutionary changes during this period. However, a focus on alternative sources of fuel, especially ethanol and biodiesel in countries such as Brazil, the US, Germany, China, and India, will likely substantially change the global balance of fuel production and use by 2020. For example, in 2007 President Bush announced the

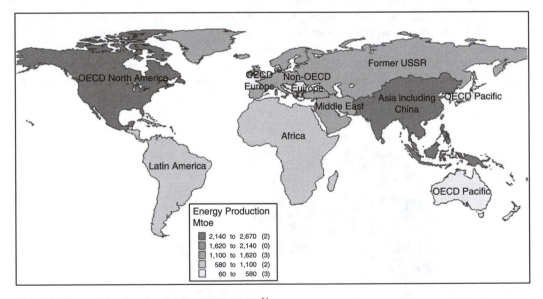

Map 1.1 Energy Production in the GMP, 2005.[51]

Source: IEA Statistics © OECD/IEA; http://www.iea.org/textbase/stats/index.asp.

Note: Energy Production = Total production of primary energy, i.e. hard coal, lignite, peat, crude oil, natural gas liquids, natural gas, combustible renewables and waste, nuclear, hydro, geothermal, solar, and the heat from heat pumps that is extracted from the ambient environment. Production is calculated after removal of impurities.[52]

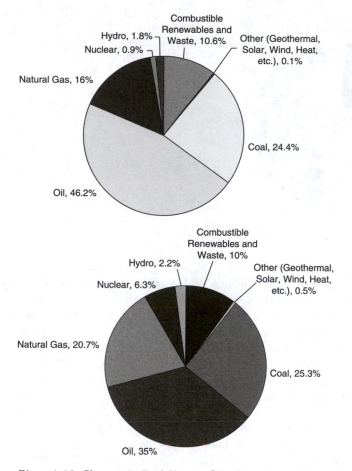

Figure 1.15 Changes in Fuel Shares of Total Primary Energy Supply (TPES), 1973–2005.[53]
Source: IEA Statistics © OECD/IEA; http://www.iea.org/textbase/stats/index.asp.

"Twenty in Ten" initiative. This initiative aims to reduce US gasoline usage by 20 percent from 2007 to 2017 by dramatically increasing the domestic production of ethanol and other renewable fuels, as well as increasing automobile fuel efficiency standards.[54]

Electricity Generation in the Global Marketplace   The production of electricity is one of the most energy-intensive industries of the GMP. It consumes almost all hydropower generation and more than two-thirds of world coal production. According to projections from the International Energy Outlook from the Energy Information Administration of the US government: "Coal and natural gas remain the most important fuels for electricity generation throughout the projection period, together accounting for 80 percent of the total increment in world electric power generation from 2004 to 2030."[55] It is important to realize that the role of certain energy resources in electricity generation differs from their role in energy production.

Although hydropower accounts for only 16 percent of world electricity generation, it is a very significant source of electricity (see Figure 1.16). Hydropower plants reduce the use of other sources of electricity during peak times. In the morning and during working hours, hydropower plants increase the stability of energy systems and play a very important role in energy balance and consumption in different regions connected by electrical networks.

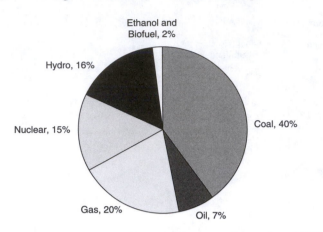

Figure 1.16 Sources of World Electricity Generation, 2005.[56]

Typically, among regions that share an electrical grid, during periods of reduced energy consumption (daily, weekly, etc.), electricity from a hydropower plant can be diverted to another region that experiences a peak in electricity consumption during this period.

EMCs are among the world leaders in terms of hydropower resources and production. China is the largest producer of hydropower electricity, accounting for 13.3 percent of the world total (see Table 1.12). As part of a national initiative, China will triple the capacity of its hydropower stations to 300 gigawatts by 2020.[57] That will be six times the hydropower capacity of Russia, which accounts for 9 percent of global hydropower resources, as of January 2008. Brazil is the leading producer of hydropower electricity in Latin America, accounting for 11.3 percent of the world total. Despite the fact that EMCs are the leading producers of hydropower, in terms of utilization of total capacity, they lag behind developed countries. For example, in Japan, 99 percent of hydropower resources are utilized; in the US, 82 percent; in Canada, 65 percent; and in Eastern Europe, 60 percent. By comparison, Russia utilizes only 20 percent. But in Siberia and the Russian Far East, where the major hydropower resources are located, only 4 percent of resources are utilized. Nevertheless, hydro energy accounts for 50 percent of Siberian energy consumption. Since 2003 India has implemented a national program to utilize hydropower energy and aims to build 50 gigawatts of hydropower stations by 2012 (which is also more than the total capacity of all hydropower stations in Russia as of January 2008).

Table 1.12 Production of Hydro Electricity, as a Percentage of World Total, 2005[58]

Country	Percentage of World Total
China	13.3
Canada	12.1
Brazil	11.3
United States	9.7
Russia	5.8
Norway	4.6
India	3.3
Japan	2.9
Venezuela	2.5
Sweden	2.4
Rest of the World	32.1

The hydro energy sector is typically owned or regulated by governments, even in developed countries. In the twenty-first century, most of these stations will be privatized, and national governments will act only as a regulator. Developments in the hydropower industry are of great economic importance, and strategists should understand hydropower plants as centers of regional economic development. According to the author's estimate, hydropower stations are typically constructed with the capacity to accommodate a 50 to 200 percent increase in economic activity in the surrounding area.

Production of Nuclear Electricity in the Global Marketplace   In terms of energy production, the most dynamic changes in the last 30 years of the twentieth century took place in nuclear energy (see Figure 1.17). Over 32 years, the role of this high-tech sector in electricity

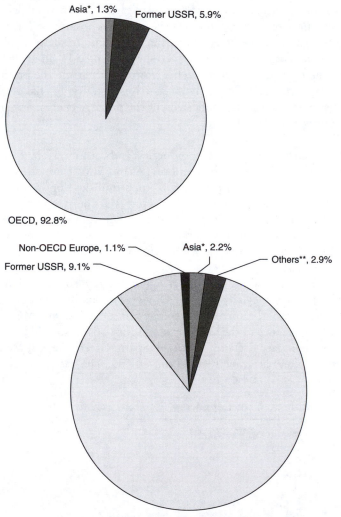

Figure 1.17 Changes in Regional Shares of Nuclear Production, 1973–2005.[59]

Source: IEA Statistics © OECD/IEA; http://www.iea.org/textbase/stats/index.asp.

Notes:
* Asia excludes China.
** Others include Africa, Latin America, and China.

generation increased by 1,363.5 percent. No other source of electricity increased by an amount even close to this figure. During this period, the role of EMCs in nuclear electricity generation has more than doubled. As of 2005, the GEM accounts for 15 percent of this industry. This trend will likely increase due to ambitious nuclear energy programs in several EMCs, including Armenia, Brazil, Bulgaria, Chile, China, the Czech Republic, Egypt, India, Israel, Jordan, Kazakhstan, Lithuania, Pakistan, South Africa, and Turkey, among others. China will achieve a "fivefold increase in nuclear capacity to 40 GWe [Gigawatts electrical] by 2020."[60] For China the nuclear industry is especially important because the country's current registered coal resources will last only until roughly the year 2100. Replacing coal as a source of electricity is a major goal of the Chinese government.

By 2007, of the ten leading producers of nuclear electricity, three were EMCs (see Table 1.13). By 2020 more than half of all nuclear energy will be produced by EMCs. Any strategic analysis of the allocation of energy-consuming industries and production facilities should take into account these countries and the growth of their nuclear programs. Typically, when the location of energy-intensive projects is under consideration, an analysis of the current balance of energy in the potential location has to be supplemented by an analysis of the energy balance of that region over the next three to five years. By the time the proposed project will be implemented in practice, the energy balance may substantially change. It is also important to consider the impact of the diversification of the primary energy resources, a key trend of the twenty-first century.

Energy Consumption in the Global Marketplace   A high production and consumption of energy is obviously not an indication of a highly efficient economy. While EMCs are among the world leaders in terms of energy resources and production, they trail developed countries by a great distance when it comes to energy consumption. However, the steady economic development of EMCs is increasing their role in global energy consumption. According to *The Economist*: "The oil price has risen mainly because of strong demand in emerging economies, which have accounted for as much as four-fifths of the total increase in oil consumption in the past five years."[61]

Figure 1.18 demonstrates the tremendous extent to which energy consumption has increased in Latin America and Asia (especially China). Obviously, this does not indicate any increase in efficiency. Nonetheless, the increasing energy consumption in EMCs does reflect their growing clout and importance in the GMP. From Figure 1.18 it should be noted that 11 EMCs (Czech Republic, Hungary, Ireland, Portugal, Spain, Greece, Korea, Mexico, Poland, Slovak Republic, and Turkey) are members of the OECD. The category "former

Table 1.13 Production of Electricity from Nuclear Energy, 2007[62]

Country Producer	Percentage of World Total
United States	29.2
France	16.3
Japan	11
Germany	5.9
Russia	5.4
South Korea	5.3
Canada	3.3
Ukraine	3.3
United Kingdom	3
Sweden	2.6
Rest of the World	14.7

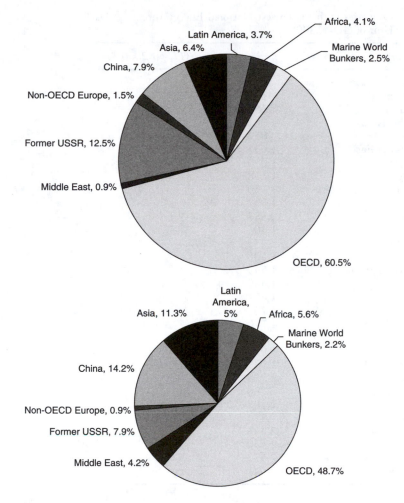

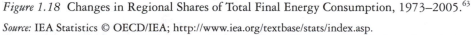

Figure 1.18 Changes in Regional Shares of Total Final Energy Consumption, 1973–2005.[63]

Source: IEA Statistics © OECD/IEA; http://www.iea.org/textbase/stats/index.asp.

USSR" does not contain the same countries in 2005 as it did in 1973, because for political reasons, the three Baltic states are no longer considered part of the "former USSR."

Energy Intensity in the Global Marketplace   Energy intensity describes total primary energy consumption per unit of GDP. An analysis of national energy intensities yields somewhat unexpected results. Within the thirty countries with the lowest use of energy per unit of GDP, there is not a single developed country and only three EMCs (Burkina Faso, Sri Lanka, and Saint Kitts and Nevis). These three countries barely meet the requirements of an EMC and are actually considered developing countries by some estimates. This illustrates the limited ability of energy intensity as an indicator of the actual energy efficiency of an economy. In the case of the countries listed in Table 1.14, a lower level of consumption of energy per unit of GDP is not the result of a national policy of energy efficiency, but of a tremendous lack of energy, underdeveloped industrial sectors, and widespread poverty.

However, as indicated by Table 1.15, high national energy intensity is not correlated with high level of economic development. No single developed country is included in the list of

Table 1.14 Thirty Countries with the Lowest National Energy Intensity (Use of Energy per One Unit of GDP), 2005[64]

Rank	Country	Energy Intensity (BTU per 2000 $)
1	Chad	187
2	Cambodia	302
3	Mali	688
4	Afghanistan	822
5	Guinea	852
6	**Burkina Faso**	1,037
7	Nicaragua	1,050
8	Bangladesh	1,118
9	Rwanda	1,150
10	Haiti	1,302
11	Uganda	1,387
12	Niger	1,405
13	Lesotho	1,471
14	Ethiopia	1,506
15	Central African Republic	1,549
16	Nepal	1,580
17	Burundi	1,651
18	Burma	1,764
19	Cape Verde	1,770
20	Cameroon	1,884
21	Macau	1,913
22	Gambia, The	1,935
23	Somalia	2,228
24	**Sri Lanka**	2,280
25	Solomon Islands	2,308
26	Laos	2,423
27	Congo (Brazzaville)	2,443
28	Sierra Leone	2,459
29	**Saint Kitts and Nevis**	2,572
30	Malawi	2,641

the thirty countries with the highest energy intensity. However, half of the countries in this table are from the GEM. Out of these fifteen EMCs, only two do not produce enough oil for their domestic consumption. This indicates that the overwhelming majority of EMCs have high energy intensity as a result of inefficient use of primary energy rather than a lack of energy, which is the case in the developing and underdeveloped countries listed in Table 1.15. Typically, developing and underdeveloped countries have outdated and inefficient technologies and as a result use much more energy than necessary per unit of production despite a shortage of energy resources.

The economies that actually use energy most efficiently are not found on the top or bottom thirty in terms of energy intensity. Tables 1.15 and 1.14 both include countries that lack a national energy strategy. Many of them totally lack energy resources, and/or modern machinery, technology, etc. All of them have standards of living far below the level of developed countries, with the exception of Kuwait and Qatar, who have high levels of energy consumption due to abundant oil reserves, and the Virgin Islands and the Netherlands Antilles, which have extremely expensive energy due to transportation costs. Both of these tables illustrate why strategists should not rely too heavily on a single indicator when assessing a country's economic maturity and business climate.

Table 1.15 Thirty Countries with the Highest National Energy Intensity (Use of Energy per One Unit of GDP), 2005[65]

Rank	Country	Energy Intensity (BTU per 2000 $)
1	Turkmenistan	14,074
2	Former Serbia and Montenegro	14,157
3	Kazakhstan	14,207
4	Russia	14,935
5	Oman	14,979
6	Seychelles	15,271
7	Jamaica	15,392
8	Singapore	15,444
9	Iceland	15,483
10	Mongolia	16,097
11	Korea, North	16,190
12	Venezuela	16,493
13	Djibouti	16,740
14	Ukraine	17,209
15	Brunei	17,952
16	Saudi Arabia	17,979
17	Iraq	18,390
18	Tajikistan	20,413
19	Trinidad and Tobago	24,361
20	Libya	24,452
21	Uzbekistan	26,919
22	American Samoa	30,788
23	Bahrain	32,337
24	United Arab Emirates	32,740
25	Syria	36,086
26	Cuba	36,847
27	Qatar	39,321
28	Kuwait	39,442
29	Netherlands Antilles	45,155
30	Virgin Islands, US	87,562

Among the largest economies in the world, Russia has the highest energy intensity (see Table 1.16). This is caused by inefficient and outdated technologies and machinery, a lack of energy strategy, and the increasing energy transportation costs in Russia's vast territory.

Since 1990 several important trends have affected global energy intensity. The most important development during this period was the formation of the GMP and the GEM. This is reflected in the decreasing energy intensity in the former Soviet Union, where the majority of countries are EMCs, transitioning from industrial to service-based economies (see Table 1.17). However, in Central and South America, where the overwhelming majority of countries are also EMCs, energy intensity has remained relatively stable. This is a result of the somewhat slower process of technological development, which itself results from a shortage of investment in science, technology, and education in this part of the world. Energy intensity increased during this period in the Middle East, where the majority of countries were in the process of industrializing their economies. North America experienced a substantial decrease in energy intensity, as did the GMP as a whole. In both cases, this is a direct result of the utilization of modern technologies and machinery, a trend that will likely continue in the foreseeable future.

Table 1.16 Energy Intensity (Use of Energy per One Unit of GDP) of Major Economies of the GMP, 2005[66]

Rank	Country	Energy Intensity (BTU per 2000 $)
1	**Russia**	14,935
2	Canada	13,825
3	United States	9,113
4	**China**	7,906
5	France	7,243
6	**Spain**	7,140
7	Germany	7,021
8	Japan	6,539
9	**Brazil**	6,312
10	United Kingdom	6,048

Table 1.17 Energy Intensity (Use of Energy per One Unit of GDP) by Region (BTU per 2,000 $), 2005[67]

Region	1990	1995	2000	2005
North America	11,878	11,440	10,117	9,282
Central and South America	N/A	6,556	6,893	6,792
Europe	N/A	8,112	7,461	7,177
Territory of the Former USSR	N/A	20,776	18,324	14,681
Middle East	13,835	14,150	14,036	15,037
Africa	6,589	6,962	6,535	6,365
Asia and Oceania	7,711	7,357	6,564	6,706
GMP	N/A	9,335	8,417	8,035

Energy Consumption per Capita   It is important to analyze energy consumption on a per capita basis, in addition to per unit of GDP. The difference in consumption per capita of the least-energy-consuming countries and the most-energy-consuming countries varies by a factor of roughly 1,000. The average of the ten countries with the lowest energy consumption per capita is only 1.032 BTU. Not surprisingly, all of these countries are under-developed and developing, with the exception of Burkina Faso, which is among the poorest of all EMCs (see Table 1.18).

Table 1.19, which lists the countries that consume the most energy per capita, consists entirely of developed countries and EMCs, with the exception of Brunei and Nauru (indicators from these two countries are always distorted by extreme wealth imbalances and tiny populations). The highest per capita consumers of energy are mostly countries rich in primary energy resources, such as Qatar, Kuwait, Norway, and Canada; countries with very high standards of living, such as Iceland, Luxembourg, and the United States; or countries with poor energy-consumption practices, due to outdated machinery and technology, such as Trinidad and Tobago. The average energy consumption per capita of the top ten countries is 856.9 BTU. In general, energy consumption per capita is directly correlated with standard of living.

From 1990 to 2005, on a regional basis, there have been some important trends in energy consumption per capita (see Table 1.20). In North America and the former Soviet Union, there is no discernable pattern. However, in Central and South America, energy consumption per capita has increased steadily, due to the industrial development of EMCs of this region, which is occurring without modern energy-saving technologies as well as slowing of

Table 1.18 Thirty Countries with the Lowest Energy Consumption per Capita, 2005[68]

Rank	Country	Consumption per Capita (BTU)
1	Chad	0.3
2	Cambodia	0.6
3	Afghanistan	0.6
4	Burundi	1
5	Mali	1
6	Somalia	1.2
7	Ethiopia	1.2
8	Central African Republic	1.3
9	Rwanda	1.3
10	**Burkina Faso**	1.4
11	Niger	1.4
12	Uganda	1.5
13	Congo (Kinshasa)	1.6
14	Tanzania	1.9
15	Malawi	2
16	Comoros	2.2
17	Eritrea	2.3
18	Madagascar	2.3
19	Nepal	2.3
20	Guinea	2.4
21	Liberia	2.6
22	Gambia, The	2.6
23	Sierra Leone	2.9
24	Lesotho	3
25	Haiti	3.3
26	Guinea-Bissau	3.7
27	Sudan	4.3
28	Kiribati	4.4
29	Benin	4.5
30	Laos	4.6

demographic trends. A similar dynamic occurred in Europe, the Middle East, Africa, and Asia. As a result, the efficiency of energy use is declining, while at the same time, energy consumption is increasing. At the beginning of the twenty-first century, some countries have started to develop national energy-saving programs, but as of 2008, they have not yielded any tangible results.

After the initial stages of capitalization in EMCs and the completion of the initial processes of industrialization in underdeveloped and developing countries, energy consumption per capita tends to stabilize and eventually decrease, due to the use of energy-saving modern technologies and structural changes in the economies of these countries.

However, the interconnected use of technologies of varying levels of efficiency in processes of production, delivery, distribution, and consumption makes it very difficult to improve the energy efficiency of a national economy as whole. It is very difficult to optimize the efficiency of installed and currently used technologies. While each individual phase of these processes can be optimized based on linear programming, the optimization of such complex interconnected processes (which consist of many different industries, companies, and projects based on a variety of technologies and sources of energy) can be done only with non-linear modeling. For this reason, the participation of professionals and economists with high-level mathematical skills are needed to craft a strategy for multi-hierarchical scenarios.

Table 1.19 Thirty Countries with the Highest Energy Consumption per Capita, 2005[69]

Rank	Country	Consumption per Capita (BTU)
1	Qatar	1,000.40
2	Bahrain	665.8
3	Trinidad and Tobago	613.1
4	United Arab Emirates	563.6
5	Kuwait	498.3
6	Iceland	489.6
7	Singapore	457.1
8	Norway	455.7
9	Canada	436.2
10	Luxembourg	431.2
11	United States	340.5
12	Brunei	314.4
13	Australia	273.4
14	Sweden	259.9
15	Netherlands	258.5
16	Saudi Arabia	252
17	Belgium	249.2
18	Finland	241.5
19	Russia	212.2
20	New Zealand	211.3
21	Taiwan	198.1
22	Korea, South	190.7
23	Austria	188.3
24	Kazakhstan	186.9
25	Bahamas, The	183.4
26	France	181.5
27	Nauru	177.9
28	Japan	177
29	Germany	176
30	Estonia	175.2

Table 1.20 Energy Consumption per Capita (Millions of BTU) by Region, 1990–2005[70]

Region	1990	1995	2000	2005
North America	277.5	279.6	285.8	280.3
Central and South America	40.7	45.2	49.7	52.2
Europe	137.2	134.5	140.4	146.4
Former Soviet Union Countries	211.4	146.5	141.3	160.4
Middle East	84.1	92.2	104.1	124.7
Africa	15.2	15	15	16.1
Asia and Oceania	25.2	29.9	31.6	41
GMP	65.9	64.3	65.6	71.8

Transportation (and even the transportation of energy itself) is one of the most energy-consuming industries in the GMP. However, significant progress has been made since the beginning of the twenty-first century, especially toward the development of more efficient vehicles. The governments of developed countries such as the United States, the EU and its member-states, as well as those of EMCs such as Brazil, China, and India, are developing national initiatives to motivate companies to develop energy-efficient technologies and machinery. The largest engine, airplane, locomotive, and automobile manufacturers are responding to these initiatives with more efficient products. Even small companies have begun to play an important role in the development of key energy-saving technologies. According to the *Venture Capital Journal*, between 2006 and 2007, roughly $220 million was invested in small companies that are developing electric cars.[71] Small countries are also developing their own strategies to use renewable and environmentally friendly technologies. Iceland is one of the best examples. In 1998 this country announced an initiative to become the first hydrogen society, and by 2007 local buses were running on hydrogen fuel cells, as were many private cars. Iceland's scientists are among the leading experts in this field.

Energy-related Environmental Pollution in the World Many countries are following Iceland's lead, and the global community is becoming more focused on protecting the environment by implementing alternative energy strategies. The most ecologically and socially responsible countries have already begun to implement technology and other measures to decrease the negative influence of their energy consumption on the environment. In most emerging-market and developing countries, these concerns have not yet resulted in high-priority national clean-energy and efficiency programs. As a result, the GEM has become responsible for a growing share of global pollution. As indicated by Figure 1.19, Asia's (and especially China's) share of global CO_2 emissions has more than tripled. Emissions of CO_2 have also increased in the EMCs of Latin America and Africa. The largest increase occurred in the Middle East, where CO_2 emissions have quadrupled since 1973.

The unique issues of economic development and environmental protection experienced by EMCs require coordinated cooperation to overcome similar challenges of their development. It would be very beneficial to EMCs to establish a multilateral institution, which would monitor, coordinate, and provide recommendations for all countries of the GEM. This organization could be known as the Global Emerging Market Monitoring and Coordinating Agency (GEMMCA).

THE FACTOR OF METALS IN THE GLOBAL MARKETPLACE

A comprehensive presentation of metal resources of the GMP is an immense task, and not the goal of this section. There are a number of encyclopedic source books and web sites that can provide the appropriate information. This section focuses on the most economically important metals for major industries of the GMP. As a result of the formation of the GEM, competition for these metals, their reserves, and their production facilities is extremely high. In coming decades, competition for these resources will only intensify, as demand for their final products will continue to increase in the GEM and the developing world. Prices for metal-based products will undoubtedly rise, and available reserves will eventually decline. This is why it is very important to strategically evaluate the scale of current production and consumption of these metals and their allocation in the GMP. The analysis of these metals is based primarily on data from the United States Geological Survey of the US Department of the Interior. The tables are only slightly modified to highlight the role of EMCs for the reader's convenience.

Aluminum Typically, major aluminum production facilities are not located in the countries with large amounts of the mineral resource for aluminum (bauxite). The process of aluminum production is extremely energy intensive. As a result, bauxite is usually delivered to countries with powerful hydroelectric plants. One of the most significant changes in the aluminum industry is the emergence of China as the leading producer of this metal, recently surpassing Russia (see Table 1.21). Its high established capacity and very low production costs practically ensure China's continued dominance of this industry, despite its very

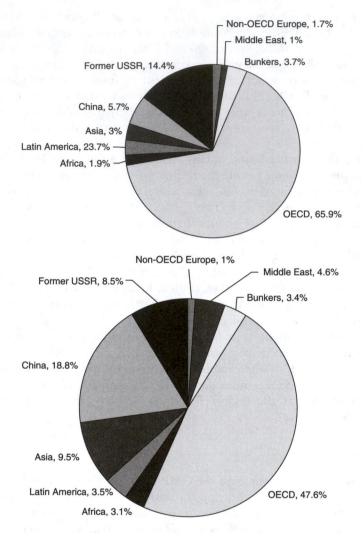

Figure 1.19 Change in World Energy-related Carbon Dioxide Emissions by World Region and Country, 1973–2005.[72]

Source: IEA Statistics © OECD/IEA; http://www.iea.org/textbase/stats/index.asp.

limited bauxite resources (only 3 percent of global bauxite reserves are located in China). This emerging Asian giant already consumes 14.3 percent of world aluminum, second only to the US. Interestingly, China produces enough aluminum for its domestic needs but still imports it from any available sources to store as reserves. This is one of many examples of China's sophisticated long-term strategy.

Copper   The overwhelming majority of reserves and production of copper come from EMCs, with Chile as the unchallenged leader (see Table 1.22). At the beginning of this century, a geological evaluation of global copper reserves using more sophisticated technology resulted in a doubling of estimated reserves. Nevertheless, because of the continuing industrialization of many developing and EMCs, the demand for copper will continue to surpass the supply. Among the leading consumers of this heavy non-ferrous metal are China, followed by the EU, the United States, Japan, South Korea, and Taiwan. Russia

Table 1.21 World Aluminum Production (Thousands of Metric Tons), 2006[73]

Rank	Country	Production*
1	**China**	8,700
2	**Russia**	3,720
3	Canada	3,000
4	United States	2,300
5	Australia	1,900
6	**Brazil**	1,600
7	Norway	1,360
8	**India**	1,000
9	**South Africa**	890
10	**Bahrain**	830
11	**United Arab Emirates, Dubai**	770
12	Venezuela	615
13	Mozambique	560
14	Germany	530
	World Total	33,100

Note: * Estimated.

Table 1.22 World Copper Mine Production and Reserves (Ordered by Production) (Thousands of Metric Tons), 2006[74]

Rank	Country	Production*	Reserves**
1	**Chile**	5,400	150,000
2	United States	1,220	35,000
3	**Peru**	1,010	30,000
4	Australia	950	24,000
5	**Indonesia**	800	35,000
6	**China**	760	26,000
7	**Russia**	720	20,000
8	Canada	600	9,000
9	Zambia	540	19,000
10	**Poland**	525	30,000
11	**Kazakhstan**	430	14,000
12	Mexico	380	30,000
	World Total	15,300	480,000

Notes:
* Estimated.
** The part of the reserve base that could be economically extracted or produced at the time of determination. The term "reserves" need not signify that extraction facilities are in place and operative. Reserves include only recoverable materials.

and Kazakhstan are not only among the leading producers but also among the leading consumers.

Nickel   Two of the most potentially dangerous metal shortages for the European and US economies are deficits of nickel and cobalt. Neither the US nor the EU has substantial natural reserves or production facilities of nickel, which has been in high demand for many years due to its use for the production of stainless steel. The importance of nickel increased substantially when major car manufacturers began production of nickel-metal hydride batteries for gasoline-electric hybrid cars at the beginning of this century. The only two countries that have actually implemented an aggressive long-term strategy in the nickel industry are Russia and China (see Table 1.23).

China's demand for nickel has grown substantially in recent years. As of 2005, it accounts for 17 percent of global primary nickel consumption.[75] China is seeking and signing long-term contracts in order to guarantee a sufficient supply for the needs of its economy and increase its share in the global consumption of nickel. Russia has a different strategy. Already one of the largest producers of nickel, Russia acquired nickel-production facilities in Canada, another leading producer. This will have important strategic implications for the United States. By 2007 Russia already accounted for 17 percent of US imports of nickel. As a result, all imports from Canada (which account for 41 percent of total US imports of nickel) are also under the control and ownership of the Russian nickel-cobalt-platinum giant—Norilsk Nickel.

Cobalt   The lack of domestic production of cobalt from primary raw materials will also have significant implications for the US and EU. The United States consumes more than 350 million tons of this heavy metal annually, mostly for engine and machinery building and aircraft production. Most imports to the US and EU are from developing countries and EMCs. The world leader by far is Congo (Kinshasa) (see Table 1.24). However, due to strategic agreements made by the Chinese government with the Congo, a substantial amount of cobalt ore goes directly to refineries in China. In 2005 China became the world's largest producer of refined cobalt. Ninety percent of cobalt ore used to produce final products in China comes from the Democratic Republic of Congo. Only one-quarter of raw materials (including scrap) for refined cobalt production comes from domestic Chinese sources.

Table 1.23 World Nickel Mine Production and Reserves (Ordered by Production) (Metric Tons), 2006[76]

Rank	Country	Production*	Reserves**
1	**Russia**	320,000	6,600,000
2	Canada	230,000	4,900,000
3	Australia	191,000	24,000,000
4	**Indonesia**	145,000	3,200,000
5	New Caledonia	112,000	4,400,000
6	**Colombia**	90,000	830,000
7	**China**	79,000	1,100,000
8	**Brazil**	74,200	4,500,000
9	Cuba	73,800	5,600,000
10	Dominican Republic	46,000	720,000
11	**Philippines**	42,000	940,000
12	**South Africa**	41,000	3,700,000
13	Botswana	28,000	490,000
14	**Greece**	24,000	490,000
15	Venezuela	20,000	560,000
16	Zimbabwe	9,000	15,000
	World Total	1,550,000	64,000,000

Notes:
* Estimated.
** The part of the reserve base that could be economically extracted or produced at the time of determination. The term "reserves" need not signify that extraction facilities are in place and operative. Reserves include only recoverable materials.

Among developed countries, only the United States and Australia have substantial natural cobalt reserves. However, due to a lower amount of cobalt per ton of raw material, extraction is much more expensive and requires very sophisticated technologies. Furthermore, there are much stricter environmental regulations in these countries, further increasing extraction costs. It appears that the US government does not have a strategy to motivate the development of cobalt production. For example, in 2006, a plant in North Carolina that produced extra-fine cobalt powder relocated to Belgium, Canada, and China.[77] Even from this decision, the role of imports from China is again increasing for the US economy.

Platinum-group Metals A global shortage of platinum-group metals will have serious strategic implications for several major industries of the GMP. Platinum-group metals include platinum, palladium, rhodium, ruthenium, iridium, and osmium. Despite the fact that the majority of readers may have never heard of some of these metals, demand for them has risen markedly, due to increasing production of catalytic converters for environmentally friendly technologies and engines. These metals will also be used heavily for the removal of organic vapors, odors, and carbon monoxide. Unlike other non-ferrous metals, which were mentioned above, the production of platinum-group metals is estimated not in millions of tons, or even tons, but in kilograms. Only five countries are major producers of these metals (see Table 1.25). Among developed countries, only the US has reserves and production facilities of platinum and palladium. But even the US imports more than 70 percent of its palladium. Thirty-seven percent of these imports come from Russia.

In a few countries, platinum is a popular jewelry metal. Japan and China are by far the leading consumers of platinum for the jewelry industry. Until 2001 Japan accounted for 25 percent of global sales of platinum jewelry. However, as the standard of living in China improved, its consumption of platinum jewelry surpassed Japan's. It is important to underline that being one of the largest consumers of platinum, China has only 0.3 percent of global platinum reserves. For industrial purposes, the US, Germany, Japan, South Korea, China, Italy, France, Brazil, Sweden, India, Iran, and the Czech Republic, among others, will compete intensely for platinum, and especially palladium. According to the US Geological Survey:

> An increase in diesel car sales in Europe can be expected to cause a strong increase in use of platinum . . . The tightening of emissions regulations in China, Europe, Japan and

Table *1.24* World Cobalt Production and Reserves (Ordered by Production) (Metric Tons), 2006[78]

Rank	Country	Production*	Reserves
1	Congo (Kinshasa)	22,000	3,400,000
2	Zambia	8,600	270,000
3	Australia	6,000	1,400,000
4	Canada	5,600	120,000
5	Russia	5,100	250,000
6	Cuba	4,000	1,000,000
7	Morocco	1,500	20,000
8	China	1,400	72,000
9	New Caledonia	1,100	230,000
10	Brazil	1,000	29,000
	World Total	57,500	7,000,000

Note: * Estimated.

other parts of the world is also expected to lead to higher average platinum loadings on catalysts, especially on light-duty diesel vehicles, as particulate matter emissions become more closely controlled.[79]

In the first quarter of the twenty-first century, the world will continue to face an increasing shortage of palladium because this precious metal will play a crucial role in the upcoming mass production of hydrogen fuel cells and converters. All major scientific advances have already been completed for this technology. Scientists and engineers are working on the development of commercially viable products. In this context, the acquisition of Stillwater Mining Company from Columbus, Montana, by Norilsk Nickel (the largest producer of palladium in the world) is an example of Russia's aggressive cross-border economic strategy.

Norilsk Nickel (Norilsk Mining-Metallurgical Concern) even during the time of the Soviet command economy, was and still is the largest producer of palladium and nickel, and one of the largest of cobalt, platinum, osmium, and gold in the world. It is one of Russia's most efficient companies and one of the most profitable in the world. Prior to the disintegration of the Soviet Union, this company, with 125,000 employees, had an annual profit of about $1.5 billion, and an annual total value of production of non-ferrous and precious metals of about $3.2 billion. The privatization of the Norilsk Concern is an example of mismanagement and possibly corruption by the Russian government. In 1996 it sold for only $170 million, and it is not even clear if this money was ever actually delivered. These numbers would be comical if it weren't so tragic for the national budget of Russia and the standard of living of its people. At that time, any company in the world, at least from this industry, would be happy to buy 10 percent of this company for $1 billion. In order to increase production of nickel, copper, platinum, or any other metals produced by Norilsk, any company would have to invest in geological explorations, the development of the mines, construction of enrichment and metallurgical plants, and development of an infrastructure (transportation, telecommunication, and housing, etc. for employees—the location of ore and raw material are far from existing housing areas). These investments require billions of dollars and substantial time. Any company would not hesitate to seize the

Table 1.25 World Platinum-group Metals Production and Reserves (Ordered by Reserves) (Kilograms)[80]

| | | Mine Production | | | | |
| | | Platinum | | Palladium | | Platinum-group Metals |
Rank	Country	2005	2006*	2005	2006*	Reserves**
1	United States	3,920	4,000	13,300	13,600	900,000
2	Canada	6,400	6,700	13,000	13,700	310,000
3	Colombia	1,080	1,000	N/A	N/A	N/A***
4	Russia	30,000	32,000	97,400	97,000	6,200,000
5	South Africa	169,000	172,000	84,900	87,000	63,000,000
	World Total	217,000	223,000	219,000	222,000	71,000,000

Notes:
* Estimated.
** The part of the reserve base that could be economically extracted or produced at the time of determination. The term "reserves" need not signify that extraction facilities are in place and operative. Reserves include only recoverable materials.
*** Included with "World Total."

opportunity to buy Norilsk Nickel, with its huge proven and registered reserves, established production facilities, and developed infrastructure.

Gold The primary value of gold in the GMP is its use as a banking metal. With the extension of capital markets to the GEM and other areas of the GMP, it is important to consider the limited production of gold. As more EMCs attempt to make their national currencies stable and convertible, the importance of gold as a banking metal is increasing. Gold reserves, together with foreign currency reserves, act as a back-up of any currency. It is different for the United States because the US dollar is the leading banking currency, and practically all countries try to accumulate it in their reserves. As a result, despite strong competition from the euro, the US dollar is still an equivalent of gold in several economic functions. Thus the US Department of Treasury has only about $47 billion worth of foreign currency reserves, which, for example, is 22.5 times less than Chinese reserves and 8.2 times less than Russian. Both of these countries keep 40 to 45 percent of their foreign currency reserves in US dollars. This is why the United States, the emitter country of dollars, does not need huge foreign currency reserves. Instead it has the largest gold stocks in the world: 261.5 million of fine troy ounces stored in Fort Knox and other vaults around the country.[81] Even though the gold standard was abolished in 1971, gold reserves still play a very important role in the global banking system, especially for currencies that are not freely convertible. Out of the eight major gold-producing countries, five are EMCs, accounting for about three-quarters of world gold production (see Table 1.26). The biggest individual gold mine, the Muruntau, is in Uzbekistan, which by many indicators can still be considered a developing country. Regardless, the GMP will not experience a shortage of gold for industrial purposes, but in terms of its role as a banking metal, gold can at least be partially replaced by platinum-group metals if it is required by the global monetary system.

Gold production is a very sensitive and often secretive issue. It is important to verify statistics by multiple sources. With increasing demand for gold from EMCs (who are most interested in holding gold as a back-up for their national currencies), some EMCs have reported very rapid increases in production, despite the fact that total world production is not increasing. According to some sources, China increased its production by 12 percent in

Table 1.26 World Gold Production and Reserves (Metric Tons), 2006[82]

Rank	Country	Production*	Reserves**
1	**South Africa**	270	6,000
2	United States	260	2,700
3	Australia	260	5,000
4	**China**	240	1,200
5	**Peru**	210	3,500
6	**Russia**	162	3,000
7	**Indonesia**	145	1,800
8	Canada	120	1,300
	World Total	2,500	42,000

Notes:
* Estimated.
** The part of the reserve base that could be economically extracted or produced at the time of determination. The term "reserves" need not signify that extraction facilities are in place and operative. Reserves include only recoverable materials.

2007, becoming the leading producer of gold in the world.[83] However, this information needs further verification.

There are other important metals, such as titanium and molybdenum, and some minerals, such as metallic uranium, which may be in shortage in the future. In general the GMP will be able to find substitutes or make alloys that can replace minerals and metals in extreme shortage. In addition to being aware of the location of reserves and existing production facilities for key metals and minerals, it is also important to analyze their capacities and percentage of use. Of course, technological advancements will likely make many existing production facilities obsolete. It is also important to realize that not all reserves are economically feasible to extract. The reserves could be located in areas with a lack of transportation infrastructure, which is the case for at least 35 percent of Russian mineral resources, which are located in permafrost above the Arctic Circle. The world has tremendous reserves of minerals on and under the ocean floor, but there are no existing technologies to efficiently exploit them. The production of metal as well as of all other natural resources as a basic economic factor is very heavily influenced by two other basic economic factors: technological development and available capital.

When evaluating natural reserves, it is important for strategists to consult several sources. Corporate reports on reserves, for instance, are not always accurate. In order to avoid taxes, companies in EMCs sometimes underreport the scale of their reserves. On the other hand, reserves may be overreported in the interest of attracting investors. It is a good idea to consult independent organizations that specialize in the particular mineral or natural resource. For example, the Society of Petroleum Engineers (http://www.spe.org/spe-app/spe/index.jsp), a professional association of energy, is a good resource when evaluating oil reserves. Evaluations based solely on company reports should always be reevaluated based on actual geological studies when possible, in order to avoid potentially serious strategic blunders.

THE FACTOR OF FORESTRY

Forestry is among the most important natural resources for any country and its inhabitants. Since the beginning of the industrial revolution in the eighteenth century, forestry has been considered only as a source of industrial production. However, by the end of the twentieth century, as concern for humankind's impact on the environment increased, forestry has become a major factor in environmental quality and health standards. With time and technological development, the ecological value of forestry will overwhelm its value as a source of timber and pulp production. For example, forestry reserves can be artificially augmented in order to prevent environmental threats such as desertification, which is a danger in roughly 32 percent of the world's territory. This could substantially improve standards of living, as population growth in areas of desertification is growing faster than the world average. Among the countries with the largest reserves of forestry, there are only a few developed countries (Canada, the US, Australia, and much further behind, ranked 22nd in the world, Sweden).

Table 1.27 lists countries with the largest forest areas. This data should also be interpreted on a per capita basis. For example, while China has the fifth most abundant forest areas in the world, this country is six times below the world average on a per capita basis. As when analyzing the allocation of all natural resources, it is important to evaluate forestry resources in terms of their location relative to existing production facilities, infrastructure, etc.

Having the largest reserves of forestry does not guarantee that a country will be a major producer of wood-based final goods. Japan, which is the 23rd country in terms of forestry, is the third-largest producer of paper and paperboard. Japan gets much more revenue from these final products than countries with larger forestry reserves that export more timber or

Table 1.27 Top 25 Countries in Terms of Forest Area (Square Kilometers)[84]

Rank	Country	Forest Area (Sq. Km)
1	Russia	8,087,900
2	Brazil	4,776,980
3	Canada	3,101,340
4	United States	3,030,890
5	China	1,972,900
6	Australia	1,636,780
7	Congo, Dem. Rep.	1,336,100
8	Indonesia	884,950
9	Peru	687,420
10	India	677,010
11	Sudan	675,460
12	Mexico	642,380
13	Colombia	607,280
14	Angola	591,040
15	Bolivia	587,400
16	Venezuela, RB	477,130
17	Zambia	424,520
18	Tanzania	352,570
19	Argentina	330,210
20	Myanmar	322,220
21	Papua New Guinea	294,370
22	Sweden	275,280
23	Japan	248,680
24	Central African Republic	227,550
25	Finland	225,000

logs (i.e. raw material). Japan exports only high-value-added final products, not raw materials. Not surprisingly, China is at the forefront of national strategies in the forestry industry as well. This is clearly illustrated by the fact that China has a quarter of the forestry resources of Russia (the world's leading country), but Russia produces only 13 percent as much paper and paperboard products as China. Russia lacks a strategy in this industry, as it primarily exports logs (without any value added) and timber, rather than more sophisticated final products. This trend is increasing, as more logs are imported to China from Russia. The percentage of total Chinese log imports from Russia increased in two years, from 43.6 percent in 2000 to 60.7 percent in 2002. It is important to note that 93 percent of these imports are of pine and larch, the highest-quality wood.[85] The strategic success of China is even more clearly demonstrated by the fact that the combined production of paper and paperboard of the two world-leading countries by forestry (Russia and Brazil) is only 28.7 percent of China's production. China has also made strategic investments in the timber industry of many countries of South America and Africa, as well as Russia. China has established more than 30 companies related to forestry and timber in these areas. Forty percent of timber consumption in China is imported. At the same time, China is developing a strategy to spare its own natural forestry from industrial purposes, and instead is developing artificial forestry farms, which account for 26 percent of the world total, covering 160 million hectares.[86]

The exploitation of natural resources without a proper strategy can do more harm than good to a national economy. When a country sells raw materials or semi-products instead of final goods, the country loses a significant amount of potential revenue. Out of the 25 leading countries in terms of forestry, 19 are emerging market, developing or even underdeveloped. In terms of production of much more profitable goods, such as paper and paperboard, out of the top 25 countries, less than half (11) belong to the GEM, and none are developing or underdeveloped (see Table 1.28). Countries that lack strategic vision sell raw materials. Sophisticated countries sell final products. A key element of successful strategy in the GMP is the use of technology, which allows the export of more sophisticated and expensive final products. In forestry, new technology has allowed byproducts to be converted into butanol—a clean, renewable fuel.

Labor Resources of the Global Marketplace

Labor is a key basic economic factor and the most important in terms of a country's future prosperity. For strategists and executives, dynamics and qualitative indicators of this factor, such as population growth or decline, literacy level, level of higher educational attainment, dynamics and development of the middle class, and the level of social unity and tolerance in society are more important than quantitative indicators. Labor resources are not only a key basic economic factor, but they are also a bridge between economic analysis and broader evaluations of a country. Strategists often make the mistake of looking at a country, region, or corporation only through the prism of economic indicators. It is important not to underestimate or fail to estimate at all the role of social, cultural, and religious issues in a society. All of these concerns are key to understanding the current and future labor market, required remuneration, and the quality of potential employees. These factors also have crucial implications for the development of a country. Low-cost, quality labor resources attract foreign investment. China is an obvious example. The overwhelming majority of foreign investment in China is not there because of the country's natural resources or its

Table 1.28 Paper and Paperboard Production (Tons), 2006[87]

Rank	Country	Tons of Production
1	United States of America	81,436,643
2	China	53,463,000
3	Japan	29,473,000
4	Germany	21,679,000
5	Canada	19,673,000
6	Finland	12,391,000
7	Sweden	11,736,000
8	Korea, Republic of	10,355,000
9	France	10,332,000
10	Italy	9,999,371
11	Brazil	8,335,000
12	Indonesia	7,223,000
13	Russian Federation	7,024,000
14	United Kingdom	6,235,000
15	Spain	5,697,000
16	Austria	4,950,000
17	Mexico	4,841,100
18	India	4,183,100
19	South Africa	3,774,182
20	Netherlands	3,471,000
21	Thailand	3,431,000
22	Australia	3,244,000
23	Poland	2,732,000
24	Norway	2,223,000
25	Belgium	1,897,000

existing production facilities. China's main lure is its inexpensive and practically unlimited number of hardworking employees. Despite the fact that China's consumer market is rapidly growing and already large, it is not a major draw for foreign investors; 80 percent of goods produced in China are export oriented.

The role of labor resources of developed countries in the global labor market is diminishing due to fast-growing populations in emerging, developing and underdeveloped countries. Out of the ten countries with the highest populations, only two are developed—the United States and Japan (see Table 1.29). Within a matter of five years, Japan's population will likely be surpassed by Mexico's.

Among the fifteen fastest-growing national populations there is not a single developed country, and only one country that barely qualifies as an EMC (see Table 1.30). The fastest-growing nations require a great deal of international support in terms of health and education, as well as the creation of conditions conducive to business activity.

Contrary to popular opinion, among the top ten countries with the most rapidly declining populations there is also not a single developed country. The high standard of living and low birth rates (below the 2.15 per women replacement rate) usually associated with developed countries are not necessarily a cause of a rapidly declining population. Also contrary to popular opinion, there is only one sub-Saharan nation, Swaziland, among the most rapidly declining national populations. Even the extreme hunger, mass disease, and

Table 1.29 Ten Largest Countries in Terms of Population, 2007[88]

Rank	Country	Population
1	**China**	1,321,851,888
2	**India**	1,129,866,154
3	United States	301,139,947
4	**Indonesia**	234,693,997
5	**Brazil**	190,010,647
6	**Pakistan**	164,741,924
7	Bangladesh	150,448,339
8	**Russia**	141,377,752
9	Nigeria	135,031,164
10	Japan	127,433,494

Table 1.30 Fastest-growing National Populations, 2006[89]

Rank	Country	Population Growth Rate (%)
1	Timor-Leste	5.35
2	Burundi	3.72
3	Uganda	3.61
4	Niger	3.24
5	**Jordan**	3.17
6	Yemen, Rep.	3.10
7	Somalia	3.08
8	Congo, Dem. Rep.	3.06
9	Eritrea	3.06
10	Benin	2.97
11	Liberia	2.91
12	Guinea-Bissau	2.88
13	Mali	2.86
14	Angola	2.78
15	Mauritania	2.73

Table 1.31 Most Rapidly Declining National Populations, 2006[90]

Rank	Country	Population Growth Rate (%)
1	Ukraine	−1.08
2	Moldova	−0.87
3	Georgia	−0.85
4	Belarus	−0.61
5	Latvia	−0.60
6	Bulgaria	−0.53
7	Russian Federation	−0.52
8	Lithuania	−0.51
9	Swaziland	−0.43
10	Romania	−0.43

low standards of living that plague much of sub-Saharan Africa do not necessarily cause rapid decline in national populations. Out of the ten fastest-declining national populations, eight are countries of the former Soviet Union (see Table 1.31). They are all from Eastern Europe, with moderate standards of living, decent health care systems, a high level of education and literacy, and a developing middle class. This regional phenomenon should be further examined from a strategic economic point of view.

Another counterintuitive trend regarding population dynamics is the rapid growth in populations in areas near deserts. The productivity of this population as a labor resource is strongly tied to the issue of freshwater resources, especially for water-consuming processes such as agriculture and chemical industries. Typically, desert areas also suffer from a short-age of energy resources, which is an issue for the labor productivity and cost of this growing segment of the world's population.

Of course there are a number of factors beyond the size of a national population that determine its productivity as a labor resource. For strategists it is important to calculate the percentage of people of working age (between age 16 and 65). Typically, in countries with high standards of living there is a high percentage of elderly people (65 and over), who are generally not considered a productive part of the labor force. However, there is an emerging trend of continued employment for people of retirement age due to improvements of health of the population of this age. Among the ten oldest national populations, there are four European EMCs—Greece, Croatia, Portugal, and Latvia. Among the top twenty, half are EMCs (see Table 1.32). This is also a reflection of improvements in health care and standards of living and longer life expectancies in the GEM.

An extremely young national population also has important strategic implications for business and government. Practically all national populations with a high percentage of people age 15 or younger are very poor, with low standards of living and low life expectancies (see Table 1.33). These countries require special attention from the global community to support the establishment of health care and education systems. These countries also require specially designed microfinance systems to help develop domestic companies. Some of these countries are already attracting foreign investment—Burkina Faso and the Democratic Republic of Congo, for example—but this investment is neither sustainable nor big enough to be a significant factor of economic development. Nonetheless, strategists have already found a way to address these countries as a market. This approach is known as the bottom of pyramid (BOP). People in these countries have the same essential needs as anyone else—basic consumer and durable goods, education for themselves and their children, etc. A strategy crafted for this particular business environment can yield substantial profit for companies in certain industries. In doing so, companies from the GMP participate in the

Table 1.32 Countries with Largest Percentage of National Population Age 65 and Above, 2006[91]

Rank	Country	Percent of National Population 65 and Above
1	Japan	20.23
2	Italy	20.22
3	Germany	19.21
4	**Greece**	18.27
5	Belgium	17.61
6	Sweden	17.38
7	**Croatia**	17.33
8	**Portugal**	17.22
9	**Latvia**	17.19
10	Austria	17.03
11	**Bulgaria**	16.85
12	**Estonia**	16.63
13	France	16.62
14	**Spain**	16.51
15	**Ukraine**	16.32
16	Switzerland	16.26
17	Finland	16.05
18	United Kingdom	16.01
19	**Slovenia**	15.74
20	**Lithuania**	15.71

Table 1.33 Countries with Largest Percentage of National Population Age 15 and Below, 2006[92]

Rank	Country	Percent of National Population Age 15 and Below
1	Uganda	50.50
2	Niger	49.03
3	Mali	48.17
4	Guinea-Bissau	47.65
5	Congo, Dem. Rep.	47.36
6	Malawi	47.33
7	Chad	47.30
8	Congo, Rep.	47.28
9	Liberia	47.20
10	**Burkina Faso**	46.99

improvement of the standards of living of these countries. The poorest countries' most desperate need is more permanent jobs.

Life expectancy is another issue worth exploring by strategists in order to properly evaluate the labor resources of a country. Among the ten countries with the lowest life expectancy, only one belongs to the GEM: South Africa. The other countries listed in Table 1.34 are underdeveloped and developing. Beyond the implications of this indicator for the labor resources of these countries, it is a further illustration of the unique needs of developing and underdeveloped countries. Many multilateral and research institutions falsely group all non-developed countries into the category of developing countries. This is extremely counterproductive, as the needs of developing and underdeveloped countries are totally different from those of EMCs. Each of these categories has substantially different business,

Table 1.34 Countries with the Lowest Life Expectancies, 2007[93]

Rank	Country	Life Expectancy at Birth
1	Swaziland	32.23
2	Angola	37.63
3	Zambia	38.44
4	Zimbabwe	38.44
5	Lesotho	39.97
6	Liberia	40.39
7	Sierra Leone	40.58
8	Mozambique	40.9
9	**South Africa**	42.98
10	Namibia	43.11

social, and political environments. If EMCs mostly seek cooperation and even fair competition with the developed world, the developing and especially underdeveloped countries seek foreign aid more than anything else. An entry strategy for companies going to underdeveloped and developing countries is also unique. Companies investing in these groups of countries have to make investments in the social infrastructure in addition to their main industrial investment. Social investment and the creation of new jobs are not only extremely beneficial to the people of these countries, but also to the companies themselves. It establishes a positive relationship with the local population and improves the lives of the company's employees, who would otherwise struggle to afford housing, health care, transportation, and education.

LITERACY

The well-educated populations of many EMCs are a major lure for foreign investment. Among the ten most literate populations, there are three EMCs: the Czech Republic, Latvia, and Estonia (see Table 1.35). Among the countries with the most illiterate populations, there is not a single EMC (see Table 1.36).

Contrary to popular opinion, developed countries do not dominate the list of countries with the highest percentage of the national population with university-level educations. Half of the top ten countries in this category are EMCs (see Table 1.37). Four of them have a higher percentage of people with university degrees than that of the US and Japan. Out of the top twenty countries with the most educated population, more than half (eleven) are from the GEM.

DISTRIBUTION OF WEALTH

The formation of the GMP, about 50 percent of which consists of the GEM (in terms of GDP PPP), has made it more difficult for strategists to understand traditional statistical data. In EMCs, average and median statistics give a less accurate portrayal of economic and social conditions for the majority of the population than equivalent data of developed countries. The numbers are distorted due to the very unequal distributions of wealth, corruption, and the diminished role of the middle class (relative to developed countries). In EMCs, standards of living of the top 10 percent and bottom 10 percent vary by a factor of at least 15 in most cases. Any indicator related to the average quality of life in an EMC (life expectancy, for example) is distorted by the substantial gap between the rich and

Table 1.35 Countries with the Highest Literacy Rates, 2006[94]

Rank	Country	Literacy Rate (%)
1	Australia	100
2	Andorra	100
3	Denmark	100
4	Finland	100
5	Luxembourg	100
6	Norway	100
7	**Czech Republic**	99.9
8	Iceland	99.9
9	**Latvia**	99.8
10	**Estonia**	99.8

Table 1.36 Countries with the Lowest Literacy Rates, 2006[95]

Rank	Country	Literacy Rate (%)
1	Niger	17.6
2	Burkina Faso	26.6
3	Sierra Leone	29.6
4	Benin	33.6
5	Guinea	35.9
6	Afghanistan	36
7	Somalia	37.8
8	Gambia	40.1
9	Senegal	40.2
10	Mauritania	41.7

Table 1.37 Countries with Highest Level of Educational Attainment (Ordered by Graduates as a Percentage of Population), 2005[96]

Rank	Country	Total University (Tertiary) Graduates	Graduates as a Percentage of Population
1	Australia	269,253	1.32
2	**Poland**	501,393	1.31
3	**Russian Federation**	1,813,340	1.27
4	**Republic of Korea**	602,701	1.25
5	France	664,711	1.09
6	United Kingdom	633,042	1.05
7	**Ukraine**	470,873	1
8	United States	2,557,595	0.86
9	Japan	1,059,386	0.83
10	Romania	156,565	0.72
11	Netherlands	106,684	0.65
12	Italy	379,933	0.65
13	Iran	366,321	0.54
14	**Philippines**	387,108	0.47
15	Germany	343,874	0.42
16	**Turkey**	271,841	0.38
17	Mexico	380,413	0.37
18	**Colombia**	131,844	0.29
19	**South Africa**	120,385	0.26
20	Vietnam	182,489	0.22

the poor and is not indicative of the conditions experienced by most people. Unlike in underdeveloped countries, where the dynamic is different, in EMCs increasing social polarization typically leads to decreased birth rates, shrinking populations, and decreasing life expectancy.

The correlations between all of these factors were the focus of the many research instates and groups, such as the Luxembourg Income Study (http://www.lisproject.org/). This project examined more than 30 countries, including 14 EMCs from Europe, Asia, and Latin America. Studies like this, analyzing a limited number of countries from all areas of the GMP, are useful for strategists to evaluate the role of a particular country or group of countries in the GMP relative to others. The general conclusions from the Luxembourg Income Study are that the poorer a country, the wider the gap between the rich and poor, the more social tension, and the worse conditions are for international business.

Among the top ten countries with the highest polarization of wealth distribution, the first four are underdeveloped, and only four are EMCs (see Table 1.38). None of them are from Europe or North America, where the standards of living are higher than those of Latin America and Africa. One of the most efficient methods of evaluating income inequality is the Gini index, developed by Italian statistician Corrado Gini in 1912. This index became especially popular at the end of the 1980s, as EMCs became more important in the international business community. The growing role of the GEM created a demand to evaluate variations in income equality. The Gini index is essentially a coefficient of income concentration; the Gini coefficient can also be used to compare different regions within a country. The Gini method is a simple means of providing a *static* picture of income distribution. However, the Nobel laureate in economics (1971), Dr Simon Kuznets developed a hypothesis that deals with the *dynamic* of income distribution. The Gini coefficient is an extremely useful method to understand income inequality. Many economists have attempted to develop an economic law that determines the distribution of income; the most successful of them are Nobel laureates Maurice Allias (awarded in 1988) and Amartya Sen (awarded in 1998). These attempts substantially built upon the Gini coefficient.

Of the ten countries with the most equitable distribution of wealth, five are developed countries and four are from the GEM. The one exception is Bosnia and Herzegovina, which is moving towards being considered a pre-emerging-market country (P-EMC). Countries with equitable distributions of wealth are much easier for companies to enter on the base of an evaluation of their human resource policy, though the benefits of low-cost labor are much harder to utilize. Nonetheless, one country on the list definitely still has a substantial supply

Table 1.38 Countries with the Most Unequal Distribution of Wealth— Gini Index, 2007[97]

Rank	Country	Gini Index
1	Namibia	74.3
2	Lesotho	63.2
3	Sierra Leone	62.9
4	Central African Republic	61.3
5	**Botswana**	60.5
6	**Bolivia**	60.1
7	Haiti	59.2
8	**Colombia**	58.6
9	Paraguay	58.4
10	**South Africa**	57.8

Note: A value of 0 represents absolute equality, and a value of 100 absolute inequality.

of cheap but quality labor—Ukraine. The appearance of Ukraine on the list of the 10 countries with the most equitable distributions of wealth is very questionable. Ukraine is a typical oligarchic market with a great deal of inequality in income distribution. The inclusion of Bosnia and Herzegovina in Table 1.39 is also very questionable. These countries are most likely on this list due to inaccurate data.

EMPLOYMENT

One of the most important indicators of a labor market is the level of national unemployment. This indicator provides an evaluation of stability, political and economic risk of investment, and has important implications for human resource policy, potential level of remuneration, etc. The general dynamics from Figure 1.20 indicate a decreasing level of unemployment in the world and in all major categories of countries of the GMP since 2004. The unemployment rate in the world economy has been steadily declining since 1997. However, the terrorist attacks on September 11, 2001, had a very negative impact on this indicator. It took another three years for the world economy to recover its positive dynamic.

Table 1.39 Countries with the Most Equitable Distribution of Wealth— Gini Index, 2007[98]

Rank	Country	Gini Index
1	Denmark	24.7
2	Japan	24.9
3	Sweden	25
4	**Czech Republic**	25.4
5	Norway	25.8
6	**Slovakia**	25.8
7	Bosnia and Herzegovina	26.2
8	Finland	26.9
9	**Hungary**	26.9
10	**Ukraine**	28.1

Note: A value of 0 represents absolute equality, and a value of 100 absolute inequality.

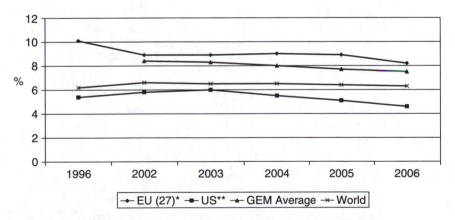

Figure 1.20 World, GEM, United States, and EU Unemployment Rates.[99]

Notes:
* Eurostat; 1996 data for EU is EU 15.
** US Bureau of Labor Statistics.

In terms of regions of the GMP, the highest unemployment can be found in the EU, which is higher than the average in the world, and even higher than in the GEM. According to the author's evaluation, as of January 1, 2008, average unemployment in the GEM is 7.4 percent, which is higher than the rate in the US, but lower than that of Europe.

Another very important indicator for an evaluation of employment is the productivity of labor. However, this indicator can be difficult to interpret. For example, the United States has a higher productivity of labor than Germany. But this indicator does not factor in the working hours of employees in these countries, which has important implications for the efficiency of a labor force. In the United States the average annual hours worked per employee is about 1,708. In Germany it is about 1,433, about 19 percent lower. These numbers demonstrate both the strong work ethic of American employees and the efficiency of German employees. Employees in EMCs actually have long working days. The top six countries by this indicator are EMCs from Asia, Europe, and Latin America. The integration of EMCs in the GMP and the unification of the global and regional labor markets increased the influence of the GEM on labor productivity of developed countries. There is a direct correlation between the number of immigrants in a developed country and the number of hours worked annually. This correlation is the cause of Italy surpassing Japan in Table 1.40, as it received an influx of workers from EMCs of Eastern and Southern Europe, especially from Balkan countries.

In an attempt to create a method to objectively compare standards of living in different countries, in 1990 the UN began publishing the Human Development Index (HDI). This highly integrated indicator incorporates statistics that reflect economic strength, inflation,

Table 1.40 Working Hours by Country (Average Annual Hours Worked per Employee), 1995 and 2006[100]

Rank	Country	1995	2006
1	**Korea**	2,658	2,357
2	**Greece**	2,154	2,052
3	**Czech Republic**	2,064	1,997
4	**Hungary**	2,039	1,989
5	**Portugal**	1,897	1,985
6	**Mexico**	1,857	1,883
7	Italy	1,859	1,800
8	Iceland	1,832	1,794
9	New Zealand	1,842	1,787
10	Japan	1,884	1,784
11	**Slovak Republic**	1,879	1,758
12	Canada	1,775	1,736
13	Australia	1,793	1,728
14	Finland	1,776	1,716
15	United States	1,733	1,708
16	United Kingdom	1,743	1,669
17	Austria	1,647	1,659
18	**Spain**	1,733	1,656
19	Switzerland	1,702	1,651
20	**Ireland**	1,875	1,640
21	Luxembourg	1,719	1,604
22	Sweden	1,656	1,601
23	Denmark	1,499	1,584
24	Belgium	1,580	1,571
25	France	1,651	1,555
26	Germany	1,534	1,433

life expectancy, access to freshwater, health care, literacy, education, electricity, as well as a number of other quality of life indicators. The HDI provides strategists with a great deal of information and can be very useful when analyzing the labor resources of an economy. On the top 25 countries on the HDI, there are six EMCs (see Table 1.41). At the bottom of the list are only developing and underdeveloped countries, with the exception of Burkina Faso, which barely qualifies as an EMC.

An analysis of indicators, less integrated than the HDI, illustrates that in some social categories, the standards of living of EMCs are not far behind those of developed countries. The clearest example of this may be life expectancy. Among the top twenty countries by this indicator, six belong to the GEM—Singapore, Hong Kong, Spain, Israel, Greece, and Malta. This also can be related to access to freshwater resources, or free or affordable higher education and health care. This means that any integrated indicator always has to be supplemented by an analysis of more specific economic and business indicators and characteristics. The HDI, for example, has flaws, as it does not illustrate the access that people of varying income levels have to an assortment of services, or specific energy-consumption patterns of different groups of people. However, there are limitations to the use of statistics to compare quality of life. As previously discussed, any average or median statistic of a given country (especially EMCs) does not take into account disparities between the rich and the poor. Socioeconomic indicators are most effective when they are analyzed from several angles and used in conjunction with extensive market research and expert consultation.

Table 1.41 HDI Ranking, 2006[101]

Highest 25 Scores		Lowest 25 Scores	
Rank	Country	Rank	Country
1	Iceland	1	Burundi
2	Norway	2	Congo (Democratic Republic of)
3	Australia	3	Ethiopia
4	Canada	4	Chad
5	**Ireland**	5	Central African Republic
6	Sweden	6	Mozambique
7	Switzerland	7	Mali
8	Japan	8	Niger
9	Netherlands	9	Guinea-Bissau
10	France	10	**Burkina Faso**
11	Finland	11	Sierra Leone
12	United States		
13	**Spain**		
14	Denmark		
15	Austria		
16	United Kingdom		
17	Belgium		
18	Luxembourg		
19	New Zealand		
20	Italy		
21	**Hong Kong**		
22	Germany		
23	**Israel**		
24	**Greece**		
25	**Singapore**		

THE NEW PARADIGM FOR GLOBAL FINANCIAL STRATEGISTS

The creation and development of the GMP tremendously increased the access of financial strategists and executives to capital from around the world. Prior to the integration of local markets into regional and national markets, a company's access to capital was mostly determined by the quality and scale of the local capital market; companies operated on a local market, using local capital in the domestic currency. This was the paradigm prior to the birth of the GMP and the formation of the global financial system. As a result of the internationalization of financial markets and their eventual globalization, new opportunities appeared for corporate leadership and even for national economies. These processes tremendously changed requirements for financial strategies. In the nineteenth century and most of the twentieth, financial strategists and executives considered foreign financial markets only in terms of uncertainty, risk, and extra costs. Debt and profit in foreign currency was always associated with extra expenses and was not desirable. Expatriation of profits made in foreign countries required expenses related to currency exchange and the difficulties in forecasting fluctuations in exchange rates and price transfers. Variations in financial regulations of different countries and even regions compounded the level of risk and uncertainty. While there is still a certain amount of disharmony among national financial and monetary systems, prior to the birth of the GMP, these systems were very disparate.

During the initial stages of international economic integration, multinational corporations were the main force driving local and national financial markets beyond domestic boundaries. With the birth of the GMP, practically every company is tied, to some extent, to the global financial market. This has created new professional requirements for financial and money managers and greatly complicated financial strategy and its development. By the late 1990s, the existence of the integrated global financial market was not fully acknowledged and understood. This made it nearly impossible to stop the global spread of what is often referred to as the Asian financial crisis. This crisis of currencies and stock markets began in 1997 in Thailand, Malaysia, the Philippines, Indonesia, and other Asian economies. It was not a national or regional crisis, however: it was global. Due to a poor understanding of the global financial system and a lack of appropriate strategy, it was not recognized as such, and its contagion spread. This crisis marched from Asia through the vast territory of Russia, ruining its national currency in August 1998 (the so-called "ruble default"), through European financial markets, finally making its way to Latin America in December 2001 with the Argentinean peso crisis. This crisis led to the recognition of the integration of the global financial system and a reevaluation of the rejuvenating role of government and central banks in this sphere. It clearly demonstrated the necessity of cooperation between national financial institutions and private business, national governments and central banks with global multilateral institutions in order to properly manage the global financial system. This cooperation can help to prevent future crises.

THE GLOBAL FINANCIAL MARKET

The global financial market requires a new dialectical attitude from executives, economists, strategists, and political leaders. This new approach requires an understanding of the appropriate balance between a high level of economic freedom and strict enforcement of widely accepted regulations, i.e. tighter monitoring, clearer international rules, global harmonization of national rules, and defined functions and responsibilities of multilateral institutions. The global financial and monetary systems are not well defined and are the most informal of all international economic regimes. It is mostly based on established practice and national laws and under-law regulations, which do not coincide with one another. Essentially, "the money and banking system of the world—usually called the *international monetary system*—is not a coherent, nor even well-organized system. There are no convenient sets of laws or regulations."[102] The international monetary system is not well organized despite the existence of the IMF, which is supposed to establish clear international financial regulations. Even international financial institutions themselves do not a have well defined role, function, or even a universally accepted legal base for cooperation with national financial systems and private companies. One of the best examples of this is the Basal Committee, which was created by the central banks of 10 Western European countries and the United States in 1974. The committee aims to encourage "convergence towards common approaches and common standards without attempting detailed harmonisation of member countries' supervisory techniques."[103] The committee has gone through several stages of development in order to promote appropriate global supervisory standards. The limited number of country members undermines the committee's goal to be a global "standard-setting body on all aspects of banking supervision."[104] Nonetheless, the Basal Committee can be very useful for banking supervisory bodies from EMCs; the secretariat of the committee and its many sub-committees are open to giving advice to representatives of any country.

Globalization actually changed traditional practices of transferring price, currency exchanges, stock market regulations, etc. Companies began to address their strategies toward the global financial market in order to increase production, profit, and market values. Strategists began to find solutions to local financial and business problems in the GMP, beyond not only local but even national borders. The combination of modern technologies and a new level of *informatization* in financial systems multiplied by slightly more transparent regulations of global financial transactions, worked to increase the speed and frequency of these transactions. As a result, at the beginning of the twenty-first century, remarkable opportunities for companies in all corners of the GMP appeared.

The integration of EMCs (with limitedly or totally inconvertible currencies) to the GMP and their cooperation with developed countries (with convertible currencies) further multiplied the complexity of the global monetary system. The global financial system is complicated by a very narrow specter of financial instruments in national capital markets of EMCs, restrictions on foreign capital, and a lack of protection of minority shareholders. However, this system has created new opportunities to use capital as a basic factor of economic development. Integration of companies and national economies to the global monetary system increases the necessity of international exchanges between different currencies, and complicates the dynamics of national currencies in comparison with each other. National emitters (such as central banks), national supervisory securities, and exchange bodies, started to face new challenges in banking, stock market and currency regulation and practice. The integration of financial systems of EMCs into the GMP expedited the rate of growth of capitalization of their national economies. It also increased financial stability and eventually decreased the number of inconvertible and limitedly convertible currencies. In order to make currencies freely convertible, financial systems more stable, and to prevent a lack of liquidity, countries began to amass foreign currency and gold reserves (see Figure 1.21). The largest currency reserves are held by countries that would eventually like to render convertible their limitedly or inconvertible currency—China, Japan, South Korea, Russia, and Taiwan. By the beginning of the twenty-first century, a few EMCs already have convertible currencies: the Czech koruna and the Hong Kong dollar, among others.

As indicated in Figure 1.22, the GEM is the main holder of foreign currency reserves; it has surpassed Canada, the EU, Japan, and the US *combined*.

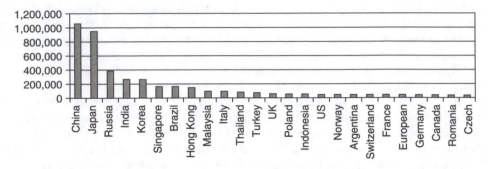

Figure 1.21 Foreign Currency Reserves in Convertible Currencies (Millions of $), January 2008.[105]

Note: Convertible currencies are defined as currencies that are freely bought and sold globally and are usable for settlements of international transactions.

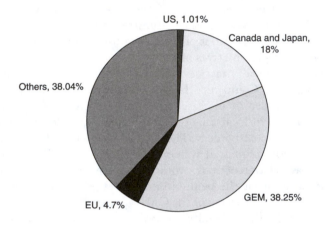

Figure 1.22 Foreign Currency Reserves as a Share of Global Total, 2007.[106]

Large accumulations of foreign currency and gold increase the value of gold stocks worldwide. Even the IMF has increased its gold assets, one of the largest stores in the world: as of October 2007, the IMF holds 103.4 million ounces of gold.[107] With the increasing instability of the GMP in 2007, countries began to increase their banking stocks of other precious metals, such as platinum and palladium. Table 1.42 shows global gold reserves special drawing right (SDR).

An understanding of the global financial market and its trends is a major requirement for strategists, especially those who would like to use globally available capital as the dominant factor of economic success in the GMP. Prior to the birth of the GEM and the integration of this market to the GMP, developed countries with excess capital competed intensely for the most interesting and lucrative investment projects. Of course, their options were restricted

Table 1.42 Global Gold Reserves Special Drawing Right[108]

	1998	1999	2000	2001	2002	2003	2004	2005
Global Gold Reserves (SDR)	1,446,450	1,575,820	1,752,930	1,915,340	2,092,440	2,379,440	2,743,060	3,285,100

Note: "The SDR is an international reserve asset, created by the IMF in 1969 to supplement the existing official reserves of member countries . . . The value of the SDR will continue to be based on a weighted average of the values of a basket including the US dollar, euro, Japanese yen, and pound sterling,"[109] evaluated on a daily basis.

to the relatively small international marketplace of the 1980s that consisted of 17 developed countries. After the formation of the GMP and the GEM, a new trend became evident—the increasing shortage of capital. Strategists stopped considering foreign currencies as an unnecessary risk and began evaluating their supplies and demands. The role of local financial markets and their authorities started to decrease as they became integrated with the global financial system. This process increased the speed of international transactions and developed a global network of foreign currency exchanges. It even created new functions for the oldest international financial institution, the Bank for International Settlements (BIS), which was established in 1930.

According to the BIS: "BIS financial services are provided out of two linked trading rooms: one at its Basel head office and one at its office in Hong Kong SAR [special administrative region].

The Bank continually adapts its *product range* in order to respond more effectively to the evolving needs of central banks. Besides standard services such as sight/notice accounts and fixed-term deposits, the Bank has developed a range of more sophisticated financial products that central banks can actively trade with the BIS to increase the return on their foreign assets. The Bank also transacts foreign exchange and gold on behalf of its customers.

In addition, the BIS offers a range of asset-management services in sovereign securities or high-grade assets. These may be either a specific portfolio mandate negotiated between the BIS and a central bank or an open-end fund structure—the BIS Investment Pool (BISIP)—allowing customers to invest in a common pool of assets. The two Asian Bond Funds (ABF1 and ABF2) are administered by the BIS under the BISIP umbrella: ABF1 is managed by the BIS and ABF2 by a group of external fund managers.

The BIS extends short-term credits to central banks, usually on a collateralised basis. From time to time, the BIS also coordinates emergency short-term lending to countries in financial crisis. In these circumstances, the BIS advances funds on behalf of, and with the backing and guarantee of, a group of supporting central banks.

The Bank's *Statutes* do not allow the Bank to open current accounts in the name of, or make advances to, governments."[110]

Unfortunately for private companies, "the BIS does not accept deposits from, or generally provide financial services to, private individuals or corporate entities."[111] The globalization of the monetary system also increased the fluctuations of exchange rates and value of different currencies. One of the major roles of financial strategists in the global environment became financial risk management. Each strategy in the GMP requires a hedging strategy as an important sub-element. Even traditional instruments against currency fluctuations, such as forward markets, money market systems, and restructuring systems, have changed. Global operations of companies have complicated traditional evaluations of labor productivity, cost production, quality of goods, and the efficiency of technology. This happened because of the necessity to evaluate all of these strategic issues within the scale of the GMP, rather than in isolated local, regional, or national markets. Debt restructuring of companies has to be analyzed by the different countries and even continents where this company and its subsidiaries operate or from which its goods and services are supplied and sold.

The increasing role, stability, and maturity of the GEM accelerated the development of banking systems in EMCs. At the initial stages of democratization and market-oriented reforms in these countries, the banking sectors were limited to state-owned banks with a few insignificant private exceptions. Economic development, processes of privatization, and increasing numbers of entrepreneurs drastically raised the need for commercial and investment-banking services. Like mushrooms after rain, many private banks emerged with small amounts of assets and capital. Typically, it takes several years, or even a couple of decades of development, for the processes of concentration and the regulation of the banking sector to see even a few sophisticated private banks established in EMCs. At the end of the twentieth century, the initial stage of development of the banking sector was completed in EMCs. National banking systems developed according to the requirements of international regulations and the needs of domestic entrepreneurs and companies. At the beginning of the twenty-first century, the combined banking assets of the EMCs are substantially greater than those of the United States—the dominant banking power of the world (see Figure 1.23). The banking systems of EMCs have begun to compete with foreign banks on their soil and to cooperate with them globally.

What is especially important for private businesses in EMCs is the fact that the growth in capitalization and assets of the banking sector is increasing the role and capacity of private financial institutions in short-term lending. However, in the bond market, private banks are still far behind state and governmental institutions. Despite the increasing maturity of the banking sector in the GEM, and the continuing growth of capitalization in these countries, the scale of domestic capital is still relatively low, and far behind the similar role of domestic capital in developed countries. This explains why the factor of foreign investors in bond markets in EMCs as of 2008 is still increasing. In some EMCs—Uruguay, Hungary, and Poland—foreign investment accounts for more than a quarter of the total domestic bond market.

THE GLOBAL CAPITAL MARKET

Financial assets of companies have become more international and in some cases global. But the liabilities of a company have been even more heavily influenced by globalization. The manner in which financial strategists evaluate the costs of preparation and development of new production facilities and the production process itself relative to income and profitability has changed dramatically. All of this is leading to constant adjustments in the theory of capitalization and its national and international practice. Capitalization is essentially the conversion of potential income into capital. However, this simple concept has been greatly complicated by the dialectical relationship between the dynamics of the global capital market and regional and national capital trends. Different patterns of global capitalization

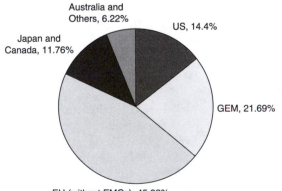

Figure 1.23 Bank Assets as a Share of the Global Total, 2006.[112]

are determining factors of national and regional dynamics of capitalization. For example, financial decline or crisis in one part of the GMP tremendously influences tendencies and even the scale of capitalization in distant national and local markets. Figure 1.24 shows stock market capitalization of the GMP as of 2006.

Rapid capitalization in the GEM positively influences global capitalization. During the last decade of the twentieth century, companies from EMCs began to be listed on major international stock exchanges in developed countries, directly or indirectly. Due to the uncertainty of domestic markets in EMCs and a lack of knowledge in developed countries about brands and even names of companies from EMCs, some were able to be listed on major stock exchanges through international depository receipts (IDR). If a company would like to be listed, for example, on the New York Stock Exchange, this company has to give a US financial institution its stock in trust and create and issue American depositary receipts (ADR) in the United States. These receipts offer potential holders the same rights as regular shareholders have, including the right to vote. Only this kind of ADR, usually called a sponsored ADR, can be listed on the New York Stock Exchange. Unsponsored ADRs issued by any US financial institution, without official relationships with the foreign company, can also be traded in the US, but only over the counter, such as on the NASDAQ (National Association of Securities Dealers Automated Quotations). The use of these instruments, among others, has expedited the process of global capitalization. Figure 1.25 illustrates the fact that the dynamics of global capitalization would be at least five times slower without the input of BRIC (Brazil, Russia, India, and China)—the leading countries of the

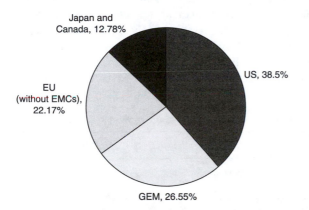

Figure 1.24 Stock Market Capitalization of the GMP, 2006.[113]

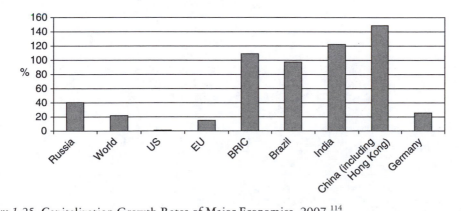

Figure 1.25 Capitalization Growth Rates of Major Economies, 2007.[114]

GEM. The rate of growth of capitalization in developed countries is far below the world average.

In developed countries, net savings as a percentage of GDP is roughly negative 1.25; in EMCs, it is 4.5 percent.[115] This ratio actually represents the current account balances of these categories of countries. As a result, domestic spending in the GEM is closely tied to GDP, which is why budget deficits are decreasing in these countries. Table 1.43 shows major net exporters and importers of capital.

Table 1.44 and Figure 1.26 provide an understanding of the scale, structure, and dynamics of global movements of capital during the first decade of the GEM's maturity, including portfolio and direct investment, and capital in national reserves. International investors still view the GEM as an area suited for direct investment. Rising capitalization of companies and listings in stock exchanges of the GEM is increasing portfolio investments, but at a pace about three times slower than in the United States. As of 2008 the dynamic of capitalization and the inflow of portfolio investment in the GEM do not coincide. Access of public companies from the GEM to international stock exchanges will change this ratio during the second decade of the twenty-first century. Outflow of capital from the GEM to other regions of the GMP will always occur, but with the increasing number of stock exchanges in the GEM and the names of major international companies appearing on these stock exchanges, the outflow in portfolio investment will decrease.

In addition to the integration of regional and national financial systems, unique regional cultural and religious traditions have also been integrated within the global capital market. This has created new challenges for executives and managers from the developed world who are unaccustomed to the idiosyncrasies of certain traditional capital-market practices. The most obvious example is the Islamic prohibition of generating profit from interest. In order to avoid violating this principle, Islamic financiers developed interest-free financial instruments known as *sukuk*. *Sukuk* returns are tied directly to purchased or constructed assets, such as equity in an existing company. The largest *sukuk* market is in Malaysia; it accounts for

Table 1.43 Major Net Exporters and Importers of Capital (Percentage of World Totals), 2006[116]

Major Net Exporters of Capital*, 2006		*Major Net Importers of Capital**, 2006*	
Country	Percentage of Global Capital Exports	Country	Percentage of Global Capital Imports
China	17.3	United States	59.6
Japan	11.8	Spain	7.8
Germany	10.1	United Kingdom	6.5
Saudi Arabia	6.6	Italy	3.3
Russia	6.6	Australia	3
Switzerland	4.6	Turkey	2.3
Netherlands	4	Greece	2.2
Norway	3.8	Other Countries (All with Less than 1.9%)	15.2
Kuwait	2.9		
Singapore	2.5		
United Arab Emirates	2.5		
Algeria	2		
Sweden	1.9		
Other Countries (All with Less than 1.9%)	23.4		

Notes:
* As measured by current account surplus.
** As measured by current account deficit.

Table 1.44 US and GEM Capital Inflows (Billions of $), 1996–2006[117]

United States	1996	1997	1998	1999	2000	2001	2002	2003	2004	2005	2006
Direct Investment	86.5	105.6	179	289.4	321.3	167	84.4	63.8	145.8	109	180.6
Portfolio Investment	332.8	333.1	187.6	285.6	436.6	428.3	427.6	550.2	867.3	832	1017.4
Other Investment	131.8	268.1	57	165.2	289	187.5	285.8	250.4	448.6	263.2	661.6
Total Capital Flows	551.1	423.6	423.6	740.2	1046.9	782.9	797.8	864.4	1461.8	1204.2	1859.6

Emerging-market and Developed Countries	1996	1997	1998	1999	2000	2001	2002	2003	2004	2005	2006
Direct Investment	148.4	191.5	187.4	213.1	211.7	225.5	182.2	199.6	272.8	361.2	422.3
Portfolio Investment	174.7	147	32.2	102.8	93.3	11.7	−10.3	91.2	141.3	214.1	211.9
Other Investment	95.4	141.1	−119.6	−77.7	−8.8	−61.6	1.8	124.7	200.5	146.3	358.9
Total Capital Flows	418.5	479.6	100.1	238.2	296.1	175.5	173.7	415.5	614.5	721.7	993.2

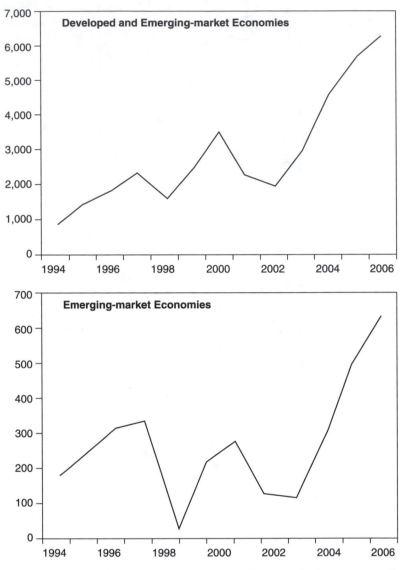

Figure 1.26 Total Capital Inflows to Emerging and Developed Countries (Billions of $), 1994–2006.[118]

two-thirds of outstanding global Islamic bonds with an estimated value of $47 billion.[119] Islamic finance is one of many challenges that capital market executives in EMCs face.

Production Facilities of the Global Marketplace

AUTOMOBILE PRODUCTION FACILITIES

Production facilities and infrastructure are important basic economic factors. For this reason, companies are rarely created in uninhabited islands, deserts, or frozen wastelands. Companies generally need existing transportation or telecommunication infrastructure, nearby human settlements, and existing production facilities. However, with modern technology, even uninhabited islands can access telecommunications infrastructure via satellites. The aim of this section is to underline internationalization and globalization of production facilities. In the GMP of the twenty-first century, it is nearly impossible to find entirely domestic production facilities, technologies without any foreign influence or elements from abroad and infrastructure not internationally connected. The global automobile industry shown in Tables 1.45, 1.46, and 1.47 is a good example of this phenomenon. Out of the 14 major production facilities of light vehicles in North America, 11 originate in Europe or Asia. Even the automobiles assembled in domestically owned production facilities contain at least 30 percent of foreign made parts and components.

Western European automobile production is just as globalized as North America. Out of the fifteen major automobile production facilities in Western Europe, eight are of direct

Table 1.45 North American Light Vehicle Production, December 2007[120]

Manufacturer	Number of Units
BMW Group	155,295
Chrysler Group	2,479,777
Daimler Group	163,468
Ford Group	2,833,230
Fuji Heavy	109,178
General Motors	4,187,635
Honda Group	1,432,731
Hyundai	250,519
Isuzu	6,529
Mitsubishi	82,544
Renault-Nissan Group	1,200,457
Suzuki	31,403
Toyota Group	1,671,009
Volkswagen	405,172
Total North American Production	15,008,947

Source: © J.D. Power Automotive Forecasting. www.jdpowerforecasting.com.

Table 1.46 Western European Passenger-car Assembly, December 2007 (Estimated)[121]

Manufacturer	Number of Units
Aston Martin	7,224
BMW Group	1,336,495
Chrysler Group	83,449
Damlier Group	1,119,760
Fiat Group	921,241
Ford Group	2,242,931
General Motors	1,430,835
Honda	239,440
Mitsubishi	66,808
PSA Group	1,973,138
Porsche	105,052
Renault-Nissan	1,470,168
Suzuki	5,372
Toyota	547,820
Volkswagen Group	2,886,093
Other	15,537
Total W. Europe	14,451,363

Source: © J.D. Power Automotive Forecasting. www.jdpowerforecasting.com.

Table 1.47 Central and Eastern Europe plus Kazakhstan, Russia, and Turkey Passenger-car Assembly, December 2007[122]

Manufacturer	Number of Units
AvtoVAZ	817,415
BMW	4,720
Fiat Group	507,542
Ford	72,870
General Motors	481,969
Honda	22,322
Hyundai Group	397,449
Mercedes-Benz	42
PSA Group	380,566
Dacia	284,761
Renault	460,491
Ssangyong	9,714
Subaru	6,893
Suzuki	195,551
Toyota	271,323
Volkswagen Group	936,895
Other	204,844
Total CEE plus Kazakhstan, Russia, and Turkey	5,055,367

Source: © J.D. Power Automotive Forecasting. www.jdpowerforecasting.com.

Note: Central and Eastern Europe includes Bosnia, Czech Republic, Hungary, Poland, Romania, Slovakia, Slovenia, and Ukraine.

foreign origin. Just as in North America, domestically owned facilities contain a significant number of foreign parts and components.

Automobile production in EMCs has experienced the same trends as in North America and Western Europe. In EMCs, high-quality and high-tech production is almost always a result of international collaboration. Out of the 16 major automobile-production facilities in the emerging markets of Eastern Europe, Russia, Turkey, and Central Asia, 13 are of direct foreign origin, from the US, Western Europe, and Asia. The automobile industry is only one of many that have been substantially globalized. Production facilities of heavy, light, and agricultural industries, low- and high-tech products, services, and industries, are the result of international cooperation and globalization. International cooperation is one of the most important factors in the creation of modern production facilities. Globalization made these facilities available to companies and consumers from all corners of the GMP.

Production facilities of the GMP are experiencing the influence of many political, economic, and global trends. With the increasing role of infrastructure, the role of production facilities as an economic factor is increasing. But it always has to be analyzed together with the most modern basic economic factors, research and technology.

Science, Research, and Technology Capabilities of the Global Marketplace

KNOWLEDGE-BASED ECONOMY

The industrial structure of global production will change radically in the twenty-first century. Science and technology will no longer function only as instruments for other industries; they will become major industries themselves. Over the past 50 years, the world has transitioned from an agriculturally based economy to an industrialized one, and then to a service-based economy. In the twenty-first century, the service-based economy has already started to be replaced by the knowledge-based economy. This will create new opportunities, higher standards of living, and the expansion of economic activity beyond planet Earth through dual and nano-technologies. Of course, the technology of the knowledge-based economy will also present tremendous threats to civilization, as it can be used for war and destruction. The economy of war and the military-industrial complex will unfortunately continue to be an indivisible part of the GMP. Newly empowered countries from the GEM will direct a substantial amount of investment toward this effort.

All of the Nordic states, including Denmark, Finland, Sweden, as well as Switzerland, are considered knowledge-based economies or knowledge economies. Among the top 10 knowledge economies, according to the World Bank's Knowledge Economy Index of 2007 (see Table 1.48), all are developed nations. Of the top 25 countries, according to this index, 7 are from the GEM, Ireland having the highest rank, followed by Taiwan, Hong Kong, and Israel. In these countries, high-tech industry, science, and education generate a substantial segment of the GDP. The position of Israel and Canada would be much higher in this ranking if they were not evaluated so high in another ranking; Israel and Canada are the top countries in terms of the ratio of their scientists who work abroad. The main recipient of these scientists is the United States. According to Professor Dan Ben-David of Tel Aviv University, "the number of Israeli academics in US universities has already reached 25 percent of the scholars still remaining in Israel."[123] The example of Israel and Canada shows how the science- and knowledge-based industries are already an integrated sector of the GMP. In some of the EMCs, such as Hungary[124] and Taiwan, in Table 1.48, knowledge-based technologies have already penetrated economies to the point that they can be considered knowledge-based societies. In February 2007 the European Federation of National Academies of Humanities discussed the role of research in knowledge-based societies, arguing that it should be the "basis for strategies; the instruments—mobility, infrastructure, cooperation—should be tuned in harmony with basic objectives."[125] At the bottom of the Knowledge Economy Index, among the 25 countries are only two (Singapore and Burkina Faso) that this book considers to be EMCs. All others are developing (Bangladesh, Nepal, and Ethiopia) and underdeveloped countries (Haiti and Sierra Leone). The placement of Singapore as the third-to-last country below the likes of Sierra Leone, Rwanda, and Zambia seriously brings into question the methodology of this index.

Technological processes of production are not the only systems that are being changed by the knowledge economy. Technology will soon integrate the human mind in a global network of knowledge. The development of the Internet is the first step in this process. Before the end of the twenty-first century, everyone will be constantly integrated as users and contributors within this network. Unprecedented availability of individual knowledge and experience will create incredible opportunities and serious challenges for human civilization in the GMP.

RESEARCH AND DEVELOPMENT

Research and development (R&D) are a central part of any strategy that seeks future prosperity for a country or company. The results of investments in this field are usually not immediately tangible and are very difficult to measure. There is still not an adequate measurement system to estimate the long-term impact of fundamental science, which produces theoretical results of long-term economic consequences. It takes time to implement the discoveries of groundbreaking and revolutionary studies for the betterment of society.

Table 1.48 The Knowledge Economy Index, 2007[126]

Rank	Country	Rank	Country
1	Sweden	56	Thailand
2	Denmark	57	Armenia
3	Norway	58	Macedonia, FYR
4	Finland	59	Mexico
5	Netherlands	60	Trinidad and Tobago
6	Switzerland	61	Belarus
7	Canada	62	Jordan
8	Australia	63	Oman
9	United Kingdom	64	Mauritius
10	United States	65	Jamaica
11	New Zealand	66	Lebanon
12	Iceland	67	Panama
13	Austria	68	Serbia and Montenegro
14	Ireland	69	Saudi Arabia
15	Germany	70	Moldova
16	Belgium	71	Tunisia
17	Japan	72	Kazakhstan
18	Luxembourg	73	Philippines
19	Taiwan	74	Peru
20	France	75	China
21	Hong Kong	76	Georgia
22	Israel	77	Colombia
23	Slovenia	78	Venezuela
24	Spain	79	Mongolia
25	Estonia	80	Guyana
26	Italy	81	Sri Lanka
27	Korea, South	82	Namibia
28	Hungary	83	Egypt
29	Czech Republic	84	Botswana
30	Cyprus	85	El Salvador
31	Lithuania	86	Bolivia
32	Portugal	87	Kyrgyz Republic
33	Latvia	88	Dominican Republic
34	Greece	89	Azerbaijan
35	Poland	90	Morocco
36	Slovak Republic	91	Indonesia
37	Barbados	92	Uzbekistan
38	Croatia	93	Ecuador
39	Chile	94	Albania
40	Malaysia	95	Paraguay
41	Bulgaria	96	Honduras
42	Qatar	97	Vietnam
43	Uruguay	98	Iran
44	Dominica	99	Algeria
45	Costa Rica	100	Nicaragua
46	Kuwait	101	India
47	Russian Federation	102	Cape Verde
48	Romania	103	Guatemala
49	United Arab Emirates	104	Syrian Arab Republic
50	South Africa	105	Swaziland
51	Ukraine	106	Kenya
52	Bahrain	107	Zimbabwe
53	Turkey	108	Tajikistan
54	Brazil	109	Senegal
55	Argentina	110	Madagascar

111	Lesotho	126	Malawi
112	Uganda	127	Mali
113	Ghana	128	Mozambique
114	**Pakistan**	129	Lao PDR
115	Nigeria	130	Bangladesh
116	Tanzania	131	Nepal
117	Mauritania	132	**Burkina Faso**
118	Benin	133	Eritrea
119	Yemen	134	Rwanda
120	Côte d'Ivoire	135	Djibouti
121	Angola	136	Ethiopia
122	Zambia	137	Sierra Leone
123	Cameroon	138	**Singapore**
124	Sudan	139	Bosnia and Herzegovina
125	Myanmar	140	Haiti

However, every generation is profoundly indebted to past scholars and governmental and business leaders who invested in the future by conducting and financing scientific research. When the British scientist Michael Faraday discovered electromagnetic induction in 1845, everyone (including himself) thought its only practical application was in circus performances. Of course, only a few decades later, thanks to the genius of Thomas Edison, Faraday's discoveries brought light and heat to homes and offices, laying the foundation for the modern economy. Due to the strong influence of scientific achievements on global economic dynamics, the World Bank developed

> a *summary index of technology* that combines a much wider range of indicators than included in other technology indexes. This index is derived from three sub-indexes that measure four dimensions of technological achievement:
>
> - The extent of scientific invention and innovation
> - The diffusion of older technologies
> - The diffusion of newer technologies
> - The intensity with which foreign technologies are employed in domestic production[127]

One of the leading countries in the world in terms of R&D spending as a percentage of GDP is Germany. At the beginning of the new millennium, Germany's prime minister, Angela Merkel, gave special attention to science policy and prepared an editorial about German priorities in scientific strategy. In this editorial she claimed, "By 2010, we aim to increase spending on R&D to 3 percent of gross domestic product. Science and research will be one of the priorities of Germany's European Union (EU) presidency."[128] But by far, the leading country in the world in terms of budgetary expenses on R&D as a percentage of GDP is the EMC—Israel, followed by the Scandinavian countries, then Japan with several other EMCs close behind, such as South Korea, Taiwan, and Singapore.[129] In terms of total expenses on science, research, and development, in 2007 China surpassed Japan and Germany and is second only to the US. Among the top 15 countries in terms of gross domestic expenditure on R&D are also India, South Korea, Taiwan, Russia, and Spain.[130] It has to be clear that the difference in expenses on science between China and the other EMCs are so large that they are barely comparable. For example, Russian spends almost 10 times less than China. Globalization increases international cooperation in this leading economic sector and developed countries, from this perspective, play a very important role in the

Tables 1.49 R&D Performed Abroad by Majority-owned Foreign Affiliates of US Multilateral Corporations (Millions of $)[131]

Economy	1994	1995	1996	1997	1998	1999	2000	2001	2002
All Countries	11,877	12,582	14,039	14,593	14,664	18,144	20,457	19,702	21,151
Asia	1,538	1,569	1,651	1,482	1,298	2,923	3,587	3,908	3,552
China	58	68	63	117	118	553	*	*	*
Mainland	7	13	25	35	52	319	506	*	646
Hong Kong	51	55	38	82	66	214	*	289	*
India	5	5	9	22	23	20	*	26	80
Indonesia	5	9	6	5	4	1	2	3	3
Japan	1,130	1,286	1,333	1,089	962	1,523	1,630	1,507	1,433
Malaysia	27	21	23	32	30	161	218	*	*
Philippines	14	23	14	12	10	31	40	48	50
Singapore	167	63	88	73	62	426	551	755	589
South Korea	17	29	34	41	29	101	143	157	167
Taiwan	110	61	75	84	55	122	143	139	70
Thailand	3	5	5	5	4	7	13	18	22
EU	8,271	8,852	9,386	9,691	10,058	11,900	12,472	11,253	12,142
Other	2,068	2,161	3,002	3,420	3,308	3,321	4,398	4,541	5,457

Notes:
Data is for non-bank overseas majority-owned affiliates of non-bank US parent companies. Majority-owned affiliates are those in which combined ownership of all US parents is more than 50 percent. Data includes R&D performed by affiliates, whether for themselves or others, and excludes R&D expenditures made by others for affiliates. EU includes 12 countries for 1994 and 15 countries thereafter. Data for 2002 is estimated.
* Suppressed to avoid disclosure of confidential information.

global distribution of scientific achievements. One of the major vehicles of this process is multinational corporations, the overwhelming majority of which originated from developed countries such as the US and EU countries. Table 1.49 shows R&D performed abroad by majority-owned foreign affiliates of these corporations.

According to calculations of the World Bank, "technological progress in developing countries between the 1990s and 2000s has been very strong."[132] It is important to underline that in the category of developing countries, in this statistic the leading role is actually played by EMCs, as they are categorized in this book. In EMCs from very different regions of the GEM, such as "Chile, Hungary, and Poland, the overall level of technological achievement increased by more than 125 percent during the 1990s."[133] However, a regional analysis of technological development in the GEM shows that in Asia and Eastern Europe, technological progress is moving much faster than in Latin America, Africa, and the Middle East. In terms of know-how, the GEM is still behind developed countries. In the global know-how market, the United States accounts for 35 percent, Japan—30, Germany—16, and Russia—only 0.3 percent.[134] Disparities in the use of patents and other technologies are shown in Figure 1.27.

An interesting tendency should be underlined: the most modern technologies spread through countries of the GEM at a much faster pace than traditional technologies. For example, Internet bandwidth more than doubled between 1999 and 2004 in middle- and lower-income countries.[135] But, the more and more expensive access is, the slower its dispersion through society.

An entry and development strategic analysis in different areas and industries of the GMP does not need to go through the same order of basic economic factors as presented in this chapter. For example, an analysis of high-tech industries has to begin with the last

Indexes, High-income Countries = 100

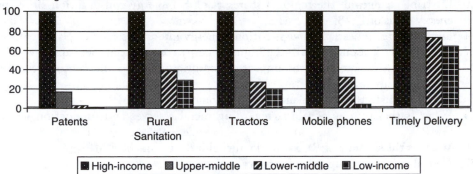

Figure 1.27 Disparities in Use of Patents and Various Technologies, 2004.[136]

(and most modern) basic economic factor, science, research, and technology. Regions and countries rich with natural resources and industries related to these resources must be analyzed with a starting point of territory and natural resources. However, any strategic analysis related to bringing businesses to a new country or region, or to increase one's presence there, should go through an analysis of all basic economic factors, followed by an analysis of major elements of management systems in these regions, countries, and industries.

Study Questions

1. What is the GMP?
2. What is the difference between the GMP and the world economy?
3. What role did technological progress play in the formation of the GMP?
4. What kind of integrated economic indicators are best to use for a strategic evaluation of the GMP?
5. What is the role of the GEM and developed countries in the GMP?
6. Why is PPP a useful indicator for a strategic evaluation of the GMP?
7. Describe the dynamics of the industrial structure of the GMP.
8. How can the Leontief method be used to analyze the GMP?
9. What are basic economic factors?
10. What are the most important modern basic economic factors?
11. What are the most important natural resources for the development of the world economy in the twenty-first century?
12. Why will the factor of freshwater resources increase in the GMP?
13. What is an example of international cooperation on the equitable use of freshwater resources?
14. What is the role of energy in the GMP of the twenty-first century?
15. Describe the dynamic of energy consumption in parts of the GMP.
16. Describe the global distribution of energy reserves. Are they equally allocated throughout the GMP?
17. What are the major sources of energy in the GMP? Describe their regional distribution.
18. Why will the global balance of fuel use and production change substantially by 2020?

19. What are the major sources of electricity generation in the GMP?
20. Describe changes in the regional shares of global energy consumption since the energy crisis of 1973.
21. Describe the highest and lowest national energy intensities.
22. What kinds of countries have the highest energy consumption per capita?
23. Describe the dynamics of the impact of energy production and consumption on the global environment.
24. Describe the factor of metals in the development of the GMP.
25. What is the strategy of China regarding metal reserves and production in the GMP?
26. What is the strategy of Russia in the nickel industry in the GMP?
27. Describe the changing role of forestry in the GMP.
28. Describe the correlation between large national forestry reserves and the production of timber and paper.
29. How do labor resources affect a country's ability to attract FDI?
30. What kinds of countries have the most rapidly declining national populations?
31. What are the implications of a very young national population for the development of a company's strategy?
32. What kind of countries have the highest literacy rate?
33. What is the Gini coefficient, and how can it be used for a strategic evaluation of a country's stability and attractiveness for FDI?
34. Describe the correlation between working hours and the productivity of labor and how this ratio influences a company's entry strategy for EMCs.
35. Describe the Asian financial crisis.
36. What is the influence on the global monetary and financial systems of the integration of EMCs in the GMP?
37. Why do EMCs have large foreign currency reserves?
38. Describe the strategy of the United States regarding foreign currency and gold reserves.
39. Describe the dynamics of the changing assets of commercial banks in the GMP.
40. Describe the dynamics of the capitalization of the GMP. Which countries have the fastest-growing rates of capitalization and why?
41. How does religion in some emerging markets influence the traditional use of capital-market instruments?
42. What is the major trend of the development of production facilities in the GMP?
43. Describe the new role of science and technology in the economy of the twenty-first century.
44. What is the Knowledge Economy Index and how can it be useful for investment strategy?
45. What kind of measure of technological development was introduced by the World Bank, and how can it be useful for a strategic analysis?

2 The Global Emerging Market

If we began with certainties, we shall end in doubts, but if we begin with doubts, and are patient in them, we shall end in certainties.[1]

(Francis Bacon, English philosopher and lord high chancellor of Great Britain, 1561–1626)

All the like us are We,
And everyone else is They.
And They live over the sea,
While We live over the way.
But—would you believe it?—
They look upon We
As only a sort of They.[2]

(Rudyard Kipling, English author and 1907 Nobel Prize winner in literature, 1865–1936)

Keynote Definitions

Emerging-market country: An emerging-market country (EMC) is a society transitioning from a dictatorship to a free-market-oriented economy, with increasing economic freedom, gradual integration within the GMP and with other members of the GEM, an expanding middle class, improving standards of living, social stability and tolerance, as well as an increase in cooperation with multilateral institutions.

Global emerging market: The global emerging market (GEM) is a new economic and political phenomenon of the GMP, encompassing EMCs and their regional blocs, which, despite varying geopolitical characteristics, are united by comparable levels of risk and developing free-market infrastructure. These factors of the GEM unify vectors of development of EMCs toward economic freedom and global integration, attracting international economic and business cooperation and competition.

Despite the fact that it has existed for about 25 years, this is the first published definition of the GEM. Economists and strategists are to a certain extent like astronomers. Astronomers do not create stars and planets; they discover, describe, and name them. Economists and strategists do their best to discover new or unrecognized trends, economic phenomena, opportunities and threats, and to explain correlations between them, describe their characteristics, and use them to increase efficiency of companies and the prosperity of nations.

Preconditions for the Birth of the Global Emerging Market

Historical Precedents of the Creation of Emerging Economies

Human civilization has gone through several turning points in history. These crucial mile-stones were almost always marked by the expansion of the frontiers of major civilizations into unknown or barely known countries and uninhabited territories, from the time of Alexander the Great and his "expeditions" deep into Asia, to the borders of Punjab; to the extension of the Roman Empire to Africa and Britain; the creation of the empires of Genghis Kahn and Tamerlane (who unified Central Asia for the first time); and to the opening of the "New World" by Columbus, among other great geographical explorations. These expeditions throughout Eurasia and the Americas spurred the emergence of new economies and subsequent opportunities and challenges.

Leaders tend to think that the borders and new frontiers of their empires will last forever. Alexander, for example, assumed that the "fusion" of his people's culture with that of conquered nations would maintain the borders of his empire. The Spanish and Portuguese royalty assumed that the economic resources and markets of the Americas would always be under the control of their protectionist duopoly. Of course, global orders never last forever. In just the twentieth century, for example, the global order went through three drastic changes: the global order prior to World War I, between the two World Wars, and after World War II.

In December 1975, the US, Canada, and the countries of Western Europe met with the Soviet Union at the Conference on Security and Cooperation in Europe. From this confer-ence, the Helsinki Accords, signed by 35 countries, officially recognized the territorial integrity and sovereignty of all European states, acknowledging and seemingly condoning the expansion of the Soviet Union into Eastern Europe following World War II. Of course, within less than two decades, the Berlin Wall fell, and the Soviet empire disintegrated into 15 independent states (all of which have since become members of the UN), radically altering the global order. During the same general period, dictatorships throughout the world, including those in Greece (1973), Spain (1975), Turkey (1982), Argentina (1982), and Brazil (1985), and the personal dictatorships of Ferdinand Marcos in the Philippines (1986) and of Alfredo Stroessner in Paraguay (1989) failed. People and political and busi-ness leaders who assumed that past global orders would become the permanent status quo ignored a basic strategic principle: nothing lasts forever. Strategists always have to try to discover and evaluate new trends with the potential to change the political, economic, and business order and redesign their strategies accordingly.

Economic and Philosophical Inevitability of the Failure of Dictatorships and Command Economies

The overwhelming majority of people living under dictatorships were isolated from the world beyond their national borders. Travel and most forms of communication (mail, radio, television, etc.) were severely restricted. Only high-level government officials and their relatives and cronies were able to see first-hand the lifestyles and standard of living enjoyed by people in free societies. In return for this privilege, as well as access to consumer and luxury goods from capitalist countries, and in order to maintain their own power, these bureaucrats endorsed the official propaganda about their "imperialist enemies."

But why was access to foreign-made goods such a coveted privilege of the top-level bureaucrats and decision-makers of dictatorships (this was correctly referred to as the *Nomenklatura* in countries of the Soviet bloc—a term that can be used for any dictatorship)?

Why did people living under dictatorships prefer used foreign cars to new domestic ones? Indeed, why did most dictatorships not even attempt to produce cars or other sophisticated consumer goods?

Command-economy dictatorships were incapable of producing these high-quality and technologically advanced goods because of the direct relationship between motivation and the availability of goods and services on one side of the equation, and freedom and variations in the quality of goods and services on the other. These relationships are the source of the fundamental distinction between command-economy dictatorships and free-market economies. Quality of life (or standard of living) is determined by the availability of quality goods and services appropriate to varying individual preferences and needs. The production of high-quality goods and services requires a high quality of labor. High-quality labor is the result of effective motivation throughout the process of production. Effective motivation, in turn, helps ensure attentive, thorough, and professional workers. A fundamental ideal of communism and a staple of all command economies is the equality of wages, salaries, and other forms of remuneration regardless of a worker's level of output. This practice removes effective incentives for worker efficiency, innovation, or leadership, and often even integrity. When motivation is removed from the process of production, the result is low-quality labor, goods, and services, and subsequently, a much lower quality of life. Furthermore, there is also a constant deficit of the various goods and services required by different individuals, which negatively affects quality of life. Consumers totally lack options. This absence of consumer choice allows goods and services to be produced and consumed, regardless of their quality. The inevitable poverty and low quality of life of command economies and dictatorships are tangible results of the suppression of motivation. Most important, beyond the political-repression characteristic of dictatorships, the results of a lack of motivation repress the freedom of individuals to make choices that determine the quality of their lives. This is the structural weakness of command economies and dictatorships as well as the fundamental distinction between them and free-market democracies.

If a dictatorship were to introduce motivation to the production processes via differentiated remuneration that reflects productive input, the ensuing variation in product quality and standards of living as well as consumer's freedom of choice would seriously contradict the ideology and relevance of the dictatorship. This introduction inevitably leads to the destruction of the dictatorship or at the very least a major revision of its ideology, such as the Chinese Communist Party's embrace of free-market principles.

Why do dictatorships always repress free thinkers? The answer to this question was given by the great philosopher Jean-Paul Sartre, Nobel laureate in literature and one of the founders of existentialism. In the following quote from *Les Mouches* (*The Flies*), King Aegistheus describes how destructive freedom can be to dictatorships: "A man who is free is like a mangy sheep in a herd. He will contaminate my entire kingdom and ruin my work."[3] Individual freedom of choice is the defining quality of a free society; any ruling structure that represses this freedom sows the seeds of its own destruction. The blunt names of the stores in the Siberian city of Krasnoyarsk illustrate the lack of freedom of choice and constant deficit of goods in dictatorships: "Meat" or "Fish"; "Shoes," "Dress," "Furniture," etc. One particular store, when it first opened in the 1960s, was called "Meat-Fish." When the shortage of meat became severe, the name changed to "Fish-Chicken." When there was a shortage of fish, the store was renamed "Chicken-Eggs," then both words disappeared for the same reason and the name was changed to "Vegetable-Fruits." Finally, it was called only "Vegetables." A more accurate name would have been "Potato-Cabbage."

In addition to ensuring an impoverished and miserable material existence for the majority of the populace, the anemic economic performance of command economies makes it increasingly difficult for the self-appointed leadership to maintain power. Poverty, combined with a lack of freedom, repression of minorities, government-sponsored nationalism and intoler-ance, and economic as well as political self-isolation create conditions that cannot be endured for very long, and that almost inevitably lead to democratic change. The form of these changes varies from country to country. However, in general, democratic changes began to occur during the same period, due to the influence of one of the most powerful global trends—democratization. The convergence of this trend with globalization and revolutions in global IT made it practically impossible for the overwhelming majority of dictatorships to resist democratic pressures. It is important, however, to point out that there are exceptions to this scenario. Dictatorships in unusually wealthy countries, typically with smaller populations, can maintain control for longer periods, primarily due to income derived from the sale of natural resources. Dictatorships and repressive regimes financed by petrodollars are an obvious present-day example. But the recent example of Iraq shows that even oil-rich dictatorships cannot last forever. Nevertheless, in most command-economy dictatorships, it becomes practically impossible to generate the revenue necessary to dominate, appease, and/or placate the public. But it was the dramatic improvement in ITs, an external factor completely beyond the control of any government, that has made it exceedingly difficult for dictatorships to exist and will likely be the proverbial nail in the coffin. Dictatorships' ability to control information has been seriously compromised. Global communication systems made it exceedingly difficult for dictators to keep their populations isolated from and ignorant to the superior standard of living that exists in free-market democracies. This was the beginning of the end for the majority of dictatorships throughout the world. Two obvious exceptions to this trend are China and Vietnam. The communist parties of these two countries introduced economic freedom and motivation to the productive process and allowed foreign investment. Subsequently, the quality of goods and services and standard of living has improved steadily in these two countries. However, in most dictatorships political unrest led to the eventual replacement of dictatorial regimes with elected leaders, democratic governments, and economic freedom. The newly elected leaders looked abroad for proven methods to create economic growth and improve the standard of living. This led to a wave of market-oriented economic reforms, the appearance of the first modern EMCs, and eventually to a new economic and political phenomenon, the GEM. In any emerging-market democracy, in order for a political regime to be sustainable, its major strategic concept should include preferences that reflect the basic needs and choices of the public. In the words of Dr Alexander Nekipelov "the problem of public preferences influence upon the strategy of economic development of a country is a permanent one."[4]

The Global Emerging Market

Initial Understanding of the Global Emerging Market as a New Economic and Political Phenomenon

The creation of the GEM cannot be given a precise date of birth. The terms "emerging stock markets" and "emerging markets" first appeared in financial literature at the end of the 1980s to describe stock, equity, debt, and security markets outside of developed countries.[5] At that time there were already 43 countries outside of the developed world with stock exchanges, and the term "emerging stock markets" referred mostly to markets in these countries. However, there were no terms used to describe the maturity of national econ-omies until the 1990s. This initial terminology demonstrated a vague understanding of the development of EMCs but not of the GEM and lacked a real theoretical framework. For example, the International Finance Corporation (IFC) considers all countries with a

GNI per capita below the World Bank's minimum requirement for high-income countries to be emerging markets (see current classifications below).[6] (For a more detailed analysis of classification systems of major multilateral institutions, see Chapter 4.) The current classification of countries by the World Bank according to 2006 annual GNI per capita is as follows:[7]

- Low Income: < $905
- Lower Middle Income: $905 to $3,595
- Upper Middle Income: $3,595 to $11,115
- High Income: > $11,115

When the IFC, by the initiative of Antoine van Agtmael, renamed the Third World Database the Emerging Market Database[8] (which would later appear as two indices: the S&P/IFC Investable Emerging Markets Index covering 22 markets, and the S&P/IFC Global Index, which covers 33 markets[9]), it incorrectly equated these two terms. Nonetheless, it was a step in the right direction toward recognizing the birth of a new economic phenomenon, which was later described as the GEM.[10]

Any attempt to classify a national economy purely by the above-mentioned limited financial approach does not explain the distinctions between different categories of non-developed countries. There are fundamental differences between those countries that have become an important part of the GMP (all categories of EMCs—economies in bloom, emerging-market democracies, oligarchic emerging markets, emerging-market dictatorships, and to a limited extent, pre-emerging markets) and those that still are not a comfortable option for foreign and even domestic businesses (developing and under-developed countries). Developing countries are in the early stages of opening up for international business, while underdeveloped countries typically have economic and business agendas that are not conducive to international business activity whatsoever. Even at the beginning of the twenty-first century, the unique needs and characteristics of EMCs and both developing and underdeveloped countries are ignored by most country classifications. Ignoring these distinctions distorts the conclusions and results of studies of the GMP. For example, a 2006 special report on EMCs in the *Economist*[11] arbitrarily blurs the lines between emerging-market, developing, and underdeveloped countries into one category, rendering all of the survey's statistics inaccurate. Due to a lack of understanding of the distinctions between EMCs and developing countries, the real emerging-market economies appeared to be less efficient than they were in reality, as the population and economies of developing and underdeveloped countries falsely augmented the population of the GEM. This also falsely reduced the productivity of labor and GDP per capita of EMCs (see Chapter 4 for a detailed analysis of current country classification systems and their flaws).

Unlike EMCs, developing and underdeveloped countries still need special attention from multilateral institutions and aid associations to prevent starvation, mass disease, and politi-cal instability. Developing countries need special attention from the international com-munity to improve their education systems, because the quality of these systems has very important implications for the future of these countries—as well as the pace of economic and political reform. They need assistance in the formation of their national economic strategies, with the goal of transitioning into the GEM. This is also an important mission of companies from developed countries and EMCs. Companies from EMCs can be especially helpful to those in developing countries, as they have a great deal of experience operating in conditions of non-developed markets. For example, China is playing an instrumental role in strategy development in Nigeria, as is Taiwan in Swaziland.

Ratings and Evaluations of the Maturity of Emerging-market Countries

A single indicator, even one as integrated as GNI or GDP per capita, cannot adequately categorize an EMC. It is very important to consider the vector of change of GNI per capita. Obviously, the pace and direction of a statistic such as GNI per capita has significant implications for a country's economic maturation. There are examples of countries that were once categorized as EMCs that have reverted to the developing and/or underdeveloped category. Take Uzbekistan and Venezuela, where the government changed the political and economic course and attitude toward international cooperation. However, even describing a country solely in terms of the vector of GNI per capita will not give an adequate basis to analyze economic maturity or a sufficient basis upon which to determine the correct categorization of development. A much more comprehensive analysis is required, such as the Strategic Comprehensive Country Classification System described in Chapter 4.

The first periodicals dedicated specifically to the study of EMCs were introduced at the World Economic Development Congress and the Joint Annual Meeting of the World Bank and IMF in October 1994 in Madrid.

The international community specifically focused its attention on EMCs in October 1995 at the World Economic Development Forum and the Joint Annual Meeting of the World Bank and IMF in Washington, DC.

Also in 1995, the US Department of Commerce and the International Trade Administration demonstrated an understanding of the new role of EMCs and organized a seminar called "Beyond Borders: Big Emerging Markets." The seminar listed Argentina, Brazil, China, Hong Kong, Mexico, Poland, Turkey, South Korea, South Africa, and Taiwan. Initially, experts debated over what exactly qualified as an EMC. Furthermore, the fact that EMCs were part of a global phenomenon—the GEM—was scarcely understood at all. Unique historical legacies make the countries of the GEM a diverse bunch, and the level of economic and political freedom and standards of living vary a great deal among them. Nevertheless, EMCs can be grouped together because of a present orientation and a long-term trend toward economic freedom and integration with the GMP. While some EMCs may temporarily veer off course (such as Venezuela, Bolivia, Zimbabwe, Belarus, and, until 2007, Turkmenistan), and the pace of progress varies, all paths in the GEM eventually lead to economic and political freedom and improved standards of living.

In order to determine the level of a country's economic maturity, its level of integration into the GMP, and whether or not it can be categorized as an EMC, strategists should consult several sources. There are a multitude of sources for data, including multilateral institutions, rating agencies, and various research organizations; the key to successfully understanding EMCs, the GEM, and the GMP is the ability to critically analyze and compare data, evaluations, and opinions from multiple sources. It is also important to understand the rationale behind the differences in ratings and opinions from various agencies regarding the same country, industry, or company. In the end strategists must draw their own conclusion regarding the status of a national economy. There are a number of organizations and agencies that regularly publish ratings and/or data that can be strategically analyzed to decide the maturity of a country. Among them are the World Bank Group (http://www.worldbank.org/), Moody's (http://www.moodys.com/cust/default.asp), Standard and Poor's (S&P) (www.standardandpoors.com), Fitch (http://www.fitch.com/), Dun and Bradstreet (www.dnb.com), the Heritage Foundation (www.heritage.org), the *Wall Street Journal* (www.wsj.com), the Economist Intelligence Unit (www.eiu.com), the Morgan Stanley Capital International Barra (MSCI Barra) (www.mscibarra.com), and others.

The World Bank Group and IMF regularly update the World Development Indicators (www.worldbank.org) and the World Economic Outlook Database, International Financial

Statistics, and Direction of Trade Statistics, among others (www.imf.org). The World Economic Forum, an annual meeting of political and economic leaders and experts from a number of fields, annually publishes its *Global Competitiveness Report* (www.weforum.org), which measures "the set of institutions, policies, and factors that set the sustainable current and medium-term levels of economic prosperity"[12] of national economies. The International Institute for Management Development (IMD) (www.imd.ch), a Swiss business school, publishes a similar annual report, *The World Competitiveness Yearbook*, which ranks national economies based on how they create and sustain the competitiveness of enterprises. There are also a number of organizations that release rankings of economic freedom annually. The Hong Kong Center for Economic Research's annual report on the *Economic Freedom of the World* and the *Index of Economic Freedom* (www.heritage.org), published annually by the *Wall Street Journal* and the *Heritage Foundation* are two of the most widely respected. Each year Transparency International publishes the *Global Corruption Report* (www.globalcorruptionreport.org), which is a reliable indicator of the openness of an economy and demonstrates its level of economic and political freedom. Major rating agencies are an excellent source of data that can be used to determine the degree to which a country is developing. S&P's offers independent national credit ratings, international indices, and risk evaluation, in addition to other extensive research. When it comes to sovereign credit risk, S&P's opinion is especially useful. This rating is so widely respected that it influences corporate credit ratings in the country where the sovereign credit risk evaluation occurs. S&P basically issues an opinion regarding possible future scenarios in a country or of a company that it is evaluating. Fitch provides a number or ratings, such as the Country Ceiling Ratings, which indicate transfer and convertibility risk. The International Credit Ratings reflect a government's ability to meet foreign or local currency commitments. Moody's has offices throughout the world in developed countries as well as in EMCs, such as Hong Kong and Singapore. One index with particularly important implications for EMCs is Moody's National Scale Ratings, which assigns an evaluation to "certain countries in which investors have found the global rating scale provides inadequate differentiation among credits or is inconsistent with a rating scale already in common use in the country."[13] Dun and Bradstreet is one of the best sources for information on particular companies that work with or within the GEM. The United States Trade Representative publishes the annual *National Trade Estimate Report on Foreign Trade Barriers* (www.ustr.gov), which is a very good indicator of a country's openness to international business activity and to its overall economic maturity. Similar agencies from other countries can also provide useful information on EMCs. The *globalEDGE*,[14] a web site of the International Business Center of Michigan University, is also a useful source. Since 2002 it has published an index and rankings that evaluate countries considered to be emerging markets by *The Economist*. Of course, all of these ratings have to be reevaluated with one's own critical analysis and compared with those of other agencies. For example, in the *globalEDGE* rating, China correctly shifted from the fifth-ranked EMC in 2002 into the no. 1 position in 2007. But the market potential indicator does not reflect the progress that India and Brazil have made; both fell in the rankings, as did South Korea, one of the most efficient EMCs in economic terms. It is also very hard to believe that Brazil is ranked below Pakistan, Saudi Arabia, and Russia, and that Russia has a lower rating for economic freedom than Hugo Chavez's Venezuela. The fact that Taiwan was not rated until 2005 (it was ranked fourth) brings into question the accuracy of all previous rankings. Most agencies also missed the signs pointing to a 2008 financial crisis. Nevertheless, the indexes incorporate the opinion of several professional publications and should not be ignored.

Strategists must compare the rankings of different agencies, find discrepancies, and understand the reasons behind them. In order to do so, one must have a great deal of theoretical and practical knowledge. It is absolutely crucial to underline the fact that all of the agencies and organizations mentioned above lack clearly defined country-classification systems upon which to base their ratings, forecasts, evaluations, etc. As a result, strategists must be very careful when these organizations and agencies describe groups of countries, such as EMCs, developing or developed countries. These categories are almost never well defined and/or based on a comprehensive methodology, which distorts the results and conclusions of these organizations and agencies regarding specific country groups. The classification system presented in Chapter 4 should be used to help organize and strategically analyze data received from the above-mentioned agencies, organizations, and institutions.

It is important to analyze not only absolute ranks of countries but also the relative rank of a country compared with others. Strategists should compare the opinions of domestic and foreign experts and analyze any discrepancies. Due to the fact that EMCs benefit from being ranked by major rating agencies—it attracts investment—many governments respond to the requirements of the major agencies. This is a direct and positive impact of rating agencies on the economic and financial situation of a country and the world. Investors can benefit from this by developing a strategy oriented to entering a country that it expects to be ranked by a major rating agency. Once the country appears on this list, its assets will immediately increase in market value.

Major Characteristics of an Emerging-market Country

What are the major requirements and characteristics that a country must have or achieve in order to be qualified as a part of the GEM? First of all, it is important to note that the process of acquiring the necessary characteristics is non-linear. As an economy develops into an EMC and continues to mature, some characteristics are gained, others are lost. From the beginning of the practical use of the term "emerging markets" by financiers, economists, and business executives (even before the creation of the term EMC), there has always been a need to understand the general characteristics of this economic phenomenon. It was especially necessary because initially, when the term was not clearly defined, "emerging stock market" and "emerging market" were used interchangeably. A typical example can be found in Margaret M. Price's (1993) *Emerging Stock Markets: A Complete Investment Guide to New Markets Around the World*. In the section "Characteristics of Emerging Markets," the author states that emerging markets "include countries experiencing or having the potential for high economic growth but facing substantial political, economic and/or market-specific risks."[15] The author's characteristics are clearly not specific enough to differentiate emerging markets from other categories of national economies. It is also important to remember that none of the key characteristics remains static in a growing national economy. Below is a list of major characteristics that all EMCs have, had, or will have at some stage during their process of economic maturation and development. While it is not necessary for all of the below characteristics to be present for a national economy to be considered an EMC, all EMCs experience the following characteristics and processes at some point in their development.

The list below shows 45 major characteristics of an EMC:

1. A difficult search for the path to democracy from dictatorship.
2. A rapid transition from a command economy to a free-market economy.
3. Often, but not always, an increasing level of political freedom.
4. A rapidly increasing level of economic freedom.
5. A brief anarchic period during the initial transition from a dictatorship to a free-market economy, which quickly ends as law and order is better enforced.
6. The replacement of a one-party system with a multiparty system (unless there were multiple parties under the dictatorship).

7. The emergence of a more transparent society.
8. An initial increase in corruption but a decrease in nepotism, and an eventual reduction of both as transparency increases.
9. The replacement of the legal framework of the dictatorship with a free-market-oriented legal system that protects private property and interests.
10. Poor protection of intellectual property rights.
11. A reduction in the differences of legal treatment of foreign and domestic businesses.
12. An initial rise in crime followed by a gradual improvement of law and order as the government gains strength.
13. A rapidly changing legal, business, and economic environment that makes investment risky, even when these changes have a positive vector.
14. A transition from a society in which rulers are above the law, to a government that is accountable to the law and society.
15. A search for spiritual tolerance and unification of different political and ethnic groups based on a rising interest in historical roots and national memories.
16. Decentralization of many economic functions from the national government to regional and local authorities.
17. Large-scale privatization.
18. Increasing productivity of labor.
19. Increasing economic growth, usually at a faster rate that the average of the GMP.
20. Deregulation of the creation and operation of businesses and other legal entities.
21. Establishment of free-market institutions such as commercial and investment banks; insurance companies; auditing, accounting, and legal-services firms, etc.
22. Creation and development of capital-market institutions (stock, currency, and commodity exchanges, trust and custodian organizations, security and exchange oversight bodies, etc.).
23. Increasing convertibility of national currency.
24. Gradual integration with other members of the GEM and the GMP.
25. Manifestations of the global trend of regionalization via increasing economic cooperation in regional blocs, and on a multi- and bilateral basis.
26. Integration of domestic regional economies within the national economy, but at a slower rate than the integration of the national economy with foreign economies, especially of developed countries.
27. Removal of the majority of remaining dictatorial restrictions on foreign investment.
28. An influx of FDI that gradually replaces foreign aid.
29. An outflow of domestic and, periodically (especially during a crisis), foreign capital.
30. Diversification from an economy predominantly oriented to natural resources and raw materials to more sophisticated and high-tech industries and services.
31. Decreasing role of the production of raw materials in GDP and exports.
32. An increasing national and personal emphasis on ecology and green technologies.
33. A general move toward a more efficient, consumer-based economic structure.
34. An expansion of the tourism and hospitality industries.
35. Increasing number and role of small and medium-size companies.
36. The existence of a positive trade balance, initially a result of inability to afford imports. As the economy matures, there is a growing need for more sophisticated goods and services that cannot be produced domestically. In general, the poorer the EMC, the more positive the trade balance.
37. Development and expansion of the middle class.
38. A proportion of roughly 15 percent to 20 percent of the population lives below the poverty line.

39. An increase in income disparities and inequality during the initial development of a market economy.
40. An increase in emigration of blue-collar workers as well as scholars and scientists (the brain drain) when national borders are first opened. Many return later, when the economy and level of freedom improve.
41. Improvements in the industrial infrastructure, telecommunications, transportation, and energy-distribution networks with significant governmental investment.
42. An exponential increase in the development of the telecom and IT industries as the demand for access to information increases dramatically.
43. A higher level of general education than in developing and underdeveloped countries and a lower level of illiteracy.
44. A major deficit of financial professionals, but a tremendous increase in the interest of students in economic and financial studies, as well as a dramatic improvement in these areas of education.
45. An increase in the acceptance of English as the language of business in parallel with local languages.

These 45 major characteristics of an EMC can be used as a checklist to evaluate if a particular country belongs to the GEM or not. However, as previously stated, a country does not need to exhibit all of these characteristics at a given time to be considered an EMC.

A critical mass of these major characteristics creates a comfortable and often attractive environment for global business, foreign investment, and international trade. Based on this understanding, it is possible to define two business, economic, and political phenomena: an *emerging-market country* and the *global emerging market*.

Classification of Emerging-market Countries

It is important to understand that there are 83 different EMCs in the world economy. However, there is only one GEM, which is a subset of the GMP. The GEM is in constant cooperation with other subsets of the GMP, i.e. developed, developing, and underdeveloped countries. In the majority of cases, EMCs differ greatly from one another in terms of their maturity, economic and industrial structure, and the development of a middle class and democratic institutions, etc. They can be classified by several different methods. The following classification categorizes EMCs based on their level of maturity during the transition from developing to developed countries (see Figure 2.1). It does not mean that every EMC has to go through the below stages of transition. Each EMC has its own "starting point." The starting point of a country considered an oligarchic emerging market may have been an emerging-market dictatorship, while another country may have started as a developing country—the category prior to the first stage of the emerging-market group of countries. In the end all EMCs are headed toward the same goal: becoming a developed country.

The GEM consists of a variety countries, some of which never before existed in history as independent states (Kazakhstan, Kosovo, etc.) or briefly existed for a very short period (Ukraine) as well as countries that have had statehood for thousands of years, such as India, China, and Russia. Regardless of the various histories of these EMCs, all of them have only recently developed conditions conducive to international business activity, and thus have only recently become part of the GEM.

A typical mistake is to combine the terms "EMC" and "GEM" to create the pseudo-term, "global emerging markets." An example of this pseudo-term can be found in the name of companies such as Global Emerging Markets (http://www.gemny.com/) and in academic databases such as the Global Emerging Market Database (http://www.pitt.edu/~ibcmod/

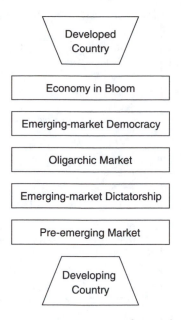

Figure 2.1 EMC Classification by Socioeconomic Maturity.

gem/), which on its homepage uses the correct term, "GEM," and the wrong term, "GEMs," interchangeably. It is very important for future analysis to understand that there is only one GEM. It is global and cannot be plural.

With the increasing economic and political power of EMCs and their regional blocs and improving levels of political stability and democracy, the role of the GEM is growing in the GMP. While in a given EMC, democracy may not be growing, it definitely is in the GEM in general. The overwhelming majority of EMCs are democratizing and liberalizing their societies. Most EMCs are also diversifying their national economies, although this trend is occurring at a slower pace. While not every EMC is undergoing this process, the majority of EMCs are transitioning from mono-industry economies dominated by a single industry, or from an inefficient industrial structure to a more efficient, diversified economy. This process requires tremendous investment and political will. Some EMCs, such as Argentina, Brazil, the Philippines, and Egypt, had a few major free-market institutions—commercial and investment banks and accounting and law firms—even prior to the internationalization of their economies. However, in general, EMCs are in the early stages of creating these institutions. Not all EMCs are constantly experiencing a high speed of economic development, but the GEM as a whole is. EMCs can have very different GDP per capita and, as a result, very different standards of living. In some cases the standard of living of an EMC may be closer to standards of developed countries, while in other cases, the standard of living may be comparable to that of a developing country. However, the GEM average GDP per head and standard of living are unique to the GEM, i.e. below those of developed countries and above those of developing countries. It is important to realize that the GEM as a whole has specific characteristics that may differ from individual EMC members of the GEM.

The GEM, as previously stated, is a new phenomenon. Professionals, experts, and even special publications dedicated to this subject often have conflicting opinions as to which countries qualify as part of the GEM. Table 2.1 shows the opinion of major periodicals dedicated to EMCs. (The opinion of *The Economist* appears in this table because until January

Table 2.1 EMC Classifications According to Professional Publications

Europe	The Emerging Markets Monitor		JP Morgan Emerging Markets Economic Outlook		S&P's Emerging Markets		Emerging Markets Investor		The Economist		Total	Change from 1994–2001
Date	94	01	94	01	94	01	94	01	94	01		
Bulgaria	x	x	x								3	
Czech Republic	x	x	x		x		x	x	x	x	8	−1
Greece			x		x		x	x	x		5	
Hungary	x	x	x		x		x	x	x	x	8	
Poland	x	x	x				x	x	x	x	7	
Portugal	x	x	x		x				x		5	−1
Russia	x	x	x				x	x	x	x	7	
Turkey	x	x	x		x		x	x	x	x	8	
Romania	x	x						x			3	+1
Slovakia	x	x			x						3	

Latin America	The Emerging Markets Monitor		JP Morgan Emerging Markets Economic Outlook		S&P's Emerging Markets		Emerging Markets Investor		The Economist		Total	Change from 1994–2001
Date	94	01	94	01	94	01	94	01	94	01		
Argentina	x	x	x		x		x	x	x	x	8	
Brazil	x	x	x				x	x	x	x	7	
Cuba								x			1	+1
Chile	x	x	x		x		x	x	x	x	8	
Colombia	x	x	x		x		x	x		x	7	
Ecuador			x				x	x			3	
Mexico	x	x	x		x		x	x	x	x	8	
Peru	x	x	x				x	x	x		6	
Panama					x						1	
Uruguay					x						1	
Venezuela	x	x	x		x		x	x	x	x	8	

Asia/Pacific

Asia/Pacific	The Emerging Markets Monitor		JP Morgan Emerging Markets Economic Outlook		S&P's Emerging Markets		Emerging Markets Investor		The Economist		Total	Change from 1994–2001
Date	94	01	94	01	94	01	94	01	94	01		
Bangladesh	x							x			2	
China	x	x	x		x		x	x	x	x	8	
Hong Kong	x	x	x				x	x	x	x	7	
India	x	x	x		x		x	x	x	x	8	
Indonesia	x	x	x		x		x	x	x	x	8	
South Korea	x	x	x		x		x	x	x	x	8	
Malaysia	x	x	x		x		x	x	x	x	8	+1
Mongolia								x		x	1	+1
Pakistan		x					x	x		x	3	
Philippines	x	x	x		x		x	x	x	x	8	
Singapore	x	x	x				x	x	x	x	7	
Taiwan (ROC)	x	x	x		x		x	x	x	x	8	
Thailand	x	x	x		x		x	x	x	x	8	
Vietnam	x	x					x	x			2	

Africa/Middle East

Africa/Middle East	The Emerging Markets Monitor		JP Morgan Emerging Markets Economic Outlook		S&P's Emerging Markets		Emerging Markets Investor		The Economist		Total	Change from 1994–2001
Date	94	01	94	01	94	01	94	01	94	01		
Africa												
Algeria										x	1	+1
Cote d'Ivoire	x			x							2	
Egypt	x			x			x		x		4	
Morocco	x			x			x	x			4	
Nigeria	x			x			x	x			4	
South Africa	x	x	x	x			x	x	x	x	8	
Middle East												
Israel		x	x	x						x	4	+1
Saudi Arabia								x		x	2	+2
Kuwait								x			1	+1
Iran								x			1	+1

2007 it dedicated its last page to emerging-market indicators.) Out of 45 countries listed in Table 2.1, only 16 countries received the consensus opinion of all five periodicals regarding their status as an EMC. This is why an analyst, strategist, or executive should study the opinion of all available rating agencies, professionals, and leading publications and draw their own conclusion regarding a country's level of maturity. Although a country may have all characteristics of an EMC, it does not mean that this market has actually "emerged" for all foreign companies. Not all companies are prepared to work in the conditions of a particular EMC.

The Genesis of the Global Emerging Market

Growing Input of the Global Emerging Market in the World Economy

The GEM is developing at a much faster rate than the world economy as a whole and faster than developed countries. More than that, the slowest developing EMCs of Eastern Europe and the former Soviet Union are still growing at a faster rate than the world economy, as indicated by Table 2.2. Since 2003 the output of emerging economies "has grown by 35 percent; the developed world's by only 10 percent. More than ever before, emerging economies are being relied upon to help lift the world economy."[16] Actually, for most of economic history, emerging economies have grown at a faster pace than developed economies. The explanation for this is simple: rising from a very low level is much easier than growing from a higher level of economic maturity. Each percentage point during the initial stages of development consists of much less economic input and output. But of course, economic crises and downturns happen more frequently in non-developed economies than in developed economies. In 2007

> for the fourth year running, all of the 32 emerging economies tracked by *The Economist* show[ed] positive growth. This is a remarkable turnabout: in every previous year since the 1970s at least one suffered a recession, if not a severe financial crisis.[17]

As is evident from the Table 2.1, *The Economist* evaluates 29 EMCs on a regular basis, not 32, as is written in the above quote, at least prior to 2007. The *globalEDGE* of International Business Center of Michigan University stated that the focus of its study is to rank "the market potential of 27 countries identified as an 'Emerging Market' by *The Economist*."[18]

Table 2.2 Global and Central and Eastern Europe/CIS Growth Outlook, 2005–2008[19]

	2005	2006	2007*	2008*
World	3.4	3.96	3.2	3.4
Euro Area	1.5	2.76	2.3	2.2
Emerging Europe	5.9	6.6	5.7	5.4
CEE5	4.2	5.6	4.9	4.5
CIS6	6.5	7.3	6.8	6.2

Notes:
Emerging Europe: CEE5, three Baltic States: Estonia, Latvia, Lithuania, CIS6, and Turkey.
CEE5: Czech Republic, Hungary, Poland, Slovakia, and Slovenia.
CIS6: Armenia, Azerbaijan, Kazakhstan, Moldova, Russia, and Ukraine.
*Forecasted. (In the author's opinion, the forecast for 2008 should be lowered due to the financial crisis.)

Clearly, even rating agencies do not have consistent positions regarding which countries qualify as emerging markets, which is important to take into consideration.

This observation is correct, not only for faster-growing economies of Southeast Asia and Russia, but also for emerging Europe—old economies, which are reemerging after communist dictatorships. This is one more indication that despite different geographical locations, all EMCs share many similar characteristics and development dynamics.

But even in terms of GDP value, the GEM has already reached, and will soon overcome, the cumulative GDP of developed countries. According to *The Economist*: "The best hope that global growth can stay strong lies . . . with emerging economies . . . [In 2007] . . . they will contribute half of the globe's GDP growth, measured at market exchange rates, over three times as much as America."[20]

As of January 2008, the input of the 83 countries of the GEM in the world economy is approaching 45.44 percent of total global output, and it will soon overcome the total GDP of developed countries. However, estimates of this figure vary substantially, due to the lack of a universally recognized structure of categorization of national economies (see Chapter 4).

According to *The Economist*:

> Emerging economies account for 30 percent of world GDP at market exchange rates (and over half using purchasing-power parity to take account of price differences). At market exchange rates they already account for half of global GDP growth. And by a wide range of measures, their weight is looming larger. Their exports are 45 percent of the world total; they consume over half of the world's energy and have accounted for four-fifths of the growth in oil demand in the past five years (explaining why oil prices are so high); and they are sitting on 75 percent of global foreign-exchange reserves.[21]

To break down the source of EMCs' 45.44 percent role in the world economy, Table 2.3 offers a list of countries that are considered by the author to be EMCs and their cumulative GDP as a percentage of global GDP in PPP.

The Business Perspective

Ideally, the leadership of EMCs should strive to develop conditions that create opportunities for their citizens to improve the quality of their lives. This is usually achieved by promoting freedom and market-oriented reforms, which eventually leads to a true freedom of choice for individuals and companies. This is the source of a high standard of living. In existential terms, the production of a variety of quality of goods and services of any company is determined by the freedom of choice of individual consumers and their preferences. But on the other hand, freedom of choice cannot exist without the production of a variety of different quality of goods and services, in order for consumers to actually have choices. Different standards of living and/or different preferences of consumers of the same purchasing power group generate differences in demands. As Kenneth Arrow, 1972 Nobel laureate in economics, stated in his famous book, *Social Choice, and Individual Values*:

> The relation of "known preference or indifference" is clearly transitive, but it is not connected since, for example, it does not tell us how the individual compares two social alternatives, one of which yields him more of one commodity than the second, while the second yields him more of a second commodity than the first.[22]

This assumption of Arrow, which may be difficult to understand at first, works only when an individual or company has the opportunity to make choices. Under command economies,

Table 2.3 EMCs by GDP in PPP (Billions of $), 2006[23]

Rank	Country and Rank by GDP PPP	GDP PPP (Billions $), 2006
1	The People's Republic of China	7,046
2	India	2,965
3	The Russian Federation	2,076
4	Brazil	1,838
5	Korea, South	1,206
6	Spain	1,362
7	Mexico	1,353
8	Indonesia	845
9	Taiwan	690
10	Turkey	667
11	Argentina	608
12	Thailand	596
13	South Africa	587
14	Saudi Arabia	572
15	Poland	554
16	Philippines	449
17	Pakistan	437
18	Colombia	374
19	Ukraine	364
20	Egypt	334
21	Malaysia	313
22	Vietnam	262
23	Hong Kong	259
24	Greece	256
25	Algeria	250
26	Czech Republic	225
27	Portugal	210
28	Chile	203
29	Romania	202
30	Peru	187
31	Ireland	181
32	Hungary	175
33	Israel	170
34	Morocco	153
35	Kazakhstan	143
36	Singapore	141
37	United Arab Emirates	130
38	Slovakia	99
39	Sri Lanka	95
40	Tunisia	91
41	Iraq	88
42	Bulgaria	79
43	Ecuador	62
44	Guatemala	61
45	Croatia	60
46	Ghana	60
47	Azerbaijan	60
48	Lithuania	55
49	Costa Rica	51
50	Slovenia	47
51	Serbia	45
52	Turkmenistan	43
53	Uruguay	38
54	Latvia	37
55	El Salvador	34

56	Estonia	34
57	Jordan	30
58	Bolivia	28
59	Qatar	26
60	Panama	26
61	Trinidad and Tabago	21
62	Albania	20
63	Burkina Faso	19
64	Georgia	18
65	Cyprus	18
66	Botswana	18
67	Bahrain	18
68	Madagascar	17
69	Macedonia	17
70	Mauritius	17
71	Armenia	17
72	Jamaica	13
73	Gabon	10
74	Moldova	9
75	Malta	9
76	Bahamas, The	7
77	Mongolia	6
78	Barbados	5
79	Guyana	4
80	Montenegro	3
81	Belize	2
82	Saint Lucia	1
83	Saint Kitts and Nevis	0.75
	Total	29,902
	Percentage of World	45.44

choices are very limited because of shortages of goods and services, especially higher-quality ones. Freedom of choice is created in EMCs by the development of a free-market economy, which responds to individual consumer demands and interests. Of course, the goal of companies entering the GEM is to generate profits. But in doing so, a wider variety of goods and services is produced, which benefits society by increasing freedom of choice for individuals. Companies seek profit by responding to the constantly differentiating demands of consumers in a free market. When a strategist positions a company in the market, an evaluation should be made of all current and potential competitors, in order to identify consumer demands that are not totally, if at all, addressed. By addressing consumer demands that current producers are not satisfying, companies increase freedom of choice, and a wider variety of goods and services is produced. This is how free-market economies address private and public interests. But first and foremost in the GEM, strategy should define and publicly announce, via a mission statement and vision, a company's social orientation and responsibilities to society and to regional and local communities, and the services that the company will provide.

Environmental Protection in Entry Strategy to the Global Emerging Market

When companies from developed countries made their first ventures in the GEM, they were barely cognizant of the potential opportunities that lay ahead. Initially, companies expanded into the GEM in search of competitive advantages that would make them more successful in their domestic or traditional markets of operations. When they unexpectedly found huge markets of consumers and producers; new, inexpensive production facilities; and access to a practically unlimited supply of cheap labor, the development and role of the GEM in the GMP grew exponentially. However, in some cases, a lack of strategic vision can turn short-term profits into long-term liabilities. Some companies took advantage of inexperienced and ineffective governments and local executives in the GEM to maximize short-term profits. In many cases, this resulted in the loss of access to markets, resources, production facilities, etc., once governments matured and the general population had a better understanding of the situation. Many companies entered EMCs when they were actually pre-emerging markets, still under dictatorship. At this time democracy was little more than a pipedream for the people of these countries. In these conditions a handshake from the dictator was practically all that was required for foreign companies to operate. The social and ecological impact of a foreign company was totally ignored. When these dictator-ships collapsed and democracy began to emerge, companies accustomed to dealing with the dictatorship made the mistake of ignoring the birth of a new social force: public opinion. In many cases freedom of speech and assembly seriously hindered the operations of a foreign company of which local populations did not approve, whether formally or informally. Ignoring the social and ecological impact of a company's activities is a reflection of a lack of strategic vision.

The experience of Tengizchevroil (TCO) in Kazakhstan is a clear example of the dangers of ignoring ecological issues. Tengizchevroil, a joint venture of Chevron, ExxonMobile, Lukarco, and KazMunayGas, produces oil from one of the world's biggest oil fields, the Tengiz in western Kazakhstan. For several years TCO spent only about one cent per metric ton of oil produced in Kazakhstan to address ecological issues, such as the disposal of sulfur byproducts from crude-oil production. TCO maintained that these byproducts were harm-less.[24] Such a shortsighted approach eventually cost them a great deal. When the national government began to focus on the environment, TCO was forced to pay much more than they would have if they had addressed the sulfur-byproduct issue from the beginning of their venture. In February 2007 the minister of ecology of the Republic of Kazakhstan threatened to suspend the operational license of the joint venture. TCO subsequently agreed to pay $300 million a year to the national government for environmental protection.[25]

Even more serious charges were brought against Shell Petroleum Development Corp. (SPDC), a joint venture of Royal Dutch Shell in Nigeria, by the national government. SPDC was forced to

> pay $1.5bn (£830m) compensation to communities affected by oil pollution in the country . . . SPDC was to compensate the Ijaw tribe in the southern Bayelsa state. SPDC has long been accused by activists of not cleaning up oil spills and complicity in human rights abuses.[26]

Increasing competition among EMCs to produce and export more energy resources has led many of them to implement less restrictive environmental policies that attract FDI from major international energy-producing companies. These shifts of FDI suddenly decrease or increase the role of a particular EMC in the global energy balance. For example, the Gulf of Mexico is experiencing a shortage of offshore drilling equipment (jack-up and deep-water rigs), as a result of multinational corporations relocating their equipment in search of more profitable projects in areas with less restrictive environmental regulations. The richest and most accessible reserves of the Gulf of Mexico have already been drilled. Many foreign companies do not want to bother with the more expensive remaining deep-water and ultra-deep-water reserves, especially because of the relatively higher environmental standards. This is further increasing the prices to lease oil rigs. It will be more difficult for the Gulf region, which produces one-quarter of US oil, to curtail its annual decline in output.[27]

In order to decrease energy shortages, many countries of the EU have enacted very restrictive domestic energy policies and aggressive foreign energy policies in order to gain access to more energy resources. One exception to this rule is Bulgaria, which has the most liberal and least environmentally restrictive energy policy in the EU. It exports some electrical energy to Turkey, among other countries, while also acting as a hub in the North Balkan region. Several pipelines already connect Bulgaria (and more are planned) with the countries of the Black, Caspian, and Adriatic seas via its Black Sea coast.

The experience of Global Fishing, a producer of seafood products headquartered in the US that operates in the GEM, offers an example from a different industry. Global Fishing was accused of illegally poaching. According to one report: "The small leg size of some Russian product sold in the United States indicated that young, undersize crab have sometimes been part of the haul."[28] One former Alaskan crabber added: "If we had landed crab like that in Dutch Harbor, [Alaska] we would have ended up in jail."[29] Any company that ignores ecological regulations takes the risk of putting short-term profits (which are generally affiliated with unacceptable levels of risk) over long-term strategy. This has very serious implications. It is unwise for companies from developed countries operating in the GEM to take advantage of the lower standards and regulations or a lack of their enforcement. In the long-term, it is not worth it.

Emerging-market Countries' Regional Integration into the Global Marketplace

International business activity is the locomotive that drives the development of the GEM, integrating the economies of EMCs with those of developed countries at an incredible pace. But among EMCs themselves within the GEM, there is not yet a great deal of political and economic integration. Even the most developed regions within individual EMCs often have more economic ties with developed countries than with nearby domestic regions. This is because developed countries are the main source of investment, modern managerial skills, and technologies, and, in some cases, even funding for operational activity, for companies in EMCs. This is a very important dynamic in the GEM and between it and developed countries.

In general, the larger the territory of an EMC is, the larger the difference in economic development among its domestic regions (see Table 2.4). This is the case in Brazil, Russia, China, Argentina, South Africa, and Ukraine. In these large EMCs, the location and deficit of the five basic economic factors (see Chapter 1) is the main cause of the disproportionate regional economic development. Natural resources, labor, and production facilities are often concentrated in certain regions, separated from one another by great distances and usually a lack of infrastructure. A domestic deficit of the two remaining basic economic factors, technology and capital, further isolates regions from one another.

By the author's estimation, 65 percent of the basic economic factors of Russia, China, and Brazil are concentrated in particular regions, isolated from each other by the previously mentioned factors. In China the natural resources are concentrated in the northwest, the production facilities in the southeast, and the cheap labor resources in the central region. More than 25 percent of China's forestry is located in the northeast, while most industrial facilities are roughly 2,000 miles south, or in Inner Mongolia. In Russia about 40 percent of all natural resources are located above the Arctic Circle, where only about 6 percent of the population resides. Most production facilities in Brazil are located in the southern part of the country, with a few exceptions on the Atlantic coast, while all natural resources, including those of the rainforests, are in central Brazil, thus separated from these facilities by thousands of kilometers. Furthermore, in all of these countries, the local population in natural resource-rich regions, in many cases, is unprepared culturally and professionally to

Table 2.4 EMCs by Size of Territory[30]

Rank	Country	Area (Sq. Km)
1	Russia	17,075,200
2	China	9,596,960
3	Brazil	8,511,965
4	India	3,287,590
5	Argentina	2,766,890
6	Kazakhstan	2,717,300
7	Algeria	2,381,740
8	Saudi Arabia	2,149,690
9	Mexico	1,972,550
10	Indonesia	1,919,440
11	Mongolia	1,565,000
12	Peru	1,285,220
13	South Africa	1,219,912
14	Colombia	1,138,910
15	Bolivia	1,098,580
16	Egypt	1,001,450
17	Pakistan	803,940
18	Turkey	780,580
19	Chile	756,950
20	Ukraine	603,700
21	Botswana	600,370
22	Madagascar	587,040
23	Thailand	514,000
24	Spain	504,782
25	Turkmenistan	488,100
26	Morocco	446,550
27	Iraq	437,072
28	Malaysia	329,750
29	Vietnam	329,560
30	Poland	312,685
31	Philippines	300,000
32	Ecuador	283,560
33	Burkina Faso	274,200
34	Gabon	267,667
35	Ghana	239,460
36	Romania	237,500
37	Guyana	214,970
38	Uruguay	176,220
39	Tunisia	163,610
40	Greece	131,940
41	Bulgaria	110,910
42	Guatemala	108,890
43	Korea, South	98,480
44	Hungary	93,030
45	Portugal	92,391
46	Jordan	92,300
47	Serbia	88,361
48	Azerbaijan	86,600
49	United Arab Emirates	82,000
50	Czech Republic	78,866
51	Panama	78,200
52	Ireland	70,280
53	Georgia	69,700
54	Sri Lanka	65,610
55	Lithuania	65,200

56	Latvia	64,589
57	Croatia	56,542
58	Costa Rica	51,100
59	Slovak Republic	48,845
60	Estonia	45,226
61	Taiwan	35,980
62	Moldova	33,843
63	Armenia	29,800
64	Albania	28,748
65	Macedonia	25,333
66	Belize	22,966
67	El Salvador	21,040
68	Israel	20,770
69	Slovenia	20,273
70	Montenegro	14,026
71	Bahamas, The	13,940
72	Qatar	11,437
73	Jamaica	10,991
74	Cyprus	9,250
75	Trinidad and Tobago	5,128
76	Mauritius	2,030
77	China, Hong Kong	1,092
78	Singapore	693
79	Bahrain	665
80	Saint Lucia	616
81	Barbados	431
82	Malta	316
83	Saint Kitts and Nevis	261
	Total	71,329,352
	Percentage of World	47.89

utilize industrial resources needed to exploit natural resources. Most productive facilities in these big EMCs are separated from the natural resources by roughly two or three thousand kilometers of uninhabited territory.

As a result of the location of resources within EMCs, companies from developed economies focus their investment and activity in certain regions of a particular EMC. Not surprisingly, the regions with the abundant natural resources tend to experience the fastest industrial growth. These regions often develop almost independently from other parts of the country, due to the lack of domestic capital and modern technology needed to integrate the productive forces of different domestic regions with the rest of the country. As a result, foreign economic interests have weakened interregional domestic economic connections in large EMCs.

A lack of domestic-regional integration is also evident in EMCs with smaller territories, such as those of Eastern and Southern Europe. Since 2004, 12 Eastern European EMCs have joined the EU. These countries are being integrated with the developed Western European member-states of the EU at a much faster rate than between each other. Even Ukraine, which is not a member of the EU, exports more to the EU than to Russia. Russia is only the seventh biggest investor to Ukraine, far behind Germany, Cyprus, Austria, Great Britain, the Netherlands, and even the United States.[31] The cumulative investment of Russia in Ukraine is only 4.6 percent of all cumulative foreign investment in Ukraine. The role of Ukrainian exports to Russia has decreased from 43 percent in 1995 to 22.5 percent of total exports in 2007.[32] The EU accounts for one-third of Ukrainian external trade.[33] According to *The Economist*, "rich economies' trade with developing countries is growing twice as fast as their trade with one another."[34] This acceleration is occurring because the removal of barriers and tariffs between different (and even neighboring) EMCs happens at a much slower pace than the removal of barriers and tariffs between EMCs and developed countries. EMCs are competing with each other for FDI from developed countries and for cooperation with them. There is a much stronger incentive to liberalize economic relations with the developed world than with other less-developed competitors, i.e. EMCs. Lower inter-industrial connections among EMCs is one of the key factors that decreases domestic interregional integration and increases international integration of EMCs' regions with developed nations and within the GMP.

In order to optimize economic development, EMCs must achieve a balance between foreign-led growth and growth initiated by internal factors. The most prosperous EMCs, such as Ireland, the Czech Republic, South Korea, and Argentina have achieved this balance. But as of 2008, many EMCs still export more raw materials than processed products. Producers of raw materials in EMCs tend to be more tightly integrated with processing companies in developed countries than they are with domestic processing companies. This prevents companies from EMCs and the EMC itself from receiving higher profits, as the profits from sales of final products are always higher than those from raw materials. This dynamic is an obstacle for more balanced economic development and faster economic and social improvements in EMCs.

Integration of the Labor Resources of the Global Emerging Market into the Global Marketplace

Labor resources of EMCs have several similar characteristics such as long working hours, higher unemployment, much lower wages, and faster growing productivity of labor relative to developed countries. On the other hand, each EMC has many unique characteristics regarding its labor resources, rooted in its distinctive economic history. For example, levels of education vary substantially, with a high level of professional and general education in Central and Eastern Europe and Russia, compared to the Indian subcontinent and Latin America. The productivity of labor resources as well as the level of unemployment and wages are also quite different among some EMCs due variations in their economic maturity. The earlier a country begins the transition from a totalitarian regime and command economy, the closer its productivity of labor, education, and wages will be to developed countries and to economies in bloom.

During the initial stages of transition to the free market, the rate of growth of product-ivity of labor is not as high as one would assume. Low levels of education and techno-logical development slow the growth rate productivity. For example, during the 1980s and 1990s, the growth rate of labor productivity in China was only about 4.5 percent. India suffered from a slow growth rate of labor productivity during the initial stages of its relatively late transition from a command economy to a free market economy. Despite the fact that it had been the largest democracy in the world for several decades, it only began to embrace the free market at the end of the twentieth century. After the initial transition period EMCs generally surge in labor productivity growth. In the first decade of the twenty-first century, the average growth rate of productivity of labor in the GEM has been roughly four times faster than that of the developed world. During this period, labor productivity has increased at an average annual rate of 8 percent in Central and Eastern Europe, China, and Russia. This is mostly a result of increasing access to modern technol-ogy and equipment, growing familiarity with free-market conditions, and improvements in motivation systems. During the same period, most developed countries experienced a slowdown in the growth of labor productivity to less than 2 percent. Some EMCs, despite their early entrance to the GEM, have not experienced rapid growth in productivity of labor. For example, Mexico has been very slow to adopt modern technologies and improve general educational levels. The growth rate of its productivity of labor has been about 1 percent, which is almost two times lower than that of the US, though still higher than that of Western Europe.

The rapid growth in labor productivity of the GEM is actually one of the causes of its higher unemployment relative to the developed world (see Figure 2.2). From another perspective, high unemployment is a cause of the rapid growth rate of labor productivity in the GEM. This can be seen in the more rapid pay increase in EMCs than in the developed world. According to the Mercer 2008 Global Compensation Planning Report, prepared by Mercer LLC, India, Vietnam, Bulgaria, Turkey, China, South Korea, Romania, and Ireland will have a higher rate of growth of remuneration than the US and other developed countries.[35]

A negative side effect of the increasing freedom that inevitably comes as countries embrace democracy and the free market is the widespread emigration of its citizens, who seek more stable economic conditions. As EMCs stabilize and economic conditions improve, émigrés usually return. In cases of the most successful economic reforms, in addition to the return of émigrés, migrants from other EMCs also come, looking for stability and prosperity. Such was the case of the Ireland, the so-called Celtic Tiger, which experienced a wave of émigrés returning to their homeland as well as of migrants from Eastern Europe at the beginning of the twenty-first century.

The liberalization of the global labor market is characterized by a similarly outward-oriented phenomenon. A tighter relationship and more open cooperation with developed countries motivates and gives more opportunities for unemployed or underemployed people in EMCs to permanently or temporarily emigrate to developed countries in search of employment. Due to their intensive and extensive work ethic, they are often willing to do any work, even if they are overqualified for the job. They compete successfully with local work power in the countries to which they emigrate. Aging work forces in developed countries also make it difficult for domestic workers to compete with younger émigrés from the GEM. When and if these émigrés find employment, a significant portion of their wages is sent back to their relatives in their country of origin, a practice called remittances. According to the International Fund for Agricultural Development:

> The driving force behind this phenomenon is an estimated 150 million migrants worldwide who sent more than US$300 billion to their families in developing countries during 2006, typically US$100, US$200 or US$300 at a time, through more than 1.5 billion separate financial transactions.[36]

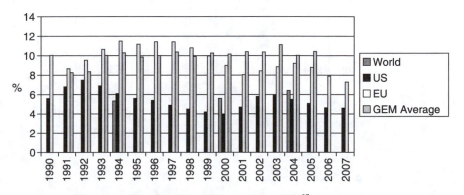

Figure 2.2 Unemployment in the US, EU, GEM, and the GMP.[37]

Many émigrés from the GEM in developed countries realize themselves not only as employees but also as entrepreneurs. With easier access to financial resources via commercial and investment banks in developed countries, they are able to implement their business ideas, know-how and even patents. A lack of capital, overpowering bureaucracy, and corruption make such achievements practically impossible in their native countries. Remittances sent home by these émigrés have a very positive impact on the standard of living of the poorest and most vulnerable segments of society in the GEM. In addition, they increase the consumption power of EMCs and the role of consumption in the GDP of EMCs. In some countries the role of remittances is comparable to the GDP itself. In Moldova remittances account for one-third of the GDP, which, as of 2007, is a record for an EMC. However, in developing countries the share of remittances of GDP can be even higher. In Guinea-Bissau remittances account for 48.7 percent of GDP. However, remittances also have a negative impact. They can contribute to inequality of income distribution, which is discussed further in the following section. Plate 2.1 and Figures 2.3, 2.4, and 2.5 present the geographical distribution of remittances and their role in the economies of different EMCs.

According to a special report from *The Economist*:

> Tim Jones of Innovaro, a European innovation consultancy, points out that Africa is about to take the lead in using mobile phones for payments and remittances, thanks to the introduction of schemes like the M-PESA money-transfer service introduced by Vodafone and Citigroup in Kenya. These allow people to send money using text messages.[38]

Income Inequality, Uncertainty, and Risk

The outflow of labor resources from the GEM to developed countries can accelerate income inequality in EMCs. The more citizens of a particular EMC emigrate to work in developed

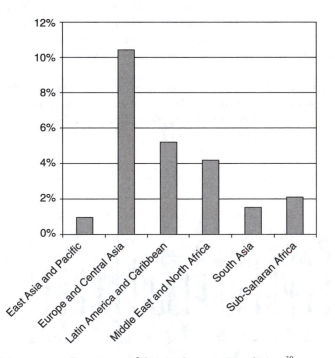

Figure 2.3 Size of Diaspora as a Percentage of Origin Country Population.[39]

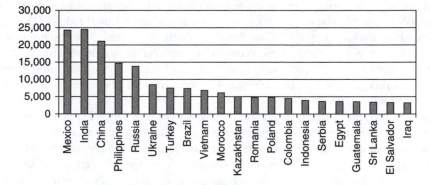

Figure 2.4 Top EMC Recipients of Remittances (Millions of $), 2006.[40]

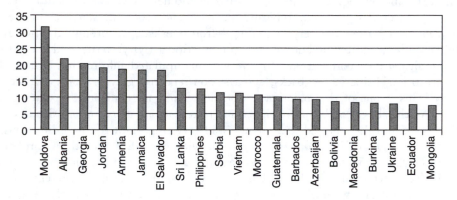

Figure 2.5 Top EMC Recipients of Remittances (Percentage of GDP), 2006.[41]

countries, the more remittances are sent to their country of origin. Their remuneration or profit in developed countries is substantially higher than in their native countries—up to 10 times more than the average remuneration. This is one factor that can contribute to increases of income-distribution inequality in EMCs.

One of the strongest factors causing increasing income-distribution inequality in EMCs is corruption and nepotism. Corruption and income inequality are directly related. As corruption increases so does income inequality, to a certain point. While there are many detailed studies of income inequality,[42] it is very difficult to apply them to EMCs because of the strong negative influence of informal and unreported underground economies. These statistics are obviously not reflected in official data. However, ultimately, as economic freedom increases, so does average income per capita, but not equally. Nonetheless, this gradually leads to a more equitable distribution of income. This process progresses at a substantially slower pace in EMCs than in developed countries (discussed further below).

The need for FDI from developed countries is helping to reduce corruption, and as a result, income inequality. Investors from developed countries seek stability and predictability in potential recipients of investment, even more so than democracy. Widespread corruption is a significant deterrent to FDI. As corruption is reduced by national governments seeking FDI, so is income inequality.

Nevertheless, the high level of corruption and unreported economic activity not reflected in official financial statistics and balance sheets of companies in the GEM causes a great deal of uncertainty and limited and/or inaccurate information for investors, companies, and entrepreneurs. Not having an accurate understanding of existing companies and the business environment or information about economic and financial processes and legal entities has a very negative impact on the initial risk of investment and operational risk in a country. This is especially the case for companies that are not officially registered. They do not pay taxes or insurance, and they put their employees and customers at an unmeasured risk. These unregistered companies greatly complicate the business environment for investors. If uncertainty is related to a lack of understanding and limited information of the economic and business reality, risk is related to lost or negative results of economic and business activity in conditions of uncertainty. In *Risk, Uncertainty, and Profit*, Frank Knight wrote: "If we are to understand the workings of the economic system we must examine the meaning and significance of uncertainty; and to this end some inquiry into the nature and function of knowledge itself is necessary."[43] Economic statistics, business reporting, and auditing and due diligence systems in EMCs are far behind those of developed countries. This is one of the identifying characteristics of countries that are not yet developed. An analysis of official governmental and business statistics from EMCs should never be made without understanding how the data was gathered. Typically, business and economic statistics in the GEM divert from reality from the very beginning—from workshops, through the processes of feasibility studies, architectural design, and construction activity, to the headquarters of the biggest multinational corporations. Incorrect or manipulated information almost always hides corruption, bribery, kickbacks, and the non-reported gray or black sectors of the economy. This is one of the major causes of inefficiency for companies operating in the GEM. All of the above conditions in the GEM create *economies of uncertainty*. Studies related to this economic reality formed entirely new and very important research directions. Any strategist, executive, or investor operating in or with the GEM should be familiar with Dr Harry Markowitz's studies on the economics of uncertainty, for which he received the Nobel Prize in economics in 1990. Uncertainty is a main focus of strategy. Without uncertainty, the future would be clear to everyone, and there would scarcely be a need for strategy and strategists. But because uncertainty is so prevalent in business, economics, and politics, it is vitally important (and extremely difficult) to forecast and predict the future. As President Franklin Delano Roosevelt said: "The only limit to our realization of tomorrow will be our doubts of today."[44]

The Current Role of the Global Emerging Market in the World

The relatively different economic, political, and geographic situations of EMCs have important implications on the speed and progress of their development. However, what allows all EMCs to be understood as a part of the GEM is the uniformed direction of their progress toward economic freedom, global integration, and in the best cases, democracy. As EMCs develop, they are beginning to become more and more integrated with one another. The global trend of regionalization, which leads to the creation of regional blocs and economic unions, furthers this process. (This trend is discussed in detail in Chapter 3.) Today EMCs are found in North, Central, and South America; Pacific and Central Asia; the Indian subcontinent; Central, Eastern, and Southern Europe; the territory of the former Soviet Union; and Northern and Southern Africa. It is impossible to over-estimate the scale of the GEM. As of January 2008, the GEM consists of 83 countries, which account for nearly 68.75 percent of the global population, and about 47.89 percent of the Earth's surface. The input of the GEM into the world's output is 45.44 percent and about 40 percent of FDI goes to EMCs. The GEM capitalization has more than doubled since 1995, growing from less than $2 trillion to more than $5 trillion in 2006. This is 12 percent of GMP capitalization,[45] up from 3 percent in 1981 and 5 percent in 1990.[46] As of 2008 (prior to the financial crisis), in terms of market capitalization, among the top three largest companies in the world are the Russian natural gas semi-state monopoly—OAO Gazprom, which surpassed another company from the GEM, China Mobile Ltd, as well as a non-GEM company, General Electric.[47] Countries of the GEM are a beacon for the remaining underdeveloped (North Korea, Democratic Republic of Congo, etc.) and developing countries (Afghanistan, Somalia, etc.) that strive to or one day will strive to build market-oriented economies.

The GEM contains all major characteristics of individual EMCs. However, collectively, there is a synergy among EMCs that creates an environment more conducive to global business. Different resources and factors attract developed countries and their companies to cooperate with and within emerging markets. The integration of EMCs into a unified GEM creates a distinct, cumulative, joined power of all EMCs that draws companies to the GEM. The integration of EMCs within the GEM is an example of the conversion of a critical mass of quantity to a new quality.

The development of the GEM decreased the importance of American, European, and Japanese business—an economic triangle that dominated the second half of the twentieth century. In terms of economic power and foreign trade, the dominant forces of the GMP in the twenty-first century are the US, the EU, and the GEM. In several categories of the production of goods and services, the GEM as a whole and even some individual EMCs have surpassed the US, individual EU member-states, and Japan. The increasing importance of the GEM can also be seen in Table 2.5, which shows the largest countries in the world

Table 2.5 Largest Countries in terms of GDP PPP (Billions of $), 2006[48]

Rank	Country	GDP PPP (Billions $)
1	United States	13,060
2	China	10,210
3	Japan	4,218
4	India	4,164
5	Germany	2,632
6	United Kingdom	1,928
7	France	1,902
8	Italy	1,756
9	Russia	1,746
10	Brazil	1,655
11	Korea, South	1,196
12	Canada	1,181
13	Mexico	1,149
14	Spain	1,109
15	Indonesia	948
16	Taiwan	681
17	Australia	674
18	Turkey	640
19	Argentina	609
20	Iran	599
21	Thailand	596
22	South Africa	588
23	Poland	555
24	Netherlands	530
25	Philippines	450
26	Pakistan	438
27	Colombia	374
28	Saudi Arabia	372
29	Ukraine	364
30	Belgium	343

economy by GDP; out of the top 10 countries in terms of GDP PPP, 4 are EMCs. Out of the top 20 countries of the GMP, 11 are EMCs. Finally, out of the top 30 countries in terms of GDP PPP, 19 are EMCs.

From the perspective of companies of the developed world, the GEM represents new markets with substantial purchasing power and new sources of labor and natural resources that can be harnessed to achieve high returns on investment. From the perspective of countries of the GEM, companies from the developed world represent sources of new investment and operational capital, managerial skills, technology, and new jobs that can lead to further economic and social development, and, subsequently, more tax revenue. This revenue provides the funding for the construction of new nurseries, kindergartens, schools, retirement communities, hospitals, theaters, athletic complexes, and other entertainment facilities, which results in an increase in the local standard of living. This leads to further integration of EMCs into the GEM and of the GEM into the GMP. This in turn improves the global optimum (see Chapter 5) of the world economy by decreasing poverty, mass disease, and migration, and improving the standard of living of all individuals through increases of global output, and international economic cooperation via the utilization of new technological advancements. This is how the standard of living of Earth's 6.5 billion people will eventually improve.

Despite the substantial risks offered by the GEM, no company in the GMP can ignore the opportunities. There are an endless number of examples of companies that went out of business after failing to compete with rivals who took advantage of opportunities offered by the GEM. The risks and opportunities offered by the GEM have also led to the rise in importance of *risk-management systems* in order to understand, evaluate, measure, and adjust in order to manage risk.

Global business risk management is one of the major functions of strategic and tactical business practices. In the past, risk was something to avoid. But the GEM has resulted in a fundamental change in how international business considers risk. While the opportunities are incredible in the GEM, risk is to some degree inherent in EMCs. Instead of avoiding risk altogether, investors utilize risk-management systems and convert new opportunities into profit and success, despite threats. (For more on risk see Chapter 8.)

The geopolitical location of some EMCs essentially ensures them a key and lucrative role as a bridge between developed countries and the GEM as a whole. Bulgaria, Turkey, Ukraine, and Spain are important crossroads between the developed countries of Europe and EMCs of Eastern Europe, the Middle East, Russia, and Africa. Mexico is an important intermediary between developed North America and Latin America. Kazakhstan is a key entrance to Central Asia and China, as is China to Southeast Asia. Azerbaijan occupies a very strategic location, the role of which will only increase when Iran's dictatorship collapses. As stability increases in Iraq, so will its strategic value; the country will play an integral role in the twenty-first-century GMP. Of course, strategic geopolitical locations are not always taken advantage of. Portugal has failed to exploit its cultural ties to the world's substantial Portuguese-speaking market, and especially with Brazil. It did not follow the lead of its neighbor Spain, which realized the potential of South America and was one of the first developed countries to establish a relationship with the newly formed economic union of the southern cone of South America—Mercosur. Due to extremely tense bilateral and multilateral relations with its neighbors, Israel has not been able to take advantage of its strategic location. Despite these difficulties, Israel is improving its economic relations with Muslim countries, such as Jordan, Egypt, Turkey, and (predominately Muslim) Albania.

The integration of the GEM into the GMP has multiple effects on both developed and EMCs. Both categories, through their cooperation, investment, and increasing international trade due to liberalized economic conditions and deregulation, have experienced acceleration in their rate of growth. This resulted in an overall acceleration of world economic development, which the world has experienced since the operational existence of the GEM in the beginning of the 1980s. The fact that the world economy has more than quadrupled in terms of GDP since 1980 is due directly to the growth of the GEM (see Figure 2.6).

Figure 2.7 shows the differences in the vector of economic development of EMCs and developed countries. Over the past 17 years, the rate of growth of the GEM has always outpaced that of the world economy and (with the exception of one year) of the US. At the same time, the dynamics of individual GEM members can fluctuate substantially. Figure 2.7 shows the example of Russia, which for seven of eight years beginning in the 1990s, during the transition from communism to a free-market economy, experienced economic recession and a serious downsizing of the national economy. Nonetheless, the GEM continued to grow at a faster pace than the world economy, despite the fact that Russia was part of the GEM. Developed countries no longer dominate global production.[49]

Integration of the GEM into the GMP and increasing industrial and economic development in EMCs due to new business opportunities, foreign investment, and trade have all

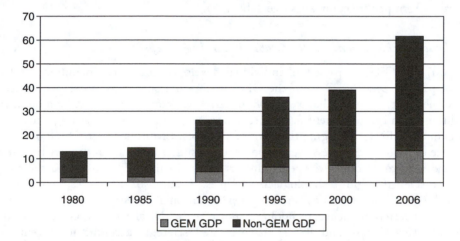

Figure 2.6 Input of GEM in Global GDP (Exchange Rate, Trillions of $).[50]

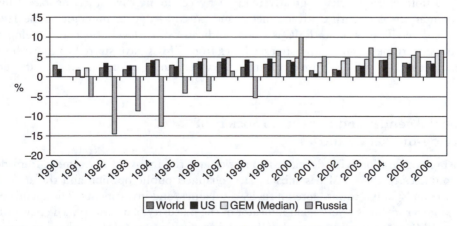

Figure 2.7 Comparison of the Rate of Growth of the World Economy with the Dynamics of Economic Development of the GEM, US, and Russia.[51]

had a tremendous influence on the societies of EMCs. These changes initiate huge shifts in the allocation of different basic economic factors. One of the most significant changes is the reallocation of production facilities, which in turn alters the scale and patterns of domestic migration. It is very important for investors in the GEM to consider the fact that urban populations are increasing at least three times faster than rural populations. This is important for companies seeking consumer markets of scale in the GEM. Because of the population growth in the GEM and increasing migration of people from villages to urban areas, the number of cities with five million people or more will increase from 41 to 59, between 2000 and 2015.[52] During the same period the number of cities of more than 10 million will increase from 19 to 23.[53] This will have a powerful impact on the world economy because the population of the GEM accounts for 68.3 percent of the global population. As a result, domestic and social dynamics in EMCs are changing the process of world social development (see Table 2.6).

In the early 1980s, prior to the birth of the GEM, 70 percent of capital invested in developing countries (many of which are EMCs today) came from developed countries as governmental aid. Due to tremendous improvements in the business environment of the GEM and increasing political stability, the private economic interests of developed countries in EMCs has skyrocketed. As a result, in 2007, 83 percent of capital invested in the GEM came from private companies (see Table 2.7).

Technological Achievements in the Global Emerging Market

As of 2007 the GEM surpassed all individual developed countries, including the US, in terms of patents pending. Within the GEM, China has surpassed Russia as the leading source of new patents. As of January 2008, in terms of patents pending, China ranks third, behind the US and Japan. Scientific and technological progress, as well as huge investments in R&D in the GEM, is changing the goals of investors. Investors used to think of the GEM as a source of natural resources, cheap labor, and consumer markets. Today, with increasing frequency, investors from developed countries invest in the GEM to utilize their highly developed scientific and technological resources. Leaders of EMCs can continue this dynamic by generating revenue from foreign exploitation of domestic resources (natural and labor) to be invested in science, technology, education, and health care. Some EMCs, such as Azerbaijan, Kazakhstan, and Russia, have created strategic accounts for revenue from natural resources (mostly oil) to be invested in the non-oil economy. The vulnerability of EMCs to unforeseen shocks is greatly reduced by economic diversification based on the implementation of scientific advancements and cutting-edge technologies. The level of economic diversification of an EMC is a good indicator of its level of overall development. National governments and corporate executives from EMCs have started to motivate their foreign partners to use their investment for new technologies and modern management systems.

National Agendas and Benefits to Society of Emerging-market Countries

Increasing cooperation with developed countries and the inflow of investment from developed countries to the GEM has substantially changed public opinion and the attitude of governments of EMCs toward foreign trade, companies, and investments. The agenda of the national government is a very good indicator of the maturity of a country. The new outlook of most EMC governments toward collaboration within the GMP is the first indicator to foreigners that they can start to explore and analyze business opportunities in these

Table 2.6 EMCs by Population, 2007[54]

Rank	Country	2007 Population Estimate
1	China	1,321,851,888
2	India	1,129,866,154
3	Indonesia	234,693,997
4	Brazil	190,010,647
5	Pakistan	164,741,924
6	Russia	141,377,752
7	Mexico	108,700,891
8	Philippines	91,077,287
9	Vietnam	85,262,356
10	Egypt	80,335,036
11	Turkey	71,158,647
12	Thailand	65,068,149
13	Korea, South	49,044,790
14	Ukraine	46,299,862
15	Colombia	44,379,598
16	South Africa	43,997,828
17	Spain	40,448,191
18	Argentina	40,301,927
19	Poland	38,518,241
20	Morocco	33,757,175
21	Algeria	33,333,216
22	Peru	28,674,757
23	Saudi Arabia	27,601,038
24	Iraq	27,499,638
25	Malaysia	24,821,286
26	Ghana	22,931,299
27	Taiwan	22,858,872
28	Romania	22,276,056
29	Sri Lanka	20,926,315
30	Madagascar	19,448,815
31	Chile	16,284,741
32	Kazakhstan	15,284,929
33	Burkina Faso	14,326,203
34	Ecuador	13,755,680
35	Guatemala	12,728,111
36	Greece	10,706,290
37	Portugal	10,642,836
38	Tunisia	10,276,158
39	Czech Republic	10,228,744
40	Serbia	10,150,265
41	Hungary	9,956,108
42	Bolivia	9,119,152
43	Azerbaijan	8,120,247
44	Bulgaria	7,322,858
45	Hong Kong	6,980,412
46	El Salvador	6,948,073
47	Israel	6,426,679
48	Jordan	6,053,193
49	Slovakia	5,447,502
50	Turkmenistan	5,097,028
51	Georgia	4,646,003
52	Singapore	4,553,009
53	Croatia	4,493,312
54	United Arab Emirates	4,444,011
55	Moldova	4,320,490

(*Continued Overleaf*)

Table 2.6 Continued

Rank	Country	2007 Population Estimate
56	Costa Rica	4,133,884
57	Ireland	4,109,086
58	Albania	3,600,523
59	Lithuania	3,575,439
60	Uruguay	3,460,607
61	Panama	3,242,173
62	Armenia	2,971,650
63	Mongolia	2,951,786
64	Jamaica	2,780,132
65	Latvia	2,259,810
66	Macedonia	2,055,915
67	Slovenia	2,009,245
68	Botswana	1,815,508
69	Gabon	1,454,867
70	Estonia	1,315,912
71	Mauritius	1,253,434
72	Trinidad	1,056,608
73	Qatar	907,229
74	Cyprus	788,457
75	Guyana	769,095
76	Bahrain	708,573
77	Montenegro	684,736
78	Malta	401,880
79	Bahamas, The	305,655
80	Belize	294,385
81	Barbados	280,946
82	Saint Lucia	170,649
83	Saint Kitts and Nevis	39,349
	Total	4,538,973,199
	Percentage of World	68.75

Table 2.7 FDI Inflows to EMCs, 2006[55]

Rank	EMC	2006 FDI Inflow (Millions $)
1	China	69,468
2	Hong Kong	42,892
3	Russian Federation	28,732
4	Singapore	24,207
5	Turkey	20,120
6	Spain	20,016
7	Mexico	19,037
8	Brazil	18,782
9	Saudi Arabia	18,293
10	India	16,881
11	Israel	14,301
12	Poland	13,922
13	Ireland	12,811
14	Romania	11,394
15	Egypt	10,043
16	Thailand	9,751
17	United Arab Emirates	8,386
18	Chile	7,952

19	Taiwan	7,424
20	Portugal	7,371
21	Colombia	6,295
22	Kazakhstan	6,143
23	Hungary	6,098
24	Malaysia	6,060
25	Czech Republic	5,957
26	Indonesia	5,556
27	Greece	5,363
28	Ukraine	5,203
29	Bulgaria	5,172
30	Serbia and Montenegro	5,128
31	Korea, South	4,950
32	Argentina	4,809
33	Pakistan	4,273
34	Slovakia	4,165
35	Croatia	3,556
36	Peru	3,467
37	Tunisia	3,312
38	Jordan	3,121
39	Bahrain	2,915
40	Morocco	2,898
41	Panama	2,560
42	Philippines	2,345
43	Vietnam	2,315
44	Ecuador	2,087
45	Lithuania	1,812
46	Algeria	1,795
47	Qatar	1,786
48	Malta	1,757
49	Estonia	1,674
50	Latvia	1,634
51	Cyprus	1,492
52	Costa Rica	1,469
53	Uruguay	1,374
54	Georgia	1,076
55	Jamaica	850
56	Trinidad and Tobago	788
57	Turkmenistan	731
58	Bahamas	706
59	Sri Lanka	480
60	Ghana	435
61	Slovenia	363
62	Guatemala	354
63	Macedonia	351
64	Armenia	343
65	Albania	325
66	Botswana	274
67	Iraq	272
68	Gabon	268
69	Bolivia	240
70	Madagascar	230
71	Moldova, Republic of	222
72	El Salvador	204
73	Saint Kitts and Nevis	203
74	Mongolia	167
75	Saint Lucia	119
76	Guyana	102
77	Belize	76
78	Barbados	36

(Continued Overleaf)

Table 2.7 Continued

Rank	EMC	2006 FDI Inflow (Millions $)
79	Burkina Faso	26
80	Mauritius	6
81	South Africa	−323
82	Azerbaijan	−601
	GEM Total as a Percentage of World Total (Approximately)	40

Note: 2006 FDI data evaluates Serbia and Montenegro as a single country.

countries. Mature EMCs see integration within the GMP as a means to resolve domestic challenges, while less mature countries look for internal solutions to domestic challenges and still embrace isolationism. The latter view is usually a transparent attempt to either recentralize power, such as in Putin's Russia and Morales' Bolivia; to revert to totalitarianism, such as Chavez's Venezuela and Mugabe's Zimbabwe; or to assert the role of religion in politics and business, such as Erdogan's Turkey.

Role of the Middle Class in Economic Maturation of Emerging-market Countries

The creation and development of a middle class is crucial for stable economic and political conditions in EMCs. The middle class plays an important role in attracting international business activity and investment. Unfortunately, in the GEM, the rich segment of the population often allocates their money and assets abroad (both legally and illegally). This capital is not used for domestic economic activity, such as job creation, which would further expand the middle class, attract foreign investors, and improve the overall stability and economic situation of the country. At the beginning of the twenty-first century, the per capita income in the 20 richest countries is 37 times higher than the average per capita income in the 20 poorest countries.[56] One of the causes of this situation is an under-developed financial sector in national economies of the GEM, and the subsequent lack of trust of the general population to these institutions. This situation is mirrored in the Global Financial Centres Index.[57] As of January 2008, out of the top ten global financial centers, only two are from the GEM (Hong Kong and Singapore). However, of all 46 ranked financial centers, there are already 16 in EMCs and the financial centers ranked from thirty-ninth to forty-sixth are all from EMCs.[58] Dublin stands out as a financial center that is oriented toward its customers' quality of life. More than any other EMC financial center, Dublin gives a great deal of attention to individual customers, not just corporate clients. Practical observations make it possible to conclude that the banking system is adequate to the needs of the general population once there are roughly 10 banks and their offices per 100,000 people. This ratio can be increased to 75 banks per 100,000 people in countries with much larger territories than average such as Russia, China, Brazil, India, Argentina, Kazakhstan, and South Africa.

Another factor that encourages people to move their personal and corporate financial assets abroad is high taxes. As of January 2008, the highest corporate tax is in Mumbai, India, with a rate of 81 percent.[59] This creates an incentive for capital to be moved abroad, which has negative implications for the development of the middle class. For EMCs, a developing and strong middle class is a key factor of stability, which eventually attracts more investment and also discourages domestic companies from sending their assets abroad.

For this reason the government has to develop programs to motivate the expansion of the middle class. If the correct programs are implemented, eventually the market itself will create the conditions necessary for the sustainable expansion of the middle class.

The development of the middle class also has positive implications for gender inequality. According to the director of one of CISCO Systems' Networking Academies (part of a global education initiative of CISCO), 30 percent of students and 20 percent of teachers of IT in CISCO Academies are women. While many assume that women do not play a significant role in the GEM, this is not the case. In some EMCs, especially those of Eastern Europe, women occupy several important leadership positions in governments as well as in technology companies. Among medical doctors, teachers, and engineers, the percentage of women in some EMCs is equal to the percentage of men.

It is also important to note that the middle class of EMCs may be very different from that of developed countries in terms of standard of living, purchasing power, etc. The effects of the middle class on politics in EMCs can be different than in developed countries. In developed countries, the middle class is the most politically active. In EMCs, the middle class often prefers the stability of the status quo, instead of the continuation of rapid political reform. For this reason, in EMCs without a tradition of democracy, once a certain level of political freedom is attained, the pace of democratic reform dissipates. This can be seen in China, Russia, Colombia, Venezuela, Ukraine, Egypt, etc.

The Future of the Global Emerging Market in the Global Marketplace

The role of the GEM in the GMP will continue to expand, at least until the end of the twenty-first century. After this period, the majority of the most mature EMCs will achieve a level of prosperity on par with median developed countries and will no longer be part of the GEM. This will obviously have a huge impact on the GMP.

In no more than a decade, a few EMCs will transition into the highest category of a country's development in the GEM—economies in bloom, and even to the category of developed country. In Europe, the Czech Republic, Greece, Portugal, Slovenia, and Slovakia will follow the lead of Spain (which is already an economy in bloom) and Ireland, which by that time will have completed the transition to the category of developed country. In Asia, Singapore, South Korea, and possibly Taiwan will also be categorized as economies in bloom. Costa Rica will be the only EMC outside of Europe and Asia to become an economy in bloom during this period. Israel, with its well-established democracy, high levels of economic freedom, and technological advancement, has the potential to make this transition as well. However, a very high level of political risk, as a result of extremely tense bilateral relations with its neighbors, inhibits the development of multilateral and regional agreements and may prevent Israel from completing the transition to developed country.

Countries with a low standard of living that lack economic and political freedom will eventually (within 10 years) initiate political and economic reforms and become part of the GEM. This even includes economies that are "repressed" according to the *Wall Street Journal* and Heritage Fund Index of Economic Freedom, such as Myanmar and Iran—nothing lasts forever. Of course, it would be equally foolish to assume that all EMCs constantly progress forward. The examples of Venezuela and Bolivia clearly indicate how progress can be stalled and even reversed. But in all likelihood, these governments will eventually realize that there is no alternative to economic freedom and integration with the GMP.

The continuation of the spread of democracy and economic freedom will lead the most successful EMCs to become developed economies. Countries that, at the end of the first decade of the twenty-first century, are considered pre-emerging market, developing, and even underdeveloped will become part of the GEM. It is important to note, however, that the GEM is not a temporary entity composed of countries in transitional phases of their development. There will always be differences in the political, economic, and technological characteristics of development of countries in the GMP, and the GEM will be made up of the relatively less developed countries in terms of their political, economic, and social maturity. These countries will always provide opportunities and challenges to developed countries. What is indisputable is that all major problems of humankind, such as poverty, hunger, unemployment, mass disease, ecological devastation, and migration, can be solved only though a partnership between national governments of different categories of countries, together with private companies and multilateral institutions. Under the influence of the GEM, problems of humankind will be both aggravated and mollified, and the global order will constantly adjust in response.

The list below shows a forecast of the Top 20 EMCs (by attractiveness of FDI), until 2020:

1. China
2. India
3. Brazil
4. Russia
5. Mexico
6. South Korea
7. Poland
8. Vietnam
9. Israel
10. Kazakhstan
11. Egypt
12. Czech Republic
13. South Africa
14. Turkey
15. The Philippines
16. Argentina
17. Ukraine
18. Romania
19. Hungary
20. Portugal

Study Questions

1. What defines an EMC?
2. What defines the GEM?
3. What is the relationship between EMCs, the GEM, and the GMP?
4. Who decides if a country has the traits of an emerging market for a particular company?
5. What would cause a country to no longer be included in the emerging-market category?
6. Describe the correlation between quality of goods and services and freedom of choice.
7. How are freedom of choice and the quality of goods and services related to the birth of the GEM?
8. What kind of free-market institutions must a country have in order to internationalize its economy, to be an attractive destination for FDI, and to be considered an EMC by foreign investors?
9. Which major rating agencies should a company consult before becoming active in an EMC?
10. Can a country that was once but is no longer considered an EMC fall into that category again? Give examples.
11. Which economy's input to world output is larger: the United States, the EU, or the GEM?
12. What are the major categories of EMCs?
13. What are remittances?
14. What makes up a larger share of the world total (in terms of percentage), GEM territory, GEM work power, or GEM GDP?

3 Ten Modern Global Political, Economic, and Technological Trends

> Democracy is the worst form of government, except for all those other forms that have been tried from time to time.[1]
>
> > (Sir Winston Leonard Spencer Churchill, the first lord of the treasury and prime minister of the United Kingdom, 1953 Nobel Prize winner in literature, 1874–1965)
>
> Democracy means simply the bludgeoning of the people by the people for the people.[2]
>
> > (Oscar Wilde, Irish author, 1854–1900)

Globalization and Democratization as Objective Trends

All economic systems, be they macro (global, regional, etc.) or micro (corporate, workshop, etc.) experience the following basic stages: formation, maturation, and eventually dissolution or drastic changes, which substantially alter the system. These processes are mostly predetermined by objective factors. When those factors have long-term implications, they define the vector of the dynamics of economic systems. Objective factors influence economic systems regardless of the wishes or efforts of politicians or executives, which can be understood as subjective factors. Objective factors are overwhelmingly beyond the control of human beings. As a simple example, regardless of how hard one tries (a subjective factor), the laws of thermodynamics, gravity, or the absence of rich natural resources (objective factors) will never be overcome.

A strategic economic analysis must begin with a study of basic economic factors (see Chapter 1) and objective global, regional, and industrial trends because these are objective influences of the GMP. Despite the subjective wishes of political leaders and executives, the quantity of oil, gold, and other mineral deposits cannot be increased; this is an objective factor. Because natural resources are limited and humankind utilizes them, the amount in the earth is decreasing. This is not only a factor but also an objective trend. Though labor resources may change over time, at a given point, literacy rates, life expectancies, and national demographics are what they are. However, subjective factors do influence economic systems to a certain extent. "Economic globalization is a contradictory phenomenon that necessarily produces, as its support, a space of flows and, as its nemesis, the importance of place, a source of objective and subjective resistance."[3] The quality of management systems determines the efficiency of the use of objective factors. For example, the amount of oil in a particular field cannot be increased, but the manner and technology by which it is extracted, enriched, distributed, etc., significantly influences the actual output of the company exploiting the field.

In order to develop and implement an efficient strategy for any company's executives or national governments, one must recognize and understand the most powerful objective trends and their hierarchical breakdown. A successful strategy will work according to these trends, not against them. Strategists must figure out how to minimize the negative impact of trends or, if possible, to harness them toward the fulfillment of strategic objectives. Like the best captains, strategists must be able to use headwinds to propel ships to their destination.

The end of the twentieth century saw drastic changes in modern civilization. Major dictatorships disappeared; the Soviet Union, the world's last empire, disintegrated; the Internet, mobile systems, and other technological achievements radically changed people's daily lives; even preparation for a manned mission to Mars began. All of these developments are the result of the influence of global trends. Global trends are objective processes that predetermine the dynamics of any economic system. The hierarchy of global trends changed during the last quarter of the twentieth century, as *globalization* and *democratization* became the two most important and influential trends. Globalization emerged from the maturation of the previously dominant trend, internationalization. Globalization "involves two main features: increasing interdependency and increasing integration. Trade is most closely associated with interdependency while capital flows and investment are most closely associated with integration."[4] The strength of the trend of globalization was multiplied by cutting-edge ITs, which eventually led to the formation of the GMP, which occurred on the border of the two millennia (discussed in detail in Chapter 1). Globalization as a trend can be understood as a process of involvement of all countries from all continents under one global order, and the GMP functions under the influence of this order. It may be impossible, in fact, to identify a single country of the world as totally separate from the GMP. Nonetheless, some professional firms and experts disagree. For example, MSCI, in 2006, considered countries of sub-Saharan Africa and Western Asia to have missed the globalization process. It is true that they are late to catch the train of globalization, but they obviously did not miss it altogether. The positive impact of globalization is obvious, but as with any new phenomenon to which people are not yet accustomed, globalization also has effects that can be seen as negative, such as environmental problems, cultural clashes, erosion of traditions, and even an influence on people's ethnicity. Nonetheless, the positive impact is unparalleled. Globalization connects all individuals, bringing billions of people the truth about freedom. The growing capabilities of globalization based on ITs have brought the reality about democratic countries to every corner of the world. No dictatorial regime, whether personal, military, or communist, could stop the spread of information at its national borders. This was the inspiration of democratic rebellions against dictatorships throughout the world, which acted as the tipping point in the collapse of the overwhelming majority of inefficient command economies. Around this time another global trend was peaking in influence—democratization, which of course experiences tremendous resistance and has a variety of paths of realization in different countries. According to a report by the National Intelligence Council of the US:

> [B]y 2015, key countries will have made some headway in building sturdier and more capable democratic institutions. Democratic institutions in Mexico, Argentina, Chile, and Brazil appear poised for continued incremental consolidation. In other countries, crime, public corruption, the spread of poverty, and the failure of governments to redress worsening income inequality will provide fertile ground for populist and authoritarian politicians. Soaring crime rates will contribute to vigilantism and extrajudicial killings by the police. Burgeoning criminal activity—including money laundering, alien smuggling, and narcotics trafficking—could overwhelm some Caribbean countries. Democratization in Cuba will depend upon how and when Fidel Castro passes from the scene.[5]

The confluence of globalization and democratization changed the landscape of the political and economic structures of the world. The subsequent new political and economic reality triggered the birth of several other global trends (which will be discussed in this chapter). At the end of the twentieth century, these trends changed the global order itself. According to the National Intelligence Council:

> All states will confront popular demands for greater participation in politics and attention to civil rights—pressures that will encourage greater democratization and transparency. Twenty-five years ago, less than a third of states were defined as democracies by Freedom House; today more than half of states are considered democracies, albeit with varying combinations of electoral and civil or political rights. The majority of states are likely to remain democracies in some sense over the next 15 years, but the number of new democracies that are likely to develop is uncertain.[6]

System of the Ten Global Trends

Ten selected key global trends of varying strength and maturity influence the political, social, economic, and technological development of modern civilization. The interaction of these trends and their influence on one another can be understood as a hierarchical system. At the top of this hierarchy are the super trends—*globalization* and *democratization*. These two global trends, enforced by advancements in IT, destroyed empires, dictatorships, and command economies, and they gave smaller and less powerful nations the opportunity to achieve their own statehood and to cooperate in the GMP—the formation of which was also a result of these trends. The collapse of dictatorships on a global scale led to the emergence of the global trend of *political disintegration*. Political disintegration indelibly changed the political map of the world. Since the 1980s new independent countries have appeared almost annually, usually with smaller and smaller populations. In an attempt to improve standards of living among their citizens, the governments of these new nation-states looked for solutions beyond their borders, causing a surge in international economic cooperation. This initial attempt of internationalization developed mostly between neighboring countries on a bilateral and multilateral basis. The liberalization of international economic relations, under the influence of the trends of globalization, democratization, and internationalization, initiated tighter political and economic cooperation between countries with relatively similar cultural, religious, political, and economic characteristics. From this process another global trend was reinforced—*regionalization*. The formation of regional economic unions, free-trade areas, and special economic and technological zones was accelerated by the global trend of *regional economic integration*, born during iterations of this process. The objective need to increase the efficiency of national economies strengthened regional economic integration of politically independent countries. Regional integration gets specific characteristics when countries that were once part of a bigger state begin to reintegrate economically, while maintaining their recently gained political independence. This occurred in Europe and is ongoing among countries of the former Soviet Union, as well as in Asia, where, for example, Singapore and Malaysia, which used to be one country, are experiencing regional economic cooperation under the umbrella of the Association of Southeast Asian Nations (ASEAN). After several iterations, the trend of regional integration and regionalization motivated the integration of regional economic blocs, unions, and zones within the GMP.

The widespread failure of dictatorships and command economies, which resulted from globalization and democratization, led to the global trend of *privatization*. The burgeoning number of privately held enterprises in national economies that were once dominated by the state catalyzed a new wave of *internationalization*. This trend, the father of globalization, was rejuvenated in new, objective conditions. The dialectic connection between internationalization and globalization is obvious; at different stages of economic development, one of them plays the leading role. In order to increase the efficiency and profitability of their companies, private entrepreneurs looked for capital from abroad, and mergers and acquisitions spread like wildfire throughout the world economy. The influence of all of these trends eventually resulted in the formation of the GMP at the edge of the third millennium.

The GMP created tremendous opportunities for international investors, immediately leading to a *shortage of capital* in international markets. While the implications of this trend are not positive, neither is it the worst global trend. A deficit of capital is only a minor obstacle in the path of globalization. The most dangerous global trend, which became evident in the less restrictive international arena of the GMP, is the rebirth of *terrorism and extremism. Revolutions in science and technology* (especially ITs) not only expedited the creation of the GMP and provided new instruments for international business, but they also gave weapons of new and very dangerous capacities to terrorists. The combination of the last two trends tremendously increased political risk in the newly formed GMP.

As previously mentioned, the influence and maturity of these ten trends vary. Some, such as democratization and political disintegration, have been influential for a long time. Their effect on society has likely already peaked. As time goes by, the influence of these two global trends is diminishing, mostly due to their successful implementation. Other trends, such as economic reintegration and global terrorism and extremism, are only approaching the pinnacle of their influence. Strategists must always be aware that the global impact and existence of some trends may not yet be detectable. However, the above-mentioned ten global trends have directed the recent dynamics of the world economy and the eventual formation of the GMP. Strategists should expect these trends to continue to influence the progress of humankind over the first quarter of the twenty-first century.

The Roots of the Global Trend of Political Disintegration

During the second half of the twentieth century, the influence and momentum of globalization and democratization steadily increased, like a snowball rolling down a hill. Democratization first emerged as a global trend in the eighteenth and nineteenth centuries due to the success of democratic principles in the United States and the democratic ideas and civil code of Napoleon, which he and his armies spread across Europe on the tip of their bayonets. These two historical phenomena established examples for democratically oriented political leaders around the world. Democratization was an especially important trend following World War II. Its influence was greatest in Western Europe, Australia, and Japan; the success of these democratic countries demonstrated to the world the strong correlation between democracy and economic strength, efficiency, and prosperity.

Modern trends in IT compounded the strength of globalization and democratization, making these trends major tools for democratic opposition forces in all countries under totalitarian regimes. In some states the leaders of ruling dictatorships endorsed and implemented market-based economic ideas and principles to prolong the lives of their regimes. This was done, for example, by the communist dictatorships in China and the Soviet Union. Why does the Soviet Union no longer exist, while the Chinese Communist Party is still in power? The basic distinction between the reforms undertaken by these two dictatorships is that in China, under the leadership and legacy of Deng Xiaoping, freedom was never implemented in the country's political sphere. Instead, forced by overwhelming famine and the impending political unrest, the Chinese Communist Party decided to implement economic freedom and market-oriented reforms, without any political concessions.

The situation in the Soviet Union was quite different. US President Ronald Reagan's epithet, the "Evil Empire," was totally accurate. The 40-year-long Cold War with the United States had focused total Soviet capacity on the development and production of weapons. In 1985, when Mikhail Gorbachev was promoted to the top of the communist dictatorship, he recognized that the overwhelming superiority of the US military and that of its North Atlantic Treaty Organization (NATO) allies made it economically impossible for the Soviet Union to maintain the path it was on. It is important to keep in mind that at this time, the strongest ally of the Soviet Union was Poland—a country with an equally feeble economy that was experiencing its own major social crisis. A total inability to satisfy the basic economic needs of its people and those of the army and military industry forced Gorbachev to propose the well-known concepts of *glasnost* and *perestroika*. These terms roughly translate to openness and economic restructuring, respectively. Gorbachev mistakenly understood glasnost as a minor cosmetic change to the Soviet political system. But the people of the Soviet Union understood glasnost as a signal that the KGB, the secret police who controlled Soviet society for more than 70 years and victimized millions, was no longer in power. The communist dictatorship lost ideological control of its people and could no longer deny the inferiority of its societal model. It is also important to consider that the Soviet army, like in many countries, including the US, did not have any political power. Just as most Soviet citizens, the majority of officers and soldiers lived in tremendous poverty. The small dose of freedom to Soviet society overwhelmed the communist regime and its devalued ideology, causing the disintegration of the world's last empire. Economic reforms developed much more slowly than expected; during the last years of the Soviet Union, they did not progress substantially.

By the early 1990s, a few of the world's political leaders hoped that the Soviet Union's communist dictatorship would diminish in power in the near future, but practically no one was prepared for its almost immediate disappearance. It was unimaginable at the time, but it was one of the first and most powerful manifestations of the then unrecognized global trend of political disintegration.

In early 1992, after the failure of the Soviet Union, 15 politically independent countries appeared overnight. All of these countries became members of the UN, and all of them eventually joined major economic multilateral institutions. The disintegration of the Soviet Union is the most profound manifestation of the global trend of political disintegration. However, the initial results of this trend were more subtle. It started to influence the world in an almost invisible way, when dictatorships became weaker, under the influence of objective and subjective factors. In 1990 the Socialist Federal Republic of Yugoslavia disintegrated into five countries, the Federal Republic of Yugoslavia, Bosnia and Herzegovina, Macedonia (though its neighbor, Greece, refused to recognize this name), Slovenia, and Croatia. This part of the Balkans was still experiencing the influence of political disintegration, when Montenegro left the State Union of Serbia and Montenegro (the successors of the Federal Republic of Yugoslavia) in 2006 and became an independent state. On February 17, 2008, Serbia, under the influence of the same trend, experienced the painful independence of the previously autonomous Serbian province of Kosovo. There are 2.2 million Kosovars, 92 percent of whom are ethnically Albanian. Kosovars have a real opportunity to improve their standard of living and to integrate economically with the GMP, and the people of Serbia also benefit. Cooperation in the Western Balkans is reaching a new level: after many years of ethnic and political conflict and uncertainty, a much friendlier relationship between Kosovo and Serbia will prevail. Serbian minorities in Kosovo can play a very important role as a bridge between these two independent states.

In January 1993 another example of the influence of the global trend of political integration took place when Czechoslovakia split through the "Velvet Divorce" into the Czech and

Slovak republics. The reach of political disintegration is not limited only to the Soviet Union, Eastern Europe, and the Balkan states, it is a trend that directs political and economic processes around the world. Also in 1993, the State of Eritrea declared its independence from Ethiopia after many years of military conflict. In May 2002, after a 27-year-long fight for its independence, Democratic Republic of Timor-Leste, which had been occupied by Indonesian armed forces, finally became the first new independent country of the new millennium. The global trend of political disintegration has to be understood as a process, not only through the result of the influence of this trend—declaration of independence. This trend influences many countries that are still unified and may continue to be unified forever. But maybe not. Strategists cannot ignore this issue.

One of the best examples of this trend as a process is the democratic votes on independence in Quebec. The people of Quebec have already expressed their opinion on the issue of sovereignty through two transparent referendums, which took place in 1980 and 1995. During the first referendum, 40.44 percent of the population voted in favor of pursuing independence from Canada, while 59.56 percent voted to keep Quebec as a province of Canada. Fifteen years later, by a margin of only 1 percent, supporters of sovereignty (49.42 percent) again lost to those who voted to keep Quebec as a province of Canada (50.58 percent). Quebec is still part of Canada, and it may always be. But no one knows what the next referendum will show if it even takes place. It's certain that Canada, like many other countries, is under the strong influence of the global trend of political disintegration.

The Kingdom of Belgium is still a unified country, but at the beginning of the twenty-first century, the gap between the provinces of Wallonia and Flanders is widening, not narrowing. When on June 17, 2008, the new Benelux treaty was signed with Luxembourg, and the Netherlands, on behalf of Belgium, it was signed also by "ministers-president of Flanders, the Walloon region, the German-speaking community in Belgium and the Brussels Capital Region." This clearly indicates that even in the international arena, Belgium does not present a singular unified voice.[7] This kingdom may continue its existence as a federation, but maybe not. Strategists cannot ignore this. It may come as a surprise to many, but the same situation exists in 18 other regions of European states. Some separatist leaders of the rich north of Italy would like independence from the less economically developed south of the country. Leaders of this idea even established a name for the northern part of Italy, the "Republic of Padania."[8] Strategists should not totally ignore this; nor should they ignore the separatist movement in the Basque Country and Catalonia, two of the most industrialized regions of Spain. Another European country, the United Kingdom of Denmark, is experiencing separatism from the regional government of a territory that is many times bigger than the mainland. Greenland, the largest island in the world, is seeking more self-ruling authority. Since 1979 this process has been in progress, amicably so, and since 2003 the Danish–Greenlandic Commission has supervised it. This commission gives recommendations on the increasing foreign-policy rights of Greenland, which already has its own national symbols. Similar processes are under way in several other European countries, as well as in Asia and in Russia. The majority of these movements in Europe unfold through peaceful and democratic means. However, in Russia and Asia, these processes often occur outside of voting booths. This was the case in Chechnya, where separatists in the 1990s practically declared war on Russia and especially on neighboring provinces such as Dagestan. Violence is a major means employed by similar separatist movements, such as that of the Tigers of Tamil, who seek the creation of their own country—Tamil Eelam—on the island of Sri Lanka. Two provinces of the country of Georgia, Abkhazia and South Ossetia, as well as the Transdnestrian Republic in Moldova, have for many years operated as independent states and seek official international recognition. For these three regions, the recognition of Kosovo is a very promising example. All of these processes and military conflicts can be seen not only as separatist movements but also as processes under the influence of the global trend of political disintegration. This approach is more accurate for strategists, who are not taking part in any of these conflicts and must evaluate both scenarios: all of these provinces can be part of unified countries or will become independent states. This is not the approach of politicians, but it is the appropriate mindset for economic and business strategists.

The result of the influence of this trend can be seen in the increasing number of countries around the world. The League of Nations, which was established by the Treaty of Versailles in 1919–1920, had 42 charter countries. The UN had 51 founding member-states who declared the establishment of this organization in 1945. Ten years later the UN already had 76 member states. In 1965 there were 117 members. In 1990, 159 countries were members of the UN; in 2000 the figure was 189, and as of January 1, 2008, the UN has 193 member-states.[9] Due to this dynamic, strategists always have to analyze the continuation of the influence of this global trend, despite what political leaders may wish.

The transition from dictatorship or command economies is not necessarily a smooth process: never is a totalitarian system instantly swapped for democracy and a free-market economy. The process ebbs and flows, and can even reverse itself, but the one constant is usually increasing economic freedom. The former Soviet Republic of Turkmenistan offers an interesting example. Following the disintegration of the Soviet Union, all 15 former Soviet Republics took their own path away from the Soviet system. The Baltic States (Estonia, Latvia, and Lithuania), which were part of the Soviet Union for only about 50 years, immediately embraced democracy and economic freedom with much success. Other countries, such as Moldova, Ukraine, Kazakhstan, and Russia, immediately began developing foundations for democracy and economic freedom—with great difficulty. These newly independent countries straddled the line between anarchy and oligarchic capitalism, where the rule of law is often subjugated to the personal interests of a super-rich minority. Countries such as Belarus (the last dictatorship of Europe), Azerbaijan, Uzbekistan, and Turkmenistan replaced the dictatorship of the communist party with personal dictatorships. In Turkmenistan the leader of the communist party, Sapurmurat Atayevich Niyazov, was "elected" president by people who never experienced anything even resembling democracy, in a country that had never experienced independence. Turkmenistan's economy (with some of the richest natural gas and oil reserves in the world) was converted into Niyazov's personal empire. He changed his name to Turkmenbashi (father of the Turkmens), ordered stamps from the US with his portrait on them, put his profile on currency and coins, replaced monuments to Lenin in every poor village with monuments of himself, renamed the major seaport after himself (from Krasnovodsk to Turkmenbashi), made the birthday of his mother a national holiday, and made a book of his poetry required reading for all students. In 1995 "Turkmenbashi" declared Turkmenistan's neutrality, maintaining an equal distance from his neighbors Russia, China, and Iran as well as the US, preventing economic activity with all of them. He firmly held on to power until December 2006, when he unexpectedly died of cardiac arrest. After a brief struggle for power, a medical doctor and minister of health under Turkmenbashi, 49-year-old Gurbanguly Berdymukhammedov, was elected president. Cautiously, he started to lead the country out of the ruin of Turkmenbashi's personal dictatorship into the democratic world. This process is extremely complicated, and every move made by the new president sends multiple messages to allies and enemies both foreign and domestic. The many business leaders who are interested in Turkmenistan (and countries in relatively similar situations, such as Azerbaijan, Venezuela, Saudi Arabia, or China) must be able to sift through the multifaceted and subtle messages from President Berdymukhammedov. One of his first moves was to open Internet cafés with free, unlimited access to the web. He reestablished the Academy of Sciences of Turkmenistan, which Turkmenbashi had abolished, and lengthened the required years of schooling from nine to ten. However, as of 2008, the poetry of Turkmenbashi was still part of the curriculum. The mass media remains in the hands of the state, but the president also appointed a third-year university student to be editor-in-chief of a major youth newspaper. The president gave the order to purchase 19,000 computers for schools and universities and has already given all universities access to the Internet. All of this took place within the first six months of his presidency. But when asked by the president of Columbia University in September 2007 if he planned on dissolving the legacy of Turkmenbashi, he replied ambiguously: "Turkmenbashi is our history." At this pace it looks like the legacy of Turkmenbashi will be similar to that of Mao in contemporary China, portraits and books of whom are all over mainland China.

The transition to democracy varies by country but is never easy. That is why the political risk of investment is so much higher in EMCs than in countries with long democratic traditions. While it may be surprising to some, most people of the world (65 percent) actually live in partially free or totally free societies. The majority of people not living in at least partially free societies are in Africa and the Middle East.

Regionalization as a Global Trend

Scientific and technological revolutions of the second half of the twentieth century have led to radical structural shifts in the world economy. This first initiated the industrialization of the world economy, and later, the development of the post-industrial, service-based economy. At the beginning of the twenty-first century, the world economy has begun a transition to the knowledge-based economy. Increasing economic growth in developed countries and their regional economic blocs required a stable source of raw materials and energy resources from abroad, since the majority of these countries could not sustain their growth by domestic natural resources. Eventually, this situation also became relevant to EMCs that achieved a relatively high level of economic maturity and began to experience a shortage of energy and raw materials. Increasing inequality in economic development between different regions of the world economy led to a new international division of labor. Growth in EMCs and developed countries could not be sustained without the expansion of key industries related to the exploration, extraction, and enrichment of raw materials in developing and underdeveloped countries. This led to a huge investment in economically underdeveloped territories, which were never before part of the world economy and were very often uninhabited, lacking basic infrastructure and modern production facilities. The allocation of investment and the development of assets in these areas began a large-scale transfer of raw materials to these newly industrializing regions. This large-scale economic shift could not and still cannot be efficient without a new regionalized form of interaction between science, technology, businesses, governments, and society within the legal framework of environmental protection.

The extraction of hydrocarbon raw materials in the deserts of the Arabian peninsula and Central Asia, in the permafrost of northern Siberia and on the shelf of the World Ocean, the development of deposits of non-ferrous metals, diamonds, and coal above the Arctic Circle, the forests in the tropical zone and the arctic taiga, and the development of fallow and virgin lands in the zone of experimental agriculture all required regionalized equipment and technologies. This technological specialization according to regional conditions is a simple way to understand the global trend of technological regionalization. In addition to the natural difficulties of exploiting resources in these environments, the fact that they are primarily located in EMCs and developing countries with insufficient infrastructures, poorly studied geological features, low population density, and shortages of skilled labor created requirements for special economic solutions, regionally suitable social and environmental programs.

Machinery and technology that is extremely efficient in one particular region may be barely functional in another. For example, innovative technologies and equipment have been implemented in the eastern part of Russia in the brown coal deposits of the Kansko-Achinskiy and Ekibastuz (northeastern Kazakhstan) basins. This technology has achieved labor productivity 20 to 25 times higher than the national industry averages of these countries. However, if these technologies were implemented in any mine in Europe or in almost any other region of the world, they would not operate at their full capacity: they would be inefficient. Geological conditions in a particular region—the reserves of natural resources such as minerals, timber, and energy—largely determine technological development. This phenomenon is a result of the influence of the global trend of the second half of the twentieth century—regionalization, which is still very powerful. It is important to underline that regionalization is definitely not restricted to science and technology used in processes of production, engineering, construction mechanics, etc. Science itself has also been influenced by this global trend, leading to the development of new theoretical disciplines such as regional geology and regional geomorphology, regional sociology, and regional economics, among other fields of study. Regionalization also has very important implications for environmental protection and revitalization.

Economic development in the Arctic zones of Scandinavia, Russia, Canada, and Alaska was particularly influenced by the trend of regionalization. These territories required specialized technology, such as frost-resistant concrete for the construction of roads, dams, and hydroelectric facilities, among many other innovations.

Region-specific approaches to economic and technological development tremendously influenced social studies and social development in areas of new economic activity, as well as the regional integration of these territories via the establishment of regional governments, unions, etc. New technologies in aircraft construction, such as a new engine that allowed direct flights between geographically remote regions, became the base for new extra-regional economic cooperation, which tremendously improved the efficiency of the GMP. Companies began to gear their products toward regional cultures, climates, and economic and business conditions and opportunities. This regionalization of products increased company market share and the efficiency of regional economies. According to Professor Lin Sien Chia of the Institute of Asia-Pacific Studies:

> The addition of more powerful engines to Boeing 747-200 series in the 1990s meant that non-stop operations were possible between Southeast Asian points and Europe . . . Additional non-stop options were feasible following the introduction of the Boeing 747-400 series (for example, between Bangkok and Singapore and Europe overflying the Persian Gulf). These technological developments provided scope for the region's carriers to pursue expansionist strategies and broaden their connections both within the region and with Northeast Asia. The increased regional feeder links gave airlines the potential to use key airports as hubs to mitigate weaknesses in Southeast Asia's route network.[10]

This global trend, which extended international business to new economic territories, was a topic of great interest among global leaders and scholars who often referred to it as regionalism:

> Early discussions about regionalism emerged from three primary sources. The first was a political-normative question about the sustainability of the nation-state as a vehicle for

effective and peaceful human governance. The second was the growth and gradual formalization of the social sciences, particularly in the United States. The third, of course, was the appearance of regional integration schemes.[11]

Some mistakenly interpret the trend of regionalization as the opposite of globalization. It is not. Regionalization is one of several processes of globalization. Regional blocs, regional economic unions, and free-trade areas play a very important role in the improvement of the GMP.

The influence of regionalization on social and economic processes, especially in EMCs and developed countries, motivated changes in governance and management systems. The founder and former president of Sony, the first global Japanese company, Akio Morita, established the term *glocalization*, to explain the relationship between regional management and governance in the GMP.[12] Corporate leaders operate on both levels simultaneously. The improvement in management systems and governmental practice in collaboration with other processes under the influence of globalization and democratization eventually led to an offspring modern global trend—*regional decentralization*. This trend is related to the decentralization of managerial functions of national governments to regional and local authorities. Dictatorships always concentrated and centralized most power in the hands of one dictator or authoritarian body. When a dictatorship falls, new democratically elected leaders focus on strategic national issues, mostly preoccupied with the democratization of society, and begin to delegate many managerial functions to regional and local bodies.

Like privatization, while the global trend of regional decentralization has been vital in the GEM, it was developed and used much earlier in the developed world—in France. Despite the socialist nature of the party of François Mitterrand, who won the French presidential election in 1981, his strategy to improve the efficiency of public administration and the national economy was to transfer many national functions to provincial authorities. In order to do so, he formed the Ministry of the Interior and Decentralization. Mitterrand's decentralization strategy was based on his belief in the need "to develop regional economic development strategies, based upon a regionalized economic plan."[13] According to Professor Michael Keating:

> The French governmental system comprises a mixture of central and local power. The Socialist Government came to power pledged to decentralization. This is being achieved through a series of laws. Yet separating central and local affairs has raised major problems. There are contradictions within the Socialists' ideology with regard to decentralization and the implementation of the programme has been slowed down.[14]

Outside of the developed world, especially in those countries under dictatorships and command economies, all governing and managerial functions were the responsibility of the national government, which is located in the country's capital city. After the fall of the dictator and/or liberalization of the economy and establishment of a free market, these functions are transferred to regional, local, and even community authorities. It is important that foreign companies that were active in the country during the rule of the dictator are aware of this trend. Those who ignore the implications of this trend and work exclusively with national or federal governments will suffer as a result. Increasing economic freedom not only weakens national and federal governments but it also empowers local communities and entrepreneurs, as well as regional and local authorities. Foreign companies should pay special attention to the local communities in which they do business. Offering assistance on local social issues can be a relatively cheap way to create an environment friendly foreign business and to avoid potential conflicts. Nobel laureate in economics Joseph Stiglitz argued that local communities were the "fourth pillar" of successful development strategies, in addition to markets, government, and individuals.[15] One successful example of this is the practice of Eli Lilly (www.lilly.com), a leading pharmaceutical company that always has offices in the capital city as well as the particular region in which it invests (especially in EMCs). The office in the capital city is responsible for the company's national strategy, while the regional office implements this strategy through sales and the development of relationships with regional and local communities and authorities. It is vital for certain industries such as pharmaceuticals, to have a good relationship with local and regional authorities and communities, as the quality of health care is usually a crucial community issue and can vary a great deal regionally and even locally.

The evaluation and measurement of the practical realization of the influence of global trends is always a subject of interest and necessity for strategists and economists. Regional decentralization does not have a widely accepted index to measure its impact as a global trend, although scholars have made several attempts to quantify this trend. In 1999 Professor Christine Kearney created the Decentralization Index, which measures "the assignment of fiscal, political, and administrative responsibilities to lower levels of government."[16] The index is based on the following nine dimensions: government structure; selection of regional executive; selection of local executive; override authority; revenue-raising authority; revenue sharing; authority for education; authority for infrastructure; and authority for policing.[17]

Regional decentralization has occurred in practically all EMCs. According to the UN Development Program, there are three challenges that arise in processes of regional decentralization:

> First, most countries are implementing reforms on an ad hoc basis, and the legal framework for decentralization is incomplete or inconsistent. Second, fiscal decentralization remains very much a work in progress. Fiscal decentralization reform is characterized by the following: one-off or piecemeal approach; lack of logical sequencing; unclear assignment of expenditure responsibilities between the different tiers of the government; ineffective local tax management; inadequate fiscal-equalization mechanisms; and inadequate regulation of local borrowing. Third, attracting and retaining professional and qualified employees in local governments continues to be a challenge. Local governments are expected to carry out decentralization, taking on new responsibilities and providing quality services. However, personnel management and employment conditions at the subnational levels have long been neglected.[18]

Indonesia introduced a decentralization plan in 2001. According to Kazuhisa Matsui, a senior research fellow from the Institute of Developing Economies of the Japan External Organization:

> Decentralization has transferred not only administrative authority but also many new vested interests from the center to regions. Local governments have become more extensive economic actors in regional economies. Regional economic actors now compete actively for such vested interests and have missed the opportunity to create market-friendly regional economies.[19]

The Trend of Regional Economic Integration

Globalization and liberalization of international economic relations created a new environment for politically independent countries. Economic isolation and autarchy led some nations to economic failure and declining standards of living. Countries that recently obtained their independence often attempt self-isolation—and suffer the inevitably negative consequences. In the euphoria of their fresh independence, political leaders often make the mistake of cutting not only political but even economic ties with its former dominant or sister countries. However, political leaders are learning from experience and past examples, and the naive concepts of autarchy and self-isolation are being replaced quickly by international economic cooperation.

International economic cooperation and trade, which increased on a *global* scale since the beginning of the 1980s, later, during the early 1990s, developed rapidly on a *regional* scale. The beacon for all countries that sought to improve regional cooperation was the European Communities, which were established in 1967, by the merger of the European Steel and Coal Community, the European Atomic Energy Community, and the European Economic Community. In fact, modern European economic integration began much earlier, when in 1958, Belgium, Luxembourg, and the Netherlands formed the Benelux Economic Union, which would be the prototype for future European integration. Benelux was formed in 1958 on the base of the Benelux Customs Union, which had been operational since 1948. In the twenty-first century, Benelux is still very much alive. In June 2008, the leaders of these three countries signed a new Benelux treaty. This agreement is no longer restricted to issues of economic cooperation. It also focuses on the harmonization of the policies on justice and law enforcement. The success of European integration and its increasing number of member-states inspired other countries to achieve a new level of economic efficiency, through economic integration or reintegration with neighboring countries.

Regional economic integration is most successful when it includes countries of different levels of economic development, and other basic economic factors such as labor and natural resources. Asymmetry in regional economic cooperation creates the incentives for tighter economic and business connections. The example of North American economic cooperation is a clear illustration of this point. The high unemployment in Mexico (relative to the United States and Canada) of people with a strong work ethic was one of the reasons for the national leaders of North America to develop intracontinental economic cooperation. Another motivating factor was the different allocation of natural resources and the asymmetric consumption of these resources among these three countries. For example, oil resources and oil consumption are distributed disproportionately in North America. It may come as a surprise to many that the largest and second-largest exporters of oil to the US are Canada and Mexico, respectively. The technological advancement of the United States was the base for the beginning of industrial cross-border cooperation with Mexico in 1965, when the US started to build production facilities in Mexican territory, using a duty-free regime for the delivery of equipment and raw materials, employing Mexicans. This cross-border regional cooperation was called the Masquerader program. The success of this program provided support for President Bill Clinton, when in 1993 he brought through Congress and signed the North American Free Trade Agreement (NAFTA). This trilateral treaty between the United States, Canada, and Mexico was developed during the time of his predecessor, President George H.W. Bush.

After the two successful precedents of NAFTA and the EU, countries from other parts of the world followed suit. The level of intensity of economic ties in different regional economic agreement varies, but the concept is always the same. In 1991 formal multilateral regional economic cooperation began between the countries of the south cone of South America—Argentina, Brazil, Paraguay, and Uruguay. Later other South American countries joined this regional economic and trade agreement, known as Mercosur (or Mercosul in Brazil), with varying statuses of membership, including Venezuela (member in waiting) and Bolivia, Chile, Colombia, Ecuador, and Peru (associate members). In Asia, ASEAN, which was established in 1967, began to intensify the economic component of its cooperation in the 1990s. Its members include Brunei Darussalam, Cambodia, Indonesia, Laos, Malaysia, Philippines, Singapore, Thailand, Vietnam, and even the isolated country of Myanmar. An interesting development is that ASEAN has begun to sign and participate in bilateral economic agreements between ASEAN as a whole and other non-member countries.

Several African regional economic unions have intensified ties between member countries, such as the Common Market for Eastern and Southern Africa (COMESA), which was established in 1994. Another African economic bloc, the Economic Community of West African States (ECOWAS), was established much earlier in 1975. In the 1990s it was rejuvenated, and its fifteen member countries began to expand their mutual trade and economic ties. The same dynamic occurred in the Caribbean Community (CARICOM), which was formed in 1973 (originally as the Caribbean Community and Common Market). As of 2008, CARICOM has fifteen full members, twelve associate members and seven observers.

It is interesting that republics of the former Soviet Union that were so eager to secede from the Soviet empire later in the 1990s established several regional economic organizations, such as the Commonwealth of Independent States (CIS), which is based on a relatively loose agreement, and the GUAM Group, which includes Georgia, Ukraine, Azerbaijan, and Moldova. These member-states signed an economic cooperation treaty in 1996. Interestingly, the member countries of GUAM are also members of CIS, together with six other countries.

The influence of globalization has increased the geographic scale of regional economic cooperation and trade. Reflecting this trend, the Asia-Pacific Economic Cooperation (APEC) became "the premier forum for facilitating economic growth, cooperation, trade and investment in the Asia-Pacific region."[20] In 1995, during a meeting in Osaka, Japan, APEC adopted the framework for the intensification of ties in the biggest economic region in the world, "the Osaka Action Agenda (OAA), which provides a framework for . . . trade and investment liberalisation, business facilitation and sectoral activities, underpinned by policy dialogues, economic and technical cooperation."[21] No one regional bloc can compete with APEC, not only in number of countries but also in terms of the economic power of its member-states, which account for 41 percent of the world's population, 56 percent of GWP and about 49 percent of global trade.[22]

APEC is only one example of the expansion of regional economic integration in the GMP. Regional trade blocs throughout the world are beginning to evolve into huge regional trade and economic areas. An obvious example is the proposed Free Trade Area of the Americas, which would extend NAFTA and Mercosur, usurping the smaller regional blocs, such as the Central American Free Trade Agreement (CAFTA), as well as bilateral and multilateral agreements among blocs and between blocs and individual countries (such as the free trade agreement between the Dominican Republic and the countries of CAFTA). In Asia several regional blocs and individual countries have begun to develop the South Asia Free Trade Agreement (SAFTA). This agreement provides the legal framework for another mega-zone, which includes 1.5 billion people. A similar trend is occurring in Africa, where the previously mentioned African trade blocs and economic agreements are in the early stages of converging into a continental free-trade area of Africa. This enlargement of the territorial and economic scale of economic integration is primarily the result of globalization, democratization, and regionalization. Countries involved in large-scale regional cooperation tear down economic barriers for each other and eliminate custom duties, tariffs, and quotas, allowing the free movement of all basic economic factors such as raw materials, manpower, and capital as well as goods and services. Businesses in these zones and areas also benefit from the harmonization of domestic legal frameworks. At the same time, companies that originate in these mega-areas receive preferential treatment (de facto and de jure), which leads to unequal conditions for companies from other parts of the world. This is a major concern for the WTO. The solution to this issue is already in regular use—intercontinental agreements, such as the signing of the framework agreement between Mercosur and the EU and their country members. "Regionalization for countries and for firms is characterized by preferential trading arrangements among countries and a regional network approach to resources, markets, and organization for firms."[23]

Regional economic integration and reintegration is a major trend of increasing efficiency of the GMP. The dialectic connections between global and regional integration will be on national and multinational agendas throughout the twenty-first century. (Particular regional economic blocs and areas and their strategic economic and business conditions will be additionally discussed in detail later in Chapters 5 and 8.)

The Trend of Privatization

A basic characteristic of a dictatorship is absolute and complete domination by the ruling body or individual dictator over the politics, culture, and economics of a society. Economic domination is generally what leads directly to the collapse of dictatorships and command economies (a detailed analysis of this process can be found in Chapter 2). Poor management of nationalized state-owned companies and the complete centralization of an economy do not generate the revenue necessary to control, placate, or appease the population. When the dictatorship falls, the nascent democratic government faces a dilemma. In general, the leadership lacks the necessary experience and knowledge to efficiently run large national companies and is incapable of doing so, while also focusing on the creation of democratic institutions. The leaders of these countries found themselves with obligations to control the majority of a country's enterprises, most of which were on the edge of bankruptcy or barely profitable. The budgets of these countries were very limited, making it difficult for democratically elected leaders to fulfill their pledges to improve the standard of living of their citizens. The transfer of ownership of state-controlled companies to private hands— privatization—was the only option to increase national economic efficiency, increase market capitalization, and improve the fiscal situation of the national government and the standard of living of its citizens. In the early 1990s, most FDI in EMCs was drawn by opportunities generated from the privatization of state-owned companies. According to Professor Bruce Wallin of Northeastern University:

> [T]he goal of privatization as contracting out is usually reduced cost, and often greater flexibility. The argument usually suggests:
>
> - government bureaucracy is inefficient and is not driven by the threat of competition, thus raising cost and lowering performance, reducing efficiency;
> - civil service and public employee union contracts limit flexibility and ability to reward performance, and to punish those who don't perform, or reassign personnel;
> - privatization eliminates corruption.
>
> Critics of privatization posit:
>
> - government workers have expertise;
> - government exists to promote goals beyond low cost;
> - the need to lower bids may lead to reduced service;
> - government loses direct control, becoming dependent on private providers;
> - "legal corruption," in the form of campaign contributions, occurs.[24]

Privatization is not a process that is restricted to the emerging and developing world. In fact, the above points were used to argue for the privatization of public services in the state of Massachusetts. Some of these arguments require further explanation. For example, it is mentioned that privatization eliminates corruption. This can be understood in the following way: when companies appear in private hands, corruption is decreased, compared with the level of corruption while a company is state owned. However, it is important to realize that during the process of privatization itself, corruption typically skyrockets.

Privatization is a complex and very important process for countries progressing from a dictatorship to a free society. While it is vital to transfer state-owned assets to the private sector in order to prevent a regression to dictatorship, this is not the main objective of privatization. Ideally, privatization should result in increasing efficiency of the national economy on the base of a net creation of jobs, the establishment of a new middle class of business owners and entrepreneurs, the creation of a competitive atmosphere between private and state-owned businesses, and a prevention of the appearance of a large wealth gap. Ideally, in an EMC the transition from a state-owned economy to a private economy (whereby more than 50 percent of GDP is produced by private or mostly private companies) takes three to seven years. A successful privatization will go a long way toward solidifying political and economic progress. The extent to which an EMC has privatized its economy is one of many indicators of its maturity.

Unfortunately, in reality, the process of privatization is structurally very vulnerable to corruption. Typically, the bureaucrats in charge of the privatization receive modest salaries that are disproportionate to the market value of the government assets that they are bringing to the market through auction or privatization tenders. Some entrepreneurs are more than willing to offer bribes worth more than most bureaucrats have been paid for their entire career of public service in order to purchase government assets at a reduced price. This is why a substantial part of state-owned assets were transferred into the hands of private entrepreneurs for a fraction of the company's market value, while the bureaucrats in charge of the privatization retire early with an unusually healthy bank account. In many cases governments actually receive only a small part of the already discounted price from the private buyer. And governments rarely enforced the agreements made with private buyers. There are some instances in which ownership of state assets was transferred to private entrepreneurs without any payment ever being delivered.

Privatization as a global trend became most powerful and practically useful, mostly during the time of the initial maturity of EMCs. As a major economic phenomenon and powerful instrument for improving the efficiency of national economies, privatization began in 1979 when Margaret Thatcher became the first female prime minister in the history of Great Britain. Her main objective was to improve the country's dismal economic situation and to increase employment. Privatization was central to her strategy; she chose her close associate David Young, who later obtained a Cabinet position, to oversee the process. Under his guidance, almost all companies of huge industries were successfully privatized, including coal, iron, steel, gas, electricity and water supply, real estate, trucking, railways, airlines, and telecommunications. Young did an outstanding job, and on average, privatized companies decreased cost production by 30 percent to 33 percent. Shipyards were able to accomplish the same jobs in the same time, but with 10 percent fewer cost expenses.[25]

Poorly managed privatization, extreme corruption, and the outright theft of government assets often provoke future governments to renationalize private but formerly state-owned assets. Although the impulse is understandable, it harms the economy. It results in low investment ratings of the country from all major international rating agencies, which leads to a great reduction of foreign investment and business activity. Privatization also has to be understood as an initial stage of the capitalization of EMC. The increasing capitalization is one of the major and most important results of privatization together with the development of private and public ownership of companies that were once state owned. In general, by the mid-1990s, about 75 percent of state-owned companies in the GEM were privatized. As a result three-quarters of the GDP of the GEM was from the input of private companies. The conversion of state-owned companies to private ownership in EMCs has made the transition from state domination to economic freedom irreversible in the GEM. Even attempts to increase the role of the state through the creation of private–state partnerships cannot be seen as a direct analogy of state ownership during dictatorial regimes. The economic nature of private–state corporations is significantly different. They work for profit, and tax revenue from these profits go toward increasing citizens' standard of living, not just military expenditures. These processes of course could not be successful without strong public oversight (such as public accounting chambers, and increasing role of the legislative branch over financial issues) and transparency. This decreases corruption or any impulse by government officials to "privatize" revenue of these corporations. The last point is important to clarify. Due to the issue of corruption, a lot of governmentally connected people with deep pockets try during privatization to privatize not a company as a whole, but particularly its profits. This means that potential buyers try to get a company below the market price—even those that were profitable before privatization. This is exactly what happened, for example, with the privatization of Norilsk Nickel (http://www.nornik.ru/en/), a company with more than $1 billion of annual profit prior to privatization (for a more detailed description of this example see Chapter 1). Another example occurred during 2002, when relatives of Bulgarian officials attempted to underpay for the privatization of Bulgartabac Holding AD (http://www.bulgartabac.bg/?&LanguageCode=en), a state-owned manufacturer of cigarettes and tobacco, which covers 85 percent of the Bulgarian market.[26] This holding consists of 22 companies, which employ about 300,000 people, mostly Turkish minorities.[27]

The initial stages of privatization in EMCs typically proceed in very difficult conditions. On the one hand, state-owned companies have to be privatized, but on the other hand, the overwhelming majority of people cannot buy even a medium-size company. It is not hard to imagine how absurd it sounded to offer to the general population, who for generations could barely afford enough food and clothing to subsist, the opportunity to purchase multimillion-dollar enterprises. In EMCs, unlike in developed countries, privatization generally goes through the following stages:

1. Employees and the general population receive some of the shares of state-owned companies for free, according to their experience, input, and years working for the company. Another version is that every citizen receives a certificate (voucher) for a certain portion of national wealth, without any distinction between people who spent their entire life working for the country, or a child who was born a day before the declaration of privatization. Both ways have their pluses and minuses. This stage can be called *mass privatization*. Typically, foreigners are not allowed to be part of this stage. However, they can participate on the secondary market by buying shares of companies or vouchers from citizens who get them for free from the state.

2. The second stage is usually conducted a few years later, when the country has gone through the initial stages of development of market-oriented reforms. It typically begins once some domestic entrepreneurs have enough initial capital to buy properties, and/or are capable of getting credit and loans from banks. This stage is usually called *cash privatization*. In this period of privatization, foreign investors actually get access to the primary market of company's shares.

Mass Privatization

In EMCs, during the initial stages of market-oriented reforms and capitalization, due to general population's lack of purchasing power, governments cannot simply auction off state assets. Instead, what the government owns (anywhere from 10 to 100 percent) can be distributed among employees of state-owned companies based on the tenure and position of each employee. Often, executives of the company get an additional 10 to 15 percent of ownership, contingent on the development and implementation of a program to increase the productivity and efficiency of the company once it is privatized during a one- or two-year period. This has generally been an ineffective means of motivation, as executives usually leave the company or sell their shares shortly after privatization. Of course, the government tries to limit special executive shares by time and other constraints to buy or sell shares, but with the mass scale of this privatization, and the strong atmosphere of corruption, it is difficult to control, monitor, and especially to enforce regulations in practice.

An alternative first stage of privatization in EMCs is to distribute a part of state-owned property equally among all citizens, regardless of age, position, or even employment status. This was the method used by the Russian Federation. On September 1, 1992, every living citizen received a voucher with a face value of 10,000 rubles. Unfortunately, due to high inflation and poor management of the privatization process, within a couple of months people had no faith in the vouchers, and many threw them away or exchanged them for bottles of vodka (worth roughly 100 rubles at the time). Most Russians were extremely pessimistic about the future. Although the vouchers represented a means to future ownership of state assets, most people were more concerned with their immediate well-being. Also, people tried to sell vouchers through any means because they were valid for only one year. In reality the expiration date was prolonged for a few months, but this did not change the situation. Some entrepreneurs (many of questionable backgrounds) wisely collected hundreds or even thousands of these vouchers, which most people thought were worthless.

During the next stage of mass privatization (the "vouchers tenders"), first priority was given to voucher holders to purchase assets of state-owned companies. In some countries the vouchers applied to specific companies, in others to all regional or national state assets. This gave entrepreneurs who had collected thousands of vouchers the ability to amass huge portfolios of state assets from voucher tenders. It also is the origin of the unprecedented disparities between the rich and poor in many EMCs. The final stage of the process of mass privatization is known as the open tenders and biddings. Typically, citizens who already held state vouchers, shares of the company, or were employees of the privatizing company participate in these tenders. Outsiders and foreigners are not allowed to participate in the initial stages of tenders and biddings, but they can buy companies or shares of privatizing companies from owners who obtained their ownership at these tenders. This basic structure of mass privatization took place during the first half of the 1990s in Czechoslovakia, Bulgaria, Romania, and some other emerging markets of Europe, in the so-called transitional economies. Table 3.1 shows in more detail mass privatization programs in Central and Eastern Europe and the CIS.

Cash Privatization

Mass privatization, above and beyond all goals mentioned above, was a simple and practical way for many countries to build initial capital markets. However, according to Zuzana Fungacova of the Center for Economic Research and Graduate Education and Economics Institute, "the functioning of capital markets in mass-privatization countries would seem to

Table 3.1 Mass Privatization Programs in Central and Eastern Europe and the CIS[28]

Country	Shares in Waves or Continuous Issue	Vouchers Bearer, Tradable, or Non-tradable	Investment in PIFs Allowed, Encouraged, or Compulsory	Independent Fund Managers or Self-managed Funds
Albania (1995)	C	B	E	I
Armenia (1994)	C	B	A	I
Belarus (1995)	C	B	E	S
Bulgaria (1995)	W	N	E	S
Czech Rep. (1992)	W	N	E	I
Estonia (1993)	C	T	A	I
Georgia (1995)	C	N/A	A	
Kazakstan (1994)	W	N	C	I
Kyrgyzstan (1994)	C	B	A	I
Latvia (1994)	C	T	A	
Lithuania (1993)	C	N	A	I
Moldova (1994)	W	N	E	I
Poland (1995)	W	T	C	I
Romania (1992)	C	B	C	I
Romania (1995)	W	N	A	Tbd
Russia (1992)	C	B	E	S
Slovak Republic (1992)	W	N	E	S
Slovenia (1994)	C	N	A	I
Ukraine (1995)	C	N	A	S

lag the development of other transition economies, which we consider to be the price for establishing capital markets only as a kind of 'by-product' of mass privatization."[29] The thousands of new owners that appeared after mass privatization became a new class of investors and developers after a few years. They were eager to pay for companies and production facilities during the next stage of privatization—cash privatization. In many cases the new private owners are restricted from raising prices of goods or services that are used by domestic consumers or producers. This was the case in the 1998 privatization of Telebras, the state-owned telephone system of Brazil, and of Israeli state-owned gas companies in 2006.

The transition from centralized economies dominated by state-owned monopolies to the free market is obviously not immediate. This period is often characterized by a decline in production as state control wanes but enterprises are not yet privatized, and it offers huge investment opportunities for entrepreneurs and companies from developed countries. Many domestic companies are so strapped for cash that they do not even have enough operational capital to maintain production and pay their employees. Foreign investors can offer relatively small loans to domestic companies so that they may continue to function. This often provides foreign companies the opportunity of eventually assuming ownership of local companies that are in desperate need of operational and investment capital, companies that struggle to repay loans. This was the process by which many multimillionaires and billionaires from developed countries, who today can be found on the *Forbes* list of the richest people in the world, made their initial fortune in the GEM.

While many EMCs have legal restrictions on foreign ownership, these limits usually apply only to certain regions or strategically or militarily important industries. There are also cases in which national governments seek to protect the livelihood of people whose income is dependent on recently privatized companies, preventing new owners from drastic restructuring and downsizing. Governments of EMCs usually put together an annual privatization plan, which lists the companies that are ready to be privatized. This can be a valuable tool for strategists who are deciding between countries for a potential direct investment. Governments typically provide very detailed information on companies included in this list. However, this information should not always be taken at face value. It is not unusual for governments to include companies that are not ready to be privatized, in order to artificially balance the national budget by falsely augmenting incoming privatization revenue.

Participation of foreign investors in cash privatization tenders and bidding often leads to the following situation: 49 percent of a company's shares being available for purchase; the other 51 percent having been distributed during mass privatization among employees and executives of the company. Typically, in this situation the foreign owner promises employees to invest in further restructuring and modernization of the company only if the employees sell the remaining shares or a controlling stake to the owner. This is usually easier in companies that are not operational at the moment of privatization due to a lack of capital or broken equipment that the company cannot afford to repair. One often-used transitional method consists of a combination of ownership by foreign investors and employees. An analogy of this kind of ownership can be found even in the United States, in Avis Car Rental Company, which in 1987 became employee-owned. In EMCs, this is usually a transitional stage of ownership, eventually leading to a shareholding company with very few owners.

A high concentration of capital and ownership are two other characteristics that usually occur with processes of privatization. When new investors concentrate ownership in their hands, they have the economic interest to improve efficiency of the company, to buy new equipment (a lack of which used to limit production), to promote and develop marketing abroad, especially in their country of origin. These new rich business owners (foreign or domestic) often become executives of the companies, try to get exclusive rights and licenses from regional or central governments, and become de facto monopolies again. A typical tactic is to promote their cronies in governmental structures and occasionally to be governmental officials themselves. They practically become oligarchs. This is the time of the beginning of oligarchic capitalism in several EMCs, such as Russia, Indonesia, Ukraine, Kazakhstan, etc. In recent history, it was the situation in South Korea and Argentina, but this is no longer the case. Oligarchy was the usual practice in ancient Greece. For all intents and purposes, it exists in some developed countries, such as Japan, where huge industrial conglomerates have a strong influence on political processes. In EMCs, at the initial stages of their development, when democracy has not firmly taken root, oligarchs are able to concentrate a considerable amount of power in their hands. The description of this process can be supplemented by the astute comments of Professors Bruce Kogut (INSEAD, France) and Andrew Spicer (University of California, Riverside). They argued that a successful privatization program depends on the development of impersonal capital markets, but

> mass privatization created the contradictory conditions of generating millions of poorly informed shareholders, with no efficient markets for the sale of the shares. The absence of financial markets created systematic pressures to move assets by illegal or non-transparent means to users who value them more. Privatization created the incentives to destroy the financial markets critical to its success . . . the functional necessity for these markets does not engender their own creation. In the absence of institutional mechanisms of state regulation and trust, markets become arenas for political contests and economic manipulation. The irony of these policies is that a principal lesson has been that market reforms cannot create viable markets, only institutional formation can.[30]

As democratic institutions mature in EMCs, the role of public opinion increases and people become more acquainted with their political rights (especially during elections), the power and influence of oligarchs tends to diminish.

The Role of Initial Public Offerings in Privatization

Following the completion of major privatization processes, new owners often still lack the necessary capital to modernize or even to make the company efficiently operational. As a result, owners in this situation often take their companies to the public market. The typical procedure is to make new issues by offering securities for sale in the primary market. This is called an initial public offering (IPO). Largely as a result of the influence of the global trend of privatization, IPOs in the GEM dramatically increased in the beginning of the twenty-first century. According to a study by Ernst & Young on global IPO activity, "the so-called BRIC countries together—Brazil, Russia, India and China—have raised $106.5 billion in 382 deals so far in 2007 [as of December 17]. More than half of those were flotations of Chinese companies, however."[31] The global value of IPOs for 2007 as of December 17 is $255 billion, and the global number is 1,739.[32] The Ernst & Young report goes on to say that

> seven out of the top ten IPOs and 14 out of the top 20 IPOs by capital raised were from emerging markets. Two out of the top ten IPOs were from Brazil, and three of the top 20 IPOs by capital raised were from Brazil. Two out of the top 10 IPOs were from China, and six out of the top 20 IPOs by capital raised were from China.[33]

Table 3.2 clearly demonstrates the steadily increasing role of the GEM in terms of numbers of IPOs as well as in raised capital. The concentration of this capital is in big IPOs in EMCs. The average size of IPOs in BRIC countries is almost twice the average size of those in developed countries (this ratio is made with the assumption that there are no IPOs in developing and underdeveloped countries). According to Maria Boutchkova (Concordia University, Canada) and William Megginson (University of Oklahoma, USA):

> Privatizations have significantly improved stock market liquidity during the last ten years [1990–2000]. On average, each additional privatization deal is associated with a 2.3 percent increase over the first year and 1.7 percent increase over the second year of the turnover ratio of the respective stock market.[34]

In general, the increasing numbers of publicly held companies in EMCs strengthens the influence of shareholders and society over business. It also improves the transparency of business transactions and eventually decreases corruption.

Table 3.2 The Role of BRIC IPOs in the GMP[35]

	2005	2006	2007
Number of IPOs Worldwide	1537	1729	1739
Number of BRIC IPOs	142	302	382
BRIC IPOs as a Percentage of World IPOs	9.24	17.47	21.97
Total Value of IPOs Worldwide (Billions $)	167	246	255
Total Value of BRIC IPOs (Billions $)	29	89.6	106.5
Value of BRIC IPOs as a Percentage of World Total	17.37	36.42	41.76

In geographic terms, companies in Europe and Asia occupy the leading positions by capital raised from IPOs.[36] The role of IPOs in raising capital in Central and South America has never exceeded 5 percent in the twenty-first century in terms of total capital raised from IPOs worldwide. It is possible to conclude that capital raised by IPOs is directly correlated to the existence of mature and deep regional capital markets.

When IPOs of different companies proceed simultaneously in several markets, a usual occurrence in the GEM, other domestic and foreign investors have the opportunity to make money through arbitrage. In this context arbitrage is the simultaneous trade of securities in different markets with the purpose of profiting from short-term price disparities. The prevalence of this practice in the EMCs is a clear illustration of the extent to which the GEM is integrated within the GMP.

It is not unusual for oligarchs to offer portions of their privately held companies to be publicly listed on stock exchanges in order to create an air of greater legitimacy. However, they often buy back these shares of their company from the market in the future. This is typically done through a "tender offer," which has a limited window in which the company can buy its own shares, usually at a premium to their current market value.

Oligarchs, or any investor with lots of cash, can also be influential in the IPOs of companies in which they do not yet hold shares. They typically do so by a process called "averaging down," whereby a potential investor with lots of cash lowers the average share price by various tactics in order to buy more of them once the price has been sufficiently reduced. Oligarchs usually try to keep most shares under their control. Often, they will put about 30 percent of their shares on the stock market, both to raise capital and to improve their image. An example of this is Skyworth (www.skyworth.com.hk/), the biggest exporter of consumer electronics in China, and the third largest producer of these goods. The company is listed on the Hong Kong Stock Exchange, but its facilities are in mainland China, in the Shenzhen Special Economic Zone, of the Guangdong province.

The Trend of Internationalization

Internationalization is one of the oldest global trends, under the influence of which globalization appeared. Internationalization has already passed the peak of its influence but is still a very relevant global trend. Under the influence of internationalization as a *trend*, internationalization as a *method* and *form* of increasing the efficiency of national economies as well as of corporations was developed and is widely in use.

Strategic Reasons to Do Business Internationally

What are the major strategic reasons for companies to internationalize? This analysis can first be done in terms of basic economic factors. Companies can internationalize in order to gain access to richer and cheaper natural resources, raw materials, or parts, and to decrease cost production by the use of cheaper, well-educated, and/or specialized labor resources. With the development of the global capital market, companies often internationalize in order to access venture capital and investment from abroad due to a domestic deficit of capital, which emerged as a result of the globalization of international markets (discussed later in this chapter). The failure of dictatorships and the birth of the GEM created a new reason for companies to internationalize—to access existing, cheap production facilities and infrastructure. This allows them to avoid the cost of constructing these facilities domestically, which would require a much larger investment. For companies that are struggling in their domestic market, one of the fastest ways to improve their competitiveness is to use existing foreign facilities and infrastructure to increase production and achieve economies of scale with cheaper products. With the growing importance of the knowledge economy, companies seek access to foreign scientific resources and researchers. The opposite concept also works; a company can make its scientific research and educational facilities available to foreign companies or individuals. This method of internationalization was used in the UK to increase the economic efficiency and stability of its universities and colleges. At the beginning of the 1960s, there were about 28,000 foreign students in Great Britain. At that time relatively new universities developed a strategy to internationalize their operations by attracting foreign students and developing branches and subsidiaries abroad. As a result, by 2002 the number of foreign students in the UK reached 225,000.[37] Through the export of education, Great Britain received £28bn in 2003–2004, more than it received from financial service exports.[38] Also, the international prestige of British universities, which was declining toward the end of the twentieth century, has improved markedly.

Quite often, companies internationalize not for cheap but unique natural resources, production facilities, skilled workers, or even final products. After the US invasion of Iraq in 2003, some brave entrepreneurs went there to obtain traditional goods that are not produced anywhere else, such as rugs and art, to sell in American and European markets.

However, it is important to realize that there are dangers associated with the process of internationalization. Companies take major political and economic risks when they create subsidiaries in unknown or unfamiliar emerging markets (discussed in detail in Chapter 8). Nonetheless, less competitive environments and cheaper production have the potential to generate very high profits, which can then be repatriated and used to increase production or reduce prices in a company's domestic market. In many cases companies that were not willing to take the risks associated with the internationalization of their operations struggle to compete in their domestic market with those companies that did internationalize. Practically, internationalization is one of the most efficient ways to increase the volume of production by decreasing cost and price, which finally increases profit and market shares of the company in its domestic market.

It is difficult to conclude by traditional means if internationalization is a proactive or reactive strategy. In the case of companies that go abroad due to a loss of competitiveness in domestic markets, it is definitely a reactive strategy. But when these same companies repatriated and reinvested their profit from abroad in their domestic market, the strategy is considered proactive. The internationalization of some companies was proactive from the very beginning. Executives with great vision and fortitude saw the potential in emerging markets very early or at least saw the successful internationalization of other companies in other industries. These executives invested in the GEM, not to save their companies, but to build markets abroad and eventually increase their domestic market share. Trade companies can go abroad just to increase sales, without investments in overseas production facilities.

Companies use different organizational forms, or "vehicles," to go international. Options include *strategic alliance* with a foreign company; *cross-border merger*; or to save time (but definitely not money), *acquisition*, whereby a company buys an existing business or facility abroad. If the acquisition is not amicable, it is referred to as a *hostile takeover*. In order to decrease investment abroad while still having a strong partner overseas, one of the most popular and efficient forms and vehicles to go abroad is the creation of an *international joint venture* (IJV) with (a) foreign partner(s). The following examples illustrate the strengths and weaknesses of the different vehicles for taking a company international.

Company A, a Canadian firm, has international aspirations but lacks the experience and know-how to expand beyond its local market. The company can use the following four options.

Option 1: Strategic Alliance

Company A could make a *strategic alliance* with Company B, which operates in a market of interest (Mexico, for example) and has an interest in expanding its operations into Canada. A strategic alliance is an agreement between two companies not to compete against each other, for example for raw materials or market share, and to provide access to each other's facilities. Company B, from Mexico, would gain access to Company A's facilities and infrastructure in Canada, and vice versa. Both Company A and Company B would theoretically gain a competitive advantage over their traditional competitors. A strategic alliance is one of the most inexpensive ways to take a company international.

An example of a strategic alliance agreement took place on February 5, 2008, when the British retailer Sports Direct announced a strategic alliance with ITAT Group. Sports Direct "operated out of 465 stores, of which 408 are located domestically, 30 in Belgium, 12 in Ireland, 11 in Slovenia and four in the Netherlands."[39] ITAT Group is a Hong Kong apparel retailer that operates in mainland China. Prior to this strategic alliance, ITAT Group had several strategic alliances with other companies, including China Resources Vanguard, Ren Ren Le, Trust Mart, Hualien, Better Life, BLC, Bailian, Wal-Mart, Carrefour, and Chongqing New Century. Sports Direct is investing about £20 million to fit out ITAT stores in China.[40] ITAT's 700 stores in 275 Chinese cities made it an ideal ally for Sports Direct's expansion into the Chinese market.[41]

Option 2: Merger

Company A could merge with Company B, which is already international. Company B will provide the know-how, experience, and infrastructure to internationalize Company A. However, this could result in the disappearance of one of the company's brands as the more internationalized company grows dominant. An example of this is the merger between the Union Bank of Switzerland and the American investment banking company PaineWebber Group, Inc., which took place in 2000. Initially, the new company was called UBS PaineWebber, Inc. But in 2003 the name of the less internationalized PaineWebber disappeared: the company's name was once again UBS, the brand of a single integrated firm.[42]

Company A could merge with a company of relatively equal size and recognition that already has a foothold in the particular market of interest. For example, Company A could seek a Mexican company with local experience, connections, and sales infrastructure that may be interested in merging with Company A in order to obtain access to its intellectual property, know-how, financial capacity, production facilities, etc. An example of a merger occurred in February 2008, when Thomson Corp.'s £7.9 billion bid for Reuters gained approval from US, Canadian, and European regulators. The goal of this merger is to create a more competitive rival for Bloomberg LP, a leading provider of financial information.

Option 3: Friendly Acquisition and Hostile Takeover

A strategic partnership or IJV may provide Company A with the financial capacity and desire to acquire control over Company B's business. If Company B accepts the offer, the acquisition will be friendly. It is also possible for Company A to acquire control of Company B without its approval, via a hostile takeover. Company A can secretly acquire a controlling interest (ownership of more than 50 percent of voting shares) of Company B on the stock market and gain the ability to hire and fire executives and make strategic decisions. In big business a hostile takeover can often be successful by obtaining a sufficient amount of voting shares that allow an investor to impede the operations of a company (much less than 50 percent). This would allow Company A to bring the business of Company B to a halt. The amount of shares necessary for a company to have a blocking stake depends on the overall distribution of shares among owners and is typically between 10 and 25 percent. For example, in February 2008, China's state-owned aluminum producer Chinalco partnered with Alcoa, an American aluminum group, to acquire a 12 percent blocking stake in Rio Tinto, a UK-listed mining powerhouse.[43] A hostile takeover is the most expensive way to take a company international. According to an article from the *Financial Times*, since 2007, there has been a rise in hostile takeovers, largely as a result of two factors:

> The first is cyclical. Many commentators fear that the latest deal making cycle that began in October 2003 . . . is nearing an end—particularly since private equity groups have pulled in their horns because of the credit squeeze, and chief executives of corporate buyers are concerned about an economic slowdown . . . The second driving force has been the proliferation of hedge funds and activist investment firms.[44]

It is not difficult to find studies and textbooks describing the advantages of international acquisition. However, it is not as easy to find information on the disadvantages of international acquisitions, though they are substantial. Being aware of these disadvantages is extremely helpful in avoiding pitfalls during and especially after the acquisition process. In *The Handbook of International Mergers & Acquisitions*, Professor David J. BenDaniel, together with the experienced executive Professor Arthur H. Rosenbloom, lists some of the most important drawbacks: cultural shock, management distance, people problems, lack of local business knowledge, poor knowledge of industry and geography.[45]

Option 4: International Joint Venture

Company A (from Canada) and Company B (from Mexico) could create an IJV forming a new legal entity, separate from both companies. By creating and supplying the initial charter capital for a separate legal entity, Company A and Company B can benefit from each other's competitive advantages, infrastructure, and unrestricted access to markets, etc., while limiting their respective liabilities. Parent companies are *not* held responsible for obligations made by an IJV. From an economic perspective, an IJV is essentially the same concept as a strategic partnership or alliance. However, from a business and legal perspective, they are significantly different because pure strategic alliances do not require the creation of a new legal entity and substantial investment. IJVs are a very efficient legal form for companies going abroad to a country in which they do not have prior experience or local relationships. Well-established local partners can create substantial advantages for an IJV. An experienced and well-connected partner can make the IJV victorious over other companies with foreign capital (subsidiaries of foreign firms or other IJVs) that have already entered the market. For this reason, some foreign companies seek partnerships with state-owned companies or companies with strong ties to the current government. There are advantages and disadvantages to this approach. When the IJV is very profitable, the government may force the foreign partner to sell all its shares to the local partner. One of the best examples of this is what happened in 1999 with Metromedia International Group, Inc. (www.metromedia-group.com) in China, when they received a letter from "China Unicom [www.chinaunicom.com.hk/] stating that a department of the Chinese government had requested termination of one of its four joint telecommunications projects."[46] (Details of IJVs as a business and legal form are analyzed in Chapter 7.)

As a result of the influence of the trend of internationalization, business has expanded beyond national borders to the point that a company's single "international" department can no longer manage the export of products and the import of raw materials to and from all parts of the world. Well ahead of the curve, in 1990, Jack Welch, the famous chief executive officer (CEO) of General Electric (GE) (http://www.ge.com/), shut down General Electric International, the division of GE responsible for international activity. Welch realized that the quantitative increase of GE's international business would make it impossible for one division to handle cross-border transactions for the other 11 GE divisions that existed at that time. Welch realized that in order to be globally competitive, all divisions of GE had to be international. A similar situation happened to the investment-banking company PaineWebber, which was once the fifth-largest United States securities firm.[47] It followed GE's lead and closed its subsidiary PaineWebber International. In the mid-1990s, Andersen Worldwide, the largest auditing and consulting professional firm in the world at the time, opened Arthur Andersen International (AAI). Andersen Worldwide, with more than 100,000 employees and 100,000 clients in 78 different countries, could not work through AAI, one small international subsidiary. AAI was insignificant and incapable of handling Andersen Worldwide's international activity, and this department closed shortly after it was opened. In the twenty-first century, the majority of multinational corporations do not have international departments. Most businesses and subsidiaries handle their own cross-border activity in the GMP. Figure 3.1 shows the number of new international firms in the GMP between 1989 and 2000. Figure 3.2 illustrates market capitalization of international firms as a percentage of total market capitalization.

In terms of foreign assets of globally operated companies, businesses from the GEM do not play a major role. The company from the GEM with the most foreign assets is Spain's Repsol YPF SA, ranked only forty-sixth on the UN list of the world's top 100 non-financial multinational corporations (see Table 3.3). The first non-European company, Petronas–Petroliam Nasional Berhad from Malaysia, is ranked fifty-fifth. Nonetheless, out of the top 100 non-financial multinational corporations, 10 are from the GEM. However, it is important to understand that almost all of these companies have a presence in the GEM, but only 10 of them register their headquarters in EMCs.

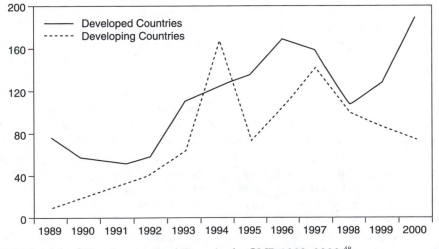

Figure 3.1 Number of New International Firms in the GMP, 1989–2000.[48]

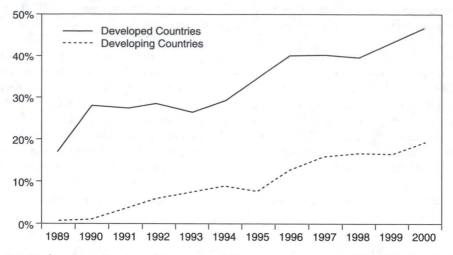

Figure 3.2 Market Capitalization of International Firms as a Percentage of Total Market Capitalization, 1989–2000.[49]

Note:
For both Figures 3.1 and 3.2: "The United States and the United Kingdom are not included in the sample due to
the classification of these countries as international financial centers. International firms are those identified as
having at least one active depository receipt program, having raised equity capital in international markets, or
being listed on the London Stock Exchange, NASDAQ, or NYSE [New York Stock Exchange]. Countries are
divided by income level following the classification of the World Development Indicators, World Bank at the
beginning of the sample period (1989)."[50]

    The Geographical Spread Index, presented in Table 3.4, is a technical but very interesting
indicator of the globalization of multinational corporations. It is calculated as the square
root of the Internationalization Index (the number of foreign affiliates divided by the
number of all affiliates) multiplied by the number of countries in which a company operates.
According to this calculation, only three of the most globalized multinationals originate in
the GEM (two companies from Spain and one from China). But this 6 percent presence is
only the beginning of the increasing role of multinationals from the GEM in the GMP.
With the rapid capitalization (see Chapter 1), there is a strong basis to expect an exponential
increase of GEM multinationals on this kind of list. Figure 3.3 indicates this dynamic,
which is already becoming visible.
    Participation of a company in the GMP does not necessarily mean that a company is
international. The overwhelming majority of territories of developed countries and EMCs
are already part of the GMP. But many companies operate locally, without even knowing
that they are part of the GMP. When a company purposefully looks for international
cooperation, receives FDI, or exports its goods and imports raw materials and parts from
abroad, this is an example of the influence of the trend of internationalization.
    Figure 3.4 represents the internationalization of national economies on a corporate level.
It is important to underline that in this figure, the authors from United Nations Conference
on Trade and Development (UNCTAD) used a classification of countries that does not
separate developing countries from EMCs. It also inexplicably separates the South-East
European countries and those of the former Soviet Union (without the Baltic States) from
developing and developed countries in a separate regional group. Clearly, the authors lack a
definitive categorization of the countries.
    The internationalization of science and technological development is proceeding even
faster than the internationalization of business and investment. As described in Chapter 1

Table 3.3 GEM Multinational Corporations from the List of the World's Top 100 Non-financial Multinational Corporations Ranked by Foreign Assets (Millions of $), 2005[51]

Ranking by Foreign Assets	Company	Home Country	Assets Foreign	Total	Transnational Index (%)	Internationalization Index
46	Repsol YPF SA	Spain	32,075	54,224	54.7	49.6
51	Endesa	Spain	28,394*	65,574	48.5	47
53	Telefonica	Spain	27,556	86,667	50.1	79.1
55	Petronas—Petroliam Nasional Bhd	Malaysia	26,350**	73,203	25.7	71.4
63	Cemex Sab De CV	Mexico	21,793	26,439	79.5	96.6
82	Singapore Telecommunications Limited	Singapore	18,000	20,748	67.4	95.2
83	CRH PLC	Ireland	17,950	19,013	79.1	93.6
87	Samsung Electronics	Republic of Korea	17,481	74,834	45.4	88.4
92	LG Corp.	Republic of Korea	16,609	50,611	49.2	91.3
98	Jardine Matheson Holdings Ltd	Hong Kong	15,770***	18,440	69.6	85.8

Notes:
The Transnational Index is calculated as the average of the following three ratios: foreign assets to total assets; foreign sales to total sales; and foreign employment to total employment. The Internationalization Index is calculated as the number of foreign affiliates divided by the number of all affiliates.
* Assets in Portugal considered domestic.
** Foreign assets data calculated by applying the share of foreign assets in total assets of the previous year to total assets.
*** Data for outside of Hong Kong and mainland China.

Table 3.4 GEM Multinational Corporations from the List of the Top 50 Multinational Financial Corporations Ranked by the Geographical Spread Index, 2005[52]

Rank	Geographical Spread Index	Company	Home Economy
16	42.9	Grupo Santander Central Hispano SA	Spain
34	30.7	BBV Argentaria SA	Spain
40	27.6	Bank of China Limited	China

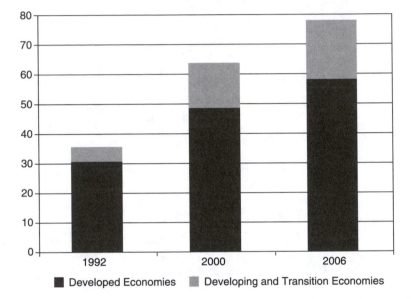

■ Developed Economies   ▨ Developing and Transition Economies

Figure 3.3 Number of Multinational Corporations from EMCs, Developed, and Developing Countries (Thousands), 1992–2006.[53]

and later in this chapter, the GMP is transitioning from a service-based economy to a knowledge economy. The new role of science in this transition practically represents the approaching second scientific-technological revolution. Recognition of this has made countries pursue inflows of foreign high-tech companies and scholars, which eventually leads to the increasing role of the scientific sector in the national economies of these countries. Prosperity in these countries is highly correlated with scientific-technological progress. The influence of internationalization in these processes is represented in Figure 3.5. Worldwide, an average 38 percent of all patents pending come from non-residents. That in itself reflects the high level of internationalization of science and technology. Out of 28 countries with the highest level of internationalization in this sector, 15 are EMCs—more than half. Fifteen countries have a higher level of internationalization in scientific studies than the world average. Two-thirds of these countries are EMCs. A high internationalization of science and technology is a further illustration of the new emerging stage of development of the GMP—the knowledge-based economy.

Deficit of Investment as a Consequence of Internationalization[54]

Prior to the birth of the GEM at the end of the 1970s, the developed world had a surplus of cash for investment. Companies and entrepreneurs had to compete for investment projects. The birth of EMCs and formation of the GEM turned this relationship upside down, creating tremendous opportunities and an unprecedented inflow of FDI, achieving a record high in 2000. Companies from the GEM sought FDI and partnership from and with companies from well-developed countries. For the majority of companies in the GEM, at the initial stage of economic liberalization, finding a foreign partner or potential owner was like a panacea from bankruptcy or dissolution. Local executives reported to their employees about successful or failed hunts for foreign investors, partners, and even owners. Equipment was stagnant, and raw materials and parts did not come due to the shortage of operation cash. This forced executives and domestic companies to totally or partially sell their assets and shares to foreign owners, often for practically nothing. It is one of the major characteristics of the initial stage of integration of companies from the GEM to the GMP—and the birth of the GMP itself. For two years the terrorist attacks of September 11, 2001, changed the situation for the worse. Investors started to take this capital back to country of origin, or to a few tax-haven countries such as Luxembourg. It was the first major impact of international terrorism on the GMP. It took five years for the FDI to rebound after the tragic events of 9/11. In 2006, for the first time, FDI inflows surpassed the previous record set in 2000.

The Economic Impact of the Global Trend of Terrorism and Extremism

The Roots of Terrorism and Extremism

Globalization brought the influence of modern Western culture and values to parts of the world with very different cultural and religious traditions. In some of these countries and regions, extremists exploit the Western presence and influence for political purposes, creating an environment hostile to foreign business and even its products. Western values and law often contradict ingrained attitudes toward women's rights and the law of the dominant religion of the land. The new wave of terrorism and extremism emerged from this clash. Conflicts of this nature are most prevalent in regions where religion was never separated from the state. This is why such conflicts basically do not exist, or at least are less intense, in Turkey, where in 1924 the great leader Kamal Atatürk effectively made Turkey a secular state. The implementation of secularism on a practical level meant the closing of Islamic courts and the Islamic educational system, and the adoption of the Swiss Civil Code. But Western values are not the only source of discord with foreign activities in regions with non-Western cultural traditions. In some countries any foreign business or cultural presence is often met with animosity, by small but fierce groups and movements. This is why there is a basis for saying that conflicts are inflamed by extremists and exploited by terrorists, who in any country do not represent the general sentiment of the population.

There are several other roots of terrorism, the most serious of which are poverty and illegal immigration. It is a well-known fact that the majority of the terrorists who committed the attacks of September 11, 2001, came from Saudi Arabia. This lends credence to well-known Saudi journalist Abid Khazindar's argument that "without development, it will be impossible to attack the root causes of terrorism; they spring from poverty, unemployment which in turn are produced by the absence of sufficient places in our universities for our young people."[55] Poverty is definitely correlated to levels of education, but

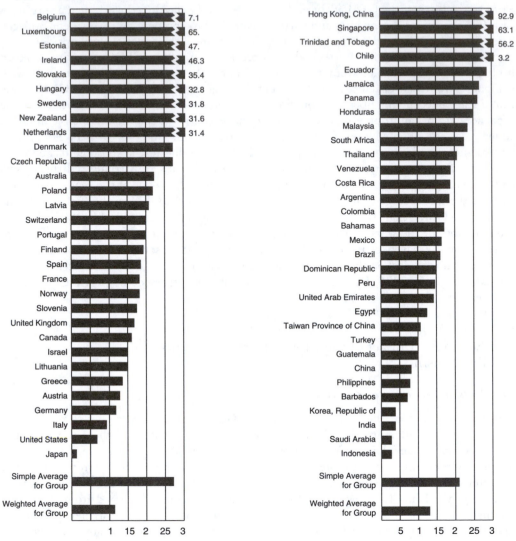

(a) Developed Economies

Belgium	7.1
Luxembourg	65.
Estonia	47.
Ireland	46.3
Slovakia	35.4
Hungary	32.8
Sweden	31.8
New Zealand	31.6
Netherlands	31.4
Denmark	
Czech Republic	
Australia	
Poland	
Latvia	
Switzerland	
Portugal	
Finland	
Spain	
France	
Norway	
Slovenia	
United Kingdom	
Canada	
Israel	
Lithuania	
Greece	
Austria	
Germany	
Italy	
United States	
Japan	
Simple Average for Group	
Weighted Average for Group	

1   15   2   25   3

(b) Developing Economies

Hong Kong, China	92.9
Singapore	63.1
Trinidad and Tobago	56.2
Chile	3.2
Ecuador	
Jamaica	
Panama	
Honduras	
Malaysia	
South Africa	
Thailand	
Venezuela	
Costa Rica	
Argentina	
Colombia	
Bahamas	
Mexico	
Brazil	
Dominican Republic	
Peru	
United Arab Emirates	
Egypt	
Taiwan Province of China	
Turkey	
Guatemala	
China	
Philippines	
Barbados	
Korea, Republic of	
India	
Saudi Arabia	
Indonesia	
Simple Average for Group	
Weighted Average for Group	

5   1   15   2   25   3

it is not true that poverty inevitably leads to terrorism. In Saudi Arabia, for example, the illiteracy rate is 21 percent and enrolment in primary schools is only 59 percent,[56] which will increase the amount of illiterate adults. As long as education is not valued, the low literacy rate will not improve. It is sad and difficult to believe that a country as rich in natural resources as Saudi Arabia can have such a poor education system. There are so many terrorist attacks on civilians in Iraq also because the illiteracy rate in this country is 26 percent.[57]

At the same time, the roots of terrorism can be found among the wealthy and well educated. According to Professor Alan B. Krueger of Princeton University:

> [C]ontrary to popular stereotype . . . uneducated, impoverished masses are particularly *unlikely* to participate in political processes, through either legitimate or illegitimate means . . . Instead of being drawn from the ranks of the poor, numerous academic

(c) South-East Europe and CIS

Figure 3.4 Transnationality Index for Host Economies, 2004.[58]

Note:
The Transnationality Index is the average of FDI inflows as a percentage of gross fixed capital formation from 2002–2004; FDI inward stocks as a percentage of GDP in 2004; value added of foreign affiliates as a percentage of GDP in 2004; and employment of foreign affiliates as a percentage of total employment in 2004.

and government studies find that terrorists tend to be drawn from well-educated, middle-class or high-income families.[59]

This does not contradict the previously stated link between poverty and terrorism. In fact, terrorists or those sympathetic to terrorist causes from middle-class or wealthy backgrounds use the poor by offering them money to participate in terrorist attacks. State sponsors of terrorism use the same tactic. For example, Saddam Hussein offered an honorarium to the surviving poverty-stricken families of recruited terrorists. According to the report of the National Commission on Terrorist Attacks Upon the United States: "Terrorism

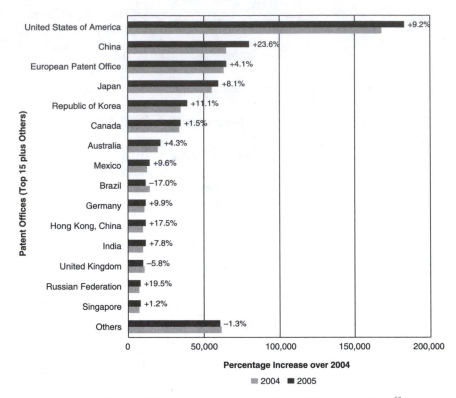

Figure 3.5 Non-resident Patent Filings as a Percentage of Total Filings by Office.[60]

is not caused by poverty."[61] There is no doubt that this is an accurate statement, but by the same token, poverty is a vulnerable environment to the poison of terrorist money and ideology.

Illegal immigration is another root of terrorism, which is directly related to poverty. Only those who are forced by extreme poverty are willing to leave their home to become illegal aliens in another country. According to a report from an independent research organization, the Center for Immigration Studies, "strict enforcement of immigration law—at American consulates overseas, at ports of entry, and within the United States— must be an integral part of our efforts to prevent future attacks on US soil."[62] Nonetheless, even legal immigrants can come to America with non-peaceful goals.[63]

Defining Terrorism

While the existence of terrorism and extremism as a global trend is obvious to even the most casual observers of international affairs, it is a particularly challenging phenomenon to analyze. Despite a practically global consensus rejecting terrorism as a deplorable and inhuman act, terrorism is actually a very controversial issue. The US Department of Defense defines terrorism as "the unlawful use of—or threatened use of—force, or violence against individuals or property to coerce or intimidate governments or societies, often to achieve political, religious or ideological objectives."[64] Even a definition as clear-cut as this is not necessarily accepted by every international and multilateral organizations and national governments. As of 2008, no one has been able to come up with a globally accepted definition of terrorism.

The League of Nations was the first international institution to attempt to create a globally approved definition in the Convention for the Prevention and Punishment of Terrorism in 1937. Although the UN has issued many conventions, some of which are relevant to international business, such as the Convention for the Suppression of Financing of Terrorism (1999) and the Protocol for Suppression of Unlawful Acts against the Safety of Fixed Platforms Located on the Continental Shelf (1988), among others, it has been unable to achieve a consensus on this term. The lack of a definition is a major obstacle for universally accepted countermeasures against terrorism. In 1999, two years prior to the tragic attacks of September 11, 2001, the UN made a resolution strongly condemning the practice of terrorism as criminal and unjustifiable. On September 28, 2001, the UN Security Council adopted Resolution 1373, which not only condemned the attacks of September 11 but also created the Counter Terrorism Committee. This committee monitors the implementation of the resolution and is made up of all 15 members of the Security Council. The UN's inability to come to a consensus on the definition of terrorism did not shield the organization from the impact of this global trend. In August 2003, a truck bomb exploded in the UN Headquarters in Iraq, killing 17 people and injuring 100. From a business perspective, terrorism can be understood as an unprovoked and intentional attack on unarmed civilians or nonmilitary targets. This approach innately covers businesspeople as well as business and economic entities.

Responses to Terrorism and Extremism

Due to the lack of a clear definition of terrorism in conjunction with several other important issues, the legal systems of the overwhelming majority of countries could not effectively prosecute and use force against terrorist organizations. The attacks of September 11, 2001 were a monumental point in the theory, legal regulation, and practice of fighting terrorism. The events of 9/11 were the catalyst for the development of antiterrorism strategies of international business, governments, and multilateral institutions.

One of the first and most important responses to the global trend of terrorism was the so-called USA Patriot Act (the abbreviation for "Uniting and Strengthening America by Providing Appropriate Tools Required to Intercept and Obstruct Terrorism"), which was signed by President Bush on October 26, 2001. In order to protect global supply chains from concealing and smuggling terrorist weapons, the US government also implemented the Customs-Trade Partnership against Terrorism (C-TPAT). Import-export companies that participate in this program can expedite the clearance process for their goods through customs and receive less intensive inspections.[65] The US Department of State also undertook special measures. In order to monitor terrorism worldwide, the Secretary of State transmits

> to the Speaker of the House of Representatives and the Committee on Foreign Relations of the Senate, by April 30 of each year, a full and complete report providing . . .
>
> A. detailed assessments with respect to each foreign country—
>   i.   in which acts of international terrorism occurred which were, in the opinion of the Secretary, of major significance;
>   ii. about which the Congress was notified during the preceding five years . . .
>   iii. which the Secretary determines should be the subject of such report; and
>
> B. detailed assessments with respect to each foreign country whose territory is being used as a sanctuary for terrorists or terrorist organizations.[66]

Note: As a base for this report, the term terrorism means "premeditated, politically motivated violence perpetrated against non-combatant targets by subnational groups or clandestine agents."[67]

Of course, any national security measures or private security activities of businesses can be seen from two points of view. In one sense they decrease international cooperation and increase business costs, but on the other hand, they give people grounds for believing that they are better protected. An example of this is the Patriot Act, which focuses substantially on the prevention and reporting systems about suspicious financial transactions that can be related to money laundering. The Patriot Act required the implementation of preventive monitoring systems. This requirement immediately increased the role of due diligence and improved the quality of the preparation of professionals for this service. Several US government agencies specialize in the prevention of money-laundering activities. Among them are the Bureau of Alcohol, Tobacco, Firearms and Explosives (ATF), United States Secret Service (USSS), Internal Revenue Service (IRS), Immigration and Customs Enforcement Agency (ICE), Customs and Border Protection Agency (CBP). As a result of their activities, a substantial amount of money, which would have financed terrorism, landed in US government coffers.

Based on the experience presented in the Figure 3.6, the US government, with the leadership of the Department of the Treasury, the Department of Justice, and the Department of Homeland Security in 2007 developed the National Money Laundering Strategy.[68]

The more that governments and the private sector cooperate, the more a country will be able to minimize the economic damage of terrorism. According to Peter Jennings, a director from the Australian Strategic Policy Institute, "the best way to defeat terrorism will involve government and business borrowing some of each other's styles of operating: Governments must learn to be more open and flexible, while business must develop greater skills in strategic analysis and war gaming."[69]

The Impact of Terrorism on the Global Marketplace

The terrorist attacks of 9/11 were much more than an assault on the United States; they were an attack against the GMP. It was the first real indication of the scale of the terrorist impact on the GMP. However, for the GMP, as well as civilization in general, it is important to realize that local and regional insurgent groups are just as dangerous as global terrorist networks. In fact local insurgents pose a particular challenge to businesses, despite the fact that their impact may be less widely felt. It is harder to monitor local terrorists and thus more difficult to prevent their attacks.

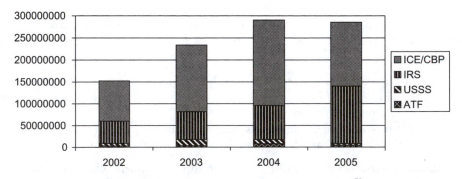

Figure 3.6 Asset Forfeiture by US Government Agencies ($), 2002–2005.[70]

The major economic impact of terrorism on the GMP is extremely wide ranging. The disruption of financial and currency markets, of global transportation systems and infrastructure, and the distortion of global prices for key commodities are only the beginning. The burden of unprecedented expenses on security and protection drives some companies to bankruptcy. The cost of maintaining commercial and corporate transpiration facilities, airplanes, and ports skyrockets as a result of terrorist activity due to increased security costs. Of course, terrorism is not only a threat to physical assets. Crucial elements of the GMP, such as the Internet and telecommunications infrastructures, are very vulnerable to attack. Terrorists can use any one of the thousands of different viruses, not to mention other cyber attacks, to harm the Internet and personal computers. Internet viruses are especially dangerous for identity fraud: in 2005 there were about 60 cases per 100,000 people. This ratio shows the vulnerability of the Internet to terrorism.

Terrorism has become one of the most important determinants and indicators of political risk of investment. Even the *threat* of terrorism prevented many potential international transactions that would have benefited the GMP. In the US alone, the direct economic impact of 9/11 was $75 billion, or a 0.75 percent reduction of the 2002 GDP.[71] It took seven years, for the total amount of FDI flows to surpass the pre-9/11 record and for the United States to become the leading recipient and source of FDI, which occurred in 2007, when global FDI outflows reached a record high of $1.82 trillion.[72] The tourism, transportation (especially the airlines), and insurance industries felt the brunt of 9/11. Unemployment had the largest rise during one month in 21 years, and 415,000 jobs were cut as a direct result of 9/11. In the hotel industry, 46,000 jobs were eliminated, and in the trade industry, 81,000 jobs were cut. The surge in unemployment and declines in the above-mentioned industries were the result of cautious consumer spending and a failure in investor confidence. Nationwide consumer spending in the US fell by 6 percent and by 11 percent in New York City during the following year. Domestic spending fell by 9 percent, and international spending by 13 percent.[73] Immediately after the attacks of September 11, US airspace was closed for two days, which resulted in a daily loss of $330 million. For the following week, by different evaluations, the loss was between $1 billion and $2 billion. Following the terrorist attacks, travel to New York City dropped by 15 percent in volume compared with the previous year (a 10 percent drop in leisure travel and a 29 percent drop in business travel). International arrivals to New York City declined by 54 percent. According to the US coordinator for counterterrorism, Ambassador Francis Taylor, New York City's estimated losses in sales were $1.7 billion, and in rent, $1.75 billion, following September 11, 2001, until the end of 2003.[74] Compared with September 2000, passenger miles were down by 32 percent, and by 29 percent for international flights. Because of this, in October 2001, airlines reduced their flights by 18 percent (compared with October 2000), leading to 140,000 layoffs. New York and New Jersey seaports were closed for two days. Freight decreased by 9 percent, and US borders with Canada and Mexico were almost shut down, which had a wide impact on the economies of both countries. For example, "the Ford Motor Company was not a direct target on September 11, but it lost US $30 million through supply chain disruptions when the US–Canada border was shut after the attack."[75] To demonstrate the scale of the negative economic impact of the closure of the US–Canada border, it is important to underline that 500,000 vehicles cross this border every day.

As a result of 9/11, the world's insurance industry parted with about $50 billion.[76] The US government, through the Terrorist Risk Insurance Act of 2002, made the following limitations: insurers have to pay the first $5 million of losses in full; if they are between $5 million and $100 billion, the insurer pays the deductible. From the remaining losses, the insurer pays 10 percent and the US government pays 90 percent. The World Trade Center in New York alone

> holds the "worst loss ever" title for numerous individual coverages, such as Workers Compensation for which the loss has been valued at $3.5 billion. Aviation loss [was] valued at $4 billion, and a combined property and business income interruption loss [was] valued at $18.5 billion and life insurance payments at a cost of $2.7 billion.[77]

It is interesting from a strategic business perspective to underline that reinsurance companies consider terrorism as an uninsurable risk. This can be explained by the difficulties to rate terrorism and to determine the credible profitable/possible maximum losses. Reinsurers usually support their position by the fact that terrorist attacks are unpredictable and can be too large in destruction. But strategists always have to be able to deal with and predict the unpredictable (further discussed later in the book). One of the leading experts in this area, Kenneth Hoggins, vice-president of William Gallagher Associates' Property and Casualty Group, provides interesting suggestions to minimize a company's exposure to risks of terrorism, such as "increasing use of videoconferencing instead of travel, limiting the number of staff members on any single flight, and conducting more vigorous background checks on contractors and employees."[78] But one of the most important objectives of global business in the struggle against terrorism is to help "to cut off money flows to terrorists."[79] Most of the money that goes to terrorist organizations goes under the cover of legal transactions. According to United States General Accounting Office, oil smuggling and illegal surcharges between 25 and 50 cents per barrel of legal oil revenues provided funds that bolstered Saddam Hussein's regime.[80] For changes in value of exports and imports in selected OECD countries see Tables 3.5 and 3.6.

The economic impact on Spain after the Madrid train bombing on March 11, 2004, and the London terrorist attack on July 7, 2005, damaged not only these countries but also all of Europe and the world economy. Even a country as far from the US as Norway experienced damage from the 9/11 attacks. The Norwegian capital market had cumulative average losses of approximately 25 percent in the 11 days after the attack. It took 107 days for the Norwegian stock market to recover, which is the second longest recovery period

Table 3.5 Changes in Value of Exports in Selected OECD Countries[81]

	Percent Change in Respective Month from 2000			Annual Percent Change		
	1 Sep	*1 Oct*	*1 Nov*	*2000*	*2001*	*2002*
Australia	−0.5	−1.4	N/A	10.6	9.7	7.3
Canada	−7.4	−10.1	−9.8	8.7	−3.4	0.6
Denmark	−8.3	−2.2	−0.5	N/A	N/A	N/A
EU-15 (ext.)	−9	−1	−8	N/A	N/A	N/A
Germany	1.3	0.7	−4.5	12.5	3.9	3.1
Japan	−11	−9	−9.2	9.4	−10	−1.3
Korea	−17.7	−20.7	−17.1	21.6	2.1	4.7
New Zealand	7.9	−0.6	−3.4	5.6	5.2	3.4
Sweden	−10.2	−3	−8.5	N/A	N/A	N/A
Switzerland	−9	4.5	−3.4	N/A	N/A	N/A
United States	−17.6	−13.6	−14.2	11.3	−5.2	−3

Source: The Impact of the Terrorist Attacks of 11 September 2001 on International Trading and Transport Activities, © OECD, 2002.

Table 3.6 Changes in Value of Imports in Selected OECD Countries[82]

	Percent Change in Respective Month from 2000			Annual Percent Change		
	1 Sep	*1 Oct*	*1 Nov*	*2000*	*2001*	*2002*
Australia	−10	−0.8	N/A	7.5	3.8	6.3
Canada	−7.1	−7	−9.3	9.5	−4.4	2.3
Denmark	−8.9	−5.6	−7.1	N/A	N/A	N/A
EU-15 (ext.)	−14	−10	−15	N/A	N/A	N/A
Germany	−3.5	−3.6	−7	10.2	1.8	3.9
Japan	−7.8	−4.6	−7.9	10.9	−3.7	−10.4
Korea	−11.9	−18.3	−18.3	20	−3.6	7.2
New Zealand	−11.6	2.7	−4.5	3.6	0.7	2.5
Sweden	−16.3	−4.3	−8.5	N/A	N/A	N/A
Switzerland	−6.3	−1.5	−12.6	N/A	N/A	N/A
United States	−15.8	−10.5	−13.8	13.5	−3.7	−1.9

Source: The Impact of the Terrorist Attacks of 11 September 2001 on International Trading and Transport Activities, © OECD, 2002.

among stock exchanges worldwide, behind the Johannesburg Securities Exchange, which took 162 days to recover.[83] In Mumbai, India, the public transportation system was attacked by terrorists twice. The July 11 attack in 2006 killed 174 people and injured 464.[84]

Despite all of the economic damage and direct business losses, the most negative impact of terrorism is psychological: the creation in the mindsets of many of barriers against globalization, liberalization, and open national borders. The mentioned decrease in tourism, and especially international tourism, is a direct result of the psychological impact of terrorism. When reported terrorist attacks occur in one part of the world, people from another part of the world will not even consider traveling to places as attractive as Madrid and London, at least for a certain period after terrorist attacks. The World Travel and Tourism Council's Crisis Committee met in London shortly after the attacks and estimated that out of the 31 million people who visit the United Kingdom each year, a drop of about 588,000 was expected—a decline of 1.9 percent from the original 2005 forecast.[85] British carriers alone lost about $475 million due to the fact that 2,500 flights, scheduled to leave only the three major airports of London, were canceled during the week following the attack.[86] London airports had to deal with all of these losses in addition to their 26 percent loss in passengers in 2001 after the 9/11 attacks, which had implications for Great Britain as well as the entire GMP. However, in 2005 the British government reacted quickly and allocated £4 million to the London Tourism Action Group for a marketing campaign. This money was spent on theatrical performances, athletic events, discount packages, etc., in order to attract tourists and the revenue they generate.

Psychological barriers caused by terrorism became real business barriers for companies from the GEM when they tried to invest in assets of high national security in developed countries. In 2006 Dubai Ports World (DP World), owned by the Dubai government, bought the British company Peninsular & Oriental Steam Navigation. For years this London-based company was a major operator of many ports in the US. When DP World became the owner of this British company, the US Congress grew anxious.[87] In order to solve the problem, DP World wisely decided to hand over control of US port operations to an American company. These fears happened despite the fact that Dubai is one of the most liberal Islamic states in the Middle East and a major trading hub of the world. It is important to underline that there is not only Islamic terrorism in the world. There are many other streams of terrorism that negatively influence the GMP. When terrorists, motivated purely by domestic issues, attacked an oil tanker in Nigeria, the eighth-largest petroleum producer in the world, oil exports were immediately reduced by 20 percent.[88] Because of this attack, Shell Oil Company removed 330 employees that were operating in Nigeria, resulting in a decline of 226,000 barrels of daily oil production.[89]

Terrorism and the Global Emerging Market

Terrorists usually seek to strike in developed countries, but in fact, it is terrorism's activity in poor countries and EMCs that allow them to be successful. This is where they find their foot soldiers, spread their propaganda, and have the best chances of getting governmental support (national, regional, or at least local). EMCs are usually the primary location for fundraising and weapons manufacturing. In most cases, EMC governments are secular, and terrorists use this as propaganda to incite extremism with the effort to make religious law the law of the state. Terrorist organizations usually have two artificially separated wings—one engaged in political battle against the government, and another engaged in military insurgency against the government. Hezbollah in Lebanon is an obvious example of this. Businesses are prime targets for terrorists in their attempts to create civil unrest and anti-Western sentiment, and to weaken secular governments. The closer a government moves toward democracy and Western values, the more aggressive and active terrorists become. Such is the case in Lebanon, Pakistan, Bangladesh, Indonesia, and Turkey, where terrorists are making last-ditch efforts to prevent the spread of prosperity and democracy. The presence of foreign companies, especially those from developed countries, for terrorists and extremists, always symbolizes the "infidels" of their domestic governments, which allow the foreign presence. Under fear of other terrorist attacks, during 2001–2002, net private capital inflows to EMCs decreased by 36.5 percent, from $167 billion to $106 billion. Certain industries are more attractive targets for terrorists, especially tourism, the world's largest industry in terms of input to GWP, which is approximately 11 percent. This industry employs 207 million people worldwide, 8.2 percent of employment in the GMP.[90] In the GEM, the role of tourism is even more important. In small EMCs such as Morocco, Lebanon, Croatia, Albania, and small island nations, tourism is the main industry. Terrorist attacks or just their threat negatively impact tourism by reducing the number of tourist arrivals and forcing the hospitality industry, including tourist companies to invest heavily in protection, decreasing profits and required foreign investment. Turkey receives 1.8 percent of worldwide tourist arrivals and is ranked twentieth by the World Tourism Organization by this indicator.[91] In spring 2006, because of terrorist attacks and threats, Turkey lost between $4 billion and $5 billion, and tourist arrivals decreased by 20 percent.[92] According to a study by the Australian Strategic Policy Institute, "in Indonesia, a 2.2 percent fall in tourist arrivals in 2002—in part reflecting the Bali bombings—led financial market analysts to predict a 1 percent reduction in national gross domestic product."[93]

Leaders of EMC understand the danger of terrorism. Counterterrorism was once on the agenda of only a few developed countries. In the twenty-first century, the leaders of EMCs such as Algeria, Pakistan, Saudi Arabia, and China; of P-EMCs such as Saudi Arabia, and even of developing countries such as Afghanistan and Uzbekistan, devote substantial resources to fighting terrorism. Laws against terrorism appear throughout the GEM, as do laws preventing money laundering and the funding of terrorist activities. For example, the CIS, an organization of 12 of the 15 former Soviet Republics, have a formal agreement on financial crimes inspired by the Office of Foreign Assets Control of the US Department of Treasury, which enforces economic and trade sanctions according to US foreign policy and implements in practice regulations against terrorist activities and the trafficking of narcotics.

Modern technology and increasing economic integration has made it possible for domestic extremists and terrorists to operate in foreign countries and to develop networks on a global scale. Terrorism has become a major factor of political risk of investment. Consequently, the development of the future global order has and will be greatly influenced by this. Terrorism will continue to be a very important and money-consuming threat for business in the twenty-first century. But increasing economic integration can be considered one of the strategies of business against terrorism. The development of private domestic businesses in Arab nations and the integration of these businesses in the GMP undoubtedly play an important role in the fight against terrorism. This strategy benefits not only the business community but also society within these countries in general.

Terrorism is a social manifestation of evil and requires complete eradication. Terrorists interpret kindness as weakness—such methodologies will not solve their malevolence. Compromising with terrorists only prolongs their ability to wage war against humanity and creates an ocean of grief and extended poverty. The existence of the plague of terrorism and extremism diverts badly needed resources from the fight against hunger. Just as barbarians destroyed ancient Rome and plunged humankind into darkness, terrorists with modern weapons can bring a global catastrophe. But the GMP has demonstrated strength to with-hold the wave of terrorism. The fast reaction of the global community helped to develop more strict regulations and to implement preventive measures and new technologies in practically every industry and region of the GMP. Despite the high cost of all these measures, during the first decade of the twenty-first century, the GMP has demonstrated steady growth and an improvement of the standards of living of the global population. What humankind needs is the development of a detailed strategy: first to prevent terrorism; second, methods of fighting and prosecuting terrorism and extremism; and third, economic and social-recovery strategies after terrorist attacks, which unfortunately will occur for the foreseeable future.

Technological Trends

As a result of the scientific-technological revolution of the twentieth century, evaluations of the current and future political, social, and economic trends cannot be accurately completed without factoring in the repercussions of technological trends. The most influential scientific and technological development in the twenty-first century is the transformation of the world economy from the predominance of the service sector to that of knowledge-based industries. This emerging transformation is a result of the approaching second scientific-technological revolution, which will determine all aspects of socioeconomic and even political development. This revolution will so profoundly change science and technology that its influence can be compared only to the scientific-technological revolution of the twentieth century. The GMP will be dominated by this revolution at least until 2050 and possibly until the twenty-second century. (The development of the knowledge economy and trends in R&D are discussed in more detail in Chapter 1, and will be touched upon throughout the book.)

This section provides a brief analysis of the most important trends in scientific research and technological development and their impact on humankind in the twenty-first century. The technological trend with the most wide-reaching impact on the GMP is the increasing penetration of radical telecommunications and cutting-edge ITs, which is creating an unprecedented level of interconnectivity throughout the entire GMP. The capabilities of these technologies do not even compare to those of the twentieth century. By the end of this century, practically everyone will have access to telecommunications and ITs of fundamentally new qualities. However, at the beginning of the twenty-first century, despite very rapid growth in penetration rates (see Table 3.7), there are still substantial portions of the global population without access to basic ITs. Figures 3.7 and 3.8 show mobile phone penetration and subscribers respectively by country categorization. Table 3.8 and Figure 3.9 illustrate similar data but for the Internet.

Technological trends respond to the social, economic, and security needs of society. Most R&D is being used to discover technological solutions to practical demands of companies and entrepreneurs. This is the major avenue of scientific achievements to the GMP. The second way involves the national budgets of countries. Typically, research and technology sponsored by national governments address problems shared by contemporary civilization, such as poverty, mass disease, migration, unemployment, terrorism, national security, and environmental protection. Even new technological achievements from the private sector reach their final utilization by the needs of the general population. More than that, military-oriented technological achievements, almost always with a certain time lag, are used in the civilian sector of the economy and finally by individual consumers. The development of scientific-technological solutions to the most challenging problems facing humankind is already underway, not only via IT but also through advancements in transportation, geological studies, civil engineering and construction, biology and genetics, and subsequently food production and health care. Some directions in scientific research, such as nano, membrane and space technologies will penetrate all industries as well as the social and private lives of individuals.

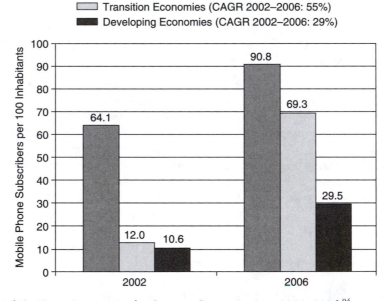

Figure 3.7 Mobile Phone Penetration by Country Categorization, 2002–2006.[94]

Notes:

The country categorization in this report is not according to the categorization used in this book. Because of this, regarding the section of EMCs and developing countries, countries from both groups are mixed together.

CAGR stands for Compounded Annual Growth Rate.

Under the category of transition economies in this chart are two countries, according to the categorization of this book, that are still developing—Uzbekistan and Tajikistan. The remaining countries are EMCs of Eastern Europe, the former Soviet Union, and Central Asia.

Table 3.7 Trends in Mobile Phone Penetration by World Region and Country Categorization, 2002–2006[95]

Economy	2002	Percentage change 2002–2003	2003	Percentage Change 2003–2004	2004	Percentage Change 2004–2005	2005	Percentage Change 2005–2006	2006
GMP	18.8	19.5	22.5	22.7	27.6	21.2	33.4	21.4	40.6
Developed Countries	64.1	8.6	69.6	10.8	77.1	8.1	83.3	9	90.8
Japan	66.2	6.3	69.3	5.8	73.3	3.8	76.1	7.2	81.6
Europe	75.2	8.3	81.4	10.8	89.7	9	97.8	6.8	104
US and Canada	47.7	10.3	52.6	14.5	60.3	8.2	65.2	15.1	75
Australia and New Zealand	63.7	11.6	71.1	14.6	81.5	11.4	90.7	15.1	95.3
EMCs and Developing Countries*	10.6	28.7	13.6	29.4	17.6	28.9	22.7	30.1	29.5
Africa	4.5	36.3	6.1	46.9	9	64	14.7	39.2	20.5
Asia	10.7	29.5	13.9	25.9	17.5	23.1	21.5	30.5	28.1
Latin America and Caribbean	18.9	23.4	23.3	36.7	31.8	35.3	43.1	24.1	53.5
Emerging Markets of Oceania	3.1	24	4.2	37.4	5.7	31.4	7.5	28	7.7
EMCs of Europe and Central Asia**	12	72.5	20.6	32.4	37.6	48.5	55.9	23.9	69.3

Notes:
* This table was redesigned on the base of the *List of Country Groupings and Sub-groupings for the Analytical Studies of the United Nations World Economic Survey and Other UN Reports*.[96] The country categorization in this report is not according to the categorization used in this book. Because of this, regarding the section of EMCs and developing countries, countries from both groups are mixed together.
**In this category, two countries, according to the categorization of this book, are still developing—Uzbekistan and Tajikistan.

Table 3.8 Trends in Internet Penetration by Region and Country Categorization, 2002–2006[97]

Economy	2002	Percentage change 2002–2003	2003	Percentage change 2003–2004	2004	Percentage change 2004–2005	2005	Percentage change 2005–2006	2006
GMP	10	14.6	11.4	19	13.6	14.5	15.6	10.9	17.3
Developed Countries	42	6.3	44.7	15	51.3	6.7	54.8	6.3	58.2
Japan	45	4	46.8	28.6	60.2	7.3	64.6	2.6	66.3
Europe	32.2	12.3	36.2	11.7	40.4	7.2	43.3	10.4	47.8
US and Canada	54.1	2	55.1	13.3	62.4	5.6	66	3.7	68.4
Australia and New Zealand	52.6	6.9	56.3	14.1	64.2	9.1	70	8.1	75.7
EMCs and Developing Countries*	4.2	27	5.3	24	6.6	26.5	8.4	16.1	9.7
Africa	1.3	42.1	1.8	44.6	2.6	43.5	3.7	27.3	4.7
Asia	4.3	28.3	5.5	24	6.8	22.6	8.4	14.8	9.6
Latin America and Caribbean	8.2	19.5	9.8	19	11.6	37.7	16	17.1	18.8
Emerging Markets of Oceania	2.8	13.5	3.2	12.2	3.6	10.5	4	10.1	4.4
EMCs of Europe and Central Asia**	4.1	78.8	7.3	52.2	11.1	17.1	13	25.6	16.3

Notes:

* This table was redesigned on the base of the *List of Country Groupings and Sub-groupings for the Analytical Studies of the United Nations World Economic Survey and Other UN Reports*.[98] The country categorization in this report is not according to the categorization used in this book. Because of this, regarding the section of EMCs and developing countries, countries from both groups are mixed together.

** In this category, two countries, according to the categorization of this book, are still Developing—Uzbekistan and Tajikistan.

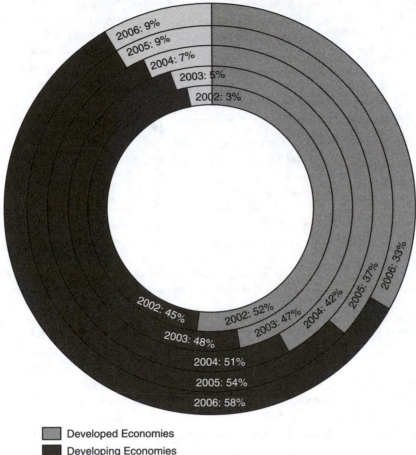

Figure 3.8 Mobile Subscribers by Country Categorization, 2002–2006.[99]

Notes:
The country categorization in this report is not according to the categorization used in this book. Because of this, regarding the section of EMCs developing and countries, countries from both groups are mixed together.

Under the category of transition economies in this chart are two countries, according to the categorization of this book, that are still developing—Uzbekistan and Tajikistan. The remaining countries are EMCs of Eastern Europe, the former Soviet Union, and Central Asia.

A 2006 RAND Corporation study sponsored by the National Intelligence Council of the United States evaluated the implementation feasibility of the following 16 most promising technological applications by the year 2020:[100]

1. *Cheap solar energy.*
2. *Rural wireless communications.*
3. *Communication devices for ubiquitous information access anywhere, anytime.*
4. Genetically modified crops.
5. *Rapid bioassays.*
6. *Filters and catalysts for water purification and decontamination.*

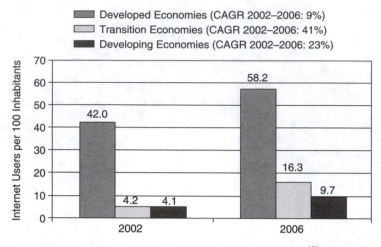

Figure 3.9 Internet Penetration by Country Categorization, 2002–2006.[101]

Notes:
The country categorization in this report is not according to the categorization used in this book. Because of this, regarding the section of EMCs and developing countries, countries from both groups are mixed together.

Under the category of transition economies in this chart are two countries, according to the categorization of this book, that are still developing—Uzbekistan and Tajikistan. The remaining countries are EMCs of Eastern Europe, the former Soviet Union, and Central Asia.

7. *Targeted drug delivery.*
8. Cheap autonomous housing.
9. *Green manufacturing.*
10. *Ubiquitous Radio-Frequency Identification tagging of commercial products and individuals.*
11. *Hybrid vehicles.*
12. Pervasive sensors.
13. *Tissue engineering.*
14. *Improved diagnostic and surgical methods.*
15. Wearable computers.
16. *Quantum cryptography.*

Note: Those technological applicants that are italicized are considered to be highly feasible or feasible by 2020 and to satisfy a strong need for a medium-size or large market without raising significant public-policy issues.

Based on evaluations of scientists from the Massachusetts Institute of Technology, the *Technology Review* offers another expert opinion on the most important emerging technologies at the beginning of the twenty-first century. This publication's annual selection (since 2001) of 10 revolutionary technologies is a very useful tool for strategists. In 2008 the *Technology Review* selected the following 10 technologies,[102] all of which represent modern technological trends with key strategic implications:

- Forecasting modeling of unexpected events.
- Probabilistic chips.
- Nanoradio.
- Wireless power.

- Atomic magnetometers.
- Offline web applications.
- Graphene transistors.
- Connectomics.
- Reality mining.
- Cellulolytic enzymes.

Detailed descriptions of these technologies can be found at http://www.technology review.com/Infotech/20249/.

When assessing global technological trends, it is very important for strategists to keep in mind that the technological development of the GMP (and especially of the GEM) is an uneven process. These disparities have roots in the educational gap between different countries and even domestic regions. This can be understood through an analysis of historical legacies and the subsequent societal attitudes toward education. Variations of this have very important implications for economic and technological development. The quality of education and the influence of technological trends are always preconditions for socioeconomic progress, especially in EMCs, developing and underdeveloped countries. Some EMCs from Asia, Africa, and Latin America suffer from educational levels below the world average. However, in other EMCs, such as Ireland, the Czech and Slovak republics, Hungary, Russia, Ukraine, Poland, etc., the educational levels are well above that average. In countries with large territories and populations, such as China, Russia, India, and Brazil, the quality of education differs profoundly by region and even ethnic group. For example, in the Chinese northwest, the quality of education is far behind that of southeastern regions of China. In Brazil a significant portion of the indigenous population in the central regions does not even speak Portuguese, the national language. Obviously, the educational levels in this region are far below the national average. Due to many years of oppression from the horribly shameful system of apartheid, the black population of South Africa has lower levels of education than the white population, in general. In many of the rural villages in Russia, children do not receive more than an elementary school education, while at the same time, some of the most respected scientists and scholars of the world are Russian.

Surprisingly, in many EMCs, an advanced level of some technologies is a legacy of the dictatorial system, which devoted most of its resources to military power, in order to protect itself from internal and external threats (the greatest of which was democracy). A strong military requires a sophisticated level of science and technology. Highly educated specialists were a necessity, especially in the fields of mathematics, physics, chemistry, and engineering. This is why countries from the former Soviet bloc and later China and Cuba have achieved relative success in education. It is important to underline the fact that investments in education by dictatorships were done to protect the regime, not to benefit the people. The fall of dictatorships throughout the world has allowed a reorientation away from mostly military use of technology toward civilian and consumer use. Not surprisingly, foreign investors have become very keen to develop high-tech industries in countries from the GEM with well-educated and relatively cheap engineers, scientists, etc. This is actually increasing the gap between the educational and technological "haves" and "have nots." Countries with rich traditions in science and education receive substantial foreign investment in this field, while technologically less-developed countries do not.

All of these disparities in education are on the one hand a major obstacle to the universal implementation of modern technologies. On the other hand, modern technological trends are so powerful that they will eventually increase the standards of living in every single region and country of the GMP, which in turn creates a virtuous cycle of gradual and constant educational and technological advancement. Figure 3.10 indicates that disparities in education lead to disparities in scientific and technological achievements. The top 30 countries in terms of patents filed by resident per unit of GDP does not only include developed countries. Half of the countries on this list are from the GEM. Twelve of the 15 EMCs are former dictatorships, which illustrates the link mentioned above between some dictatorships and some scientific achievements. As of the beginning of the twenty-first century, the fastest-growing input of science relative to GDP is in China—a country still controlled by the Chinese Communist Party.

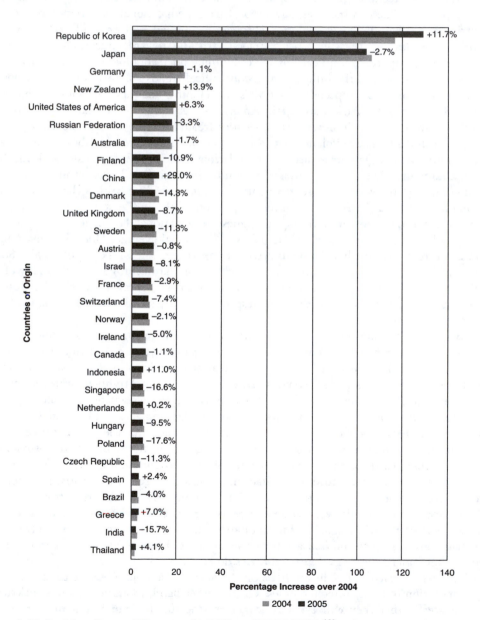

Figure 3.10 Resident Patent Filings per $1 Billion of GDP (PPP).[103]

According to a study from the RAND Corporation, the twenty-first century will be revolutionized by "the growing effect of multidisciplinary technology across all dimensions of life; social, economic, political, and personal. Biotechnology will enable us to identify, understand, manipulate, improve, and control living organisms (including ourselves). The revolution of information availability and utility will continue to profoundly affect the world in all these dimensions. Smart materials, agile manufacturing, and nanotechnology will change the way we produce devices while expanding their capabilities. These technologies may also be joined by 'wild cards' . . . if barriers to their development are resolved over time. The results could be astonishing. Effects may include significant improvements in human quality of life and life span, high rates of industrial turnover, lifetime worker training, continued globalization, reshuffling of wealth, cultural amalgamation or invasion with potential for increased tension and conflict, shifts in power from nation state to non-governmental organizations and individuals, mixed environmental effects, improvements in quality of life with accompanying prosperity and reduced tension, and the possibility of human eugenics and cloning."[104]

When developing a strategy for a particular entity (corporation, government, or multilateral institution), it is absolutely crucial to analyze the impact of key technological trends. Political and economic goals can be achieved faster and more efficiently if the right technological means are selected. The decades of success of the Microsoft Corporation (www.microsoft.com/), based on the ability of Bill Gates in the 1970s[105] to foresee technological trends in personal computers and the "information superhighway," is an obvious illustration of this. As a result of Gates' strategic vision and recognition of these key trends, Microsoft had huge strategic advantages over its competitors in the development of personal computers and Internet technologies. The strategic selection of the right trends and development of a scientific-technological policy for its research and implementation can bring great personal and commercial success—and almost always a positive social impact. A sophisticated scientific-technological strategy significantly accelerates the fulfillment of its objectives and goals. Corporate scientific-technological policy, which is part of general corporate strategy, should be developed with an orientation toward basic economic factors of production, as well as the social and environmental impact of the company's activity.

Study Questions
1. What are objective factors? How are they related to corporate or national strategy?
2. Describe the balance between objective and subjective strategic factors.
3. How are global trends related to objective and subjective factors?
4. Why is it important for strategists to recognize, describe, and evaluate global trends?
5. Are modern global trends equally powerful? Describe the relationship among them.
6. Describe the roots of globalization as a trend.
7. Describe the relationship between the global trends of democratization and globalization.
8. Describe the confluence of these two trends on corporations and national economies.

9. Describe the dialectical connection between internationalization, globalization, and democratization.
10. Describe the roots of regionalization as a global trend. Describe the relationship between regionalization and globalization.
11. Describe the relationship between the global trends of democratization and privatization.
12. How are democratization and privatization related to the trend of a global shortage of capital?
13. How is the democratization of the GMP related to the rebirth and empowerment of terrorism and extremism?
14. Describe global trends not analyzed in this chapter and their significance for the GMP.
15. Describe the impact of different global trends on the disintegration of the Soviet Union.
16. How can an analysis of global trends be useful in the forecasting stage of strategy development?
17. Why is the global trend of political disintegration important for corporate strategy development and revision?
18. Describe recent examples of the influence of the global trend of political disintegration.
19. Describe the major examples of the influence of the global trend of economic reintegration.
20. When and why did privatization become a global trend?
21. Describe the economic conditions under which privatization is an effective national strategy.
22. Describe the major stages of privatization.
23. Describe the difference between mass privatization and cash privatization.
24. When is mass privatization an efficient national strategy?
25. Describe how initial public offerings are related to privatization.
26. What are the strategic reasons for a company to go international?
27. What is the difference between strategic alliances and IJVs?
28. Describe the difference between mergers and acquisitions.
29. Why is the number of multinational firms increasing in the GMP?
30. What kind of legal and economic forms can a company use to go international?
31. In what category of countries is the number of multinational corporations growing fastest, and why?
32. How is internationalization related to the GEM and trends in FDI flows?
33. How are the roots of terrorism and extremism related to problems of the GMP?
34. Describe the major economic impact of terrorism on the GMP.
35. How is international terrorism changing the production costs in private business?
36. In which industries does terrorism create the most damage?
37. How do insurance and reinsurance companies consider the risk of terrorism? Why?
38. Describe the different impacts of terrorism on developed countries and EMCs.
39. Describe the correlation between science, technology, and regional development of the world economy. Provide examples.
40. Describe regionalism as a global trend.
41. How is the global trend of regionalization related to decentralization of managerial functions of central governments? What is its impact on private business?

42. Describe the relationship between regional decentralization and democratization.
43. What is the knowledge-based economy? How is it related to the major global trends?
44. What is the major goal of corporate technological development?
45. How does the level of education in different countries influence the internationalization of the national economy and its technological development?

4 Strategic Country Classification of the Global Marketplace

> The proposed good, said I, through which oligarchy was established, was indeed excess of wealth, wasn't it?[1]
>
> (Socrates, 469 BC–399 BC)

> Be assured, fellow citizens, that in a democracy it is the laws that guard the person of the citizen and the constitution of the state, whereas the despot and the oligarch find their protection in suspicion and in armed guards.
>
> (Aeschines, Greek statesman and orator, 389 BC–314 BC)

> Whenever you have an efficient government you have a dictatorship.
>
> (President Harry S. Truman, Lecture at Columbia University, April 28, 1959)

The Strategic Necessity for Country Classification Systems

The political and economic classification of countries has always been on the agenda of politicians and scholars. One of the first attempts to classify the world was the use of the term "ecumene" by the ancient Greeks to describe the world as they knew it. The known world of that time can be separated into two general categories. The ancient Egyptian economy, especially of the Ptolemaic period, was fundamentally different from that of ancient Greece, which was organized around city-states based on market principles and individual property rights. According to Professor Darel Tai Engen of California State University, San Marcos, "unlike the large kingdoms of the Near East, Greece had a free-enterprise economy and most land was privately owned."[2] Conversely, the Egyptian economy was based on "large palace or temple complexes," which "virtually monopolized anything that can be called 'industrial production' as well as foreign trade . . . and organized the economic, military, political and religious life of the society through a single complicated, bureaucratic, record-keeping operation."[3] Later, at the end of the fifteenth century, civilizations of the ecumene became the core of a new category—the "Old World," due to the European discovery of the "New World," the territories of which eventually became distinct countries.

Military conflicts and post-war status quo usually result in new divisions of countries on a political basis. During World War II, for example, the world was divided between the Allies (United States, Great Britain, France, and the Soviet Union) and the Axis powers (Germany, Italy, and Japan) and their respective satellites. This division of the world lasted only until the end of World War II, when the Cold War divided the global community into capitalist, socialist, and neutral (or the Third World) camps, which, again, was based on political issues. Neutral countries became part of much bigger group, known as the "Third World," a term that became associated with poor, non-developed countries. The logic behind this association is obvious—the majority of these countries rejected free-market principles. The further the nation was from implementing free-market principles, the more impoverished its people were. Growing polarization between capitalist and socialist countries eventually climaxed with the fall of the Berlin Wall in 1989, destroying at once the relevance of the three categories of this classification—capitalist, socialist, and Third World countries. In general, divisions of the world based on politics last for a much shorter period than classifications based on economic, social, cultural, and religious factors. The shelf life of other attempts at classification systems during this period, for example, those based on a division between market-oriented and non-market-oriented economies, also proved to be limited. This concept was no longer appropriate following the failure of the communist system in 1990. After only a few years, it became clear that every national economy of the world was at least partially market oriented (with the exception of North Korea). Even the communist dictatorships of Cuba, Vietnam, and China have enacted some level of market-based reforms. While political factors cannot be the sole determinants of classification systems, they are still relevant. For strategic purposes, it is important to distinguish countries under repressive regimes from free countries. However, the economic systems of the most repressed countries, such as Iran, Cuba, Belarus, and Zimbabwe, are still generally market based. While there is practically a global consensus regarding the legitimacy of market-based economics, the modern GMP still comprises 192 countries with very diverse levels of maturity. (See the Classification Glossary at the end of this chapter for a clarification of key terms such as classification, category, indicator, index, and rating.)

Corporate and political leaders, strategists, analysts of rating agencies, and international investors constantly have to classify countries based on differences in levels of social and economic development as well as political and investment climates. Through an analysis of these issues, strategists and executives attempt to classify countries for their own practical needs, such as political, economic, sovereign and country risk of investment, as well as business and technological risks (For a detailed analysis of risk, see Chapter 8.) The most common approaches are to rely on country classifications from major multilateral institutions such as the UN, the World Bank, the IMF, and the WTO or to consult leading rating agencies. This chapter aims to prove that a lack of a clearly defined country classification system in multilateral institutions has made them unreliable resources for strategists and executives.

The Flawed Country Classifictions of Major Multilateral Institutions

One would assume that global multilateral institutions classify countries by specific factors, based on a comprehensive methodology with clearly defined categories, and are thus an appropriate reference for strategists to use as a guideline for vital strategic decisions. Unfortunately, this is not the case. Among multilateral institutions there are no universally accepted criteria upon which to base country classification systems. Even within individual multilateral institutions, there are no unambiguous definitions of the different categories of countries used in their statistical reporting and analytical materials. As a result, their categories overlap and are only vaguely defined. The same country can be found in different and seemingly exclusive categories. Furthermore, the definition of these categories has not remained constant over time. The use of the category "developing countries" is a clear indication of this fact. During the Cold War, in economic terms, the world was basically divided into three groups of countries—developed, command economy dictatorships, and developing countries (also known as Third World countries). Initially, these groups were based on a blend of economic and political criteria. Multilateral institutions, for political reasons, never used the term "communist dictatorship." Prior to 1979, the IMF, for example, divided the world into "industrial," "developing," and an "intermediate group called 'more developed primary producing countries.' "[4] Obviously, this classification and its categories became obsolete at the beginning of the post-industrial period of global economic development, when service- and later knowledge-based sectors became the more advanced, efficient, and in some countries, dominant sectors of national economies. Following the end of the Cold War, developing countries essentially became a geographic category, with no economic or political basis. According to multilateral institutions, all countries in South America, Asia, and Africa fell into this group. Eastern European countries became known as "transition countries," without any explanation of the economic and strategic differences between this category and the category of developing countries. Countries of the former Soviet Union, which vary substantially in terms of economic and social development, were practically uncategorized. They were generally referred to by the title of their loose economic bloc—the CIS. From an economic perspective, this grouping is not logical. The level of socioeconomic development of some CIS countries is much closer to that of so-called transition countries than to that of other CIS countries. The economic indicators of Ukraine, Belarus, and even Russia, for example, much more closely resemble those of the Eastern European countries and the Baltic States (considered transition countries) than indicators of the Central Asian republics of the CIS. Logically and semantically, transition countries should refer to all EMCs and developing countries, as they are all in some stage of transition.

It will come as a surprise to many that as of 2008, the category of EMCs, which professionals and academics have widely used since the end of the 1980s, is not an official country group according to the UN. Other economic multilateral institutions use this category in a completely arbitrary manner—sometimes as a synonym for developing countries and transition countries, other times, as a unique category. The lack of a universally accepted definition and category of EMCs and of a standard comprehensive country classification system has resulted in an overwhelming amount of misleading statistics and studies. Even within individual reports from Bretton Woods Institutions, statistics on EMCs contradict one another. The majority of Bretton Woods Institutions and their analytical groups have essentially ignored the two new economic phenomena studied in this book—EMCs and the GEM, significantly inhibiting the process of understanding and evaluating the entire GMP.

The World Bank Group Approach

Economic history or the history of country classification systems is not the main focus of this book or this chapter, but in order to analyze the flaws of contemporary attempts, it is necessary to at least have an understanding of the evolution of multilateral institutions' attitude toward this issue. The World Bank Group (WBG) has always needed to distinguish between countries that qualify for preferential loans and technical assistance and those that do not. Prior to 1987 the WBG's country classification system was based solely on its operational lending activity. Since 1970 the WBG has used GNI per capita as a basis for lending decisions. In 1975 the International Bank for Reconstruction and Development (IBRD) became the only division of the WBG to establish a GNI per capita bracket to determine a country's loan eligibility. The International Development Association (IDA), another division of the WBG, continued to base its decisions only on a GNI per capita ceiling. Over time the range of the IBRD bracket has increased in order to reflect increasing standards of living and inflation in countries that receive its loans. In 1975 its GNI per capita bracket was between $521 and $1,075. By 1988 the bracket rose and widened to $1,071–$2,200, surpassing the GNI per capita minimum mark of $1,000. In 2006 the bracket increased to $1,736–$3,595.[5] Such a wide range is the result of the very different economic situations of the countries that receive IBRD loans (all of which this book classifies as EMCs). In 1987 the WBG developed and used its first country classification system, which consisted of four categories based on GNI per capita thresholds. According to the WBG,

> the economies whose per capita GNI falls below the Bank's operational cutoff for "Civil Works Preference" are classified as low-income economies; economies whose per capita GNI is higher than the Bank's operational threshold for "Civil Works Preference" and lower than the threshold for 17-year IBRD loans are classified as lower-middle income economies; and those economies whose per capita GNI is higher than the Bank's operational threshold for 17-year IBRD loans and lower than the threshold for high-income economies are classified as upper-middle income economies.[6]

Due to increasing standards of living and inflation, changes of these income per capita thresholds are such that what was considered high income in 1987 (more than $6,000) was considered only upper middle income ($2,466–$7,620) by 1990. What was lower middle income in 1987 was considered low income by 2006. It can be challenging to determine whether a country's classification has changed due to real growth or inflation.

Tables 4.1 and 4.2 are based on the WBG classification of countries by income per capita. There is no doubt that this statistic is an important indication of a country's economic development, but it is not adequate as the only criteria to classify a country. Countries considered to be EMCs by this book can be found in all of the four major income brackets of the WBG, from low income (Mongolia, Pakistan, and Vietnam), to lower middle income and upper middle income (the majority of EMCs fall in these two categories), and finally to high income (the Bahamas, Bahrain, Malta, South Korea, Singapore, Slovenia, among others).

The WBG also uses its classification of countries by income per capita as a base for other categorizations. In studies of the WBG, the term

> "developing economies" has been used to denote the set of low and middle income economies. Bank publications with notes on the classification of economies state that the term "developing economies" . . . does not imply either that all the economies belonging to the group are actually in the process of developing, nor that those not in the group have necessarily reached some preferred or final stage of development.[7]

Based on the WBG's own explanation, it is difficult to find any strategic use for this category. The WBG itself even concedes, "[c]lassification by income does not necessarily reflect development status."[8]

The WBG does use the term "emerging markets," if rarely, in some of its reports and studies, but basically as a synonym for developing economies; never does the WBG describe

Table 4.1 Dynamics of WBG GNI per Capita Brackets ($)[9]

	1987	1990	1995	2000	2006
Low Income	≤ 480	≤ 610	≤ 695	≤ 760	≤ 905
Lower Middle Income	481–1,940	611–2,465	696–2,785	761–3,030	906–3,595
Upper Middle Income	1,941–6,000	2,466–7,620	2,786–8,625	3,031–9,360	3,596–11,115
High Income	> 6,000	> 7,620	> 8,625	> 9,360	> 11,115

Note: "Income classifications are set each year on 1 July. These official analytical classifications are fixed during the World Bank's fiscal year (ending on June 30), thus countries remain in the categories in which they are classified irrespective of any revisions to their per capita income data."[10]

Since the implementation of this classification system, the categorization of many countries has fluctuated back and forth, due mostly to changing GNI per capita brackets rather than changes in development or maturity levels of a given country.

Table 4.2 Sample of Fluctuating Classification of the WBG[11]

Country	1987	1988	1989	1990	1991	1992	1993	1994	1995	1996	1997	1998	1999	2000	2001	2002	2003	2004	2005	2006
Albania	N/A	N/A	N/A	LM	LM	LM	L	L	L	LM	L	LM	LM	LM	LM	LM	LM	LM	LM	LM
Bulgaria	N/A	N/A	LM	LM	LM	LM	LM	LM	LM	LM	LM	LM	LM	LM	LM	LM	LM	LM	LM	UM
Armenia	N/A	N/A	N/A	N/A	LM	LM	L	L	L	L	L	L	L	L	L	LM	LM	LM	LM	LM
Barbados	UM	UM	H	UM	UM	UM	UM	UM	UM	UM	UM	UM	UM	H	UM	H	UM	UM	UM	H
Brazil	UM	LM	UM	UM	UM	UM	UM	UM	UM	UM	UM	UM	LM	LM	UM	LM	LM	LM	LM	UM
Equatorial Guinea	L	L	L	L	L	L	L	L	L	L	L	LM	L	L	L	L	L	UM	UM	H
Georgia	N/A	N/A	N/A	N/A	LM	LM	L	L	L	L	LM	L	L	L	L	L	L	LM	LM	UM
Indonesia	L	L	L	L	L	L	LM	LM	L	LM	LM	L	L	L	L	L	LM	LM	LM	LM
Korea, Rep.	UM	UM	UM	UM	UM	UM	UM	H	H	H	H	UM	UM	UM	H	H	H	H	H	H
Latvia	N/A	N/A	N/A	UM	UM	LM	LM	LM	LM	LM	LM	LM	LM	LM	UM	UM	UM	UM	UM	UM
Lithuania	N/A	N/A	N/A	N/A	UM	LM	LM	UM	UM	LM	LM	LM	UM	LM	UM	UM	UM	UM	UM	UM
Malta	UM	UM	H	UM	UM	UM	UM	UM	UM	UM	UM	H	UM	H	UM	H	H	H	H	H
South Africa	LM	UM	UM	UM	UM	UM	UM	UM	UM	UM	UM	LM	UM	UM	LM	LM	LM	UM	UM	UM

Notes:
L: Low Income
LM: Lower Middle Income
UM: Upper Middle Income
H: High Income

the differences between the two of them. There is no official WBG definition of the term "emerging markets." As a result, the category of developing economies includes countries with a high level of economic maturity alongside the least developed countries of the world (categorized as underdeveloped countries in this book and explained later in this chapter). For example, the geographic category of developing economies "Middle East and North Africa" includes Egypt, which is definitely an EMC by any understanding of the term, and countries such as Djibouti and Syria, which only barely qualify as developing countries.[12] The geographic classification used by the WBG consists of the following categories: East Asia and Pacific (24 developing economies), Europe and Central Asia (26), Latin America and the Caribbean (29), Middle East and North Africa (14), South Asia (8) and sub-Saharan Africa (48).[13] It is a totally unsystematic classification and does not provide any serious basis for strategic economic analysis because each of the six geographic categories includes countries of very different economic maturity, political stability, economic freedom, risks, etc. Of all the WBG country classifications, the GNI per capita classification is the only approach that can be of any use to strategists. However, as previously stated, a classification system based solely on GNI per capita brackets cannot accurately categorize countries of the GMP.

The International Monetary Fund Approach

Like the WBG, the IMF's country classification is muddled and unsystematic. The IMF's country classifications have at times been based on temporary political and economic situations. The energy crisis of the 1970s led the IMF to classify countries based solely on whether they were oil producers or oil consumers:

> [In] December 1979, the Fund adopted a basic scheme for classifying countries in which oil trade played a dominant role. The staff at that time had proposed a tripartite scheme that would have divided the world into industrial, major oil-exporting, and non-oil developing countries . . . Following an extended discussion in which some oil exporters objected both to being singled out and to the apparent implication that they were not developing countries, the Executive Board decided that there should be two broad groups—industrial and developing—with the latter divided into oil-exporting and non-oil.[14]

This classification "scheme" was a mistake for many reasons. First, the list of oil-producing countries is not constant due to the discovery of new oil fields, which happens somewhat regularly. Second, the energy balance can change as a result of the influence of technological progress, such as the development of alternative energy sources, as well as under the influence of new geological discoveries of natural gas and coal. Third, changes in industrial structure can alter the position of a country in the international energy balance; an exporter of oil can become an importer of oil, and vice versa. The IMF realized its own shortsightedness, as that classification system "was retained until January 1985, when the oil/non-oil distinction was relegated to a subsidiary status."[15]

In 1997 the IMF revised its classification system, mostly in an attempt to reflect the new economic reality created by the birth of the GEM. Its updated classification system attempted to take into account the

> advanced stage of economic development these economies [EMCs] have now reached. In fact, they all now share a number of important industrial country characteristics, including per capita income levels well within the range indicated by the group of

industrial countries, well-developed financial markets and high degrees of financial intermediation, and diversified economic structures with relatively large and rapidly growing service sectors. Rather than retaining the old industrial country label, the expanded group is labeled the "advanced economies" in recognition of the declining share of employment in manufacturing common to all of these economies.[16]

According to this statement, the IMF's revised country classification places the most mature EMCs (economies in bloom) in the same category as developed countries. This in and of itself is not a strategically sound grouping, as there are several key distinctions between economies in bloom and developed countries. What is even more strategically unsound is that the IMF does not actually stick to this revised classification. Sometimes the IMF considers EMCs to be advanced economies, while in other cases they are considered emerging markets. Sometimes they are even referred to as developing economies.

The IMF has yet to establish a clear definition of EMCs. As a result, despite its attempt to update its country classifications, its statistics on EMCs, advanced economies, developing countries, etc., are not comparable from report to report and even among different charts in a given report, because the countries included in these groups vary considerably. Categories overlap one another and as a result, are of limited use to strategists. In one table from the IMF's Global Financial Stability Report, EMCs are listed by continent and include "Other Emerging Markets and Developing Countries . . . together with Hong Kong SAR, Israel, Korea, Singapore, and Taiwan Province of China."[17] This is an obvious contradiction of the 1997 revised country classification. But in the IMF World Economic and Financial Survey, "Public Debt in Emerging Markets," the category "Advanced Economies" includes EMCs such as Hong Kong, Taiwan, Korea, Cyprus, and Israel.[18] The same category also includes Portugal, Greece, Spain, and Ireland, which many agencies (as well as this book) consider EMCs. Later in the same report, some countries that were previously classified as EMCs are evaluated as developing countries, including those that are obviously EMCs, such as China, India, and Turkey. These EMCs are included in the same category as all sub-Saharan African states despite the fact that many of these countries are of a fundamentally different development status. While some are definitely EMCs, such as South Africa, for example, many of them are still underdeveloped. Later in this report, a different categorization appears—countries in transition. This category includes Central and Eastern Europe, the CIS, and Mongolia. It is not clear why Mongolia is in this group, as it is not a member of CIS and has many characteristics that distinguish it from these countries.

The 2007 World Economic Outlook of the IMF includes equally muddled distinctions between the categories of advanced economies, emerging-market economies, and developing countries (see Table 4.3). Countries are divided by the following distinctions: *economic* (advanced economies, major advanced economies, newly industrialized Asian economies, other EMCs and developing countries); *geographic* (Africa, sub-Sahara (strangely considered separate from Africa), Central and Eastern Europe, CIS (which includes Mongolia without a satisfactory explanation), Developing Asia, Middle East, and Western Hemisphere); *analytical* (source of export earnings, external financing source, net debtor countries by debt-servicing experience, countries with arrears and/or rescheduling during 2001–2005); and *other groups* (heavily indebted poor countries (HIPCs) and Middle East and North Africa). HIPCs are countries that qualify for the HIPC initiative of the IMF and WBG, which aims to ensure "that no poor country faces a debt burden it cannot manage."[19] The wide variety and overlap of these categories indicate the IMF's lack of a comprehensive, country classification system. Like the WBG, the IMF's classification is totally unsystematic and should be used by strategists with caution.

Table 4.4 is an attempt by the IMF to clarify the term "advanced economies." The

Table 4.3 Classification by World Economic Outlook Groups and their Shares in Aggregate GDP, Exports Goods and Services, and Population (Percentage of Total for Group or World), 2006[20]

	Number of Countries	GDP		Exports of Goods and Services		Population	
		Advanced Economies	*World*	*Advanced Economies*	*World*	*Advanced Economies*	*World*
Advanced Economies	30	100.0	52.0	100.0	67.7	100.0	15.3
United States		37.8	19.7	14.6	9.8	30.7	4.7
Euro Area	13	28.2	14.7	42.8	28.7	32.2	4.9
Germany		7.4	3.9	13.3	8.9	8.4	1.3
France		5.6	2.9	6.1	4.1	6.3	1.0
Italy		5.2	2.7	5.2	3.5	6.0	0.9
Spain		3.5	1.8	3.3	2.2	4.5	0.7
Japan		12.1	6.3	7.4	5.0	13.1	2.0
United Kingdom		6.2	3.2	6.9	4.6	6.2	0.9
Canada		3.4	1.7	4.7	3.1	3.3	0.5
Other Advanced Economies	13	12.4	6.4	23.6	15.8	14.5	2.2
Memorandum							
Major Advanced Economies	7	77.6	40.4	58.2	39.1	73.9	11.3
Newly Industrialized Asian Economies	4	6.5	3.4	13.8	9.3	8.4	1.3

		Other EMCs and Developing Countries	*World*	*Other EMCs and Developing Countries*	*World*	*Other EMCs and Developing Countries*	*World*
Other EMCs and Developing Countries	143	100.0	48.0	100.0	32.9	100.0	84.7
Regional Groups							
Africa	48	7.0	3.4	7.7	2.5	15.3	12.9
Sub-Sahara	45	5.4	2.6	5.8	1.9	13.9	11.8
Excluding Nigeria and South Africa	43	2.9	1.4	2.8	0.9	10.3	8.7
Central and Eastern Europe	14	7.1	3.4	13.1	4.3	3.4	2.9
CIS	13	8.0	3.8	10.1	3.3	5.2	4.4
Russia		5.4	2.6	6.9	2.3	2.6	2.2
Developing Asia	23	56.3	27.0	38.7	12.7	61.9	52.4
China		31.4	15.1	22.0	7.2	24.2	20.5
India		13.1	6.3	4.1	1.3	20.5	17.4
Excluding China and India	21	11.7	5.6	12.6	4.1	17.1	14.5
Middle East	13	5.9	2.8	14.5	4.8	4.3	3.6
Western Hemisphere	32	15.7	7.6	15.9	5.2	10.0	8.5
Brazil		5.4	2.6	3.3	1.1	3.4	2.9
Mexico		3.7	1.8	5.5	1.8	1.9	1.6
Analytical Groups							
By Source of Export Earnings							
Fuel	23	13.3	6.4	26.5	8.7	10.9	9.2
Non-fuel	120	86.7	41.6	73.5	24.1	89.1	75.5
of Which, Primary Products	21	1.7	0.8	2.2	0.7	4.1	3.5

(Continued Overleaf)

	Number of Countries	Other EMCs and Developing Countries	World	Other EMCs and Developing Countries	World	Other EMCs and Developing Countries	World
By External Financing Source							
Net Debtor Countries	121	54.1	26.0	48.4	15.9	64.8	54.9
of Which, Official Financing	34	6.1	2.9	3.8	1.2	14.0	11.8
Net Debtor Countries by Debt-Servicing Experience							
Countries with Arrears and/or Rescheduling during 2001–2005	51	10.2	4.9	7.6	2.5	19.0	16.1
Other Net Debtor Countries	70	43.9	21.1	40.8	13.4	45.8	38.8
Other Groups							
HIPCs	30	2.0	1.0	1.2	0.4	8.3	7.0
Middle East and North Africa	19	7.8	3.8	16.6	5.5	6.4	5.4

Table 4.4 Subgroups of the IMF Classification "Advanced Economies"[21]

	Other Subgroups					
Major Currency Areas	Euro Area		Newly Industrialized Asian Economies	Major Advanced Economies	Other Advanced Economies	
United States	Austria	Ireland	Hong Kong SAR	Canada	Australia	Korea
Euro Area	Belgium	Italy	Korea	France	Cyprus	New Zealand
Japan	Finland	Luxembourg	Singapore	Germany	Denmark	Norway
	France	Netherlands	Taiwan Province of China	Italy	Hong Kong SAR	Singapore
	Germany	Portugal		Japan	Iceland	Sweden
	Greece	Slovenia		United Kingdom	Israel	Switzerland
		Spain		United States		Taiwan Province of China

column "Major Advanced Economies" includes countries that belong to the Group of Seven leading economies of the world (G7), which, since the 1997 addition of Russia, is known as the G8. For reasons that are not totally clear, the column "Newly Industrialized Asian Economies" separates the four Asian economies, which are then repeated in the column "Other Advanced Economies." According to this table, the IMF classifies 30 countries (including Taiwan and Hong Kong, which the IMF does not consider independent countries) as advanced economies.

The IMF also categorizes 143 countries in the group of "other emerging market and developing countries," with the explanation: "The group . . . includes all countries that are not classified as advanced economies."[22]

Table 4.5 Other EMCs and Developing Countries by Region, Net External Position, and HIPCs, according to the IMF's 2007 World Economic Outlook[23]

	Net External Position		HIPCs		Net External Position		HIPCs
	Net Creditor	Net Debtor			Net Creditor	Net Debtor	
Africa				Mali	*		*
Maghreb				Niger	•		*
Algeria	*			Senegal	*		*
Morocco		*		Togo	•		
Tunisia		*					
Sub-Sahara	*			**Central and**			
South Africa				**Eastern Europe**			
Horn of Africa				Albania		*	
Djibouti		*		Bulgaria		*	
Ethiopia	•		*	Croatia		*	
Sudan	*			Czech Republic		*	
Great Lakes				Estonia		*	
Burundi	•		*	Hungary		*	
Congo, Dem. Rep. of	*		*	Latvia		*	
Kenya	*			Lithuania		*	
Rwanda	•		*	Macedonia, FYR		*	
Tanzania	•		*	Malta		*	
Uganda	*		*	Poland		*	
Southern Africa				Romania		*	
Angola	*			Slovak Republic		*	
Botswana	*			Turkey		*	
Comoros	•						
Lesotho	*			**CIS**			
Madagascar	•		*	Armenia		*	
Malawi	•		*	Azerbaijan		*	
Mauritius	*			Belarus		*	
Mozambique, Rep. of	*		*	Georgia		*	
Namibia	*			Kazakhstan		*	
Seychelles	*			Kyrgyz Republic		*	
Swaziland	*		*	Moldova		*	
Zambia	*		*	Mongolia		•	
Zimbabwe	*			Russia	*		
West and				Tajikistan		•	
Central Africa				Turkmenistan	*		
Cape Verde	*			Ukraine	*		
Gambia, The	*		*	Uzbekistan	*		
Ghana	•		*				
Guinea	*		*	**Developing**			
Mauritania	*		*	**Asia**			
Nigeria	*			Bhutan		•	
São Tomé and	*		*	Cambodia		•	
Principe				China	*		
Sierra Leone	•		*	Fiji		*	
CFA Franc				Indonesia		*	
Zone				Kiribati	*		
Benin	*		*	Lao PDR		*	
Burkina Faso	•		*	Malaysia	*		
Cameroon	*		*	Myanmar		*	
Central African	•			Papua New		*	
Republic				Guinea			
Chad	*		*	Philippines		*	
Congo, Rep. of	•		*	Samoa		*	
Côte d'Ivoire	*			Solomon Islands		•	
Equatorial	*			Thailand		*	
Guinea				Tonga		•	
Gabon	•			Vanuatu		*	
Guinea-Bissau	*		*	Vietnam		•	
				South Asia			
				Bangladesh		•	

(Continued Overleaf)

Table 4.5 Continued

	Net External Position		HIPCs		Net External Position		HIPCs
	Net Creditor	Net Debtor			Net Creditor	Net Debtor	
India		*		Peru		•	
Maldives		*		Uruguay		•	
Nepal		•		Venezuela	*		
Pakistan		•		**Central America**			
Sri Lanka		•		Costa Rica		*	
				El Salvador		•	
Middle East				Guatemala		*	
Bahrain	*			Honduras		*	*
Iran. I.R. of	*			Nicaragua		*	*
Kuwait	*			Panama		*	
Libya	*			**The Caribbean**			
Oman	*			Antigua and		*	
Qatar	*			Barbuda			
Saudi Arabia	*			Barbados		*	
United Arab	*			Belize		*	
Emirates				Dominica		*	
Yemen, Rep. of	*			Dominican		•	
Mashreq				Republic			
Egypt		*		Grenada		•	
Jordan		*		Guyana		*	*
Lebanon		*		Haiti		*	*
Syrian Arab		*		Jamaica		*	
Republic				St Kitts and		*	
				Nevis			
Western				St Lucia		*	
Hemisphere				St Vincent and		•	
Mexico		*		the Grenadines			
South America				Suriname		*	
Argentina		*		Trinidad and	*		
Brazil		*		Tobago			
Bolivia		•	*				
Chile		*					
Colombia		*					
Ecuador		*					
Paraguay		•					

Notes:
Dot instead of star indicates that the net debtor's main external finance source is official financing.

Mongolia, which is not a member of the CIS, is included in this group for reasons of geography and similarities in economic structure.

Even the IMF's approach to geographical categorization is unsystematic (see Table 4.5). According to the 2007 World Economic Outlook,

> the regional breakdowns of other emerging market and developing countries—Africa, central and eastern Europe, Commonwealth of Independent States, developing Asia, the Middle East and Western Hemisphere—largely conform to the regional breakdowns in the IMF's International Financial Statistics. In both classifications, Egypt and the Libyan Arab Jamahiriya are included in the Middle East region rather than in Africa. In addition, the World Economic Outlook sometimes refers to the regional group of Middle East and North Africa countries, whose composition straddles the Africa and Middle East regions. This group is defined as the Arab League countries plus the Islamic Republic of Iran.[24]

Classification based on membership in the Arab League does not have economic logic and is only barely politically logical. It is a category based on ethnicity, but the addition of Iran contradicts even this rationale, seemingly making this category religion based. However, many Muslim countries of the world and even of this region are not included in the category.

The IMF's approach to country classification is deeply flawed and of very limited strategic value. That its classifications have a financial orientation is logical; it attempts to group countries in terms of external debt and sources of export earnings. However, its classification by industrial development is totally insufficient, and an analysis of sources of export earnings is better suited to the WTO.

The World Trade Organization Approach

The WTO has the most unsystematic approach of all multilateral institutions. In the documents and agreements of the WTO, countries are divided into three categories: developed, developing, and least developed. The WTO allows countries to define their own status as developing or developed. Developing and least-developed countries receive preferential treatment and provisions. These countries can get special treatment for their protectionist measures during the initial period of their membership and are eligible for technical assistance from the organization. They are also usually allowed more time to implement WTO agreements. Since the WTO functions as a "club" of countries, other country-members can question the self-assigned developing status of any country. The WTO considers countries to be "least developed" based on the opinion of the UNCTAD. As of 2006 this category includes 50 countries, which are considered to be extremely disadvantaged and as a result receive special treatment from the international community (further discussed in "The United Nations Approach" section of this chapter below). The term "emerging markets" practically does not exist in the documents of the WTO, which is a disservice to countries of all categories and confuses the policy of the WTO itself.

The United Nations Approach

As the preeminent multilateral organization, one would assume that the UN would have a comprehensive country classification system. In reality, the classification system of the UN is outdated and very bureaucratic. First, countries are divided geographically into the following continents and regions:[25]

Africa

- Eastern Africa
- Middle Africa
- Northern Africa
- Southern Africa
- Western Africa

Americas

- Northern America
- Latin America and the Caribbean

    —Caribbean
    —Central America
    —South America

Asia

- Central Asia
- Eastern Asia
- Southern Asia
- South-Eastern Asia
- Western Asia

Europe

- Eastern Europe
- Northern Europe
- Southern Europe
- Western Europe

Oceania

- Australia and New Zealand
- Melanesia
- Micronesia
- Polynesia

Second, they are divided into developed and developing regions:[26]

Developing Regions

- Africa
- Americas excluding Northern America
- Caribbean
- Central America
- South America
- Asia excluding Japan
- Oceania excluding Australia and New Zealand

Developed Regions

- Northern America
- Europe
- Japan
- Australia and New Zealand

Third, separate from the previous two classifications, there is the category of least-developed countries,[27] which is based primarily on economic factors:

Least Developed Countries

- Afghanistan
- Angola
- Bangladesh
- Benin
- Bhutan
- Burkina Faso
- Burundi
- Cambodia
- Cape Verde
- Central African Republic
- Chad

- Comoros
- Democratic Republic of the Congo
- Djibouti
- Equatorial Guinea
- Eritrea
- Ethiopia
- Gambia
- Guinea Bissau
- Guinea
- Haiti
- Kiribati
- Lao People's Democratic Republic
- Lesotho
- Liberia
- Madagascar
- Malawi
- Maldives
- Mali
- Mauritania
- Mozambique
- Myanmar
- Nepal
- Niger
- Rwanda
- Samoa
- Sao Tome and Principe
- Senegal
- Sierra Leone
- Solomon Islands
- Somalia
- Sudan
- Timor-Leste
- Togo
- Tuvalu
- Uganda
- United Republic of Tanzania
- Vanuatu
- Yemen
- Zambia

Fourth, the UN has the following three categories, which largely overlap the previously mentioned groups:[28]

- landlocked developing countries;
- small island developing states.

Although neither classification is directly related to the topic of this book, both definitely have economic and strategic implications for these countries and companies operating with or within them. The final category, transition countries and its two subsections,[29] also significantly overlaps the previously mentioned categories.

Transition Countries

CIS

- Armenia
- Azerbaijan
- Belarus
- Georgia
- Kazakhstan
- Kyrgyzstan
- Moldova
- Russian Federation
- Tajikistan
- Turkmenistan
- Ukraine
- Uzbekistan

TRANSITION COUNTRIES OF SOUTH-EASTERN EUROPE

- Albania
- Bosnia and Herzegovina
- Croatia
- Montenegro
- Serbia
- The former Yugoslav Republic of Macedonia

As previously stated, "transition countries," logically and semantically should include all non-developed countries. Nevertheless, in the category transition countries, the three Baltic States are not included, nor are those countries of Eastern Europe that have already became members of the EU. From a political perspective, excluding these countries may make sense, but in terms of economic development, the majority of Eastern European countries and the Baltic States share many mutual economic characteristics with those in the UN category of "transition countries." At the same time, among those evaluated as transition countries, some should be considered developing. Among the countries in this group that lag behind in terms of economic development are Tajikistan, Uzbekistan, Moldova, Belarus, and Bosnia and Herzegovina. This category lacks any economic or business basis and is of little, if any, use to strategists.

There are a number of flaws with UN's approach to country classification. First of all, regarding the regional classification, all of Europe is considered a developed region, as is North America. In Europe this totally ignores the level of economic development of European countries such as Albania, Belarus, Kosovo, and Moldova, which by no means can be considered developed. The same argument can be made regarding Mexico, but in order to avoid this discrepancy, the UN uses the term "Northern America" (instead of North America), which does not include Mexico.

Second, in the official documents of the UN, the terms "developed" and "developing countries" and regions are commonly used. However, the UN neglected to provide a theoretically based, unambiguous definition of these categories. In the "composition of macro geographical (continental) regions, geographical sub-regions, and selected economic and other groupings,"[30] the UN admits that

> there is no established convention for the designation of "developed" and "developing" countries or areas in the United Nations system. In common practice, Japan in Asia, Canada and the United States in northern America, Australia and New Zealand in Oceania, and Europe are considered "developed" regions or areas. In international trade statistics, the Southern African Customs Union is also treated as a developed region and Israel as a developed country; countries emerging from the former Yugoslavia are treated as developing countries; and countries of Eastern Europe and of the Commonwealth of Independent States . . . in Europe are not included under either developed or developing regions.[31]

The classification of the South African Customs Union as a "developed region," which consists of South Africa (indisputably an emerging market), Botswana (considered an emerging market in this book), Lesotho, Namibia, and Swaziland (almost universally evaluated as developing countries) seems totally arbitrary. The category of transition countries is also poorly defined. The UN states only " 'countries in transition from centrally planned to market economies' is a grouping used for economic analysis."[32] It is hard to believe, but *the* global institution of the world does not have a comprehensive system by which to classify its country-members.

The UN category of least developed countries has a more clear definition (at least relative to other UN country categories). Since 1971 the UN has

> denominated "least developed countries" [LDCs] a category of States that are deemed highly disadvantaged in their development process (many of them for geographical reasons), and facing more than other countries the risk of failing to come out of poverty. As such, the LDCs are considered to be in need of the highest degree of attention on the part of the international community.[33]

In 2003 UNCTAD established three qualifications to be met by a country in order to be considered least developed:

• "low income, in the light of a three-year average estimate of the gross national income per capita (under $750 for cases of addition to the list, above $900 for cases of graduation)";
• "weak human assets, as measured through a composite Human Assets Index"; and
• "economic vulnerability, as measured through a composite Economic Vulnerability Index."[34]

Typically, international aid to least developed countries is related to the improvement of the foreign trading systems; the development of the financial sectors based on bilateral, regional, and multilateral aid; and technical assistance.

Observations of Multilateral Institutions' Country Classification Systems

The country classifications of all major multilateral institutions are obviously deeply flawed. First of all, they lack a well-defined methodology based on established criteria and as a result are unsystematic. Second, terminology and categories are not synchronized among these institutions, largely the fault of the UN, which, as the major multilateral institution, has not used its authority to do so. Third, the terminology in these classifications is substantially outdated and does not reflect the reality of the twenty-first century. Fourth, EMCs are not officially or clearly defined in any of these institutions. The classifications of the UN and the WBG do not include a classification of EMCs. EMCs are included in several different categories, and the same country is often found in multiple groups in the classification of a single institution. The IMF is the only multilateral institution to officially use the term "emerging market"; however, it does so without a clear definition. Countries included in this group are also found in other IMF categories. The classification systems of these institutions are not in touch with the practical requirements of the international business community, national governments, and even of the needs of these institutions themselves. As a result, multilateral institutions' ability to make fair and efficient decisions regarding the provision of international aid, loans, and technical assistance is undoubtedly hindered. For global and regional multilateral institutions, a country classification system is the foundation upon which its strategic decisions are made. Understanding the distinctions between different categories of countries is absolutely crucial in order to optimize limited resources of these institutions. Unlike emerging markets, developing and underdeveloped countries still need special attention from multilateral institutions and aid agencies to prevent starvation, mass disease, and political instability. Developing countries need assistance to improve their education systems and create an entry strategy for their transition to the GEM. Multilateral institutions cannot ignore the need for clear definitions of emerging markets, as well as of developing and underdeveloped countries. It is important not only for the global business community but also for the poorest people and countries, who need special attention from political and business leaders of the world.

Alternatives to the Classifications Systems of Multilateral Institutions

Multilateral institutions alone are clearly not an adequate resource for country classification systems. There are a number of private agencies and research organizations (see Chapter 2) that provide ratings of countries based on specific practical needs. However, to offer alternatives to the approach of multilateral institutions, the following example from a major rating agency follows in this chapter.

One of the most reliable and respected private rating agencies, S&P, together with Citigroup, one of the largest international financial conglomerates in the world, developed a country classification system based on their own practical needs. The Standard & Poor's/ Citigroup Global Equity Index divides countries "into two major regions—the Developed World and the Emerging Composite. The objective of the Developed World/Emerging Composite split is to segregate countries according to the relative size of their economic output per capita."[35] The index is based on the following criteria:

1. "Annual per capita gross national income (GNI) falls in the high-income category, defined by the World Bank, for the most recent three consecutive years.
2. The market should exhibit financial depth; the ratio of the country's equity markets to its gross domestic product should be high. In recent years financial depth has increased around the world and has far outpaced the growth of gross domestic product. However, for a country to be considered truly developed both income levels and gross market capitalization should be high.
3. No broad-based discriminatory controls against non-domiciled investors for the most recent three consecutive years.
4. The country's stock markets should exhibit characteristics of developed markets in terms of transparency, depth, market regulation, operational efficiency, and absence of broad-based investment restrictions . . ."[36]

This index is based primarily on evaluations of the financial sectors of a country's national economy. It does not take into account a number of other key indicators of development, such as political and economic freedom, business infrastructure and industrial development, social stability, level of technological development, etc. While in many cases classification systems made by rating agencies and private research organizations may be based on a more clearly defined methodology than those of multilateral institutions, they are usually focused primarily on the practical needs of these organizations. As a result, they are rarely comprehensive in nature and scope. However, they are very useful references for strategists regarding specific issues and can be used in conjunction with other evaluations to form a more comprehensive system. For example, financial characteristics of country classifications can be refined and supplemented by a classification of capital markets or a classification of countries by the use and efficiency of individual financial instruments:

> As an alternative to using a stochastic macroeconomic model to define a country's risk, it may be worthwhile to consider market appraisals of countries' risk as has been done by Daniel Kohler of the Rand Corporation. He discovered that many countries' bonds are traded in an international market located in Switzerland. Using data relating to transactions in this market he was able to classify countries with respect to risk class.[37]

But rating agencies and research organizations tend to group countries of different levels of economic maturity and political stability into the same category. Even the widely respected surveys published by the Economist Intelligence Unit arbitrarily blur the distinctions between emerging-market, developing, and underdeveloped countries, rendering the statistics regarding certain categories from these surveys inaccurate. Reports on EMCs often make them seem less efficient than they are in reality, due to an overestimation of their population, which falsely reduces per capita productivity of labor and GDP.

Due to the lack of accurate classifications, strategists should develop their own classification systems based on indicators and evaluations specific to their practical and theoretical needs. However, when compiling these indicators, they must be very meticulous in order to avoid errors that will distort results and lead to inaccurate conclusions. Strategists must cater to the needs of the entity for which they are developing the classification system. Different types of entities have different needs for country classification systems.

National governments need classification systems for a better understanding of their country's position in the GMP, to study and implement the successful strategies of countries with similar characteristics, to optimize their international humanitarian aid programs, to improve economic and trade relations, and to develop strategies toward countries of different levels of maturity. Governments of developed countries need to know which nations are the least developed (underdeveloped countries) in order to optimize aid and assistance; which countries would benefit most from and are prepared for liberalized trade regulations and freer movement of labor, resources, and capital (EMCs); and which countries are capable of collaborating on anti-monopoly and money laundering regulations, and of harmonizing monetary and fiscal policies to avoid double taxation toward businesses and individuals working in multiple countries (developed countries). Governments of EMCs also require country classification systems in order to develop their domestic and foreign economic and trade policies. Companies from EMCs now operate not only domestically but also in other EMCs, developing, underdeveloped, and even developed countries.

Multilateral institutions play a crucial role in helping governments achieve these goals. They have to provide channels for developed countries to improve relationships among themselves, as well as with emerging-market, developing, and underdeveloped countries. They need to help direct assistance from developed countries to non-developed countries, focusing and coordinating aid to help the neediest people. Multilateral institutions are also best equipped to develop mutually acceptable rules of business and economic cooperation in the GMP.

For *companies* from any category of country, it is extremely important to have an understanding of the level of economic development and business conditions of a country in which they are going to invest or deal with businesses and governmental agencies from that country. They need to understand systematic and national credit risk, the quality of banking institutions, the general investment climate, and the standard of living of potential employees, counterparts, and consumers in these countries. For this and many other reasons, country classifications focusing especially on economic and business maturity, political stability, and standards of living are important for companies from all countries.

The Strategic Approach to Country Classification

The comprehensive approach to country classification is derived from the gnoseology of the emerging-market categorization. Typically, country classification begins with an analysis of two integrated indicators—GDP and GDP per capita (or GNI per capita). A strategic approach to country classification requires the analysis of a much wider spectrum of indicators. As the 1975 Nobel laureate in economics Tjalling Koopmans, together with the great economist John Michael Montias, wrote:

> [I]n general, we believe the new circumstances invite approaches to the comparison of economic systems that altogether avoid prior classification according to the grand "isms" and instead start from comparisons of organizational arrangements for specific economic functions. Among these we should wish to consider the coordination of production activities by distinct organizations, the accumulation and utilization of means of production of new or existing types, the research and development for new methods and means of production, the distribution of currently produced goods and

services among the participants and beneficiaries of the system, the maintenance of aggregate stability, and the protection of individuals from harmful effects of the economic actions of others.[38]

Even an approach as wide reaching as Koopmans and Montias' still relies solely on economic issues. Countries cannot be classified only by an analysis of economic and financial indicators and basic economic factors. This kind of approach is simple economic determinism, which undervalues the role of cultural, religious, and ethnic traditions and to some extent, political interests. An analysis of such issues is one of the first steps in the development of a country classification system. However, political, social, environmental, cultural, and technological issues all have to be taken into consideration through an analysis of the maturity and role of the middle class, social unity, religious freedom and tolerance, etc. All of these issues have to be part of a truly comprehensive country classification system. Strategists must also be aware of the vector of the dynamics of all of these indicators and must keep in mind that positive vectors can always be reversed or redirected. Large, diverse, multicultural, and multireligious societies are especially vulnerable to such reversals of progress. Society is like a human being: in order to function best, it must be happy and healthy. It occasionally happens in modern history that disunited, weak, and unhappy societies can revert from a path to freedom and progress back to dictatorship and repression. People of these countries usually do not demonstrate social optimism. Stronger and more unified societies with a developing and expanding middle class usually look for a strong leader who will continue to lead a country toward freedom. Strategists must be careful when they are not from or are not familiar enough with the region or country that is being analyzed. In such cases, issues have to be evaluated from domestic and foreign points of view, especially regarding the country's bilateral relationships with its neighbors. For these reasons, it is extremely important to evaluate cultural, social, and political issues, despite the fact that they are very difficult to quantify and compare. Even national and regional characteristics such as climate and weather (both innate aspects of the basic economic factor of territory) have important implications for economic and social development, and must be analyzed.

Nonetheless, when developing a country classification system, it is always easier and more efficient to start with indicators that can be quantitatively measured, according to which countries can be unquestionably ranked. This gives strategists more credibility and a solid base to build upon when the quantitative approach has to be supplemented by a qualitative approach. This is the opposite order by which strategy is developed. In strategy, first it is better to develop qualitative objectives to provide an orientation, followed by quantitative goals to meet these objectives. A system of quantitative and qualitative political, economic, financial, and technological indicators provides the morphology of a country—a system of characteristics and internal structure by which it operates as a unified sociopolitical, economic, and technological entity. All of these factors and indicators have to be analyzed within the national cultural and religious environment.

Indexation of Countries by Industrial Structure

In the last quarter of the twentieth century, leading countries began to move beyond the industrial stage of their economic development to a service-based economy. An economy can be considered service-based (or post-industrial) when the value added of service industries surpasses at least 50 percent of the national GDP.

Table 4.6 is compiled primarily from 2005 WBG statistics. Out of the 143 countries with available data, 91 already have post-industrial economies. In more than 30 countries,

Table 4.6 Services Value Added as a Percentage of GDP, 2005 (Unless Noted Otherwise)[39]

Rank	Country	Services Value Added as a Percentage of GDP
1	**Hong Kong**	90.72
2	Luxembourg	83.32
3	Djibouti	79.08
4	France	76.88
5	United States*	76.67
6	**Panama**	75.98
7	Belgium	74.93
8	**Latvia**	74.46
9	**Greece**	73.98
10	Netherlands	73.55
11	Denmark	73.54
12	United Kingdom	72.79
13	**Portugal**	72.49
14	Lebanon	71.21
15	Italy	70.88
16	Sweden	70.7
17	Switzerland*	70.36
18	**Mexico**	70.17
19	Australia*	69.62
20	Germany	69.44
21	Iceland*	68.41
22	Belize	68.22
23	Japan*	68.14
24	Austria	67.78
25	**Estonia**	67.75
26	**Jordan**	67.58
27	Finland	67.53
28	**Spain**	67.22
29	**South Africa**	67.12
30	Canada**	66.42
31	**Singapore**	66.14
32	**Mauritius**	65.72
33	New Zealand***	65.67
34	**Hungary**	65.58
35	Suriname	64.8
36	**Poland**	64.57
37	Bosnia and Herzegovina	64.49
38	**Slovak Republic**	64.49
39	**Turkey**	64.45
40	**Brazil**	64.01
41	Slovenia	63.4
42	Senegal	63.2
43	**Croatia**	62.69
44	Dominican Republic	62.09
45	**Serbia**	61.83
46	**Montenegro**	61.71
47	**Costa Rica**	61.39
48	**Jamaica**	61.22
49	**Lithuania**	60.53
50	**Ireland***	60.22
51	**Uruguay**	60.01
52	**El Salvador**	59.77
53	**Bulgaria**	59.7
54	**Tunisia**	59.69
55	**Czech Republic**	58.81

(Continued Overleaf)

Table 4.6 Continued

Rank	Country	Services Value Added as a Percentage of GDP
56	Paraguay	58.63
57	Moldova	58.46
58	Guatemala	58.32
59	Peru	58.03
60	Macedonia, FYR	57.74
61	Namibia	57.71
62	Sri Lanka	57.15
63	Côte d'Ivoire	57.02
64	Zimbabwe	56.95
65	Georgia	56.46
66	Russian Federation	56.39
67	Madagascar	56.33
68	Zambia	56.33
69	Korea, Rep.	56.32
70	Morocco	55.92
71	Albania	55.7
72	Ukraine	55.34
73	Norway	55.06
74	Argentina	54.99
75	Romania	54.86
76	Eritrea	54.79
77	Honduras	54.63
78	Kenya	54.44
79	Benin	54.38
80	India	54.37
81	Gambia, The	54.25
82	Bolivia	53.84
83	Kazakhstan	53.67
84	Nicaragua	53.42
85	Philippines	53.41
86	Colombia	53.27
87	Timor-Leste	53
88	Bangladesh	52.63
89	Pakistan	51.3
90	Mozambique	49.74
91	Belarus	49.29
92	Egypt, Arab Rep.	49.01
93	Ecuador	47.79
94	Chile	47.7
95	Cameroon	47.35
96	Mauritania	47.05
97	Malawi	45.86
98	Thailand	45.85
99	Guinea	45.76
100	Kyrgyz Republic	45.66
101	Burundi	45.14
102	Iran, Islamic Rep.	45
103	Tajikistan	44.78
104	Botswana	44.52
105	Guyana	44.47
106	Uzbekistan	43.2
107	Swaziland	42.84
108	Uganda	42.53
109	United Arab Emirates	42.03
110	Indonesia	42.01
111	Lesotho	41.28

112	Nepal	40.83
113	**China**	40.11
114	Ethiopia	39.82
115	**Malaysia**	39.58
116	Trinidad and Tobago	39.58
117	Afghanistan	39.42
118	**Ghana**	39.39
119	Mali	39.26
120	Cambodia	39.1
121	**Vietnam**	38.17
122	Comoros	37.99
123	**Mongolia**	37.51
124	Rwanda	37.28
125	Tanzania	37
126	Bhutan	36.71
127	Sudan	36.59
128	**Armenia**	35.21
129	**Gabon**	33.76
130	Togo	32.41
131	**Algeria**	30.09
132	Sierra Leone	29.68
133	Guinea-Bissau	28.06
134	**Azerbaijan**	27.69
135	Congo, Dem. Rep.	27.55
136	Lao PDR	25.72
137	Congo, Rep.	25.42
138	Chad	24.87
139	Central African Republic	24.76
140	Nigeria	19.87
141	Angola	18.74
142	Liberia	18.24
143	Equatorial Guinea	2.94

Notes:
*2004 data.
**2002 data.
***2001 data.

two-thirds of GDP comes from the service sector. The role of service industries in GDP is an important indication of the economic maturity of a country. However, it does not present an absolute picture of the level of national economic development. Countries with national economies dominated by the service sector include countries of a high level of economic maturity (Hong Kong, the US, Denmark, etc.) as well as national economies that were never industrialized and are not highly developed (Djibouti, Belize, Eritrea, etc.). Countries such as Armenia and Azerbaijan, which rank near the bottom of this table, are in fact more advanced in economic terms than countries such as Djibouti, Belize, and Eritrea. The fact that an economy is based more heavily on industrial rather than service sectors does not necessarily mean that it is less developed. However, a country's services value added as a percentage of GDP does have important strategic implications, and should be part of a country classification system. However, it must be supplemented with several other indicators, such as an evaluation of the technological development of the national industrial base (Table 4.7).

Table 4.7 Percentage Share of Modern-tech Sectors in Total Manufacturing Value Added, 2005[40]

Rank	Country	Machinery and Equipment	Office, Accounting, and Computing Machinery	Electrical Machinery and Apparatus	Radio, Television, and Communication Equipment	Medical, Precision, and Optical Instruments	Motor Vehicles, Trailers, Semi-trailers	Total Percentage Share of Modern-tech Sectors
1	Hungary	3.7	4.4	10.1	45.7	1.1	9.6	74.6
2	United States	3.9	6.4	2.3	44.5	3.1	4.7	64.9
3	Korea, South	7.7	2.6	2.3	37	0.7	8.1	58.4
4	Japan	5.4	13.2	21.9	4.4	1	9.6	55.5
5	Singapore	1.3	0	2.9	44.2	1.9	0.2	50.5
6	Sweden	9.3	0.3	2.4	22.5	2.8	12.6	49.9
7	Malaysia	2.3	0.3	5.5	32.7	0.7	3	44.5
8	Germany	14.2	1.9	7.5	4.1	3.7	11.9	43.3
9	Finland	9.2	0	3.4	27.3	1.7	1.2	42.8
10	France	7.9	0.8	4.8	10.9	4.2	13.2	41.8
11	Czech Republic	12.3	1.2	5.7	2	1.5	15.1	37.8
12	Austria	12.8	0.3	4.5	5.2	2.1	6	30.9
13	Ireland	1.2	12.9	5.9	1.2	8.7	0.6	30.5
14	Turkey	7.7	0.3	2.6	9.9	0.2	8.6	29.3
15	Mexico	3.4	2.2	2.9	2.8	0.7	17	29
16	Portugal	5	0.4	1.7	7.7	1.2	12.2	28.2
17	Denmark	12.8	1.6	5.3	1.4	5.1	1.6	27.8
18	United Kingdom	8.1	2.6	2.8	3.6	3	6.5	26.6
19	India	6.7	0.8	9.4	1.8	0.9	6.6	26.2
20	Poland	7.6	0	4.7	3.2	1.7	7.6	24.8
21	Italy	11.2	0	4.3	2.6	2.9	3.4	24.4
22	Belgium	5	0.4	4.7	2.3	0.5	10.4	23.3
23	Canada	7.2	1.1	1.3	3.2	1.1	8.4	22.3
24	Spain	7.7	0.2	4.6	1	1	7.6	22.1
25	Brazil	5.4	2.4	4.4	3.1	2.1	4.6	22
26	Bulgaria	16.1	0.3	4	0.9	0.4	0.3	22
27	Romania	5.7	0	3.9	0.5	0.8	11.1	22
28	South Africa	6.4	1.6	1.3	1.7	0.4	9	20.4
29	Malta	1.1	0.2	2.6	13.4	2.9	0.1	20.3
30	Armenia	9.9	2	0.5	0	7.9	0.2	20.5
31	Lithuania	4.4	0	4	10.6	0.3	0.9	20.2
32	Australia	4.1	0.5	4.2	2.5	1	7.6	19.9
33	Norway	8.3	3.6	2.2	2.3	1.8	1.6	19.8
34	Netherlands	7.2	0.6	1.7	6.2	0.6	2.4	18.7
35	Luxembourg	8.4	0	1.8	2.5	0.3	0.8	13.8
36	New Zealand	6.1	0.1	3.6	1.1	0.4	2.3	13.6
37	Croatia	4.7	0.2	5	1.3	0.7	1.6	13.5
38	Argentina	5.4	0	1.3	0.8	0.4	5.3	13.2
39	Egypt	5.9	0	4.2	0	0	0.7	10.8
40	Estonia	3	2.1	1.5	1.5	2.4	0.3	10.8

Source: © Dr Vladimir Kvint, 2008.

Indexation of National Economies' Technological Maturity

An evaluation of the role of a country's modern-technological manufacturing sectors provides an adequate base to analyze the technological development of a national economy. In Table 4.7, the percentage share of six modern-tech sectors in total manufacturing value added is analyzed in 40 countries. All six of these sectors are somewhat knowledge-based and thus require a certain amount of technological sophistication. The most technologically advanced industry among the six selected is radio, television, and communication equipment. Logically, the economies with the highest level of technological development will have the highest share of these modern-tech sectors in total manufacturing value added.

Table 4.7 illustrates the extent to which the leading countries of the world are already transitioning from post-industrial to knowledge-based economies. It is not surprising that the US and countries with technologically advanced economies, such as Japan, Germany, Finland, and France, are among the leaders. What is surprising to most is that Hungary is the highest-ranked country in terms of the role of modern-tech manufacturing sectors, and that it has substantially surpassed the US by this indicator.

For many years Hungary has concentrated on the production of information and communication technologies. By share of these technologies in total manufacturing output, Hungary is far ahead of other emerging markets of Eastern Europe—countries such as Poland, the Czech Republic, and even Russia (in Russia, this sector accounts for only 10 percent of manufacturing output).[41] Hungary's production of information communication technology per capita is especially impressive, which is equal to $0.8 million. By comparison, production of IT per capita in the EU is $0.6 million.[42] Hungary, a relatively small country of about 10 million people, accounts for 2.4 percent of global exports of telecom appliances; its share in the global export of television receivers is 2.2 percent.[43] Hungary's very impressive success in this industry is the result of a national technological strategy, an efficient regional concentration of production facilities, and its territorial proximity to other European countries. Several world-class companies partially backed by foreign investors are located in Hungary such as Tungsram (http://www.tungsram.hu/tungsram/english/index .html), an electro-technical company with hundreds of years of experience and Videoton (http://www.videoton.hu/), a provider of electronics manufacturing services.

In Table 4.7, out of the 40 countries evaluated, 23 are emerging markets. However, it is important to note the limited availability of statistics in multilateral institutions for several EMCs, which prevented the evaluation of several countries that would have made this list, such as Taiwan and Hong Kong, Russia, Israel, and China. Only 13 countries in the world (of those with available statistics) reached the level of technological development whereby modern technologies account for more than 30 percent of their total manufacturing value added. Hungary and the US are the only two countries in which at least two-thirds of manufacturing value added is accounted for by modern technologies. A complete list of the ranking of these countries by this indicator is not included, but it is useful to know that in countries such as Peru, El Salvador, and surprisingly for many, Greece, modern-tech sectors account for less than 10 percent of manufacturing value added. In the near future, these sectors will act as a platform for further development of super-high technologies of the twenty-first century in the most advanced countries.

The use of and investment in super-high technologies, such as nanotechnologies, membrane technologies, alternative energy production and technologies, etc., are also an important indication of the technological development of a national economy. As of 2006 the US accounts for the largest share of investment in nanotechnology, followed by Japan, and then Germany, the United Kingdom, France, China, Russia, South Korea, Canada, and Australia.[44] Countries that compete for leading positions in this revolutionary industry made a strategic decision to invest in high-school programs teaching nanotechnologies. As this industry continues to develop, there will be more available and reliable statistics for strategists, which will allow the comparison of the first results of the race on this new scientific technological road. According to Dr James Canton, CEO of Institute for Global Futures:

> [N]anotechnology may become an essential large-systems strategic competency that will require coordination among all sectors of society in order to become a force for enhanced social productivity. This technology is fast emerging. Nanotechnology may well shape the sustainability and wealth of nations, organizations, and entire industries in the future. A central concern here is the necessity for us, together as a nation, to plan today to meet the readiness challenges that most certainly will lie ahead.[45]

Other evaluations of a country's level of technological advancement include an analysis of the national use and production of alternative sources of energy, such as ethanol, bioethanol, nuclear-generated electricity, etc. It is also of strategic value to be aware of potential threats posed by certain technologies in the hands of governments that are perceived as adversarial to the international community. The most obvious example of this is the attempts by non-democratic regimes such as North Korea, Syria, and Iran to obtain nuclear technology. At the same time, there are several countries that are technologically capable of developing and producing nuclear technologies for civilian and non-military purposes, including EMCs such as Algeria, Egypt, Indonesia, South Africa, and Taiwan. There are a few independent agencies that monitor the strategic concern of nuclear programs of the world, for instance, the Stockholm International Peace Institute and FirstWatch International.[46] The best way to evaluate the extent to which a country's nuclear capabilities are perceived as a threat to the international community is to monitor the level of a country's cooperation with the International Atomic Energy Agency (IAEA) and whether or not the country has signed the Nuclear Nonproliferation Treaty. Among the non-threatening, nuclear-capable countries, Kazakhstan should be given special credit. It inherited a substantial nuclear arsenal from the Soviet Union, making it the first Muslim country with nuclear weapons. Admirably, Kazakhstan voluntarily transferred its nuclear weapons to Russia. This illustrates the entirely peaceful orientation of Kazakhstan's nuclear program.

Evaluation of National Environmental Protection

In addition to an analysis of the industrial structure and level of technological sophistication, a country's attitude toward environmental protection is also a crucial part of a comprehensive evaluation of its level of development. One of the best resources for such an evaluation is the Environmental Sustainability Index, developed by the Yale Center for Environmental Law and Policy and the Center for International Earth Science Information Network of Columbia University, in collaboration with the World Economic Forum and the Joint Research Centre of the European Commission. This index is based on an analysis of five major components: environmental systems; reducing environmental stresses; reducing human vulnerability; social and intuitional capacity; and global stewardship.[47] According to this index, the Nordic states are among the most environmentally sustainable countries. The seven lowest-ranked countries on this list all suffer under repressive political regimes, leading to an interesting correlation between freedom and environmental protection. The ranking of a country on this index has significant implications for its level of development, and it (or similar evaluations) should always be taken into account when developing a country classification system. Another evaluation of the level of national environmental protection can be done through an analysis of environmentally related tax revenue as a percentage of total tax revenue. The OECD made such a study;[48] however, its methodology was not comprehensive enough, and its results do not necessarily illustrate the quality of national environmental protection.

A Synthesized Rating of National Technological, Economic, and Social Advancement

One of the more difficult aspects of developing a country classification system is the formation of a rating that synthesizes a number of different indicators. A synthesized rating allows strategists to make quick and/or preliminary strategic evaluations of the level of political, economic, and technological development of a country, to compare different groups of countries, and to create coefficients in investment and risk-management processes. The development of a synthesized country-rating system based on multiple integrated indicators has challenged economists, mathematicians, and strategists for at least 50 years. Nonetheless, a truly comprehensive method was never achieved.

The best-known attempt to do so was based on national consumption levels, developed more than 50 years ago by the economist Merrill Kelley Bennett, a professor from Stanford University.[49] But the Bennett method has several weaknesses, the most glaring of which is its inability to accurately evaluate countries with wide disparities in development. The method is based on the following: the best indicator in any classification has to be divided by the worst one. If the best is 1, for example, and the worst is 50, then 1 has to be divided by 50. This approach is useful only to evaluate and precisely rank the most developed or the most underdeveloped countries of the world. For example, an evaluation of the GDP per capita of the US, Denmark, Sri Lanka, and El Salvador through the Bennett method will likely not yield reliable results, as the huge variance of indicators skews the relative ratio among the countries.

This problem in the Bennett method appeared because of the use of an *algorithmic summary* of country-specific indicators of an index, where particular indicators are calculated relative to one another. His general approach is reflected in the following algorithm, which has been changed slightly according to the goals of this chapter:

$$P = \sum_{k=1}^{N} P_k \cdot W_k,$$

where P is a synthesized indicator, P_k is one of the five specific indicators listed below, W_k is the weight (i.e. importance) of indicator P_k, and N is the total number of indicators (in this case, 5). W_k is defined as the relative weight of each of the five indicators listed in Table 4.8.

Table 4.8 Integrated Indicators and their Weights

Indicator	Weight
Modern-tech Manufacturing Index	1
Knowledge Economy Index	1
Service-based Economy Index	0.7
Economic Freedom Index	0.7
GDP per Capita (PPP) Index	2

Source: © Dr Vladimir Kvint, 2008.

Bennett never used these particular indicators himself, but this book proposes them to address the practical needs of strategists and economists.

Countries are organized by P in descending order. This method of ranking countries is presented in the Table 4.9.

The limitations of the Bennett method can be avoided by supplementing the algorithmic summary with an *algorithmic multiplication* function (the Kvint algorithm[50]).

$$\hat{P} = 1000 \cdot \prod_{k=1}^{N} P_k^{W_k},$$

where $\hat{P}$ is the product of multiplication. The coefficient 1,000 is included in the algorithm only to avoid very small numbers with several decimals.

Using a synthesis of these two mathematical models, a more comprehensive country ranking system is developed in this book by an analysis of five key indicators (listed in Table 4.8.) that reflect the level of technological and socioeconomic development. Algorithmic multiplication uses the same indicators and their relative weights according to strategic importance.

The data for these indicators were collected for 50 countries, with varying levels of economic maturity. Among these indicators, only the Modern-tech Manufacturing Index, compiled from the database of the United Nations Industrial Development Organization (UNIDO), was specifically developed for this book. Unfortunately, from most countries of the world, it is a challenge to find reliable and complete statistics for the indicators used in this algorithmic model. Several national governments do not supply multilateral institutions with the necessary information. For this reason, countries of great strategic importance such as China and Russia are not included in Table 4.9 and Table 4.7. The basic information for the knowledge- and service-based economy indices and the GDP per capita index were taken from public sources (the World Bank and the CIA World Factbook). Every year the *Wall Street Journal* and the Heritage Foundation compile the Index of Economic Freedom. However, it should be noted that the evaluations and rankings of economic freedom are questionable for several countries relative to the position of other countries in the index. The following points are a few examples of questionable evaluations. It is extremely hard to accept the fact that Taiwan has a level of economic freedom seven positions below that of Mauritius and six positions below that of Bahrain. Furthermore, it is hard to rationalize a significantly higher evaluation of the level of economic freedom in Armenia than of Norway and the Czech Republic. The amount of corruption alone in Armenia and Georgia makes it impossible to have a higher ranking than Hungary or Slovenia (especially by 48 positions). The ranking of Armenia 75 positions above Georgia and 79 positions above Azerbaijan is also hard to accept. Azerbaijan, an emerging-market dictatorship, has one of the highest levels of corruption in the world yet is ranked above India and Croatia. It is difficult to believe that Iran has a higher level of economic freedom than Turkmenistan. Finally, the evaluation of Portugal below Uganda or of France below Oman and Kuwait is very disputable. As a result of such questionable rankings in the 2008 Index of Economic Freedom, it is not the only resource used for final evaluations of the level of economic freedom in this book.

In Table 4.10, countries are ranked by the average of both algorithmic methods mentioned above. Countries that received identical average scores were differentiated based on evaluations of the level of national environmental concern. The accuracy and proximity of results of these two different algorithmic methods is surprisingly high. Six countries (Sweden, United States, Italy, Belgium, India, Jordan) received identical evaluations from both methods. Six other countries have minimal differences in the two evaluations that do not change their

Table 4.9 Synthesized Country Rating of Technological, Economic, and Social Advancement (Kvint's Country Rating)

Kvint's Rank	Country	Based on the "Bennett" Algorithm	Kvint Algorithm	Average of both Algorithms
1	Sweden	1	1	1
2	Denmark	6	2	4
3	United States	4	4	4
4	Finland	8	3	5.5
5	Norway	7	5	6
6	Japan	9	8	8.5
7	Canada	11	9	10
8	Netherlands	13	7	10
9	Ireland	5	16	10.5
10	Australia	10	13	11.5
11	Germany	12	11	11.5
12	United Kingdom	16	10	13
13	Hungary	15	12	13.5
14	Luxembourg	3	24	13.5
15	France	14	15	14.5
16	Austria	17	14	15.5
17	Turkey	27	6	16.5
18	Belgium	18	18	18
19	Korea, South	19	17	18
20	Singapore	2	34	18
21	New Zealand	22	19	20.5
22	Italy	21	21	21
23	Spain	20	23	21.5
24	Czech Republic	23	20	21.5
25	Portugal	24	22	23
26	Malaysia	28	25	26.5
27	Estonia	26	30	28
28	Poland	30	26	28
29	Mexico	29	28	28.5
30	Lithuania	31	27	29
31	Greece	25	36	30.5
32	Bulgaria	33	29	31
33	South Africa	32	31	31.5
34	Brazil	35	33	34
35	Romania	36	32	34
36	Croatia	34	35	34.5
37	Argentina	37	39	38
38	India	38	38	38
39	Armenia	42	37	39.5
40	Jordan	41	41	41
41	Colombia	43	42	42.5
42	Egypt	45	40	42.5
43	Malta	39	50	44.5
44	Cyprus	40	50	45
45	Peru	44	47	45.5
46	Indonesia	50	43	46.5
47	Morocco	47	44	45.5
48	Sri Lanka	48	46	47
49	Algeria	49	45	47
50	El Salvador	46	48	47

Source: © Dr Vladimir Kvint, 2008.

relative positions in the table. In general, smaller countries have wider differences between the Kvint algorithm and the Bennett-based algorithms. For example, there is a 32-point difference for Singapore, a 21-point difference for Luxembourg, and an 11-point difference for Ireland and Malta. This can be explained by the fact that in smaller countries, only a few technological innovations can have a substantial impact on the efficiency of a national economy. This is also illustrated by the fact that for all of these differences, the result calculated by the Kvint algorithm is significantly higher than that of the Bennett-based algorithm.

The Synthesized Country Rating of Technological, Economic, and Social Advancement is extremely useful in the development of a country classification system, as well as for a number of other strategic purposes. It is very helpful for companies that seek cross-border investment in high- and modern-tech sectors of foreign economies. It is also useful for companies from countries that have not yet reached the stage of a knowledge-based economy but would like to gain advantages by investing and outsourcing in foreign countries with a high level of science and technology. The GMP of the twenty-first century poses new challenges for executives and strategists to evaluate risks of investment in EMCs, which by technological characteristics can be ahead of developed nations. There is a new trend—FDI from EMCs is going to science-based industries of developed countries. It is practically a new direction of outsourcing. Unlike the initial stage of development of this phenomenon, when companies from developed countries outsourced to emerging markets in order to decrease cost production and cost service, later, companies from EMCs began to outsource knowledge-based production to developed countries because it is less expensive and less time consuming than building these industries domestically. All business leaders in the GMP are in need of new criteria and country-rating systems to correctly reflect the new economic reality.

The Strategic Comprehensive Country Classification System

An analysis of all of the previously mentioned indicators (political, economic, business, technological, and environmental) via different rating and index systems creates a foundation to classify countries through the algorithmic development of a set of rules that lead to a comprehensive country classification system of the GMP in a limited number of steps. This classification system is only a base upon which strategists, economists, and executives should make further analyses. Unlike other indexes that were used as a base, this country classification system deals not only with quantitative indicators and ratings, but also with largely qualitative indicators, such as evaluations of political systems and social climates. As a result, despite the use of many quantitative approaches, this classification should be questioned and analyzed by strategists, depending on their perspectives and practical needs. In fact, one of the main goals of this chapter is to initiate such discussions and studies.

The categorization of this classification system uses some groups that have been widely accepted for many years, such as superpower, developed, developing, and underdeveloped countries. Some categories, such as EMCs, became widely accepted only at the end of the twentieth century. Other categories, wealthy nations and emerging-market democracies, may not have been used as categories in any classification, but can be found as terms in economic and business literature. However, some of categories are totally new terms, such as *economies in bloom*, *technologically advanced economies*, *oligarchic emerging markets* and *emerging-market dictatorships*. This country classification system has several important qualities. First, unlike many prior attempts, this system does not include any countries in multiple categories. Second, no categories overlap. Third, this classification is not determined purely by economic factors. Political, social, and cultural characteristics, in addition to economic indicators, play an important role. For example, higher levels of economic and political freedom, religious tolerance, and environmental protection explain why some countries with substantially higher GDP per capita are classified below countries with lower GDP per capita. The openness of a country to international investment and its level of integration within the GMP were heavily weighted in the country classification process. The specific qualifications of an EMC are described in detail in Chapter 2, but additional observations of characteristics will be presented following the Integrated Country Rating.

The classification of non-EMCs is not a major focus of this book, but without their classification it is difficult for strategists and executives dealing with these countries to understand the role of EMCs and the GEM in the GMP, and to compare EMCs with countries of other categories. A comprehensive country classification and ratings system creates not only a systematic framework for strategic analysis, but it also elucidates the regionalization of the GMP and the gnoseology of the development of different types of regional blocs, unions, and economic areas and zones. The classification below logically begins with the most developed countries and ends with countries that are economically and politically lagging behind. This classification does not provide a global rank of countries outside of categories in which they are listed. It is made only within categories, because an overall ranking straight through all categories in this methodology would arbitrarily increase the ranking of countries in categories classified first, and disadvantages to those classified in the last category. In the categories of developing and underdeveloped countries, the higher the rank, the closer the nation is to the category of P-EMCs. The comprehensive classification system consists of the following structure:

- Developed Countries

    —Economic Superpower
    —Technologically Advanced Economies
    —Wealthy Nations

- Emerging-market Countries

    —Economies in Bloom
    —Emerging-market Democracies
    —Oligarchic Emerging Markets
    —Emerging-market Dictatorships
    —Pre-emerging Markets

- Developing Countries
- Underdeveloped Countries

Table 4.10 Kvint's Integrated Country Ratings, 2008

Developed Countries		
Rank within Category	*Superpower*	*Integrated Rating*
1	The United States of America	2
Rank within Category	*Technologically Advanced*	*Integrated Rating*
1	Sweden	5.25
2	Denmark	5.7
3	Finland	5.71
4	Iceland	5.75
5	Norway	5.8
6	Japan	5.85
7	Australia	6.17

8	Canada	6.75
9	Netherlands	6.92
10	United Kingdom of Great Britain and Northern Ireland	7.5
11	Austria	8
12	France	8.67
13	Germany	8.83
14	Belgium	9.08
15	New Zealand	10.08
16	Italy	11.83

Rank within Category	Wealthy Nations	Integrated Rating
1	Luxembourg	13.5
2	Switzerland	13.7
3	Lichtenstein	13.8
4	Bermuda	14.2
5	Andorra	14.4
6	San Marino	14.7
7	Monaco	14.7
8	Holy See (Vatican)	15

EMCs

Rank within Category	Economies in Bloom	Integrated Rating
1	Hong Kong SAR	2.75
2	Czech Republic	4.1
3	Ireland	4.8
4	Slovakia	6.38
5	Singapore	6.63
6	Hungary	7.38
7	Taiwan, Republic of	7.63
8	Israel	9.25
9	Slovenia	9.25
10	Costa Rica	9.75
11	Portugal	10.2
12	Korea, Republic of	10.7
13	Spain	12
14	Greece	14.8
15	Malta	15.5

Rank within Category	Emerging-market Democracies	Integrated Rating
1	Cyprus	4.66
2	Estonia	4.7
3	Bahamas, The	5.5
4	Barbados	6
5	Mauritius	8
6	Latvia	8.5
7	Panama	9.5
8	Uruguay	9.75
9	Mexico	10
10	Brazil	10.08
11	Croatia	11
12	Chile	11.6
13	Lithuania	12.6
14	Argentina	12.67
15	Poland	12.83
16	Turkey	14.42

17	South Africa	15.67
18	Botswana	17
19	Bulgaria	17.5
20	Peru	18.3
21	Romania	19.58
22	Albania	20
23	Colombia	20.5
24	Trinidad and Tobago	21
25	Thailand	21
26	Jordan	22.8
27	Jamaica	23
28	Macedonia, The Former Yugoslav Republic	24.5
29	Serbia	25.25
30	India	25.92
31	Guyana	26.75
32	Ghana	27
33	Ecuador	28.25
34	Saint Kitts and Nevis	28.5
35	Philippines	28.6
36	Montenegro	28.75
37	Guatemala	29
38	El Salvador	29.3
39	Algeria	29.7
40	Georgia	30
41	Armenia	30.2
42	Saint Lucia	35.5

Rank within Category	Oligarchic Emerging Markets	Integrated Rating
1	Russian Federation	2
2	Malaysia	2.83
3	Kazakhstan	3.33
4	Ukraine	4
5	Belize	4.17
6	Indonesia	4.67

Rank within Category	Emerging-market Dictatorships	Integrated Rating
1	Bahrain	4.4
2	United Arab Emirates	5
3	Egypt	5.2
4	Qatar	5.4
5	Morocco	6.2
6	Pakistan	6.2
7	Azerbaijan	6.4
8	Moldova	6.6
9	Gabon	6.8
10	China	7.2
11	Vietnam	8.8
12	Turkmenistan	9.8

Rank within Category	P-EMCs	Integrated Rating
1	Tunisia	2.25
2	Mongolia	4
3	Madagascar	4
4	Sri Lanka	4
5	Bolivia	4
6	Iraq	5.5

| 7 | Saudi Arabia | 5.75 |
| 8 | Burkina Faso | 6.5 |

Developing Countries

Rank within Category	Developing Countries	Integrated Rating
1	Brunei Darussalam	3
2	Paraguay	4
3	Seychelles, Republic of	5
4	Oman	8.33
5	Namibia	8.75
6	Antigua and Barbuda	9
7	Fiji	11.5
8	Cook Islands	13
9	Kuwait	13.67
10	Suriname	14.67
11	Cape Verde	15
12	Dominican Republic	15
13	Palau	15
14	Bosnia and Herzegovina	15.5
15	Lebanon	17
16	Kosovo	17.3
17	Nicaragua	17.5
18	Honduras	18
19	Swaziland	19.33
20	Belarus	19.5
21	Senegal	19.75
22	Kyrgyzstan	21
23	Nauru	21
24	Cameroon	22.5
25	Zambia	24.25
26	Kenya	24.9
27	Uganda	25
28	Côte d'Ivoire	25.75
29	Venezuela	25.9
30	Cuba	26
31	Grenada	26
32	Congo, Republic of	26.75
33	Iran, Islamic Republic of	27
34	Maldives	27
35	Equatorial Guinea	27.25
36	Benin	27.5
37	Cambodia	27.75
38	Dominica	28
39	Libyan Arab Jamahiriya	28
40	Papua New Guinea	28.33
41	Mali	28.5
42	Timor-Leste	28.5
43	Mauritania	29.75
44	Nigeria	30
45	St. Vincent and the Grenadines	30
46	Syrian Arab Republic	30.67
47	Angola	31
48	Mozambique	31.25
49	Tanzania, United Republic of	31.5
50	Bhutan	32
51	Bangladesh	32.5
52	Marshall Islands	33
53	Nepal	33.25

54	Djibouti	33.33
55	Tajikistan	34
56	Vanuatu	34
57	Uzbekistan	34.25
58	Yemen	35
59	Chad	37
60	Micronesia, Federated States of	38
61	Lesotho	38.67
62	Haiti	40
63	Afghanistan	41
64	Ethiopia	42
65	Samoa	44.5
66	Tuvalu	51
67	Sao Tome and Principe	60
68	Kiribati	67

Underdeveloped Countries

Rank within Category	Underdeveloped Countries	Integrated Rating
1	Gambia, The	4.75
2	Lao People's Democratic Republic	4.85
3	Myanmar	5
4	Tonga	5
5	Eritrea	5.2
6	Guinea	5.75
7	Malawi	6.25
8	Rwanda	6.5
9	Sudan	7.67
10	Togo	9
11	Sierra Leone	9.5
12	Burundi	10
13	Niger	10
14	Central African Republic	10.25
15	Korea, North	10.67
16	Guinea-Bissau	11.25
17	Zimbabwe	11.75
18	Comoros	12
19	Congo, Democratic Republic of	14.67
20	Liberia	15.33
21	Solomon Islands	16
22	Somalia	18

Source: © Dr Vladimir Kvint, 2008.

Observations of the Superpower Category

The *superpower* category includes only countries of such political power, economic strength, and stability that they influence the behavior of all other countries, relationships between countries, regional organizations, and the general global order and its subsystems. The United States is the only country that qualifies for this category. Although many argue the opposite, a global order dominated by one superpower—a unipolar system—is more likely to lead to peace and prosperity. There are many historical examples to illustrate this, such as the relative peace and prosperity of ancient Rome, the unprecedented peace and prosperity following the end of the Cold War, and the violent and tense climate of the Cold War period.

It is possible that the US may be joined by China in the superpower category in the near future. The twenty-first century has already witnessed the rise of several regional superpowers (Russia, Germany, Brazil, South Africa, etc.). There can be superpowers of unique or abundant resources: Russia, Canada, and to some extent Saudi Arabia can be considered energy superpowers on the basis of their use of natural resources such as natural gas, oil-sands, coal, or oil. As the prime minister of Canada, Stephen Harper, said in a June 2007 speech in Berlin:

> [I]ndeed, it is no exaggeration to call Canada an "emerging energy superpower" and a "global mining giant." We are the fifth largest energy producer in the world. Third in global gas production. Eighth in global oil production. Second in the generation of hydro-electric power.[51]

It is possible to expect the emergence of freshwater superpowers, which will be able to dictate preconditions in order to cooperate with those who desperately need this resource. There is also the potential rise of a superpower that lacks a defined territory but is unified by violent ideology and modern technology. The rise of all of these superpowers will profoundly complicate the GMP and the global order. However, this classification system considers only the US to be a true superpower. By an integration of all major indicators such as GDP per capita (PPP), distribution of national wealth, role of knowledge-based technologies, level of political and economic freedom, role in the GMP, and level of environmental protection, the United States' dominance is unparalleled. Its dominance is unquestionable, not only by a quantitative approach but also through a qualitative approach, meaning it is more than its input to GWP—the structure of its national economy, productivity of labor, social cohesion, strength of the middle class, etc. This is despite the fact that the United States has relatively low ratings on environmental protection.

Observations of the Technologically Advanced Economies Category

The order within the category of *technologically advanced economies* is mostly (though not totally) based on the Synthesized Country Rating of Technological, Economic, and Social Advancement. Certain countries occupy higher positions than basic economic statistics would indicate due to high evaluations of national environmental concerns, efficient industrial structures, and a high role of modern-tech industries as a percentage of GDP. For example, Iceland, a country with very limited national resources, has achieved a GDP per capita much higher than other countries on the list due to its efficient and modern industrial structure and its leadership in industries such as hydrogen and the production of other alternative energies. Norway, having the highest GDP per capita among countries of this subcategory, is behind Sweden, Denmark, the United States, and Finland because of its less efficient industrial structure with the dominant role of oil-related production and lower (except compared to the United States) evaluations of environmental protection. Finland also has a more equitable distribution of income than Norway. Unlike Finland, Norway has four people on the 2008 *Forbes* Billionaire List. Wealth distribution is evaluated with a 0.5 coefficient, relative to other indicators. The more equitable the national distribution of wealth, in general, the higher the country's integrated rating.

Developed countries can also be grouped by the stage of the structural development of their economies (countries with one or two dominant industries such as Norway or Switzerland, countries with ethnic or social conflict such as Belgium, and countries that are still at the stage of industrialized nations, and the few that are already closer to qualifying as knowledge-based economies).

Observations of the Wealthy Nations Category

Countries in the subcategory of *wealthy nations* are mostly (though not entirely) ranked by their GDP per capita (PPP) and national wealth. Luxembourg occupies the highest position among wealthy nations according to the Synthesized Country Rating of Technological, Economic, and Social Advancement, and it has a more equitable distribution of income than Switzerland, which has 11 people on the 2008 *Forbes* Billionaire List. Switzerland is the only wealthy nation with individual citizens on this list. The leading country of this group, Luxembourg, is also the second-ranked country in the world in terms of the role of services in GDP. Some wealthy nations, such as Lichtenstein and the Holy See (Vatican City), do not provide multilateral institutions with updated information, which complicates strategic analysis. These are the only two countries on this list in which the analysis is done mostly on estimations and extrapolations from outdated information.

The World Bank, in its 2005 report, *Where Is the Wealth of Nations? Measuring Capital in the Twenty-First Century*, establishes a de facto classification of wealthy nations that differs from the classification that this book uses. The World Bank's methodology does not take into account GDP per capita and levels of national technological advancement: rather, the defining indicator is wealth per capita. Table 4.11 lists the 10 wealthiest countries according to this study. By the classifications of this book, most of the World Bank's wealthiest nations fall into the categories of superpower, technologically advanced economies, and wealthy nations. Also, the World Bank ignores the wealth of small countries such as Lichtenstein, Bermuda, Andorra, San Marino, Monaco, and Vatican City. It is important to note that despite the fact that this report was made in December 2005, the information in the table is based on data from 2000.

Wealthy nations have very stable economic characteristics, but assets in the banks of these countries fluctuate more than in other countries. During periods of global instability (following the September 11, 2001, terrorist attacks, for example), bank assets in these countries usually increase; during periods of stability, they tend to decline. These countries are havens for international investors and financial speculators. It may seem counterintuitive, but a few small underdeveloped countries (Tonga, for example) and developing countries (Nauru), as well as the emerging-market democracy of Panama also act as financial havens.

Table 4.11 World Bank's List of the 10 Wealthiest Countries, 2000[52]

Rank	Country	Wealth per Capita ($)
1	Switzerland	648,241
2	Denmark	575,138
3	Sweden	513,424
4	United States	512,612
5	Germany	496,447
6	Japan	493,241
7	Austria	493,080
8	Norway	473,708
9	France	468,024
10	Belgium-Luxembourg	451,714

Observations of the Emerging-market Countries Category

It is clear from the *Integrated Country Ratings* presented in Table 4.11 that the GEM and EMCs play a core role in the GMP. They act as a bridge between developed countries and developing and underdeveloped countries. The GEM helps to unify the world and suppress the existing polarization between wealthy and poor nations. Without EMCs, the tension between wealthy and poor nations would be much more intense, and it would be practically impossible to form a global consensus on any major issue. The global order, which has been forming during the first decade of the twenty-first century, would be totally different and likely not functional at all without countries of the GEM.

Observations of the Economies in Bloom Category

The most advanced countries of the GEM are grouped in the category of *economies in bloom*. By some evaluations and indicators, these countries can already be considered developed. In fact, by many of the Integrated Country Rating indicators, some economies in bloom were ranked above many developed countries, and even above the superpower, the United States. Such indicators included evaluations of economic freedom (Ireland, Taiwan, Portugal, Israel, Czech Republic) and the role of services in the national economy (Hong Kong SAR, Greece, Portugal, Spain, Taiwan). The production of raw materials does not play a dominant role in any of the countries of this category, and they all have strong financial sectors. Some of these countries, such as Hungary, Taiwan, the Czech Republic, Korea, and Ireland, are also ahead of developed countries in terms of the role of science-based technologies. In Hungary, Korea, Singapore, Ireland, Taiwan, and Portugal, modern-tech sectors play a larger role in the national economies than in many developed countries. In terms of national environmental protection, Costa Rica, Ireland, Portugal, Slovakia, and Israel rank ahead of developed countries, according to the Environmental Sustainability Index.[53] But, by the overall integrated rating, these countries are still slightly behind developed countries. This will not be the case for long. The dynamics of progress in these countries will allow some of them to qualify as developed countries by the second decade of the twenty-first century. It is clear that Ireland, the Czech Republic, Hungary, and Korea, as well as Portugal and Greece, will be the first economies in bloom to transition to the category of developed countries. The issue that may inhibit this transition for countries such as Israel, Taiwan, and Hong Kong SAR, is related to their bilateral relationships (Hong Kong and Taiwan with mainland China, and Israel with its neighboring countries). If it were not for this major issue, these countries would also likely transition to the category of developed countries by the next decade. The issue for nations such as Spain, Greece, Slovenia, and Costa Rica is primarily overregulation of business activity, which can be solved relatively simply. High taxes (including those related to environmental protection) are a problem for many economies in bloom. In some of these countries, for instance, Hong Kong, Spain, Korea, and Israel, there is a significant wealth gap. Ten of the fifteen countries in this category have citizens whose billion-dollar fortunes are disproportionate to the scale of national economies, an indication of an inequitable distribution of wealth. Compared to the majority of developed countries, economies in bloom have relatively high levels of poverty, a smaller middle class, and, subsequently, a wider gap between rich and poor. Costa Rica is behind many other economies in bloom in terms of GDP per capita but compensates for this with better environmental conditions, as well as a much lower cost of living. This category is a beacon for all other emerging-market and developing countries. Economies in bloom are equal competitors with developed countries in many industries, especially in financial services, hospitality, and modern, high-tech, and knowledge-based sectors. In terms of GDP per capita (PPP), there are three emerging markets and one developing country ranked above the United States. Out of fifteen economies in bloom, nine are members of the EU, four are in Southeast Asia, one in the Middle East, and one is in Latin America. The UN classifies several countries of this category as transition countries. However, in this book not all transition countries classify as economies in bloom. Several of them qualify as emerging-market democracies, emerging-market dictatorships, and oligarchic emerging markets. Many others, such as Belarus (the last remaining dictatorship in Europe), Kyrgyzstan, Bosnia, and Herzegovina and Tajikistan, qualify as developing countries.

Observations of the Emerging-market Democracies Category

The remaining emerging-market subcategories are primarily ranked based on the level of political and economic freedom. The highest levels of economic freedom among *emerging-market democracies* are found in Chile, Mauritius, Barbados, Cyprus, and Estonia. In this category, by definition, there is not a single country without a sustainable democracy and a multiparty system. There people have and utilize the right to elect their executive, legislative, and judicial branches of government. No country in this category has an absolute monarchy. While there is a country with a monarchy included in this category (Thailand), the monarchy is constitutional, without significant direct executive power. In all emerging-market democracies, the law is not only declared but also enforced, and protection of human rights, if not well established, is at least increasing. Standards of living are also steadily improving. All of this is closely linked to an emerging and growing middle class, based on positive dynamics of most economic indicators. Among the emerging-market democracies with the most equitable distributions of wealth are Croatia, Estonia, Barbados, and Trinidad and Tobago. A high standard of living and a well-established middle class also exists in Cyprus, but the level of income distribution is not very equitable, illustrated by the fact that this small nation of fewer than 800,000 people, as of 2008, has 10 billionaires. Albania, Poland, Turkey, and Uruguay have benefited from some of the most rapidly growing middle classes in this category.

Despite the fact that these countries are far from perfect, the vectors of the most important integrated indicators have positive dynamics; all of these countries have relatively well-developed business infrastructure. Countries in this group are found in Europe (13), Asia (7), Africa (5), and the Americas and the Caribbean (17). Despite the huge geographic dispersion, emerging-market democracies share the majority of characteristics and even their scale on a per capita or per unit of GDP basis. Countries of this category have a relatively equitable distribution of income, at least when compared with all countries in less-developed categories. Not a single country of this category has a convertible currency, but they all have relatively stable financial indicators, and inflation is generally under control. They freely cooperate with political and economic multilateral institutions and do not have serious conflicts with one another. The majority of them do not have militarized border conflicts, with a few exceptions, such as Serbia and Armenia. There is hope that the declaration of independence of Kosovo and its recognition by many countries will mitigate its tension with Serbia. The Armenian–Azerbaijanian military conflict does not seem to have a quick solution, but the intensity of the conflict does not substantially influence the economies and business climates of these countries. The border dispute between India and Pakistan has been under control during the first years of the twentieth century. The only country in this category with provinces attempting to break away is Georgia. However, the democratically elected government and president of this country are trying to peacefully solve this problem with the autonomous regions, Abkhazia and South Ossetia.

Out of the 42 emerging-market democracies, 13 are considered to have a modern technological industrial base. Among the technological leaders of this category are Turkey, Mexico, India, Poland, and Brazil. In this category the service sector accounts for the most significant portion of GDP in Panama, Latvia, Jordan, Estonia, and Mauritius. All emerging-market democracies have a strong orientation for the development of a market economy and capital market infrastructure. The average level of internationalization of these countries' economies is higher than that of countries in all the following categories. Many countries of this category are among global leaders in terms of environmental protection and environmentally related taxes (Uruguay, Guyana, and Argentina). Surprisingly, in terms of taxes as a percentage of total tax revenue, the leading country is Turkey. These taxes in Turkey are substantially higher than in developed countries.

Observations of the Oligarchic Emerging Markets Category

Since the time of their reign in ancient Greece, oligarchies had become an almost forgotten economic category, and their traditional role in history was interrupted for some 2,000 years. Unlike in ancient Greece, where oligarchs included political leaders and their family members as well as distinguished military heroes, in the modern world, the majority of oligarchs are just nouveau riche with huge fortunes (especially compared with the general population) who want to influence government for their own selfish interests. At the end of the twentieth century, the failure of dictatorships in several countries brought oligarchs back into the political and economic arena of several EMCs. The resurgence of oligarchs in these countries was a result of poorly managed transitions from dictatorships to market-based economies in countries with a lack of democratic traditions, very high levels of corruption, and inexperienced political leaders. There are oligarchs in countries that are not included in this category, such as Bulgaria, but their role is declining and much less significant than in *oligarchic emerging markets*. Elected leaders in countries without democratic traditions did not receive the right advice during the initial stages of privatization, and as a result, vast amounts of property and wealth that were built by several generations of de facto slavery and serfdom transferred, almost immediately, to the hands of a few nouveau riche who were close to inexperienced and/or corrupt decision makers.

The past Bulgarian situation described above is very similar to the situation in Russia that appeared under the presidency of Boris Yeltsin. His advisors wrongly recommended that he transfer ownership of state assets to a handful of people who eventually became oligarchs. The logic was that this transfer of assets would make democratic reforms irreversible. These advisors lacked strategic vision. Not only did it put Russia's newly born democracy completely in the hands of oligarchs but it also created a situation in which democratic reforms weakened and were unable to withstand the pressure of oligarchs in the free political system. The total lack of an understanding of strategic steps from dictatorship to the free market demonstrated by Yeltsin's advisors put the majority of Russians in total poverty—after only a few months. The galloping inflation of 1992 wiped out everyone's life savings. Society became completely polarized, with a few wealthy oligarchs and the overwhelming majority in utter poverty. And thus, all of those people who were tired of communist dictatorship and ready for capitalism turned against this kind of free market that had rendered them instantly poor.

The first step oligarchs took to assert their power was to buy TV and radio stations, newspapers, and magazines. They used these major media outlets to promote their own selfish motives. This was the initial stage of the undermining of new democratic institutions. It should not be surprising that 15 years later, by numbers of billionaires, Russia has surpassed traditional free-market countries such as the United Kingdom, France, Italy, and

Japan combined, becoming second only to the United States. Although Vladimir Putin, the successor to Boris Yeltsin and Russia's second president, has been widely criticized, he does deserve credit for managing to substantially decrease the influence of oligarchs over the political process in Russia. However, he did not fight oligarchy as a system and over-emphasized the idea of state-controlled economy. As a result, at the end of the first decade of the twenty-first century, Russia is practically a state-dominated economic system, which is substantially different from state capitalism, as well as from communism. Despite President Putin's attempt to diminish the political role of oligarchs, there is statistical proof that as of 2008, Russia is the no. 1 oligarchy in the world. According to *Forbes*, in the Russian parliament (the Lower House—the Duma—and the Upper House—the Federation Council) there are 12 billionaires, with a total fortune of $41 billion.[54] This does not take into account the fortune of the many multimillionaires in the Russian congress. By the number of super-rich people in the legislative branch, Russia has surpassed the US and every other country of the world. Furthermore, among Russian regional governors, there is at least one billionaire—Roman Abramovich, the governor of the northeastern-most region of Russia, Chukotka. Mrs Yelena Baturina, wife of Yuri Lushkov, mayor of Moscow, is also a billionaire.

Contrary to popular opinion, oligarchic capitalism is not a purely Russian phenomenon. Very similar processes occurred in several Asian nations during their initial stages of market development 20 years earlier than in Russia. In the relatively economically free environment of Indonesia, President Suharto concentrated tremendous assets in the hands of a few people, including his direct relatives and even himself. Indonesia

> had long presented neo-liberal orthodoxy with difficult paradoxes. The protracted metamorphosis of power in which authoritarian rule and state capitalism were colonized and harnessed to the interest of a pervasive politico-business oligarchy in the 1980s and 1990s took place as Indonesia's integration with global financial and capital markets deepened and became more intense.[55]

The situation was similar at some point in economic history in the Philippines, Malaysia, and Singapore, and in other countries in this part of the world, which developed between the Chinese and Soviet communist dictatorships and the free-market system of Japan and the United States. As Dr Barry Gills explains, "popular demands for change represent a real challenge to both the domestic authoritarian-oligarchic power structure of PWEAC [post-war East Asian capitalism] and its crucial geopolitical underpinning and external orientation."[56] It is possible to conclude that oligarchy is innate to semi-dictatorial countries. At certain points in time, the majority of East Asian nations, as well as some pieces of the Soviet empire, such as Russia, Kazakhstan, and Ukraine, went or are still living under these conditions. Oligarchy as a stage and type of economic development is not exclusive to Russia and Asia. Belize, a small Latin American nation with fewer than 300,000 citizens, is experiencing a similar process.[57]

Because of the concentration of huge assets in the hands of a small group of people in the midst of widespread poverty (despite moderate GDP per capita), social tension and an underdeveloped middle class are typical characteristics of oligarchic emerging markets. A lack of religious and cultural tolerance is another problem in these countries, which has a negative impact on foreign entrepreneurs and investors who operate in this environment. All of these factors have to be taken into strategic consideration. Oligarchy is usually a short-term phenomenon. Several countries that do not belong to this category were qualified as oligarchic markets in recent history, such as Colombia, which is now an emerging-market democracy. By the middle of the twenty-first century, the six countries that are considered oligarchic emerging markets will most likely be emerging-market democracies. This transition can be painful for its citizens, as well as for foreign investors in these nations, despite the fact that the majority of these countries have some very attractive basic economic factors.

Observations of the Emerging-market Dictatorships Category

"Market economies" and "dictatorships" may at first seem like incompatible terms. In reality, *emerging-market dictatorships* are among the most attractive destinations for foreign investors; China is the most obvious example. As previously mentioned, foreign investors seek stability, which is one of the most typical characteristics of emerging-market dictatorships. For this reason only a few traditional democracies—the US, the United Kingdom, and possibly the Netherlands—can compete with China in terms of attractiveness for FDI. "Economic freedom" and "dictatorships" are also not antonyms. According to the Index of Economic Freedom of 2008, Bahrain, an emerging-market dictatorship, is ranked above countries with long traditions of capitalism, such as Belgium, Germany, and even a social democracy such as Sweden. The 12 countries from this category are not homogeneous in terms of type and level of dictatorial repression. Even countries such as Moldova, Morocco, and Pakistan, which have relatively moderate politically systems, often use non-democratic instruments to promote some businesses or pressure others. Countries of this category can be divided into three groups based on their dictatorial roots. One group consists of Bahrain, United Arab Emirates, and Morocco, which are still monarchies with extremely limited rights for elected officials, and of countries such as Qatar, which totally lack elected officials. Another group is made up of those countries that are slowly emerging from their communist past, such as Azerbaijan and Turkmenistan, or countries such as Moldova, Vietnam, and China, where the communist party is still in power. One can argue that in these countries, leaders were "elected" by bodies or even parliaments. However, this does not mean that these countries are not dictatorships. This can be seen in the examples of countries such as Azerbaijan, where the president inherited the presidential "throne" from his father, as well as under communist party systems, where so-called elections are actually appointments. These "modern dictators" are not much different from those of ancient Rome, where the Senate appointed dictators. The third group includes the two African nations, Gabon and Egypt, which are formally democracies with elections but have been ruled by the same leaders for decades. In fact, as of 2008, the president of Gabon, El Hadj Omar Bongo Ondimba, has been in this office since 1967 and is one of the longest-serving heads of state in the world.[58]

The power of the democratization trend significantly limits the time of dictatorial regimes. In 2007 Turkmenistan received a new leader (as described in Chapter 3) who is somewhat progressive and is already installing positive political reforms. The Moldavian and Vietnamese communist parties have changed substantially since the twentieth century. Unfortunately, reversals of progress are also possible. After its succession from the Soviet Union, Azerbaijan was, for a short period, a semi-democracy. However, as of 2008 there is a moderate semi-dictator, who practically inherited this position directly from his father. But formally speaking, in Azerbaijan, Moldova, and even in Morocco, Pakistan, Vietnam, and Turkmenistan, some democratic institutions are in place, despite the total lack of a politically competitive environment and strong intervention of dictatorships in private business, to the extent of breaches of contract, a major indicator of political risk of investment.

In economic terms, these countries are also diverse. Some of them, such as China, Azerbaijan, and Pakistan have pretty balanced industrial structures. Moldova is among the leaders of this group in terms of the role of service in GDP. These countries have different national policies toward environmental issues, but none of them has made environmental protection a national priority. The high evaluation of environmental sustainability of Gabon is related to the ratio of its population (about 1.5 million) to its large territory, which is about the size of the US state of Colorado. All countries of this group have moderate standards of living but an underdeveloped and in some cases weak middle class.

Strategically, these countries are attractive mostly due to their basic economic factors, such as natural gas and oil in Turkmenistan, Azerbaijan, Bahrain, United Arab Emirates, and Qatar; abundant resources for the tourism industry (mineral waters, beaches, historical sites, etc.) in Vietnam, Egypt, Morocco, and Gabon; and lower cost and hardworking labor resources in China, Vietnam, and Pakistan. The technological level of development of these countries varies. Some of them, such as China, Pakistan, and Egypt, are very competitive in several modern industries, while others, such as Gabon and Moldova, lag far behind. The trend of the twenty-first century for state support of these industries is related to outsourcing. Governmental investment can act as seed money, which attracts FDI to industries and businesses of potential interest for outsourcing. In countries of the lower categories of the Integrated Country Ratings, outsourcing is gravitating to technological industries, rather than only unskilled services. All emerging markets are transitioning from their dark dictatorial past to the bright future of free-market democracy. Strategically, this is the light in which emerging-market dictatorships should be understood.

Observations of the Pre-emerging Markets Category

At the bottom of the group of emerging markets are countries that are not yet full emerging markets but are no longer developing countries. These countries fall into the category of *pre-emerging markets*, or frontier economies. This is usually a brief stage, early in the process of creating conditions conducive to international business. Membership in international organizations or unions can be the tipping point that pushes a country toward conditions that attract international business.

Several countries in Africa with nascent but relatively stable democracies in the near future may qualify as pre-emerging market countries (P-EMCs), such as Mozambique, Nigeria, and Uganda. The ability to attract foreign capital is a strategic achievement toward becoming an EMC. For many of these countries, FDI comes from EMCs, not developed countries. EMCs such as China and India have invested substantial sums in Africa in order to gain access to strategic and cheap natural resources. P-EMCs are not only in Africa; some of the lower income countries of Asia and Latin America also fit into this category. P-EMCs are definitely, by the majority of indicators, ahead of developing countries. The most advanced countries of this group, Tunisia and Mongolia, will likely skip the oligarchic and dictatorship stages of development and by the end of the first quarter of the twenty-first century will be among emerging-market democracies. Madagascar and Sri Lanka are also on this path but are slightly behind. Iraq, which at the beginning of the twenty-first century was under one of the most isolated and brutal dictatorships, already has democratically elected branches of government. Despite internal military conflicts, the economy of this country is developing, and not only around oil industries. It is possible that by 2025 it will be an emerging-market democracy; of course, this is assuming that it will remain a unified country. Even in the case of political disintegration, some parts of the country will be democratically oriented. Unfortunately, Bolivia is headed in the opposite direction. It was once considered an emerging-market democracy but is now only a semi-democracy with pre-emerging economic market conditions. As of 2008, FDI is fleeing the country under the political threat of nationalization and expropriation, which are the most integrated indicators of political risk of investment. There have been some attempts to build electoral bodies with limited power in Saudi Arabia, which will likely eventually be an emerging-market dictatorship. For the Saudi Arabian monarchy, this would be substantial progress, and it would be very beneficial for foreign investors as well as for the people of the country. Burkina Faso is an outlier in this group, but its government has demonstrated very positive intentions; moreover, it is the leader in terms of environmental sustainability in this category. All of these countries already have a limited level of basic business infrastructure in place. Due to the high risk in P-EMCs relative to other emerging markets, several strategists use the term "frontier economies/countries" to describe nations of this group.

The IFC, one of the five divisions of the WBG, but the only one designed to work with the private sectors of national economies, has used the term "frontier countries" since 1997 (the most recent available criteria is from 2004[59]). According to the IFC's qualifications, "frontier country" is not an equivalent term to "P-EMC." Among those that were considered by the IFC as frontier countries at some time are Serbia and Montenegro, Pakistan, Nigeria, China, and India. The IFC basically uses frontier countries as a loose synonym for both emerging-market and developing countries, which is similar to the arbitrary and deeply flawed classification systems found in most multilateral institutions.

All countries of the GEM share the basic quality of economies that welcome foreign investment and have modest to high levels of internationalization. Even countries that may be experiencing reversals of progress, such as Bolivia, are still not anywhere near cutting off international ties and legally restricting FDI. All countries of the GEM have a certain level of economic freedom, are relatively politically and environmentally sustainable, and as of 2008, none of them (except Iraq) is experiencing a civil war. As of 2008 no EMC is under arms embargo by the UN.[60] However, China continues to be under the embargo declared by the EU on June 27, 1989, as a response to the events of Tiananmen Square. US regulations also control some defense articles and services toward China, Cyprus, Iraq, Pakistan, and Vietnam. It is important to reference embargo lists of the UN, EU and US State Department when engaging in business in foreign countries with which one is not very familiar.

EMCs require advice regarding the modernization of their economies, the operations of major social democratic institutions (elections, media regulations, promotion of religious freedom and tolerance, economic freedom, and liberalization of business), and the stabilization of their political and economic systems. They need assistance in the improvement of their international cooperation of domestic businesses and advisory services for foreign companies that come to these countries during their initial stage of international cooperation. Global institutions can help to improve the monetary and financial systems of EMCs.

Observations of the Developing Countries Category

Prior to the birth of the GEM, the category of *developing countries* was the largest group of countries (125), and all non-developed countries generally fell into this category. According to Professor Peter Stearns of George Mason University, "the fact that full industrial revolutions proved to be rare after 1950 misled some observers into lumping all nonindustrial societies into the then common category of 'developing nations.'"[61] As previously described, from this category appeared the majority of EMCs, including several economies in bloom. As of 2008 developing countries account for only 6 percent of GWP and falling, as many of these countries begin the transition to P-EMC status. There are a couple of unusual cases of regression from P-EMC to developing-country status, such as Venezuela and Turkmenistan (under Turkmenbashi).

"Developing countries" is one of the longest used but most vaguely defined terms in international economics. Multilateral institutions use this term to describe almost all countries below the developed category. This categorization does not provide strategists, economists, or executives with any real orientation and creates serious problems when making strategic decisions. As a result, some countries do not get enough attention from the international community, while others, which have progressed beyond the developing stage, unnecessarily get privileges of developing countries. This means that the limited amount of capital in multilateral institutions does not go to countries with the most pressing need for it. According to the classification system presented in this book, developing countries still comprise the most countries, with 68 national economies situated between EMCs and related subgroups and underdeveloped countries. Characteristics shared by countries of this category are lower GDP per capita, widespread poverty, a weak but existing middle class, technologically outdated enterprises, and a complete lack of knowledge-based industries. They all seek international cooperation and FDI and already have experience and cooperative relationships with multilateral institutions. Political freedom is not a defining characteristic common to countries of this group. Nonetheless, most of these countries have some elements of political and economic freedom. Several countries of this group will not be in this category for long and will be considered P-EMCs and emerging-market democracies (Kosovo, Kyrgyzstan, Kenya, and Uganda). Some of them are experiencing a reversal of progress (Venezuela and Bangladesh, for example). Some countries of this group are open dictatorships: Belarus, Tajikistan, Syria, and Iran. Some developing countries are under international embargos and sanctions, which obviously has important strategic implications. Developing countries tend to have high levels of political risk of investment as a result of civil disobedience and unrest, the potential for physical damage to foreign property, and the threat of expropriation and nationalization. An increase in these risks is what caused countries that were considered emerging markets in the past, such as Venezuela, to be reclassified as developing countries. In the case of Venezuela, a change in political orientation negatively redirected the vector of its economic development. At the same time, countries that for years were considered absolute dictatorships, such as Cuba, Bangladesh, Afghanistan, and Ethiopia, may be considered emerging markets by the year 2020 or even earlier.

Developing countries require assistance from multilateral institutions in order to improve education and medical systems, establish and modernize business infrastructure, and to prepare small and medium-size domestic companies for international economic cooperation and competition.

Observations of the Underdeveloped Countries Category

It is difficult to undermine the social, economic, and technological progress that humankind has experienced since the last quarter of the twentieth century. The best examples of this can be seen in the 50 countries that the UN classifies as least developed countries. According to the classification system of this book, more than half of them have progressed beyond the point of *underdeveloped* and are now developing by major social, economic, and political indicators. Examples include Angola, Cape Verde, Bangladesh, and others. Two least developed countries (Madagascar and Burkina Faso) are classified in this book as pre-emerging markets. Political freedom is severely repressed in underdeveloped countries. Dictatorship, self-isolation, war, and civil unrest are often responsible for underdevelopment and poverty. In many underdeveloped countries, the borders are sealed, forcing people to live essentially as prisoners. In addition to these least developed countries, the only monarchy in the Pacific, Tonga, and the dictatorships of North Korea and Zimbabwe are also included in the category of underdeveloped countries. However, 19 least developed countries have not experienced the recent progress enjoyed by much of humankind and still qualify as underdeveloped countries. These are countries that are very slow with market-oriented reforms.

The World Bank's presentation of the poorest countries (see Table 4.12) in a December

Table 4.12 World Bank's List of the 10 Poorest Countries in the World (Statistics from 2000)[62]

Rank	Country	Wealth per Capita ($)
1	Ethiopia	1,965
2	Nigeria	2,748
3	Burundi	2,859
4	Congo, Rep. of	3,516
5	Niger	3,695
6	Nepal	3,802
7	Guinea-Bissau	3,974
8	Mozambique	4,232
9	Chad	4,458
10	Madagascar	5,020

2005 report is also substantially outdated, not only because it was based on statistics that were six years old (from 2000). The progress that has been made in countries such as Madagascar (which is a P-EMC, according to this book) is not reflected in this list. Countries such as Nigeria, Nepal, and Chad are in much better economic conditions than several countries that the World Bank does not include on its list of poorest counties, such as Somalia, Solomon Islands, Liberia, Comoros, Sierra Leone, Rwanda, Sudan, Togo, and Zimbabwe (which has declined tremendously during the first decade of the twenty-first century). It is also very hard to accept that North Korea, a country in which people live in total poverty, is not included on the World Bank's list. At the same time, this book and the World Bank report both consider countries including Eritrea, Burundi, and Guinea-Bissau to be among the poorest nations.

Human rights and political freedom are still only a dream for the majority of people in underdeveloped countries, though in some cases extreme hunger inhibits any thoughts beyond daily survival. In this category there are absolute dictatorships, such as Zimbabwe, which was once considered an emerging market, but due to the dictatorship's economic mismanagement and repression of political freedom, it has fallen to the bottom of list of underdeveloped countries. However, a positive signal did come from this country in March 2008, when competitive presidential and parliamentary elections took place. President Mugabe, who at that time had already been in office for 28 years, was definitely not happy with the results, the announcements of which he forced to be postponed indefinitely. It should not surprise anyone that the most self-isolated country in the world, North Korea, is considered to be underdeveloped. All human capital is used by the North Korean dictator for the protection of his regime and the development of weapons of mass destruction. Once this brutal dictatorship finally collapses, the people of North Korea will be able to convert military production for civilian purposes and in a relatively short period of time will be able to substantially increase their standard of living. Political and especially business leaders still owe a debt to the people of underdeveloped countries. Indifference and the shortsighted selfishness of national leaders are what keep people in underdeveloped countries without hope. Living on one or two dollars per day, a total lack of freedom, and ethnic cleansing are common in most countries in this category. What for the majority of humankind is thought of as part of a dark, far-off past, for the people of Myanmar, Sudan, Rwanda, Comoros, Niger, North Korea, Zimbabwe, Liberia, Sierra Leone, and Somalia is a tragic reality. The Democratic Republic of Congo is the only country in the world, where officially, as of 2008, the GDP per capita (PPP) is less than one dollar per day. Nonetheless, strategists should realize that even countries with such low purchasing power need food, medical supplies, and early education. International humanitarian aid always has a material form. Some companies can and should have an orientation to help provide these products for the aid agencies of the international community. This requires companies to develop strategies for low-cost production of goods and services.

From the point of view of business strategy, for many years countries of this group were not on the corporate agenda due to their extreme poverty and their citizens' low purchasing power. With the birth of the GMP and the subsequent increase in competition, companies are starting to develop strategies to address markets of these countries, which are on the bottom of the world pyramid in terms of income. This strategy, known as the BOP, has been successful when companies take into consideration the basic needs of the population of these countries and their extremely limited purchasing power. According to Professor C.K. Prahalad, BOP strategies are "based on small unit packages, low margin per unit, high volume, and high return on capital employed. This is different from large unit packs, high margin per unit, high volume, and reasonable return on capital employed."[63] In his highly influential book *The Fortune at the Bottom of the Pyramid*, Professor Prahalad explains that unlike consumers in developed countries, people at the bottom of the pyramid (the overwhelming majority of people in underdeveloped countries) tend to have inconsistent sources of income. They therefore cannot afford to put their limited resources toward large purchases, even if it is cheaper and more convenient in the long run. It is more economical for these consumers to purchase goods for a given day.

Underdeveloped countries require a great deal of coordinated assistance from multilateral institutions in order to address major social issues such as access to freshwater, prevention of starvation and the spread of mass disease, improvement of literacy, access to energy, emigration, etc.

Evaluation of International Business Infrastructure

The comprehensive country classification system presented earlier in Table 4.10 is based on evaluations of a national economy's political, social, economic, and technological development as well the level of internationalization. For companies interested in going abroad, this classification system should be supplemented by an evaluation of the business infrastructure of the foreign country of interest. An evaluation of a foreign country's business infrastructure will give the company an idea of how it would potentially operate in an unknown or barely known environment. Beyond the investor's interest in particular basic economic factors, in order to be successful in a foreign country, an investor typically needs reliable investment and commercial banks, insurance companies, and auditing, accounting and law firms. Without these institutions, operational management and strategic development are close to impossible.

When a company first enters a foreign country, it needs to open bank accounts in order to allocate the initial cash for operational activity or for registered (charter) capital. It is always safer to open an account in a well-known bank, or a division of such a bank, especially in EMCs. Finding an operational branch of such a bank is one of the first steps undertaken by the financial department of a company when entering a foreign country. It is not unusual for a reputable international bank to have a joint venture with a local bank instead of its own operational branch. The worst-case scenario is when there is not a single well-established bank with an operational presence in the foreign country. During the first decade of this century, this was the case in Albania, where until 2007 no major foreign bank had an operational office. As of 2008 there is the American Bank of Albania (http://www.albambank.com/), which, despite its name, did not have a single dollar from any US bank. However, some shares of this bank belonged to the Albanian-American

Enterprise Fund, a private bank established with US government support. It was better than nothing, and the majority of foreign investors in Albania, as well as those from Kosovo, which lacked any major international banks, cautiously opened accounts in this bank. Companies in foreign countries also need to raise capital for the initial investment. In order to do so in emerging-market and developing countries, insurance against political risk is almost always required. When international insurance and reinsurance companies have a presence in the particular country, obtaining the necessary insurance is easier. The best and biggest US publicly held company focusing on political insurance is American International Group (AIG). If AIG has a branch or subsidiary in a country, one can assume that the decision makers at AIG are very familiar with this country and can make fast and reliable decisions regarding political risk. Companies in foreign countries must also be prepared to deal with unknown laws of the land, legal codes, and under-law regulations.

The presence of major international law firms is extremely helpful in navigating unknown and unanticipated legal complexities that may arise in a foreign country. Companies need legal advice and support beginning with the development of an entry strategy and continuing on a daily operational basis. The presence of firms such as Baker & McKenzie (www.bakernet.com/), White and Case (http://www.whitecase.com/), Skadden Arps (www.skadden.com/), or Clifford Chance (www.cliffordchance.com) is a very positive indicator for the business environment of a country. Their presence is crucial for the successful development of joint-venture agreements, strategic alliances, or for the drafting of bylaws of a subsidiary company in a foreign country. These globalized law firms experience their own strategic challenges, such as maintaining a global presence while still being able to adapt to local laws and operate efficiently in different markets.

Any purchase of foreign properties, participation in the privatization of state-owned enterprises, or merger and acquisition requires assistance from reliable auditing and accounting firms that can verify all financial statements of the business being purchased. Typically, companies rely on the presence of branches of the "Big Four," which are PricewaterhouseCoopers (www.pwc.com), Deloitte Touche Tomatsu (www.deloitte.com), Ernst & Young (www.ey.com), and KPMG (www.kpmg.com), the four largest accounting and auditing firms in the world. When a company buys a business in a foreign country, especially an EMC, and the current owner presents an auditing opinion issued by an unknown firm, the buyer will instantly request due diligence of not only the company that it is interested in buying, but also of the unfamiliar auditor. For this reason, the Big Four are extremely successful in EMCs.

Table 4.13 Index of International Business Infrastructure

Rank	Country	Score	Rank	Country	Score
1	United States	31.5	14	Mexico	15.5
2	Germany	20.5	15	Canada	14
3	China	19.5	16	Netherlands	14
4	United Kingdom of Great Britain and Northern Ireland	19	17	Poland	14
			18	Russian Federation	14
5	France	18	19	Malaysia	13.5
6	Switzerland	18	20	Taiwan, Republic of	13
7	Japan	17	21	India	13
8	Italy	16	22	Thailand	13
9	Brazil	16	23	Austria	12.5
10	Australia	15.5	24	Korea, Republic of	12.5
11	Hong Kong	15.5	25	Argentina	12.5
12	Singapore	15.5	26	Belgium	12
13	Spain	15.5	27	Philippines	11.5

28	South Africa	11.5	83	Malta	3.5
29	Indonesia	11.5	84	Slovenia	3.5
30	Sweden	11	85	Algeria	3.5
31	Czech Republic	11	86	El Salvador	3.5
32	Ireland	11	87	Estonia	3.5
33	Turkey	11	88	Jamaica	3.5
34	United Arab Emirates	11	89	Jordan	3.5
35	Luxembourg	10.5	90	Lithuania	3.5
36	Hungary	10.5	91	Gabon	3.5
37	Portugal	10.5	92	Cameroon	3.5
38	Chile	10.5	93	Dominican Republic	3.5
39	Colombia	10.5	94	Honduras	3.5
40	Venezuela	10	95	Iran, Islamic Republic of	3.5
41	Greece	9.5	96	Kenya	3.5
42	Vietnam	9.5	97	Nigeria	3.5
43	Bahrain	9	98	Paraguay	3.5
44	Israel	8.5	99	Uganda	3.5
45	Slovakia	8.5	100	Zambia	3.5
46	New Zealand	8	101	Barbados	3
47	Norway	8	102	Ghana	3
48	Kazakhstan	8	103	Latvia	3
49	Ukraine	8	104	Trinidad and Tobago	3
50	Finland	7.5	105	Bolivia	3
51	Peru	7.5	106	Bangladesh	3
52	Romania	7.5	107	Bosnia and Herzegovina	3
53	Egypt	7.5	108	Libyan Arab Jamahiriya	3
54	Saudi Arabia	7.5	109	Tanzania, United Republic of	3
55	Bulgaria	7	110	Zimbabwe	3
56	Panama	7	111	Albania	2.5
57	Lebanon	7	112	Botswana	2.5
58	Uruguay	6.5	113	Macedonia, The Former Yugoslav Republic of	2.5
59	Bahamas, The	6			
60	Pakistan	6	114	Madagascar	2.5
61	Qatar	6	115	Angola	2.5
62	Denmark	5	116	Iceland	2
63	Bermuda	5	117	Georgia	2
64	Monaco	5	118	Moldova	2
65	Croatia	5	119	Congo, Republic of	2
66	Cyprus	5	120	Maldives	2
67	Ecuador	5	121	Mozambique	2
68	Côte d'Ivoire	5	122	Nepal	2
69	Guatemala	4.5	123	Nicaragua	2
70	Morocco	4.5	124	Papua New Guinea	2
71	Sri Lanka	4.5	125	Lao People's Democratic Republic	2
72	Brunei Darussalam	4.5			
73	Lichtenstein	4	126	Malawi	2
74	Costa Rica	4	127	Armenia	1.5
75	Mauritius	4	128	Saint Lucia	1.5
76	Serbia	4	129	Burkina Faso	1.5
77	Azerbaijan	4	130	Iraq	1.5
78	Tunisia	4	131	Afghanistan	1.5
79	Kuwait	4	132	Antigua and Barbuda	1.5
80	Oman	4	133	Fiji	1.5
81	Senegal	4	134	Kyrgyzstan	1.5
82	Uzbekistan	4	135	Namibia	1.5

(Continued Overleaf)

Table 4.13   Continued

Rank	Country	Score	Rank	Country	Score
136	Syrian Arab Republic	1.5	167	Mauritania	0.5
137	Yemen	1.5	168	Palau	0.5
138	**Guyana**	1	169	Sao Tome and Principe	0.5
139	**Montenegro**	1	170	Seychelles, Republic of	0.5
140	**Saint Kitts and Nevis**	1	171	Suriname	0.5
141	Belarus	1	172	Central African Republic	0.5
142	Cambodia	1	173	Comoros	0.5
143	Cape Verde	1	174	Solomon Islands	0.5
144	Equatorial Guinea	1	175	Togo	0.5
145	Haiti	1	176	Holy See (Vatican)	0
146	Mali	1	177	**Mongolia**	0
147	St Vincent and the	1	178	Bhutan	0
	Grenadines	1	179	Cuba	0
148	Swaziland	1	180	Dominica	0
149	Congo, Democratic	1	181	Kiribati	0
	Republic of		182	Micronesia, Federated	0
150	Gambia, The	1		States of	
151	Guinea	1	183	Nauru	0
152	Rwanda	1	184	Samoa	0
153	Sierra Leone	1	185	Tajikistan	0
154	Cook Islands	1	186	Timor-Leste	0
155	Andorra	0.5	187	Tuvalu	0
156	San Marino	0.5	188	Vanuatu	0
157	Belize	0.5	189	Burundi	0
158	**Turkmenistan**	0.5	190	Eritrea	0
159	Benin	0.5	191	Guinea-Bissau	0
160	Chad	0.5	192	Korea, North	0
161	Djibouti	0.5	193	Liberia	0
162	Ethiopia	0.5	194	Myanmar	0
163	Grenada	0.5	195	Niger	0
164	Kosovo	0.5	196	Somalia	0
165	Lesotho	0.5	197	Sudan	0
166	Marshall Islands	0.5	198	Tonga	0

Source: © Dr Vladimir Kvint, 2008.

After 20 years of the influence of the global trend of internationalization on EMCs, several of them have business infrastructures that can compete with those of developed countries. While there are only two EMCs (China and Brazil) among the top ten countries in the Index of International Business Infrastructure, among the first thirty, more than half are EMCs (see Table 4.13). Among EMCs, every single one has the presence of the majority of business-service companies and firms. Among P-EMCs, only Mongolia, as of 2008, does not have a single commercial bank, auditing, accounting, or law firm. Among the sixty-eight developing countries, only four do not have the presence of major international commercial banks, insurance, law, or auditing and accounting firms. In underdeveloped countries, out of the twenty-two countries, twelve lack the presence of these business services. This shows that the country classification system employed in this book gave a relatively similar result to that of an evaluation of the presence of international professional business services. Divisions between developed, emerging-market, and developing and underdeveloped countries exist, are serious from a strategic point of view, and always have to be taken into strategic consideration.

Classification Glossary

Classifications systems are based on evaluations of various indicators. Indicators are the base of the rating system and indexes. Within ratings and indexes there are ranks; within classifications systems, categories or groups of countries are developed. Ranks also exist within these categories, and categories are developed based on the rating system. The organization of the categories composes the classification system. Classification is a system of categories, and ranks are within categories.

Study Questions

1. Why do strategists and executives need country classification systems? What are the practical needs for this?
2. Describe the classification systems of the major multilateral institutions.
3. What are the practical needs of the WBG for a country classification system?
4. Does the WBG distinguish between emerging markets and developing economies?
5. What is the country classification used by the WBG for practical purposes? Describe its accuracy and usefulness.
6. What are categories used in the classification system of the IMF? What are the major flaws of this classification system and its categories?
7. How do the country classification systems of the WBG and the IMF differ?
8. Describe the WTO's country classification system and what it uses as its basis.
9. Describe the major characteristics of the classification system of the UN.
10. Describe the UN's category *transition country*.
11. What is a least developed country? What role does it play in the country classification systems of major multilateral institutions?
12. Is the category "EMCs" an official category of any multilateral institution? Is there a universally accepted definition of this term among these agencies?
13. Describe the practical needs of rating agencies of a country classification system. How can such classification systems be useful for private business?
14. Why do national governments of different categories of countries need country classification systems?
15. Describe a comprehensive approach to country classification.
16. How can the industrial structure of a national economy be used as a base for a country classification system?
17. How can the level of technological development of a country be used to classify it?
18. Are all developed countries ahead of EMCs in terms of the technological development of their national economies?
19. Describe the Synthesized Rating and its usefulness for country classification systems.
20. How can an algorithmic summary be used as a part of a country classification system?
21. Describe the difference between the algorithmic summary of the Bennett method and the algorithmic multiplication function of the Kvint method.
22. What are the major characteristics of the Strategic Comprehensive Country Classification System?
23. Describe the structure (categories) of the Strategic Comprehensive Country Classification System. Describe the basis for these categories.
24. What makes a country a *superpower*?
25. Describe the difference between *technologically advanced economies* and *wealthy nations*.
26. How is a country's categorization related to the Synthesized Country Rating?

27. How does global economic stability influence the financial stability of *wealthy nations*?
28. Describe the category *economies in bloom*.
29. How is the category *economies in bloom* related to the UN category *transition country*?
30. What are the major characteristics of *emerging-market democracies*?
31. Is there a geographic basis for the category of *emerging-market democracies*?
32. Describe the defining characteristics of an *oligarchic emerging market*.
33. Is there a geopolitical basis for the category of *oligarchic emerging markets*?
34. Is it possible for a free-market system to function under a dictatorship?
35. Why are *emerging-market dictatorships* strategically attractive to international investors?
36. Which category has a higher risk of investment—*emerging-market dictatorships* or P-EMCs?
37. Describe the difference, if any, between *frontier economies* and P-EMCs.
38. What are the major differences between EMCs and *developing countries*?
39. Is it possible for a country from the category "EMC" to be reclassified as a *developing country*? What would cause such a reclassification?
40. Is a repressive political system the only characteristic of an *underdeveloped country*?
41. Describe the BOP approach and how it relates to corporate strategy.
42. Describe the "business approach" to country classification.
43. Describe the major characteristics of the Index of International Business Infrastructure. What is this index based on?
44. How can the Index of International Business Infrastructure be used in corporate strategy?
45. Describe the relationship between classification systems, categories of countries, and country ranking.

5 The Emerging Global Business Order

[G]overnment is not the solution to our problem; government is the problem. From time to time we've been tempted to believe that society has become too complex to be managed by self-rule, that government by an elite group is superior to government for, by, and of the people. Well, if no one among us is capable of governing himself, then who among us has the capacity to govern someone else?[1]

(Ronald Reagan, US president, 1911–2004)

The idea of the Reagan era that "government is the problem" just isn't going to get us anywhere. In such a complicated society as we have, you have got to have some kind of responsible, representative national authority to define priorities and allocate resources. That we can "get government off our backs" and privatize everything is at best an illusion, at worst an invitation to rapacity by selfish private interests[2]

(J. William Fulbright, US senator, 1905–1995)

Keynote Definitions

The global order: The *global order* is a political and economic system of cooperation that emerges organically or as a result of the influence of multilateral institutions, superpowers, and other nations, though not necessarily by cooperative means. The global order provides customary procedures, allowing the avoidance of conflict while promoting stability and sustainable development by offering countries, regional blocs, and corporations a means to negotiate disputes amongst themselves and to develop mutually beneficial solutions to global challenges.

The global business order: The *global business order* is a subsystem of the global order that provides a relatively stable framework for cooperation between businesses with global, regional, and national institutions, allowing the evolutionary development of the GMP. It is a set of customs by which corporations compete and cooperate with other businesses in the GMP, exploiting opportunities offered by it without violating human rights, national interests, or regional and global standards.

Genesis of the Global Order

The terms *international order, world order, global order*, and all their variations (*new world order*, etc.) have been on the agenda of thinkers, scholars, and political leaders throughout modern history. According to Professor Lynn Miller of Temple University (Philadelphia, USA), this issue has existed for several centuries:

[T]he game of international politics is played in the normative framework, which provides the parameters within which international actors compete for power and influence. That framework is not an accident of nature but a human invention, created to rationalize and order the relevant social and technological capabilities of increasingly sovereign actors some 350 years ago and consciously enlarged and adapted to respond to changes in those capabilities ever since. It therefore should be regarded not merely as a footnote or an afterthought in the analysis of international politics but as the ordering, ideal structure that both shapes international behavior and makes its evaluation possible.[3]

The global order is, in fact, much more than a framework for "the game of international politics." After the millions of deaths suffered in the two world wars and the extreme tension of the Cold War, national leaders, strategists, and scholars have come to understand the global order differently. It is not only a framework for international politics but also for peaceful economic, technological, and business cooperation and collaboration toward the resolution of the major challenges that face civilization—hunger, mass disease, poverty, and international terrorism, among others. Politicians are far from the only participants in the global order. The corporate world also plays a crucial role. Due to the unifying impact of the GMP, corporations have reached the stage of development in which their leaders and strategists understand the importance of collaboration with national governments and multilateral institutions to expand global prosperity for the sake of humankind, as well as for their own business interests. In general, corporations are intrinsically selfish, as their primary function is to make a profit. However, the current situation, in which only 1.5 billion out of the world's 6.5 billion people are part of the corporations' market of buyers and clients, is not sustainable. With the increasing productivity of labor derived from cutting-edge technologies, corporate overproduction is a realistic possibility. This could cause global, national, and regional recessions, not to mention economic crises that would make the Great Depression of the 1930s look mild. In order to prevent this kind of economic disaster, it is very important for business leaders and strategists to rethink their role in the improvement of the standard of living of billions of people, with the ultimate goal of making them capable of becoming active participants in the GMP. Corporate executives and strategists are awakening to the link between improvements in standards of living and potential growth in their markets, and eventually their profits. This selfish mindset will actually be the most productive way for business leaders to understand their social responsibility as a function of business success. In the GMP, social responsibility and business success go together. The corporate world's strategic understanding of global responsibility arose over centuries of painful experiences for all those involved—corporations, governments, and individuals.

At the end of the eighteenth century, financiers discussed the concept of an international order because they needed international cooperation with creditors and lenders from other countries. This concept was also interesting to financiers because of the importance of stability for international financial transactions. Unlike politicians, who may have been able to exploit instability and uncertainty and gain for themselves and even their nations, financiers rely mostly on stability to function efficiently. However, they can also profit from instability.

The false and unproductive idea of a small group of elites running the world has fascinated conspiracy theorists for centuries. Beginning with legends about the origins of the Masonic movement several centuries ago, the creation of international clubs and the membership of national leaders in private international organizations have always been the object of suspicion. Even in the twenty-first century, a period of unprecedented enlightenment and IT revolution, some still believe in the existence of secret organizations that run the world.

Many point to international organizations and think-tanks such as the Bretton Woods Committee or the Council on Foreign Relations. In actuality, these organizations are open. Their members are prominent scholars, economists, politicians, business leaders, etc., who use these organizations to discuss and advocate solutions to global challenges.

A common source of fascination and speculation of conspiracy theorists are the words and symbols found on the US one-dollar bill and Great Seal. Dan Brown's bestseller *The Da Vinci Code*, which speculated a great deal about the meaning of the dollar bill's design and that of the Seal, briefly brought this issue to the forefront of pop culture. Strategists should always ignore such "pop" explanations. A direct clarification is provided by the United States Department of Treasury:

> [T]he eye and the pyramid shown on the reverse side of the one-dollar bill are in the Great Seal of the United States . . . The Department of State is the official keeper of the Seal. They believe that the most accurate explanation of a pyramid on the Great Seal is that it symbolizes strength and durability. The unfinished pyramid means that the United States will always grow, improve and build. In addition, the "All-Seeing Eye" located above the pyramid suggests the importance of divine guidance in favor of the American cause. The inscription ANNUIT COEPTIS translates as "He (God) has favored our undertakings," and refers to the many instances of Divine Providence during our Government's formation. In addition, the inscription NOVUS ORDO SECLORUM translates as "A new order of the ages," and signifies a new American era.[4]

Although these symbols have existed for almost 230 years (the US government officially adopted the Great Seal in 1782), the idea of a "new order" has never ceased to fascinate conspiracy theorists and the general public. It became especially interesting as the twentieth century ended. The reason for this is obvious, as at this time the world was entering a period of unprecedented change, with increasing levels of internationalization and interconnection. The number of countries has grown, and global challenges have been complicated, requiring an updated world order. The global order with which humankind entered the twenty-first century has its roots in the order developed at towards the end of World War II, in 1944. Four years later, when the Cold War began, the post-World War II order changed and became less efficient for humankind, which was divided into three camps—the capitalist, communist, and non-aligned countries. At one point this was the new world order, but newer political and economic developments, as well as global challenges, have brought national and corporate leaders, heads of multilateral institutions, and strategists to seek a newer and more efficient global order. This order must correctly reflect the current and future levels of development and improvement of humankind as well as its upcoming challenges.

Strategists, of course, cannot afford to make the mistake of believing in the existence of a nefarious, all-powerful secret global body. This would completely undermine the role of strategists and executives, and it would imply that they are mere figureheads for these secret organizations, making them ineffectual and insignificant. In reality, strategists work in and collaborate with many important international organizations, think-tanks, and corporations. While corporate and governmental strategy is, in general, tightly guarded, the "copyright" of strategic activity almost always becomes public knowledge. Corporations attempt to keep their strategies, or at least some parts of them, unknown to the public and, of course, to their competitors until a certain point. If corporate strategy becomes publicly known prior to its implementation, competitors will inevitably find ways and means to make it obsolete. Multilateral institutions also keep certain aspects of their strategies out of the public eye. This usually relates only to issues concerning the fight against terrorism, narcotic and human trafficking, national secrets of member countries, etc. However, because of the nature of these institutions, most aspects of their strategies are available to the public.

Contrary to what conspiracy theorists might imagine, global orders are generally the result of humanitarian visions of leaders and strategists to establish a mechanism to prevent international conflicts, promote stability, and to address the major challenges facing humankind that cannot be solved or handled by national governments alone. There are certain challenges that national governments are innately unequipped to handle, due to conflicts between national interests and global or regional needs. As a result of increasing shortages of various natural resources, such conflicts will be a major challenge for the global order in the twenty-first century. The freshwater resources of some countries, for instance, originate primarily from foreign sources. In cases like this, the ability of people to satisfy their most basic need depends on the beneficence of foreign governments, which at any moment could divert freshwater flows to their own industrial or other purposes. This issue was discussed in greater detail in Chapter 1, but is mentioned in this chapter as an obvious illustration of the need for international cooperation.

It is very important to underscore the fact that international cooperation should consist of a collaborative relationship among multilateral institutions, national governments, and the private sector. A supernational world government is not a productive or sustainable idea. Any form of an executive supernational government has deep roots in the ideas of dialectical liberalism and neo-Marxism, "which aims merely to harmonize rather than to eliminate differences in the pursuit of equality."[5] This approach is significantly softer than Karl Marx's, but it is no more practical. For the emerging global order of the twenty-first century to be sustainable, national governments must play a dominant role. Multilateral institutions should focus on the coordination of national governments and the private sector toward the resolution of global issues. However, multilateral institutions need to be able to make executive decisions, primarily on the basis of consensus, as it is key that national authority not be undermined. There are some cases in which decision making by overwhelming majority is required. Protection of national sovereignty comes at a cost, as international bodies that require a consensus can be very inefficient. The UN General Assembly is an obvious example of this fact. Due to numerous conflicts of interest among its 192 member-states, the decisions of this body act only as recommendations. In order to skirt this managerial challenge, in situations of great importance, executive decisions can be based on a supermajority (also known as a qualified majority), which requires two-thirds of all votes. Supermajorities will play a key role in the emerging global order in issues related to security and the survival of civilization.

New global orders often appear or are reorganized from previous orders after wars or major discoveries (the geographical discoveries of the fifteenth century, for example). The development of a new global order is almost always challenged by politicization and conflicts of national interests. In attempting to solve these conflicts, be they of political, human rights, or economic nature, there is often a tendency to advocate for the creation of a global executive government. As previously discussed, this is completely undesirable. However, the need to resolve these challenges, in addition to the influence of objective and subjective factors, is the basis upon which global orders are formed. Ideally, the global order should be oriented toward the achievement of the global optimum, which can be understood as the equilibrium balance of the interests of all participants under the global order—national governments and regional bodies, multilateral institutions, corporations, as well as those of individuals. Obviously, the global optimum is an ideal that is extremely difficult (if not impossible) to achieve. Nevertheless, the closer humankind comes to it, the more efficient, prosperous, and equitable civilization will be. The global optimum is a serious theoretical issue with very important practical implications. It provides a strategic path that the development of the global order should follow. The search for this path and the triggering events of the new global order, its design, and functions have their own dynamics.

In the twenty-first century, civilization faces unprecedented challenges and problems that cannot be solved or even mitigated without coordination under a new, more efficient global order. The cataclysmic capabilities of humankind as a result of the spread of nuclear technologies and other weapons of mass destruction, as well as the increasing danger of technogenic disasters, require a global order for the survival of humankind and the prevention of the annihilation of civilization. In a time when five of the six and a half billion people of the world live in relative or total poverty, global coordination is needed in order to fight poverty, for humanitarian as well as practical purposes. The increasing liberalization of international relations in a world in which the gap between wealthy and underdeveloped nations is growing exponentially requires global coordination to monitor and regulate international migration. The surge in international and global cross-border movement of people and labor raises the risk of pandemic outbreaks of disease, the prevention and management of which can be done only through global coordination. The liberalization of international financial and economic relations and the global integration of both require a global order to help harmonize national regulations according to worldwide standards. Global coordination is absolutely necessary to counter new threats, such as international terrorism and the growing influence of religious extremism. The protection of the environment and the management of natural disasters both global and regional require harmonized international efforts. The global order should be understood as a means of improving the efficiency of civilization as a whole—it is not merely an economic or financial issue. National policies should be coordinated to promote world peace, social cohesion, prosperity, and the widespread penetration of the most important and useful technologies and knowledge. None of these issues can be addressed without a global order appropriate to the conditions of the twenty-first century. Without properly crafted functions of current and new multilateral institutions and some obligations upon national governments to coordinate their efforts with these institutions, the global order will not be able to achieve any of the aforementioned objectives. However, global and national leadership should try to reach these exceedingly difficult objectives; even attempts to do so will have a positive impact on humankind. Quite often, the process of reaching a worthwhile goal is no less important than its actual fulfillment.

Bretton Woods Institutions of the Global Order

In the twenty-first century, strategists, as well as global and national political and business leaders, tend to be very critical of the existing global order, which is a derivative of the recommendations of the Bretton Woods Conference. This book is no exception. However, despite this well-founded criticism, it is important to acknowledge and respect the visionaries from around the world who met in 1944 in the small town of Bretton Woods, New Hampshire. Officially called the UN Monetary and Financial Conference, but almost universally known as the Bretton Woods Conference, the meeting engineered the global political and economic order to be implemented immediately after the end of the war. Although the Allied forces would fight the fascists from Germany, Italy, and Japan for more than a year, the participants of the conference already considered these enemies as future business partners and even political allies. The post-war global order would likely have been different if Joseph Stalin, the leader of the Soviet Union at the time, decided to send his representative to Bretton Woods. As a powerful member of the Allies, the Soviet Union was asked to participate and Stalin initially accepted this invitation. However, he later changed his mind. This conference gave birth to the IMF, the IBRD (the major institution of the WBG), and the UN (all known as the Bretton Woods institutions). The conference also designed the International Trade Organization, whose charter was completed in 1948, but the United States Congress never ratified the creation of this organization, due to its reluctance to give a foreign organization the ability to affect US foreign trade policy. Nonetheless, this organization was established 50 years later, in 1994, and became operational in January 1995 as the WTO. The post-World War II international gold standard system was also introduced at Bretton Woods. The conference participants' vision is quite impressive. Although they were probably not looking much more than 10 or 20 years into the future, the majority of the global-order principles that they created functioned for 50 years.

The broad strokes of the global political order under which humankind lived until the last decade of the twenty-first century were designed in February 1945, in the vacation palace of the Russian imperial family in the Black Sea coastal town of Yalta. The three leaders of the anti-Nazi coalition, US President Roosevelt, UK Prime Minister Churchill, and the Soviet dictator Stalin, marked their spheres of influence in post-war Europe, the Pacific Rim, and even in continental Asia, in countries such as Mongolia and China. The Yalta Conference reinforced recommendations of Bretton Woods and made a date for the inaugural meeting of the UN, in San Francisco, later in the year: April 25. "The Yalta Declaration contains a number of ambiguous formulas that served to bridge the gap between the positions of the US, Britain, and the Soviet Union vis-à-vis the post-World War II global order."[6] The Potsdam Conference of July 1945 should also be mentioned, but the focus of this conference was mostly the post-war development of divided Germany. This meeting already demonstrated the serious disagreement between the UK and the US on one side, and the Soviet Union on the other. Potsdam was the first indicator that after the war, the world was headed toward a bipolar global order. Nonetheless, neither the Yalta nor Potsdam Conference had as significant an influence on the global economic order as did the Bretton Woods Conference.

Several alterations of the Bretton Woods global economic order were made: first, at the beginning of the Cold War, in 1948; second, in 1971, when the gold-dollar standard system failed and was abolished. It failed because dollar reserves outside of the United States substantially surpassed the value of US gold reserves. The most substantial changes to the global order occurred at the end of the Cold War, with the failure of communism.

By the end of the 1980s and the beginning of the 1990s, the world had undergone drastic changes. The colonial system was destroyed, along with apartheid in South Africa. Dictatorships throughout the world collapsed. The Soviet Union, the world's last empire, disintegrated into 15 independent states. The Cold War was over, the Warsaw Pact no longer existed, and by 1997 three former Soviet Republics—the Baltic States—had already joined NATO, along with most of the former Soviet bloc countries. During this period the number of independent countries tripled. UN membership expanded from 1945's 44 charter members to 192 members. The world has clearly gone through profound changes since the Bretton Woods Conference. Without these changes, a third world war likely would have taken place at some point. However, the global order and its regulating bodies, established in 1944, are no longer suited to the economic, business, and political reality of the twenty-first century. Furthermore, IT of the twenty-first century has multiplied the capacity of global institutions to coordinate the efforts of countries, regional bodies, and corporations, and the order needs to be reorganized appropriately.

According to the agreements between their member countries, a Board of Governors manages the activity of each Bretton Woods institution. For example, in section two of the Articles of Agreement of the IMF, it states:

[A]ll powers under this Agreement not conferred directly on the Board of Governors, the Executive Board, or the Managing Director shall be vested in the Board of Governors. The Board of Governors shall consist of one Governor and one Alternate appointed by each member in such manner as it may determine.[7]

For the management of operational activity, these organizations have executive boards. According to section 10 of the IMF's by-laws:

[T]he Executive Board shall have prepared for presentation to the Board of Governors an annual report in which shall be discussed the policies and activities of the Fund and which shall make recommendations to the Board of Governors on the problems confronting the Fund. The Executive Board shall review, as part of the annual report, the functioning of the international monetary system, including the adequacy of global reserves, the conduct of the business of the General Department and of the Special Drawing Rights Department, as well as the performance of financial services by the Fund, including the administration of resources contributed by members.[8]

For many years this was a moderately successful structure. However, as of the beginning of the twenty-first century, shares of different countries in the voting of these multilateral institutions are outdated, and do not represent the reality of the twenty-first century, the functions of these institutions have not been appropriately updated, and there is not enough coordination among multilateral institutions, in addition to other factors. Every year from the last week of September to the first week of October, the Joint Annual Meeting of the World Bank and IMF is conducted. At the meeting, the results of the previous year are accepted and the plan for the upcoming year is approved.

The key architect of the Bretton Woods system was the great British economist John Maynard Keynes (1883–1946), arguably one of economics' most important figures. In his speech on July 22, 1944, at the conclusion of the Bretton Woods Conference, he declared:

[F]inally, we have perhaps accomplished here in Bretton Woods something more significant than what is embodied in this Final Act. We have shown that a concourse of forty-four nations is actually able to work together at a constructive task in amity and unbroken concord. Few believed it possible. If we can continue in a larger task as we have begun in this limited task, there is hope for the world.[9]

The annual meeting of the Bretton Woods Committee is basically the successor to the original Bretton Woods Conference.

The current system of multilateral intuitions is clearly not a world government. The decisions of the UN General Assembly, for example, are merely recommendations and can be (and often are) ignored. It is heard but not listened to. Furthermore, the General Assembly focuses primarily on international governmental relationships, and much less on economic, financial, or business issues. The UN Security Council is a much more powerful body, but as the name suggests, it also does not directly focus on economic, financial, or business issues. Some topics with which it deals, such as terrorism and nationalism, certainly affect business and economics. Because these integrated factors of political risk affect not only businesses but also the UN itself, a relatively unified global front has been formed to counter these threats. Regardless, it is very difficult for the Security Council to reach consensus, and that is without having to listen to the voices of most countries of the world.

The power of the UN General Assembly and Security Council is clearly limited. Even so, they both still play a significant role in the current global order and will continue to do so in the new, emerging global order.

The new dynamics and qualities of the influence of objective and subjective factors have rendered traditional multilateral institutions and their operational activity inefficient under twenty-first-century conditions. For this reason, leaders of the member countries of these institutions seek new functions and structures of multilateral institutions, coordination among them, and cooperation with national governments and corporate leadership.

Dynamics of the Global Order

The birth and maturation of the emerging global order of the twenty-first century is the result of the collaboration of two processes with very different characteristics—evolution and revolution. In the twenty-first century, the world economy has been almost totally reorganized and integrated into the GMP, which is an entity of great complexity and dynamism. It consists of global, regional, national, and local elements, as well as industrial and corporate structures. The relative weight of and relationships among these elements constantly changes over time. Some countries that for many years were relatively insignificant players are beginning to assume major roles in the emerging global order, while the importance of some traditional powers is declining. The appearance of countries that did not previously exist (such as Kazakhstan) and their rise to regional and global importance, due to various factors such as unique and rich natural or technological resources, has led to further complications. New and rising powers are increasingly challenging the dominance of global and regional players. Shifts in the importance of specific industries, multinational corporations, and multilateral institutions also increase complexity. All of this requires a new global order that reflects these changes and their dynamics. The dynamics of the GMP leave the global order in constant disequilibrium. While there may be a status quo, it is only temporary.

The global order reflects characteristics of the GMP and the global workplace but at the same time influences them. As is clear from the country classification system (presented in Chapter 4), at the end of the first decade of the twenty-first century there is only one superpower—the United States—that can be seen as the center of the highest economic strength, efficiency, and relative social balance. It is undisputedly the most influential country of the global order. However, the example of the Soviet Union illustrates that the dominance of a superpower can be fleeting when it experiences drastic declines in its efficiency, the relevance of its ideology, and then inevitably its power in the global arena. Although the global order of the first decade of the twenty-first century has been essentially a unipolar, hegemonic system, the United States is not immune to the possibility of losing its status as the global superpower, especially in a world as complex and dynamic as that of the twenty-first century. Rising regional superpowers, which can be thought of as centers of high efficiency with ideologies and visions of the global order that differ from that of the global superpower, are already challenging the dominance of the US in certain regions but not on a global level. Processes of regionalization have led to a situation in which regional superpowers are not restricted to individual countries. The EU can be considered a regional superpower, although it is very different from all others. It is based not on national interests, but on the regional interests of almost 30 nations. This is a radically new phenomenon of the emerging global order. Although the EU is not a sovereign body, it has institutions that unify member countries to the extent that together they constitute a European government with loose functions and power. To a certain extent, this government is developing and implementing a European business order through under-laws and regulatory practices, such as common bankruptcy (described in many documents, such as the Lisbon Strategy for growth and jobs) and anti-trust rules (described in the treaty establishing the European Community). From this point of view, the EU is very different from the UN, which does not have such integrated power and sovereignty over its member countries. As the economic clout of regional superpowers grows, they are demanding with increasing assertiveness that the United States reduce its influence in different regions and structures. Neighboring countries of regional superpowers find themselves in tenuous situations because of the interplay between the global power of the US and the refusal of regional powers to delegate authority. The vacillating allegiance of neighboring countries between these competing powers increases the complexity, dynamism, and imbalance of the global order. After September 11, 2001, the leadership of the United States developed its own conceptual response to the challenge of rising regional super-powers. Stefan Halper, a senior fellow at the Centre of International Studies at Cambridge University, and Jonathan Clarke, a foreign-affairs scholar at the CATO Institute, described the following principles that they believe were developed by the neo-conservative administration of George W. Bush:

1. "Analyze international issues in black-and-white, absolute moral categories. They [the Bush administration] are fortified by a conviction that they alone hold the moral high ground and argue that disagreement is tantamount to defeatism.
2. Focus on the 'unipolar' power of the United States, seeing the use of military force as the first, not the last option of foreign policy. They repudiate the 'lessons of Vietnam,' which they interpret as undermining American will toward the use of force, and embrace the 'lessons of Munich,' interpreted as establishing the virtues of preemptive military action.
3. Disdain conventional diplomatic agencies such as the State Department and conventional country-specific, realist, and pragmatic analysis. They are hostile towards nonmilitary multilateral institutions and instinctively antagonistic toward international treaties and agreements. 'Global unilateralism' is their watchword. They are fortified by international criticism, believing that it confirms American virtue.
4. Look to the Reagan administration as the exemplar of all these virtues and seek to establish their version of Reagan's legacy as the Republican and national orthodoxy."[10]

The widely held critical attitude of these authors toward President George W. Bush's administration aside, the political and economic conditions and the global order within which this administration worked made it difficult for alternative strategies to be effective, especially given the tremendous influence of the new threat of global terrorism. Nonetheless, this strategy can be considered an extension of the Washington Consensus, as they do not contradict one another, unlike the so-called Beijing Consensus, both of which are described in detail later in this chapter.

The Global Business Order in the Dynamics of the Global Order

Strategists should be aware of the fact that as of 2008, no regional superpower, not even China, represents a serious challenge to the United States' global dominance. Nevertheless, during the last three-quarters of the twenty-first century, such a challenge is very likely to emerge. This will undoubtedly destabilize the global order. Given this dynamic, the unipolar global order that emerged after the Cold War will most likely remain intact until approximately 2025–2030. At this point, one or even several regional superpowers may challenge the role of the United States as the sole global superpower, and a bipolar or, most likely, a multipolar global order and its subsystem, the global business order, will emerge. The development of the GMP and the birth of the global workplace in conditions of a multipolar world will require a global business order, the rules and conditions of which will be incompatible with the current structure. The global business order is a new phenomenon. As of 2008, in economic and business literature, this phenomenon remains undefined, although the term has appeared on a few occasions, without an explanation of its role and significance. The following quote is an example: "Since 1947 successive GATT rounds lowered macroeconomic trade barriers throughout the world, facilitating the integration of domestic economies into a global business order based on internationally deregulated capital markets, which nonetheless remained rooted in the multinational corporation's host state."[11] Some authors refer to the international economic order, but their explanations of this term as it relates to the global order show that they are actually speaking about the global business order:

> [A] new international economic order has in fact emerged. However, it was not produced by the political will of government but by the needs and perceptions of the marketplace. If I were to pick three groups of actors who have contributed more to the emergence of the new Global Order than any other, it would be central bankers, financial regulators, and credit agencies. They have already laid the foundation of a new financial architecture and will continue to build upon it, brick by brick, to meet market demands. If governments want to act, they should prompt and facilitate the work of these agents of change . . . The only practical way to deal with the profound changes taking place in the structure of the global economy is not to impose on it a new architecture. Instead, what is required is to balance the profound changes that have already occurred in the global economic and financial system with an equally profound restructuring of domestic economies.[12]

In referring to a new paradigm, Dr Michael Gavin, author of the above quote, is also rejecting the need for structural changes in the managerial bodies of the GMP which will implement this paradigm in practice. The global business order requires the activity of new institutions, which will be primarily oriented toward the coordination of private businesses with one another, with national governments and government-oriented Bretton Woods multilateral institutions. The collaboration of these institutions with private business is particularly necessary in the sphere of finance. The impact of the GEM on the global financial system has been very significant with the growing role of derivative instruments, pension and mutual funds, and currency markets throughout the GMP. The use of these instruments in the GEM requires regulation by national governments as well as multilateral institutions.

The global business order and its structures have to be geared for cooperation between companies and traditional agencies from the business world with multilateral institutions and governments. They also have to face the threats, both ongoing and yet to emerge, that will influence the global order of the twenty-first century. In addition to the threat of terrorism, the emerging global business order has to be oriented to face another, more organized, though less threatening challenge—the formation of international cartels that control strategic natural resources. This challenge first emerged in 1960, upon the creation of the most powerful international intergovernmental cartel, the Organization of the Petroleum Exporting Countries (OPEC), which accounts for about 40 percent of worldwide oil production.[13] Its member countries include oil-exporting states from the Middle East, Africa, and even Southeast Asia and Latin America. By controlling the production of one of the most crucial natural resources, OPEC is tremendously influential in the global business order as well as in the global order. The interests of this cartel are totally selfish, and they completely contradict the promotion of global prosperity and the global optimum. OPEC's stated mission is to coordinate

> oil production policies in order to help stabilise the oil market and to help oil producers achieve a reasonable rate of return on their investments. This policy is also designed to ensure that oil consumers continue to receive stable supplies of oil.[14]

From this mission statement, it is clear that OPEC's first priority is the return on investment of its member countries. Stabilizing the oil supply of the world is an afterthought, generally ignored during world energy crises. During such times, in order to increase prices, OPEC member countries decrease production and exports or do not use existing capabilities in order to reduce oil supplies and raise prices.

There is a danger that other strategic natural resources will be cartelized in the twenty-first century. Several major producers of natural gas, such as Iran and Russia, are attempting to develop an OPEC-like natural gas cartel. An informal group known as the Gas Exporting Countries Forum (GECF) has already formed to discuss this issue. Among its participants are Algeria, Bolivia, Brunei, Egypt, Equatorial Guinea, Indonesia, Libya, Malaysia, Nigeria, Oman, Qatar, Trinidad and Tobago, the United Arab Emirates, and Venezuela. Norway is considered an observer.[15] Iran and Russia, the two leading natural gas producers, play a leading role in the development of this group. The formation of such a cartel would be very dangerous for the global business order because it would place 40 percent of gas production and 75 percent of reserves under the governmental control of about 15 countries.[16] If such an organization is actually created, the emergence of cartels controlling other important natural resources such as freshwater reserves, basic food commodities, or precious medals such as palladium (more important for technological and hydrogen energy production than jewelry), is quite possible. One of the most dangerous precedents was the 2008 proposal of "Thailand, the world's biggest rice exporter . . . to form an OPEC-style cartel with Laos, Myanmar, Cambodia, and Vietnam to give them more control over international rice prices."[17] The governments of several countries interpreted this proposal as a serious threat. In order to prevent the formation of a rice cartel, the government of Japan sent thousands of tons of rice to countries such as the Philippines as aid and released rice from its national stocks into the regional and global market.[18] The cartelization of the GMP would be a very negative development for the efficiency of the global business order. The function of these organizations is hostile to global prosperity. The global order has to be oriented toward the use of all possible political and economic mechanisms to prevent the creation of new cartels and limit the influence of existing ones. The new architecture of multilateral institutions in the twenty-first century will reflect many global challenges—the threat of terrorism and the cartelization of the GMP, among others.

Due to these challenges, the role of national governments in the global business order will increase compared to its decline during the romantic liberalism of the last quarter of the twentieth century. The wave of economic liberalization that swept across the world following the end of the Cold War began to recede after the "Asian" crisis of 1997 (actually, a global one). Proponents of romantic liberalism, such as Voltaire's character, Candide and several other more contemporary "experts," undermined the role of national governments, to the extent that despite having the ability to prevent contagion, governments were hesitant to intervene in financial markets. As a result, the crises crossed national borders and even oceans. Only after this experience did governmental and financial leaders, scholars, and strategists start to reevaluate the role of government in a globalized world. Romantic liberalism is beginning to give way to a new dynamic of global economic affairs, with a growing role for national interests and national governments structured to reflect these interests. Although it may not yet be evident by the first decade of the twenty-first century, the end of the period of romantic liberalism has already begun. Rising regional powers will decrease the unipolar dominance of the United States and increase the role of protectionism around multiple regional poles that are appearing.

Regional unions and blocs are already forming around these new regional poles. Members of regional blocs are constantly reevaluating the balance between their relationships with global and regional superpowers and reshuffling their allegiances accordingly. Central European countries, such as the Czech and Slovak republics and Poland, have to find a balance between the US and Germany—the regional superpower of Europe. The EU itself is a new pole in the global order. Latin American countries balance the weight of US influence with that of their regional superpower, Brazil. The situation in Asia is even more complex: countries have to deal with the influence of four regional superpowers—China, India, Russia, and Japan—as well as that of the United States. Pakistan's increasing position as one of the first Muslim nations with nuclear power will make the regional equilibrium even more difficult to sustain. The liberalization of international relations and especially of international trade has made it possible for *regional economic organizations* to expand at an unprecedented pace, and there are more than 100 regional economic organizations in the GMP, with varying levels of integration. The addition of new member countries affects the politics, economics, and business of all parties involved, and the dynamics of expansion of regional economic organizations have important implications for the global order. The strength and influence of regional organizations such as the EU, NAFTA, Mercosur, ASEAN, etc., vary substantially and are reflected in their respective roles in the GMP. However, the relative dynamics of these organizations change as membership expands to include neighboring countries and agreements are signed with economies of no geographic proximity. NAFTA, for example, has free trade agreements with Jordan, Chile, and several other countries. The dynamic and uneven development of regional blocs and unions complicates the GMP, the GEM, the relationships among countries of different categories, and the global order.

Regional blocs and unions are usually self-organized, and their development is a function of their own continued survival and improvement. A lack of balance in economic and technological development within regional blocs leads to their disintegration unless the economic, social, business, and technological situation is improved in the relatively less-developed member countries in order to maintain a balance. Development tends to be uneven within regional economic organizations, causing further disruption and disequilibrium. As this process continues, it increases the integration of member countries of regional blocs in the GMP. A key factor determining the extent to which a regional economic organization is integrated within the GMP is its relationship with neighboring countries. The more similar neighboring countries are to those of the regional economic organization, the more likely the organization is to have liberalized economic and financial relationships with its neighbors and eventually to add them as full country members. The larger a regional economic organization, and the more liberalized its relations are, the more integrated it is within the GMP. During periods of global economic liberalism, the practical significance of rapidly expanding regional blocs comes into question. In general, the more open the GMP and global workplace, the looser are regional economic organizations. One of the best examples of this is the 2008 formation of the Union for the Mediterranean. It was established by 43 countries, with very different agendas, including Muslim and Christian nations as well as Israel. It is great that the leaders of these diverse nations are meeting and working together, but their ability to come to a consensus regarding the most important issues is dubious. On the other hand, during times of reduced global economic integration, regional organizations are tighter, stronger, and more relevant. The more regional economic organizations are integrated with the GMP, the less complicated is the global order, making it less region specific and more oriented toward global issues.

The size of regional blocs is usually proportional to the size of its member countries but is limited by geographical and political conditions. The more similar the political system of a country and the closer it is geographically to the regional economic organization, the more likely that country is to join. Regional blocs are experiencing two very different and somewhat contradictory dynamics—internal integration between current country members (and their businesses) and external integration. The economic necessity of external business integration makes regional blocs intensify cooperation with countries that do not have mutual borders with the bloc and are even on different continents. Such integration between regional blocs as a whole and with other individual countries complicates the global order and the missions of its institutions. The demolition of economic barriers within regional economic organizations has linear characteristics and is typically proportional to the square of the territory of the regional economic organization and its country members. In terms of the GDP of its country members, this proportion is cubic. Bigger economies integrate at a slower pace within regional blocs, as they tend to already be more integrated with the GMP. At a certain level, these two different dynamics lead to the complete integration of some regional blocs within the GMP and the global workplace. The integration of individual corporations to regional blocs and to the GMP occurs at a much faster pace than that of national economies.

The varying rates of development of individual countries as well as of different regional blocs can be seen as a threat to the current global order, but also as a process that makes the current order sustainable. For example, the global order reflects the strong influence of the US as a superpower. But it is also influenced by the rising power of China and other regional powers such as India, Russia, Brazil, and Germany. By 2025 the role of South Africa and Egypt as regional superpowers will also be significant. Democratic reform in Iran would likely allow it to become a regional superpower as well. At the beginning of the twenty-first century, Iran, like North Korea, represents a regional as well as global threat, but it does not have any economic and social characteristics of a superpower. BRIC—Brazil, Russia, India and China—is a group of countries that many see as a bloc and even as a regional organization, however neither of these terms actually apply and no formal organization actually exists. The first time the leaders of these countries gathered in a formal setting was during the July G8 summit in Japan. The BRIC cannot be considered a regional organization, as these countries are spread among three continents. Nevertheless, they share similar characteristics, and their role in the world should not be underestimated. The collective output of these countries is about $15 trillion, which is more than the output of the US. The BRIC accounts for about 25 percent of GDP and 45 percent of the global population. In an attempt to be ahead of the game, Dow Jones established the BRIC 50 Index, "a blue-chip measure that includes 50 of the largest and most actively traded stocks in these countries. The China portion of the index is made up of offshore stocks-H-shares and US-listed ADRs/ADSes"[19] (American Depository Receipt/Shares, discussed in Chapter 8). Some experts have even expanded this grouping to BRICS, which also includes South Africa. From a strategic point of view, these countries cannot create a workable bloc. They should be analyzed as a part of the GEM. Regardless, all of the developments described above will influence the global order and change its configuration, but they will not threaten its existence as a mostly unipolar world. The hegemony and the major global multilateral institutions will deal more with balancing regional superpowers between one another.

The Evolution of the Global Order

In the unipolar global order of the early twenty-first century, a temporary balance has been achieved through the formation and development of regional blocs, usually built around regional superpowers. There are also some regional blocs, such as ASEAN, that do not have a regional superpower among their member countries. ASEAN was formed largely to counter the influence of Asian regional superpowers. Liberalization and the fall of barriers to globalization increase entropy, which can be understood as a process of increasing disorder initially, followed by the disappearance of some elements of the status quo that are never recovered. One manifestation of this is the disintegration of countries into smaller economies, during the chaotic process of the disappearance of dictatorial or imperial systems, and their integration into the GMP. The influence of this trend is waning but still significant (see Chapter 3). The self-organization around regional poles can be understood as part of the process of achieving a temporary balance in the unipolar global order. Regional self-organization has led to the creation of new organizational forms in the GMP—different types of regional economic organizations. Regionalization, primarily under the influence of the similarly named global trend, is leading to a reorganization of the GMP, which can be understood as one of the major characteristics of its *evolution*. Strategic conclusions can be drawn from the application of the morphological principle of evolution to the organizational structure of the emerging global business order. Usually, new organizational bodies appear organically, in an unsystematic process. Not surprisingly, during the initial development of any new economic and business organizational structure, more governance structures appear than are necessary for the functioning of an efficient system. Later, as a formal system begins to emerge, redundancies decrease through a process that can be understood as *oligomerization*—a process of simplification by the reduction of a structure's units and subunits. The result is a much more efficient and sustainable system with fewer executive bodies. This is the process that is under way at the beginning of the twenty-first century, during the formation of the new global order and the emerging global business order. Regionalization and political disintegration have been occurring for decades. Barring any ecological or technogenic catastrophes, both forces will continue to influence the GMP and the current global order for some time.

The basic regional structure of the global order will continue to exist until the middle of the century, but it will become increasingly unstable, especially from 2025–2050, when the formation of several global industrial-sectoral markets will collide with regional blocs in the GMP. This will happen as a result of the substantial changes in the traditional economic and south–north and east–west trade routes and axes. Due to the fact that alternative energy technologies lag behind practical needs, in the first quarter of the twenty-first century, Russia has continued to be a major source of oil and gas for Europe. Pipelines will continue to operate from east to west. They will also run east of Russia to Korea, China, and even Japan. Pipelines are also already in development from Kazakhstan to China, and from Turkmenistan and Azerbaijan toward Europe, as alternatives to Russian oil and gas. Vertical connections will also continue, as oil will flow from the Middle East and Africa to Europe, northwest to the US and northeast to China. Outsourcing and offshoring are developing along similar north–south connections, from the Indian subcontinent in the south to the US and Europe in the north. Knowledge-based technologies and intellectual property will head in the opposite direction, from the high-tech industries of the US and Europe to less-developed countries of Asia and Africa. In the second quarter of the twenty-first century, these traditional axes will change. Hydrocarbon resources in Russia, Nigeria, and even in some Middle Eastern countries (though not Saudi Arabia and Iraq) will dwindle, and new geological discoveries will not occur at the rapid pace of the twentieth century. The efficiency of alternative energy technologies such as bioethanol and nuclear power production will increase, and they will eventually replace hydrocarbon resources as the primary fuel. Any diversification of sources of hydrocarbon from different countries or its partial substitution by alternative sources of energy leads to a decreasing dominance in the energy sector of oil- and natural gas-rich countries, bringing more balance and stability to the GMP. Eventually, this will lead countries to leave cartels such as OPEC and possibly initiate the creation of new ones. Bio-energy is not only a more environmentally friendly source of energy than oil and gas, but it will also lead to a modernization of global political and economic relations. Increasing standards of living and costs of production in India and China will eventually make the outsourcing patterns of the early twenty-first century less economical. The global orientation of international business and economic connections will be much more diversified; as a result, the traditional north–south and east–west patterns and corridors will be less visible in the GMP. Nonetheless, they will still be of strategic significance. For corporate strategy, it makes sense to develop international relations along these corridors to exploit the already well-developed infrastructure and agglomeration effect, which occurs when multiple companies of different industries complement each other in a particular territory or region, reducing the expenses of all parties involved in the project or regional development.

Due to global trends, almost the entire world economy has been integrated within the GMP. By a similar process the GEM is expanding, as more countries embrace principles of free-market economics and become emerging markets. This is occurring at a faster pace than the most advanced EMCs' (economies in bloom) transition into the developed world. More developing (and even some underdeveloped) countries are becoming emerging markets because it requires fewer resources and time to transition from the status of developing to emerging than it does from emerging to developed. This dynamic is also causing imbalance in the world economy. However, processes are only one perspective from which to analyze the impact of the GEM on the global order. It should also be analyzed in terms of the static structure of the GEM, which is a stabilizing force in the GMP. Because the GEM is classified between rich developed countries and poor developing countries, it acts as a buffer between these two categories and reduces tension. Without the GEM, inequality in the GMP would be so overwhelming that it would lead to revolutionary changes that could destroy the global order. The maturation of the GEM provides another basis for the continuation of the major characteristics of the current global order until the middle of the twentieth century. At the same time, the GEM's rapid expansion decreases the stability of the world economy. For the short term, the GEM reduces tension in the GMP and increases stability, but in the long term, it increases instability. The global order has to reflect this dichotomy. The continued enlargement of the GEM coupled with the appearance of new countries and the subsequent expansion of the GMP and its sectorial markets further complicates the global order. However, the appearance of new countries under the influence of the trend of political disintegration has already slowed. The wave of transitions of developing countries to the GEM should also slow in the second quarter of the twenty-first century. As a result of these two dynamics, the evolutionary widening of the GMP will also slow down.

The Revolution of the Global Order

During the Cold War, the world was relatively balanced. There were two superpowers and the global order was organized around the balanced tension between them. This gave the false impression that the global order would last forever, because of the damage (nuclear war) that many assumed would inevitably occur in order for one side of to overcome the other. How did this global order, based on the balance of two competing nuclear powers change? Despite the consensus among experts that the loss of the bipolar balance between the United States and the Soviet Union would have devastating consequences, the end of the Cold War came about in a mostly peaceful, but *revolutionary* reorganization of the global order. This leads to the paradoxical conclusion that *balance in the global order inhibits revolutionary development and subsequent progress.* An asymmetrical global order emerged in place of the symmetrical order of the Cold War. Common sense usually argues that imbalance is dangerous, but it was the main path to progress. While it is counterintuitive, an asymmetric global order is actually more efficient. However, without the revolutionary changes, i.e. the failure of the overwhelming majority of national communist systems, including the Soviet Union, this new global order would not exist. The disappearance of the Soviet Union was the entropy of the Cold War global order. Without this, the global order would not have changed.

The emergence of the new global order allowed the GMP to form and mature. The failure of the old global order led to the fall of barriers of national economies. The fall of the Berlin Wall is the most striking symbol of the collapse of many political and economic barriers during this period of radical change at the end of the 1980s and beginning of the 1990s. These changes were triggering events toward tighter international economic integration; they resulted in the eventual formation and maturation of the GMP. Starting in the last quarter of the twentieth century and the first decade of the twenty-first, the failure and disintegration of the Soviet Union was actually not the beginning of the failure of the global order set by the Bretton Woods Conference. It began much earlier, when, under the influence of global trends, dictatorships disappeared throughout much of the world and international economic integration began to increase. The disappearance of the Soviet Union was the culmination of these processes.

At the end of the twentieth century, only formal changes were made to the global order, and international economic integration reached the level of the formation of the GMP. However, the nature of the relationships in the world economy did not change prior to the twenty-first century. At this point, there had not been enough time for political and corporate leaders, and especially for bureaucrats of multilateral institutions, to grow into their new roles. The new opportunities and challenges became clear to strategists and to political, economic, and business leaders only during the first decade of the twenty-first century. According to Steven Bernstein:

> The immediate post-cold war period marked an interregnum: a brief honeymoon of optimism for a renewed multilateralism and new global bargains among old foes as well as rich and poor. International economic institutions gained in authority, a host of global issues largely buried beneath cold war priorities began to receive a serious political hearing, and a new engagement with civil society in global affairs promised to extend the reach and legitimacy of institutions of global and regional governance . . . But a *global* world where transactions, ideas and even human beings cannot easily be blocked at borders' edges, requires a reconstitution of multilateralism, at a minimum and perhaps even a shift to a new paradigm of governance altogether.[20]

Global multilateral institutions were initiated by the Bretton Woods Conference to establish, promote, and sustain a post-war global order. For 40 years this order remained relatively intact. But as a result of the tremendous changes that occurred at the end of the 1980s and 1990s, such as the destruction of the bipolar global balance, these institutions could no longer operate efficiently enough without altering their functions. As of 2008 they are beginning the process of reform, with the aim to reflect new developments, such as the existence of the GMP and the new role of EMCs that were non-existent at the time of the

Bretton Woods Conference. Nonetheless, the GMP and the global community in general need multilateral institutions such as the UN, the World Bank, and the WTO, but the existence of the IMF as an institution separate from the World Bank is questionable. For the special needs of the global business community, more diverse multilateral institutions are needed. The number of multilateral institutions will grow to reflect the increasing level of economic and business integration in the GMP, as changes in any part of the world influence the overwhelming majority of other regions and industries.

Another important organizational form is the international and global non-governmental organization (NGO). According to Professors David Held, Anthony McGrew and David Goldblatt:

> Although governments and states remain, of course, powerful actors, they now share the global arena with an array of other agencies and organizations. The state is confronted by an enormous number of intergovernmental organizations (IGOs), international agencies and regimes which operate across different spatial reaches, and by quasi-supranational institutions, like the European Union. Non-state actors or transnational bodies, such as multinational corporations, transnational pressure groups, professional associations, social movements etc., also participate intensively in global politics. So too do many subnational actors and national pressure groups, whose activities often spill over into the international arena. Thus, the global arena can be conceived of as a polyarchic "mixed actor system" in which political authority and sources of political action are widely diffused . . . This conception alone challenges the conventional Westphalian, state-based or realist characterization of the global political order.[21]

NGOs play an increasingly important role in the emerging global order. These organizations are funded by voluntary donations by private parties that support their humanitarian missions and orientation for the resolution of the most challenging problems of humankind. The following box offers a quick glance at the different types of NGOs and their missions.

Established in 1984, International Medical Corps "is a global, humanitarian, non-profit organization dedicated to saving lives and relieving suffering through health care training and relief and development programs."[22]

Founded in 1961, the Academy for Educational Development "is a nonprofit organization working globally to improve education, health, civil society and economic development—the foundation of thriving societies." It has more than 250 programs serving people in more than 150 countries.[23]

Founded in 1971, Médicins Sans Frontières/Doctors Without Borders "is an independent international medical humanitarian organization that delivers emergency aid to people affected by armed conflict, epidemics, natural or man-made disasters, or exclusion from health care in nearly 60 countries."[24]

Formed in 1995, Oxfam International "is a confederation of 13 organizations working together with over 3,000 partners in more than 100 countries to find lasting solutions to poverty and injustice."[25]

The NGO Committee on Migration is an organization with the goal "to encourage the promotion and protection of migrants and their human rights, in accordance with the United Nations Charter."[26]

It is also important to mention the function of the International Olympic Committee in the global community due to the role of athletics in humankind's development.

Technology is an increasingly important instrument in the formation of the global order and its subsequent influence on world affairs. Consider, for example, the power of the company Google, which accounts for nearly 60 percent of all Internet searches and therefore information flows.[27] In the relationship between corporations and global institutions, dialectics are very evident; the GMP influences these organizations and companies and vice versa. This is also true regarding the relationship of the GMP with all multilateral institutions and NGOs, the majority of which represent the global business community as well, which are all part of the global business order. Revolutionary changes in the global business community at the end of the twentieth century became the objective conditions for the birth of the global business order. According to Indu B. Singh, an author of several books on technological trends:

> The global business community is beset by incessant change. In general, the change in global business is largely the consequence of significant economic and technological revolutions of the post-industrial society. The cumulative result of these revolutions is leading the way to: (a) a new world economic order, (b) creation of the global economy and market, (c) heightened importance of electronic business communications, and (d) the blurring of industry boundaries and competitors.
>
> Two important economic and technical changes made during the 1990s will further revolutionize the business community. They are: (a) the growth of transnational corporations and (b) the integral use of global networks to meet the revolutionary needs of transnational corporations. These changes will redefine the global business order and the nature of global business communications . . . Underlying the growth in the transnational corporation, global economy and markets will be the increased requirement for moving information around the world. In today's global business environment, the global networks and the value-added services they provide are critical to successful business strategies. Whatever the business, corporations in the future will run that business on the network.[28]

When the global order loses the support of the global and regional superpowers, its influence and sustainability immediately decrease, as do the institutions that represent and implement the order. This inevitably leads to the decline and disintegration of the global order, triggering the eventual development of a new order. Who is in charge of the global order? When the representatives of 44 nations met in Bretton Woods, they did not concoct a secret, self-serving organization. The delegates of this meeting were scholars, visionaries, and governmental officials. The meeting was open to all Allied member countries. The Bretton Woods Committee, which some conspiracy theorists cite as a secretive body, is actually a very open organization. Detailed information and data about all major multilateral institutions and international think-tanks is available via the Internet. Conflicts, disasters, etc., throughout the GMP and in the world make the absence of a global, all-powerful institution obvious and instead indicate the existence (barely) of poorly coordinated monitoring authorities of global processes. Multilateral institutions of the global order are unable to prevent global, regional, and industrial crises and are actually quite dysfunctional. The global order needs improved coordination among its established institutions, as well as new, more effective institutions. Mankind's technological achievements have created a base for such a global order. The harmonization of national laws, by-laws, and constitutions of regional economic organizations and other regional bodies would enable the development of a global order with specific political and economic priorities as well as the technological and legal capabilities to implement them. As of 2008 the global order is an informal political, social, and economic phenomenon with a shortage of efficient institutions, challenging its sustainability. Nonetheless, it is not an institutional phenomenon and is more objective than subjective, due to the fact that it is the reflection of mostly objective global trends, basic economic factors, and realities of a social and cultural nature. There is no single multilateral institution, including the UN, that has the definitive "global order" document, to implement in practice, and the preparation of such an order is not on the agenda of any multilateral institution. However, all multilateral institutions should develop documents with an orientation for their member countries that establishes the principles and objectives of the global order. A compendium of these documents would be a base for a universally accepted doctrine of the global order. Is it good for humankind that strategists and leaders have not developed a doctrine of the global order's principles and priorities? It would be better for the global community if there were an annual study of the global order, which could provide an orientation for multilateral institutions, governments, and corporate and NGO leadership. Multilateral institutions, of course, can present several different observations reflecting the status quo, and even make forecasts. One of the first such forecasts was the global forecast for the year 2000, developed in the 1970s under the auspices of the UN with the leadership of the Nobel laureate in economics, Wassily Leontief. The destiny of this document is not unusual—not a single international leader even considered employing it for practical needs. The global community is always forced to deal with many challenges with limited resources. Humankind needs to develop a coordinated and globally accepted order in which to use these resources and priorities for the resolution of major challenges and global problems. In this way, the global order as a doctrine is definitely needed. This doctrine should not be understood as a directive but as an orientation. It should be used to organize the activity of multilateral institutions and national governments behind consensus or majority-backed goals. If the global order can emerge organically through international structures and national governments, the doctrine should be a document that lays out principles that are endorsed by a qualified majority of multilateral institutions and national governments. This document would be very useful for corporate strategists, especially during the development of the corporate vision (see Chapter 6).

Objective and Subjective Factors Influencing the Global Business Order

The global order of the first quarter of the twenty-first century has predetermined the global business order, until 2025–2030. Prior to this period, the appearance of new countries on the political map of the world, the maturation of the global workplace and the GMP, and the appearance of new technologies will most likely require revision of the global order, and the priorities of the doctrine of the global order, which will most likely exist by that point, will have to be rethought and changed accordingly. Insofar as the interests of international business are concerned, the current global order is one of the best and most prosperous in history. The widespread liberalization of the GMP that occurred after the Cold War will continue, albeit at a slower pace. The role of national governments as regulators (a subjective factor) is increasing. However, it will not reach the point where national governments negatively intervene in private business on a large scale. One key improvement in the global order will be the emergence of a global component in corporate strategies oriented to the resolution of major challenges facing civilization. This will lead to the development of another influential factor in the global order: a trilateral relationship between global institutions, national governments, and corporations. This trilateral relationship will be a result of the influence of objective factors that shape the global order and its subsystems. For example, the limits and eventual depletion of certain elements of basic economic resources (such as hydrocarbon reserves) will have a major impact on the global order and its subsystem—the global business order. Resource shortages have the potential to entirely reconfigure the global order. If leading oil- and gas-producing countries were to suddenly run out of these resources, their role in the GMP would change, and the global order would readjust accordingly. Despite short-term signals in the GMP regarding the influence of oil-rich countries from the Middle East, their role and influence is actually quite limited and in some cases insignificant. Examples of other objective factors that will have a strong influence on the emerging global order are the capacity of the environment to withstand the negative impact of industry, natural and technogenic disasters, or the outbreak and pandemic spread of infectious disease.

Subjective factors also shape the global order. The impact of these factors can be both positive and negative. Examples of negative subjective factors are global terrorism, religious extremism, and intolerance, all of which can lead to war. An important positive subjective factor is the increasing cooperation among national governments and multilateral institutions, especially concerning environmental protection, hunger, and poverty. A few examples of this include the establishment of consensuses, such as the UN Millennium Project, the Doha Development Agenda, and the Kyoto Protocol. Although none of these multilateral agreements was universally accepted, they nonetheless had a significant positive impact on the global agenda, which is itself a subjective factor of the global order. During the first quarter of the twenty-first century, it is likely that the Kyoto Protocol (a legally binding document unifying nations' approach to international emissions trading and a clean development mechanism) and the Doha Agenda (a mandate on negotiations and implementation in agriculture and service industries of developing countries and EMCs) will be updated, overwhelmingly accepted, and used as a guideline for the development and reorganization of institutions of the global order. Multilateral, regional, national, and corporate organizational structures, which themselves are all parts of the global order, are also subjective factors that influence it.

The Factor of Global Trends

Ten key modern global trends and their influence were analyzed in detail in Chapter 3. The aim of this section is to underline their role as objective factors on the emerging global order. The majority of these trends have a positive influence on the GMP. Even trends that create challenges, such as the increasing shortages of natural resources, actually create positive incentives. Such shortages force the business world to allocate resources toward the development of alternative sources of energy, substitutes for raw materials, and other environmentally friendly technologies. The knowledge-based economy will play a crucial role in developing these technologies, making it possible for even small countries to be among the leaders in these fields. The best example of this is Iceland, the first country to develop a hydrogen-based national economy. The knowledge economy is analyzed throughout this book, but in this section, it is important to understand its implications for the emerging global order. As the great visionary Peter Drucker put it, the world needs "to develop an economic theory appropriate to a world economy in which knowledge has become the key economic resource and the dominant, if not the only, source of comparative advantage."[29] Knowledge-based technologies are the major answer to environmental challenges. Humankind will not reduce production. In fact, as the population grows, the production of necessary foodstuffs, goods, and services will continue to increase. The best option is to change the technological base of production to improve efficiency and reduce its impact on the environment. This is the only rational method for protecting the environment without compromising world needs. Eventually, as a result of the penetration of knowledge-based technologies, the emerging global order will restrict the use of non-environmentally friendly technologies. Knowledge-based technologies are the foundation for resolving of other global challenges, such as pandemics and poverty. All of these issues appeared on the global agenda at the end of the twentieth century. The collapse of most dictatorships allowed the establishment of a global consensus on the importance of human rights and human values, the only perspective from which global challenges should be strategically understood if they are to be eventually overcome. While some may argue that a global consensus on human rights does not yet exist, it must at least be conceded that the mindset of leaders is moving in the direction of accepting this as the highest priority.

The Global Optimum

As early as the 1970s, the idea of a global optimum was under discussion amongst scholars and world leaders, including representatives of dictatorial regimes. Unfortunately, the mindset of many economists and strategists regarding the global optimum was backward. Their priorities were the resolution of major international challenges, such as nuclear pro-liferation, the establishment of agreed-upon national borders, international trade and tariffs, and the strengthening of national economies in the competitive environment of the bipolar world. While these are clearly important objectives, the most important issue of all—the quality of life of individuals—was ignored. Dictatorial concepts of the global optimum were heavily influenced by a general disdain for human rights and the tension of the Cold War. The protection of human rights, routinely violated by repressive regimes, was a subject of political debate and was nowhere near a globally accepted value.

The failure of the bipolar global order provided the opportunity to establish a nearly global consensus on human rights, placing the quality of individuals' lives as the top priority of the pyramid of the global optimum (see Figure 5.1). For the most part, the emerging global order is already centered on the concept of the global optimum. The highest priorities of the global agenda are essentially based on the need to improve the quality of life of every individual on the planet. The focus has shifted to issues such as the prevention of epidemics of infectious diseases, the discovery of solutions to poverty and famine, universal access to freshwater and basic education, as well as the resolution of other challenges that threaten human dignity, such as issues of migration and unemployment. The strengthening of national economies and their regional and global integration leads to the continued improvement of international trade and business cooperation, subsequently bringing humankind closer to the global optimum. However, these positive developments are only a base upon which the standard of living of every human being will eventually be improved: this is a pyramid that stands on its base. The concept of the global optimum asserts that global progress cannot be made if it comes at the expense of individual citizens. The con-tinued improvement of the standard of living for people in developed countries, as well as of those in EMCs, cannot come at the expense of individuals in developing and underdeveloped nations. This is the basic vision of the great Italian–Swiss economist Vilfredo Pareto (1848–1923). He developed the "Pareto Optimum," which is based on *ophelimity*, a term invented by Pareto that can be understood as "economic gratification." In Pareto's words:

> We will say that the members of a collectivity enjoy *maximum ophelimity* in a certain position when it is impossible to find a way of moving from that position very slightly in such a manner that the ophelimity enjoyed by each of the individuals of that collect-ivity increases or decreases. That is to say, any small displacement in departing from that position necessarily has the effect of increasing the ophelimity which certain indi-viduals enjoy, and decreasing that which others enjoy, of being agreeable to some, and disagreeable to others.[30]

In accordance with Pareto's ideas, the global order must be organized so that economic development occurs without negatively affecting any individuals. Although this idea was developed roughly a century ago, the critical mass of political, economic, and technological achievements have only recently emerged to enable it to become a fundamental and practical concept of the global order. Pareto's understanding of maximum ophelimity is the most efficient and equitable understanding of the global optimum, although some scholars, such as his contemporary Johann Gustav Knut Wicksell (1851–1926), criticized Pareto for confusing the social optimum with competitive equilibrium.[31] This could be understood as a confusion during Pareto and Wicksell's time, but in the twenty-first century, with the increasing priority of improving the well-being of individuals and the devastating consequences of the violation of national interests, the Pareto principle is more applicable than ever. New technologies, information systems, the harmonization of statistical and reporting systems, and the experience of global institutions have made it more possible than ever before to control and monitor the implementation of the Pareto Optimum by the appropriate number of dimensions of the GMP. "Steuer [1986] showed that the size of the Pareto Global Optimum set typically grows with an increasing number of constraints, variables, and objectives for a general multiobjective optimization problem."[32] What would happen if Pareto's maximum ophelimity were achieved on a global scale—meaning that no one's quality of life could be improved without coming at the expense of someone else's? In such a hypothetical situation, technological innovation, such as improved productivity of arable land, advancements in genetic engineering of food, technological solutions to draughts, etc., could expand the boundaries of maximum ophelimity. Although Pareto's ideas are theoretical, they have practical implications. Future global orders must be organized in such a way that economic development occurs without creating tension and social conflict.

Economists and sociologists have developed several guidelines by which to achieve new levels of global prosperity and bring civilization closer to the global optimum. The Washington Consensus, a term as widely known as it is criticized, is an example of such a path to future prosperity. John Williamson, an economist from the Peterson Institute of

Figure 5.1 The Global Optimum in the Global Business Order.
Source: © Dr Vladimir Kvint, 2008.

International Economics (Washington, DC) (http://www.petersoninstitute.org/), proposed this term in 1989 as a summary of the development theories advocated by Washington-based multilateral institutions. Although it originally referred to Latin America, it eventually became associated with the general development policies of Bretton Woods institutions for non-developed countries. According to a 2002 speech by Dr Williamson, the Washington Consensus consisted of the following 10 points:

1. "Fiscal Discipline. This was in the context of a region where almost all the countries had run large deficits that led to balance of payments crises and high inflation that hit mainly the poor because the rich could park their money abroad.
2. Reordering Public Expenditure Priorities. This suggested switching expenditure in a pro-poor way, from things like indiscriminate subsidies to basic health and education.
3. Tax Reform. Constructing a tax system that would combine a broad tax base with moderate marginal tax rates.
4. Liberalizing Interest Rates. In retrospect I wish I had formulated this in a broader way as financial liberalization, and stressed that views differed on how fast it should be achieved.
5. A Competitive Exchange Rate. I fear I indulged in wishful thinking in asserting that there was a consensus in favor of ensuring that the exchange rate would be competitive, which implies an intermediate regime; in fact Washington was already beginning to subscribe to the two-corner doctrine.
6. Trade Liberalization. I stated that there was a difference of view about how fast trade should be liberalized.
7. Liberalization of Inward Foreign Direct Investment. I specifically did not include comprehensive capital account liberalization, because that did not command a consensus in Washington.
8. Privatization. This was the one area in which what originated as a neoliberal idea had won broad acceptance. We have since been made very conscious that it matters a lot how privatization is done: it can be a highly corrupt process that transfers assets to a privileged elite for a fraction of their true value, but the evidence is that it brings benefits when done properly.
9. Deregulation. This focused specifically on easing barriers to entry and exit, not on abolishing regulations designed for safety or environmental reasons.
10. Property Rights. This was primarily about providing the informal sector with the ability to gain property rights at acceptable cost."[33]

The Washington Consensus came under attack by anti-globalization protestors and several prominent scholars, including Joseph Stiglitz, Nobel laureate in economics (2001). In response to such criticism, Dr Willamson argued:

> [S]ome of the most vociferous of today's critics of what they call the Washington Consensus, most prominently Joe Stiglitz . . . do not object so much to the agenda laid out above as to the neoliberalism that they interpret the term as implying. I of course never intended my term to imply policies like capital account liberalization . . . monetarism, supply-side economics, or a minimal state (getting the state out of welfare provision and income redistribution), which I think of as the quintessentially neoliberal ideas.[34]

The neoliberalism to which Dr Williamson refers can be understood as the process of liberalization of the world economy, which took place at the last quarter of the twentieth century. The negative result of this was the subversion of the role of national governments, which is especially dangerous in times of global crises. The roots of these ideas can be traced to Nobel laureate in economics Milton Friedman, though in practice his ideas were often vulgarized.

In 2004, Joshua Cooper Ramo, a member of the Council of Foreign Relations, described an emerging alternative to the Washington Consensus, which he called the "Beijing Consensus." He underlined the economic success of China and the importance of its progress, not only for China itself but also for other states that would like to model their development on China's rapid economic growth. He discusses the possibility of the replacement of the Washington Consensus by the Beijing Consensus. In his words:

> To the degree China's development is changing China it is important; but what is far more important is that China's new ideas are having a gigantic effect outside of China. China is marking a path for other nations around the world who are trying to figure out not simply how to develop their countries, but also how to fit into the international order in a way that allows them to be truly independent, to protect their way of life and political choices in a world with a single massively powerful centre of gravity. I call this new physics of power and development the Beijing Consensus. It replaces the widely-discredited Washington Consensus, an economic theory made famous in the 1990s for its prescriptive, Washington-knows-best approach to telling other nations how to run themselves.[35]

He goes on to describe the "continuing US failure" to expedite "a shift from power politics to moral politics."[36] This statement really calls into question the legitimacy of Cooper Ramo's entire argument. Even the harshest critics of the United States are not so naive as to expect the communist dictatorship of China to have a foreign policy based more on "moral politics" than that of the US. In fact, the strategy of China's dictatorship seems to be based solely on "power politics," with a total absence of any observable morality.

Mr Cooper Ramo is very critical of the Washington Consensus, but he never gives a concrete outline of the Beijing Consensus' policies. China's strategy has definitely resulted in a substantial increase in economic development and improvement in the standard of living of the Chinese people. And it is quite possible that Chinese economic output will equal and even surpass that of the United States. However, there is no indication that the standard of living in China will even approach that of the US. Furthermore, although the Chinese Communist Party has implemented basic economic freedom, political freedom is obviously non-existent in China. Using the Chinese example as a development model for emerging-market, developing, and underdeveloped countries would represent a major shift in priorities away from valuing individual lives to valuing economic statistics. The Beijing Consensus is heavily influenced by economic determinism, which is, as previously discussed, an inappropriate perspective by which to strategically understand the world. Economic determinism played a substantial role in the outgoing global order of Bretton Woods, but the new order has to place human rights and the individual's quality of life at the top of its agenda; economic prosperity is only a means to this end. This is especially important as the emerging global order is and will be experiencing the strong influence of several negative subjective factors and trends. The subjective factor that represents the greatest threat to the global order is the impact of global terrorism and extremism. According to Professor Francis Fukuyama of Johns Hopkins University:

> In the international system, stateness has been under attack and eroded de facto for a variety of reasons. States throughout the less-developed world are weak, and the end of the Cold War led to the emergence of a band of failed and troubled states from Europe

to South Asia. These weak states have posed threats to international order because they are the source of conflict and grave abuses of human rights and because they have become potential breeding grounds for a new kind of terrorism that can reach into the developed world. Strengthening these states has become vital to international security but is one that few developed countries have mastered.[37]

Unfortunately, for most of the twenty-first century, this global challenge will not be resolved. The terrorist attacks of September 11, 2001, accelerated the decline of romantic ideas of complete liberalization of international economic and trade relations, which began during the Asian crisis of 1997. This was the moment when humankind began to understand that the plague of terrorism cannot be stopped by words and scolding. The good will of humankind has to be reoriented to fight back against individuals, institutions, and national governments that even slightly support terrorism and extremism. It further underlines the fact that the value of human life has to be the top priority for the emerging global order. The negative economic impact of terrorism is analyzed in Chapter 3; the focus of this section is to remind strategists that this factor is always crucial to consider during the development and implementation of strategy in any country or region. It is especially important for businesses or investments related to or allocated in countries with state-supported or -sponsored terrorism and their neighboring countries. Unfortunately, even countries halfway across the globe are vulnerable to the destructive impact of state-sponsored terrorism.

An evaluation of the new objective and subjective factors of the global order that appeared at the end of the twentieth century, as well as a reevaluation of traditional factors of the global order, illustrate the changing balance of power between countries and regions in the GMP and have led to the emergence of the global business order. They also indicate the changing balance between the global order and the global business order, in which the role of politics is less central but still important. The formation and functioning of the GMP have created the need for a new global order and a new global business order, particularly tailored to the twenty-first-century GMP.

Triggering Events of the Formation of the Emerging Global Business Order

Several triggering events demonstrated that the global order envisioned at Bretton Woods required more than cosmetic changes. The first major signal of the eroding relevance of Bretton Woods institutions was the failure of the gold-dollar standard system in 1971, when the US declined the request of France and other European nations to fulfill its obligation to unlimitedly convert dollars into gold at a fixed rate. While

> the last vestiges of gold were not purged from the system until after the gold window was shut for official international transactions in 1971, the US gold stock had little (if any) effective influence on the behavior of money supply after World War II.[38]

However, due to the role of the United States in the world economy and of the dollar as the dominant reserve and banking currency, this first Bretton Woods crisis was solved, at least for the following 30 years. Only the birth of the euro and the growing regional role of the currencies of several emerging regional superpowers—the Japanese yen, the Chinese yuan, the Russian ruble, and the new Brazilian real (introduced in 1994)—reinforced the currency shortcomings of the Bretton Woods global order. Some regional currencies that appeared can actually strengthen the role of the dollar. For example, if Persian Gulf countries such as Bahrain, Qatar, the United Arab Emirates, Oman, Kuwait, and Saudi Arabia were to establish a regional currency, which is a realistic possibility, it would undoubtedly be related to the dollar, though not pegged. This is because all of the economies of these countries rely on exports of crude oil, which is globally traded in US dollars. Any changes in the dollar would inevitably influence this regional currency. In general, the unification of currencies on a regional base, which could happen in Latin America, Africa (Afro currency), and among the countries of Oceania, could lead to a reform in the global business order, as shared currencies are always the result of regional integration and the influence of the continuation of this process. However, none of them would pose a challenge to the dollar's role as the ultimate banking currency.

The failure of most dictatorships and the subsequent demolition of barriers to internationalization increased the interdependence of national economies and led to one of the most active periods in business history. This period was one of the most important triggering events for the development of a framework to guide the continuing internationalization of business culminating in its eventual globalization. The increasing intergovernmental economic relations among newly free-market-oriented countries and with governments and businesses of the developed world created a virtuous cycle of increasing momentum. EMCs were in desperate need of investment, governmental aid, and a new level of cooperation with multilateral institutions. This process would not have taken place had the developed world not aggressively sought the best investment opportunities in newly emerging markets. The increasing internationalization of business led to the emergence of globalized corporations, i.e. companies with more foreign than domestic affiliates. The most globalized of these operate in almost half of the countries of the world. Among them are not only global delivery and logistics companies such as Deutsche Post AG and natural resource-oriented ones such as the Royal Dutch/Shell Group or Total—a multinational energy company headquartered in France—but also high-tech companies such as IBM and Philips Electronics and food producers such as Nestle (see Table 5.1).

This phenomenon has not been restricted to the developed world. Several corporations from EMCs, some of which operate in more than 30 countries, have also become globalized. According to the 2007 UN World Investment Report, 17 corporations based in EMCs rank among the world's top 100 most-internationalized companies (see Table 5.2). Although they are not among the top companies of this list, the dynamics of internationalization will surely raise the rankings of corporations from EMCs and increase their numbers on these

Table 5.1 Top Ten Multinational Corporations Ranked by the Number of Host Countries and the Geographical Spread Index, 2005[39]

Rank	Corporation	Home Economy	Number of Host Countries	Geographical Spread Index*
1	Deutsche Post AG	Germany	103	93.1
2	Royal Dutch/Shell Group	United Kingdom, Netherlands	96	71.1
3	Nestle SA	Switzerland	94	93.9
4	Siemens AG	Germany	85	79.6
5	BASF AG	Germany	84	80.8
6	Bayer AG	Germany	76	75
7	Procter & Gamble	United States	72	74.9
8	IBM	United States	66	77.3
9	Philips Electronics	Netherlands	62	67.7
10	Total	France	62	65.3

Note: * The Geographical Spread Index is calculated as the square root of the Internationalization Index (the number of foreign affiliates divided by the number of all affiliates) multiplied by the number of countries in which a company operates.

types of evaluations. The strategic significance of globalized companies from EMCs will continue to grow.

The rise of globalized companies has created new strategically significant implications for human resource executives and search companies. Human integration has become a major trend for these global companies' human resource departments, which have to coordinate the integration of thousands of employees from a multitude of countries, cultures, ethnicities, religions, etc., toward shared goals and ethics. This has created a new global business culture, an important quality of the emerging global business order. The most successful globalized companies have become integrated within the business systems of foreign countries in which they operate, to the point that they are essentially *multi-domestic organizations*. Local people, who use their products and services and even work for them, do not see these corporations as foreign entities. Multi-domestic organizations often name their local subsidiaries in the language and preferences of the local culture. In some cases people are not even aware that these companies are foreign entities. Globalized companies can also be seen as an important factor for the prevention of international conflict because they are typically very influential, combining the interests of nations, companies, and individuals throughout the world. Countries in business with one another usually engage in open conflict only as a last resort. These are just a few of the important qualities of globalized companies that strategists should take into account.

Increased internationalization of businesses illustrated the absence of appropriate global regulations to optimize this process. The need for new global institutions to cooperate in real time to regulate international financial, currency, and inter-banking transactions has became obvious. The Bretton Woods multilateral institutions (especially the IMF) were overwhelmed by these unanticipated economic and business needs. Instead of adapting to the new reality, they continued to use traditional outdated methods that were mostly

Table 5.2 Top Multinational Corporations from EMCs from the List of the Top 100 Multinational Corporations Ranked by the Number of Host Countries and the Geographical Spread Index, 2005[40]

Rank	Corporation	Home Economy	Number of Host Countries	Geographical Spread Index*
51	Cemex SA	Mexico	35	58.1
60	Mittal Steel Company NV**	Netherlands	32	55.7
61	Samsung Electronics	Republic of Korea	32	53.2
65	Flextronics International Ltd.	Singapore	30	52.1
76	LG Corp.	Republic of Korea	24	48.4
77	Telefonica	Spain	24	43.5
80	Singtel Ltd.	Singapore	24	24.5
81	Acer Inc.	Taiwan	23	39.3
85	Neptune Orient Lines Ltd.	Singapore	20	35.3
90	Lukoil	Russian Federation	19	26.1
92	Repsol YPF SA	Spain	17	24
93	CRH PLC	Ireland	16	38.7
94	Lenovo Group	China	15	37.6
95	Hutchinson Whampoa	Hong Kong	15	36.8
97	Orient Overseas International Ltd.	Hong Kong	14	32
98	Endesa	Spain	14	25.6
100	Hon Hai Precision Industries	Taiwan	13	32.1

Notes:
*The Geographical Spread Index is calculated as the square root of the Internationalization Index (the number of foreign affiliates divided by the number of all affiliates) multiplied by the number of countries in which a company operates.
**The source for this table did not reflect the fact that Mittal Steel Company is now part of Arcelor Mittal.

oriented for relationships with governmental institutions and did not reflect in their functions the full capacity of modern technologies and opportunities of the GMP. According to Professor Steven Bernstein of the University of Toronto, during this period, "global institutions simultaneously face challenges to their legitimacy and increasing demands to widen their scope and authority in response to material and social forces associated with globalization."[41]

Two almost completely independent, international spheres emerged—the global business world and the world of intergovernmental and multilateral institutions. Due to the Bretton Woods institutions' inability to adapt to these developments, the practical need for new global institutions became clear. The practical needs of businesses acted as a trigger for the accelerated development of three new phenomena—the GEM; the global workplace; and the GMP, which unified the GEM and the global workplace. None of these phenomena would exist without the technological advancements achieved in response to the interests of international business. Some authors evaluate the role of technology in the reengineering of the global business order to such an extent that they refer to the new "techno-economic paradigm," the major features of which are:

- "New forms of organizational 'best practice'
- New skill profiles affecting worker quality/quantity
- New 'product mix' through new technology
- New innovation trends (radical & incremental) to use new low-cost technology
- New patterns in investment locations—changing comparative advantage
- Growth of small innovative firms in rapidly growing technology sectors
- Concentration by large firms in new sectors—growth, diversification
- New patterns of consumer behavior, consumption and economic distribution"[42]

Technologies such as the Internet, the concentrated result of many scientific, knowledge-based developments that were almost unknown, became essential tools for global businesses in a matter of five years, especially in the globalization of financial markets of derivatives and futures and options operating in real time.

The delayed reaction of Bretton Woods institutions and the increasing need for cross-border cooperation among businesses without appropriate regulations by global institutions accelerated the creation of regional economic organizations. The internationalization of national economies, initiated by national governments of developed countries and EMCs as a means of increasing national economic efficiency, accelerated this process. These organizations were primarily business oriented. By the middle of the 1990s, regional organizations became substantially more efficient for many economic, business, and financial functions than global Bretton Woods institutions. This triggered all parties to initiate the development of a new framework for a more effective global business order, which then became an unrecognized reality.

Another triggering event was the realization by the business community of its social responsibilities. This understanding developed rapidly and became a global issue as multinational corporations were forced to come to terms with widespread public backlashes from countries and communities in which they operated irresponsibly. The birth of the GMP and the development of global business triggered a more intense level of competition, forcing businesses to seek new, untapped markets. This led to the development of strategies to exploit the purchasing power of the so-called BOP. While the individuals of this market may have very limited purchasing power, as an aggregate, its no fewer than two billion people represent a huge potential market. The emergence of BOP strategies is another trigger for the development of a global business order that will make this market more conducive to international business and protect individuals from exploitation as result of BOP-oriented strategies. Corporate social responsibility has already become a major characteristic of the emerging global business order.

Another major triggering event occurred in 1997, with the so-called Asian financial crisis, the global impact of which the Bretton Woods system did not prevent or manage. The Bretton Woods institutions, especially the IMF, failed largely because they incorrectly classified the crisis as a regional (Asian) one. In fact, the "Asian" crisis was just the beginning of a global financial crisis that finally ended in December 2001, in Argentina. The IMF also failed due to its emphasis on working primarily with national governments. It almost entirely ignored the private sector, even powerful, privately held currency funds, such as George Soros' Quantum Fund. The GEM, which, at that time, was still in its infancy, experienced tremendous damage as a result of the global order's traditional institutions' inability to prevent this crisis. The GEM was not even acknowledged by multilateral institutions. As of 2008, 11 years later, its existence still has not been adequately presented in the country classification of these agencies (see Chapter 4), which is another trigger of the need for reform of Bretton Woods institutions. It is also an obvious reason for the necessity of a new multilateral organizational structure that focuses specifically on sustainability and improvement of the global business order. Such an organizational structure could be known as the Global Business Coordinating Council (GBCC).

As a result of all of these events, there is a burgeoning need by businesses for professionals—especially strategists and economists—who can understand and anticipate new trends in the GMP and the upcoming global business order. As a result, the requirements for business education have changed. Companies need universities and business schools to produce graduates specially trained to work with and within the GMP and the GEM during their continuing internationalization and globalization. The global business order has already begun to emerge in response to these triggering events.

The Changing Roles of Multilateral Institutions in the Global Marketplace

Many events and power shifts among countries and regional organizations of the GMP have not been reflected in the functions, structure, and relationships of multilateral institutions with one another and with national governments and corporations. Representation of emerging superpowers such as China, India, Russia, and Brazil has not duly increased, and the growing importance of regional economic organizations is totally unrepresented in the activities and structures of the Bretton Woods institutions. As of 2008 the minor changes proposed by the managerial bodies of the World Bank and IMF do not adequately reflect the new reality of the GMP. These changes, which mostly evince a reshuffling of voting shares in favor of EMCs, ignore the role of regional economic organizations in the global workplace and GMP. Even the implementation of these moderate changes proposed by the executive directors of the World Bank can be done only by decision of the Board of Governors. However, the current members of this board at any particular time will not be very enthusiastic about giving more power and voting authority to representatives of other member countries from the GEM. No one on the Board of Governors wants to lose influence. Nevertheless, this change is inevitable and will most likely begin by the end of the first decade of the twenty-first century. More than that, no multilateral institution yet takes into account the existence of the GMP and the GEM (see Chapters 2 and 4).

The emerging global business order should reflect the changing balance of power in the world; a fundamental shift in the focus of these institutions is necessary. For example, rather than cooperating with the governments of EMCs, these institutions should cooperate primarily with the private sector, the GEM as a whole, and regional economic organizations. Currently, their main role is to provide cheap, below-market-rate loans and advice and expertise to the governments of non-developed countries. In some EMCs, the IMF helped to stabilize financial conditions, reduce inflation, establish financial market institutions, and bring national currencies closer to convertibility. However, most often, IMF loans did more to pad the pockets of corrupt bureaucrats and officials than to improve the lives of ordinary people. Loans that were not illegally appropriated by bureaucrats were used to artificially balance current accounts. This was done at the expense of future generations, who will have to repay the debt service of the increased foreign sovereign debt for years to come.

IMF-supported currency boards were also ineffectual. A currency board is

> a monetary regime based on an explicit legislative commitment to exchange domestic currency for a specified foreign currency at a fixed exchanged rate, combined with restrictions on the issuing authority—the currency board—to ensure the fulfillment of its legal obligation. This structure implies that domestic currency be issued only against foreign exchange and that it remain fully backed by foreign assets. Thus, it eliminates traditional central bank functions like monetary regulation and the lender of last resort.[43]

In most cases, attempts by the IMF to overrule domestic banking and financial institutions of EMCs ended in painful failure. For example, despite the IMF's establishment of a currency board in Argentina, the Asian financial crisis eventually spread to this country in 2001. Although it originated in Thailand in 1997 and was observable four years before it affected Argentina, the currency board did not anticipate it and did little to prevent its contagion to Latin America. As a result, inflation skyrocketed and the peg of the Argentine peso to the dollar disappeared. In Indonesia many experts were strongly against the creation of a currency board in 1999 because it was widely believed that the Indonesian dictator General Suharto would not be in office for much longer.

Only a couple of months after the establishment of the Indonesian currency board, the Suharto dictatorship collapsed, along with its currency board. The IMF currency board in Bulgaria was more effective, perhaps because it was established after the country was already relatively financially stable. After a mild financial crisis, the currency board successfully restricted the activity of inexperienced government financiers. It was also helpful in attracting FDI, which increased largely as a result of its existence. It continues to function, even after Bulgaria joined the EU in 2007, and will continue until it joins the European Economic and Monetary Union. Despite the Bulgarian example, currency boards are not necessary for a country to improve its financial and monetary situation. Ireland and Turkmenistan are great illustrations of this, as their financial and monetary situations vastly improved without their accepting a single dollar from the IMF. They were able to establish financial stability, resulting in improvements in the standard of living of their people. Ireland became one of the leading emerging markets of the world.

According to Dr Kurt Schuler "IMF-supported currency-board arrangements have been implemented in Argentina (est. 1 April 1991, abandoned 6 January 2002), Djibouti (est. 1949), Estonia (est. 20 June 1992), Lithuania (est. 1 April 1994), Bosnia (est. 1 August 1997), and Bulgaria (est. 1 July 1997).

There are several non-IMF-supported currency boards—mostly in former British colonies (see History of Orthodox Currency Boards below), such as Hong Kong, Bermuda, the Cayman Islands, the Falkland Islands, Gibraltar, and the Faroe Islands (part of Denmark).

Characteristics of a Currency Board

The main characteristics of a currency board are as follows.

Anchor currency: The anchor currency is a currency chosen for its expected stability and international acceptability. For most currency boards the British pound or the US dollar has been the anchor currency, though for some of the recent currency-board-like systems, the anchor currency is the euro. The anchor currency need not be issued by a central bank; a few currency boards have used gold as the anchor currency.

Convertibility: A currency board maintains full, unlimited convertibility between its notes and coins and the anchor currency at a fixed rate of exchange. Though an orthodox currency board typically does not convert local deposits denominated in its currency into the anchor currency, banks will offer to do so for a small fee.

A currency board has no responsibility for ensuring that bank deposits are convertible into currency-board notes. That is the sole responsibility of banks. The currency board concerns itself only with the notes and coins that it issues. Unlimited convertibility into the anchor currency means that in an orthodox currency board system, no restrictions exist on current-account transactions (buying and selling goods and services) or capital-account transactions (buying and selling financial assets, such as foreign bonds).

Reserves: A currency board's reserves are adequate to ensure that all holders of its notes and coins can convert them into the reserve currency or commodity. Currency boards often hold reserves of 105 or 110 percent of their liabilities, rather than just 100 percent, to have a margin of protection should the bonds they hold lose value.

Profits: Unlike bonds or most bank deposits, notes and coins do not pay interest; they are like an interest-free loan from the people who hold them to the issuer. The issuer's profit equals the interest earned on reserves minus the expense of putting the notes and coins into circulation. These expenses are typically less than 1 percent of assets per year. In addition, if the notes and coins are destroyed, the issuer's net worth increases, because liabilities are reduced but assets are not. Typically, the profits from a currency board left after paying all the board's expenses are roughly 1 percent of gross domestic product (GDP) a year.

Using currency issued by a currency board rather than using foreign currency, such as US dollars, directly captures seigniorage [the net revenue derived from issuing currency] for the domestic government. Also, use of a domestic currency board issue rather than a foreign currency satisfies nationalistic sentiment . . .

Relation to banks: Just as a currency board has no share in the profits of banks, it has no responsibility for acting as a lender of last resort to protect them from losses. Bank failures have been rare in orthodox currency-board systems. They have, however, been common in the recent currency-board-like systems, which have inherited many banking problems from the central banking systems that preceded them. Historical experience suggests that lenders of last resort usually create more problems than they solve, because their existence encourages banks to be less prudent than they would otherwise be. Accordingly, the best policy is to let troubled banks fail.

Though a currency board holds 100 percent or slightly greater foreign reserves, banks in a currency-board system are not required to imitate the currency board. Like banks in a central banking system, their reserves in excess of legal minimum requirements typically equal only a few percent of their liabilities. Another way to say this is that in a currency-board system, the monetary base (M0) has 100 percent foreign reserves, but broader measures of the money supply such as M1 (currency in circulation plus demand deposits) or M2 (currency in circulation plus demand deposits plus time deposits) do not have 100 percent reserves."[44]

The IMF practice of allocating quotas is also obsolete, unfair, and ineffectual. The Bretton Woods Formula, which the IMF still uses to determine voting share, does not reflect today's GMP. Many countries have fewer votes than they should. For example, as of 2008 China only accounts for only 3.66 percent of IMF votes, despite the size and influence of its economy. Similar discrepancies exist in the percentage of votes of Russia (2.69), Mexico (1.43), South Africa (0.85), and Turkey (0.55).[45] Bretton Woods institutions and leaders of its member countries already recognized the potential danger of this and have been seriously discussing this issue since 2006. According to award-winning journalist Emad Mekay:

> Officials of global organisations and rich nations rarely admit it but civil society groups and developing countries say the sad fact has not changed: multilateral bodies meant to help create a global community are in fact undemocratic. From the World Trade Organization (WTO), the International Monetary Fund (IMF), the World Bank and the United Nations, to Interpol and the World Health Organization (WHO), dozens of international agencies now work to regulate world trade, telecommunications, transportation, labour, business, health and the environment, among other issues. In almost all of those bodies, poor and powerless nations, like Somalia and Afghanistan, are under-represented while the rich and powerful, like Britain and the United States, operate with almost unchecked authority and overwhelming power . . . Directors from rich countries now control more than 60 percent of the votes at the World Bank and IMF, while the US administration has veto power over any extraordinary vote requiring a super-majority. Even in institutions like the Geneva-based WTO, which theoretically operates under consensus and technically gives each member country veto power, practice is different. Some 28 of the WTO's 146 member nations do not even attend most of the organisation's meetings for the simple reason that they lack the resources to set up diplomatic missions in the expensive Swiss city of Geneva. But those countries still figure as part of the consensus when decisions are made.[46]

The WBG does not allocate its loans proportionally to the poorest nations, even according to its own classification using income per capita. It considers China to be a lower-middle-income country, yet it allocates far more loans to China than it does to the extremely poor countries of sub-Saharan Africa and Southeast Asia (see Table 5.3). One might argue that because of China's huge population and its huge amount of poor people, it makes sense for it to receive more attention than other countries. This argument is refuted by the data in Table 5.3, which presents World Bank lending on a per capita basis. The 10 underdeveloped countries and one developing country in Table 5.3 receive less lending per capita *combined* than China. Every project that the World Bank finances in China could easily be financed by Chinese national reserves, which are the largest in the world. The World Bank has demonstrated the same questionable use of financial aid to several other countries that are not poor. For example, in 2008 the World Bank decided to finance 10 percent of a public financial education program in Russia. This is not logical due to the fact that Russia not only has the third-largest foreign currency reserves in the world but also allocates hundreds of billions of dollars into several other funds, as a result of its wealth of cash generated from the export of natural resources. The limited resources of the World Bank should go to the poorest nations of the world, such as Somalia, Sudan, and the Democratic Republic of Congo, which received such insignificant amounts of lending per capita that they were not included in Table 5.3.

The IMF also does not use its limited resources in a manner appropriate to the needs of the world's poorest people. Its reserves are not even as large as China's. As of 2008 the IMF's total financial resources are worth \$362 billion,[47] a figure dwarfed by China's foreign

Table 5.3 World Bank Lending (Comparison of China to Selected Underdeveloped and Developing Countries) ($), 2007[48]

Country	Total World Bank Lending ($), 2007	World Bank Lending per Capita ($), 2007
China	167,508,000,000	127.69
Central African Republic	100,000,000	24.42
Eritrea*	74,000,000	16.31
Burundi	120,000,000	15.32
Liberia	40,500,000	11.98
Gambia, The	12,000,000	7.73
Rwanda	70,000,000	7.57
Lao People's Democratic Republic	40,750,000	7.07
Malawi	70,000,000	5.32
Niger	70,000,000	4.86
Guinea	26,200,000	2.85
Bangladesh	379,000,000	2.63

Source: © Dr Vladimir Kvint, 2008.

Note: * 2005 data.

currency reserves alone, which are worth over $1 trillion. This does not take into consideration the $160 billion official reserves of Hong Kong[49] (larger than the reserves of the majority of European nations), which is, of course, part of the People's Republic of China. In fact, in addition to China, Taiwan, Russia, and South Korea all have larger reserves than the IMF (see Figure 1.21).

So-called "help" from the IMF, World Bank, and African Development Bank has caused the external debt of sub-Saharan countries to reach $218.5 billion as of 2008.[50] Most of this money was stolen by kleptocrats, never reaching those who desperately needed it. Without debt-relief, future generations will be overwhelmed by these obligations. In 2005, at the initiative of the G8 and the then prime minister of the United Kingdom, Tony Blair, 100 percent debt relief was granted to 18 countries, mostly in Africa and a few from Central and South American (Bolivia, Guyana, Honduras, and Nicaragua).[51] The United States is by far the largest contributor of official development assistance in absolute numbers; however, several European countries and Japan contribute more as a percentage of GNI.[52]

While the WBG does work with the private sector, it is struggling to compete with private banks, despite its below-market interest rates. Many companies of the GEM prefer private bank loans because of the WBG's constraining, bureaucratic safeguard policies. There is another strange practice of the World Bank—it penalizes countries for making payments ahead of the agreed-upon schedule, which obviously discourages borrowers from increasing their payments to the World Bank. As a result, money that the Bank could use to help struggling countries remains in the coffers of governments that do not necessarily need it. Changing this regulation should be a first priority, and it can be achieved simply by abolishing a bureaucratic barrier.

Other multilateral organizations monitor and regulate the business infrastructure of the GMP. These include the International Telecommunications Union (www.itu.int), Air Transport Association (www.iata.org), the International Labor Organization (www.ilo.org), the World Health Organization (www.who.int), and the UN Environment Programme (www.unep.org). Some of these organizations are part of the UN System of Organizations, while others are independent multilateral organizations or non-governmental global institutions. All of them, despite their business-related nature, work primarily with governments, the UN, and to a much lesser degree, with private businesses. This pattern should be changed according to the emerging global business order.

However, there is one exceptional organization, the International Chamber of Commerce (ICC) (www.iccwbo.org). "The ICC World Council is the equivalent of the general assembly of a major intergovernmental organization. The big difference is that the delegates are business executives and not government officials."[53] This organization is underestimated and underutilized by the global business community but can be a very powerful instrument to promote the global business order.

The new role of the Bretton Woods institutions should be to coordinate the activity of private businesses, international and global NGOs, and national governments to address the needs of the world's poorest people. The projects of highest priority should relate to freshwater access, alternative energy development, the prevention of epidemics, and famine alleviation. Another important objective of the new global business order will be to minimize risk in the GMP. In developing and underdeveloped countries, Bretton Woods institutions will still play a role in helping governments prepare and implement proper economic, financial, and business regulation.

The increasing regionalization of the GMP, especially in the GEM, requires a new role of the World Bank: dealing with regional economic organizations. One of the solutions to this issue will be the development of new regional banks that work within the framework of major regional blocs as well as with their territorial subsystems. One of the oldest regional banks in the world is the Inter-American Development Bank, which was established in 1959. Its mission is to "contribute to the acceleration of the process of economic and social development of the regional developing member countries, individually and collectively."[54] An example of a legally independent subsystem of the Inter-American Development Bank is the Andean Development Corp., a regional development bank that has loaned hundreds of millions of dollars to the governments of Colombia, Peru, and Venezuela, mostly to fund infrastructure projects.[55] More regional subsystems are beginning to emerge, such as the Mercosur Development Bank, the creation of which has been a topic of discussion in the meetings of the member countries of Mercosur.[56] The Caribbean Development Bank is a regional bank that has been operational since 1970.[57] These banks and their regional equivalents throughout the world will be instrumental in the motivation and practice of regional and sub-regional cooperation between companies of its country members. The major customers of these banks are businesses that focus on infrastructure and social development. Issues such as poverty, migration, and mass disease are high on their agenda. Their role has been increasing since the beginning of the twenty-first century, and this trend should continue. Regional banks and other financial, multilateral, credit, and microcredit institutions act as important mechanisms for the prevention of inter-regional crises and conflicts.

As in most institutions, there is a desire within the Bretton Woods system to maintain the status quo. This has been the case with past global orders. However, when global conditions change and the leaders of the current global order fail to adapt, it only expedites its destruction, as the global order becomes less and less relevant. Rather than resisting change, it would behove the current leaders, while they are still in power, to take an active part in the process of reforming multilateral institutions to meet the requirements of the emerging global order. As the economic dominance of countries changes so too does the global order.

New Authorities of the Global Business Order

First, current institutions have to change according to the new realities, balance of power, and ethics or international relations. These changes have to be substantial, to the extent that some of these institutions will no longer be required in the global arena, in response to the new, long-term global agenda. One of the most vocal critics of multilateral institutions is Steve Forbes, who is quoted in the article below:

> [Forbes argues] "if you didn't have the IMF, then lenders and investors would pay more attention" to the riskiness of their loans to developing nations. Left alone, investors and banks could have sorted out the Asian and Latin American crises better than the IMF did, Forbes said. Forbes also expressed skepticism about the IMF's sister agency, the World Bank, and of the US Agency for International Development.[58]

Second, there are several international organizations and de facto institutions such as the G8 meetings, the Bretton Woods Committee, and the World Economic Forum that already play an important role in focusing the opinion of the global community, especially global business leaders, on the major issues facing civilization. These institutions should be formally (de jure) institutionalized. In order for this to occur, mechanisms of practical implementation for the recommendations of these organizations should be developed through multilateral institutions and/or national governments.

G8 and its Likely Enlargement

The annual meeting of the heads of states and governments of the most powerful nations is a key part of the emerging global order. In 1975 the presidents and prime ministers of the six leading democratic countries (the United States, the United Kingdom, West Germany, Italy, France, and Japan) established an annual meeting under a rotating presidency to discuss global issues, such as energy security and global economic stability. This meeting became known as the Group of Six (G6). In 1976 the prime minister of Canada was invited, and it became the G7. After the disintegration of the Soviet Union, the president of the Russian Federation was invited, and the meetings became known as the G7 plus one: the Russian leader participated only in political, not economic, events. Since 1998, when Russia became a full member, the summit has been known as the G8. This group totally ignores the interests of several very powerful and important EMCs. It should expand to include countries such as Brazil, China, India, and South Africa, as well as possibly Egypt and Mexico. The role and function of the meeting of the expanded group (G14) should change to become a formal institution. The global community will accept the suggestions of this enlarged group with much less resistance and wider support on all levels of the decision-making processes. Although the G8 is a non-institutional group, its decisions and recommendations influence all multilateral institutions. It is possible to agree with those who argued that when China and the Soviet Union, two regional superpowers that are outside of the G8, were not included in the leadership of major multilateral institutions, they were practically excluded from the global order. When countries of such expansive territory and population are not part of the global order, the word "global" is a misnomer. China's inclusion in the major economic multilateral institutions

> raised key questions for both theory and practice as well as the prospect that the neoliberal international economic order might expand to include the two largest economies that had stood outside the order—China and the Soviet Union—and hence become a global economic order.[59]

This idea was expressed while the Soviet Union still existed, but the contents apply to today's Russia as well. Were the G8 to expand to include major EMCs, its unanimous decisions would have to be implemented by all multilateral institutions. Decisions and resolutions of the G14 would represent the opinions of the leaders of the most powerful countries of the world, the majority of which were democratically elected. The G8 also needs to increase its transparency, the relative lack of which has led some to consider it a conspiratorial and exploitive hegemon. For example, Professor Alison Bailin of the University of Toronto proposes

> a theory, called group hegemony that explains how a few wealthy countries, namely the G7, maintain the liberal economic order, and how the rules governing this order help perpetuate the disparity between rich and poor countries. The theory holds that the G7 replaced the US as the hegemon in the late 1970s. The G7 provides the public good of global economic stability. The Group responds to crises that directly influence G7 economies or threaten the perpetuation of the world economic order. The G7 does not prevent global problems nor govern the world order on a daily basis. It acts as a global government of last resort—a crisis manager—when other institutions prove inadequate to maintain world order. The G7 supplies resources, such as an international means of payment, large open markets, foreign investment, and funding for international institutions. These goods serve to entice the majority of countries to participate in and abide by the rules governing the world economic order. The group hegemon thus preserves its privileged international position by providing enough goods to integrate the wealthy and poor in to the world-system without changing the systemic distribution of power. The theory of group hegemony concludes that the wealthy few maintain the *global economic order* [emphasis added] and impart an institutional stability to the inequitable system.[60]

A casual examination of G8-meeting agendas clearly contradicts Professor Bailin's assertion of this organization as an exploitive hegemon. For example, at the 2007 G8 meeting in Heiligendamm, Germany, leaders of the G8 countries agreed to "stand by their commitment to considerably increase their official development assistance for Africa by 2010: by US$25 billion each year" and to pledge "US$60 billion a year over the coming years to fight HIV/AIDS, malaria and tuberculosis, especially for prevention programmes and to strengthen health systems in the least developed countries."[61]

The participation of key EMCs in "Group" meetings would fully represent the consensual opinion of the world. If the G8 were to become a formal institution, its power and transparency would increase. The influence of decisions of traditional Bretton Woods institutions would also increase, as they would implement "G14" resolutions. Its institutionalization will be a key element in the construction of the emerging global order. At any rate, institutionalization has to be accomplished not by increasing bureaucracy, but by making the implementation of G8+ decisions obligatory for existing multilateral institutions. This can be done by making changes to the by-laws and charter treaties of these institutions, where these countries already play a leading role.

The Bretton Woods Committee

For decades multilateral institutions had no agency by which to monitor and report to major donors (member countries) and offer a second opinion about the activities and plans of these institutions. Bretton Woods institutions were not only without a body to provide criticism, but they also lacked an organization to advocate certain activities and proposals. Finally, in 1983, to address these needs, the Bretton Woods Committee was established, upon the recommendation of two former US Treasury officials—Secretary Henry H. Fowler and Deputy Secretary Charles E. Walker. The mission of the committee is to "increase understanding of the World Bank, IMF, WTO and the regional development banks and their efforts to spur economic growth, alleviate poverty and improve financial stability."[62] The committee consists of economists, financiers, prominent business leaders, and politicians from around the world. The Bretton Woods Committee meeting takes place the day before the Joint Annual Meeting of the World Bank and IMF in the same location, so that its members do not have to travel just for the meeting. The Joint Annual Meeting is usually in Washington DC, the headquarters of both of these multilateral institutions and of the committee. Occasionally, these meetings take place outside of Washington, in different cities around the world.

Every meeting of the Bretton Woods Committee includes the participation of top-level officials from various countries, including the secretary of state and secretary of the treasury of the United States. After reports from the president of the World Bank, the managing director of the IMF, and the director-general of the WTO, there is usually a discussion and question and answer session. Following this, the committee makes its decision based on a consensus of the participants regarding the budgets of the Bretton Woods institutions and contributions of country members it will support for the next fiscal year. Two of the most impressive meetings were in July 1994 and in July 2004, when the anniversaries of the original Bretton Woods Conference were celebrated. Several participants from the original 1944 conference were at both of these meetings.

The Bretton Woods Committee also has as a subsidiary, the International Council, which includes in its membership top financial, business, and political leaders from around the world. The main function of this council, as well as of the committee itself, is to advise and monitor Bretton Woods institutions and political leaders of country members regarding these institutions' activity and to suggest alternatives, when warranted. There have been several Bretton Woods Committee annual meetings that took place outside of Washington and beyond the borders of the United States. In 1994 this meeting, as well as the Joint Annual Meeting of the World Bank and IMF, took place in Madrid. In 1998 these meetings occurred in Hong Kong, one year after the United Kingdom handed it over to the People's Republic of China. The reason for this location was to evaluate the functioning of Hong Kong's financial institutions and companies under Chinese authority. Each annual meeting of the World Bank and IMF, as well as of the Bretton Woods Committee, that occurs outside of Washington, DC, is used to verify a specific aspect of the global order.

With the increasing importance of the GEM, the Bretton Woods Committee began to give more attention to EMCs. On January 25, 2008, the Bretton Woods Committee, in partnership with the Center for Emerging Market Enterprises of The Fletcher School of Tufts University (Massachusetts), held a conference entitled "Strengthening Capital Markets in Emerging Market Countries." At this meeting, the lack of definition of an EMC and the implications of this for multilateral institutions and the global business community were discussed. As an indication of the openness of this organization, the entirety of this conference, including speakers' PowerPoint presentations, is available at the Bretton Woods Committee's web site (http://www.brettonwoods.org/events.html).

World Economic Forum

After the first 30 years of the Bretton Woods institutions, it become apparent that their major shortcoming was the absence of cooperation with the business community, scholars, and individual visionaries. The failure of the gold standard system in 1971 made these shortcomings obvious—the missions of Bretton Woods institutions were not in tune with the new objectives of humankind. These objectives were mostly related not to the interest of victorious countries of World War II, but to individuals around the world, through the resolution of issues related to poverty, mass disease, migration, and similar damaging issues (see Chart 5.1). More than that, leaders of these multilateral institutions were not familiar with these objectives, or were at least not focused on their implementation. Several attempts were made to change the situation. One of the first such attempts was the establishment in 1968 of the Club of Rome. Its original agenda focused only on Western European issues, but its mission has evolved to "act as a global catalyst of change that is free of any political, ideological or business interest."[63] The Club of Rome is still operational, but by the beginning of the 1970s, it had lost the momentum to establish itself as a permanent organization for global issues. In 1971 the German-born professor Klaus Schwab took and fully implemented the idea of an annual meeting of powerful leaders, strategists, and thinkers when he established the World Economic Forum (http://www.weforum.org).

"The World Economic Forum was first conceived in January 1971 when a group of European business leaders met under the patronage of the European Commission and European industrial associations ... Klaus Schwab ... chaired the gathering which took place in Davos, Switzerland. He then founded the European Management Forum as a non-profit organization based in Geneva, Switzerland, and drew European business leaders to Davos for their annual meeting each January. Initially, Professor Schwab focused the meetings on how European firms could catch up with US management practices.

Professor Schwab's vision for what would become the World Economic Forum grew steadily as a result of achieving 'milestones'. Events in 1973, namely the collapse of the Bretton Woods fixed exchange rate mechanism and the Arab–Israeli War saw the annual meeting expand its focus from management to economic and social issues, and political leaders were invited for the first time to Davos in January 1974. Two years later, the organization introduced a system of membership, which were 'the 1,000 leading companies of the world.' "[64]

In addition to its annual meeting, conducted in the Swiss resort town of Davos, in the last week of January and first week of February, the World Economic Forum also conducts region-specific meetings in different parts of the world, throughout the year. The activities of the World Economic Forum now fully live up to its name. However, it is definitely a non-institutional organization, as there is no multilateral institution required to implement its recommendations. Its decisions do not have any executive power. Despite its global importance, it is almost impossible for individuals that are not related to leading corporations or governments of powerful countries to participate in the annual meeting of this organization. Even leading companies are limited to only a few participants. The registration cost alone is thousands of dollars. Nevertheless, governmental officials, corporate leaders, and strategists always try to participate in this event. Through discussions, they can understand or reshape their vision of the upcoming future, and it is an ideal place to convene brief and informal meetings with top leaders. The Davos event is one of the best networking events in the world. Finally, people come to Davos to test their ideas, or to promote them, by influencing key decision makers. Any strategist or top executive has to pay close attention to this event. At a minimum, it is one of the best ways to develop an understanding of the upcoming global agenda. An example of the impact of the agenda of the World Economic Forum on corporate strategy can be seen in the experience of Marsh & McLennan Companies, a "global professional services firm providing advice and solutions in risk, strategy and human capital."[65] Its president and CEO, Mr Michael Cherkasky, participated in the 2007 Annual Meeting of the World Economic Forum, which discussed "climate change and the implications on business processes and disclosure."[66] After this meeting, Mr Cherkasky expressed the following opinion: "As with all risk, management of climate change should not be treated as an 'add-on' to a company's operation. It must be part of an integrated planning that goes into establishing business processes and operations in the first place."[67] This is an example of the correct strategic culture and exemplifies how strategists should react to the agenda of the World Economic Forum and how this agenda influences the strategy of the leading firms of the world.

The World Economic Forum is one the most exclusive and elite organizations of all non-institutional elements of the global order, second only to the Bilderberg group meetings, which are discussed later in this chapter. Before the advent of the Internet, information about the meeting was barely accessible to the public, and outsiders can still only find a limited amount of information on its web site and in media coverage.

The Council on Foreign Relations

The Council on Foreign Relations is an independent, non-partisan foreign policy think-tank and membership organization established in 1921.[68] Its mission is to be

> a resource for its members, government officials, business executives, journalists, educators and students, civic and religious leaders, and other interested citizens in order to help them better understand the world and the foreign policy choices facing the United States and other countries.[69]

Notable members of its board of directors include former US Secretary of State Madeline Albright, former US Secretary of State Colin Powell, and former US Secretary of the Treasury Robert Rubin, among others. It is difficult to consider this organization a truly global think-tank in light of the fact that membership is restricted to US citizens.

Many conspiracy theorists wrongfully characterize the Council on Foreign Relations as a nefarious global authority, arguing that

> if one group is effectively in control of national governments and multinational corporations; promotes world government through control of media, foundation grants, and education; and controls and guides the issues of the day; then they control most options available. The Council on Foreign Relations (CFR) and the financial powers behind it . . . promote the "New World Order," as they have for over 70 years. The CFR is the promotional arm of the Ruling Elite in the United States of America. Most influential politicians, academics and media personalities are members, and it uses its influence to infiltrate the New World Order into American life.[70]

This quote contradicts itself. People from many strata of society—politicians, academics, and media personalities, who do not have any shared interests—are obviously not promoters of the ruling elite. This unfounded opinion actually makes accusations without any evidence, which is quite typical for conspiracy theorists.

The Council on Foreign Relations has several affiliated organizations, such as the World Affairs Council of Oregon, the Cleveland Council on World Affairs, among many others. Participants of the meetings of these councils include regional leaders, scholars, and corporate strategists. All of these organizations have the goal of developing and sharing an understanding of the processes of the global arena based on the opinion of experts with diverse points of view. They do not actually formulate their own opinion. All regional councils and affiliated clubs (such as the Channel Club in Santa Barbara) operate as venues for learning and networking. In this sense they are extremely useful, but they do not directly influence the global order or even the national order of the US. However, the Council on Foreign Relations, which has offices in New York and Washington, is different, only because of its very well-known and well-connected members and its powerful board of directors.

One of the Council's previous presidents, Leslie Gelb, during an appearance on the popular *Charlie Rose Show* said, ". . . you [Charlie Rose] had me on [before] to talk about the New World Order! I talk about it all the time. It's one world now. The Council can find, nurture, and begin to put people in the kinds of jobs this country needs. And that's going to be one of the major enterprises of the Council under me."[71] If conspiracy theorists can find anything in this quote supporting their ideas, they can find it anywhere.

The Trilateral Commission

The global energy crisis at the beginning of the 1970s and the peak in tension of the bipolar world during the Cold War gave birth to several think-tanks that are still operational, such as the Club of Rome and the World Economic Forum. During the same period, in 1973, another organization was founded—the Trilateral Commission. This organization is a think-tank with a mission and message similar to that of the Council on Foreign Relations. The major distinction between this commission and the Council on Foreign Relations is geopolitical. The Council on Foreign Relations is an overwhelmingly American organization, while the Trilateral Commission is an international group founded by private citizens of "Japan, Europe (European Union countries), and North America (United States and Canada) to foster closer cooperation among these core democratic industrialized areas of the world with shared leadership responsibilities in the wider international system."[72] The influence of this commission is also mostly intellectual, as it promotes certain ideas via their meetings and publications. Both of these institutions are think-tanks that do not directly participate in any capacity of the development and operations of the global order. They should not be considered anything other than idea-creating organizations, as they are not institutionalized and no multilateral body implements their recommendations or ideas.

Nonetheless, some connect the Trilateral Commission to the Bilderberg group, one of the most confidential forums related to the study, monitoring, and evaluation of the global order. This forum has no executive power, but dozens of very important people participate in the club's meetings; several participants are quite active in meetings of both the Bilderberg group and the Trilateral Commission. EMCs have a disproportionately small presence at Bilderberg events. Participation is by invitation only, and the logic behind the list of invitees from EMCs is not totally clear. Of the very few representatives from EMCs that have participated in these meetings, most are not particularly influential. The majority of countries of Latin America, Africa, and the former Soviet bloc have never known representation in the group's annual meeting, although the 2007 meeting did take place in an EMC: Turkey. While still in office, the majority of leaders of Bretton Woods institutions have not participated in Bilderberg meetings. Despite the fact that some members of the media participate, publicly available official information about this group is very limited. As a result, any information about the Bilderberg group is almost entirely second hand, and strategists should be cautious regarding its validity.

The Institutionalization of the Global Business Order

None of the organizations previously mentioned (Bretton Woods Committee, the World Economic Forum, the G8, the Council on Foreign Relations, and the Trilateral Commission) are institutionalized. However, established multilateral institutions such as the World Bank, IMF, and WTO do pay attention to the results and recommendations coming from the meetings of these groups. Because the role of these organizations has not been officially acknowledged or institutionalized within the structure of the global order, many worry that the global order is secretly manipulated by these closed organizations of elites. While this is obviously not the case, their influence is significant.

Institutions should be developed to reflect the new realities of the GMP, and to present a unified voice and coordinate the activity of EMCs. Such an institution could be known as the Global Emerging Market Monitoring and Coordinating Agency. The influence of several regional economic organizations, even outside of the GEM, has substantially increased, creating the need for a new multilateral institution to represent their interests and to coordinate their activity and regulations. The Dutch economist who in 1969 became the first winner of the Nobel Prize in economics, Jan Tinbergen (1903–1994), argued, "because an effective international order requires institutions at the regional as well as the world level, decision-making bodies at the regional level can be established prior to institutionalizing a decision-making capability at the world level."[73] Tinbergen proposed the establishment of regional institutions to represent certain groups of countries in a world-governing organization. Keeping in mind national interests and democracy, it is difficult to believe that any country would agree to have its global interests represented solely by a super-governing institution. Tinbergen proposed a regional level of bureaucracy to act as an intermediary between the national interests of a group of countries and the global governing structure. The implementation of such a super-governing bureaucracy does not seem feasible, even in the distant future. However, the existence of regional organizations and their governing, coordinating, or monitoring bodies—depending on the level of regional integration—does suggest the possibility of some type of supranational bodies. But no regional organization has the ability to rule the national governments of its member countries. The highest level of integration exists in the EU, where there is a division of functions between national governments and EU executive and legislative bodies. However, when tighter political integration was proposed in the unified European Constitution, the people of France and the Netherlands roundly rejected it in the referendum of 2005. Later, in December 2007, the repudiated continental Constitution was replaced by a looser European law of land. On December 13, 2007, EU leaders signed the Treaty of Lisbon, thus bringing to an end several years of negotiations about institutional issues. This treaty "amends the current EU and EC treaties, without replacing them. It will provide the Union with the legal framework and tools necessary to meet future challenges and to respond to citizens' demands."[74] Even this much looser approach to a framework (not even a law) of political-regional integration for some still takes too much power from national governments and their citizens, who have much less influence on supranational bodies than on their national governments. This was proven during the June 2008 rejection by public vote in Ireland of the Treaty of Lisbon.[75] This example shows that globalization has two major limitations—national interests and national democracies. Beneath these two visible limitations, there are more powerful basic limitations—economic interests, which apply to nations and corporations. While analyzing this conflict of interest, strategists enter the field of geoeconomics and should always consider that the global order is a result of the dialectical relationship between geopolitics and geoeconomics. The upcoming global order will be based more on geoeconomics and the global business order than on geopolitics. At any rate, the global order of the twenty-first century already reflects the growing importance of regions. In the words of Dr Manoranjan Dutta, a professor of economics at Rutgers University (USA):

> [T]he global order of a free and perfectly competitive market economy certainly remains the ideal, but it continues to elude us. Given the necessary conditions, the global order will forseeably become real. Until then, the next best option is a marriage between regionalism and globalism, and thus, geo-economics has become the order of the day.[76]

The emerging global business order will have a hierarchy of global institutions with different functions, authorities, and structures. Membership in these organizations will be based on a mixture of representatives of regional executive bodies and national governments. NGOs will be represented, as will associations representing corporate interests, such as international chambers of commerce, exporter-importer associations, organizations of entrepreneurs, etc.

Another publication of Jan Tinbergen's, *The Need for an Ambitious Innovation of the World Order*, continued to promote the idea that the relevance of national governments is declining in comparison to supernational world-governing bodies. He argues that

> since business has been much more successful in overcoming narrow national points of view than have governments, most politicians, and the general public, it may be useful to look at the world from a *management scientific* viewpoint. This implies that we try to answer the question how the activities necessary to provide mankind with the goods and services needed for maximum welfare have to be organized without the *precondition* of the existence of nation-states.[77]

Unfortunately, world and national leaders experienced the repercussions of the subversion of national governments' authority during the global spread of the "Asian" crisis. Again, it is important to underline that it is more productive to have a partnership between global and regional multilateral institutions, national governments, and corporations than a global super-government. Such a partnership is a keystone of the emerging global order as well as of the global business order.

Major Characteristics of the Emerging Global Business Order

There is no single organization that dictates or even monitors the current global business order. It is a result of developments of global political, economic, and business systems, most of which are objective. It is a set of customs that all participants of the GMP and global workplace have to agree upon, de facto—obviously not de jure. However, those rules that a country accepts via its membership in multilateral global and regional institutions, such as the UN, World Bank, etc., must be respected and obeyed. For example, until the 1990s Switzerland was not a member of the UN, and it therefore did not have to accept UN regulations and decisions. The most stable characteristics of the GMP and its major global systems have to be monitored and reflected in the activity and functions of global and regional multilateral organizations, national governments, NGOs, and even popular movements. Does global society need a single, unified organization to monitor and guide the global order? This will be an intensely debated issue for much of the twenty-first century. Modern technology would enable such an organization to communicate efficiently, and the scale of global threats has increased to the point where a unified voice and force may be necessary to protect global civilization. Whether the creation of such an organization is politically feasible is not yet clear. The development of only a monitoring agency with the function of making suggestions for global strategy is more likely to come to power than an organization somehow resembling a global government.

The rise of the GEM has created a significant impetus for changes in the global order and its subsystem, the global business order, which is of great influence on the global workplace and global supply chains. This influence can be seen in the new industrial and regional structure of the world economy, which mirrors shifts in production, demand, and consumption of traditional resources. The high growth rate of several EMCs, especially China, India, and Russia, and increasing standards of living in most countries is causing a shift in energy consumption from developed countries to the GEM. According to Fatih Birol, the chief economist at the International Energy Agency:

> We are entering a new world energy order. Today, demand for oil is dominated by China, India, and even by the Middle East countries themselves. The main actors of the recent past—namely the OECD countries, rich countries, the United States, Europe, Japan—their time is passé. It's over.[78]

A new global energy order, as a subsystem of the emerging global order, is definitely under development; however, Birol's conclusion is a simplification of reality. It does not take into consideration technological achievements and the growing role of alternative energy resources as a substitute for traditional sources. The global order has always been about access to various natural resources, but this pattern may be altered in the twenty-first century due to scientific advancements in nuclear, hydrogen, and bio-energies. In the context of the knowledge-based economy, vital economic needs and substantial investment in science may change this situation.

The role of the US, the lone superpower in the global order, will likely shrink. This will occur as regional superpowers from the GEM, such as China, India, Brazil, South Africa, Egypt, and possibly Russia, rise. The result will be a multipolar world, with the influence of the existing superpower significantly reduced. How will this affect global security? Will it make for a more stable world? History indicates the opposite. Hegemonic periods, dominated by a lone superpower (the hegemon), are typically times of relative peace and prosperity. The rules of engagement are clear, and the authority of the hegemon is unchallenged. This has clearly been the case since end of the Cold War. It was also the case during the time of the Roman Empire. Bipolar world orders are typically very tense and far less prosperous. History and economic data show that political, economic, and business cooperation between the two powers are kept to a minimum, as was the case between the US and the Soviet Union following World War II. In 1960, at the peak of the Cold War, the US input to GWP was 38.5 percent,[79] making it without question the dominant economic power. However, the bipolar global order was a poor environment for the internationalization of business, which substantially inhibited its development, due to the existence of the Soviet Union, a superpower of limited economic strength. While the US was unquestionably dominant in economic terms, it was not a hegemon. At the beginning of the twenty-first century (2006), the input of the US in GWP is much less—27 percent[80]—but its dominant role as the hegemon is practically indisputable. The global order during a unipolar system is more clearly defined; a country that accounts for only a quarter of GWP in the unipolar world is more powerful than one that was unchallenged in economic terms in a bipolar world. For corporate strategy, the unipolar global order creates a more predictable and stable business environment under which it is far easier to develop and implement long-term corporate strategy.

Potential conflicts in the new multipolar global order are numerous. The implementation strategy in one country or the emergence of a hostile dictatorship in another nuclear power could lead to a hot or cold war. A new kind of global power, without a formal government or defined territory, but unified by terrorist ideology, may also be a major threat to global security in the twenty-first century. This is the type of situation that Professor Peter Drucker described when he wrote:

> [T]he twenty-first century will surely be one of continuing social, economic, and political turmoil and challenge, at least in its early decades. What I have called the age of social transformation is not over yet. And the challenges looming ahead may be more serious and more daunting than those posed by the social transformations that have already come about, the social transformations of the twentieth century.[81]

Some EMCs could challenge the existing global order, resulting in a drastic restructuring of it, and subsequently of the global business order. The most economically powerful EMCs or a group of them will likely confront the developed world and direct the creation of a new global order. The power of the GEM will increase significantly at the expense of developed countries; the voice of the GEM in multilateral institutions will grow substantially. Representation of the GEM will increase in the UN Security Council, where the GEM already plays a substantial role but is a minority (Russia and China are the only permanent members from the GEM. The other members are developed countries: the United States, Great Britain, and France). Notably absent from the Security Council are representatives of Latin America, such as Brazil; of the one billion people of Africa, such as South Africa; of the Muslim world, such as Egypt; of the one billion people of India; and of Japan and Germany the most advanced economies of Asia and Europe, respectively. As they continue to develop, GEM nations and regions will gain an increased representation and voice in the executive bodies of the World Bank, the IMF, and the WTO and its regional subordinates. The new global order will reflect the growing importance and power of the GEM. The various centers of economic power of the GEM will be the regional superpowers of the twenty-first century, each with different levels of democracy and economic and military capacities and goals. These variations will allow the GMP to flourish but will also represent serious challenges to its existence. Global threats such as mass disease, climate change, global terrorism, etc., will likely encourage cooperation among competing regional superpowers.

The role of P-EMCs such as Bolivia, Iraq, and Saudi Arabia will also increase in certain industries and regions in the new global order. Bolivia is a particularly interesting example, because as of 2008 its orientation is difficult to characterize—toward the GEM and democracy, or toward declining economic and political freedom. Its movement to the left has been influential in Latin America, and as a result, in the global business order. The emerging global order should represent the interests of countries with certain shared characteristics that require special attention in the new conditions of the twenty-first century. For example, the existing Alliance of Small Island States (www.sidsnet.org/aosis/index.html) should deepen and expand from its role as a lobbying organization to a political, economic, and business bloc of countries without shared borders, but facing common challenges. The mission of such an alliance should be oriented to the development of solutions to the challenges facing these nations, such as the threat of rising sea levels, which will endanger the actual existence of many of these nations. An organization that does not exist, but should be formed, is a formal association of landlocked countries. These states are particularly disadvantaged due to the growing importance of international trade in economic development. As of 2008 there is an informal group of landlocked developing countries within the framework of the UN. These countries need to form an executive body to enhance their coordination and cooperation in the promotion of understanding by the global community and multilateral institutions of the issue of not having access to the world ocean, which creates disadvantages in their participation in international trade and the division of labor. There are a few instances in which countries are separated from the coast by only a few hundred meters of territory of neighboring countries. This is the case for Moldova, which is blocked by Ukraine. Neighbors of these countries should be appealed to, in order to provide corridors to the coast for nearby landlocked states. This is an example of ethics in international economic relations. When a landlocked country is a member of a regional economic organization, it has to be an imperative to provide these member countries with access to the coast, which will eventually benefit all members of the regional economic organization, as well as the global marketplace.

There are still a few nations in the world without statehood, like that of the Kurds, which consists of more than 25 million people.[82] The emerging global business order should develop a way to reflect the special economic needs of these nations and their businesses, without, of course, ignoring Pareto's principle. The global business order of the twenty-first century and its monitoring and coordinating executive bodies need to have global information and technological structures that optimize business cooperation toward scientific and technological progress for the betterment of humankind. A unified country classification system and terminologies, harmonized national laws, regulations, and standards will be important stabilizing characteristics of the emerging global business order.

Will the new global order and global business order require a world government—a kind of conglomerated union of nations and economic multilateral institutions with greater executive power than their Bretton Woods antecedents? Some authors are strong advocates of such a government. For example, Jean L. Cohen, a professor of political science at Columbia University, wrote:

> We have entered a post sovereign, decentered world order . . . a cosmopolitan legal system regulating global politics actually exists and . . . it is *already* constitutionalized . . . To the systems theorist who elaborate this approach, the key development is the emergence of a world society out of the old international order . . . The idea is that international society has gone global, shifting from a segmental form of differentiation to a set of relations between many functionally differentiated global systems, of which the political subsystem is only one. Functional differentiation has also occurred within that subsystem, overlaying and undermining the previous order of "international society" composed of sovereign territorial states . . . this order is composed not of states but of components of states along with nongovernmental civil actors. From this perspective as well there is a proliferation of law making in world society independent of national governments' consent or control. But here the claim that a constitutional global legal system already exists (which regulates global politics) involves a shift from the external sociological to the internal legal perspective concerned above all with the production of legal validity. Accordingly, the focus is on hard, not soft, law—on the legal system, not on the mere proliferation of regulations. Nevertheless, on this approach too, the discourse of sovereignty must be abandoned.[83]

This argument basically promotes a kind of global constitutional governance. The so-called Asian crisis has already demonstrated the danger of national governments not playing a role in international business. The idea of global governance is not desirable for the majority of nations because the implementation of this idea would lead to an unelected super-government unaccountable to the people of its country members. The authority of the global order versus that of national governments is a very delicate issue. People are uncomfortable with the idea of ceding the power of their democratically elected national leaders to unelected and relatively unknown global authorities located outside of their

borders. It should not have been a surprise when the people of Europe, who have traditionally been the leaders of international integration and democratic movements, enthusiastic-
ally voted against the European Constitution. Global government and world governance
always drew a great deal of suspicion from people fearful of some kind of international
conspiracy that subverts national interests to the nefarious interests of a mysterious group of
elites. This fear is one of the explanations of the failure of the EU to implement its
constitution, and even the great difficulties experienced by the EU with the Lisbon Treaty.
As of the first decade of the twenty-first century, the majority of other regional economic
organizations and political unions based on territorial proximity have not even attempted to
implement regional authorities with elements not only of economic but also political power
over nations.

The major challenge for multilateral institutions—including the World Bank, IMF and
the WTO—is to not merely continue practices of the twentieth century that concentrate
activity on the resolution of domestic and international problems of various countries. In the
twenty-first century, the focus must be on global issues that will not appear on the agenda of
national governments without the leadership of multilateral institutions in the framework
of the new global order.

Study Questions

1. Describe the connections between the global order and corporate social
   responsibility.
2. Describe the importance of the global order for corporate strategy.
3. How, when, and where did the post-World War II global order develop?
4. Describe the global order and its dialectic relationship with national and corporate interests.
5. How is the scale and availability of basic economic factors related to the global
   order?
6. What was the Bretton Woods Conference, and how did it relate to the global
   order of the twenty-first century?
7. How has the existence of the GMP changed the global order, and vice versa?
8. Based on historical evidence, which is more sustainable—a unipolar or multipolar global order? Describe the strengths and weaknesses of each.
9. What distinguishes a global superpower from a regional superpower? Describe
   the dynamics between these entities.
10. How is the regionalization of the world economy reflected in the global order?
11. Describe the connections between the existence and maturation of the GEM and
    the global business order.
12. Describe the types of organizations that influence the development of the global
    order.
13. How are multilateral institutions monitored and supervised?
14. Describe the necessity, efficiency, and validity (or lack thereof) of a global super-
    government or global authority.
15. Describe the relationship between the global optimum and the quality of life of
    individuals.
16. What was Vilfredo Pareto's contribution to the theoretical base of the global
    optimum and global business order?
17. Describe the major characteristics of the Washington Consensus and how it
    relates to the current global business order.

18. Describe and evaluate alternative ideas and theories to the Washington Consensus.
19. Describe the major triggering events for the development of the global business order.
20. How is corporate social responsibility a trigger for the development of the global business order?
21. Describe the role of Bretton Woods institutions in the global business order.
22. What is a currency board? What role do they play in the global business order?
23. Do Bretton Woods institutions and their managerial bodies reflect the current role of EMCs in the global order and the GMP? Why?
24. Describe the role of the most influential non-institutional international organizations in the emerging global business order.
25. Describe and evaluate the argument for the enlargement of the G8. How would this affect its role in the global order?
26. Describe the Bretton Woods Committee and its role in the sustainability and development of the global business order.
27. How are the World Economic Forum, the Council on Foreign Relations, and the Trilateral Commission related to the global business order?
28. Describe the correlations between the global order and the global business order.

6 Global Economic Strategy

By three methods we may learn wisdom: First, by reflection, which is noblest; second, by imitation, which is easiest; and third, by experience, which is the bitterest.

(Confucius, 551 BC–479 BC)

Tactics, evolutions, and duties may be learned in treatises, but the science of strategy is only to be acquired by experience, and by studying the lessons of the campaigns, of the great captains. These lessons have been to keep one's forces united; to leave no weak part unguarded; seize with rapidity on important points; and to inspire terror at the reputation of your arms, which will at once maintain fidelity and secure subjection.

(Napoleon, 1769–1821)

These two geniuses directly contradict each other. While one refers to strategy and the other to wisdom, they are addressing the same subject. Strategy is wisdom with a defined vector of attack and an understanding of resource limitations.

Keynote Definitions

Strategy: Strategy is a system of finding, formulating, and developing a doctrine that will ensure long-term success if followed faithfully. It is the result of a systematic analysis of the environment and existing forecasts for future circumstances based on a strategic mindset, deep knowledge, and intuition. The final product of the analysis is a formal strategy that consists of a new *forecast*, *mission statement*, *vision*, and long-term *objectives and goals* with a particular scenario to be implemented via the *strategic plan* with a strategic system to monitor its implementation. Strategy is a guideline to selected objectives for the future through chaos and the unknown. It is wisdom with a defined vector of attack and an understanding of resource limitations.

Strategist: The strategist is a wise, disciplined, and optimistic professional with a strategic mindset, vision of the future and intuition, armed with a forecasting methodology to utilize deep knowledge of the entity and a wide understanding and firm grasp of global trends.

The Strategic Mindset

Strategy is the most philosophical and theoretical yet practical element of success. Strategic success can be the result of many years of experience and extensive knowledge, or of a fresh young mind with an unconventional point of view, free of intellectual inertia. Sound strategy is a constant process of rethinking and reevaluating. Whether at work, at play, or at rest, the strategist is always strategizing. Its development is the privilege of top-level decision makers, as well as professionals who dedicate their efforts to formulate, monitor, redesign, and update strategy. It is the apex of management. Its development is the most exclusive managerial function, and with it comes the greatest amount of responsibility. Strategy is an extremely powerful tool. A strategy based on a bulletproof theory and intensive analysis can lead an entity from disorder and failure to the top of its field. On the other hand, a strategy that is not tailored to the particular situation or is theoretically flawed can lead a company at the top of its field to disorder and failure. The strategist may very well hold the future of a company or country in his hands, which is obviously an incredible amount of pressure and responsibility. The wrong strategy will bring about the collapse of the entire strategic framework, along with all that went into its development and implementation. The organizational structure and management systems implemented, personnel hired, resources allocated, and day-to-day operational activity all become irrelevant and obsolete when the strategy behind them fails.

In order to truly understand strategy one must develop a strategic mindset. It is difficult to grasp the practical and theoretical significance of the keynote definition presented at the beginning of this chapter, if one's mind is not already strategically oriented. A successful strategy cannot be discovered, developed, or even fully understood with a traditional mindset. Daily needs and routines train the mind to be operational, short-term, and nonstrategic. The first step to becoming a strategist is a deep reorientation, retuning, and reformatting of one's thought process in order to eventually develop a strategic mindset. The benefits are enormous. The success of practically every great leader or visionary is largely the result of a well-tuned strategic mindset. One of the best examples of such a leader is the great visionary Konrad Adenauer. He occupied high-ranking positions in pre-Nazi Germany and was among the very few German leaders who immediately and completely rejected Hitler's ideas of National Socialism. He was exiled and later forced into a prison camp because his mindset conflicted with the short-sighted opinion of the majority. Contrary to the "common sense" of millions of his compatriots, eventually his vision and steadfastness were validated when he became the first chancellor of West Germany.[1] Regarding the importance of the strategic mindset, Chancellor Adenauer said, "we all live under the same sky, but we don't all have the same horizon."[2] His example demonstrates not only the challenges of formulating an accurate strategic vision of the future, but also the importance of sticking to this vision, regardless of the opposition one faces. Even in the face of imprisonment and death imposed by the power structure of his country, Konrad Adenauer refused to stray from his vision. Strategists should have a firm grasp of global trends, with the ability to set objectives and goals accordingly and to devise the most efficient paths to the beacons of their vision of the future, before everyone else catches up.

US Air Force Col. John R. Boyd, the famous military strategist and fighter-plane designer, offers a practical understanding of the strategic mindset as "a mental tapestry of changing intentions for harmonizing and focusing our efforts as a basis for realizing some aim or purpose in an unfolding and often unforeseen world of many bewildering events and many contending interests."[3] Practically, the beginning of this description paraphrases the well-known idea that strategy is a science requiring an artist's touch. In this case the artist's touch is the strategic mindset, which interprets and connects facts in a way that those without this mindset cannot. A trained strategic mindset is able to listen, understand, and select the best opinions and advice of other experts. Some (especially those in the military) believe that strategy is primarily a martial field. A colleague of Col. Boyd's, a professor of national security policy in the Department of National Security and Strategy at the US Army War College, Col. Harry Yagger, argues that

good strategy development requires the military professional to step out of the planning mindset and adopt one more suited for strategic thinking. In the strategic mindset, the professional military strategist embraces the complexity and chaos of the strategic environment and envisions all its continuities and possibilities in seeking to create favorable strategic effects in support of national interests.[4]

In fact, in recent history, civilians typically develop strategy according to national interests, which uniformed strategists then convert into military doctrine. In the twenty-first century, the overwhelming majority of strategists are civilians. However, very few of them were actually trained to be strategists. Keeping this in mind, Professor Yagger's position is understandable—strategic practice and theory are an important part of the curriculum in military colleges and universities. In business schools, however, strategy is only one of many courses and is not a major. This situation is beginning to change. As of 2008, several universities have started to provide strategy as a major, such as the University of Rochester, which created a major in economics and business strategies.[5]

Two Approaches of Strategic Thinking

Within the strategic mindset, there are two basic approaches. The first approach will be referred to as *new dimensions strategy*, which requires the ability to think not just beyond an entity's current agenda but also to be able to recognize and analyze radical paths to success, even if they would fundamentally alter the current activity of the focus entity. From the practically infinite possibilities, the strategist must select a strategic objective, to which a substantial part of the entity's resources will then be dedicated. It would be wrong to say that all of the entity's resources are dedicated to the selected strategic objective, because when an established company finds a new approach, at least for the short term, it continues to use some resources for its existing operations. Typically, new dimensions strategy is not designated as the primary approach in books on strategy. Most books steer the reader toward the improvement of current functions, without exploring radically new options. This book considers such an approach, which is referred to as an *improvement strategy*, secondary to a new dimensions strategy. Unlike a new dimensions strategy, an improvement strategy is based primarily on systems analysis of the entity's subsystems, elements, and functions, and their interactions. In *The Mind of the Strategist: The Art of Japanese Business*, Kenichi Ohmae, director of McKinsey & Company and a leading strategic analyst, gives the following description of strategic thinking, which specifically describes an improvement strategy:

> In strategic thinking, one first seeks a clear understanding of the particular character of each element of a situation and then makes the fullest possible use of human brainpower to restructure the elements in the most advantageous way. Phenomena and events in the real world do not always fit a linear model. Hence the most reliable means of dissecting a situation into its constituent parts and reassembling them in the desired pattern is not a step-by-step methodology such as systems analysis. Rather, it is that ultimate nonlinear thinking tool, the human brain. True strategic thinking thus contrasts sharply with the conventional mechanical systems approach based on linear thinking. But it also contrasts with the approach that stakes everything on intuition, reaching conclusions without any real breakdown or analysis.[6]

One of the best practical examples of a successful improvement strategy is General Electric's development and adoption of Six Sigma—a process to define and measure efficiency in manufacturing explained below.

"Six Sigma is a highly disciplined process that helps us focus on developing and delivering near-perfect products and services.

Why 'Sigma'? The word is a statistical term that measures how far a given process deviates from perfection. The central idea behind Six Sigma is that if you can measure how many 'defects' you have in a process, you can systematically figure out how to eliminate them and get as close to 'zero defects' as possible. To achieve Six Sigma Quality, a process must produce no more than 3.4 defects per million opportunities. An 'opportunity' is defined as a chance for nonconformance, or not meeting the required specifications. This means we need to be nearly flawless in executing our key processes.

Key Concepts of Six Sigma

At its core, Six Sigma revolves around a few key concepts.

Critical to Quality: Attributes most important to the customer
Defect: Failing to deliver what the customer wants
Process Capability: What your process can deliver
Variation: What the customer sees and feels
Stable Operations: Ensuring consistent, predictable processes to improve what the customer sees and feels
Design for Six Sigma: Designing to meet customer needs and process capability"[7]

Practically, GE's Six Sigma provides a means to describe the standard deviation from constrained limits, which ideally is as small as possible. It is a strategic methodology of specific scope to find and analyze problems, and in doing so, increase the efficiency of products in respect to customer needs. It is a pure improvement strategy that companies throughout the world have adopted. An efficient improvement strategy will lead to a new generation of products and services or to a substantial reduction in production costs via a more effective combination of basic economic factors. One of the drawbacks of this strategy is that it prevents a company from aggressively looking for strategies of revolutionary opportunities.

The first approach to strategic thinking, *new dimensions strategy*, focuses on finding and evaluating new spheres of activity. The second approach, the *improvement strategy*, focuses on optimizing existing functions.

Profitability is a key function of effective strategic management. One method that strategists can use to improve profitability is the application of natural laws (physics, chemistry, and other natural sciences) to improve the efficiency of business processes. For example, the ideas of Ilya Prigogine, who won the Noble Prize in physics in 1977 for his "contributions to non-equilibrium thermodynamics, particularly the theory of dissipative structures,"[8] have many practical strategic applications. A "dissipative structure" is basically one that is far from its equilibrium, such as a company with low profitability or a government with unbalanced accounts. In both cases, these entities have to strategically reorient themselves toward outside, international cooperation. An inefficient company has four basic economic options—it can be divided, it can raise investment by selling partial ownership and reorganize or rightsize itself using this income; or it can be downsized. If none of these first three steps is taken, Prigogine's theory predicts that the company will eventually cease to exist. In terms of thermodynamics, the inflow of investment can be understood as the energy needed to sustain the structure. The fourth option is a managerial one: the company can change its strategic leadership, improve its management system, and in doing so, attain the energy required to sustain the company.

Stages of the Strategic Thought Process

The *exploration of the two strategic approaches* is the first stage of the strategic thought process. The second stage is the *selection* of one of them. The third stage of the strategic thought process, the *stage of enlightenment*, employs long-term vision and analytical skills to sift through the less important factors and focus exclusively on those of strategic significance. In other words, the main focus of this stage is to find the enlightening key idea of the strategy. At this stage, strategists need a mental spotlight that projects and focuses all intellectual capacity on the key idea. The fourth stage is the *strategic evaluation and development* of the fundamental idea selected in stage three. This is the stage where the flesh and bones of the strategic idea are formed (see Figure 6.1).

Characteristics of the Strategic Mindset

In order to be able to focus all of one's intellectual capacity on the enlightening key idea, strategists have to be both *rigid* and *flexible*, depending on an analysis of the dynamics of external and internal factors. Strategists should always be *open to feedback* from users of their strategy and to forecasts and strategic ideas of others. However, no idea from outside the strategist's mind can be rejected or accepted without a serious reevaluation, always from a *long-term perspective*. The strategic mindset has to *project* and *refocus* all signals that appear from studies and analyses of other experts or from day-to-day life *toward one mission*, which has to be achieved through a successful strategy. The *reevaluation of the past, extrapolation of known trends, and exploration of the future* are the daily activities of strategists. At all stages of strategic development and implementation, the reexamination of accomplishments and facts is routine. This should also be done in order to prevent the repetition of previously diagnosed mistakes. However, routines are extremely dangerous for strategists; they are a practical manifestation of intellectual inertia. In an effort to counteract such forms of

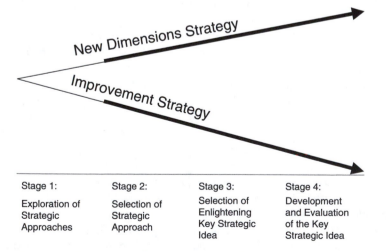

Stage 1:	Stage 2:	Stage 3:	Stage 4:
Exploration of Strategic Approaches	Selection of Strategic Approach	Selection of Enlightening Key Strategic Idea	Development and Evaluation of the Key Strategic Idea

Figure 6.1 Stages of the Strategic Thought Process.

Source: © Dr Vladimir Kvint, 2008.

inertia, Eric Schmidt, CEO of Google, one of the most successful companies of the first decade of the twenty-first century, formally requires his employees to dedicate 20 percent of their activity to non-operational, innovative efforts. This has undoubtedly helped establish a strategic mindset in Google's employees and has been a significant factor in the company's consistently cutting-edge technological offerings. The strategic mindset has to constantly strive to look beyond daily routines in order to *connect the past directly to the future*, building an invisible road from the known to the unknown. This cannot be done without a blend of *analytical skills* and *artistic creativity*. The strategic mindset always has to be oriented toward the optimization of resources on the path to success—not the maximization of the result, which in some cases can actually be harmful. Optimization is the main path to success. The achievement of sustainable success is one of the most important elements of the strategic mindset. Leaders with a strategic mindset think of the ultimate victory not as the destruction of their competitors but as the prevention of competition by rendering their competitors obsolete; unnecessary competition is an inefficient use of an entity's resources.

The need for strategy, as a profession or professional orientation, first emerged from the vital needs of military leaders, who were responsible for the lives of thousands of soldiers as well as the well-being of their nations. Logically, the roots of strategy are in military applications. Over the past 200 years, strategy has become a theoretical and practical weapon in politics, economics, business, and any activity that requires a *long-term vision* and the ability to find and allocate resources to achieve sustainable success. For strategists, *sustainability of success* is a crucial issue. Strategy is not about the temporary achievement of objectives and goals; it is about long-term, sustainable success. The definition of long and short term is relative. Typically, corporate strategy is not developed for a period shorter than three years. Five- and 10-year strategies are common for multinational corporations. If a company tries to develop a strategy for a shorter period, the time of strategy development may be longer than the period of its use, making it outdated at the moment of its implementation. For this reason, the "current time" of the moment of the beginning of strategy development is six months ahead of real time. Strategists should envision the external and internal environment of the entity in six months and take these conditions as the starting moment for strategy development. In 1812 Napoleon, at great expense, captured Moscow. However, due to a lack of resources, he was not able to hold it. After only a few weeks he left the city. This is an example of one of the most brilliant strategic minds in history focusing only on victory instead of on long-term sustainable success. He won every battle on his way to Moscow but lost the war and almost his entire army. Like Napoleon's experience in Russia, the US's "shock and awe" strategy in Iraq in 2003 was initially very successful. Saddam Hussein's regime was promptly dismantled; however, it very quickly became apparent that the US did not have a strategy to sustain this success. Tremendous resources and the lives of thousands of US soldiers and Iraqi citizens have been the cost of this strategic miscalculation. The same idea applies to business. Without a strategy that focuses on long-term, sustainable success, finding and occupying a new niche in the marketplace or utilizing a new technology will achieve only a temporary victory.

In the words of professors Thomas H. Davenport, Marius Leibold, and Sven Voelpel:

> [T]he key elements of a strategy mindset can also be described as a set of mental spaces occupying individuals' minds at any particular period of time. Fauconnier describes mental space as providing a medium in which cognitive activities can take place, i.e. the partial cognitive structures that emerge when we think and talk. And it is in these mental spaces that domains are defined, reasoned, changed, and merged for purposes of understanding and action. Furthermore, mental spaces are inter-connected and can be modified as thought and discourse unfold.[9]

Once an individual develops a strategic mindset, it is a tool that will never be lost as long as it is in practical need and regularly used. Dr Gilles Fauconnier, a professor of the University of California, San Diego, mentioned in the above quote, is a leading authority of cognitive psychology and the study of the mindset. The mental spaces described by Dr Fauconnier must be oriented in such a way as to be able to distinguish between a company that is on the verge of falling apart versus one that is going through an extremely challenging time but has a long-term future. To those without a strategic mindset, these two companies may appear to be in very similar situations. In reality, they are in fundamentally different situations in that one company has a strategy that will lead it out of a difficult period, and the other does not. An entity can operate only temporarily without a strategy. Such entities are like boats with a cracked hull—they may be able to stay afloat for a brief period, but it is only a matter of time before they sink to the bottom of the ocean. Companies enjoying success without a strategy are in a precarious situation. They allocate their resources to expanding the production of highly sought-after goods or services, unaware of technological advancements or crossovers from other industries that (combined with the right strategy) will create substitute products—and their company's obsolescence. There are numerous examples of this type of short-sighted success. Think of all of the software companies that have moved into the hardware, mobile, or telephony business and put the dominant company of these industries out of business. Contrary to popular opinion, strategy is not needed only during times of crisis—when a country is at war, or when a company encounters a threatening situation. This could not be further from the truth. One of the great challenges of success is resisting the drift toward complacency.

The Three Axes of Strategic Thought

Strategists always have to explore both approaches of strategic thinking and decide if the situation facing an entity calls for a revolutionary strategic change or a reevaluation and revision. Regardless of which strategy is chosen, all strategic thought occurs within the following three axes: *time, cost,* and *space.* The nature and dynamics of time and space are typically thought of as the realm of physics. Actually, this dilemma is a fundamental concept of strategy. Napoleon theorized that "strategy is the art of making use of time and space. I am less concerned about the later than the former. Space we can recover, lost time never." Almost a century after Napoleon, in 1905, Albert Einstein developed a slightly more complex explanation, which eventually became known as the Special Theory of Relativity. In 1908 the mathematician Hermann Minkowski made a geometric illustration for Einstein's theory (see Figure 6.2), which developed the concept of "spacetime" by combining the three dimensions of space, with time as the fourth dimension.[10] Einstein and Minkowski's work has very practical implications for strategists. However, contrary to the concepts of physics, time and space, in political, economic, and business strategy, can be intertwined beyond the concept of spacetime, to the point of these axes becoming interchangeable. Strategists must understand time as the space for strategic development. Strategy is developed only in time, while space is where most resources are allocated. Strategists should understand space as more than just territory. Strategy is the product of the multiplication of time, costs, and space, where space can be understood as the developed and implemented strategic ideas. Time can be understood as the developmental space of strategy during the allocation of all resources in strategic non-physical space. Unlike in economics, in strategy, resources are not necessarily physical; they can be intangible, such as information, or strategic ideas, paths, or methods to achieve success. Even the most practical self-made billionaire will describe the development of strategy (stage four) as beginning with an idea and ending with an idea, although the evaluation may lead the strategist to a refined idea or a radically new one. From the perspective of information theory, ideas are just new information in various forms. Of course, the implementation of any strategic idea must be feasible given limited resources. For entrepreneurs, strategy is always about the idea, with time as a key factor.

All strategic ideas should be seen through the prism of intuition, without which an evaluation of the three axes of strategic thought is of limited utility. For the strategic mindset it is impossible to overestimate the role of intuition. While quantitative analyses are extremely important, intuition is a key part of the strategic thought process. Intuition is the grandmother of all great strategies; without it, the development of a vision, the direction of quantitative analyses, and an efficient strategic management system are nearly impossible. Intuition will develop with experience and/or with a conscious fine-tuning of the mind toward strategic analysis.

The Professional Strategist

Now that the approaches, stages, and characteristics of the strategic thought process have been presented, the next logical step is to describe *who* the strategist is. This begins with an examination of the strategic departments of major corporations, although not all corporations have this department, even in the twenty-first century when strategy has become a proven instrument to success. Who are the employees in these departments, and what do they do? Strategic branches, or strategic initiative departments (as they are sometimes known), of multinational corporations and even of medium-size companies typically have two types of employees. The first is very experienced, connected, and knowledgeable. In addition to being extremely informed about the field, industry, and region in which they work, these people generally have a deep knowledge of geography, political science, political economy, economics, business, and technology, among many other fields. However, experience and knowledge are only half of the equation. Strategic departments are usually not capable of generating truly revolutionary ideas without young employees. These people have an understanding of the entity for which they work and make up for their lack of experience with their ability to think outside of the box and seek the new horizons to which Konrad Adenauer referred. One of the most important qualities of young strategists is the boldness, guts, or in the words of New York-based strategists, "chutzpah" to disagree with their highly accomplished and respected colleagues. The most innovative and successful corporate strategies are usually the result of the collaborative efforts between these two types of employees, especially in new fields (such as the GEM). There are exceptional cases in which young or old strategists have some qualities of both types of strategists. For small and family-run businesses, with their limited resources, it is a significant challenge to find even two employees with the aforementioned qualities to develop and implement strategy. Typically, in these companies, strategy is the work of the owner, top-level management, and possibly an accountant or engineer. Due to limited resources, strategy is updated only periodically, which puts such companies at a disadvantage to larger competitors that can constantly reassess and reevaluate their strategy. However, a great strategic idea or revolutionary business concept can bring tremendous success to businesses that begin as small or family run. The best and most-known examples of this are Wal-Mart, Microsoft, and Google.

The strategist is like an astronomer. An astronomer does not create stars, comets, or planets; he discovers them and interprets their significance for the universe and for the Earth. In the same spirit, strategists explore and analyze the GMP, to discover and understand new trends and their impact on particular companies, countries, new markets, and the GMP itself. The strategist acts as a navigator, guiding a company, government, or any legal entity from the present to a future destination, anticipating, avoiding, and reacting to the unknowable obstacles of the future. Most strategists do not develop new products, technologies, standards, etc., rather, they are adept at homing in on practical applications and potential. The strategist is not involved in operational, day-to-day activity. Present-day activities are already the past for the strategist. Nonetheless, strategists should be in regular contact with operational managers, in order to get feedback from them about challenges and requirements for the company. Strategists must anticipate and forecast potential events, placing themselves no fewer than six months in the future and taking this moment as the present. All forecasts have to be made from this time-based platform. All events within the immediate six months are already the past as far as the strategist is concerned. This does not apply to strategists focusing on stock and currency markets. In these markets of extreme uncertainty, strategy applies to everything beyond one month; an accurate prediction of an event in money management five months ahead of time is a major feat. Strategists have to be as precise as possible with their predictions. This is what makes strategy so difficult—the more precise a strategist's prediction, the more likely it will be wrong. One failed prediction is all that is necessary for a strategist to lose credibility. In this sense, the strategist is like a minesweeper; his first mistake is often his last. A strategist will be successful only if he can see the moment of conception. In other words, success for a strategist is based on the ability to recognize the very beginning of a trend and predict its implications, before competitors are able to. A successful strategy provides a vision of and a roadmap to the future, and in the best-case scenario, even specific event predictions.

The Strategist's 15 Rules

The following 15 rules can act as an aid and guideline for the development and use of the strategic mindset. A practical set of rules can be especially helpful for strategists when they are in an environment with which they are not entirely familiar, such as strategists from developed countries who deal with the GEM. EMCs are characterized by significantly more uncertainty than markets of the developed world, where the rules of engagement are well established. The strategist's 15 rules can also be used as algorithmic tools to guide the discovery, formation, development, and implementation of strategy, especially in markets with high levels of uncertainty and risk:

- Rule 1: Strategists can never rely on common sense alone.
- Rule 2: The majority is very often strategically wrong.
- Rule 3: Strategically, the present is already the past.
- Rule 4: The strategist must learn from history.
- Rule 5: Nothing lasts forever.
- Rule 6: Inertia is the strategist's greatest adversary.
- Rule 7: Strategists should not fall into predictable patterns.
- Rule 8: A successful strategy cannot be dishonest.
- Rule 9: Strategists must make systems out of chaos.
- Rule 10: An asymmetric strategic response is more efficient than a symmetric one.
- Rule 11: The strategist must always be an optimist.
- Rule 12: Always overestimate the competitor.
- Rule 13: Innovation can provide huge strategic advantages.
- Rule 14: The strategist should optimize limited resources, using time as the determining factor.
- Rule 15: Strategists must figure out what their clients need, not what their clients want.

The strategic rules selected and described below may seem rigid and uncompromising, but they are presented in this fashion to give a clearer understanding of how to use them efficiently. The prerequisite for the use of all of these rules is wisdom—something that does not necessarily depend on one's age.

Rule 1: Strategists Can Never Rely on Common Sense Alone

Common sense generally leads to the very opposite of an accurate forecast and insightful strategy. Conclusions based on common sense ignore the very deep and complicated processes that lie beneath the surface of an issue and can be made by anyone. As the philosopher Hegel said, the quintessential—that is the pure, highly concentrated essence of a phenomenon—is not what lies on the surface. Strategy must go beyond what is obvious to everyone. It should be based on an intense, interdisciplinary analysis of environmental, political, economic, business, and technological systems and factors that determine possible outcomes. The functions of these systems are too complex to be understood, let alone predicted by common sense. In fact, great strategic ideas are very often rejected by common sense, which is based on habitual knowledge of the status quo. A great strategic idea rejects customary knowledge through the implementation of new and different methods of production, or a previously unknown good or service.

One of the best examples of a revolutionary strategy rejected by common sense is the vision of Bill Gates. In 1975 he founded Microsoft based on the idea that "the computer would be a valuable tool on every office desktop and in every home."[11] At the time, single-person computers were extremely expensive, occupied entire rooms, and were used exclusively by research institutions and companies. According to the common sense of 1975, Gates' ideas were unrealistic. Bill Gates experienced the pressure of common sense, and the subsequent lack of attention to his "impractical" ideas:

> [D]uring the PC industry's infancy, the mass media paid little attention to what was going on in the brand-new business. Those of us who were enthralled by computers and the possibilities they promised were unnoticed outside our own circles and definitely not considered trendy.[12]

However, history and the immense fortune he has acquired have vindicated his revolutionary vision. Common sense does not only reject strategies based on unanticipated technological advancements. There are many examples of very simple strategies that are initially rejected but prove lucrative once implemented. For example, the mail-order DVD business model of Netflix was initially proposed to and rejected by Blockbuster, which did not think that people would want to receive movies via mail. Practice proved otherwise, and in 2006 Netflix's quarterly profit more than doubled.[13] Ironically, in an attempt to compete with Netflix, Blockbuster now offers an almost identical service. The idea of disregarding common sense may seem strange, but it is crucial for the development of long-term strategy. Albert Einstein may have put it best when he said that "common sense is the collection of prejudices acquired by age eighteen."

Rule 2: The Majority is Very Often Strategically Wrong

Much like the strategic rejection of common sense, a strategist must accept the seemingly counterintuitive notion that when it comes to strategy, the majority is almost always wrong. Conclusions based on comprehensive and intensive analysis almost always defy the popular opinions of society, which are based primarily on common sense. After all, the majority of society has not invested substantial time and energy, combining knowledge with intense analysis and research to find the solution to a particular challenge. The majority has a collective knowledge but lacks the ability to extract the "diamonds" or truthful and far-sighted strategies for the future from this mountain of empty ore. When strategists find such diamonds they must hold on to and embrace them without hesitation. It is the responsibility of the strategist to convince skeptical decision makers and the non-believing majority that a particular strategy is the right scenario for the future. Once a strategy is finally successfully implemented, the majority will inevitably forget about the opposition it mounted and the strategist who created it. They again will be weary of accepting unusual predictions and revolutionary strategic ideas. The most innovative strategies almost always face derision from the majority. The general population lacks the specific knowledge, experience, and dedication of strategists, who usually have focused their professional life on the resolution of a particular challenge. The majority does not refer only to mainstream society. Corporate strategic decisions are often the result of collaboration between executives and the board of directors but are rarely endorsed by a consensus. Any truly revolutionary strategy will initially experience rejection from most people who did not invest their time in its development. The various parties involved will often hold divergent views on the strategic direction that ought to be pursued. Quite frequently, such disagreements will lead to changes on the board of directors.

The story of almost every successful entrepreneur fully endorses this rule. For example, in 1963, when Leslie Wexner came up with the idea to create a global business by selling women's clothing, many thought he was joking. More than 40 years later, the Limited Brands (www.limitedbrands.com)—which include Victoria's Secret, Bath & Body Works, Henri Bendel, among others—are thriving, and Leslie Wexner is one of the richest people in the world. This is an indisputable confirmation of his strategic vision and his company's status as a premier global brand with a large and expanding presence in the GEM.

In fact, a possible indication of a strategy being correct and surprising to competitors is a reaction of shock and disbelief from the majority. The annals of history are filled with numerous examples of this. The "Iron Chancellor," Otto von Bismarck, the great strategist who unified Germany during the late nineteenth century, astutely said, "a government must not waiver once it has chosen its course. It must not look to the left or right but go forward." A good example is the biblical story of Moses. What would have happened if Moses had listened to the voices of the majority? He was a great leader because he believed deeply in and was committed to very unusual advice. He brought his people through the wilderness, and his legacy has lasted for thousands of years. The modern strategist will most likely never have as reliable an advisor as that of Moses. Nevertheless, a strategist must be prepared to maintain faith in their strategy when it is widely rejected. According to Eric Schmidt, the CEO of Google, "the story of innovation has not changed. It has always been a small team of people who have a new idea, typically not understood by people around them and their executives."

Rule 3: Strategically, the Present is Already the Past

For the strategist, the present is already the past. A successful strategist's professional thinking will always be three to five years ahead of everyone else's. As no one has invented a time machine, strategists must travel to the future using only their mindset. The future cannot be understood only by an analysis of current events. Such an approach will result in outdated forecasts that are nothing more than the extrapolation of current trends. It takes sunlight eight minutes to travel to Earth; thus, images of the sun are always from the past.

The same applies to business, economics, and politics—without intensive systematic study and contemplation, the past is all that can be observed.

One of the simplest ways to illustrate this rule is to return to the issue of "spacetime." A simple illustration of the mathematician Dr Hermann Minkowski's light cone, which he developed to illustrate Einstein's Special Theory of Relativity, is a great way to visualize the position of the strategist (see Figure 6.2).

The lower cone represents past spacetime, while the upper cone represents future space-time. At the moment when strategists give the "creative touch" to a new strategy, they are at the vertex of these two connected cones. New strategies are developed at the point where the past and the future meet. This conception of time is very useful for strategists.

Rule 4: The Strategist Must Learn from History

The position of the strategist in Minkowski's light cone, between the future and the past, increases the importance of studying history when forecasting future scenarios. While strategists should not merely extrapolate current or past trends, ignoring lessons from history altogether is even worse. Some strategic ideas are extremely appealing but have been unsuccessfully attempted by many strategists throughout history. Using a concept that has failed in practice over and over is a foolish waste of resources. One inventor from Florida, John Kanzius, claims he has figured out how to create enriched hydrogen from burned saltwater. This would essentially create a basis for a perpetual motion machine—an idea that has never been successfully implemented since its initial proposal in the Middle Ages. However, the possibility always exists that what did not work in the past or was unsuited to wide-scale implementation may be efficient in new economic and technological conditions. Keeping this in mind, historical lessons have to be revisited and analyzed intensively, within the context of emerging trends and technological developments. What was impossible to do 15 years ago in countries such as China due to low levels of education or purchasing power may be a requirement, as of 2008, to stay in business. Another example of this is the use of bioethanol as a fuel for cars. This idea was rejected even at the end of the twentieth century,

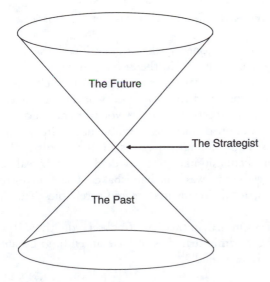

Figure 6.2 The Strategic Position between the Past and the Future.

Source: © Dr Vladimir Kvint, 2008.

but was reborn in the twenty-first century and is spreading throughout the world. It has already become a requirement to use a blend of gasoline and ethanol in the EU, China, Japan, and several US states. Many countries and other US states have encouraged the use of this blend, which is far more environmentally friendly than gasoline. New technologies give the opportunity to farmers in remote rural areas to produce bioethanol as a fuel from communal agricultural waste and decaying forestry. Biofuel technologies that were once roundly rejected by the majority are now in great demand.

Rule 5: Nothing Lasts Forever

The strategist's job is most difficult when an entity is presently enjoying success. In these cases, even when it appears that conditions are changing, most would prefer to maintain the status quo. This mentality is particularly prevalent among those responsible for operational activity. To these people, strategists represent a threat to their success and stature. They tend to have the "if it ain't broke, don't fix it" mentality.

When executives and entrepreneurs make strategic decisions about the future, they have to balance current profits (especially when profits are high and the company occupies a leading position) with potential future profits and threats. All executives report to shareholders, and all entrepreneurs analyze their past quarter or year. These analyses are all based in the past. Nonetheless, executives and entrepreneurs cannot afford to make the mistake of assuming that success in the past will guarantee success in the future. Nothing lasts forever. For this reason it is necessary—though very difficult—for executives, in spite of current success, to invest money in the future. This is why smart leaders will cut R&D expenditures last. They must be willing to replace practices that have been successful in the past with new, unproven methods as they anticipate changing conditions. It is generally easier for new companies and those that are currently unsuccessful to develop and accept strategies for the future. For example, when Google first appeared with its highly disruptive technology, it was not hard for its executives and strategists to envision the future; they did not have the baggage of past success to inhibit strategic decision making. As of 2008 Google's share of the search-engine market has grown to 65.1 percent,[14] more than nine times that of Microsoft, a company that was once synonymous with cutting-edge computer technology. Microsoft has been forced to come to terms with the fact that market dominance, like everything else, does not last forever.

In the GEM, changes usually occur much more frequently than in developed economies. This even applies to issues that are relatively unchanging in the developed world, such as the national legal framework. In the GEM, legal systems are in almost constant change. A major mistake that many executives and investors from the developed world have made in the GEM is to rely too heavily on political connections. In the volatile and uncertain environment of the GEM (compared with developed countries), established political connections can very suddenly become useless. Many foreign investors in Turkmenistan lost large sums of money when the dictator Turkmenbashi unexpectedly died and they realized that the only thing protecting their investments was his handshake. These investors learned—painfully—that in the long term, legal documents are more reliable than the handshake of a dictator.

As the Roman philosopher Marcus Fabius Quintilian (AD 35–96) observed, "thus, if we say that the world had a beginning, we must admit that it is to have an ending; because every thing that has had a beginning, must have an end."[15]

Rule 6: Inertia is the Strategist's Greatest Adversary

Inertia is a major obstacle for innovative strategic ideas. Once an entity becomes accustomed to day-to-day operations, it is extremely difficult to accept change. This is why chief operating officers (COOs) are typically very averse to radical ideas, especially when things are going well. The implementation of a new strategy could undermine a COO's successful career. This is a further illustration that employees who focus on operational issues are, by nature, opponents of strategists.

When an entity does not have a strategy, inertia inevitably sets in. The entity becomes accustomed to its activity and does not explore alternatives, even in the face of declining demand for its product, service, or function. This is another case in which the laws of natural science have useful strategic applications. In terms of strategy, Newton's First Law of Motion (the law of inertia) can be interpreted in the follow way: when the influence of all factors is balanced, it is almost impossible to increase economic efficiency. Equilibrium is the adversary of strategic improvement. Innovative strategic ideas are applicable to an entity only when it lacks balance or the status quo is changing. Newton's Second Law of Motion can also be applied to strategic situations, but only in cases where the entity is unbalanced and strategists have to find the net influence of different forces acting upon the entity and the ratio between this and the entity's size. For example, in large companies, small changes in the balance of relevant political, social, and economic forces do not have much of an impact. Strategists have to figure out how forces can be changed and strengthened to redirect the entity toward its current or new strategic objectives and goals.

Strategic investments in an entity are successful until the point at which the entity moves from balance to imbalance. In order to change the strategic direction of an entity at equilibrium, imbalance must be created via a strategic force, such as a revision of law and under-law regulations, changes in investment inflows, the implementation of new technologies, etc. The larger the entity, the more difficult it is to overcome inertia. For this reason, it is easier for individual entrepreneurs and small businesses to change their activity and implement new dimensions strategies. Small businesses and entrepreneurs from the developed world were the first to take advantage of the enormous opportunities in EMCs. In many cases, it was émigrés returning to their homelands, which were in the initial stages of establishing free markets. These émigrés, with their connections and knowledge of their motherland, were light-years ahead of major corporations from developed countries, many of which were ignorant to the strategic opportunities in the GEM. In general, the first entrants to the GEM were less influenced by inertia in their methods of thinking and in practice. Nevertheless, after overcoming the initial challenges of establishing a business in a new and foreign environment, many of these people found themselves in balanced entities, under the influence of inertia.

For strategists there is a dialectical contradiction between balance and sustainability on one hand, and imbalance and improved efficiency on the other that plays an important role in the development, implementation, and monitoring of strategy. An imbalanced economic and business system is more dynamic, but not sustainable. For this reason strategists attempt to bring balance to entities through systematization. However, once balance is reached, the strategist has to anticipate imbalance, and prepare the appropriate strategic update. This process is very challenging and often requires the use of mathematical methods, which is difficult because the dynamics of balance and imbalance are non-linear and thus not easily modeled.

Rule 7: Strategists Should Not Fall into Predictable Patterns

The strategist should never be afraid to use unconventional ideas. In fact, these are often the most effective paths toward success. Unfortunately, when an unconventional strategy brings success, it will become widely adapted and implemented by competitors. Strategists must anticipate their opponents' adaptations. Napoleon was always an advocate of unconventional strategies. But his experience illustrates the dangers of falling into a predictable pattern. His strategies became widely known, and eventually, his opponents used them against him. Strategists should always be aware of what their opponents are and are not expecting.

Rule 8: A Successful Strategy Cannot be Dishonest

Strategy can be amoral, but it cannot be dishonest. The same applies to strategists. The means by which strategic objectives are achieved can be amoral but not dishonest. Why don't corporations with innovative technologies share them with their competitors? Morally, shouldn't life-saving technologies be as widely available as possible? Restricting the use of such technologies may be immoral, but it is not dishonest. Nevertheless, regardless of the moral quality of a strategy, or the type of entity for which it is being developed, without honesty the strategy will never be successful, at least in the long term. However, without a strong sense of morality, the strategy will likely die long before implementation, or it will at least be less efficient. Typically, the morality of a strategy has to be addressed in the mission statement or vision. The consequences of strategies that lack morality include the wrong and untruthful message to society, income-distribution inequality, and low-quality goods and services as a product of the strategy. The strategist has to respect and feel responsible for those whom the strategy will affect. According to Dr Nicole Immorlica, of Northwestern University, and Mohammad Mahdian, a researcher for Yahoo, "a strategy for a player is a function that outputs an announced preference list for any input preference list. Hence the truthful strategy is the identity function."[16] This statement supports the simple idea that an entity's announced mission statement and vision should predetermine its real strategic objectives and goals, otherwise, the entity will mislead society. The same idea applies to a governmental system of strategy: "economic policy cannot be independent from targets, which society advances."[17] However, it is not unusual for company leadership to ignore society, its customers, and even its shareholders, and focus only on misleading its competitors by a public announcement of a fake vision or objectives. This may be controversial, but it is not an unusual practice.

In the mid-1980s two young European entrepreneurs went to Brazil looking for business opportunities. They found a serious think-tank that was seeking to expand its consulting activity in Europe. The young entrepreneurs presented themselves as the owners of a major European consulting company. They signed an agreement with the Brazilian think-tank, on behalf of a European company that existed only in their minds. Later, upon returning to their country, they legally established a consulting company. The Brazilian think-tank eventually realized that these entrepreneurs were dishonest and found better partners. They also opened a legal case against the two Europeans because at the moment when the agreement was signed, the European consulting company did not exist, and all information presented about it was fraudulent. The agreement was nullified and the two entrepreneurs did not get anything out of their efforts but a bad reputation and large debts for their travel and legal fees. They understood the opportunities that the GEM presented, but they did not anticipate the emergence of an age of complete accountability, whereby even companies lacking familiarity and connections with the international business community have the ability to access information that eventually brings all dishonesty to light. The great

Russian military and spiritual leader of the thirteenth century, Grand Prince Alexander Nevsky (1219–1263) of Great Novgorod said, "God is not in power, but in truth." In strategy, power and truth are not mutually exclusive. The winning strategy has to be both powerful and truthful.

Rule 9: Strategists Must Make Systems Out of Chaos

Strategists always deal with chaos, because the future is unknown and thus unsystematized. Depending on which of the two strategic approaches is selected, the level of uncertainty with which the strategist will deal varies substantially. New dimensions strategies involve absolute uncertainty and chaos. Everything is unclear; from total chaos, strategists have to find the best and wholly innovative strategic idea and develop the appropriate strategic management system for the implementation of this idea. Chaos is what separates the strategist from the idea upon which the strategy will be based. The second approach— improvement strategy—involves substantially lower levels of uncertainty. Regardless of the approach that is selected, various levels of chaos and uncertainty are unavoidable. Strategists work on the edge of chaos, bridging the gap between current systems of production and unknown strategic possibilities of the future. According to Dr Shona Brown, an executive of Google, and Dr Kathleen Eisenhardt of Stanford University, "being at the edge of chaos means being only partially structured. The intuition behind the edge of chaos is that change occurs when strategies and their related organizations are sufficiently rigid so that change can be organized to happen but not so rigid that it cannot occur."[18] Strategists guide an entity through several stages of strategic improvement and development. When an entity first enters the ocean of chaos, driven by the sail of the new strategy, and chaos is then preliminarily systematized for the foreseeable future, it is the point at which strategists have to be flexible enough to correct or adjust certain characteristics of the strategy.

Strategists should not be influenced to choose improvement strategies over new dimensions strategies because of the lower amount of chaos. Chaos is unavoidable. Consequently, risk management is a major part of strategy. Even the smallest amount of uncertainty immediately and substantially increases risk. Strategists in the GMP cannot avoid risk and must be prepared to face it. This is especially true for all strategies that deal with the GEM, an environment that, relative to the developed world, is less known and predictable and has a greater variation of characteristics among its economies. Risk management is largely about managing chaos by creating systems and recognizing patterns. Those who try and avoid risk altogether will never be victorious. To say the least, any strategy not oriented to address risk is not grounded in reality.

The strategist must tackle every issue with a systematic approach in order to find relationships and correlations between facts and events that appear to be unrelated. The strategist must create order from chaos, guiding a company from a murky present to bright future objectives. Analyzing issues within a systematic context is the most effective way of achieving this. Without a systematic approach and "without strategy to focus effort, chaos can ensue as people pull in a variety of directions."[19] Employees always need a leader who is able to choose a single direction from the multitude of options and lead the entity in the corresponding direction. Executives can do this through intuition, talent, and definitely with the right strategy.

Strategists attempting to systematize chaos must be prepared for unpredictable challenges. No strategy is perfect, and no one can predict all potential threats. At the same time, strategists cannot be so consumed with preparing for threats that they are unable to take advantage of unexpected opportunities. If strategists think their strategy is perfect, they are either completely out of touch with reality or naive. Typically, executives and strategists are better prepared to face threats than opportunities. As a result, they are incapable of taking advantage of unexpected fortuitous situations because the windows of opportunity will open only for a brief period. When strategists fail to seize an opportunity, it is safe to assume that their competitors will not.

Rule 10: An Asymmetric Strategic Response is More Efficient than a Symmetric One

A strategic response can be either symmetric or asymmetric. The most effective reactive strategy is almost always asymmetric. Symmetric reactions essentially take the same strategic approach as one's opponent, which is predictable and allows the competitor to stay at least one step ahead. It is a typical false cliché of strategic thought that "if a strategy worked for competitors, it will work for us." However, the strategy was successful for the competitor with distinct characteristics operating under different conditions, such as unique technological resources, employees, raw materials, market segment, etc. Repeating a strategy that was efficient for a competitor will not achieve the same success, if any. This approach is an example of the bandwagon effect, where companies do not carefully analyze and create their own strategy, but simply adopt strategies that have recently achieved success. For example, rising gasoline costs in the summer of 2008 led to a wave of promotions offering gas cards to customers, from companies such as General Motors, Hotels.com, and Callaway Golf Co., among many others.[20] Some of them should think about different options: for instance, instead of providing a debit gas card, simply reduce prices or offer cash back. The symmetric strategy basically repeats what competitors have done, which is rarely successful and never catches competitors off guard. Furthermore, it is difficult to redirect consumers by offering the same product as competitors. While it is crucial to understand the strategy of one's competitor, this alone will not produce a winning strategy. An asymmetric strategic response, on the other hand, puts competitors under pressure to reevaluate their strategy. An asymmetric response produces goods and services that will actually attract customers away from competitors or will open a new market niche. Successful asymmetric strategies eventually become the base for symmetric responses in the next iteration of competition.

In January 2002, Airbus surprised Boeing—its biggest competitor—when it announced that production of the A380 would begin. The A380 can fly 8,000 nautical miles and carry 500 to 800 passengers at a speed approaching mach 0.9. Boeing executives felt very threatened, as they were far behind on a similar project (the symmetric response). Boeing strategists instead proposed an asymmetric response. They argued that the upcoming expansion of the EU from 15 to 27-plus members would increase the frequency of European flights. They predicted that this would increase the demand for medium-range commuter planes rather than long-range, high-capacity planes. Boeing focused its resources on the production of the next-generation Boeing 737, a plane more suited for European travel. By 2004 the 1,500th next-generation 737 was delivered to ATA Airlines, reaching this milestone faster than any other commercial airplane in history. This is a great example of a successful asymmetric response.

Another example of an asymmetric strategy is Linux Corporation's response to Microsoft's release of the Vista operating system in January 2007. Linux is a producer of an operating system for computers, comparable to Windows or Mac OS X.[21] Rather than try to develop a similar program, Linux chose to develop a revolutionary project to "shift the desktop's purpose from a 'file manager view' used to display a static set of icons to a dynamic, contextual project management tool."[22]

An asymmetric strategic response can be particularly effective for companies in EMCs when a major competitor merges with or is bought by a multinational corporation. Many multinational corporations do not have a global strategy. In order to establish a presence in emerging markets, these companies often purchase a local company and make it a subsidiary. Such subsidiaries tend to be barely integrated with the multinational corporation. In general, executives of these corporations expect market conditions in their segment of the emerging market to remain the same. At the very least, they do not expect unusual steps from local existing competitors of their subsidiary. This provides other domestic companies with the opportunity to make an unexpected, asymmetric response. Strategists of multinational corporations should always anticipate such asymmetric responses from domestic competitors when establishing new subsidiaries by acquisition. In the GEM, multinational corporations should always use asymmetric entry strategies when possible. For example, when a company that produces home appliances acquires a subsidiary in an EMC that has successfully sold refrigerators in its national market, an asymmetric strategy would be to redirect the specialization of the subsidiary into a new niche market that still uses the existing production facilities, such as the production of freezers. These products are not widely used in emerging markets, but demand for them is increasing. Because of worries about food shortages in many EMCs and developing countries, people are buying more food than they can consume at once; these supplies, of course, must be preserved.

Rule 11: The Strategist Must Always be an Optimist

The strategist has to be an optimist. When facing powerful competitors, strategists must realize that strength is always relative. Strategists must focus on finding stronger responses to powerful challenges. When the implementation of strategy does not go well or a competitor unexpectedly announces a very efficient strategy, the strategist must maintain optimism and patience in the face of these threats. Former heavyweight boxing champion Mike Tyson once said: "Everybody has a strategy until I hit them."[23] Strategists have to be able to endure the punches thrown at them by market forces, and especially from their competitors.

Pessimism is a major barrier to successful strategic decision making. For strategists there is nothing worse than when a strategy that proves to be completely accurate over time was not implemented due to a lack of faith from executives or decision makers. It is easy for the strategist to become extremely pessimistic when this happens. When executives or a board of directors accept a strategy, they are hopeful and optimistic, but the strategist is fearful and overcome with responsibility and pressure. According to Dr Svend Frolund,

> there are two extreme implementation strategies for constraint evaluation. A *pessimistic* strategy will evaluate the constraints before dispatching a message. An *optimistic* strategy will concurrently dispatch a message and evaluate the constraints. If the constraints are not satisfied, an optimistic strategy "rolls back" the message dispatch.[24]

However, there is one area in which strategists can benefit from pessimism—cost. In general, strategists should anticipate unexpected costs of strategy implementation. Unfamiliar conditions in EMCs turned many strategists away prior to even a detailed evaluation of opportunities in these markets. Often, EMCs have very limited financial resources and issues with profit repatriation, which discouraged many strategists before they evaluated the abundant natural resources and huge market potential for these countries.

Even in the face of tremendous challenges and uncertainty, Russian and American strategists remained optimistic about their space programs. As a result, in 1961 the Soviet Union sent the first man (Yuri Gagarin) into orbit, and in 1969 the US sent Neil Armstrong to the moon. These achievements would not have been accomplished without the optimism of the Russian rocket scientist Sergei Korolev and President Kennedy. Strategists must maintain their optimism throughout all stages of development and particularly during implementation, when a great deal more people are involved with the proposed strategy. They also have to be averse to implementing the many unnecessary changes that are often proposed when major strategies are put into practice.

Unlike executives, strategists do not directly unify employees, although they must think about the consolidation of people around the proposed strategy. Executives, the board of directors, or the government manage the actual consolidation. Once they accept the strategy, it is their responsibility to unify stakeholders behind the strategic idea. A qualified majority of people will follow leaders during difficult times if the leader is steadfast and optimistic. In strategy, steadfastness is next of kin to victory.

Rule 12: Always Overestimate the Competitor

Strategists should always overestimate the resources and abilities of their competitors. One will almost never know the exact resources available to competitors, or their strategy for optimizing those resources. More than that, *a weak competitor is not necessarily a defeated competitor.* As the very experienced military and civilian consultant Dr Steve Osborne wrote, "a common mistake is to underestimate competitors and overestimate your own capability. When in doubt, give the advantage to your competitor. The consequences of overestimating a competitor are less than the consequences of underestimating."[25] Overestimating will prevent being caught off guard as a result of either a miscalculation of resources or an unanticipated, extremely efficient resource-optimizing strategy. Prior to the Battle of Alesia in 52 BC, Julius Caesar found out that he had one-fifth the warriors of the Gauls. The leader of the Gauls, Vercingetorix, was a talented commander. Caesar allocated his very limited resources in an innovative and unusual way and developed such an unanticipated strategy that he won the battle decisively. As a result, for the next six centuries, present-day France was part of the Roman empire.

Rule 13: Innovation Can Provide Huge Strategic Advantages

Strategists must always search for innovative ideas and figure out methods and organizational vehicles by which to implement them in their particular field. Innovation can come in many forms, such as advances in science and technology, management systems, etc. Julius Caesar used innovative construction methods and advancements in munitions to achieve military success. Napoleon exploited advancements in artillery to defeat his opponents. Cornelius Vanderbilt used advancements in railroad wheels and breaks to create a vast commercial empire. J.P. Morgan amassed a huge fortune and revolutionized the financial system by developing modern investment-banking practices.

Strategists read the same web sites, newspapers, and magazines as millions of others, but their focus is oriented toward the use of innovations as vehicles to success. Again, strategists must draw on knowledge from many fields. Typically, macroeconomics, microeconomics, and management systems are all taught as separate disciplines. The strategist must combine knowledge from all of these fields, among others. The development of a successful strategy requires an extremely eclectic mind. As a result, business education should be redesigned on a multidisciplinary basis, synthesizing macroeconomics, microeconomics, statistics, applied mathematics, political science, systems analysis, and managements systems with a strategic focus. Many academic programs that focus on strategy narrow its scope, focusing exclusively on "the relationship between politics and military power including the preparation, the threat and use of force, and its latent presence in international politics."[26] This is far from a complete description of the modern requirements of strategists. Regardless of the entity for which a strategy is being developed, geographical, political, social, military, economic, business, and technological issues all must be covered in order to be successful in choosing the right strategic approach and scenario.

Rule 14: The Strategist Should Optimize Limited Resources, Using Time as the Determining Factor

Rule 3 dealt primarily with the dialectic relationship between time and space. Rule 14 focuses on a dialectic issue that is always on the strategist's agenda. One of the fundamental dilemmas for strategists regarding the implementation phase is deciding between reducing time at the expense of resources, versus conserving resources at the expense of time. This basically comes down to the relationship between capital investment and the time required for a recovery of this investment. For this dilemma, time is the factor that determines the strategic cost effectiveness of any decision. By increasing capital investment, the implementation phase is shortened, and production—based on the newly implemented strategy—can begin sooner. Economizing time is the first law of strategy. This law can apply to the ratio of time and space (discussed in rule 3) and the ratio of resources and time. It is especially applicable in the context of the unyielding onslaught of competition in the GMP; saving time, even at the expense of extra resources, increases the likelihood of an entity being ahead of its competitors in a new market niche, in their reaction to changing conditions, etc. Essentially, during the implementation phase, an entity should allocate extra resources to reduce the time of this phase, if during the time saved the company can produce goods and services (according to the new strategy) that will cover the extra resources allocated or will position the company ahead of strategically important competitors. The mathematical approach and calculations of this issue are presented later in this chapter in the strategy implementation section. Strategists always have to remember that unlike popular opinion, time is not on anyone's side. Strategists should always find methods by which to make any time related competitor's advantage obsolete. Ideally, strategists should find methods to use the resources of their competitors to optimize the expenditure of an entity's time and resources.

Rule 15: Strategists Must Figure Out What their Clients Need, not What their Clients Want

Working under contract for a client is a very challenging undertaking. In many cases, the client will not understand the situation from a strategic perspective. After strategists conduct an intense study of the client's situation, they may find that the client's vision is flawed, and what the client wants is not what will provide long-term success for the client and its entity. The strategist must not be influenced by the client's way of thinking. A lack of imagination, from which some clients may suffer, can be contagious, and will prevent the development of a successful strategy.

The strategist must avoid the clip mentality—an attractive image of the strategy or its scenario not founded in substantive thought. When the strategy is sold, the client may realize that they are not receiving what they initially wanted or were promised. Nevertheless, when presenting a strategy to executives or clients, it should be as streamlined as possible, focusing only on ideas that are absolutely crucial to the implementation of the strategy, unless the client asks the strategist to elaborate on particular issues. It is not necessary to explain the intellectual development of the strategy or any other superfluous information to clients: unnecessary details take away from the core of the strategic scenario. Clients should always be presented with a *short executive summary* of the core ideas of the

278 Global Economic Strategy

strategy and the results of its implementation. The entire study should be available, but in many cases it would be uninteresting and overwhelming to clients, especially when the client is a board of directors. When trying to convince a client, it is important to get to the point. Any mathematical formulas used in the development of a strategy should be used only to convince decision makers of the limitation of their resources and what they *cannot* do. It is generally not a good idea to use mathematics to prove what should be done. This is especially true in the executive summary. People tend to have an aversion to mathematical formulas. It is usually best to explain the concept in words and graphics.

Strategists must achieve a balance between clarity and complexity in the presentation of a strategy. The more complex and hard to understand a strategy, the more difficult it is for competitors to develop countermeasures. However, complexity also makes it more difficult to promote and gain support. Strategy must be well understood by those who are responsible for the implementation, but in order to gain widespread support, slogans are very useful. Slogans can convey a strategy's gist without going into detail. Slogans act as a popular version of the mission statement, with minimum information and maximum appeal. Strategists working internationally, especially within the GEM, have to factor in language comprehension to their presentations. They should generally prepare presentations at least in two languages— the national language and English. Cultural issues are extremely important to take into consideration during the presentation of a strategy. Native speakers have to be consulted regarding the connotations and associations of every single symbol in the presentation. Once a strategy is approved and implemented, it no longer belongs to the strategist—it belongs to clients, executives, and the world.

Some of General Cohen's rules are based on the same general principles of the strategist's 15 rules of strategy recommended by this book. However, some of them are not mentioned in this book and can be useful. The rules "Seize the Initiative and Keep It" and "Exploit Your Success" are particularly useful during the phase of strategy implementation.

In addition to the strategist's 15 rules, it is important to mention that a strategy's area of influence is usually wider than the targeted area. In the overwhelming majority of cases, strategy can be improved during the process of implementation by putting together a number of different details that were not visible during a strategy's stage of formation and development. Testing a strategy is like testing a nuclear bomb. In real conditions, it is tested the day it is dropped.

For a comparison of the strategist's 15 rules presented in this book, it may be of interest to the reader to examine other authors' rules of strategy, such as the "10 Essential Principles of Strategy," according to Major General of the US Air Force, Dr William A. Cohen:

1. The Fundamental Principle: Commit Fully to a Definite Objective.
2. Seize the Initiative and Keep It.
3. Economize to Mass Your Resources.
4. Use Strategic Positioning.
5. Do the Unexpected.
6. Keep Things Simple.
7. Prepare Multiple, Simultaneous Alternatives.
8. Take the Indirect Route to Your Objective.
9. Practice Timing and Sequencing.
10. Exploit Your Success.

System of Strategy

Hierarchy of Strategy

Strategy is a systematic phenomenon. By its nature, it is multidisciplinary. By its influence, it is multidimensional, and by its structure, it is hierarchical. With the birth and development of the GMP and the GEM, the system of strategy has become more complex, with more hierarchical levels. Globalization has led corporate strategists to develop not only an international but also a global level of strategy. Additionally, multinational and even medium-size corporations develop strategies for regional economic blocs (international regional strategy). These levels were always prominent in the development of governmental foreign-policy strategies, but national economic strategies were traditionally developed without a global aspect practically until the twenty-first century. Multilateral institutions such as the IMF, World Bank, WTO, etc., have almost always missed a key aspect of strategy—the international regional level. This is largely because multilateral institutions do not have any formal mechanism that deals with regional economic organizations and do not cooperate with many of them. The national level of the system of strategy can be broken down into sectorial (industrial) and regional aspects. However, a typical mistake of national strategists is to ignore the strategies of domestic and foreign corporations operating within their borders. Ignoring this strategic aspect decreases the efficiency of both corporate and national strategies. By including the corporate aspect within an entity's national strategy, cooperation between corporations and governments will inevitably improve. It is absolutely necessary in order to increase the role of corporations in the resolution of major national and regional challenges. The final or initial level of the system of strategy (depending on the strategic approach) is the unit strategy, which applies to corporate subsidiaries, regional and local authorities, and governmental departments (ministries, agencies, etc.).

Globalization influenced all strategists throughout the world to develop global strategy for all multilateral institutions, national governments, and for almost all businesses, even medium-size and small companies, if they are looking for opportunities and threats on the GMP. Global strategy of national governments and internationalized companies required multilateral levels in the strategic hierarchy. The international level did not disappear as a result of the birth of global strategy. It continued to exist as an important stratum. The trend of globalization and the increasing role of international regional economic organizations made it necessary to develop an international-regional stratum within the strategic system. In this strata, the issue of company or country on a bilateral or multilateral level typically develops, but in the frame of regional economic organizations. The national stratum was and is a prominent part of governmental and corporate strategy. Only the integration of businesses to the GMP made this level necessary even for smaller companies. National strategy has to be developed in two dimensions—regional (in terms of domestic regions) and sectoral (industry). Any entity has to develop its pure internal strategy, which for businesses is the corporate strategy. Medium-sized and, obviously, large corporations need to have business strategy for all of their units, and that strategy should be developed under the influence and in correspondence with the overarching corporate strategy. The described dimensions and layers can be understood as the structure of the strategy system; the ideal corporate strategy should encompass all of them (see Figure 6.3).

Correlation between Strategy, Tactic, and Policy

A systematic approach to strategy requires a clearly defined understanding of all of its aspects and strata. The relationship and distinction between strategy, tactic, and policy is

Figure 6.3 System of Strategy.

Source: © Dr Vladimir Kvint, 2008.

often a stumbling point for students. This is not surprising, as in economic and strategic literature, it is possible to find descriptions that totally contradict one another. Quite often policy is presented as the practical implementation of strategy. In this case, it is difficult to explain where tactics fit in, and what the difference is between tactics and policy. In some sources, especially in business literature, business policy and business strategy are treated as synonyms, with tactics presented as the practical implementation of strategy or policy. In this book, policy, strategy, and tactics are three distinct but related aspects of strategic management. The distinction is the following: once strategy is approved and becomes the orientation of an entity's practice, the tactic dictates the daily, monthly, and annual implementation. Policy is the aggregate of the strategy and the tactic. Strategy + Tactic = Policy.

Development of Strategy

Stages of Strategy Development

Scanning and Forecasting External and Internal Environments

When developing a new strategy or revising an existing one, strategists should begin with an analysis of existing and well-recognized trends relevant to the entity, monitoring the dynamics of their influence. More important, strategists have to be able to anticipate trends that are not yet recognized and plan accordingly for their influence. Strategists do not create trends—they discover existing ones. But the most innovative and successful strategies are based on analyses of undiscovered trends. It is of equal importance to understand and analyze the relationships between different trends—how they influence each other, the GMP, and any relevant industries and regions. At the corporate level of strategy, key trends should be used as a guiding vector for the strategy-development process. This is one of the first priorities for executives and strategists.

The process begins with an analysis of global trends. This is followed by an evaluation of industry and regional trends. Typically, corporations monitor industry or sectoral trends but ignore regional ones. This often leads to serious mistakes, as well as competitive losses in the location of their corporate facilities. Analyses of regional trends can be easily obtained from local and regional governments. Even in EMCs, the majority of governments develop their own socioeconomic and technological forecasts. The analyses of global, regional, and industrial trends are then used to make a global *forecast*, followed by regional and industrial *forecasts*.

The most important function of an industrial forecast is the projection of the activity of major competitors for the next one to five years. Special attention should be given to the possibility of the appearance of newcomers in the sector, from "next door" industries. Strategists should also analyze possible openings for newcomers in terms of potential windows of opportunities for their own entity. The next step in a sectoral forecast is related to products and services. In this part of the forecast, the trends that have to be monitored the most closely are technological. The strategist should be very familiar with the technology of the industry and be able to predict—with the help of professional engineers and scientists—the possibility of the development of substitute products and services. The appearance of such products and services is the most threatening and resource-consuming issue for an entity. Finally, an industrial forecast has to include forecasts of technological issues related to suppliers.

Regional forecasts typically begin with an analysis of social and political dynamics. This is not restricted to the regions/communities in which the entity operates—trends in neighboring areas should also be monitored. Regional dynamics also have to be analyzed on an inter-sectoral basis. Forecasts have to focus on trends that could cause major changes in industries of the region. New business opportunities tend to appear when other industries in the region close facilities or open new ones. These changes quite often result in access to cheaper raw materials and parts when new facilities open, and opportunities to acquire existing production facilities in the case of bankruptcies and closures. Strategists also have to analyze regional industrial development in terms of potential threats. For example, a company's ability to attract and retain talented employees may be compromised when an industrial giant unexpectedly allocates production facilities in close proximity, offering higher remuneration for talented professionals. Finally, the main priority of regional forecasts is to monitor changes in the market. For the majority of companies, the regional location of their production facilities is the same as the regional market for their products. Tendencies in consumer behavior, in standards of living, new industrial development, etc., should always be monitored, as they can potentially shrink or expand market shares of the company.

The ultimate result of all of this activity is a company-specific forecast that describes the most relevant global, industrial, and regional trends for current and future corporate activity. For strategists working with or within the GEM, this process is especially challenging because of the rapid pace of changes relative to the developed world. Also, it is far more difficult in the GEM to obtain accurate information from the governments of many EMCs. This creates a very high level of uncertainty and makes accurate forecasts very difficult. Some EMCs and especially developing countries still restrict access to political, economic, and technological information, which is openly available to the public in the developed world. In many EMCs and even more so in developing and underdeveloped nations, the Internet is not yet a major source of reliable day-to-day information. All of these reasons inhibit strategists' ability to discover crucial changes and trends.

A key function of the forecasting phase is the scanning of the external and internal environment (see Figure 6.4). Basic economic factors are the major limitations that should be evaluated during this process. Unlike an analysis of the internal environment, a scan of the external environment should begin with an evaluation of natural resources and environmental limitations. This should be followed by a forecast and scan of labor resources and existing production facilities or capital (depending if the forecast is industrial or regional). The final factor of the external environment to be analyzed is technological and scientific achievement, which, as previously discussed, during the monitoring of the global trends is the most important dynamic to observe. During the preparation of an industry-specific forecast, the major issues are related to an analysis of trends in competitors' development, forecasts of potential improvements in the industry's major products and services, and finally a forecast of suppliers' potential activities. Regional forecasts are primarily related to socioeconomic characteristics of the community targeted by the company, or in which its facilities are located. A very important element of regional forecasts is the production of companies in nearby areas that belong to different industries. Often, this stage of forecasting can lead a company to new and cheap raw materials that are waste or the byproduct of companies in different industries across the region. This regional production forecast can also open potential consumer markets for the company. Finally, regional forecasts should analyze the future performance of the regional market.

Once global, industrial, and regional forecasts or their updates have been prepared, strategists should develop entity-specific forecasts. During this phase, the major focus is the reevaluation or scanning of the internal environment of the entity in order to spot any resource shortages that may be relevant for the forecasting period. In this process, the order in which basic economic factors are analyzed is different from that of the external scanning process. The first step is an evaluation of the entity's technological and scientific resources, how they relate to emerging technological trends, and what these trends mean for the company in terms of opportunities and threats and the educational attainment of its employees in terms of exploiting new scientific-technological advancements. The next basic economic factor to be evaluated is the entity's existing production facilities and corporate infrastructure. This should also be done in the context of upcoming trends and changes that may be influential during the forecasting period. Capital, employees (labor resources), and finally raw materials and parts (natural resources) currently used by the entity are the final basic economic factors to be evaluated. This order illustrates that the most important issue for a company-specific forecast is technology, which can influence all other basic economic factors of a company's internal environment. The development of the *company-specific forecast* is actually the first stage of *strategy formulation*.

Unfortunately, in practice many corporations do not complete company-specific forecasts. However, investment-banking equity groups and hedge funds are more strategically focused on monitoring trends and almost always prepare industry-, country-, and company-specific forecasts. They then develop strategies based on these forecasts, which are protected as proprietary information. Equity groups and hedge funds are like vultures, constantly on the lookout for weak companies, for which they see great strategic potential. They buy these companies, change their management, reengineer the company, make them successful, and sell them at a high profit. The success of hedge funds and equity groups of investment-banking companies demonstrates the effectiveness of an intense and constant focus on monitoring trends and developing forecasts based on their analysis—from global, industrial, national, regional, and even local perspectives. Regardless of the stage of one's strategy, the strategist must continue to monitor trends. However, following the approval of a strategy, the strategist typically narrows the focus to trends related to the approved strategy. After only a few months, the monitoring of trends widens its scope. This is especially related to technological discoveries, revolutionary political changes, new or aggravated environmental issues, and natural or technological disasters that have major technological, economic, political, environmental, and business implications.

Strengths, Weaknesses, Opportunities, and Threats

The process of scanning the external and internal environment and the initial preparation of a company-specific forecast and the mission statement, vision, and objectives is similar to the strengths, weaknesses, opportunities, and threats (SWOT) analysis created by Albert S. Humphrey of the Stanford Research Institute.[27] Understanding SWOT is very important when developing a strategy. However, while SWOT may have a nice ring to it, it is best to start one's analysis with the external environment, i.e. opportunities and threats, rather than the strengths and weaknesses (the internal environment). Discovering opportunities should be the priority in the scanning of the external environment. While it is obviously important to anticipate threats, not being able to take advantage of an unanticipated opportunity can actually be more harmful. Strengths and weakness (the internal environment) and available resources should all be analyzed within the context of what is needed to exploit potential opportunities. So, while the name may not be as catchy, an opportunities, threats, strengths, and weaknesses (OTSW) analysis is actually a much better method of creating the strategic vision and objectives, as it more efficiently prevents a company, country, etc., from being unprepared for opportunities or threats. It is especially useful for the GEM, where both opportunities and threats are immense. An OTSW analysis will provide time advantages for companies to recognize opportunities and identify threats, and allow them to be positioned ahead of competitors in the marketplace.

The OTSW approach can be especially useful for companies with high appetites for risk, such as a company from the developed world seeking opportunities in Iraq. While Iraq is beginning to show signs of improvement in its political stability and business climate, it is still clearly *under fire*—meaning that it is in a state of war and armed civil unrest. Trade

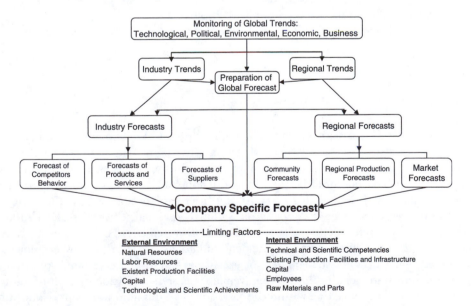

Figure 6.4 Stages of Development of Business Strategy: Scanning and Forecasting External and Internal Environments.

Source: © Dr Vladimir Kvint, 2008.

companies are usually better suited to operate in markets with such high levels of instability; it is less risky to buy and sell products than it is to invest. However, when a company becomes more familiar with a country, gains local experience, develops a relationship with national and local authorities, and better understands the local culture and consumer behavior, it is only logical for the company's strategists to evaluate investment opportunities. Below is an example of an OSTW analysis related to trade and investment in a country under fire—Iraq:

- Opportunities:

  —gradual political and economic stabilization;
  —possible diversification of company's export to Iraq;
  —company's import development of specific Iraqi products.

- Threats:

  —terrorism;
  —regional instability;
  —corruption;
  —inflation;
  —currency inconvertibility;
  —barriers to expatriation of profits.

- Strengths:

  —excess capacity of existing production facilities;
  —extra inventory;
  —new sources of inexpensive raw materials and parts.

- Weaknesses:

  —high prices due to production costs for the majority of Iraqi population;
  —deficiency of bilingual (Arabic–English) employees;
  —poor knowledge of Iraqi culture, consumer behavior, and educational system.

Strategy Formulation

MISSION, VISION, OBJECTIVES, AND GOALS

Mission Statement   The mission statement is the first practical document created as a result of analyses and forecasts of the external and internal environment. The mission statement is the simplest and most straightforward way to communicate the essence of a business venture to consumers and potential partners. The mission statement has to describe the *service* that the company will deliver to society. It is a brief explanation of how the entity will satisfy the interests and needs of society on a global, regional, or local scale. Unlike the following stage of development—vision—the mission statement is oriented exclusively for outsiders of the entity. The mission statement should never describe how employees are remunerated, what benefits shareholders or executives enjoy, the company's profitability, etc. The mission statement is also not an avenue to express ambition or to highlight one particular product or service line within the company. The mission statement is a document that has to be prepared for the long term. Companies make substantial investments to tie the mission statement to the company brand; it is not a document that should be constantly revised to reflect new products or service lines. Skyworth, a leading consumer-electronics developer and manufacturer, is publicly held and listed on the Hong Kong Stock Exchange. In 2002, the Skyworth mission statement expressed the desire to be the no. 1 consumer-electronics company. Declarations of ambition such as this do not belong in the mission statement. Potential consumers, partners, etc., seek the leading companies of their respective industries. Declaring the desire to be a leading company tacitly concedes that one's products or services are not the best on the market and draws outsiders to question their assumption of the quality of the company's goods and services. It is especially important for companies such as Skyworth, which sells expensive, high-end electronics, to present themselves properly to consumers. Skyworth revised its mission statement in 2003 as part of an improvement of its entire strategy.

In only a few sentences, the mission statement should convey what industry the company belongs to, what region, and the *reasons for the company's existence*, i.e. what this particular entity's value is for buyers and customers. Every successful company, even those with ordinary products or services, occupies a unique niche in the market. Companies must compete for this niche from the moment of the development of its entry strategy. As the great German leader and "Iron Chancellor" Otto von Bismarck said: "All treaties between great states cease to be binding when they come in conflict with the struggle for existence." It is clear from these words that the reason for existence is one of the most vital issues for the company, and they will be willing to sacrifice anything for this. From this perspective, the mission statement also addresses employees, but only for one reason—to ensure their understanding of the entity's service to its country, society, and customers. The mission statement has to clearly explain the company's uniqueness—how it differs from others, and even from its subsidiaries, which may have similar functions but different locations. For example, despite the fact that the Marriott Marquis Hotel—located in the theater district of Manhattan—and the New York Marriott East Side are separated by roughly five blocks, they both have unique mission statements. Although the mission statement must cover a lot of information, it is important to keep it as short as possible. It should not exceed 275 words; an ideal target is roughly 150 words.

For strategists to write a mission statement is like consolidating, in very simple words, their major strategic idea. For many years in developed countries the mission statement was not a particularly important aspect of the strategic process. It was almost ignored in the business plan and during strategy development. In many cases, it was written at the last minute by an accountant after completing the Form 10-K annual report required by the US Securities and Exchange Commission. Since the formation of the GMP and the subsequent groundswell of international competition, the situation has changed drastically. The importance of the mission statement has substantially increased; it is the first message from the entity to all outsiders. The mission statement is often the base for an entity's slogan, logo, etc. Most important, the drafting of the mission statement is a key stage in strategy development and a major guideline for all subsequent steps. Although the intended audience of a mission statement is not shareholders, executives, and employees, one of its functions is to unite all of them behind the implementation of the company's responsibilities to society. Foreign companies' mission statements receive a great deal of attention in the GEM, the population of which is less familiar with international companies than that of the developed world. As a result they have to be crafted with particular care, especially taking into account local culture, religion, and foreign-language comprehension. The majority of the GEM's population has a limited understanding of foreign languages, including English.

By the end of the twentieth century, practically all leading corporations began to invest time and resources in the formulation of the mission statement. Many even hired outside consultants to rewrite or create their mission statement. As a result of this increased attention, the quality of mission statements has improved noticeably. The progression of the mission statement of Dow Jones & Company is indicative of this general trend. Prior to its recent revision, the Dow Jones mission statement stated the following:

> Publish the world's most vital business and financial news and information—in any form, time or place—to create the greatest value for our customers, employees and shareholders and for the benefit of free people and free markets. Also publish high-quality community newspapers.[28]

This mission statement includes several typical mistakes. Most important, it is not directed to the proper audience, as indicated by the declaration to "create the greatest value . . . for employees and shareholders." The target audience of a mission statement should be outsiders, not employees and shareholders of the company. As of 2008 Dow Jones's mission statement has been revised and substantially improved: "to be the world's best provider of business content and information services across all consumer and enterprise media channels."[29] This mission statement is definitely addressed to the global community, which is the appropriate audience. Nonetheless, some ambitions are apparent. Despite the widely acknowledged importance of the mission statement, there are still some major companies that have not revised their mission statements appropriately. For example, Merrill Lynch's 2006 annual report does not even mention a mission statement.[30] This may actually be an improvement from the very poorly written mission statement in its 2001 annual report:

> Our goal is to be a leader in our chosen markets: wealth management, global markets and investment banking, and asset management. Our future is about growth—growth built on a culture of excellence. A culture that extends from how we think, to how we behave, to how we measure performance. By achieving excellence—in everything we do, every time we do it—we will deliver the full value of Merrill Lynch for our clients, shareholders and employees.[31]

First of all, it begins with an explanation of a goal, which should not be included in the mission statement: all goals should be stated in the goal-setting stage of strategy formation. As previously stated, the expression of ambition in the mission statement is never a good idea. Second, there is no mention of ethics or fair play in financial markets, which are of great importance. Merrill Lynch learned this the hard way from the serious legal trouble in which it found itself in 2002.[32] To be fair, this mission statement does have some positive aspects, such as its focus on the future and corporate culture. However, it does not describe how these elements are related to their customers. It also makes the mistake of speaking about shareholders and employees.

Vision   Following the mission statement, the vision of the entity is the next part of strategy formulation. Unlike the mission statement, the vision, as a document, is intended for both outsiders and insiders of the entity. Many of the aspects that mistakenly appear in the mission statement actually belong in the vision. By including them in the vision, the mission statement is streamlined, brief, and focused on the perception of the company by outsiders. The vision is the philosophy of the entity. Typically, in an entity's vision describes ideology and principles. Regarding its importance, it is best to defer to Bill Gates, one of the most successful business leaders of the twenty-first century:

> People often ask me to explain Microsoft's success. They want to know the secret of getting from a two-man, shoestring operation to a company with 17,000 employees and more than $6 billion a year in sales. Of course, there is no simple answer, and luck

played a role, but I think the most important element was our *original vision* [emphasis added].[33]

In addition to the entity's philosophy, the vision should address how the leadership of the company will benefit employees and shareholders. However, it should not include quantitative estimations such as the amount of production, market share, or even worse, profitability that the company would like to achieve. These issues belong in the company's objectives and goals. Vision is the best place to briefly describe the social responsibilities of an entity. Unlike in the mission statement, in which an entity's service to society is described, social responsibility should be described in the vision, as a part of the philosophy, principles, and priorities of its strategy. In the vision, the priorities of a company need to be mentioned. The principles of a company's business ethics and culture should be part of the vision. The vision should be a concise digest of all of the above topics, and should consist of no more than 900 words. Outsiders will never read an overly lengthy vision—and outsiders are still one of its main audiences. Detailed explanations of the key aspects of the vision should be reserved for later phases of strategy development. According to Professor Willie Pietersen of Columbia Business School:

> [I]t is a common misconception that a firm can simply invent a new direction for itself in vacuum, express it in a galvanizing vision statement, and implement it the next day. If only life were so simple . . . it is essential to develop key insights first and *then* develop a vision statement based on those insights . . . A company's vision and its strategy are intertwined. A vision statement, after all, is an extension of a firm's winning proposition—an aspirational statement of where that winning proposition can take them in the future. To treat them as separate entities is a serious mistake.[34]

Professor Pietersen's characterization of vision as an indivisible part of strategy is quite accurate. The key insights to which he refers come from a scanning of the external and internal environment. More than being a part of strategy, the development of a company's vision has to occur after the mission statement and prior to the formation of objectives and goals. It functions as a bridge between the brief mission statement and the more comprehensive objectives. A company's mission statement and vision lay the philosophical foundation for a company's objectives and goals. It is a logical progression from the mission statement, to the vision, to the objectives and goals. A revision of any of these elements of strategy formation requires all subsequent and previous elements to be revised as well.

As the vision is a public document, it should not overtly include any information that the company needs to keep secret from its competitors. A certain level of secrecy is crucial for any successful strategy. As Sun Tzu said: "All men can see these tactics whereby I conquer, but what none can see is the strategy out of which victory is evolved." Once a strategy becomes public, one must anticipate symmetric and asymmetric responses from competitors.

Objectives, Goal Setting, and a Strategic Plan   *Objectives* mark the beginning of a strategy's substantiation. Building upon the mission statement and vision, the objectives present the qualitative orientation, priorities, and aim of a strategy. This phase of strategy formation must describe where the entity will be following the successful implementation of the strategy. Objectives provide the qualitative orientation for the goal-setting process. The mission statement, vision, and objectives together form the strategy's concept. The selection and enrichment of objectives is usually the first stage in which strategists face criticism and arguments when presenting to executives and the board of directors, as these documents clearly present changes in the direction of the entity's strategy. The section of objectives in the strategy development as a document can vary from bullet points to several dozen pages of documents, describing all objectives in details. Regardless of the document's length, it should be presented only in qualitative terms, although due to a common misconception of the distinction between objectives and goals, this is often not the case. How does one define the appropriate strategic objectives? More so than an analysis of resources, competitors, etc., wisdom is the light that guides the direction to strategic objectives. Strategists will struggle to progress through the strategic development process without this very important quality.

Goal setting is the first part of strategy that presents quantitative targets for production, sales, employees, etc., for the implementation of a strategy. Building on all previous stages of strategy formation, goal setting provides a measuring stick to guide the further stages of strategy development and implementation. If a strategy will require a company to downsize or expand its business, goal setting is the phase of development in which this should be detailed. All goals are set within the context of an entity's resource limitations. The great Chinese thinker Confucius argued "when it is obvious that the goals cannot be reached, don't adjust the goal; adjust the action steps." Confucius' words are inspiring but have little relevance in the practical world of strategy. Strategists have to be flexible. Natural or technogenic disasters, unexpected technological developments, changes in the consumer behavior, or the appearance of a substitute product may make the initial goals set impossible to reach or obsolete. In these cases, doing anything but reevaluating the entity's goals is an inefficient use of resources. In extenuating circumstances, strategists may even be forced to reevaluate strategic objectives.

Once the mission statement, strategic vision, objectives, and goal setting are complete and preliminarily approved, the next step in the strategic process is the selection of at least *three scenarios* by which to reach the approved goals and objectives, and finally to develop a strategic plan. Economic-mathematical analyses are very useful for selecting these three scenarios, and determining which will be most successful. This type of analysis is also a very effective way to determine which scenarios will not work due to limited internal or external resources. The most important limitations are those of the external environment, as they are beyond the control of an entity, unlike internal resources which can be augmented if necessary. The external environment is a systematic risk. Some experts believe that this type of risk is mostly unpredictable. Contrary to this point of view, it is actually possible to predict systematic risk, although it cannot be managed. Mathematical models can be used to forecast and provide insight on processes of the external environment that have both linear and non-linear characteristics. Conceptual and optimizational mathematical modeling should be employed to verify the feasibility of a strategic scenario, in terms of resource and time limitations. For example, imitational mathematical economic models are very good at narrowing down possible strategic scenarios. However, some experts argue that "it is more important whom one imitates rather than how."[35] These models are inevitably influenced by the quality of information provided and the biases of the strategist. The quality of the strategist and their strategic mindset also plays a role in the interpretation of the results of modeling. One data set can result in a multitude of different conclusions. In order to avoid misinterpretation, a hierarchic system of different mathematical models of sectoral and regional conditions should be used. Imitational models are also every effective, especially for eliminating unworkable scenarios.

A *strategic plan* is very different from an operational or annual plan. The strategic plan must be more flexible, allowing for adaptations to future conditions. The strategic plan constructs an entity-specific framework under which the five basic economic factors are analyzed. This provides an analysis of the scale of raw materials and parts, labor avaibility, capital (in the form of a large-scale budget), and production facilities necessary to meet the goals of the strategy. One of the most important elements determining the strategic location of a company is the availability of existing infrastructure, especially rail, water, and air transportation, as well as communications and high-tech infrastructure. But the key element of a strategic business plan is a schedule. A workable time frame should be established for everything from the entry strategy to the exit strategy, including all basic economic factors, their allocation, and combinations for use of the production of goods and services. Strategic planning consists of a "hierarchy of endeavors . . . starting at the largest, the strategic plan, followed by the portfolio, the program, the project, and even the sub-project."[36] Typically, in large entities—corporations, political parties or governments, etc.—the strategic plan combines several projects as part of strategy development and implementation. One of the first and best examples of strategic planning was the Program Evaluation and Review Technique (PERT). The Virginia-based consulting company Booz Allen Hamilton Inc. (www.boozallen.com/) created this strategic planning method for the US Navy Special Projects Office, for the planning of the development and construction of the first US submarine-launched nuclear-armed ballistic missile, Polaris, in 1958. As of the twenty-first century, the PERT approach has been revitalized with modern computers and IT. It is also important to include leadership within the strategic plan, in the form of a schedule and recommended incentives for effective implementation. The strategist must monitor the implementation of the strategic plan, as well as figure out how to avoid unanticipated obstacles as they arise and how to deal with those obstacles that are unavoidable.

Figure 6.5 presents a visual aid of all required strategic documents from the stage of strategic forecasting to the development of a strategic plan. When strategists present a strategy, all of these documents should be delivered to clients, executives, the board of directors, governments, etc.

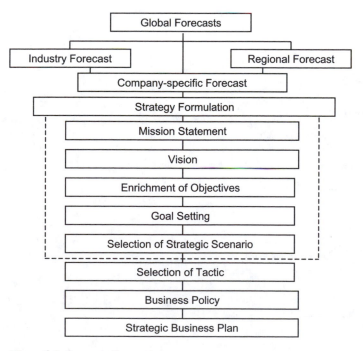

Figure 6.5 Strategy Formation.

Source: © Dr Vladimir Kvint, 2008.

Selection of Strategic Scenario, Tactic, and Policy

The three strategic scenarios can basically be understood as low risk, moderate risk, and extreme risk, each of which provides potential returns relative to the risk level. The extreme-risk scenario usually requires all resources that the entity can obtain, within reason. For each of these three scenarios the strategist develops an aggregated, tactical bloc, which consists of three possible tactics. So, when presenting a strategy to a client, board of directors, etc., the strategist should provide three strategic scenarios, with a total of nine possible tactics. From these options, decision makers select a single strategic scenario and a single tactic for its implementation, which are the base for the strategic policy. At this point all elements and subsystems of the policy are substantiated with specific details, coming together in the entity's strategic plan.

Figure 6.6 illustrates the process of selection of strategic scenario, tactic, and policy.

Strategic Factors and Limitations for Businesses Entering Emerging Markets

Quantitative Limitations

Once a policy is preliminarily approved to be a subject of further, detailed strategic and tactical development, all resource limitations must be intensively reanalyzed. This analysis uses conceptual and mathematical modeling, beginning with the preliminarily approved policy, followed by the tactic, all in terms of the approved strategic scenario.

The following is an example of how conceptual modeling can be used to analyze resource limitations. Assume that a corporation is planning on entering a region in an emerging

Figure 6.6 Selection of Strategic Scenario, Tactic, and Policy.

Source: © Dr Vladimir Kvint, 2008.

market with a policy involving new technology, which will be referred to as a regional technological policy. The technological base of the policy has to be very closely scrutinized, as it is a major determinant of the required resources. In this case, the regional technological policy P in k region may be implemented by means of a multitude of strategies and accordingly, a multitude of tactics. In this case:

P_k is a multitude of possible scenarios of the regional technological policy in k region;

p_k^j is j scenario of the regional technological policy in k region;

Q_k^j is a multitude of scenarios in the k region according to j regional technological policy;

q_{ik}^j is i strategy in k region according to j policy;

Z_{ik}^j is a multitude of tactics according to i strategy, j policy in k region;

z_{sik}^j is s scenario of tactic according to i strategy, j policy in k region;

$\in$ is the Greek symbol meaning "element of."

Based on these descriptions, the following hierarchy of correlation can be presented to decision makers as a possible strategic scenario in region k of an EMC:

$$z_{sik}^j \in Z_{ik}^j \Leftarrow q_{ik}^j \in Q_k^j \Leftarrow p_k^j \in P_k$$

where:

k is the index of the region;

j is the index of the regional technological policy;

i is the index of the strategy of the preliminarily selected policy;

s is the index of the tactic of the preliminarily selected strategy.

Based on the above conceptual model, a system of optimizational models can be formed. The purpose of this model is to maximize the economic impact within the context of resource limitations of the scenario of the policy and the corresponding scenarios of the strategy and tactic. The model for selecting the optimal tactic is the following:

$$\max \sum_{s} f(z_{sik}^j) \times \eta_{sik}^j,$$

where:

$f(z_{sik}^j)$ is the integral social and economic effect from implementation of the selected tactic, according to i strategy, j policy, in k region. The effect is oriented to the main objectives of the corporation's regional technological policy;

η_{sik}^j is the Boolean variable, the value of which describes choice according to tactic: 1 if s tactic was selected, 0 in all other cases. (The Boolean variable is named after George Boole, the great British mathematician and philosopher. It is used to hold the integer values 0 or 1, or the C++ literals true and false.)[37]

In the view of interchangeability of the versions of the policy, limits are needed:

$$\sum_{s} \eta_{sik}^j = 1 \; \forall \; i, j, \text{k}.$$

Besides these, there can be other limited resources:

$$\sum_s \partial_\ell(z_{sik}^j) \times \eta_{sik}^j \leq R_k^e \ \forall \ \ell, i, j,$$

where:

$\partial_\ell (z_{sik}^j)$ is expense of resource ℓ during the implementation of s tactic;
R_k^e is maximum expenditure of resource ℓ in k region. "Resource" can be understood very widely—from basic economic factors to the influence of environmental, labor, and even cultural limitations.

The following model can be used to select the optimal strategy out of the three scenarios presented to the board of directors:

$$\max \sum_i U(q_{ik}^j) \times y_{ik}^j,$$

where:

$U(q_k^j)$ is the integral social and economic effect with the single intensive exploitation of i scenario of strategy with j scenario of the regional technological policy;
y_{ik}^j is 1 if i strategy was selected, 0 in all other cases;

$$\sum_1 y_{ik}^j = 1;$$

$$\sum_1 h_e(q_{ik}^j) \times y_{ik}^j \leq D_e.$$

After that, the selection of the optimal scenario of the company policy in the particular region can be done according to the following model:

$$\max \sum_j c(p_k^j) \times x_k^j,$$

where:

$c(p_k^j)$ is the integral social and economic effect from implementing j policy in k region;
x_k^j is 1 if the policy was selected and 0 in all other cases;

$$\sum_j x_k^j = 1;$$

$$\sum_{j} m_e(p_k^j) \times x_k^j \le N_e.$$

The given model is according to the simplified case when there is a rigid hierarchical order in the model "company regional entry policy ⇒ strategy ⇒ tactic." In other words, one strategy, and one entry policy scenario may be implemented simultaneously. Besides that, the same tactic may be according only to one strategy, and the same strategy may be according only to one scenario of the policy. In reality, more complicated cases may take place. In these situations, the given models should be modified accordingly.

However, even this simplified situation allows one to proceed to executing the concrete calculations for choosing the most profitable version of the regional entry policy (after formulating all necessary normative information, describing all versions of the multitudes of scenarios of regional policy, strategy, and tactic, and defining the type of functions of the effect of f, U, c; functions of e, h, m resource expenditure and of R, D, N limits).

Any entity can use this modeling system to compare the effectiveness of a particular strategy in two regions of the same country, or between two countries with different limitations of resources. For example, region k_1 may be attractive due to its inexpensive and appropriately trained labor resources, while region k_2 may have much cheaper and more widely available energy resources. In this case, the index of strategy for region k_2 will be i_1, and will be oriented towards employing inexpensive work power, and to increase the production of the company based on this work power. Index i_2, for region k_2, due to its cheap energy, but shortage of available labor resources, will be oriented towards the use of energy and should be based on the use of automation and robotic systems. In this case, index f_3 can be the symbol for the increasing energy use per one employee, etc. This is how optimal models of a company's strategy for a particular region should be developed. Then strategists and decision makers have to compare the entry strategies for the two different regions.

The next stage in the strategic process is the implementation phase. However, this is assuming that the entity already has an appropriate management system. If not, the development of a strategic management system is the next priority (see Chapter 7).

Qualitative Limitations

Quantitative analysis should always be supplemented by qualitative evaluations, which are of equal importance for strategic success. The many opportunities in GEM and the GMP have brought executives and strategists of companies operating exclusively in domestic markets to a crossroad; they can allocate their resources domestically, as they have throughout the history of their company, or they can allocate resources in countries and regions of the GEM, an unfamiliar, but potentially very lucrative market. Any venture into the GEM should keep in mind the following issues:

- A foreign venture should make input to improve the level of economic development in the host country. The local population should benefit from a foreign company's activity. At the very least, the local population should not be harmed. In order to ensure this, corporate leaders should be willing to seek compromises with trade unions. Unresolved grievances of trade unions can be serious obstacles to strategic success.
- Foreign companies should ensure that global or foreign culture coexists with local culture. For example, fast-food franchises should adapt their standard menu to accommodate local tastes, limitations, and preferences. This is in the interest of the company, the host country, and the GMP.

- The entry strategy of a company to the GEM must be developed within the context of the political system and the basic economic factors—including business infrastructure and level of technological development—of the particular EMC or its region.

Another limitation that concerns many companies when investing in an EMC is that potential subsidiaries or branches in the GEM will be isolated from the major global business hubs, such as New York City, London, Tokyo, etc. Actually, there are already several major global business hubs in the GEM, such as Moscow, Beijing, São Paulo, Mexico City, and Singapore. In fact, subsidiaries in these GEM hubs may be more closely connected to global business trends than subsidiaries in developed countries that have relocated to suburban campuses in order to cut costs. Advancements in telecommunications and IT have definitely reduced the importance of location. However, suburban headquarters do not benefit from the creative energy that exists in major cities, as there tends to be less social or professional interaction among executives and managers of different companies. From a different perspective, the exodus of the companies from major cities does not bode well for these cities. Many of the best high-tech and financial companies have already left New York City. Even the New York Stock Exchange has considered relocating. This would have a profoundly negative impact on the creative sprit of what is the capital of the world.

For research companies of different scientific fields, it can be very fruitful to be within close proximity to each other, slightly removed from major urban hubs, in what are now called scientific parks. Historically, Silicon Valley can be considered the first scientific park, where many technological and later research and educational institutions were established. This happened over a matter of decades, though it was not planned. In the beginning of the 1960s, the same technological agglomeration took place outside of Boston, along Route 128 which later became the catalyst of the "Massachusetts Miracle" technological-based development. One of the earliest examples of a planned "think-tank town," was Akademgorodok, established in 1957, where the Siberian Branch of the Russian Academy of Sciences is headquartered along with dozens of other research institutions from all spectrums of science, technology, and social studies. This academic town is located 20 km outside of the Siberian city of Novosibirsk. All institutes share facilities, including clubs, restaurants, discussion halls, etc. Scholars benefit tremendously from interdisciplinary exchanges, as they are kept up to date on cutting-edge academic thought and activity throughout the world. This center has been a pioneer in many research fields. For example, the leader of the Siberian economic school, Dr Leonid Kantorovich, won the 1975 Nobel Prize in economics. It is very important for strategists to have the opportunity not only to collaborate with leading scholars of their specialization through the Internet and publications, but also to interact with them, as well as with researchers from other fields, face to face and share the spirit of innovative ideas.

In 1980 Professor Michael E. Porter of Harvard University and the head of the Institute for Strategy and Competitiveness proposed a method of evaluating strategic factors that focuses primarily on the "five competitive forces." This is an important but incomplete evaluation of strategic factors, based mostly only on common sense. The free-market conditions of the GEM are obviously extremely competitive, as it is open to companies from any part of the GMP. A new, innovative competitor can enter an EMC and render the product for which a strategy is being developed obsolete or substantially change the bargaining power of consumers and suppliers. Porter's five competitive forces (listed here)[38] are a necessary aspect of the process of scanning the external environment, but they are only part of the preliminary stages, when the company is choosing the country or region to allocate its resources:

1. Bargaining power of suppliers.
2. Bargaining power of buyers.
3. Threat of new entrants.
4. Threat of substitute products.
5. Existing competitors.

An analysis of these forces is also good practice for setting the mind of decision makers to a strategic tune. These forces are related only to competitive advantages and disadvantages and do not provide enough information for an informed decision about the political and financial (exchange rate, taxes, etc.) environments. For these reasons, once a decision maker comes to the stage of the practical development of strategy and its implementation, it is important to follow stages of the processes mentioned earlier in this chapter, including, of course, quantitative evaluations of all limitations.

Strategy of Subordinate Units

Whether the entity is a multinational corporation with its various subsidiaries or a national government with its various ministries and committees, regional bodies, etc., it is important for subordinate units to develop strategies under the guidance of the organization's strategy. Subordinate strategies can be more precisely tailored to the conditions of the subordinate unit and can focus on very specific technological and organizational trends that may be too narrow for corporate-level strategies. In many cases, multinational corporations request that their units develop strategy without offering any guidance. Feedback provided to subordinate units is often related only to resource limitations, rather than revisions of strategic concepts. This generally results in a corporate strategy that is basically an uncoordinated and even contradictory summary of its various unit strategies, making it very difficult to provide leadership. This *siloed* approach to strategy is actually quite prevalent among multinational corporations. However, to call such an approach a strategy is an abuse of the term; it is actually an indication of a lack of corporate strategy. In order to prevent a strategy from becoming siloed, executives and strategists should maintain an open line of communication with their subordinates, especially regarding implementation. Nonetheless, it would be naive to assume that it is even remotely possible to avoid conflicts of interest between corporate leadership and its subsidiary leadership. Conflicts typically occur over the amount of resources, investment allocated to the unit during development, the amount of time allotted for implementation, and finally, over sales territories, for which subunits may compete among one another. Corporate leadership often questions the unit leadership's projections of productivity and efficiency, arguing, for example, that the average rates in emerging markets are five times higher than those suggested by the unit leadership. The unit leaders will counter that this level of productivity is possible, but only with substantially higher levels of corporate investment. The basic conflict is over the ratio of expected production profitability and time versus investment and emerging-market shares of the subsidiary. The more familiar the board of directors is with the unit leadership, the more influence they will have, making it easier for them to argue successfully for the allocation of the necessary resources for the proposed unit strategy. Annual evaluations of strategy are always aggravating times for the leadership of these two levels, especially when objectives are not being met. When the unit meets objectives and operates efficiently, there is still conflict, though of a different nature; corporate leadership wants to appropriate higher shares of the unit's profits to the corporate budget. For obvious reasons, the unit leadership will always be loath to support this. While, to a certain extent, these kinds of conflict are unavoidable, they can be substantially mitigated through coordinated development of unit and corporate strategy, which benefits both parties. Strategists have to be aware of these conflicts during the process of strategy development and especially during implementation, when the conflict usually intensifies, regardless of the level of success. From the perspective of employees, it is important to pose questions to superiors regarding the strategy of their particular unit (branch, ministry, etc.), as well as the overall strategy of the company or government. This increases employees' knowledge of their organization and demonstrates their seriousness and ambition to superiors.

Consultant and author Clive Reading astutely described the importance of the existence of a strategy for each unit of an organization:

> The old idea of strategy, as an ivory tower exercise handed down for the managers to implement, just does not work. The leadership team and the managers have to be their own strategists. The practitioners have to be planners. Therefore they need a system that they can follow, that will be comprehensive and exhaustive, yet understandable. They need a model that simplifies the situation, but does not ignore the complexities.[39]

In an attempt to diversify the company and to constantly search for more profitable activity, GE, like other large multinational corporations, has subsidiaries in a wide range of industries. Nevertheless, among subsidiaries as diverse as GE Power Generation and the National Broadcast Corporation, there is a shared strategic business culture understanding of success and failure. Typically, if any division of GE is not in the top two in the world in its industry, it is considered a failure. When GE Insurance Solutions did not reach these criteria, GE sold it in 2006 for $6.8 billion to Swiss Re.[40]

Strategy Implementation

Initially, it is difficult to get support for a strategy when it exists only on paper. People are generally critical of ideas that may require change. It is much more difficult to get a strategy approved than it is to gain support for it while it is being implemented and is beginning to deliver results. Some strategists overemphasize the process of implementation, often misinterpreting the strategic plan as a foundation for achieving goals. Goals are actually developed before the strategic plan, under the guidance of the mission statement and vision. The strategic plan lays out a timetable of goals for the implementation of the strategic objectives.

It is very important for strategists to understand the social dynamics and personalities of the actors who will be responsible for implementing the strategy. Successful implementation of a strategy is not only determined by economic and technological factors but also the personal influence of key decision makers plays a substantial role. The strategist should have a good understanding of their principles and mindsets. When possible, it is a good idea to forecast the reactions of key decision makers. The strategy implementation process is illustrated in Figure 6.7.

Time-sensitive Resource Analysis

A time-sensitive resource analysis is an evaluation of the correlation between increases in capital investment and the reduction in the duration of the strategy-implementation phase. It is a very useful tool for strategists. This analysis is closely related to the economy of time. Despite the fact that many economists consider that first law of economics to be "the greater the demand the higher the price,"[41] in strategy, both categories—demand and price—can

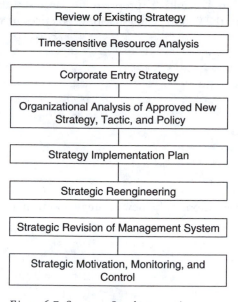

Figure 6.7 Strategy Implementation.

Source: © Dr Vladimir Kvint, 2008.

be fundamentally changed under the influence of time. For this reason the *first law of strategy is the law of economizing time.*

As mentioned in Rule 14, the ratio of time and expenses or investment is among the most important strategic dilemmas that strategists deal with in all stages of development, implementation, and monitoring of strategy in terms of the strategic investment recovery period. This ratio should always be evaluated in terms of the first law of strategy. The following example demonstrates the implications of the law of economizing time by evaluating the economic efficiency of accelerating the strategy-implementation period by investing more resources. The formulas used in this evaluation can be employed for a quick and preliminary evaluation of a time versus resource investment ratio for the implementation of a strategy by executives, boards of directors, and strategists themselves.

During the first stage of this evaluation, the annual economic impact of the implementation of the new strategy is calculated using the following formula:

$$E_{ann} = \left[\frac{Y_2 - Y_1}{Y_1} \times \Pi_1 + \frac{C_1 - C_2}{100} \times Y_2 \right] - E_s C_d^i$$

where:

E_{ann} is the annual economic impact;

Y_1, Y_2 are the volume of goods sold the year before and after the implementation of the new strategy and technology ($1,000);

C_1, C_2 are the investment per $1.00 of goods sold before and after the implementation of the new strategy and technology (in cents);

Π_1 is the profits from goods sold before the implementation of the new strategy and technology ($1,000);

E_s is the appropriate (standard) coefficient of economic effectiveness of capital investment (0.18, this coefficient means that the return on investment should take no longer than five and a half years, which in general is appropriate for large strategic projects. It can be changed according to the country's regulations, practices or the corporate entity's strategy).

In this case,

$$\left[\left(\frac{Y_2 - Y_1}{Y_1} \right) \times \Pi_1 + \left(\frac{C_1 - C_2}{100} \right) \times Y_2 \right].$$

$_\Delta\Pi$ is the annual increase in profits

where:

C_d^i is the costs of development and implementation of the new strategy and technology ($1,000);

$$C_d^i = C_i + C_d$$

where:

C_i is the cost of development and C_d is the cost of implementation.

The annual economic impact gives an idea of the extent of the economic effectiveness of the development and implementation of the new strategy and the required technology with consideration given to all the costs.

The effectiveness of these costs can be defined according to the following formulas:

$$E_e = \frac{_\Delta\Pi}{C_d^i} = \frac{\left[\dfrac{Y_2 - Y_1}{Y_1} \times \Pi_1 + \dfrac{C_1 - C_2}{100} \times Y_2 \right]}{C_i + C_d}; E_e > E_s;$$

where:

E_e is the estimated coefficient of cost (investment) effectiveness.

While, cost (investment) recovery time is:

$$T = \frac{C_i + C_d}{\Pi},$$

where:

T is the cost-recovery time in terms of years.

If, to reduce the cost-recovery time (T), one minimizes development and implementation costs (C_d^i) as much as possible, thereby making E_e larger than E_s, the time factor would not be accounted for. The completion time of the cost-recovery period of the new strategy and technology (T) is then postponed. The time factor is very significant in economics and strategy (this book considers time economization to be the most important law of strategy and economics), because it strongly affects the growth rate of the entity. The overall economic benefit of the new strategy implementation, which will be accumulated over a long period of time, is not proportionate to the benefit gained in the initial stages, starting from the beginning of the implementation process.

In this case, the problem transfers to the evaluation of the time factor with varying implementation costs. Nonetheless, in considering increasing investment to accelerate the implementation of a new strategy and the required technology with the aim of reaching the period of sales of goods produced based on the strategy, one should not require the condition of increasing the absolute sum of costs of this process. Instead, one should increase costs in a time unit of the implementation period that would intensify all operations at this stage of the development and implementation of strategy and the preparation of production. But since increasing expenses in the time unit will require an increase of total costs and there-fore, the cost-recovery time, the challenge is to determine the optimal limits that will make increasing implementation costs economically effective. For example, Y_1, Y_2 = $300,000 and $400,000 respectively. C_1, C_2 = $0.90 and $0.75 respectively; Π_1 = $1,200,000. In this case, the increase in profit after the implementation of the new strategy and new technology will equal:

$$\Delta\Pi = \frac{(Y_2 - Y_1)}{Y_1} \times \Pi_1 + \left(\frac{C_1 - C_2}{100}\right) \times Y_2 = \$406,000.$$

Assume that the costs of development and implementation of the new strategy and new technology amount to $1,015,000; concurrently,

$$C_d^i = C_i + C_d = \$675,000 + \$340,000.$$

In this case, cost (investment) recovery time will equal:

$$T_1 = \frac{C_d^i}{\Delta\Pi} = \frac{\$1,015,000}{\$406,000} = 2.5 \text{ years.}$$

Processes of development, implementation of strategy, and the period of investment recovery can be presented graphically, which is always useful for meetings with top execu-tives and board of directors, for mutual discussion and understanding (see Figure 6.8).

Where T_1' (time of strategy development) is two years, and T_1'' (time of strategy imple-mentation) is one and a half years. The total time of development, implementation, and strategic investment recovery is six years.

Assuming that the implementation costs (C_i) increase by $160,000, that is:

$$C_d^{1i} = C_i + C_d^1 = \$675,000 + \$500,000 = \$1,175,000.$$

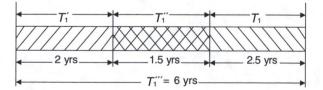

Figure 6.8 Schedule of Strategy Development, Implementation, and Strategic Investment Recovery.

Source: © Dr Vladimir Kvint, 2008.

Meanwhile, cost (investment) recovery time gets longer:

$$T_2 = \frac{C_d^{1i}}{\Pi} = 2.9 \text{ years.}$$

This means that due to intensification of the time of the strategy implementation on the base of increasing investment the time of strategy implementation decreases by 0.6 years (see Figure 6.9).

However, by the second scenario, to increase the time recovery period by 0.4 years, executives, by this decision, decrease the initial economic efficiency of the strategy. But the increased time of expense recovery, executives, by this method, decrease the period of strategy implementation. Because of that, the company starts to sell goods produced on the base of new technology and strategy 0.6 years earlier and as a result final strategy efficiency will improve. The economic effect of this can be calculated by the following order (formula):

The sum of the effect equals:

$$E_{add} = \Pi \times T = \$406,000 \times 0.6 = \$243,600$$

where:

$$T = (T_1 + T_1^{\Pi}) - (T_2 + T_2^{\Pi}).$$

Despite increasing costs and increasing the cost-recovery period in the second scenario, additional profits that will be obtained by the end of the six-year period equal:

$$\Pi_2 = E_{add} - {}_{\Delta}C_i = \$243,000 - \$160,000 = \$83,600$$

where:

$$C_i = C_i^1 - C_i.$$

Thus, in some instances it is useful to increase strategy implementation costs on the condition that as the result of this increase there will be a decrease in the implementation time period. But the total amount of this time decrease will exceed (by absolute numbers) the decrease of the cost-recovery period.

This is a simple method for strategists to present suggestions that by increasing expenses during the time of the implementation of an entry strategy for the benefit of earlier appearance on the market and earlier sales of the goods produced on the base of the new strategy and technology. This method of estimation is also good for executives when they present strategy to the board of directors.

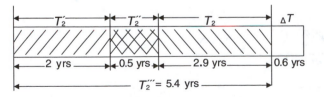

Figure 6.9 Schedule of Intensification of Strategic Investment with Accelerated Period of Strategy Implementation by 0.6 Years.

Source: © Dr Vladimir Kvint, 2008.

In addition, it is important to underline that the uncalculated affect is much bigger, due to the fact that when a company, because of the faster period of implementation of the entry strategy, appears earlier on the marketplace, competitors may lose the initiative to enter the market with the same product. As a result, the company will have a much wider niche for its goods, and will have the opportunity to increase production with lower competition for some time. Reducing the implementation period is even more effective in EMCs. Seeing that a company has already entered the market, many competitors will not even attempt to enter this EMC. In many EMCs, competition is less intense between companies from developed countries. Consumers in these countries become familiar with the first company to enter their market with quality products (relative to local purchasing powers) and are reluctant to change their allegiance. Brand loyalty is particularly strong in the GEM. It is not uncommon for goods to be referred to by brand name, rather than proper names. For example, copy machines are generally referred to as Xeroxes and in many Eastern European countries in the 1980s, VCRs were known as Panasonics, regardless of which company actually produced them.

Corporate Entry Strategy

Strategy implementation provides a framework for the entry strategy and subsequent tactical steps. Entry strategy in the GEM differs a great deal from entry strategy in developed countries. In the developed world, with minor adjustments, successful entry strategies can be effectively replicated in other foreign markets. In the GEM, if an entry strategy is not crafted to the specifics of the particular EMC, it is likely to fail. It is crucial to locate and target the demographic that will likely be most responsive to the new product. In the GEM, the majority of the population, even the middle class, may be considered poor in terms of purchasing power and economic interests by developed-country standards. However, these standards are largely irrelevant in the GEM, where people's purchasing power should not be underestimated. BOP strategies can be very effective in the GEM. The success of an entry strategy in an EMC is largely a result of finding the most responsive segment of society, which is likely very different from a company's experiences in developed countries.

Marketing and advertising studies can be very helpful in offering insight into the specifics of EMCs. They are absolutely necessary for the development of a successful entry strategy. It is very difficult for foreign executives, who have spent all of their life in developed countries, to understand cultural traditions and consumer preferences of different EMCs. Initially, multinational corporations relied completely on experienced executives from developed countries to lead their ventures in the GEM. Eventually, most realized that it was extremely difficult for foreigners to understand the complex cultural and religious traditions and unfamiliar consumer behavior in EMCs. In the twenty-first century, most multinational corporations employ executives from the EMC in which they are operating, people who are already familiar with the idiosyncrasies of certain EMCs. Corporations usually train important employees from EMCs in their education facilities and headquarters. Not only does this help the corporation to better understand consumer behavior, but it also appeals to the protectionist instincts of EMCs, which are much more willing to work with native-born executives than with foreign executives. However, financial and investment departments of companies are a different story. Domestic owners prefer foreign professionals from developed countries to run these departments. In the end, an entry strategy is only as good as the company's strategic understanding of cultural and religious traditions, and consumer preferences of the EMC in which it would like to operate. Ignorance of these issues will inevitably lead to failure.

The process of acquiring partners and allies in a new market is a crucial issue that should be dealt with in the entry strategy. Establishing these relationships can be time-consuming, but it is extremely important in the GEM. Despite the large territories and populations of many EMCs, the purchasing power is often not as large as that of many developed countries. Protectionist policies (and in some cases, lax intellectual property laws that allow domestic companies to copy international brands) have allowed some domestic companies to establish brands that are more recognized in their native countries than some of the most famous global brands. This makes the implementation of entry strategy into certain markets very difficult for foreign companies without some form of cooperation with domestic entities.

The delayed entry of Starbucks into the Russian market is an illustration of the difficulties of penetrating EMCs. In Russia, Starbucks has struggled to achieve the success that it has enjoyed in much of the world, primarily because of a flawed entry strategy. As a result, two domestic brands that offer consumer experiences very similar to Starbucks have already firmly established themselves as the leaders of the Russian coffee-shop market. Many in the West are under the false impression that "it will take time to build a coffeehouse culture in Russia similar to that now seen in the UK and US."[42] In fact, Russia has a very long tradition of coffee drinking, beginning in the Russian Renaissance of the eighteenth century, when Peter the Great brought the coffeehouse culture (in addition to other traditions) to Russia from Western Europe. This tradition was reinforced by immigration from neighboring states such as Azerbaijan, Armenia, Georgia, Uzbekistan, and other Central Asian and Baltic States, which have centuries of coffee-drinking tradition. Unlike executives and strategists from the developed world, domestic entrepreneurs were well aware of the coffee-drinking tradition in Russia, which is why every corner in Moscow and St Petersburg is occupied by a Koffee Haus and Choklotnitza—not by a Starbucks. The Russian market is very big, and Starbucks still has an opportunity to gain access to it, but its delayed entry will make this process more difficult than it had to be. The September 2007 opening of the first Starbucks store in Russia, just north of Moscow, was a non-event. According to Adrian Blomfield, a Russian correspondent for the British newspaper *Telegraph*, "much richer and far more brand savvy, Russians can barely muster an indifferent shrug now that another American landmark, the Starbucks coffee chain, has arrived."[43] Had Starbucks followed the examples of McDonald's in Moscow or Burger King in Warsaw, it likely would have enjoyed similar success. These two franchises employed well-crafted entry strategies for these markets and as a result, enjoyed a great deal of success. The leadership of McDonald's was initially skeptical of the extra expenses needed to set up shop in Moscow—which was done through its Canadian branch—but quickly realized that the free public relations the company enjoyed as a result of the global media coverage of the opening more than made up for it. As of 2008, McDonald's can be found in Moscow, St Petersburg, and even in Siberia; it is a household name in the entire GEM.

Many multinational corporations from developed countries do not have an understanding of local traditions and culture in EMCs, causing them to miss out on huge potential profits. While to a certain extent there is a trend of cultural convergence, whereby people of the GEM are beginning to adopt consumer behavior characteristic of parts of the developed world, nation-specific traditions will always be an important factor for entry strategies in EMCs. The most successful multinational corporations will be those that can integrate local traditions with global brands and products. Coca-Cola for example, sells its products made famous in the United States throughout the GEM, but it also has brands targeted specifically for local populations, such as Limca in India. Success in the GEM is closely related to understanding local consumption traditions, which are usually driven by cultural and religious norms.

An important part of an entry strategy is the development of a system of strategic motivation, strategic monitoring, and control. At this stage, an understanding of cultural and religious differences has to be taken into consideration. A system of motivation has to be specifically adapted to local business practices. Otherwise, the motivation will be ineffective and the strategic business plan will not be properly implemented.

Quite frequently, leaders of corporations do not make a distinction between the entry strategy, which should be a very detailed and precise document, and the tactic. This, however, is not the case among the premier executive strategists, such as Jack Welch:

> [Y]ou have to be careful in China, and you have to use certain cautions because it's going to be a tough, long way. Tactically I'm not particularly in favor of making large investments in China at present, but I'm very much in favor of taking a very determined entry strategy, being patient, and being there when the time is right.[44]

From this statement it is clear that the executive makes a firm distinction between a tactic of a currently used strategy and upcoming strategy, the entry stage of which likely is just being developed.

Tactic

The tactic is developed in order to determine how to handle the major challenges of implementation. Policy consists of a strategy and a tactic. Three tactics should be prepared: one with minimum level of risk and lower results, one with a moderate level of risk, and one with an extreme level of risk, which is feasible but requires a large amount of resources. The tactic is a detailed roadmap for strategy implementation; it is more meticulous and focused as a document than an entry strategy. In terms of its scope, the tactic covers all details of strategy development, implementation, the formulation of strategic management systems, and the most secretive aspect of a policy—the exit strategy (discussed later in this chapter). One of the most important functions of the tactic is as a guideline for chief executives' regular monitoring of the effectiveness of the strategy. At the same time, a tactic is not as detailed as an operational plan. The tactic is an aggregate document, the elements of which are described in the operational plan. Many authors confuse tactic and strategy, mistakenly citing objectives as a separate, non-innate part of strategy. For example, William E. Rothschild, the author of several books and articles on strategy, wrote: "What do you want to achieve or avoid? The answer to this question is your objectives. How will you go about achieving your desired results? The answer to this, you can call strategy." In fact, Rothschild is not actually speaking about strategy—he is speaking about a tactic. More specifically, he is referring not only to a tactic, but also to a strategic plan, tactical implementation, and finally the operational plan. Otherwise, objectives cannot be achieved.

The tactic plays a crucial role in strategic success. As the ancient Chinese military strategist Sun Tzu said: "Strategy without tactics is the slowest route to victory. Tactics without strategy is the noise before defeat." Sun Tzu is absolutely correct. A strategy without a tactic will not be successful; at the very least, its implementation will be slow and unsystematic. A tactic without a strategy will most probably lead the entity that follows it to a disaster and market failure. This point was expressed very eloquently by the great statesman and strategist, former US Secretary of Defense, William Cohen:

> Years ago, another academic strategist, writing about marketing strategy, claimed that good tactical implementation can overcome a bad strategy. That notion is ridiculous. If the strategy is bad or wrong, the only thing good tactical implementation will do is

make a bad strategy result in something worse. The bad strategy may succeed, but it would be better if it failed.[45]

As a document, the tactic can be referred to as an implementation plan. However, in this case, implementation has a much wider meaning. It includes the implementation in practice of every job during development and implementation. Strategic reengineering is an important part of the tactic as a document. This can be understood as "a complete restructuring of technical services operations."[46] The practice of reengineering became very popular in the 1990s. Several consulting companies specialized in this, such as Andersen Consulting, which later continued this service under its new name, Accenture. For example,

> Accenture enabled pump and valve manufacturer KSB to improve, streamline and optimize its business processes in addition to implementing SAP R/3. KSB now outperforms its peers and has outsourced its application management to Accenture as part of its drive to achieve high performance.[47]

In this particular case, reengineering is a product of Accenture but a tactical element for the company KSB. When the results of reengineering are successfully implemented, the entity moves on to the next stage of the tactical implementation of the strategy. According to the results of reengineering and an evaluation of the current success of the strategy implementation, the company should strategically revise its management system. The final tactical stage of strategy implementation is the monitoring and controlling of the strategy realization, which continues until the end of the current strategy. At this point, the previously developed exit strategy should begin to be implemented.

As important as a tactic is, tactical success without a strategic understanding of the future is a direct route to failure. Any success that is achieved without spending time and effort to define a strategy is like treating the symptoms instead of the disease. A detailed analysis of tactic is not one of the aims of this book. However, all elements described above of strategy development and implementation are a guideline for the development of the tactic.

Cultural and Religious Environment of Strategy Development and Implementation

Globalization has very important cultural and religious implications that must be understood by strategists operating in the GMP. Its critics often argue that it is causing a global conversion of cultures that dilutes the authenticity and uniqueness of local culture. In fact, strategists have to take into consideration two paradoxical cultural dynamics: a global conversion of cultures and, at the same time, an embrace and protection of local cultural idiosyncrasies. While English has practically been established as the standard means of communication in the GMP, there are several regional languages of great importance— Spanish in Latin America, Russian in territories of the former Soviet Union, and Arabic in the Middle East and North Africa. In addition, there are languages that represent significant markets of people dispersed throughout the world—the francophone market (extends to every inhabited continent), the German market (several European and African countries), the Portuguese market (Portugal, Brazil, and several African countries), the Italian market (Italy, Ethiopia, Eritrea, and Albania), and the Arabic market (the Middle East and the Arabic diaspora throughout Europe, Africa, and North America). The GMP has created a need for widespread comprehension of key foreign languages and comprehension of foreign cultures. Nevertheless, English is the language of business. As editor-in-chief of *Forbes*, Steve Forbes wrote:

English is the language of economic opportunity . . . If you know English, the Information Age is your friend. If you know English, the doors of opportunity are wide open. But if you don't, you're stuck—and in danger of being left behind.[48]

The same goods, services, and technologies are being used throughout the world, which is contributing to further global integration and unification and is both a factor and a consequence of the GMP. The GMP accelerates global progress, because innovation and new ideas become widely accepted and implemented. Cross-cultural exchange of ideas and technology is also a consequence and factor of the GMP. It creates a process of constant evolution and optimization of strategies and operations. This process is leading to the creation of a more unified, peaceful, and tolerant world. But at the same time, different political and ideological environments and varying consumer behavior throughout the GMP present a challenge to the process of global integration and strategists trying to build success in this changing environment. This requires companies to have a global strategy that takes into account differences in consumer behavior in national and regional markets.

Cultural convergence is a two-way street. The success of corporate global strategy is related to the reflection of the growing influence of the GEM business cultures and its conversion with well-established business ethics and practices of companies from developed countries. A great example of this phenomenon is ArcelorMittal, the world's largest steel-producing company, owned by the British–Indian Mittal family. This family used a hybrid of Indian and British values to become one of the most successful family-owned and operated businesses in the world. Their success is reminiscent of the DuPont family in America in the nineteenth century, when they merged French ethics with American business culture. The business culture of the Mittal family should be studied by executives throughout the world, not just those from India, or the GEM. When the Mittal family purchased Arcelor, a leading European steel company, it was one of the first examples of *insourcing* by an emerging-market company in the developed world as a new global trend, which can be defined as "an allocation or reallocation of resources internally within the same organization, even if the allocation is in different geographic locations."[49]

Another significant cultural trend is related to the mass culture of the US as a superpower—Americanization. Behavioral norms of the US have spread throughout the GMP and global workplace. For example, diplomas on the walls of executives' offices in Albania or Brazil are a symbol of interaction with partners and clients from US companies. It used to be the case, prior to the influence of this trend, that people from the GEM kept their awards and diplomas at home, not displaying them in corporate offices. However, there are limits to Americanization, even on small-scale issues. In the US, it is not uncommon when buying a car to kick the tires as a kind of perfunctory test of the car's quality. This is not advisable in many EMCs, especially Ukraine, Moldova, and Georgia. When looking at a new car, if someone were to kick the tires in one of these countries, the salesman would likely (at the very least) kick that person back! The aim of this joke is just to give an idea for foreign investors that even day-to-day behavior varies substantially among cultures and can be the source of misunderstanding, if they are not accounted for. As the saying goes, the devil is in the detail. Professional behavior is a summary of many small cultural issues to which foreigners have to be sensitive in order to develop a positive business atmosphere.

McDonald's is often portrayed as an instrument of Americanization of foreign countries. To a certain extent, McDonald's is one vehicle through which American consumer culture has spread throughout the world, but its international success is based on its ability to cater to local tastes and preferences, often with the help of local partners. McDonald's does not enter new markets expecting to replace local cuisine with hamburgers—such a strategy would inevitably result in failure. In fact, McDonald's corporate strategists develop a variety of entry strategies in EMCs in accordance with regional, national, and local cultural and religious values. For example, in Muslim countries, McDonald's provides halal food, as well as kosher menus in Israel. Another important part of McDonald's global strategy is to always hire local people and to use local traditions and culture in its advertising. The successful application of McDonald's strategy is related to its ability to cater to local tastes and preferences. This is the model for strategists that are developing entry strategies for countries of the GEM. The diversity of the GEM and the role of cultural traditions are much stronger and more relevant than in developed countries, which have reached a much higher level of cultural conversion.

Culture as a Strategic Risk Factor

The variety of different cultural, historical, and religious traditions and the ethics of business practices pose certain challenges and even threats to international investors and companies, which can be referred to as cultural risk. This basically refers to the cultural gap between a foreign investor, merchant, or entity and the society of a potential recipient of investment or business activity. The greatest challenge comes in understanding the mentality of people with completely different cultural, religious, and historical traditions. The very different political and business cultures of EMCs compared to developed countries deeply affect peoples' mentality. For example, words such as democracy, elections, public opinion, etc., that are universally embraced in developed countries have completely different connotations in the populations of EMCs. Many of these people have not rejected democracy outright, but associate it with the chaotic transition period after the fall of dictatorships leading to and during the liberalization of command economies. Furthermore, what to strategists and executives from developed countries may seem like an oppressive dictatorship covered in transparent democratic slogans may be a tremendously positive step forward from the brutal dictatorship that people were once forced to endure. The legacy of dictatorship deeply affects the business culture of the GEM. Many foreign managers and executives will be shocked by the lack of initiative of employees in EMCs. This is a result of generations of risk-averse behavior that understandably occurred under dictatorships. In many EMC societies, there is only one correct answer—whatever the boss thinks.

The rapid pace of urbanization in the majority of EMCs furthers the cultural gap faced by foreign strategists. Large portions of urban populations have just arrived from provincial villages. These people experience a double culture shock—one with the more sophisticated urban culture (museums, theatres, libraries, etc.) of city life, as well as the shock of dealing with foreigners and interacting with international culture for the first time. This is the source of a great deal of conflict between foreign executives and managers and their local blue-collar employees.

The best way for foreign companies to handle cultural risk is not to try and change the mentality of local populations. This is a gradual process that happens slowly as they interact with different types of people. What has to be an integral part of a successful entry strategy is for foreign companies to make the effort to understand local traditions, histories, and political and business cultures. Foreign companies must be willing to change their typical practices in order to work more efficiently in and with the local society.

It is also very important that strategists of foreign companies do not misinterpret backwards political and business cultures as a reflection of a society's knowledge of high culture, such as art, literature, film, etc. An entry strategy for the GEM has to be developed with respect to the very deep literary and artistic traditions, especially in EMCs such as Russia, those of Eastern Europe, Argentina, and India. Strategists should expect that many people with whom foreign businesspeople will interact will be very knowledgeable about high culture of the world. American strategists may not be familiar with writers that Europeans (and most people of the former Soviet Union) grew up on, such as the French novelist Guy de Maupassant or the German writer Eric Marie Remarque. It would be very difficult to find Latin American executives that are not intimately familiar with the works of the Colombian Nobel laureate in literature, Gabriel Garcia Marquez, or the Brazilian author Jorge Amado. It would be equally difficult to find Chinese executives and strategists who do not embrace the teachings of the ancient philosopher Confucius. Any leaders unfamiliar with the Italian political philosopher and Renaissance man Niccolò Machiavelli will struggle to be successful in the Byzantine business cultures of the Balkans and the Maghreb. EMCs' high culture and especially literature should be studied by foreign executives and strategists as it can be a very effective means of bridging cultural gaps during the implementation of strategy.

There are many examples of the disastrous results of a failure to address cultural strategic risks. The theme parks of Walt Disney Co. were very successful in the US and even Japan, but due to an entry strategy that inadequately evaluated cultural factors, initially failed miserably in France. In 1992 Disney opened a theme park outside Paris that failed to meet projected earnings and attendance and lost a great deal of money. Disney made the mistake of assuming that the French would spend the same amount of money on entertainment, pay the same entrance fee, and enjoy the same food as Americans and Japanese. All of these cultural assumptions were strategically wrong; Disneyland Paris became successful only after making certain adjustments, such as serving alcohol, which would be inappropriate according to US cultural norms in similar circumstances.

Cultural risk is an especially important aspect for entity-specific strategy development and implementation. This does not only apply to entities that are located in foreign countries. It can also apply to consumer culture in certain industries toward particular products and services. For example, in January 2007, when Microsoft released its newest operating system, Microsoft Vista, it was the result of the development and implementation of Microsoft's strategy for several years to combat Apple computers. They gave substantial attention to make sure that Vista would be simpler and take less time to load. Microsoft also used a tactical step—to delay the day of release of Vista in order to build up anticipation of this product by customers, and to increase initial demand. Without evaluating the success or failure of the Vista operating system, this example is very appropriate for introducing a new product into EMCs, where people first need to be familiarized with the existence of the product; second, have to believe that it is easy to use; and third, that people will anticipate the product for some time before they are able to purchase it.

Exit Strategy

Even the most successful strategies come to a point at which, due to changing conditions or needs, the transition must begin to a new strategy. If a strategy is failing, or the strategist can see a failure in the near future, the strategy has to be ended. Even very profitable businesses have to have an exit strategy in case they would like to sell their business or merge with others during peak profitability. Successful strategists will be prepared for this moment and employ the exit strategy, which is mostly developed during strategy implementation. Nonetheless, exit strategy is the most forgotten part of the strategic system. The majority of companies do not have pre-prepared exit strategies. A survey by Massachusetts Mutual Life Insurance Company (MassMutual) found that 67 percent of small businesses do not have an exit plan or a plan for exactly when and how to sell the business.[50] In some companies executives and strategists think that they are "too good" to need an exit strategy. When they unexpectedly encounter a situation needing such a strategy, they find themselves completely unprepared. This is especially the case regarding liquidation exits, one of several types and methods of leaving the marketplace. This is exactly what happened in May 2002 to the largest professional auditing and consulting firm in the world (at that time), Arthur Andersen, LLP, with more than 100,000 employees and about 100,000 clients in almost 80 countries. Its leadership could not imagine that they would be forced out of business and their Certified Public Account license would be revoked by the US Securities and Exchange Commission, per a court decision. The liquidation of this firm was sudden and very harmful to current and former employees, as well as for many clients. It was only the absence of an exit that allowed the firm's conviction in the first place, as four years later by decision of the Supreme Court, this decision was overturned.[51] By that time, out of the 100,000 employees, there remained only a couple hundred. If an exit strategy had existed, Arthur Andersen would have been prepared for such a situation and could have defended itself from the initial accusations, preventing the liquidation. Instead, years of litigation resulted in the destruction of the company's once highly respected name.

Another example of the tremendously negative consequences of not having an exit strategy is the experience of Metromedia Fiber Network Inc. This group was part of John Kluge's (a great business visionary and one of the richest entrepreneurs and executives in the history of the United States) "empire." "The Group has international operations in Europe and Japan. On 08-Feb-2001, the Group merged with SiteSmith, Inc. On 20-May-2002, the Group filed for reorganization under Chapter 11 of the United States Bankruptcy Code."[52] This bankruptcy happened to a company that was once very successful, only because it lacked an exit strategy from a market that became no longer lucrative. The desire to hold on to the business, no matter what, is a major barrier to the right and properly timed exit from a market. Due to the high volatility of the GEM compared with the developed world, an exit strategy definitely has to be prepared no later than during strategy implementation, because the exit period of companies in the GEM is significantly shorter. Companies that do not prepare exit strategies will in many EMCs be prey for raiders.

It is no less important to have an exit strategy for owners of small and family-run businesses, because, unfortunately, life is a time-sensitive issue. "The idea that someday, someone else will be running your business may be a difficult one to consider,"[53] but it is an issue that must be addressed prior to the development of an exit strategy. This allows owners to transfer their business to relatives, friends, or colleagues, preventing the immediate liquidation of the entity to which they dedicated their life. As Steve Robbins said in his article "Exit Strategies for Your Business": "It's not enough to build a business worth a fortune; you have to make sure you have an exit strategy, a way to get the money back out."[54]

For partnerships an effective exit strategy that prevents liquidation is to sell some shares to outstanding employees in order to raise the capital necessary to prolong the firm's existence, though with an extended partnership. Typically, the name of the partnership will change as a result. In legal terms the previous firm exits the market and is replaced by the new partnership. Some partners may prefer to have an exit strategy related to the full sale of their rights and shares. In these cases, it is important in the preparation of the exit strategy to have measures preventing loss of clients and market share. The most successful exit strategy for companies under private ownership is the preparation of an initial public offering. Other exit strategies can be related to a long-term vision to merge with certain competitors or to create a joint venture with them.

One of the main functions of the exit strategy is to deal with exit barriers, which "can be economic, strategic, or emotional factors that keep companies from leaving an industry even though they are earning a low—or possibly negative—return on their investment."[55] Among the major reasons for these barriers can be a strategic vacuum that prevented the company from developing an exit strategy prior to the emergence of major problems. These barriers include long-term contracts with buyers or suppliers, tenants, long-term lease agreements, the termination of which leads the company to huge compensation for counterparts of the agreements. Strategic exit barriers can also be the result of special agreements with trade unions, the cancellation of which can bring a company immediately to court and arbitration, resulting in huge compensations for grievances. A corporation may not have enough resources to become a new entrant in nearby industries or regions, practically preventing an exit from its current area of activity. Successful corporations employ their exit strategies as a result of the monitoring of internal and external policy. Otherwise, the company's exit is usually caused by unexpected threats. Ideally, the strategists will be prepared for any of these scenarios and can just take the *exit strategy* from the shelf, which should be developed far in advance, usually prior to the beginning of the strategy implementation. A successful exit strategy is no less important than an entry strategy for complete victory. To a certain extent, without a successful exit strategy, the strategy cannot be totally successful. As governor, George W. Bush said regarding the conflict in Kosovo in April 1999 (prior to his election as president): "Victory means exit strategy, and it's important for the president to explain to us what the exit strategy is." Unfortunately, when US military forces very successfully took over Iraq, US leadership obviously did not have either a strategy to maintain success in Iraq or a strategy for exiting. Very soon after the first victorious days, this became apparent. In some stages of corporate activity, exit strategy is the most important part of strategy. This is especially the case when owners, shareholders, or executives decide to sell their business. The better the exit strategy, the higher the market price of the company at the moment when ownership changes. In this case, the exit strategy has to bring the company, like an admiral brings a ship for a parade, with a raised flag, in the best possible condition.

Study Questions

1. Describe the characteristics of the strategic mindset.
2. Describe the two approaches of strategic thinking and the differences between them.
3. What are the stages of the strategic thought process? Describe each one.
4. Describe the qualities and background of a professional strategist.
5. Why is the traditional way of thinking not useful during processes of strategy development?
6. Why is inertia one of the greatest adversaries of strategic thinking?
7. Describe symmetric and asymmetric strategic responses—give examples.
8. How is the optimization of resources related to strategy development and implementation?
9. Describe the correlation between time and resources in strategy development and implementation.
10. Which is more efficient—spending more resources in a shorter period of time during strategy implementation or spending fewer resources but over a longer period time?
11. Describe strategy as a system.
12. What is the correlation between strategy, tactic, and policy?
13. Describe the major stages of strategy development.
14. How is forecasting related to strategy development?
15. Describe the scanning of the external and internal environment. What is the difference between the two? Which should be done first, and why?
16. Describe a SWOT analysis. Why should the order of the stages of this analysis be changed?

17. Describe major elements of strategy formulation.
18. What is a mission statement? What is its role in strategy formulation? What should it convey?
19. What is the difference between a mission statement and vision? Why is it necessary to have both of these documents in the process of strategy development?
20. What is the major function of vision as a stage and document of strategy formulation and development?
21. Describe the difference between objectives and goals.
22. What is a strategic plan? Is this plan (as a document) part of an entity's strategy?
23. Describe quantitative and qualitative strategic factors of strategy limitation.
24. What is a time-sensitive resource analysis? Describe the dialectic relationship between resources and time in the strategy-implementation process.
25. Describe an entry strategy. At what point is the entry strategy developed?
26. What is the role of the tactic in the policy and strategy implementation?
27. Describe cultural and religious traditions as a strategic factor.
28. Describe the importance of an exit strategy. At what point should an exit strategy be developed?

7   Strategic Management Systems

When you become a leader, success is all about growing others.[1]

(Jack Welch, former chairman and CEO of General Electric, b. 1935)

From a management standpoint, it is very important to know how to unleash people's inborn creativity. My concept is that anybody has creative ability, but very few people know how to use it.[2]

(Akio Morita, cofounder of the Sony Corporation, 1921–1999)

Concept of a Strategic Management System

One of the most important qualities for a strategist to have is a systematic mindset. It is of equal importance for strategists to apply this mindset to management. However, if masters in business administration (MBAs) and even experienced executives were asked to describe a management system, or to be more precise, to cite the major elements of a management system, the answer would likely reveal a completely unsystematic understanding of management. The knowledge gained from an MBA and years of experience as an executive cannot be fully exploited without an ordered understanding of management systems. All information relevant to the strategist's activity should be organized within the mental framework of the management system. Understanding the basic elements of a management system—the managerial function of motivation, basic organizational structures, and indicators of the efficiency of the decision-making process, etc.—is of immeasurable value to a strategist.

A strategic systematic understanding of management begins with an explanation of its major elements, within the context of its two basic processes—formation and implementation. If a strategy has already been developed and a corporation's board of directors has approved the allocation of resources accordingly, what is needed to implement this strategy? The answer to this question is the first element of a management system: *leadership*. Even if the corporation is flush with cash, has a wealthy investor to finance the next step, and the board is in unanimous agreement, nothing will be accomplished without strategic leadership. Immediately following the approval of a strategy, or, ideally, during the discussion of the new strategy and its tactical implementation, a leader or a small group of top executives should be selected to head the new project. What is the first step for this leader or group? Some argue subordinate directors and managerial staff should be hired. However, this will provoke a flurry of detail-oriented questions from the human resource department. Why two executives versus three or one? Why five managers, not seven? What is the required level of education? Why two assistants and one secretary and not one assistant and two secretaries? The leadership is not ready to deal with these minute issues. Prior to hiring people, the *organizational structure* has to be developed and approved; at that point the process of hiring *executives, managers, and staff* according to this structure should begin. The next element to be developed is the formal *decision-making process*, i.e. the responsibilities, rights, and division of power among members of the managerial team. Once the first three elements—the organizational structure, requirements for executives and managers and staff, the establishment of the decision-making process—are formalized, funding should be allocated for *managerial tools, aids, and information systems*, including office space, supplies and most important, IT. In correlation with this, requirements for information have to be developed as the "raw materials" for the decision-making process and at the same time the only "product" of the functioning of the strategic management system.

Once all of these elements are developed, their role in the major functions of the management system should be detailed. The three most important functions of a strategic management system are strategic *planning*, *motivation*, and *control*. The system of the major elements and functions of strategic management is presented in Figure 7.1.

Finally, prior to a strategy's becoming part of the policy being implemented, the strategist must figure out what organizational forms (vehicles) can be used to bring the management system and the approved strategy itself into practice. This is the process by which new entities and subsidiaries are established.

Major Elements of a Strategic Management System

Strategic Leadership

Strategic Leadership in Strategy Formulation

Beginning with the initial stages of strategy development, leadership is a key issue. It is up to leaders to put the development of a new strategy or the improvement of an existing one on the entity's agenda. Furthermore, without leadership a strategy cannot be implemented and definitely will not succeed. One of the fundamental dilemmas for the leadership of any

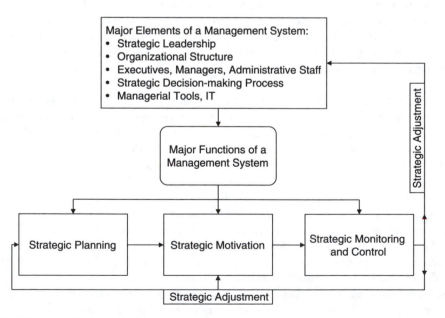

Figure 7.1 Concept of a Strategic Management System.
Source: © Dr Vladimir Kvint, 2008.

organization is how to balance attention between operational, tactical, and strategic issues. When leaders ignore current events, it tends to result in declining performance and subsequently, the loss of the leadership position. However, as previously stated in Chapter 6, for strategists the present is already the past. Evaluations of current and annual results can be a major obstacle for leaders to give attention to strategic issues. Leaders who lack a strategic orientation will inevitably be criticized for their lack of vision. Leaders must achieve a balance between current and future needs of the entity. As Brent Davies, Professor of International Leadership Development at the University of Hull, put it, "strategic leaders are concerned with not just managing the now but setting up a framework of where the organization needs to be in the future, setting a direction for the organization. The function of strategy is to translate the moral purpose and vision into reality."[3] The larger the organization, the more it is internationalized and operates on a global scale, the more important it is for the leadership to focus on long-term strategic issues. When the leadership of a large or small entity decides to enter an EMC, this decision is innately strategic. It is closely tied to issues of substantially higher risk (political, economic, and business) and uncertainty than in the developed world. For many leaders, routines and assumptions acquired from operations in developed markets will be a serious impediment to success in the GEM. Even technology that operates effectively in the conditions of a developed market will often not function properly in emerging markets due to variances in the quality of raw materials, climate, and training of employees regarding the maintenance of equipment, etc.

It is not unusual, even in giant multinational corporations, for the leaders that head the early stages of strategy formation to transition into a small strategic group that focuses on the development of strategic scenarios for the future. The nature of leadership in small groups and large corporations is undoubtedly very different. The first challenge for corporate leaders is to find out how to be at the same time a global corporate leader and a leader of a small strategic group. While some may assume that within these small strategic groups, the professional strategist is the leader, in reality this is not typically the case. Usually, the leader of these groups is the deputy of one of the top corporate executives—president, CEO, or executive chairman. These deputies typically divide their time between operational and strategic issues. Even when chief strategists have high-ranking positions in the corporation, such as the vice-president for strategic affairs, it does not mean that reporting to the chief executive or president of the corporation is not at least a weekly routine. The chief strategist regularly reports to the leader of the corporation. However, corporate leaders often make the mistake of interpreting strategic ideas from the chief strategist under the light of corporate operational preferences and problems.

Chief executives usually spend more time on operational issues and tend to be more influenced by operational officers. More than that, in many medium-size and especially small corporations, the chief executive and COO are the same person, and the position of chief strategist does not exist. This strategic challenge can be overcome only by leaders with a powerful strategic vision; these leaders alone have the ability to bring long-term success to their entities. Quite often, the leaders who supervised the development of the entry strategy also conduct its implementation and continue their leadership role during the operations of the implemented strategy. This results in the somewhat inefficient situation in which strategists are in charge of operational or at the very least tactical activity. Having a mindset oriented to long-term strategic issues, they are usually not very efficient as operational executives. This causes the entity to miss opportunities and can even result in its failure, despite the fact that it developed and implemented the proper strategy. Leaders who were closely involved with the development and implementation of the strategy tend to be attached to the current scenario to the point that they suffer from tunnel vision, failing to see new opportunities in the marketplace and new technological advancements. In order to avoid this, an entity of any size should have two top-level officers who are both responsible for current success and for strategic issues. Once the strategy is successfully implemented, the responsibilities of these two leaders should be split, with one assuming the role of the CEO—i.e. managing the entity's activity according to current and operational objectives—and the other assuming the role of the chief strategist—i.e. initially monitoring the progress of the current strategy as well as heading the development of strategic revisions. This structure applies only to leaders of existing entities.

The primary influence on the unit or subsidiary leadership comes from the corporate or parental body leadership. However, unit leaders can also influence corporate or parental strategy. The theory of strategic contingencies developed by D.J. Hickson, professor of organizational analysis at the University of Bradford (UK), suggests that "the power of a sub-unit depends on three factors: (1) expertise in coping with important problems, (2) centrality of the subunit within the workflow and (3) the extent to which the subunit's expertise is unique rather than substitutable."[4] Most unit leaders tend to think of their particular strategy as being unique and non-substitutable. However, in reality the extent to which unit strategies are valued by their parental strategy is usually related to the personal influence of the unit leader, the distinctiveness of the mission of the unit and its products, and the importance of the product for the corporation's production of "ready to go" goods and services. When the unit leader has a high level of personal influence with corporate leaders and is in charge of unique and important products, he or she is often promoted to the corporate level. Unit leadership can also influence corporate leadership in cases when units and divisions have stronger leaders than there are at the corporate level. This situation is often the cause and result of siloed strategic management systems, which almost inevitably hinder the competitiveness of an entity.

In cases when the unit has a remote location in an EMC, its strategy is usually much more independent and specified. The leaders of units that achieve success in these situations have a great deal of leverage during annual corporate meetings. They tend to occupy their position for a long time, whether they like it or not. Corporate leadership usually assumes the unit's success is a result of the specific conditions of the country within which the unit is located and its relationship with local political and business leaders. Corporate leaders are skeptical of these particular unit leaders being able to replicate their success on the corporate level. However, unit leaders in this situation are in a very strong position if the corporation decides to expand its activity in the GEM to EMCs with similar political and economic conditions.

There are a number of unique issues that arise in cases of the strategic leadership of not-yet-existing entities. The greatest benefit of leading such entities is the ability to completely focus on strategic issues. At this point, strategic leadership and leadership are practically one and the same. As soon as the strategy is developed and the implementation process begins, operational problems tend to take the leadership's attention away from strategic issues. There are also unique characteristics to strategic leadership in EMCs, depending on whether the executive is local or a foreign expatriate. While local executives try to use the specific and unique local and regional characteristics, foreign expatriates usually try to implement strategies that have been efficient in developed countries. This approach is generally less effective due to substantially different conditions in the GEM. However, expatriate executives have other advantages, especially when the parent company is in a developed country. Expatriate executives tend to be much better at securing funds for the subsidiary and using reporting systems, and tend to be more adept with financial strategy. Despite the fact that domestic entrepreneurs have a better knowledge of local conditions and deeper connections, foreign executives in EMCs also tend to more actively address national and regional social issues, business ethics, environmental protection, etc.

Strategic Leadership in Strategy Implementation

The first responsibility of strategic leadership during the strategy implementation phase is the development and implementation of the major elements of a management system, of which strategic leadership is an innate part. This process starts with the formation of the organizational structure, including the strategic organizational structure, according to objectives and vision of the entity's strategy. Strategic leadership is a crucial element of success from the beginning of strategy development to the exit from the current strategic scenario. According to Mike Friedman and Benjamen Tregoe in their book, *The Art and Discipline of Strategy*: "The twenty-first century demands, as has no other, that corporate leaders create both strategic literacy and a robust process to ensure strategic constancy."[5] Leadership has to develop a collective, well-organized mindset shared by all employees involved in the processes of strategy development and implementation. According to Thomas Davenport, Marius Leibold, and Sven Voelpel, in *Strategic Management in the Knowledge Economy*:

> "Systemic thinking" is the basis of this mindset, i.e. understanding of a phenomenon within the context of a larger whole. The recent great shock to strategic management has been that systems cannot be understood by analysis. The properties of the parts are not intrinsic properties, but can be understood only within the context of the larger whole. Accordingly, systems thinking does not concentrate on basic building blocks, but rather on basic principles of organization—it is the whole that determines the behavior of the parts.[6]

Successful leadership in the development and implementation of this collective mindset is an important means by which modern civilization has achieved technological progression. Nevertheless, for heads of strategic departments, it is not very productive to develop strategy solely from the point of view of a unified system. Strategy as a system always contains elements of the strategic scenarios of its units, as well as sub-strategies developed for particular programs and projects. For example, governments develop a national strategy for 10 to 15 years in the future, as well as sub-strategies on energy independence, ecological protection, etc. Companies develop sub-strategies on certain vital issues such as the supply of unique materials, etc. Strategy should be understood in terms of its overall system as well as its innate elements. The success of strategic leadership is closely related to the ability to assimilate the knowledge, suggestions, and strategic proposals of leaders of units and subsystems. Many authors, such as Friedman and Tregoe, describe leadership as a synthesis of art and science:

> A crucial lesson we have learned over many years of strategy engagement is that strategic leadership requires a combination of art and discipline. By art, we mean thinking that is creative, out of the box, and blue sky. Examples include the creation of alternative strategic visions for top team assessment, new product development, the crafting of what-if scenarios, the identification of decision-making criteria, and the design of a new culture that is strategically aligned. Creativity is also required in other activities such as communicating the strategy and supporting ownership of and commitment to it . . . Discipline is essential, both in the thought processes involved in strategy and in its execution. For example, it is not easy to craft and implement a plan that may include hundreds of projects and thousands of subprojects as the prerequisites to strategy implementation. Difficult too are the needs to ensure consistency of decision making throughout the organization; keep focused when so many options are available for

consideration; and regularly to monitor, review, and update strategy when operational or financial imperatives are knocking at the door.[7]

In fact, leadership is a science that must be used with artistic creativity, according to the leader's vision of the future.

Organizational Structure

The organizational structure is the blueprint of the construction and operation of the entire management system. The strategic organizational structure is very different from the operational structure. The prior term is generally related to two different issues—the development of an organizational structure specifically for processes of strategy implementation or for the development of corporate strategy in general (the strategy of organizational development itself). An organizational structure is a form of a management system, and its major functions. Its structure determines the requirements for all subsequent elements of a strategic management system and the efficiency of managerial functions.

Organizational structures have to be designed in such a way as to reflect the characteristics of the environment in which the entity operates. The organizational structure of an entity operating in an EMC has to take into account the level of uncertainty and risk found in these markets, as well as local political and economic conditions—especially the level of economic freedom. Likewise, a country's civil and financial laws, corporate and financial regulations, and established reporting systems must also be accounted for in an entity's organizational structure. An entity's organizational structure has to both reflect its own strategic objectives and be an effective bridge for cooperation with outside authorities.

Strategists from the developed world have to be mindful of the impact of the legacy of command-economy systems on organizational structures in the GEM. Companies in EMCs lose a lot of potential foreign investment because their strategies are still influenced by the vestiges of old organizational structures. Entrepreneurial spirit and freedom in the decision-making process is rising in EMCs, but most organizational structures do not yet reflect it. One of the lingering influences from command economies is an excess of unnecessary positions in the organizational structure. This is a significant hindrance to the decision-making process, one that's very common in Balkan countries and small Latin American countries, such as Uruguay and Paraguay, as well as in the Philippines and Egypt. It is also a function of the relatively poor remuneration and meager salaries for managers and staff, which leads companies to hire more people—complicating the organizational structure—rather than intensifying the workload of a smaller group of managers. Managerial functions are often widely dispersed and the organizational structure has too many elements. Governments of EMCs often suffer from the same poorly organized structures. It is exceedingly difficult for the myriad of deputies, ministers, and even prime ministers to be effective because they do not have full authority even in the areas of their designated responsibility, as the duties of a number of other vice-presidents, deputy prime ministers, and prime ministers overlap.

Another issue in EMCs is a general preference for vertical subordination instead of dual responsibility, which is a major characteristic of modern organizational structures. Under modern structures, such as matrix organizational systems, there are double and even triple reporting systems from employees to operational and functional superiors. For example, a senior engineer in a workshop has to report to the head of the workshop according to the administrative line of responsibilities, and to the chief technologist of the corporation regarding engineering issues. Employees in the strategic department often have triple responsibilities—to the head of the strategic department, to the head of a particular branch of the company for which they are developing a strategy, and to the chief professional in their area of expertise (chief technologist, chief economist, etc.). The situation in the GEM is starting to improve, especially in countries such as India, China, the Czech Republic, Hungary, Estonia, and even Colombia and Bahrain. Furthermore, organizational structures in countries such as Taiwan and Singapore—especially those oriented to strategic innovation—are often more efficient than the traditional organizational structures of corporations from developed countries.

There are several key concepts for the formation and role of the strategic organizational structure. According to Professor Robert Mockler of St. John's University's Graduate School of Business, the

> somewhat paradoxical view of organization structure—that the formal structure is and is not important—is only one of many multinational strategic management paradoxes. However, the paradox exists only if one insists on too formal a solution. When viewed from a contingency perspective, the solution to organization, as in other task areas, is that the preferred form is a basic structure (for example, a three-way matrix organization) flexible enough to be tailored to each business unit's needs . . . This perspective enables developing an organization that balances situation factors: the firm's core competencies, the local country, the global scope of operations, the changing competitive market, the business processes, the people, the communications systems, and other relevant situation factors. One result of this is that organizations often change over time as situation factors change.[8]

In EMCs, the organizational structure traditionally plays a more important role, with less room for flexibility than in developed countries. The organizational structure is an anchor of stability. Foreign investors can use it as a base for the understanding of corporations and the influence of national authorities on corporate leadership. At the same time, during the transition from command economy and dictatorship to the free-market economy and democracy, the organizational structure of governments and heads of state rapidly changes due to fluctuations in the role of the state in the economics and business. In general, managerial functions decrease and regulating functions increase. Organizational structures have to reflect this transformation processes. One would assume that privatization and the decreasing number of state-owned entities and businesses would lead to changes in the governmental organizational structure. However, in practice, it is quite different. Despite the decreasing number of state-owned companies and managerial authority of the government over businesses, it does not necessarily lead to a decreasing number of bureaucrats and state officials. In countries such as Russia, Ukraine, Pakistan, Azerbaijan, and Greece, regulatory bodies have mushroomed. They are mostly oriented to collect bribes, by creating artificial barriers for companies. In some countries this problem is so endemic that it is more accurate to describe it as a racket, rather than mere bribe collecting.

Many argue that the implementation of strategic management systems should begin with managerial functions, prior to the organizational structure. In fact, it is practically impossible to delegate managerial functions and make a management system operational before the implementation of the organizational structure. In the words of Professor John C. Camillus of the University of Pittsburgh:

> Discussing the planning and control system without considering organizational structure is inappropriate, if not impossible. Sociologists tend to view *control* and *structure* as synonymous. In a management control system, organizational structure serves as a key determinant of what is appropriate. The structure of organizations directly affects the

processes and perspectives of formal strategic planning ... Organization structure therefore represents a set of variables or choices that top management can influence or make that are fundamentally related to the planning and control system and also clearly affect the organization's performance. In short, in order to describe top management's responsibilities, it is necessary not only to consider the design of the planning and control system but also the chosen form of organizational structure.[9]

Professor Camillus should not be taken literally without considering the differences in processes of strategy development and strategy implementation. The development of strategic management systems quite often starts with an analysis of strategic managerial functions, because the strategic management system and the organizational structure are organized according to effective realization of strategic managerial functions. However, the implementation of strategic management systems always starts with the organizational structure as a form that must reflect the internal characteristics of the strategic management system.

It should be emphasized that a strategic organizational structure is not oriented to operational management. It is oriented to the formation, development, and implementation of strategy. A strategic organizational structure is not a closed-ended system. In existing organizations, it should have connections with operational management and should function under the general executive bodies—the president, CEO, the board of directors, etc. Copying American organizational structures, the majority of EMCs establish a board of directors. In EMCs this model is more popular than the British one, where the organizational structure is oriented around the executive-chairman, a combination of chairman of the board and CEO. The advantages and drawbacks of these systems will be described later in the section on the decision-making process.

Executives, Managers, and Staff

Once the organizational structure is developed and approved by the appropriate authorities, the leadership should begin to hire or reallocate executives, managers, and support staff. In non-existent companies, leaders of the strategy-development process will occupy the executive positions in the new entity. In existing corporations the leadership of parental companies or the leadership at the corporate level will be responsible for the selection and appointment of executives of new subsidiaries and units. It should go without saying that every single executive be a leader by nature. While heads of departments or subsidiaries may be the subordinates of corporate executives, they still must lead their employees. In the words of Robert Mockler, a professor of management at St John's University Graduate School of Business:

> In practice, it is often difficult to distinguish between managers and leaders. In general, managers guide, staff, and control an enterprise's operations ... That is, they manage a new or existing enterprise within a short- to medium-range perspective. Managers also plan and guide plan implementation, and so at times must inspire and energize or led and show the way. Managers, therefore, need some leadership skills and must perform some leadership tasks. Leaders, on the other hand, create visions and inspire (show the way), lead by example (by going before), and energize a firm and its people within a longer-range perspective. They also have to do some managing (guiding and controlling), when enterprise-wide crises arise ...[10]

In the developed world, it is typical to hire executive-search firms and consultant companies to find executives and top managers. In EMCs this is not usually the case. In many EMCs executive-search firms have not been established, or executive-search companies from developing countries have not yet established branches. Since the beginning of the twenty-first century, in some cases, executive-search companies have started to fill these niches. Nonetheless, it is still common practice that the search for executives is the sole responsibility of leaders of the existing bodies. Unfortunately, nepotism and corruption often take place during this process. New executives are appointed based not on their qualities, but on their relationship with the entity's leadership. Their personal loyalty is an enabler and base for corruption. After the birth of the first EMCs in the 1980s, a young new generation of executives began to arise. They were less influenced by the legacy of their country's history, which led to positive changes in the management of companies in the GEM. This generation of executives grew up and climbed the ranks during the time of transition from dictatorship and command economy to democracy and a free-market economy, a time of drastic structural changes to society. As a result of this transition, the political leadership of the old regime was replaced with a new generation of leaders with business experience. However, the situation in the business community not in political structures is quite different. While the business arena may change drastically, the cast of characters generally remains the same. It is practically impossible to immediately replace executives and managers despite the fact that their mentalities may be completely out of date. Eventually, the younger generation of lower-level executives inherits leadership positions, as they are quicker to adapt to the new business environment than the old guard. This is usually preceded by a period of reshuffling of the business leadership of the old regime, as executives move from company to company. This can be seen as a by product of inexperienced and rapidly changing ownership, as businesses seek new sources of capital. In general, EMCs and companies that operate in these markets experience a shortage of qualified, experienced, and responsible domestic executives and managers. For this reason, it is practically impossible during mergers or acquisitions to prevent the loss of talented and experienced executives and managers who will be useful for the company's new strategic direction.

For decades, at the beginning of their careers, executives in EMCs were trained professionals in the industry or field of their corporation's activity. For example, in the mining industry, practically 100 percent of the heads of companies are mining engineers; in machinery-building companies—mechanical engineers; in restaurant franchises—culinary experts, etc. This is not the case in the United States or Western Europe, where top executives are mostly educated in finance, law, and economics, rather than in the particular field of the company. The majority of top executives in EMCs are not trained to manage people and finances, or to navigate legal situations. This is inefficient on a number of levels; they are not putting their education and expertise to use, and they were not trained for what they are actually doing. During the transition to free-market economies in EMCs, many institutions and departments of continuing and professional education, which provide current and future executives with knowledge of managerial finance, accounting, business, and civil law, etc., began to appear. Among the young generation in EMCs, unlike during the times of dictatorship, the most appealing academic paths are related to finance, business, and law. Engineering has become much less popular. It also led to changes in remuneration between financiers, economists on one side, and engineers and teachers on the other, who, unfortunately, lost their prestige in society.

The first priority of newly hired executives is to become very familiar with the strategy, the implementation of which was behind their hiring. It is not very common, but occasionally some members of the strategic team find themselves appointed to top executive positions. Following an intense study of the entity's strategy, the next step for newly hired top executives is to find their deputies and other subordinates—heads of units and chief professionals. This is where the first conflict of interest usually occurs. Corporate and parental company leadership influences leaders of subsidiaries and units in the hiring of deputies, while at the same time, domestic leaders and executives also experience the push from local regional and even national authorities to hire their colleagues and even their cronies. Compromise during this phase will often result in lower efficiency of the entry strategy and even the failure of the strategy implementation altogether. Once all the necessary executives are in place, the next step is to hire managerial staff, assistants, executive assistants, secretaries, and even corporate chauffeurs. Unlike in the developed world, where corporations use limousine or car services, in the GEM, companies usually keep a chauffeur on the staff, due both to a lack of efficient car services and the prestige of having a corporate chauffeur.

The system of remuneration for executives and managers in EMCs is much less sophisticated compared to that of the developed world, but most important, it is less diversified. Typically, people with the same title in different organizations have the same remuneration. The processes of IPOs and the development of publicly held companies in EMCs are leading to the systematization of remuneration for executives and other employees. This is also leading to a paradox—strategists are much less established, and the profession is much less common in the corporate world and even in governmental structures of emerging markets. This is especially true for consulting companies, which can be found in only a few EMCs. Their practice and services are still much less popular and less respected than in the developed world. Despite the fact that executives in the developed world have much better professional education and more extensive experience in free-market conditions, they still use consulting services far more than executives from EMCs. Corporate leaders in EMCs typically believe that using consulting services implies that they do not know what they are doing or how to achieve success. They have trouble believing that executives and owners of the highest reputation in the US, Great Britain, and Japan do not take a step without listening to their strategists and getting a second opinion from outside consulting firms. Even a person as highly respected as Jack Welch, the former president of GE, would not make a strategic decision without first checking with GE's department of strategic initiative and outside, independent consultants. When a major strategic decision fails, the board of directors and shareholders will demand to know whose idea the move was, and why they did not consult with outside strategists. Executives in this situation will likely find themselves in need of a job.

There are special requirements in EMCs regarding administrative staff. Typically, there are two basic requirement for applicants—computer application skills and English proficiency. In certain parts of the GEM, administrative employees need more extensive foreign-language skills. For example, in Albania, due to its proximity to Italy, many companies require that their executive assistants speak Italian as well as English. In Brazil many secretaries are required to speak Spanish, the language of most neighboring countries, in addition to English, and of course, their native tongue, Portuguese. In India this is not a major issue since most of the country is equally comfortable with their native tongue and English.

In the GEM, executive-education programs and masters in business administration programs are among the most prestigious academic paths for young students. It is impossible to find a university in an EMC without a business and economics major. The study of law is also very popular among the younger generation. The wide presence in EMCs of firms that offer professional services, such as accounting and auditing, business consulting, and legal services (mentioned in Chapter 4) is increasing the demand for people of this profession and motivating the popularity of these degrees. Traditionally in EMCs, the role of higher education is well recognized because during dictatorships it was one of the primary paths out of poverty.

One of the major difficulties in finding executives and managers in EMCs is the lower professional ethics and integrity due to the legacy of dictatorship and a lack of understanding of the role and importance of strategy and its precise implementation. All of this has created huge opportunities for graduates and young professionals from the developed world to build their career in EMCs. This is due especially to the fact that strategic education in such countries lags behind developed standards and practical needs in EMCs. For this reason, a trend is already beginning to emerge wherein more and more graduates of American and Western European universities look for opening positions in managerial and even executive structures of companies in EMCs, where the number of these positions is increasing 10 times faster than in developed countries. The rate of growth for these positions in EMCs has been 20 to 40 percent annually during the first seven years of the twenty-first century. Demand for professionals, especially those trained to work with or within EMCs, is sky-high due to the fact that there is no single university in the developed world that has management in emerging markets as a major, despite the fact that hundreds of universities throughout the world already have courses related to emerging-market studies. Graduates who would like to be employed in a strategic department or in strategically important positions have to think about themselves from the point of view of employers and must develop an appropriate mindset. According to a publication from the Harvard Business School:

> [A] strategic mindset in HR [human resources] offers important benefits on many levels—such as greater profitability for your company, access to needed resources for your HR department, and personal advantages such as more opportunities for career advancement and lower levels of on-the-job stress.[11]

The attitude described in this quote is very helpful, not only for finding employment but also for increasing productivity and usefulness as a part of a strategic and managerial team.

Strategic Decision-making Process

The strategic decision-making process is the prerogative of top-level managerial bodies and executives. From the moment decisions are made about the development of a new strategy or for a new strategic scenario of an existing one, top executives and boards of directors are fully responsible for the acceleration, funding, analysis, and implementation of the strategy. These obligations are the major responsibility of the chairman of the board and the board of directors. In EMCs, the development of a board of directors as an institution is leading to their increasing role in this process. While monitoring the development and implementation of strategy is the responsibility of executives, evaluation and acceptance of the new strategy is the responsibility of the board of directors. Attention to strategic development and implementation is among the key criteria during the process of evaluating executives and hiring new ones.

There are several unique characteristics to the decision-making process in EMCs. First and foremost is a general lack of initiative in subordinates, especially regarding bringing strategic ideas and suggestions to top executives. This is the legacy of dictatorships and command economies, from which all emerging markets come. Understandably, people living under these conditions become very risk averse and believe that taking the initiative is an unnecessary risk. As a result, it is difficult for executives to get an understanding of the success or failure of an existing strategy and the needs for the development of a new or updated one because their employees are hesitant to be critical. Managers and executives are often afraid to take responsibility and be proactive. There is a proverb in many EMCs that basically says initiative is punishable. As a result, even the smallest issues are gradually pushed up the chain of command—eventually forcing top executives to deal with a myriad of insignificant, time-wasting issues. Expatriates working as top executives in companies from EMCs very often become overwhelmed with unimportant day-to-day issues. They are forced to motivate subordinates to take on responsibilities and make decisions, or punish them for not doing so. Unfortunately, the fear of being punished by bosses for taking initiative and making decisions without consulting a superior is deeply ingrained in people who spent most of their lives under dictatorship. This results in decision-making processes that are rigid and restrictive of employees in many cases. A lack of freedom in the decision-making process becomes a base for corruption and nepotism. Bosses will often place their cronies and close relatives below them, valuing obedience over competency. In some EMCs, the decision-making process and organizational structure are dominated by such relationships. It is extremely difficult to reform these processes and structures. People's options are limited, and they are willing to do whatever is necessary to keep their jobs, even bribing their bosses. For those from the developed world, it is hard to imagine employees going to their bosses on payday to give them 10 percent of their wages, but this is not unusual in some EMCs. This is one of the reasons why it is very important for pay to be deposited directly to bank accounts, not distributed in cash. A cash economy in general is a petri dish for corruption. Another lingering effect of dictatorships on the decision-making process specific to EMCs is the large number of deputies of chief executives. Responsibility for major strategic issues is so widely dispersed that it complicates evaluations of implemented strategies as well as making it difficult to deliver a company-wide systematic understanding of new strategic ideas to the board of directors. As a result of many unnecessary positions, the strategic decision-making process is significantly slower than it could be. However, companies from the GEM are beginning to accept more modern organizational structures and decision-making processes, which will benefit them greatly, especially during the initial stages of strategy formation and development.

An efficient strategic decision-making process requires detailed descriptions of the strategic rights and responsibilities among top executives and boards of directors—who is responsible for strategy monitoring and evaluation? Who is responsible for proposing strategic decisions related to the beginning of strategy development and implementation? What is the division of strategic responsibilities between the board of directors and corporate executives and between corporate executives and their subsidiaries and units? All of these issues have to be clearly explained when formalizing the decision-making process. This is also an appropriate point at which to formalize the basic ethics of a company. Professor Laure Paquette of Lakehead University in Ontario, Canada, presents the following rules regarding business ethics and the decision-making process:

> [1] keep it simple and keep it honest . . . [2] . . . When it comes to goal selection, go with the flow of events, not against it, unless you are very early in the process . . . If you cannot go with the flow, try to divert it or redirect to use that momentum to reach your own goals . . . [3] . . . Watch the timing of your strategy . . . take the time to assess if a better time might not be just around the corner . . . [4] . . . Watch for unintended consequences flowing from your actions . . . Unintended consequences have to be managed; you cannot afford to ignore them.[12]

Nevertheless, many companies do not have a formal structure of the strategic decision-making processes, i.e. who initiates this process, how strategic orders go from one layer of the entity's management system to another, who has responsibility for the decision-making process on the corporate level and its coordination with local, regional, and national authorities of the country in which the strategy is developed and implemented. Subsidiaries of foreign companies in EMCs have even more complicated issues related to strategy development. They have to coordinate their strategic priorities and processes with parent companies abroad, as well as with regional and national authorities of the country where their facilities are located and with their suppliers and buyers in the GEM, the developed world, and maybe in developing countries as well. These problems are innate characteristics of matrix organizational structures. Often, employees of professional departments of corporations (departments of technology, patents pending, human resources, etc.) are responsible and have to report to the head of the subsidiary in the GEM, to the respective supervisory department of the parent company in a developed country, etc. In many cases, large multinational corporations unify professionals from different subsidiaries in several countries to create a task force while all professionals also continue to work in their offices. Cutting-edge video teleconferences practically teleport employees from around the world to the same conference room.

In the GEM, large companies tend to operate according to the same organizational structures and decision-making processes as small companies. Regardless of the size, most companies from the GEM tend to be very slow to accept Western practices in their decision-making processes. Even in the developed world, the strategic decision-making process is not a priority to boards of directors, nor is it on the daily schedule of top executives, although it should be. Business schools do not place sufficient emphasis on the value of a well-defined and formalized strategic decision-making process.

Incorporating Global Risk Management in the Strategic Decision-making Process

For any company operating in the GEM, the decision-making processes must be oriented to deal with risks, especially the political, business, and technological varieties. Greater political risk is a result of the government being more involved in business activity, which always runs the risk of breached contracts. Due to the complex history of privatization in EMCs, the risk of expropriation and nationalization is substantially higher than in developed countries. These issues apply not only to investment and FDI, but also to trade and operational activities of companies.

The formalization of the strategic decision-making process for companies entering emerging markets should begin prior to an evaluation of basic economic factors (see Figure 1.10), with an analysis of major rating- and credit-agency evaluations of country risk, sovereign risk, national credit risk, etc. All of these issues have to be analyzed in terms of the objectives and goals of the company until the point of the development of an entry strategy. It is important to keep in mind that there are noticeable differences in analytical methods used to determine national credit risk in EMCs by different rating agencies and multilateral institutions. Disparities in their ratings cannot simply be ignored. The reasons for these discrepancies have to be identified and understood. The significance of these differences is amplified when institutional and even public investors use this information to make investment decisions. Publishing the results of these analyses can mislead members of the business community who are not very knowledgeable about the GEM. In addition, for professionals working with the GEM, the results of these different analyses often lead to more questions than answers. The decision-making process in corporations that work domestically, prior to entering the GEM, has to be altered. New people, who are familiar with the particular EMC, have to participate in this process, as well as executives who will supervise this activity abroad, and managers and professionals, who most likely will work in the EMC, at least during the establishment of the subsidiary.

Risk-management analyses should always be revised to reflect shifts in local, regional, and national governance, regulations, and practice. However, the first priority of risk management is to analyze technological advancements that have implications for the cost of production, possible substitute goods, etc., and report to the board of directors. In EMCs, decisions regarding risk often lie not with the board of directors but with shareholders, who are generally more influential in the GEM. This can be particularly complicated when governments are substantial shareholders, which is more common in the GEM than in the developed world. Even when private minority owners do not have a controlling share, in such mixed state–private ownership companies, their input quite often goes ignored for strategic decisions. Foreign companies and entrepreneurs who would like to invest or cooperate with such companies have to take this issue into consideration.

The strategic decision-making process regarding business risk in EMCs is especially important for companies listed on a stock exchange in an EMC. The regulating agencies of these exchanges still on one hand do not have enough control over them, and on the other hand, the agencies can change the rules so frequently and in such unexpected directions that the strategic decision-making process cannot respond fast enough. This is one of the reasons why high risk and uncertainty are major factors of the strategic decision-making process for companies not only in this market, but even for those that are heavily involved in this market from beyond its national boundaries. Any strategic decision should factor in forecasts of the dynamics of changes to laws and under-law regulations. For this reason, it is not unusual to invite government officials or those with strong connections to authorities to participate in board of directors meetings. This is a key explanation as to why remuneration for members of the board is usually relatively high in EMCs and will sometimes exceed the salaries of their primary occupations. Foreign participants in board of directors and especially owners who do not participate during strategic decision meetings have to be aware of the high personal influence of top-level officials if they take part in strategic decisions. But their opinion is not always the best one to use as the base of a strategic decision. Their loyalty to the corporation is always an issue for close examination. However, the more shares any board member has, the greater their loyalty to the corporation will generally be.

Because of the higher risk in the GEM, the decision-making process in EMCs should always take into account unexpected *force majeure*, which is related to extraordinary situations such as unforeseen political, economic, business, technological and environmental changes, disasters, and catastrophes. The World Bank defines *force majeure* as

> any event beyond the reasonable control of the Project Company, the occurrence of which could not have been reasonably foreseen, and typically includes: war, whether declared or not; revolution; riot; insurrection; strikes (except strikes by employees of (a) the Project Company, (b) the Contractor and/or its subcontractors, or (c) any other company undertaking any part of the operation and maintenance of the Project); invasion; armed conflict; hostile act of foreign enemy; act of terrorism; sabotage; radiation or chemical contamination; ionizing radiation; act of God; explosion; flood; storm; tempest; earthquake; plague or other serious epidemics; and which: (i) causes material and unavoidable physical damage or destruction to the Project or, without limitation, its toll facilities or functions; (ii) materially delays the scheduled time of completion of the Project without opportunity to otherwise repair the schedule; or (iii) materially interrupts the full and regular operation of all or any material portion of the Project, including without limitation its toll collection facilities or functions. Notwithstanding the foregoing, the inability of the Project Company to pay money as required by the Loan or other documents, by itself, constitutes a Force Majeure Event.[13]

This relates to issues to which the corporation must react but can predict only with great difficulty, if at all, and is practically powerless to change: a *coup d'état*, the sinking of a shipment of important cargo, or the occurrence of technogenic or natural disasters, etc. Despite the fact that many of these incidents or disasters are practically impossible to predict, the functioning of the decision-making process in *force majeure* situations has to be described in advance in as much detail as possible. Quite often the strategic managerial approach to *force majeure* processes is detailed in the exit strategy.

Managerial Tools, Aids, and Strategic Information Technology

In addition to a shortage of well-trained executives and capital, management systems in the GEM also experience a lack of modern ITs and even office supplies. This causes certain behavior that would be completely unheard of in the developed world. For example, when executives in the GEM move from office to office, it is not uncommon for them to bring their chairs with them. The quality of executive offices in EMCs varies a great deal. Foreigners should be prepared to encounter the most opulent and technologically advanced executive offices in the world, as well as facilities that would not even qualify as offices in the developed world. The production of office furniture is an underdeveloped industry in EMCs, with a lower quality of products. In many EMCs, roughly 90 percent of office supplies are imported. Leading IT companies are very active in EMCs. The most successful companies in the GEM employ the products and services of these IT companies.

Despite breakneck growth in IT, it is hard to argue with Dr Gary Hamel, a professor of the London Business School, who said "management is out of date . . . Like the combustion engine, it's a technology that has largely stopped evolving, and that's not good."[14] The theory of management systems and strategic management in general has not adapted to reflect technological advancements or the new challenges and opportunities in the GMP and the GEM. Nonetheless, a few companies, such as Cisco Systems, have specialized in IT for strategic management and have come up with several technological solutions that have been successfully implemented in parts of the GEM. However, many governmental and corporate executives underestimated the value of this technology and have not allocated the necessary funds to purchase these expensive but very efficient products, such as comprehensive technology infrastructure and wireless initiatives that support the policy objectives of the particular entity provided by Cisco. Clients of Cisco include national presidents and prime ministers, heads of governmental agencies, as well as executives and board members of leading companies. Unfortunately, the majority of corporations in EMCs cannot afford the service of companies such as Cisco or IBM. Cisco's TelePresence System,[15] for instance, is expensive but can save money and reduce the corporation's environmental impact by allowing executives to collaborate as if they were in the same conference room despite being thousands of miles apart. Entities in the GEM often lack IT systems and have to do their best with incompatible computers, software, printers, scanners, etc. However, the trend is clear. Big and medium-size companies are attempting to catch up with the standards of developed countries. The new generation of IT is increasing the capability and efficiency of office technologies of the twentieth century. This is occurring with PERT, which initially revolutionized the strategic-planning function in the middle of the twentieth century. By the end of the twentieth century, more complex technologies appeared, such as COSO (Committee of Sponsoring Organizations), which was developed in 1985. COSO is a system of corporate guidance for the development of internal control systems over fraudulent financial reporting, the use of various financial instruments such as derivatives, risk management, among other functions. Among the major sponsors of this system are the American Accounting Association, the American Institute of Certified Public Accountants,

Financial Executives International, The Institute of Internal Auditors, and the Institute of Management Accountants.[16]

The Internet, to which top-level executives in the GEM barely had access at the beginning of the twenty-first century, is universally available to the offices of most companies as of 2008. This is the most efficient and inexpensive source of reliable strategic information. However, the Internet and e-mail bring also bring challenges to top executives, especially in EMCs, with the lack of initiative of subordinates. Some executives get as many as 400 e-mails per day, most of which they do not need. Everyone who sends these e-mails thinks that their concerns are of the utmost priority and expects an immediate response. But of course, the executives are totally overwhelmed by so much e-mail. This is a good opportunity to use motivational systems by rewarding those who make the appropriate decisions on their own and punishing those who bring every single issue to the top of the pyramid of the decision-making process in order to avoid or share responsibility.

Subscriptions to major business publication such as *Forbes, BusinessWeek, Fortune*, and *The Economist* have also increased tremendously in the GEM. Many of these magazines are published in the major languages of the GEM—Mandarin, Hindi, Russian, Spanish, Arabic, and Portuguese, and even languages of smaller nations—Bulgarian, Czech, and Filipino.

Information is the raw material of the decision-making process. To be able to analyze a myriad of sources, types, and forms of information, strategists must employ strategic Rule 9 (see Chapter 6) and systematize their approach. For example, economic information should be organized according to the order of basic economic factors (starting with natural resources, followed by labor and capital resources, infrastructure, production facilities, and technology). Indicators of basic economic factors have to be analyzed in the context of political, economic, and social systems. Management systems have to be analyzed by the order of their major elements (organizational structure, executives, decision-making process, etc.) and functions. When systematizing various sources and types of information, it is crucial for strategists to focus on dynamics, in order to discover, recognize, and describe technological, environmental, economic, and political trends. GDP growth rate is an important indicator for displaying the basic trend of economic development. This dynamic illustrates the health of an economy; GDP per head is an integrated indicator of the efficiency of a national economy; the GDP shows its scale.

As access to strategic information increases in the GEM, so too will the efficiency of strategic management systems. This also applies to companies in the US, Western Europe, and Japan, which also suffer from a lack of accurate strategic information about the EMCs. It is not always easy to get access to updated and properly translated laws and under-law regulations which, of course, can have major implications for strategy formulation and other decision-making activities. Continued advancements in IT will greatly increase the efficiency of strategic management systems throughout the world. As professors Robert Galliers and Dorothy Leidner from the London School of Economics and Baylor University (USA), respectively, stated:

> [T]he subject of strategic information management is diverse and complex. It is not simply concerned with technological issues—far from it in fact. The subject domain incorporates aspects of strategic management, globalization, the management of change and human/cultural issues which may not at first sight have been considered as being directly relevant in the world of information technology.[17]

While the Internet is improving access to information, executives from EMCs still suffer from a lack of professional strategic analyses, which hinders the efficiency of their management systems. They are often unwilling to pay for access to proprietary reports that are widely used in the developed world. Nevertheless, even in the GEM, the role of IT departments in corporate management systems is rapidly expanding:

> Information can now be delivered to the right people at the right time, thus enabling well-informed decisions to be made. Previously, due to the limited information-gathering capability of organizations, decision makers could seldom rely on up-to-date information but instead made important decisions based on past results and their own experience. This no longer needs to be the case. With the right technology in place to collect the necessary data automatically, up-to-date information can be accessed whenever the need arises. This is the informating quality of IT . . . with the growth in the usage of IT to support information provision within organizations, the political nature of information has come into sharper focus. Gatekeepers of information are powerful people; they can decide when and if to convey vital information, and to whom. They are likely to be either highly respected, or despised for the power that they have at their fingertips.[18]

Regardless of the implications of the growing importance of IT on office politics, the impact of the use of modern ITs is undeniably positive. It benefits corporations, not only by improving access to information but also by improving communication among its worldwide subsidiaries and reducing travel costs and the stresses endured by employees as a result of extensive international travel. Society benefits from this via reductions in the carbon footprint of corporations.

Functions of Strategic Management Systems

When establishing an entity's strategic management system it is very important to divide the processes of its formation from those of its operations. There are several functions of management systems that can be understood as stages of the decision-making processes (planning, motivation, and control), or can be divided among major professional areas of the management system (accounting, finance, legal, etc.) or among internal and external corporate governance (governmental relations, supervising of subsidiaries and units). There are easily hundreds of different functions that managerial bodies are supposed to fulfill. However, they are all essentially part of the three major functions, without which management systems, and especially strategic management systems, cannot be considered fully operational: strategic planning, strategic motivation, and strategic monitoring and control. If any one of these major functions does not operate properly, neither will the other two, and the entity will suffer as a result.

Strategic Planning and the Strategic Plan

The product of the strategic-planning process is the strategic plan as an executive document. This document is the pinnacle concentration of all elements of strategy and its implementation, presented in a timetable, and it is among the most proprietary and secretive corporate documents. It details all current and future corporate activity of strategic importance. The strategic plan is prepared not only in terms of time but also in terms of resource allocations for specific objectives. Of equal importance to the strategic plan as a document is the process of strategic planning itself. According to Leonard Goodstein, Timothy Nolan, and William Pfeiffer, authors of several books on strategic planning:

> [T]o be successful, a strategic planning process should provide the criteria for making

day-to-day organizational decisions and should provide a template against which all such decisions can be evaluated . . . All too often, strategic planning is seen as a top-management exercise that has little or nothing to do with the actual running of the organization.[19]

The authors of this quote correctly state that strategic planning does not deal with daily decisions; it only suggests criteria, formats, and rules for operational activity. The difference between the strategic and operational plan is that the strategic plan has a quarterly or annual timetable, as opposed to the daily, weekly, and, in some cases, monthly timetable of the operational plan. The same authors of the above quote go on to describe the distinction between strategic planning and planning:

Planning is the process of establishing objectives and choosing the most suitable means for achieving these objectives prior to taking actions . . . in contrast, we define strategic planning as "the process by which the guiding members of an organization envision its future and develop the necessary procedures and operations to achieve that future."[20]

The strategic plan should have three major sections—strategy development, strategy implementation (including the entry strategy), and the exit strategy. This document describes only activities, events, and preliminary and final results of strategic relevance. Board members and executives have to be regularly updated or briefed with the implementation of the strategic plan. According to IBM's "The Global CEO Study, 2006," industry-leading companies ("outperformers") place almost twice as much importance upon "the business model" than companies that are less efficient and less competitive. According to this study these "underperformers" place twice as much emphasis on operations relative to "outperformers." This example, which is based on operating margin growth over five years, is a clear illustration of the improved results entities achieve when they value strategic issues over operational ones.[21]

For corporations that have a strategy department, it is their responsibility to develop and monitor the strategic plan. For these departments strategic planning is a daily activity. In corporations without such divisions, strategic planning is a discrete (not continuous) activity. Executives, managers, and professionals have other responsibilities and deal with strategic planning only during the processes of strategy development and implementation. On a governmental level, strategic planning takes the form of national programs, which can be developed for specific industries and regions. Governments of EMCs are actually more familiar with this concept from the planning processes and documents of command economies. However, it should come as no surprise that plans made under command economies were totally lacking in strategy and were largely not even based in reality.

Strategic Motivation

Without a motivation system, it is impossible to implement any efficient strategic plan. In the words of C. Davis Fogg, an experienced executive and author:

[A]lthough strategic planning may seem a sterile, intellectual analytical process, it's not . . . the human element is critically important. Strategic planning requires the organization's intimate and enthusiastic involvement, often using formal and informal teams, in providing information, making decisions and successfully implementing them.[22]

It is obvious that in order for the development of a strategic plan to be efficient, motivation is required. But without motivation, the successful implementation of this plan is impossible. The specifics of strategic planning largely determine the details of the systems of motivation. The motivation system functions according to the qualities and mechanisms of motivation, which is developed during the stage of entry strategy preparation. First and foremost, this system has to inspire employees involved in the processes of strategy development and implementation to orient their mindset toward a strategic way of thinking (described in detail in Chapter 6). In the words of the famous Japanese strategist Kenichi Ohmae:

> Strategic thinking in business must break out of the limited scope of vision that entraps deer on the highway. It must be backed by the daily use of imagination and by constant training in logical thought processes. Success must be summoned; it will not come unbidden and unplanned. Top management and its corporate planners cannot sensibly base their day-to-day work on blind optimism and apply strategic thinking only when confronted by unexpected obstacles. They must develop the habit of thinking strategic-ally, and they must do it as a matter of course. Ideally, they should approach it with real enthusiasm as a stimulating mental exercise. To become an effective strategist requires constant practice in strategic thinking. It is a daily discipline, not a resource that can be left dormant in normal times and tapped at will in an emergency.[23]

Formalizing the strategic motivation system includes establishing a system of daily incentives for employees, especially those who are responsible for strategy development and implementation. The formal system is presented in a document, where all suggestions about motivation and incentives are developed and described. It includes all moral, social, and financial instruments of motivation of individual employees and groups of employees. Spe-cial recognition and awards should be granted to those who go above and beyond in creating and implementing strategic ideas.

One of the main challenges of motivational systems in the GEM is the already discussed lack of initiative. This has implications for all major functions of management systems. It obviously makes it very difficult for executives to delegate operational decisions to man-agers. One of the main objectives of management systems in the GEM is to break the following two ironclad rules of management that still linger from dictatorships:

1. The boss is always right.
2. In all other cases, see Rule No. 1.

In an attempt to destroy this mentality and encourage an independent, initiative-taking attitude, the mayor of a city in an oil-rich province of Russia officially prohibited the use of the following phrases by any employee when meeting with superiors:

- "I don't know."
- "Why would I need that?"
- "That's impossible."
- "That would cut into my lunch break."
- "That's not my responsibility."
- "My secretary made an error."
- "I don't recall your telling me that."

This example illustrates how in EMCs, positive reinforcement of strategy needs supplemen-tation from a system that has negative repercussions for employees. In establishing motivational systems, many executives and managers overemphasize financial incentives and ignore social incentives, which can be powerful. It goes without saying that employees will respond to changes in their pay. However, managers should also consider the effectiveness of social incentives, such as public recognition of accomplishments and mistakes. Under dictatorships, managers and executives developed a tendency toward cautious privacy. Accomplishments of individual employees were not celebrated. However, it was not unusual for mistakes to be publicly punished. This is beginning to change; managers and executives are starting to use tools such as diplomas and certificates of appreciation. In EMCs it is not uncommon for executives of state companies with private shareholder partnerships to have former state officals on the board of directors, who still take a bureaucratic approach to the strategic decision-making process. They understand how to punish people but not how to positively motivate them.

A strategic motivation system consists of a set of methods, procedures, and instruments to efficiently implement strategic plans in practice. The most difficult and important function is to motivate executives, managers, and even professionals to think strategically, to permanently develop a vision of the future. In the words of Michael McGrath, a well-known author and CEO of Thomas Group, Inc.:

> [A]n effective core strategic vision can motivate people to work not just smarter but also harder. If the engineers have confidence that management knows where the company is going and has a good vision of the future, they will put in the extra effort to ensure that the company gets there with new products at the right time. Nothing helps motivate a product development team better than a crisp, well-thought-out strategic vision. If a development team lacks confidence in a company's vision, it is difficult to keep the members committed. The dilemma is how to communicate the core strategic vision. If a company tells everyone its strategic vision, competitors might learn about it. This points out one of the differences between core strategic vision and product strategy. The vision does not describe specific details. While it can be of some help to competitors, it is not specific competitive intelligence.[24]

This statement describes a very special kind of motivation—when strategic ideas, vision, or a strategic plan can motivate people to follow it and to be strategically creative. Motivation is not only related to financial and morale incentives; ideas can sometimes also be a powerful means of inspiration for employees to demonstrate their initiative.

Strategic Monitoring and Control: Evaluating Strategy and Strategists

Once a strategy has been developed, approved, and is beginning to be implemented, the strategist must monitor this process, noting successes and failures, and incorporate the information in the next strategic step. In order to do so, the strategist must gather feedback from the executives and managers who implement the strategy. Feedback is used to make any necessary corrections and updates to the approved strategic scenario. Just because the strategic scenario is constantly updated does not mean that the strategy and its strategic plan are constantly changing. The major elements of the strategy (mission, vision, objectives, and goals) remain unchanged. However, some aspects of the strategic business plan can be shifted in order to make the strategy more effective and virile. It is also important during the monitoring of all stages of strategy formation and implementation to find any mistakes or the use of any incorrect or misleading information. COSO (described earlier in this chapter) is widely used for this purpose, especially by the Big Four auditing firms, including PricewaterhouseCoopers. The COSO system has similarities to GE's Six Sigma. However, while Six Sigma is related to management quality of manufacturing, COSO primarily addresses information and reporting risk management. The implementation of this system during the stage of the strategic development of the management system can prevent inefficient, unethical, and misleading business operations. Quite often, operational executives and even chief risk officers do not understand that they could avoid a lot of problems in their day-to-day activity if operational risk were analyzed during the strategic development of organizational structures, the decision-making process, and IT systems of entities. For example, cases such as the Enron Corporation implosion, due to misreporting, and the 2007–2008 case of trader Jerome Kerviel of Société Générale—the France-based corporate and investment banking company—whose unmonitored activity resulted in losses of €4.9 billion, would never have occurred or would have been caught immediately if a system of monitoring and control had been designed during the stage of strategic management development. Some authors think that it is unnecessary and even impossible to differentiate strategic planning from strategic motivation and both from control. The words of Dr John C. Camillus, professor of strategic management at the University of Pittsburgh (USA), explain this point of view:

> [C]ertain kinds of planning and control activities are so intertwined that it is difficult to label them as one or the other. My approach to design sidesteps the subjective and somewhat unnecessary task of categorizing activities such as defining the organizations mission or raison d'être as either planning or control. It is a planning activity in that it charts the future directions of the organization. It is also a control activity in that it limits the range of businesses or programs that the organization can consider.[25]

Professor Camillus misses the point that for practical strategic management, it is absolutely necessary for efficiency in processes of strategy development, planning, and control to divide these functions. Otherwise, it is impossible to structure a strategy, the responsibilities, and rights among decision makers, and the decision-making process. In political, economic, and business life, it is very difficult to find issues that are strictly divided, even by invisible borders, but strategists and executives divide them for analytical and managerial purposes. For example, it is practically impossible to divide political, economic, and business risk from one another, but for purposes of allocation, evaluation, and management, the analytical division is necessary.

An important part of strategic monitoring and control is the regular evaluation of executives and managers responsible for strategy as well as the strategy itself. Ideally, the people who carry out this evaluation have a level of separation from those who develop the strategic plan. However, this is usually only possible in large organizations. As a result, in small organizations, it is even more important to understand planning, motivation, and monitoring and control as separate functions. Strategy implementation has to be closely monitored, in order to be aware of the need for any adjustments or revisions. Strategy assessment is one of the elements of effective control and monitoring. Strategic adjustment based on control and monitoring findings is the beginning of the improvement of strategic planning, if not the entire strategy. IT can be helpful in carrying out this function. According to author Michael Reed:

> Information and communication control systems are designed and implemented in such a way that total and complete transparency of organizational behavior becomes a realizable, if not realized, managerial aspiration. While poor design, system overload and operational breakdown are routine aspects of organizational life . . . the "drive to

automate," underpinning managerial rationality in the domain of technological change, is well taken to the extent that it highlights the control imperatives at the ideological and political core of the latter. The managerial desire to "transmit the presence of the omniscient observer and to induce compliance without the messy conflict-prone exertions of reciprocal relations" (Zuboff 1988: 323) may be corrupted and deformed by all sorts of cognitive, political and cultural contingencies.[26]

A key aspect of monitoring and control is evaluating the individuals involved in the strategy's development and implementation. The implementation of a new strategy is a very risky time for an executive and board of directors—there is always the danger that the strategy could fail. In order to successfully monitor the implementation of a strategy, executives and the board of directors must have a clear understanding not only of the strategy but also of the strategist who developed it. How intelligent, experienced, innovative, practical, etc., is the strategist? One of the most important characteristics to look for in a strategist is integrity. There is nothing more dangerous than a strategist who promises to deliver more than they have proven to be possible through intense research. Some strategists are not entirely dishonest but will give recommendations that they have not fully researched. In these cases, an executive need not see a pattern of arbitrary decisions from a strategist. If a strategist proposes even one unstudied recommendation, he should not be trusted with the future of a company. Unlike executives, strategists do not have the luxury of being able to promise something that they will not necessarily be able to deliver. Executives will do so to make themselves stand out in interviews or elections. Such behavior is completely inappropriate for a strategist, especially since a baseless recommendation will be implemented by the hard (and wasted) work of other people. The strategist must give practical advice that can be implemented. The best strategy is always just shy of perfect. Nevertheless, perfection is what strategists have to strive to achieve.

International Joint Ventures as a Strategic Organizational Vehicle of Globalization

The GMP created unprecedented opportunities for private and public companies to operate globally. Foreign trade is flourishing, and since 2002 the rate of growth of foreign trade has surpassed the growth rate of GWP (see Figure 7.2). GWP has also grown steadily over the

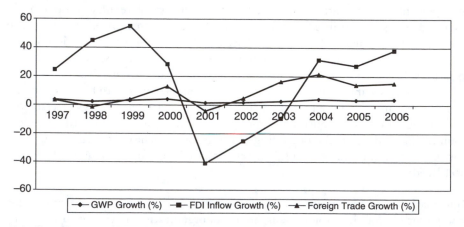

Figure 7.2 Growth Rate of FDI, GWP, and Foreign Trade.
Source: © Dr Vladimir Kvint, 2008.

past 15 years due to new opportunities related to the establishment of the GMP. Prior to the formation of the GMP, in order to participate and compete internationally, companies developed many different organizational and legal forms (vehicles) to take their products, services, and investments abroad. All of these business forms, such as international agreements of cooperation, trade contracts, cross-border mergers and acquisitions, and the establishment of IJVs became even more efficient with the birth of the GMP. The liberalization of international trade, the establishment of rules by the WTO—already accepted by 153 countries—the harmonization of regulations for competition and even production by major countries and regional groups (such as the EU, NAFTA, etc.), as well as within regional economic organizations, made the global workplace more productive and more predictable and the GMP more open for goods and services throughout the world. All of this increased the role of cross-border transactions, trade, and investment, which developed on a faster track than the growth of domestic economies' investment and trade.

Economic Genesis of the International Joint Venture

Among the major organizational business forms of global operations, the last one to fully develop was the IJV. IJVs are primarily new legal entities established by two or more parent companies from two or more countries. In most cases, one of the partners is from the country where the joint venture is located. It is important to underline that the establishment of a new legal entity does not result in the disappearance of the parent companies, which does occur in mergers and acquisitions. In some cases, this term can refer to strategic cooperation agreements between partners from two or more countries without the establishment of a new legal entity. IJVs are particularly efficient when companies operate in political, economic, and business systems with very different characteristics from those with which one or more of the parties is familiar. They became especially relevant when dictatorships started to fail around the world, and roughly 100 countries began establishing free-market economies and opening themselves to international business. This basically marked the birth of the GEM. Companies from the developed world started to create IJVs with partners from countries that were once closed to foreigners. For example, prior to 1976 there was not a single dollar of foreign investment in China. In all 15 republics of the former Soviet Union, there was no foreign investment until 1987. Even India, the biggest democracy in the world, had very strict regulations that inhibited foreign businesses from entering its market. This was, of course, a result of its strict emulation of the Soviet economic model. Many other dictatorships throughout the world restricted foreign investment. In Greece, Turkey, Portugal, Spain, Brazil, and Argentina, foreign investment existed only on a very small scale. The transition to a free-market economy did not happen suddenly in any country. Restrictions were gradually removed, slowed by many legal and economic limitations along the way. However, the greatest barriers were invisible; they existed in the mindset of people whose countries were slowly emerging from isolation and dictatorship. The overwhelming majority of attempts by American, Western European, Japanese, and Australian investors to enter these markets failed.

During the initial internationalization of what would become the GEM, between 1988 and 1992, out of every hundred companies from Europe and the United States that attempted to enter emerging markets in Eastern and Southern European countries, the former Soviet Union, Latin America, India, and China, only eight ended up being successful. It should be noted that "successful" means nothing beyond a signed IJV agreement. Ninety-two could not even accomplish this.

An analysis of the reasons for the failure of IJVs from 1988 to 1992 yielded somewhat surprising results (see Figure 7.3). The most commonly cited reason was related to difficulties

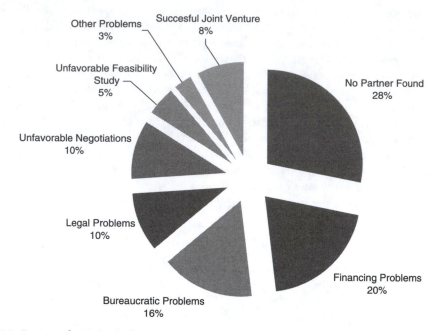

Figure 7.3 Reasons for Failure of IJVs, 1988–1992.

Source: © Dr Vladimir Kvint, 2008.

in finding the right partner in the foreign market. The new class of entrepreneurs in EMCs was extremely inexperienced, with no track record in an international business context, and with a wealth of superstitions and false images about foreigners. They were all victims of many years of dictatorial propaganda and brainwashing. Entrepreneurs and executives from the developed world were also partially to blame for their inability to find appropriate partners. They also had no experience conducting business operations in these parts of the world. They were often unable to convince local people of the benefits of signing an IJV. And local entrepreneurs and regular people were not totally off base with their suspicions. It was not unusual for foreigners to try to take advantage of local people and their inexperience. As a result, an invisible wall of distrust appeared between both parties, leading to the failure of almost 30 percent of IJV agreements.

The second major reason was related to financial challenges. Financial obstacles during that time included currency inconvertibility in all EMCs, strict regulations of cross-border transactions and repatriation of profits, as well as overregulation of foreign currency circulation. In the majority of EMCs, repatriation of profits in inconvertible currencies was illegal. Profits had almost no financial value to foreigners. But some entrepreneurs started to bring these inconvertible currencies abroad or to privately convert them in EMCs. Foreigners demanded the currencies of EMCs, despite their inconvertibility, because the domestic purchasing power of these currencies was stronger than that of convertible currencies. Several factors brought this about—the official price for raw materials was usually several times lower in domestic currencies than in foreign ones. The same applied to food, fertilizer, timber, and construction materials. Some entrepreneurs recognized this situation and began collecting inconvertible currencies, which they would exchange at a very favorable rate for themselves.

Financial obstacles were compounded by the fact that there was no operational presence of worldwide recognized commercial and investment banks in the overwhelming majority of EMCs at that time. Their representative offices in these countries did not have the right to carry out any operational activity related to customer service and investment. Their purpose was only to monitor the situation and develop relationships with the rising business class and governmental authorities.

The third most commonly cited cause of failure for IJV agreements was bureaucratic barriers. This was again mostly related to the mentality of governmental officials and employees of regulating bodies and their inexperience. They were more afraid to give permission than to not. Their inhibition to cooperate could be overcome only via bribes, which people from the law-abiding countries of the developed world were not comfortable with.

The next most commonly cited reason for failure was related to legal issues. Although many restrictions were lifted and foreign capital was allowed to operate, legal regulations in these countries were still far from being conducive to foreign business. More than that, in some countries, any operations involving a foreign currency were considered illegal. Some foreigners understood how lucrative these markets could be and tried to make speculative investments in local currency (although they were inconvertible) but found out that this was also considered illegal. This led to the wide scale use of barter trade. Foreign companies, even without investment, just selling goods and services to EMCs without convertible currency, would earn a profit. They reinvested these profits in the local currencies into goods and commodities such as oil, coal, fertilizers, etc., which they would then sell to companies from the developed world to finally get hard, convertible currency. Despite all of the barriers and extra effort required, companies that took the risk of providing their product for markets with inconvertible currencies made huge profits. Another legal issue that can lead to the failure of an IJV agreement is the rapidly changing legal systems in EMCs. This is especially dangerous to foreigners because there is often a lag time between the establishment of these laws and their translation into English and other foreign languages, making it very difficult for foreigners to adhere to them.

During this period, many negotiations were ruined from the onset because each side was unfamiliar with the other's traditions and business ethics. For entrepreneurs from many EMCs, especially at that time, a verbal promise meant a lot, and they did not have much respect for signed papers. American lawyers tend to want to put all details on paper. The result was awkward and embarrassing negotiations for both sides.

At that time, results of feasibility studies were not a common cause of failure of IJV negotiations for several reasons. First of all, competition in emerging markets between companies from the developed world was very low. Second of all, the level of profitability was so high that as long as the company could successfully sign a joint venture agreement, it was almost a given that it would be profitable. During that period feasibility studies were not a significant part of IJV negotiations. It was more important to develop a trusting relationship, familiarize both parties with the respective business, and negotiate cultures.

By 1993, not being able to find a partner as a cause of the collapse of IJV negotiations decreased substantially from 28 percent in the previous study to 15 percent (see Figure 7.4). This was the result of several factors. First of all, regulations in EMCs substantially changed, making it significantly easier for companies from the developed world to operate. In most EMCs, for example, it was no longer required to get special permission from national authorities to form an IJV and many companies were already creating wholly owned subsidiaries or acquiring domestic companies during privatization processes. Nonetheless, if a company decided to form an IJV with a local partner(s), the procedure was the same as incorporating any other business. Partners from both sides of the negotiating table had already become more familiar with each other. In addition, currency issues became less contentious. However, the bureaucratization of EMCs continued. A certain level of anarchy in some EMCs led to an increased role of government officials, giving them more

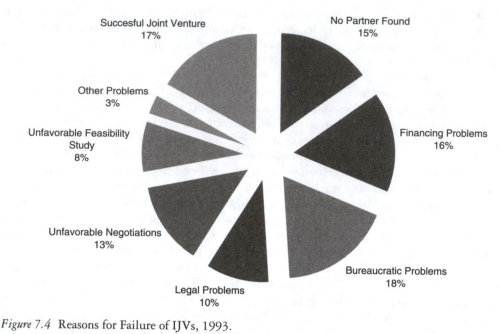

Figure 7.4 Reasons for Failure of IJVs, 1993.
Source: © Dr Vladimir Kvint, 2008.

opportunities to collect bribes. Bribe seeking by bureaucrats created a great deal of artificial barriers for foreigners. Despite the continued existence of these challenges, among others, after several years of internationalization in the GEM, the success rate of IJV negotiations more than doubled from 8 percent to 17 percent (see Figure 7.4).

By 1998 the reasons cited for failure began to coincide with the challenges faced during the formation of any new business entity (see Figure 7.5). Of the six major causes of failure during joint venture negotiations, three were essentially taxation issues. This indicates that the focus during negotiations was not only on possible opportunities for IJVs but also on the actual financial success of these ventures. Licensing and property-law issues became a regular topic of discussion during IJV negotiations. As of 2008, in the overwhelming majority of EMCs, it is still a very difficult process to obtain ownership not only of companies and their production facilities but also of the land where these facilities are located. In the majority of EMCs, it is more common for foreign investors to accept long-term land leases or concession agreements in place of outright land ownership. This is a serious issue during IJV negotiations that has put off many investors, especially individuals interested in real estate. Although a more recent study has not been conducted, anecdotally, one can make the conclusion that by the beginning of the twenty-first century, IJVs as an organizational and legal form of global business had practically completed the process of maturation.

The Letter of Intent or Memorandum of Understanding for International Joint Venture Establishment

The most important document of an IJV is the IJV agreement, which is usually based on the first document signed by potential partners—the letter of intent (LOI) or memorandum of understanding (MU). These non-binding documents are very important for future business relationships between partners and are generally used as a guideline for the IJV agreement. Although there are some exceptions, the LOI or MU is a non-binding, legally unenforceable

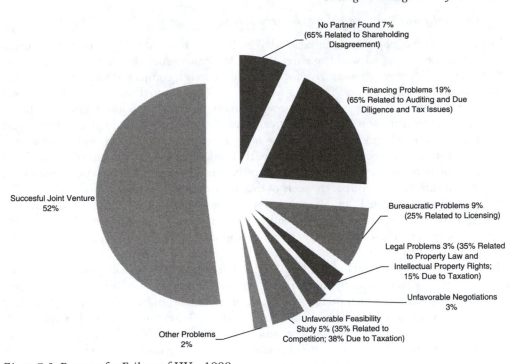

Figure 7.5 Reasons for Failure of IJVs, 1998.

Source: © Dr Vladimir Kvint, 2008.

document. In most cases, the LOI or MU is the result of successful initial negotiations between potential partners. This document is used first of all to express an interest in further developing the business relationship to the level of the creation of an IJV, and second, to agree upon an agenda for future follow-up meetings. In some cases it will include a schedule for the introduction of all parties to each other and for the drafting of the IJV agreements. Despite the fact that these documents are non-binding, they basically affirm both parties' obligations to continue the development of their cooperation with each other, establishing a certain level of loyalty and trust. Signing the LOI or MU is an important step in the creation of a successful IJV.

The LOI or MU should include the official legal names and addresses of the potential partners of the IJV. The names of the partners must match the names under which they are legally registered. The companies represented by the negotiating parties must be registered before the LOI or MU is signed. These documents should also include a clear description of the potential IJV's objectives and fields of activity. Some negotiators try to keep the objectives of the future activity of the company very general. There is an upside to this—when several objectives are mentioned in the agreement, later, the company will be more flexible in changing the direction of its business activity. On the other hand, the initial negotiations will be less focused. Nevertheless, in general, it is not a good idea to apply too many limits to potential IJV activities.

In both the LOI/MU and the IJV agreement, the role of each party must be clearly set forth—briefly in the LOI/MU and extensively in the IJV agreement. The schedule for the establishment of the IJV found in the LOI/MU does not appear in the IJV agreement. Nonetheless, the IJV agreement includes different schedules, such as the investment to registered capital ratio, the delivery of equipment, etc.

International Joint Ventures' Market-entry Strategy

IJVs became such a popular organizational vehicle in EMCs and as an approach for companies from the developed world to enter the GEM because they decreased uncertainty, as well as the political and economic risk for all parties. Foreign companies from the developed world gained experienced local partners who were well connected with national and local authorities. Domestic companies also provide them with existing production facilities, access to infrastructure and natural resources, and the ability to obtain licenses to access these resources. Furthermore, they already have appropriate personnel and can be very helpful in hiring key people to help deal with local, regional, and national authorities. Domestic partners, on the other hand, through their international foreign counterparts get easy access to direct and indirect channels of distribution for their goods and services in the GMP, as well as operational capital, with lower interest rates relative to the conditions they would get from domestic commercial banks. Foreign companies also provide them with modern ITs and cutting-edge management systems. All of these reasons explain why IJVs have been quite successful.

For the first 20 or so years of the GEM's existence, IJVs were usually the result of the creation of new legal entities by foreign and local partners. Later, on some occasions a new type of IJV appeared in which partners from one or more foreign countries established their own joint venture in the GEM, without a local partner. This usually occurs between partners with many years of experience operating in the GEM. In this case, people who years ago would have been partners are hired just as employees. Another new trend in IJVs is insourcing, as previously discussed, when companies and individual entrepreneurs from the GEM establish joint ventures in developed countries.

All IJVs can be divided into two major groups—equity related and non-equity related. Whenever a separate legal entity is established, this involves an equity-related IJV. The establishment of a long-term agreement on shared activity in EMCs by corporations and entrepreneurs of different national origins is a non-equity-related IJV. They can be created in order to share access to raw materials or amicably share markets for their goods and services. The most common form of joint venture involves the creation of a new legal entity by foreign and domestic parent companies. In order to attract foreign investors, governments of EMCs developed a wide spectrum of incentives, from tax exemptions to governmental investment in infrastructure, special regimes for profit expatriation and the import of parts and raw materials, with or without lower custom duties and quotas, etc. In order to be recognized by a government as an IJV, there is typically a minimum amount of foreign investment required. In some countries for a joint venture to be considered international, it must have a minimum of $100,000 of FDI. Another typical requirement is that a percentage ownership by the foreign partner cannot be less than 30 percent. If it is less than 30 percent, then it is treated as a domestic entity, which has its advantages and disadvantages. In many cases an IJV forms at the end of a merger or acquisition. It never arises from a hostile takeover.

Key Factors to Consider When Making an International Joint Venture

The first step for a foreign investor contemplating an IJV is to make a series of decisions as to what kind of industry, in which country, and in what particular region it seeks to invest. The reasons for foreign investment have substantially changed since the initial stages of the globalization of business. While traditional reasons, such as lower production costs and the search for new markets, still exist, new factors have appeared. The consumer of the twenty-first century demands quality products at reasonable prices. Thus, companies must produce goods of high quality at modest cost or lose their competitive advantage. This means that it is practically impossible to succeed with an entry strategy in the GEM to produce low-quality products while reducing production cost.

The location of an IJV within a particular EMC is a very important strategic issue. In the overwhelming majority of EMCs, territories and regions have different jurisdiction, tax regulation, and structure in terms of local and regional governmental authorities. The first priority is to learn about the existence of any territories of special jurisdiction such as free trade zones, special economic and technological zones, domestic offshore, technological parks in a potential location. In many EMCs, in order to attract foreign companies, the government and even regional authorities develop free trade zones near seaports and around large air-transportation hubs. EMCs have also been eager to develop special gambling or technological zones. This trend took off in southeastern China in the 1980s in places such as Shenzhen and Guangzhou. China also has other territories with special economic regulations and authorities, such as Hong Kong SAR. One of the most well-known territories of special management and regulation outside of China is the Interoceanic Region Authority in Panama. On some occasions, when a country transitions from developing to emerging-market status, the leadership of the country overestimates opportunities for territories of special regulations. For example, in the 1990s, the Republic of Georgia declared the entire country a free economic zone. Soon the government recognized that it needed taxes to finance its budget, and this regulation was officially abolished. Later, in the twenty-first century, Georgia more reasonably established a free economic zone in the Black Sea port of Poti.[27] It is always preferable for an IJV to be located in territories of special regulation.

Whether the IJV prospers depends in part on the resources available where it is located. For example, the initiator of an IJV may enter a new market with a chemical technology that consumes large amounts of water. The location of the IJV obviously must be able to provide a steady supply of suitable water, which would eliminate several potential locations. The expenses required for production in a location that suffers from water shortages would make production extremely difficult to render profitable. The same holds true for an investor entering a market with an energy-intensive technology. It is crucial for investors to have detailed knowledge about the resources of potential locations for IJVs. A mistake frequently made by electro-technical companies or clothing manufacturers is to select a new market and simply assume that they can readily acquire a cheap labor force because of the low cost of living. In many EMCs and developing countries, there is a shortage of skilled workers and relatively low unemployment rates. This causes the wages necessary to recruit competent workers to rise much higher than initially expected.

There are several important factors to consider when deciding on the location of an IJV, such as the development of the region (international or domestic), the presence or absence of capitalist institutions, and availability of necessary services. The level of development of the region's capital and financial infrastructures, the host nation's trade and distribution systems, and the level of development of its telecommunications, transportation, and energy services are also key factors. For example, while China is one of the world's richest countries in terms of labor, the low cost of this resource has often been offset by costs resulting from its poor and unreliable transportation systems, which make it difficult to obtain such resources. Because most foreign companies are located in free economic zones in coastal cities, they find it cheaper to import resources from nearby countries rather than transport them from inland China. Another important factor is the level of development of the social infrastructure in and around the region of the potential IJV. It is important to anticipate where employees will live, eat, and find entertainment, the availability of hotels, dormitories, apartment buildings, cafeterias, restaurants, movie theaters, cleaning services, etc.

Management Systems of International Joint Ventures

The economic and business nature of an IJV predetermines its management system. Significant pitfalls can appear during initial negotiations and preparation of the IJV agreement, which is one of the three major documents of IJV operations. The other two documents are the IJV by-laws, which are for the most part a reiteration of the IJV agreement (except for some temporary issues related to the establishment of the company) and IJV permission for operations from authorities of the IJV's location. The major managerial issues for IJVs are mostly related to the representation of partners on the board of directors of the IJV and in its executive structure. Typically, the ratio of representation on the board of directors reflects the ratio of initial registered capital of the IJV. This does not mean that boards of IJVs are dominated by the foreign partners. In most cases, foreign partners hire reputable domestic people to represent them on the board of directors. Intense discussion usually occurs about two positions—the chairman of the board of directors and the CEO. The final decision is always the result of a compromise between all parties involved. It is more typical for the foreign partner to keep the chairman of the board (non-executive) position for themselves, conceeding the CEO position to the domestic partner for themselves or their nominee. Some positions are relatively easy to determine. It is common practice for the partner from a developed country to nominate someone from their own country to the position of chief financial officer, because EMC financiers are less familiar with international transactions and the requirements of regulating authorities of developed countries. The continuing internationalization of the GEM and its workplace will eventually lead to the situation whereby financial officers are also from EMCs.

Strategic decisions regarding the establishment of new IJVs must be consistent with the internal policy of the company considering an IJV. It is possible to use computer models to make a decision regarding an IJV, in a process guided by experience, wisdom, and the strategist's rules mentioned in Chapter 6. Modeling allows one to choose from a variety of potential scenarios and from an infinite number of possible outcomes.

An alternative to an IJV is a wholly owned venture. Sometimes wholly owned structures rather than IJVs are the best vehicles to faciliate a transaction. This is particularly true when those involved expect that the goals of IJV partners may diverge after a certain period or when a company seeks unadulterated control to better integrate the subsidiary into the parent company's production, sales, and marketing plans. The establishment of an investment by a new wholly owned subsidiary is often a complex and costly process, but the advantages described above may make the problems worth addressing. In the decision-making process, one must consider how difficult or easy it will be to acquire the knowledge typically supplied by IJV partners to operate alone in a foreign market.

International Joint Venture Business Negotiations as a Decision-making Process

Executives of all entities—whether governments, small private businesses, or multinational corporations—must engage in the negotiating process at some point. But in IJVs, due to the nature of this organizational form, negotiating is almost a day-to-day activity. In the strategic management of IJVs, the negotiating process begins once the board of directors, by request of executives or of its own accord, decides to develop a new strategy or revise an existing one. This process cannot begin, and a new strategic scenario cannot be implemented in practice, without extensive discussion of this issue among all relevant parties. Due to the participation of partners from different countries, this discussion more resembles a negotiating process than a typical board meeting. Negotiations among IJV partners frequently unravel for several basic reasons. When two parties have equal knowledge of the market, negotiations can become overwhelmed with detail, unreasonably prolonging the process. Another cause of extensive negotiation is the inability to resolve the question of how much each participant will invest. A lack of candor between partners can be a major issue as well. Too often, partners from developed countries spend considerable money on negotiations and travel only to discover that their partners have misled them, or vice versa. Many companies, for instance, claim to be very profitable when they have earned absolutely nothing. This situation is mostly a result of differences in reporting and accounting systems in EMCs and especially in developing countries. Prospective IJV partners should request documentation supporting claims of past profitability, which should be audited in accordance with internationally accepted accounting standards. Partners should agree on an auditor or a third-party *fairness opinion* and decide who, when, and how the service will be paid for. One needs to be aware of the poor quality of a great deal of financial information in the GEM. The accounting systems in the GEM, while improving, in many cases do not provide a realistic appraisal of products or assets. In some EMCs concepts such as *current market value* or *liabilities* barely exist. The difficulty in obtaining accurate financial data makes independent auditors all the more necessary. For this reason, parent companies' IT and systems of collecting and analyzing data should be substantially improved and upgraded when making an IJV. In general, prospective investors who would like more information about a company from the GEM than what is included in formal reports are more likely to get accurate data from lower-level executives—team leaders, heads of workshops, etc. When information is reported from lower to higher levels via several strata of the managerial hierarchy, data are intentionally or unintentionally doctored. Where possible, all data provided by the local company should be supplemented by data from national and regional authorities.

While foreigners who are victims of fraud are able to seek litigation, the amount of the settlement or judgment will probably not justify the costs and the injury to the plaintiff's reputation in the international business community. A better approach is rigorous, up-front due diligence. Foreign investors in IJVs have to try to find ways to compromise with their partners from the GEM. Even if foreigners manage to get the upper hand through the courts, depending on the EMC and the level of law and order in the country, this may not translate to a settlement in real business life, which, in some cases is unfortunately still resolved with bullets. The American businessman Paul Tatum, former co-owner of the Radisson Slavyanskaya Hotel in Moscow, was gunned down near the hotel in 1996, after complaining about several threats following a long series of disagreements with his local partners.[28]

The leadership's ability to understand cultural differences often determines the success or failure of an IJV. This is certainly true regarding IJV agreement preparation to the board of directors meeting of existing IJVs. Cultural differences can play a major role in the outcome of this meeting. Subject to the limitation of all generalizations, there are some basic cultural stereotypes to note. For example, Germans tend to approach the negotiation process in a thorough, systematic, but sometimes rigid manner. This results in the need for a high degree of preparation, as well as clarity and precision in communications. French and Belgian negotiators have been known to shift the course of negotiations, preferring to discuss different options of general principles before considering the specifics, which is actually a very good approach for strategic negotiations with partners from the GEM, who themselves very often fluctuate too much. The British have been known to be informal in style—flexible and open to suggestions. The danger of this approach in the GEM is that suggestions from their EMC counterparts can be too unrealistic and overly optimistic. Chinese partners may appear tediously slow to US businesspeople, who may at their peril become impatient and press their partners too aggressively toward closure. Japanese negotiators often demand a close interpersonal relationship characterized by mutual trust, whereas US partners often view the development of personal relationships as needless and even harmful. It is not unheard of for partners from Korea to assent and nod their head throughout negotiations out of politeness; in the final moment, however, they will reserve the right to say no. On entering negotiations, partners from the developed world and from the GEM must be aware of the differing nuances in approaches to bargaining and should try to understand the other party's expectations.

Reliance on trust as a substitute for a formal agreement requires either strong cultural norms, under which trust is so institutionalized as to be a viable proxy for a contract, or a history of ongoing relations between the parties of the IJV. In such instances, mutual confidence compensates for a cultural environment of mistrust. Therefore, where the partner's culture is resistant to a formal contract, it may be advisable to replace the formal contract process with a negotiation and planning process.

International Joint Venture Management System Implementation: The Ignition of Strategy

The implementation of the management system of an IJV, as with any entity, begins with the approval of the organizational structure. Like many elements of an IJV, this structure is typically a compromise, between the norms of EMCs and those of developed countries. Typically, the organizational structure of an IJV is more centralized than that of companies in developed countries. Matrix systems are less common. At the beginning of its establishment and operation, an IJV typically hires many foreigners to move this project ahead. In some EMCs, authorities, by various means (pleasant and not so pleasant), motivate companies to hire more domestic executives and managers. It is common for IJVs to employ foreigners from developed countries as executive assistants, due to their knowledge of business ethics in developed countries and their native grasp of English.

IJVs have greater flexibility in remunerating employees compared with domestic companies, as they can pay in the domestic currency or foreign currencies. Most employees view such an option favorably, which makes it easier to attract more talented staff. Economic, cultural, and social differences must be considered when setting salary levels for local employees. For example, the average Russian or Ukrainian worker is often better educated than their US counterpart and can be an excellent employee given the proper conditions. But the average salary of a Ukrainian employee is far below that of a US employee. Employers can supply amenities, such as apartments, which are difficult to afford or are in short supply in many EMCs, to fill some of the gap. Such amenities represent excellent ways to motivate workers and strengthen relationships between employer and employee. However, there are a number of financial obstacles that IJVs in the GEM have to deal with, such as a deficit of convertible currency, a limited number of financial institutions whose guarantees can be accepted in developed countries, and a scarcity of cash. The risk of fraud, related to banking transactions, which was a serious problem in the 1990s, made many European and especially American banks at the beginning of the twenty-first century substantially decrease the number of corresponding accounts in emerging-market banks. In turn, this significantly complicated trade transactions between companies from the GEM and developed countries. Without corresponding accounts, for companies from EMCs, even operational loans for 24 to 48 hours became unavailable. In big, international commercial banks, of all transactions, those related to EMCs account for 2 to 5 percent. These banks have no desire to compromise their financial reputation by having problems in corresponding relations with banks from EMCs. From this point of view, IJVs are in much better situations than the majority of domestic companies of the GEM. They can still operate with foreign counterparts, care of their parent companies abroad, or using their guarantee. Some of them have even had IPOs in developed countries or have been listed there via depository receipts (ADR or IDR). Few banks in the GEM accept Western letters of credit because they lack working capital. Even if banks do accept letters of credit, some lend only a part of the required amount. A common (but decreasing in prevalence) practice for addressing this problem is for foreign firms to buy raw materials from companies in the GEM and pay for them with equipment instead of cash, pursuant to a predetermined agreement. This kind of transaction is called countertrade, and is a kind of export-import operation without the direct involvement of currency.

Another form of international lending has the local manufacturer pledge a title documenting interest in a precious metal or other commodity to a bank in a third country, a practice that permits the borrower from the GEM to acquire foreign-made machinery and equipment. As the business begins to generate profit, the borrower repays the loan, and upon full payment is returned the pledged title.

An important point to determine for an IJV is the share of initial capital investment each party contributes. This has very important implications for the IJV, such as determining the division of profits. Foreign parent companies should calculate the purchasing power of currencies from emerging markets during the negotiations and recognize the value of any contributed property.

From the time of entry-strategy implementation, the board of directors of the IJV gathers at regular scheduled intervals, though less often than the board of directors of domestic companies in the developed world. This is mostly due to the travel required for foreign partners. To mitigate travel costs, IJVs often use IT service companies, such as Cisco. There has been substantial progress in teleconferencing technologies, which has helped to reduce travel costs for IJVs. Nonetheless, in general, face-to-face board meetings take place no less than once every 45 days. A typical mistake made by foreigners from the developed world is to invite the CEO to be a member of the board of directors. This obviously makes it very difficult when the board of directors has to evaluate the CEO's performance, especially since in many EMCs, boards of directors have to conduct their decisions on the basis of a consensus. This is the typical situation that results in golden parachutes for fired CEOs.

During the initial stages of the implementation of IJV management systems in the GEM, it is not unusual to have to deal with issues regarding the confidentiality of proprietary information. This is especially related to decisions and materials of the board of directors. In some industries, foreigners have limited or no access to certain materials of strategic national importance. In other cases, governments and local authorities require certain information to be reported that compromises the confidentiality of the board's decisions. If the IJV is created with a government as a partner, and if the state controls more than 50 percent of shares, in some EMCs foreigners are not allowed to be chairman of the board or CEO. This has to be taken into consideration during the formation and preparation of the by-laws of the IJV. Of course, the by-laws cannot contradict the law of the land in which the IJV operates.

The decision-making process in IJVs is typically more efficient than that of domestic companies in the GEM. IJVs usually have much less managerial staff and executives compared with domestic companies of EMCs with similar output. Office discipline, office supply, and IT are almost always much higher in offices of IJVs. This is usually not the case in the offices of IJVs that are the partnership solely of companies from the GEM. Nevertheless, IJVs in the GEM are still kind of a centaur—a hybrid of developed and GEM practices and traditions. Clashes related to different cultural backgrounds of employees, to different languages and the subsequent miscommunications are a daily occurrence in IJVs. Nonetheless, this centaur is still powerful and very much alive. A key issue for IJVs is the relationship between parent companies, which are usually of different cultural backgrounds, especially during the time of IJV strategy development and implementation. This relationship is often further complicated by the cultural environment of the location of the IJV, which may be different than that of both parent companies. To allow the IJV to function efficiently, it is best if the parent companies have direct control only at the time of strategy formation and goal setting of the IJV. The authority of parent companies is a very delicate issue because legally, the IJV is an independent entity, not a subsidiary. It is especially delicate when the parent companies do not have a shared understanding during processes of strategy formation—especially the determination of objectives and goals.

As the GEM continues to develop and mature in economic terms, a somewhat paradoxical trend is appearing; EMCs are aggressively seeking foreign investment but are offering less and less special treatment to foreign companies. Companies with foreign capital are still and will continue to be treated somewhat differently from purely domestic companies of EMCs, be it de facto or de jure. IJVs will continue to be a very popular organizational vehicle for expanding a company's international activity and the reasons for their failure, presented in the analysis of the 1998 IJV activities in the EMCs, will most likely not change substantially.

Study Questions

1. Describe the major elements of the strategic management system.
2. What are the differences between the order of development of a strategic management system and the order of its implementation?
3. Describe the strategic role of leadership for multinational corporations.
4. Describe the differences between operational leadership and strategic leadership.
5. Describe the major conflicts of interests between operational and strategic leaders.
6. Describe the differences and conflicts of interest between strategic leadership on the corporate and unit levels. How does this influence the success of the corporation?
7. What are the major differences between the strategic leadership of a yet-to-be-formed corporation and a corporation that is revising its strategy?
8. Describe the difference in approach to corporate strategy development of executives from EMCs with that of foreign expatriates.
9. How does the organizational structure affect the functions of a management system?
10. Describe the major differences in the typical organizational structure of EMCs and developing countries.
11. How do EMCs search for and hire executives and managers? How does this differ from typical practice in developed countries?
12. Describe the differences in characteristics in executives from EMCs versus those from developed countries.
13. How are the systems of remuneration different for executives and managers in EMCs versus in developed countries?
14. Describe the differences in requirements of administrative staff in developed countries versus in EMCs.
15. How do office and professional ethics differ in developed countries and EMCs?
16. Describe the differences in the decision-making process for operational management versus strategic management.
17. Describe the differences and similarities in the decision-making process for developed countries versus EMCs.

18. Describe the specifics of risk management in the decision-making process in EMCs.
19. Describe the specifics of information as an element of management systems.
20. Define and describe the major functions of management systems.
21. Explain the differences between strategic planning and the strategic plan.
22. Describe the differences and similarities in strategic planning in developed countries versus in EMCs.
23. Describe the role of strategic motivation as a determinant of the success of any entity.
24. What is the difference in the motivation of initiative of managers in developed countries and EMCs?
25. What is the role of control and monitoring in the success of strategy implementation?
26. In what way are IJVs an efficient strategic form of the globalization of business?
27. Describe the dynamics and reasons for failed attempts at establishing joint ventures in the GEM.
28. What is the role of a LOI or MU in the formation of a joint venture? What is the difference between a LOI and an IJV agreement?
29. How do foreign and domestic partners complement each other in the formation and functioning of IJVs in the GEM?
30. Describe the approach to determining the location of an IJV in the GEM.
31. Describe the specifics of management systems and types of risk that should be taken into account for IJVs in the GEM.
32. Describe the specifics of business negotiations in the process of establishing IJVs.
33. Describe the role of cultural differences in the success and failure of IJVs.
34. Describe the process and specifics of IJV management-system implementation in the GEM.
35. Describe the main document that must be obtained prior to the operations of an IJV.

8   Investment Strategy for the Global Emerging Market

An investment in knowledge pays the best interest.

(Benjamin Franklin, 1706–1790)

Money is like a sixth sense without which you cannot make a complete use of the other five.[1]

(W. Somerset Maugham, English author, 1874–1965)

Keynote Definitions

Foreign direct investment: The roots of the economic nature of foreign direct investment (FDI) grow from competitive opportunities abroad, workforce of appropriate quality, available capital, effective management systems, and know-how and technology, all of which lead to a high level of return under a manageable level of risk, according to a comprehensive feasibility study and strategy.

Risk of FDI: Risk of FDI is an innate characteristic of cross-border business related to the threat of predictable or unpredictable negative changes of the external environment or of a company's internal resources, with manageable and unmanageable consequences leading to potential losses.

Reasons for Cross-Border Investment

Economic Nature of Foreign Direct Investment

In general, strategists, corporate executives, professional investors, and entrepreneurs will not seek foreign investment opportunities when there are equally lucrative prospects in their familiar and stable domestic workplace. It is only natural to invest in the known rather than venture into the unknown. It is natural to invest in stable domestic political, economic, and business conditions during times of an economic boom. It is natural to avoid uncertainty and the inevitable risk that comes along with this. Risk of cross-border direct investment from developed countries to the GEM and developing countries always involves higher levels of uncertainty and a limited ability to manage risk according to corporate interests and strategy. This obviously leads to potential threats and losses. In a perfect world, an investor's domestic market would provide ample basic economic factors—rich and abundant natural resources, inexpensive highly qualified labor, easily available capital at reasonable rates, well-developed transportation, telecommunication, and free-market infrastructure, etc. National and local authorities would create a friendly investment climate with tax holidays, and competition would not be overly intense. These conditions would almost guarantee a high return and an absence of investment risk. Unfortunately, perfect investment conditions do not exist in any country or region. Most regional and national leaders, however, will at least promote the image of having some of these conditions in order to motivate investors and entrepreneurs to enter their territories. The reasons for this are obvious. Political leaders know that investment and entrepreneurial activity lead to high employment, improvements in standards of living, high consumption, and a subsequent high rate of economic growth, which—most important for political leaders—ensures the support of the population.

In reality, if a country or region with such an ideal investment climate were to appear, it would be a haven for investors for only a very brief period. Domestic and foreign investors would be drawn to the territory like bears to honey; the surge of investment and business activity would create an extremely competitive environment. Before long many investment projects would fail. This oversimplified scenario illustrates an important point—the sooner a company goes after an opportunity, the more likely it is to succeed. It is always easier for the earlier entrants to a market to obtain concessions, contracts, exclusive agreements, etc. Not all, but a few of the first companies to enter emerging markets prospered immensely as a result of the tremendous need in these countries for cutting-edge technology, modern managerial skills, and operational capital. In addition to there being little serious competition, national and regional governments offered the first foreign investors lax regulations, liberal tax regimes, exclusivity, etc., which investors who came later did not enjoy. Investors seek certain conditions and are willing to go anywhere in the GMP or global workplace to find them.

From this basic concept, one can understand the economic nature of FDI. The roots of the economic nature of FDI grow from competitive opportunities abroad (which do not exist domestically); workforce of appropriate quality; available capital; effective management systems and their organizational forms, know-how and technology; all of which lead to a high level of return under a manageable level of risk, according to a comprehensive feasibility study and strategy. The economics of FDI explain what drives investors into unfamiliar and frontier business environments.

An influx of FDI and its increasing accumulation are very important indicators that a country is becoming an EMC and its dynamics have a positive vector. Many countries prior to their "emergence" did not receive a single dollar of FDI for a number of reasons. Dictatorships tried to completely control the domestic economy, which allowed the rulers to be above the law and unaccountable, when it dealt only with domestic investors. In the overwhelming majority of developing countries, conditions are barely or not at all acceptable for foreign investors—simply opening the door for them legally is not good enough. FDI requires the existence of free-market factors or capitalist institutions and a reasonably developed legal framework that protects the assets, property rights, and know-how of foreigners. The host developing country needs to create incentives for foreign investors to enter. Multilateral institutions should play a central role in this process.

A very difficult barrier that inhibits FDI in developing countries is the mentality of leaders, potential employees, and society. For many years people in underdeveloped and developing countries have been receiving foreign aid, not investment. A major challenge for foreign aid, in any form—food, services, or equipment—is related to its proper distribution. Unfortunately, in many cases governments have not made the efficient management of the distribution of equipment and other types of foreign aid a major priority. The same equipment, when in the form of FDI, requires that users and executives in the host country adopt a new attitude, because FDI is driven by the invisible power of private interests. A business- and efficiency-related mentality cannot appear by decree overnight; it takes time. It is very important for the leadership of country-recipients to understand that foreign investors from developed countries and domestic investors have to deal with issues that they never faced in the developed world. It is a major challenge for leaders of emerging markets and their corporations receiving FDI to recognize that the first priority of foreign investors is to earn a profit. While benefiting the recipient country may also be a motivation of FDI, it is usually secondary. It is very difficult for members of the government of some EMCs to understand that FDI is not politically motivated, but profit driven. This is the major difference between foreign aid and foreign investment. Countries that are accustomed to receiving foreign aid often struggle to provide the conditions necessary to attract private foreign investment.

Initially, foreign investors from developed countries sought destinations of new opportunities—which later became EMCs—for lower cost production and cheap labor (without requirements for social benefits) and abundant natural resources with lax ecological regulations. As developing countries matured and became EMCs, foreign investors began to reevaluate the situation. They realized that the benefits available in these markets involved more than just cheap labor and less restrictive ecological requirements. EMCs also offer less competition, exclusive agreements (for some time, which keep competitors away), and untapped markets with growing consumption power. One of the strongest incentives drawing investors from developed countries to EMCs became the ability to hire more people for less money. The global average number of employees per $1 million of FDI originating from the US is 5.5 (see Table 8.1). In developed countries, for this amount of investment, a US company is able to hire an average of only 4.7 employees. But in the GEM a US company can hire 7.2 employees for the same amount of FDI (EMCs are listed in Table 8.1

Table 8.1 Employment in US Foreign Affiliates and US Outward FDI Stock, by Sector, 2003[2]

Region/Sector	Employees (Thousands)	Outward FDI Stock ($ million)	No. of Employees per $1 Million of Outward FDI Stock
World			
Total	9 657.5	1 769 613	5.5
Primary	199.5	85 473	2.3
Mining, Quarrying, and Petroleum	181.0	85 473	2.1
Manufacturing	4 989.2	371 078	13.4
Services	3 973.4	1 176 957	3.4
Developed Countries			
Total	5 983.1	1 266 350	4.7
Primary	56.7	42 876	1.3
Mining, Quarrying, and Petroleum	55.5	42 876	1.3
Manufacturing	2 760.6	280 874	9.8
Services	1 755.8	835 881	2.1
Developing Countries			
Total	3 550.4	489 865	7.2
Primary	107.3	37 506	2.9
Mining, Quarrying, and Petroleum	92.1	37 506	2.5
Manufacturing	2 099.9	88 369	23.8
Services	779.6	333 917	2.3
South-East Europe and CIS			
Total	32.1	2 511	12.8
Primary	4.3	1 253	3.4
Mining, Quarrying, and Petroleum	4.3	1 253	3.4
Manufacturing	15.1	266	56.8
Services	4.8	325	14.8

Source: UNCTAD, FDI/TNC database (www.unctad.org/fdistatistics).

as developing countries, due to UNCTAD's previously described poor country classification system—see Chapter 4). By this indicator, the highest ratio in the GEM is found in the EMCs of Southeast Europe and the former Soviet Union (CIS), where US companies can hire 2.72 times more people than in developed countries.

The greater number of employees in the GEM per unit of investment is one of several incentives for strategic investors to go overseas. They are also motivated by the increasing consumption power of people in EMCs, who account for about 68 percent of the global population. In order to cash in on these new potential consumers, employees, and resources, foreign investors flocked to a number of different sectors in the GEM. From 1990 to 2005, the stock of foreign investment in service sectors of the GEM increased by a factor of nine. During the same period, FDI stocks in the production of food, beverages, and tobacco increased in the GEM by a factor of five. In one of the most attractive sectors of the GEM—mining of natural resources and petroleum production—foreign investment stocks increased by a factor of 9.9. The greatest increase of cumulative foreign investment in the GEM occurred in services of private businesses, which grew by a factor of 38.4.[3] This huge increase of investment can be explained by the virtual non-existence of private businesses under the reign of dictators in the former Soviet bloc and in many Latin American and Asian countries.

Despite the wealth of opportunities in the GEM, success is not automatic. Even successful investment projects will inevitably encounter serious challenges. Strategists should not make the mistake of expecting immediate returns on FDI in the GEM, especially in construction, real estate, and other big projects. Returns can be very high, but the speed at which this occurs is often not as fast as anticipated. In cases of widespread failure, foreign investors are not the only party harmed. In response to many failed FDI projects in the GEM and the subsequent outflow of FDI and even of domestic investment, Nobel laureate in economics Dr Joseph Stiglitz argued that countries should motivate long-term rather than short-term capital. In his words, "the regulation or taxation of inflows helps to limit outflow surges: if there is less short-term money in the country, there is less that can leave when expectations change and inflows turn into outflows."[4] As the GEM continues to mature and stabilize, and EMC governments intervene less in private business affairs, FDI is flocking in. As of the first decade of the twenty-first century, EMCs are still competing for foreign investment, but in the future this situation will likely be reversed. The increasing experience and sophistication of domestic investors in the GEM adds to the likelihood of such a situation. The twenty-first century will see the role of the GEM in the GMP continue to rise, partially as a result of its increasingly sophisticated domestic investors. Domestic investors of EMCs are already making the investment environment of the GEM more competitive. Nevertheless, investors always compete for the most lucrative projects in the GEM.

Rationale to Invest in the Global Emerging Market

Prior to the birth of the GEM, there were very few opportunities for large-scale investments with high long-term yields outside of the developed world. During this time there was a shortage of investment opportunities. Investment firms and individual entrepreneurs competed for any project with the potential for at least a moderate level of return. Most of these opportunities were found in developed countries such as the United States, Canada, some nations of Western Europe, Japan, Australia, and New Zealand. In the beginning of the 1980s, the situation abruptly changed for most investors. The birth and formation of the GEM and the GMP opened up an unprecedented amount of opportunities, causing national and regional governments of EMCs to compete among themselves for investors. Large losses in developed markets, such as the burst of the dot-com bubble in 2000 and 2001, directed even more investment to the GEM. Unfortunately, in the case of the dot-com bubble, the GEM was experiencing the tail end of the Asian financial crisis, which ended up affecting Russia, Argentina, and practically the entire GMP. Nevertheless, the trend of increasing investment to EMCs continued. Political leaders of these countries see FDI as a means to convert national resources into socioeconomic prosperity. For the authorities of EMCs, FDI represents an immediate source of employment. Table 8.2 illustrates the logic behind this assumption.

From another perspective, businesses owners in EMCs sought foreign investors as partners to make their production facilities more efficient and provide access to operational capital and consumers in developed markets. Some owners looked to foreign partners for a legal means to relocate their capital abroad, into foreign bank accounts or as FDI in countries with well-established legal protection of private assets. In doing so, these owners created what was essentially a personal hedge against any unfavorable changes in the mood of their national governments. As for the people of EMCs, they correctly saw FDI as a ladder out of unemployment, poverty, and in many cases starvation. Political leaders and businesses of EMCs began hiring professional consulting firms, usually headquartered in developed countries in order to create strategies to attract FDI and prepare their businesses for international cooperation.

This initiated the development of various economic mechanisms and organizational forms to lure FDI, such as free economic and technological zones, free trade zones, tax and custom duties exemptions, tax-free manufacturing zones, special privileges for IJVs, etc. These strategies were successfully implemented in countries such as China, Brazil, Singapore, Taiwan, Korea, Mexico, as well as the Balkan and Southern and Eastern European states, such as Croatia, the Czech and Slovak Republics, Hungary and Poland. These incentives played a very influential role in the great expansion of the traditional marketplace and workplace via the formation of the GEM and the GMP. The lack of experience of political and business leaders of the GEM as well as of investors from the developed world in these new markets caused the failure of a great deal of investment in EMCs (see reasons for IJV failure in Chapter 7). Nonetheless, those ventures that were successful provided such a powerful example of high profitability, that the entire international business community

Table 8.2 Employment Related to Inward FDI, Most Recent Year (Thousands of Employees)[5]

Economy	Year of Most Recent Data	Host Economy Employment of Foreign Affiliates (Thousands of Employees)	Share of Foreign Affiliate's Employment in Total (%)
China	2004	24,000	3.2
Czech Republic	2004	620.4	15.9
Hong Kong	2004	543*	22.1
Hungary	2000	606.7	22.4
Ireland	2004	149.5**	50.6
Madagascar	2003	193.8***	2.4
Poland	2000	648.3*	6.1
Portugal	2002	150.4*	4
Singapore	2004	157.6****	47
Slovenia	2004	64	8
Sri Lanka	2004	415.7*****	5.6

Notes:
*Data refers to majority-owned affiliates only.
**Total permanent full-time employment in the manufacturing and internationally traded service sectors.
***1998.
****Data refers only to the manufacturing sector.
*****Approval data.

became oriented to exploring opportunities between developed countries and EMCs. From the perspective of companies from the developed world, these markets were wide open. Competition was almost non-existent. Returns on investment were several times higher than that in developed countries. The size, scale, and availability of natural resources are radically different in the GEM than in the developed world. In general, natural resources can be exploited for a much longer time in the GEM, as a result of their greater abundance, lack of exploration and the initial willingness of EMC governments to attract foreign investors with lax labor and ecological regulations.

To the dismay of their competitors, corporations and individual investors that seized these opportunities began to return to their domestic markets with capital, resources, products, and profits made in EMCs, rather than reinvesting in host countries. Businesses that achieved success in the GEM were able to significantly reduce production costs and subsequently the prices of their goods and services in traditional markets via economies of scale, cheaper productive labor and natural resources. This marked the beginning of modern outsourcing to the GEM. The motivation behind this movement is usually to reduce labor and operational costs, increase productivity, and gain access to new technologies. Beginning in the last quarter of the twentieth century, some companies also begin using outsourcing to take advantage of differences in time zones, which allowed them to serve customers around the clock. The typical industries that are outsourced involve these cost and service advantages, such as human resources, real estate and account management, IT, manufacturing, product design, software and web development, and marketing and advertising. According to 2007 A.T. Kearney Global Services Location Index™, the destinations of most outsourcing are India, China, Malaysia, and Thailand. In 2007, the largest recipient of outsourcing in Latin America is Brazil. In Europe the large recipient of outsourcing is Bulgaria.[6] A specific form of outsourcing is offshoring to countries or territories with less restrictive regulations. This applies primarily to the banking and insurance sectors. It is important for strategists to be aware of the fact that outsourcing and offshore outsourcing relocate routine operations from the main facilities and headquarters, allowing higher quality and better paid employees and managers to concentrate on "value-ad" tasks and more important strategic issues. FDI established highly efficient production facilities in EMCs, generating cheaper and larger amounts of goods and even services for markets in the developed world. The companies that lost to these brave risk takers had no choice but to reassess their strategies, which were usually oriented to avoiding risky foreign ventures altogether.

The surge in FDI outflows from the developed world created the need for entry strategies specifically crafted for EMCs. The overwhelming majority of investors who pursued opportunities in these markets without entry strategies designed for local conditions failed. The simple conversion of strategies that were effective for decades in foreign developed countries consistently crashed and burned in EMCs, despite the lower competition, cheaper and qualified labor resources, abundant raw materials, and production facilities that are available, though in need of modernization.

Adapting to the new realities of the GMP has been extremely challenging for strategists from North America, Western Europe, Japan, and Australia. The historical experience of American companies in the 1950s and 60s in Japan—at that time the country of new opportunities with a unique business culture—was not applicable in the diverse cultural and ethical traditions in the GEM. Initially, strategists did not have a term for countries that eventually became known as emerging markets, nor were they aware of the many shared characteristics of these countries regarding FDI, as the concept of the GEM was not yet developed. Professionals did not have any prepackaged strategies to help their clients in these new markets. The need for strategists specifically trained for opportunities in these distant countries of unique cultural, political, economic, business, and technological conditions became apparent. Strategists and consultants with the expertise and connections in countries—which slowly started to become known as emerging markets—were highly valued and remunerated by investors, who, to their own surprise, became not only international but also global business players. FDI became a catalyst that jumpstarted EMCs onto the path toward prosperity. Countries that first realized the potential of FDI and actively sought it—such as China, Turkey, Brazil, Hungary, and Poland—eventually achieved a cumulative effect. Global investors recognized these countries as poles of investment growth and increased their presence accordingly, developing more and more projects. As a result of this trend, combined with domestic progress in EMCs, by the first decade of the twenty-first century, these countries became leaders among national recipients of FDI, surpassing the majority of developed countries. Figure 8.1 shows the top EMC recipients of FDI in 2006.

However, in order for FDI to actually work as a significant economic factor of development, it must reach the level of roughly $1,000 (in purchasing power of the early 1990s) per inhabitant in the recipient country or region. This is obviously easier to achieve in less populated countries, and extremely difficult in countries with large populations such as China, Brazil, India, Indonesia, Russia, Mexico, etc., where FDI per capita is nowhere near $1,000. In these countries, in order to make FDI a substantial economic factor, governments and national strategists channeled FDI to certain regions and coordinated it with other forms of private, public, and governmental investment in order to create an agglomeration effect. The establishment of special economic and technological zones was one of the most successful means by which to concentrate investment in specific regions. China did not invent this practice—several different zones of economic initiative existed in the United States prior to the Chinese experience—but China was and is the undisputed leader among EMCs. In terms of using these zones to regionally focus FDI, China's success is unparalleled throughout the world. In its southeast region, China developed several special economic and technological zones, such as the Shenzhen Special Economic Zone, which opened in the spring of 1980. Free economic zones such as Shenzhen and the Shenyang Economic and Technological Development Zones account for about 85 percent of Chinese exports. In fact, 90 percent of Chinese territory has actually never received FDI.

Many EMCs and their domestic regions have incorporated the Chinese export-oriented model into their economic development plans. For example, the Indian state Tamil Nadu exports one-third of its $29 billion net state domestic product.[7] By the beginning of the

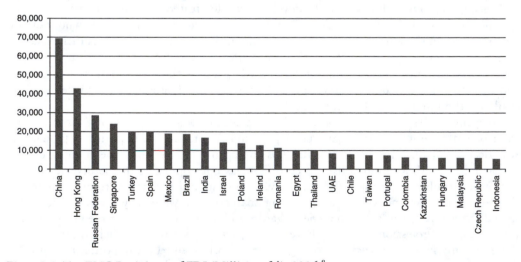

Figure 8.1 Top EMC Recipients of FDI (Millions of $), 2006.[8]

twenty-first century, in the Dominican Republic exports from special economic zones accounted for 80 percent of all exports and for almost all manufactured exports.[9] This situation exists in many other EMCs, including the Czech Republic and Hungary. FDI accounts for "half of China's exports—compared to 45 percent for Malaysia, 38 percent for Singapore, 31 percent for Mexico, and 15 percent for South Korea."[10] National strategists of EMCs should keep in mind that FDI does not have as direct an impact on standards of living as domestic investment, because profits from FDI are usually repatriated to its country of origin, while profits from domestic investment typically do not leave the country. With or without special economic zones, FDI became an important factor in the growth of exports from EMCs.

In 2006 the global average of FDI inflows as a percentage of GDP was about 2.84. There were 97 countries that received a higher percentage of FDI inflows relative to GDP, 49 of which were EMCs. In Table 8.3, it should come as no surprise for strategists that Luxembourg had FDI inflows more than three times the value of its GDP. This figure consists mostly of money from abroad deposited in bank accounts in Luxembourg, which qualifies as FDI only in legal, not economic terms. These FDI inflows are mostly "mailbox" investments. Bulgaria—where the share of FDI to GDP is 16.4 percent—is one of several EMCs in which FDI began to play an important role in the twenty-first century. The same can be said for Serbia and Panama. Countries in which the role of FDI is more than 10 percent of GDP (including mailbox investments like those in Luxembourg and Switzerland) have a national "niche-sector" strategy to attract foreign investment. Panama, for example, is a well-known, legitimate offshore bank haven, the result of its successful national strategy. Some countries, such as Turkmenistan, attract investment with their natural resources, while others, such as Costa Rica, attract investment both via natural resources and well-established banking institutions. Israel has accumulated substantial foreign investment in its high-tech industry. The Baltic republic of Estonia has a diversified spectrum of industries that draw FDI, from machinery building to the transportation sector. Large EMCs, such as Russia and especially China, despite their huge populations, attract more FDI (as a

Table 8.3 FDI Inflows as a Percentage of GDP, 2006[11]

Rank	Country Name	2006
1	Luxembourg	304.9
2	**St Kitts and Nevis**	42.4
3	**Malta**	28
4	Iceland	24.8
5	**Jordan**	22.8
6	Grenada	22.7
7	**Hong Kong, China**	22.6
8	St Vincent and the Grenadines	20.1
9	Equatorial Guinea	19.3
10	Seychelles	18.8
11	**Singapore**	18.3
12	**Bulgaria**	16.4
13	Gambia, The	16.1
14	**Serbia**	16
15	Belgium	15.7
16	**Panama**	15.1
17	Djibouti	14.1
18	Guinea-Bissau	13.8
19	**Georgia**	13.7
20	**St Lucia**	13.2

percentage of GDP) than the GMP average. Experts who argue that FDI plays an important role primarily in developing countries and EMCs contradict the statistics (see Figure 8.2). Among countries of the Eurozone (not included in Figure 8.2) the average role of FDI is about 3.8 percent of GDP, a higher share than in most EMCs. Furthermore, in Iceland and Sweden, the percentage of FDI in GDP is 25 and 7 respectively.

When analyzing FDI statistics, strategists should always be aware of the influence of financial factors. The widening gap in the exchange rate between the two most important currencies of the world, the US dollar and the euro, is increasing the role of FDI outflows from the US. For example, US companies' investments in Eastern and Southern European EMCs that adopted the euro as their official currencies or have national currencies pegged to the euro will yield higher returns than investments outside of the 16 Eurozone countries and countries heavily influenced by the Eurozone. The stronger the euro is, the higher the value of existing US assets in the Eurozone, but the more costly to make new investments. A weaker dollar also makes the domestic facilities of US companies more attractive for FDI. In addition to evaluating the role of FDI in GDP, it is useful to analyze the role of FDI in GNP. Unlike GDP, GNP takes into account all forms of income and wages including corporate profit, rent, indirect business taxes, and unincorporated personal income.

Gauging Foreign Investment Risk in Emerging Markets

Risk simply cannot be avoided in the GMP of the twenty-first century. *Risk of FDI is an innate characteristic of cross-border business related to the threat of predictable or unpredictable negative changes of the external environment or of a company's internal resources, with manageable and unmanageable consequences leading to potential losses.* Executives and strategists have come to realize that if they are not willing to deal with a certain level of risk, their competitors will be. The need to be able to deal with risk has led to the development of risk-management systems. Instead of avoiding risk, executives and strategists use these systems to measure, adjust, and manage it. Risk management is a daily practice of strategists, not just operational managers responsible for FDI in the GEM. Rising interest rates and changing national strategies can negatively influence the inflow of investment to EMCs and their performance. It is especially apparent when companies based on FDI go through IPO processes. Leaders of EMCs tend to give more attention to FDI and the activity of foreign banks, mostly ignoring foreign portfolio investment firms and their activities in national stock exchanges, despite the fact that this investment also brings capital to the country. A

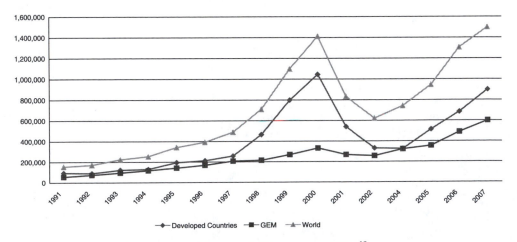

Figure 8.2 FDI Inflows by Category of Country (Millions of $), 2006.[12]

lack of governmental attention to FDI and related portfolio investment can redirect capital from a net inflow to an outflow. This redirection was described in an analysis of Dr Frederick S. Mishkin, a member of the board of governors of the US. Federal Reserve System: "A dominant phenomenon in emerging-market countries is a *sudden stop*, a large negative change in capital inflows, which, as a general rule, appear to contain a large unanticipated component."[13] Such a reversal is a serious threat for domestic financial systems of the EMCs and does not necessarily benefit developed countries. Investors who went overseas often could not have efficiently invested this capital domestically. This is especially the case with FDI done by émigrés in developed countries; they tried to use their advantages in terms of native language, experience, and connections in their country of origin.

All strategists, investors, or cross-border entrepreneurs have to develop a risk-management system related to FDI (see Chapter 7). It should be seen as an indispensable part of a strategic risk management system. The development and implementation of a strategic management system can be done through the following stages in the concept of strategic management:

- Risk identification.
- Risk measurement.
- Determination of risk aversion.
- Management of unavoidable risk.
- Systematic evaluation and monitoring of risk.
- Adjustment of strategic management system.

Successful strategists classify risk in several different ways in order to evaluate and manage it. The most fundamental classification is based on an entity's ability to change or manage risk. In this regard, risk is typically separated into two categories:

> *Systematic or country/region specific*—risk that is usually considered to be non-probabilistic, unpredictable, and unmanageable.

> *Unsystematic or company specific*—risk that is probabilistic, and therefore can be predicted, evaluated, and managed.

Systematic Risk in the Global Emerging Market

The generally accepted definition of systematic or country/region-specific risk presented above is actually quite problematic. Many risk factors that are usually included in this category, such as investment-related decisions by national governments and regional authorities, can be predicted with reasonable accuracy and thus are probabilistic. However, it is almost impossible to manage country-specific or systematic risk. It is the privilege of the country's citizens, by democratic means, such as state elections, political parties' campaigns, etc., to influence the decision-making process of the national leadership. In most developed countries—including the US—corporations do attempt to promote their interests in governmental structures, via specially registered lobbying organizations, which often hire former government employees and officials. However, this activity generally provokes a negative backlash from society. It is important to understand the distinction between influencing and managing the governmental decision-making process. In the majority of EMCs, the registration of lobbying companies still does not exist. Attempting to manage systematic risk by influencing governments through non-registered unofficial lobbyists is a very risky and publicly controversial maneuver. According to the practice of FDI strategy, *systematic risk or country/region-specific risk is predictable, though mostly not manageable.*

Systematic Risk of Foreign Direct Investment

Due to the widely accepted paradigm that systematic risk is unpredictable and unmanageable, project and direct investors entering an EMC considered to be of high risk will not be able to obtain full insurance against country-specific/systematic risk. It is a substantially uninsurable risk. However, almost three decades of experience in EMCs has led insurers to provide insurance for certain issues related to systematic risk. These issues are usually evaluated by a few specific integrated indicators of political and economic risk. The prism of these indicators can help to partially insure the activity of a company inside a risky country. Corporate management is able to make predictions about the dynamics of conditions and consequences of their strategic decisions and develop a risk-management system to mitigate different risk factors. Insurers, as well as corporate leaders, mostly deal with company-specific, unsystematic risks. Insurers will not issue policies against changes of government, revolutions, etc. However, by factoring in systematic risk, many will issue policies for certain government actions that are unfriendly to business, such as the nationalization or expropriation of properties or profits, changes in credit policy or the convertibility of the national currency, etc. These issues are typically covered by political risk insurance.

Role of Rating Agencies

When strategic investors or corporate leaders are considering making a foreign investment—especially in countries with unfamiliar political and economic conditions—they usually seek the opinion of major rating agencies and experts. Several reliable rating institutions have established themselves in the business communities of the GEM. Among the most respected are S&P, Moody's, and more recently, Fitch Ratings. In addition to the proprietary information and services of these professional companies, which must of course be purchased, there are several public sources of national investment and business climate evaluations, such as the World Bank, the WTO, and regional development banks (the European Bank for Reconstruction and Development, Inter-American Development Bank, etc.). Furthermore, there are many non-profit organizations, publications, think-tanks, etc., that provide useful information for investors moving into unfamiliar markets (see Chapter 2). The investment ratings of all of these agencies should not be taken as indisputable facts—there will always be certain characteristics of a particular project that these evaluations do not take into account. Most agencies evaluate different types of risk, without rating countries for the specific purposes of an investor.

In addition to regularly updating national investment grades, investment-rating agencies such as S&P also evaluate the grades of particular currencies, types of investment instruments, foreign debt, etc. A revision of an investment grade by a major agency is very important news for strategists and investors. For example,

> on April 30, 2008, Standard & Poor's Ratings Services raised its long-term foreign currency sovereign credit rating on the Federative Republic of Brazil to "BBB–" from "BB+," and its long-term local currency sovereign credit to "BBB+" from "BBB." Brazil is the 14th sovereign whose foreign currency debt has been raised to investment grade. The upgrades reflect the maturation of Brazil's institutions and policy framework, as evidenced by the easing of fiscal and external debt burdens and improved trend growth prospects.[14]

There are substantial differences in the evaluation of particular countries and investment instruments, even among the major investment rating agencies. For this reason, investors should always consult the opinion of as many rating agencies as possible. In addition to rating agencies and the previously mentioned sources, investment-banking companies themselves have branches and professionals devoted to evaluating investment-grade levels. According to the Royal Bank of Canada's corporate and investment-banking arm, RBC Capital Markets, as of 2008 roughly 50 percent of EMCs have an investment grade, meaning that they endorse them as destinations for investment.[15] RBC Capital Markets considers countries with a rating of Ba1/BB+ and below to be sub-investment grade. Among countries included in this category are Argentina, Colombia, Venezuela, Egypt, Ukraine, Philippines, and Indonesia. It considers EMCs with at least Baa3/BBB– rating to be of investment grade—Mexico, Chile, Russia, South Africa, Poland, Hungary, and China, among others.[16]

The assignment of an investment grade to an EMC does not mean that there is no serious political, economic, or any other type of risk for incoming FDI. A high return on investment may be a result of an underdeveloped legal framework and/or less environmental regulation than in developed countries. In some cases, systematic risk is high, but there are special laws protecting foreign property, in order to attract FDI. The existence of such specific protection of foreign property and its enforcement is one of the main distinctions between EMCs and developing countries. Foreign companies are very hesitant to invest in countries that do not have enforced legal protection of foreign property and/or ownership rights for the land itself. A lack of transparency in capital markets and the absence of branches or subsidiaries of major global commercial and investment banks, auditing firms, and insurance companies also drive foreign investment away. In these cases companies do not feel comfortable raising capital in the country in which they are investing.

There are several institutions and universities that evaluate national political, economic, and business investment conditions. One of the most useful of these evaluations for foreign investors is the "Doing Business Project," done annually by the World Bank (see Table 8.4). It evaluates the national climate for almost every facet of conducting business from the moment of registration to closing procedures. Among the 10 major indicators evaluated, particular attention should be given to the World Bank's rating of issues related to employment, relationships with banks ("getting credit"), obtaining licenses, and property registration.

By the integrated indicator of Table 8.4 ("Ease of Doing Business Rank"), of the nine countries with the best business conditions, three are emerging markets—all of which are economies in bloom. In fact, the country with the best business conditions in the world is the emerging market of Singapore. There is not a single emerging market among the bottom 15 of the "Ease of Doing Business Rank"; they are all underdeveloped and developing countries, according to the Strategic Comprehensive Country Classification System (see Chapter 4). This is an illustration of the superior free-market infrastructure available to businesses in the GEM as opposed to that of the developing and underdeveloped world. One of the drawbacks of this index, and practically all comprehensive ratings, is that they are based on data from previous years. Business conditions in the GEM are far from static. In a relatively short period, countries can make substantial improvements. Many 2008 ratings have not taken into account positive changes in Turkmenistan, for example. Unfortunately, business environments can also worsen, which is happening in countries such as Zimbabwe, Venezuela, Bolivia, and Myanmar. Nevertheless, before making an investment in an unfamiliar country, it is a good idea to consult the World Bank's "Ease of Doing Business" evaluation.

The IMD located in Lausanne, Switzerland, developed an index called the World Competitiveness Scoreboard,[17] which should also be consulted while crafting an investment strategy. This index describes the business environment of a country by evaluating several

Table 8.4 The World Bank "Ease of Doing Business Rank," 2008[18]

Economy	Ease of Doing Business Rank	Starting a Business	Dealing with Licenses	Employing Workers	Registering Property	Getting Credit	Protecting Investors	Paying Taxes	Trading Across Borders	Enforcing Contracts	Closing a Business
Singapore	1	9	5	1	13	7	2	2	1	4	2
New Zealand	2	3	2	13	1	3	1	9	16	13	16
United States	3	4	24	1	10	7	5	76	15	8	18
Hong Kong	4	13	60	23	58	2	3	3	3	1	15
Denmark	5	18	6	10	39	13	19	13	2	30	7
United Kingdom	6	6	54	21	19	1	9	12	27	24	10
Canada	7	2	26	19	28	7	5	25	39	43	4
Ireland	8	5	20	37	79	7	5	6	20	39	6
Australia	9	1	52	8	27	3	51	41	34	11	14

indicators in four major categories: economic performance, government efficiency, business efficiency, and infrastructure. As of 2008, the US has the highest score, but Singapore and Hong Kong occupy the next two positions. Ireland is ranked twelfth. Unlike the World Bank index, which evaluates business conditions in 178 countries, the World Competitiveness Scoreboard ranks only 55 economies. The country with the lowest competitiveness is Venezuela. There are a number of questionable evaluations in IMD's ranking. For example, Croatia is ranked far below the Philippines, Colombia, Romania, and even Russia and Turkey, which is difficult to accept. Also, New Zealand ranks 11 positions below Australia, despite the fact that these two countries have very similar business environments. Regardless, a few points of contention are not enough to discredit an index. Good strategists will inevitably find flaws in indices that attempt to comprehensively evaluate countries. Strategists should always consult several different sources in addition to completing their own detailed analysis, specifically tailored to their potential activity. At this stage of the strategic investment process, strategists should focus on between three and five recipient countries or regions. The final selection of the recipient country or region should be determined primarily by the strategist's own analysis.

System of Investment Risk Analysis

Where does a strategic investment risk analysis begin? Many argue that the first issue to evaluate is financial risk, as investment is inevitably tied to finance issues. This is actually false. Imagine a country with the perfect investment climate. Now imagine that the government that supports the current financial regulations is in danger of losing control of the country to an isolationist movement that wants to nationalize the entire economy and expel foreign entrepreneurs and property owners. The investment climate of that country is all of a sudden far from perfect. Financial conditions are heavily influenced by politics. The extensive history of failed and successful investments in developing countries and EMCs clearly indicates that the first evaluation must be of political risk. However, an evaluation of political risk is far from an adequate foundation upon which to base one's final investment decision. The system of investment risk evaluation is predominantly based on four types of risk: *political, economic, business,* and *technological*. Issues such as environmental risk, corruption, etc., can be understood as aspects of indicators of the four risk categories. Environmental regulation is obviously a governmental function and therefore an indicator of political risk. Corruption can be considered an indicator of both political, economic, and— to a certain extent—business risk (as a practice).

In business and investment practice, it is difficult to distinguish between these four categories of risk. For this reason, in Figure 8.3, the circles representing the major elements of risk overlap. However, for analytical purposes, they should be divided in order to systematically evaluate risk.

Political risk is a function of a country's political system; on the regional level, it is a function of the policy of regional authorities. Economic risk is a function of a country's economic system. Business risk is based on the quality of a country's free-market infrastructure. Technological risk is a function of a country or region's education system, its science and technological achievements, and societal attitudes toward education (see Figure 8.4).

Political Risk of Investment

The GEM revolutionized attitudes toward risk. Prior to the appearance of EMCs, executives and strategists would refuse to make a foreign investment in a country where there was even a hint of political risk. However, in the twenty-first century, managing political risk is a

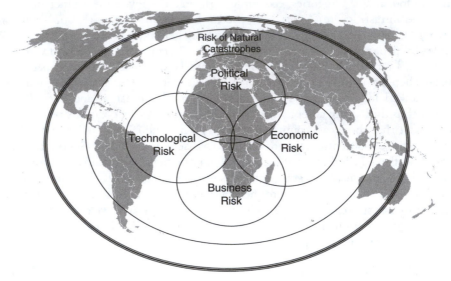

Figure 8.3 Emerging-market Risk System.
Source: © Dr Vladimir Kvint, 2008.

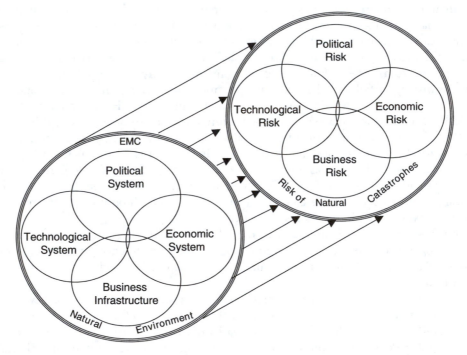

Figure 8.4 EMC Systematic Risk Evaluation.
Source: © Dr Vladmir Kvint, 2008.

fundamental aspect of executive leadership in the GMP. An evaluation of political risk always begins with an analysis of the opinions of the major rating agencies described above. Although they may employ different methodologies, most rating agencies have specific evaluations of political risk, which are often referred to as national credit risk, sovereign risk, political stability indices, or country risk. All of these evaluations focus on a country's political stability and the attitude of its political leadership toward domestic and foreign business. Some of the most well-respected evaluations of political risk include the Economist Intelligence Unit's Country Risk (www.eiu.com), the Eurasia Group and PricewaterhouseCoopers evaluation of political stability (www.eurasiagroup.net/), and the World Bank Governance Indicators (www.governancematters.org), which is based on voice and accountability, political stability, government effectiveness, regulatory quality, rule of law, and control of corruption—a few of several indicators of political stability.

At this point, the strategist usually returns to the basic question—which country belongs to the GEM, and which does not? An analysis of different points of view on political risk of investment can determine the categorization of a country. If its risk is extremely low, it may indicate that the country already has stability and maturity and is already in the developed category; or perhaps it has left the category of emerging-market democracy and is now in the category of an economy in bloom, such as the Czech Republic. Alternatively, political risk in a country could increase to such a level that it is no longer an EMC, which is what happened in Venezuela under President Hugo Chavez.

When any entrepreneur or corporate strategist decides to invest in the GEM, he or she typically seeks an outside source of financing; only a few investors will use their own resources for FDI. In most cases, entrepreneurs or corporations seek financing from investment-banking or venture capital companies, to whom they present a feasibility study of the project or a strategic business plan. Obtaining financing from an investment bank has become an extremely competitive endeavor, especially for greenfield projects. Greenfield investments are projects that do not involve existing facilities. Not surprisingly, greenfield projects tend to have much higher risk levels than FDI in existing production facilities or mergers and acquisition. Nonetheless, between 2002 and 2006, the number of greenfield projects worldwide more than doubled, according to UNCTAD. The fastest-growing sectors for greenfield FDI projects are related to the development of business services, the number of which more than tripled during this period. A trend that is worth taking note of is the decline in greenfield projects in unhealthy industries such as tobacco (see Table 8.5).

Table 8.5 Number of Greenfield FDI Projects by Sector/Industry, 2002–2006[19]

Sector/Industry	2002	2003	2004	2005	2006
Primary	267	568	374	469	492
Energy	267	568	374	469	492
Manufacturing	3,319	5,682	6,121	6,011	6,369
Food, Beverages, and Tobacco	432	710	772	693	744
Food and Drink	420	685	757	676	734
Tobacco	12	25	15	17	10
Textiles	275	419	588	409	498
Wood and Wood Products	129	229	202	203	183
Wood Products	65	105	96	100	73
Paper and Packaging	64	124	106	103	110
Chemicals and Chemical Products	394	722	716	607	649
Pharmaceuticals	117	208	203	200	195
Biotechnology	54	64	86	90	85
Chemicals	223	450	427	317	369
Plastics and Rubber	149	273	302	328	341
Building Materials, Ceramics, and Glass	81	169	182	191	214
Metals/Mining	234	472	411	598	469
Machinery and Industrial Goods	159	351	441	474	565

(Continued Overleaf)

Table 8.5 Continued

Sector/Industry	2002	2003	2004	2005	2006
Electrical and Electronic Equipment	571	998	1,107	1,194	1,160
Electronic Components	136	229	273	307	313
Semiconductors	132	218	245	183	224
Telecom Equipment	121	173	184	292	282
Consumer Electronics	122	249	228	236	195
Business Machines and Equipment	60	129	177	176	146
Motor Vehicles and Other Transport Equipment	661	942	970	905	955
Automotive Equipment	254	377	354	328	331
Auto Components	283	425	446	404	406
Other Transport Equipment	23	41	51	49	57
Aerospace	101	99	119	124	161
Consumer Products	234	397	430	409	591
Services	2,117	3,193	3,650	3,962	4,952
Hotels, Tourism, and Leisure	352	525	480	406	480
Telecom Services	138	170	180	238	275
Financial Services	384	638	643	793	1,101
Business Activities	1,170	1,732	2,211	2,400	2,918
Real Estate	127	236	226	262	487
Business Services	221	374	458	493	692
IT and Software	646	908	1,160	1,172	1,232
Logistics and Distribution	176	214	367	473	507
Health care	73	128	136	125	178
Total	5,703	9,443	10,145	10,442	11,813

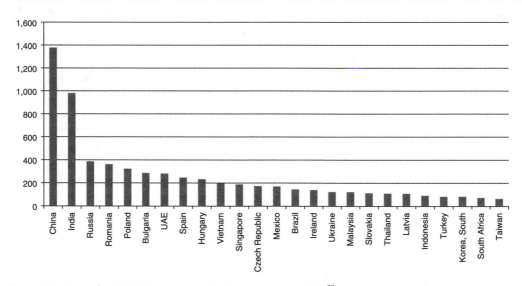

Figure 8.5 Greenfield FDI Projects by EMC Recipients, 2006.[20]

Despite the fact that the political risk of greenfield projects in the GEM is obviously higher than that of other forms of FDI, greenfield investment is increasing at a faster rate in the GEM than in the rest of the world. Among the leading EMC recipients of greenfield investment are China, India, Russia, Romania, and Poland. During this period there have been surprisingly few greenfield FDI projects in other big EMCs such as Indonesia, Turkey, and South Africa. This is likely a function of these governments not providing incentives for this type of investment.

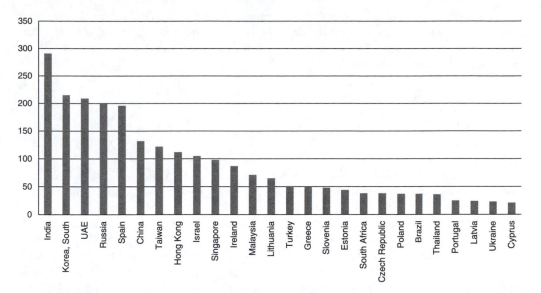

Figure 8.6 Greenfield FDI Projects by EMC Investors, 2006.[21]

During the twenty-first century, EMCs became not only recipients of greenfield FDI projects (see Figure 8.5), but also investors themselves (see Figure 8.6). Among the EMCs that are most aggressively investing in greenfield projects abroad are India, South Korea, Ukraine, Spain, Russia, and China. The role of China during this period would be much higher, but its government limited the outflow of FDI to $10 billion. However, in May 2007 China's State Administration of Foreign Exchange increased the limit of Chinese FDI abroad by three times to $30 billion.[22] Figure 8.6 does not reflect this recent development, but the 2007 outflow of greenfield FDI statistics most certainly will. The government of China made this decision largely in the interest of gaining access to natural resources in EMCs and developing countries as well expanding its investment in the developed world. According to the US–China Economic and Security Review Commission:

> China's government is now adding at least $500b a year to its foreign assets, and perhaps up to $600b. Right now, China's sovereign wealth fund—the China Investment Corporation (CIC)—manages a relatively small share of the total stock of Chinese investment abroad. It is likely to account for a large share going forward.[23]

The underwriter of any investment project seeking public capital in the GEM will almost certainly insist upon obtaining insurance against political risk. In one of the best-case scenarios, investment banks will issue a letter of preliminary approval contingent upon the acquisition of political risk insurance. How can project leaders obtain such insurance? In the 1980s, at the dawn of the GEM, this was an almost insurmountable challenge. By the end of the twentieth century, it became a regular practice of a few multilateral institutions, governmental agencies, and private insurers. Among multilateral institutions the premier provider of political risk insurance is the Multilateral Investment Guarantee Agency (MIGA) (www.miga.org). Established in 1988, it is the youngest agency of the World Bank Group. It offers three basic services: political risk insurance, technical assistance, and dispute mediation. MIGA has several limitations for providing political risk insurance. It restricts its guarantees issued annually by total amount, amount within a particular country, and by amount issued to certain sectors/industries. MIGA—like most insurers—will not issue guarantees for more than 90 percent of total project investment. This means that investors cannot completely rely on the insurance of MIGA and must do their best to adjust and manage risk on their own. MIGA helps investors and lenders deal with political risks by insuring against losses relating to:

- currency-transfer restrictions;
- expropriation;
- war and civil disturbance;
- breach of contract.[24]

As of 2008, MIGA issues guarantees for projects in 147 countries (all of which are classified by MIGA as "developing countries") for up to 15–20 years. "Equity investments can be covered up to 90 percent, and debt up to 95 percent. MIGA may insure up to $200 million, and if necessary more can be arranged through syndication of insurance."[25] Since 1988, MIGA has issued a total of 885 project guarantees and $17.4 billion in coverage. Forty-one percent of MIGA's gross outstanding portfolio is issued for projects in the poorest developing and underdeveloped countries, although due to its unsystematic country classification, this statistic is an approximation. With a gross exposure of only $5.3 billion,[26] despite the fact that MIGA is a global agency, it has very limited resources even compared with some of its equivalent national agencies.

Long before the establishment of MIGA, several countries created agencies to promote their investments abroad, in order to increase the efficiency of their national economies. The largest national agency providing insurance against political risk for companies investing abroad is a US government agency, the Overseas Private Investment Corporation (OPIC). Congress established it in 1971

> to enable US businesses to invest and compete in emerging-market countries around the world. As the pioneer of government-backed political risk insurance, direct loans, guaranties and equity funds, OPIC has helped mobilize and facilitate more than $177 billion in US private capital investment. It has done so at no net expense to the American taxpayer and without the loss of US jobs.[27]

OPIC provides insurance against political risk for the following reasons:

- To cover possible damage or loss relating to:

  —tangible assets such as trucks, manufacturing, or drilling equipment;
  —value of investment;
  —earnings or return of the investment.

- To obtain or attract financing in the face of risk.
- To deter long-term losses through OPIC's advocacy.[28]

In 2007 "OPIC supported 110 projects involving small enterprises, which accounted for 79 percent of the agency's 139 projects."[29] OPIC political risk insurance can cover individual projects up to $250 million with a maturity as long as 20 years.[30]

"OPIC's capital, allowance, retained earnings, and reserves available for insurance at both September 30, 2007, and 2006 totaled $1.7 billion. Charges against retained earnings could arise from (A) outstanding political risk insurance contracts, (B) pending claims under insurance contracts, and (C) guaranties issued in settlement of claims arising under insurance contracts . . . [regarding political risk insurance] OPIC insures investments for up to 20 years against three different risks: inconvertibility of currency, expropriation, and political violence. Insurance coverage against inconvertibility protects the investor from increased restrictions on the investor's ability to convert local currency into US dollars. Inconvertibility insurance does not protect against devaluation of a country's currency.

Expropriation coverage provides compensation for losses due to confiscation, nationalization, or other governmental actions that deprive investors of their fundamental rights in the investment.

Insurance against political violence insures investors against losses caused by politically motivated acts of violence (war, revolution, insurrection, or civil strife, including terrorism and sabotage).

Under most OPIC insurance contracts, investors may obtain all three coverages, but claim payments may not exceed the single highest coverage amount. Claim payments are limited by the value of the investment and the amount of current coverage in force at the time of the loss and may be reduced by the insured's recoveries from other sources. In addition, in certain contracts, OPIC's requirement to pay up to the single highest coverage amount is further reduced by stop-loss and risk-sharing agreements. Finally, losses on insurance claims may be reduced by recoveries by OPIC as subrogee of the insured's claim against the host government. Payments made under insurance contracts that result in recoverable assets are reported as assets acquired in insurance settlements.

OPIC's Maximum Contingent Liability at September 30, 2007, and 2006 was $3.4 billion and $3.7 billion, respectively. This amount is OPIC's estimate of maximum exposure to insurance claims which includes standby coverage for which OPIC is committed but not currently at risk. A more realistic measure of OPIC's actual exposure to insurance claims is the sum of each single highest 'current' coverage for all contracts in force, or Current Exposure to Claims (CEC). OPIC's CEC at September 30, 2007 and 2006 was $2.4 billion and $2.5 billion respectively."[31]

During the 1998 ruble default in Russia, the government of Russia froze all accounts of foreign companies and indefinitely suspended foreign debt payments by banks and enterprises. All foreign investment banks and companies suffered huge losses, except those with guarantees from OPIC or those who had OPIC as an investment partner. The Russian government made sure that all of these companies were reimbursed accordingly. In any case in which a change in government attitude leads to the nationalization or expropriation of foreign properties, OPIC immediately reimburses companies with political risk insurance relative to their insured assets. Furthermore, OPIC negotiates with the government on behalf of the insured investor.

Equivalent agencies to OPIC operate in several countries, including a number of emerging markets such as Albania, Bulgaria, and Spain. The rationale behind the establishment of these agencies in the GEM is to help their domestic clients deal with political risk and to provide a competitive edge against foreign companies from the developed world. The Spanish organization CESCE was actually established a year earlier than OPIC, in 1970, "with the primary aim of facilitating the internationalization of Spanish companies."[32]

Quite frequently, American businessmen and companies and foreign leaders are not well informed about OPIC. For example, US companies interested in investing in Bulgaria in the middle of the 1990s were not familiar with OPIC and did not fully utilize its resources and services. They were unaware that OPIC offered political risk insurance for US investors in

Bulgaria. Many US and Western European companies were also ignorant to the fact that OPIC provides financing for promising projects abroad. National governments of other EMCs were equally unaware. For this reason OPIC often ends the year with surplus cash.

Besides multilateral and national agencies, political risk insurance can also be obtained from private companies. The largest provider of this service is AIG (www.aig.com), which operates in more than 130 countries.[33] AIG's menu of political risk insurance protects against

> confiscation, expropriation, nationalization; currency inconvertibility and non-transfer; terrorism, sabotage, war, insurrection, rebellion; government act, law order, or decree; contract frustration, sovereign, non-performance, or payment default, and wrongful calling of contract guarantees and bonds. Coverage can be tailored to the insured's requirements for a broad range of overseas exposures, including equity investments, physical assets, cross-border loans, or contracts for goods and services.[34]

AIG is the leading private provider of political risk insurance but is only one of hundreds of private insurance firms offering this service. Many of them consider this to be a very profitable business, especially when they have branches on the ground in EMCs and developing countries and are very familiar with local conditions.

Any company that seeks political risk insurance from MIGA, OPIC, AIG, or any other national or private insurance agency has to go through an evaluation process. Despite the differences among these agencies and service providers, in the end all of them evaluate political risk of a potential project in the GEM by the following major integrated indicators:

- risk of expropriation and nationalization;
- risk of civil disobedience and property vandalism;
- risk of currency inconvertibility;
- risk of terrorism;
- risk of governmental breaches of contracts.

Each particular provider of political risk insurance uses different indicators to evaluate integrated risk factors. For certain countries, in addition to the major indicators listed above, agencies and insurance firms will analyze several other issues, such as bilateral relationships with neighboring states or violations of international treaties such as the Nuclear Nonproliferation Agreement. Providers of political risk will also evaluate a country's domestic political system—the existence and enforcement of constitutional law, democratic institutions, and regularly scheduled democratic elections, etc. There are a number of international organizations that evaluate political freedom, which can be very useful during this process, such as Freedom House International (www.freedomhouse.org). The Combined Average Ratings of this organization evaluates political freedom in every country, based on the legitimacy of elections and existence of pluralism, civil liberties, rule of law, and individual human rights.[35] These rankings can be a good indication of political risk of investment, although they should not be the only source of information when assessing this risk. Some of Freedom House's rankings are questionable. For example, Albania has held legitimate elections since 1998, is politically stable, and is experiencing rapid economic development, and yet in the 2007 evaluation, it is ranked in the same category as Bolivia, Nicaragua, Niger, Seychelles, and Papua New Guinea. It is also hard to accept the fact that Estonia is placed in the same category as the US, the UK, Norway, and Switzerland. In Estonia, it is difficult for most native-born, non-ethnic Estonians to get citizenship. Although there is undeniably a high level of economic freedom, political freedom is still below the level that exists in the US, UK, etc. These rankings also do not take into account the recent progress that has been made in Turkmenistan, which is included in the same category as Sudan, Cuba, and North Korea. Turkmenistan and even Uzbekistan should be ranked ahead of countries such as Belarus and Iran. It is also questionable that Iran is ranked higher than Iraq, a country that has had several legitimate elections. As with any ranking or index, it is important to use one's own experience and opinion to make analyses and conclusions.

It is also very important to keep in mind that the political desires of people of the GEM are very different from those of people in developed countries. In the GEM, people are often willing to concede some elements of political freedom in return for stability and economic freedom. People tend to be resistant to change and the uncertainty that comes along with it. As a result, soft dictatorships such as those in China and Vietnam maintain the support of most people because they provide a stable future and the economic freedom that allows gradual improvements in standards of living. However, one should not make the mistake of overestimating the staying power of "communist" dictatorships. In *Capitalism and Freedom*, the great economist and Nobel laureate Milton Friedman wrote "communism would destroy all of our freedoms . . ."[36] In fact, Milton Friedman had it backward—freedom destroys communism. The developing free markets in the communist dictatorships of Vietnam, China, and even Cuba are much more likely to destroy the communist political systems than the communist political systems are to destroy free markets. It is only a matter of time before the level of political freedom catches up to the level of economic freedom already established, especially in China, Vietnam, and even Belarus.

In order to minimize political risk, companies should be in direct contact with the national leaders of the country in which they are considering investing. It is also important to be cognizant of the relationship between the country of origin of the company and the country in which it would like to invest. The best way to establish and improve ties with foreign leaders is through bilateral governmental or semi-governmental cultural and business councils, such as the US-ASEAN Business Council (www.us-asean.org), the US-Taiwan Business Council (www.us-taiwan.org), etc. The Business Council for International Understanding (BCIU) (www.bciu.org) is another very good vehicle for meeting governmental officials from potential investment-recipient countries. The BCIU was established by President Dwight Eisenhower after he saw the many mistakes made by American businessmen as a result of not understanding intergovernmental relations. The BCIU sets up meetings between its members and US ambassadors from abroad while they are visiting the US, and between foreign governmental leaders with the US business community while they are visiting the US. The BCIU also annually presents the Dwight D. Eisenhower Award to a leader of global business. The award ceremony is a major networking event that is useful for business leaders.

In addition to political freedom and stability, another important factor is the quality of law enforcement. Unfortunately, in many EMCs laws look great on paper, but are not enforced. In these cases, law is nothing more than friendly advice. It is very risky to deal with countries that are under UN, NATO, US or EU embargo. Companies that invest in such countries in violation of restrictions will likely be put on lists compiled by different international and national bodies that monitor dual-use high-tech products. Several companies that invested in projects related to Iranian weapons programs, in spite of UN sanctions, have encountered substantial negative repercussions. However, embargos do offer opportunities (with special legal permission or authorized contracts) for companies that provide certain goods and services, such as health care and baby food, pharmaceutical needs, clothing, etc. This is a legitimate practice that can be very lucrative and socially beneficial.

All integrated indicators of political risk, the practices of political risk insurance agencies/firms, as well as the respect that political risk insurance receives from national governments should be taken into consideration during the stage of strategy formulation. An evaluation of political risk should be done during the entry-strategy development. This will prevent cases in which top executives decide that the level of political risk is too high after already having invested a great deal of resources in strategy development and implementation.

Of all integrated indicators of political risk, strategists should be most sensitive to the risk of expropriation. If a political leader even mentions this, without making any practical attempts to expropriate foreign property, that country's political risk immediately increases and it will be much more expensive for any investor in that country to obtain political risk insurance. For this reason, as of 2008 the cost of political risk insurance in countries such as Venezuela and Bolivia is exorbitant. Any government that, for whatever reason, explores the possibility of nationalizing private assets or renationalizing formerly state-owned companies that have been privatized will instantly increase the political risk of investment in their country. The same applies to national governments that attempt to take control of shares belonging to foreign partners of an IJV, a situation that has occurred at some point in China, Russia, Ukraine, Indonesia, Malaysia, Bolivia, and Ecuador, among others. Civil disobedience and widespread violence on the streets can lead to damage of physical assets and properties of foreign investors, even when the unrest has nothing to do with the foreign company's activity. Like the possibility of expropriation, the prospect of civil disobedience immediately increases political risk and the price for insurance against it.

Currency inconvertibility is another major factor of political risk. The overwhelming majority of EMCs have national currencies that are not convertible. In order to avoid this issue as a risk for foreign investors, some countries have attempted to completely replace their national currencies with a convertible foreign currency, such as the US dollar or the euro. For example, the US dollar is the currency in El Salvador and Ecuador, as well the primary currency in Panama. Montenegro, which is not a part of the Eurozone, has accepted the euro as its official currency, as have Kosovo and even the wealthy nation, Andorra. By adopting foreign convertible currencies, the leadership of these countries immediately improved their national political risk climate. A few EMCs, such as the Czech Republic, have reached the level of economic and political maturity whereby its currency is generally accepted as convertible. The national currencies of some EMCs are accepted as convertible by a few other countries, though are not considered to be convertible currencies worldwide. This is the case for the currencies of South Korea and China—"the Monetary Board of the Bangko Sentral ng Pilipinas (Central Bank of the Philippines) approved the inclusion of the Chinese renminbi (RMB) and the Korean won (KRW) in the list of currencies convertible with the central bank."[37] In order to decrease political risk, some countries are attempting to establish their national currency as a regionally convertible currency. During the 2007 and 2008 St Petersburg Economic Forums and the 2008 G8 Summit in Japan, leaders of Russia declared their intent to do so with the ruble. Currency convertibility risk is always a significant factor for FDI in EMCs, especially for companies that generate their revenue from domestic consumers. There are a number of complications that arise when dealing with non-convertible or limitedly convertible currencies, especially regarding the repatriation of profit. This issue is discussed further in Chapter 7 (regarding IJVs) and in Chapter 1 (regarding capital as a basic economic factor).

Tragically, during the twenty-first century another factor of political risk—terrorism—became a major obstacle for FDI. EMCs are particularly vulnerable to this factor (see Chapter 3). In some parts of the GEM, there is always the danger of financial support for terrorism being disguised as legitimate FDI or other investment transactions. In order to prevent this risk factor, the participants of the 1989 G7 meeting suggested the establishment of the Financial Action Task Force (FATF), "an inter-governmental body whose purpose is the development and promotion of national and international policies to combat money laundering and terrorist financing."[38] As of 2008 there are 32 full member countries of FATF, including 13 EMCs.[39] Additionally, two regional economic organizations—the EU and the Gulf Cooperation Council—are also full members. Two other EMCs, India and South Korea, are observers. Among the associate members are several regional organizations and other financial monitoring agencies, such as the Asia/Pacific Group on Money Laundering. The FATF publishes an annual list of "Non Cooperative Countries and Territories." The list consists of countries and territories with financial systems that are vulnerable to exploitation by money launderers and terrorist financiers. Before making a foreign investment or engaging in international transactions, it is important to make sure that a potential recipient country is not on this list. In the best-case scenario the country is a member or associate member of FATF. As of 2008, after the removal of Nigeria (2005) and Myanmar (2006), there are no countries on this list.[40]

Breach of contract is the final integrated indicator of political risk of investment. This is primarily a legal issue. In most cases this risk falls under economic risk of investment. However, when the government is one of the parties of a contract, this issue is an aspect of political risk. In order to reduce potential partners' fears of contract breach, some governments will prepare investment agreements or assign conditions to a greenfield FDI project in such a manner as to make it very difficult for future governments to violate contractual obligations. In cases when governments do not take such precautions, agreements are vulnerable to the whims of future governments or even of current superiors. Strategists drafting contracts without the participation of a governmental partner should still prepare preventive measures against governmental meddling. In the GEM it is not unheard of for the government to interfere—for its own reasons—with a contract between two satisfied private parties. Contracts in which one of the parties is a partially state-owned company are particularly vulnerable. This risk factor applies mainly to IJVs and companies that are engaged in a *product-sharing agreement*. This type of agreement is typically used by companies developing, producing, and enriching natural resources, such as oil, natural gas, coal, non-ferrous metals, fertilizer, etc. When the government is not involved in a breach of contract, this factor should be analyzed as an economic risk of investment.

In order to devise strategies to attract FDI, governmental officials of EMCs should evaluate national political risk from the perspective of a foreign company and analyze the practice of political risk insurance agencies and firms. Governments of non-developed countries have to take measures to improve their public image regarding risk. This can be done simply by making governmental or legislative declarations to protect foreign investors from expropriation and nationalization. Such action can even be made illegal. Furthermore, governments can declare that they will not interfere with agreements between domestic or foreign companies, especially if they have certain contracts, such as product-sharing agreements. British Petroleum was forced to deal with such interference with a product-sharing agreement in Russia in 2006–2008. Governments can develop—and promote internationally—long-term programs to increase the convertibility of the national currency. The same idea applies to a firm, public denouncement of any terrorist attempts against foreign businesses. Due to the fact that only national governments can manage systematic risk, a major priority of non-developed countries should be the reduction of national political risk according to the practice of major agencies and insurance firms.

INVESTING IN COUNTRIES IN STATES OF WAR

The highest levels of political risk and instability are related to countries in a state of war. According to a report by the International Action Network on Small Arms, Saferworld, and Oxfam International, from 1990 to 2005, the cost of wars and civil conflict in 23 African countries alone amounted to $284 billion.[41] Some EMCs that are not officially in a state of war devote a substantial part of their national budgets to military purposes. According to the CIA, of the top 20 countries in terms of military expenditures, 11 are EMCs. These are Brazil, China, India, Israel, Mexico, Russia, Saudi Arabia, South Korea, Spain, Taiwan, and Turkey. These are likely rough approximations, as the exact military expenditures of countries such as China, Israel, Russia, and Saudi Arabia are not widely known. However, there are many humane business opportunities in countries that are "under fire," including the delivery of medicine, medical equipment, pharmaceutical products, food, educational materials, construction of social infrastructure, roads, restoration of damaged facilities, etc.[42] In some cases, despite the very high risk, investing in countries or regions at war can be very fruitful for investors and the people of the recipient country.

As cynical as it may seem to say, war is often very profitable for media companies. During the first Persian Gulf War, CNN correctly predicted that land-based telecommunication infrastructure would be destroyed and invested in a cutting-edge satellite video telecommunication system. Audiences around the globe relied on CNN for up-to-date broadcasts from the battlefield, as it was the only network that could broadcast in real time. Needless to say, this proved to be a very profitable investment for CNN; it also made CNN the primary supplier of first-hand news to people around the world.

The rebuilding process that follows a war is obviously an extremely lucrative time for construction and contracting companies who address vital needs of the surviving population. Many companies have made substantial profits by providing much-needed services in Serbia, Bosnia Herzegovina, Albania, and Iraq. Post-conflict economies offer great opportunities for young entrepreneurs with a relatively small amount of cash, as governments and people are in desperate need of many services. Small governmental contracts can be very profitable. Some companies are specifically oriented toward post-conflict processes of redevelopment, such as Kellogg Brown and Root (www.kbr.com), a subsidiary of Halliburton (www.halliburton.com), which is playing an important role in the reconstruction of Iraq. DynCorp (www.dyn-intl.com/), a subsidiary of CSC (www.csc.com), specializes in assisting nascent democracies establish law and order. It has recruited, trained, and deployed more than 5,000 civilian peacekeepers and police trainers to 11 countries, including Haiti, Bosnia Herzegovina, Afghanistan, and Iraq, on behalf of the US Department of State.

Economic Risk of Investment

Economic risk is a function of the likelihood of governmental intervention in business that reduces economic freedom, especially in times of an economic crisis. It is distinct from political risk, in that political risk is a function of governmental policy toward private business and does not factor in the economic-crisis issue. For example, when a country cannot pay its foreign debt, causing a default, the economic risk of a country substantially increases. Instances of national default are very dangerous for business. Economic risk is essentially an intermediary between political risk and business risk. Although these two risks may be difficult to separate, for analytical purposes it is helpful to understand them as distinct categories.

In general, the higher the level of economic freedom, the lower the economic risk of investment, although this correlation has limits. There is a well-defined role for the government as a regulator of private business activity. Without this limited level of governmental involvement—to prevent monopoly and corruption—the private business arena can become anarchic, increasing economic risk. The private sector needs governments to establish and enforce rules of the workplace and marketplace. A country whose government is not strong enough to enforce its laws will have a very high economic risk of investment. This is why companies are often more willing to invest in countries with dictatorships—China,

Vietnam, Bahrain, Chile during Pinochet's rule, etc.—than in EMCs with nascent democracies that still struggle to enforce the law.

Economic risk of direct investment or project investment is primarily a systematic, or country/region-specific risk. Unlike business risk, economic risk is mostly related to the external economic environment in which a company has to operate, or in which a greenfield FDI project is implemented, such as the quality and availability of industrial infrastructure, such as transportation and telecommunication facilities and access to energy, freshwater resources, etc. A substantial part of economic risk is *legal and regulatory risk*, i.e. how domestic law protects foreign and individual property rights, know-how, intellectual property, etc. These issues can be evaluated as part of political as well as business risk, but due to the fact that economic and business laws and under-law regulations are a function of the government, they should be evaluated as part of economic risk. Under-law regulation and governmental practices are part of regulatory risk. Economic risk, like political risk, is related to the role of the government in the economic and business realms of a country. Many integrated ratings of economic risk, such as country risk, sovereign risk, and national credit risk are a combination of various indicators of political and economic risk. None of these evaluations provides an adequate explanation as to why certain indicators are taken into consideration while others are ignored. Some country-risk indices include sovereign risk as an element of country risk, but in others, the reverse is the case.

In terms of provincial and territorial authorities, regional risk is a mix of indicators of political and economic risk. However, unlike country risk, among the indicators of regional risk are those that describe business and even technological risk. In practice, when companies try to get a country-risk evaluation from professional firms and consulting companies, they usually get forecasts containing a mixture of political, macroeconomic, and business indicators and variables. A typical example of this is the product of the Economist Intelligence Unit's Country Risk Service. It is a

> two-year forecasting service that monitors risks in 120 key markets. It is designed for commercial bankers, institutional investors and corporate executives who invest in both emerging and developed markets. The service measures political, economic policy and economic structure risks as well as currency, sovereign debt and banking sector risks. In-depth forecasts are provided for up to 180 macroeconomic variables for each country.[43]

Among the indicators included in this evaluation are country, currency, and banking-sector risk. According to the opinion of the Economist Intelligence Unit, as of March 2008, among the fifteen least risky countries (by economic risk), there are two emerging markets— Singapore and Hong Kong—both of which have a better evaluation than the United States. Many other professional evaluations of this category include three to five EMCs such as Ireland, Estonia, and Bahrain. According to the same rating, among the most risky countries are only two emerging markets and one pre-emerging market (from lowest to highest risk)—Ecuador, Jamaica, and Iraq. The Economist Intelligence Unit's evaluation of Syria, Myanmar, and Sudan as less risky investment destinations than a country undertaking painful, though democratic reforms, such as Iraq, is questionable.[44] This can be partially explained by investor preference for stability, which is the case in Syria, but definitely not in Sudan or Myanmar. Some country-risk indices, like *Forbes*' "Best Countries for Business" (formally the Capital Hospitality Index) are mostly a summary of a few selected macroeconomic and financial indicators, which are more of a reflection of economic development than of investment risk.[45] According to the approach of this book, sovereign risk is part of economic risk, not business risk. It is primarily related to the activity of central banks, which to a certain extent function according to state policy. There are several sources for sovereign risk evaluations, such as Global Insight (www.globalinsight.com), a consulting firm specializing in risk forecasting.

The following list covers the most important issues to be examined when evaluating a country's economic risk categorized by various factors.

Economic factors include:

- Membership in multilateral, international economic organizations (World Bank Group, WTO, IMF, regional economic organizations such as Mercosur, Shanghai Cooperation Organization, GUAM, ASEAN, European Bank for Reconstruction and Development, etc.).
- Relations with Paris Club of official creditors (www.clubdeparis.org).
- Laws on the protection of private property, foreign investment, cross-border transactions, etc.
- Cross-border investment and trade barriers (duties, quotas, export import licenses, non-tariff barriers).
- Existence of Most Favored Nation status or Normal Trade Relations status.
- Capital asset pricing regulations.
- Tax law and tax code (profit tax, export-import tax, profit-repatriation tax, international and bilateral double taxation agreements).
- Existence of special economic and technological or free trade zones.
- Intensity of competition in the national marketplace and presence of major competitors.
- Patent, trademark, copyright, and know-how protection.
- Compliance, confidentiality, and enforcement of regulatory regimes and economic and business laws.
- Existence of nepotism, corruption, and rackets.
- Hostile takeovers and corporate-raid practices.
- Nationalism and its effect on legal and commercial practice.

Economic infrastructure factors include:

- Adequacy, quality, and cost of telecommunications:

    —Local, long distance, and international telecommunications channels.
    —Telecommunication penetration.
    —Access to satellite and mobile communications.
    —Access to Internet, data communications links; local area network capacity.
    —Access to services of global telecom providers.

- Transportation infrastructure:

    —Quality and extent of highways and secondary roads.
    —Access to air, rail, or water transportation.
    —Freight forwarding and customs clearing services.
    —Quality and cost of transportation services.

- Energy (availability, reliability, and cost of energy for commercial and residential use).

Social-infrastructure factors include:

- Access to medical services:

—Presence of major medical insurance companies.

- Access to hospitality services (hotel availability, quality, and pricing).
- Existence and penetration of restaurants, quality of nutrition for local and foreign personnel.
- Cultural infrastructure (movie theatres, theatres, galleries, clubs, etc.).

Industrial structure factors include:

- Analysis of the maturity and growth potential for:

    —Heavy industries (mining, metallurgy, machinery building, etc.).
    —Consumer-oriented industries (textiles, clothing, etc.).
    —Agriculture and food processing.
    —Service-related industries.
    —Knowledge-based industries.

Education and science factors include:

- Availability of quality elementary and high school education.
- Availability of quality bachelor- and master's-degree education.
- Existence of scientific and technological parks and their relations with business.

The overwhelming majority of these economic factors are part of country-specific systematic risk evaluation. Corporate strategists and executives cannot develop a system to manage these risks. However, they can make strategic countermeasures by taking into account political risk to make adjustments according to corporate strategy, interests, and capacities. Each factor requires an analysis not only from the point of view of its influence on a company's capabilities, resources, income, and profit, but also its implications on a country's sustainability and predictability. For example, a country's membership in multilateral institutions and international regional economic organizations is relevant from a monetary perspective, as well as for forecasting a company's future in the economic environment of a potential recipient of FDI. If a country is a member of the World Bank or IMF, it means that the leadership of this country took certain obligations upon itself that have to be followed by all national institutions. This definitely helps corporate strategists and leaders to understand the conditions in which they will operate in the foreseeable future. Some global multilateral or regional organizations are difficult to classify as purely economic or political. From the perspective of corporate strategy, it makes more sense to classify these kinds of organizations as economic ones. Among such organizations are the EU, Shanghai Cooperation Organization, the African Union, the Andean Community, among many others.

Special attention should be given to membership in organizations of state-owned or -controlled banks, creditors, and donors. Quite often, the new leadership of a country would prefer not to recognize debt made by previous governments, according to international agreements with foreign state banks. This is often the case when a newly elected democratic government is forced to deal with foreign debt accumulated by a past dictatorial regime in order to finance its own luxurious lifestyle and pad the pockets of corrupt bureaucrats. Unfortunately, many young democracies have had to deal with this issue. In order to protect themselves, state bank creditors created the Paris Club (www.clubdeparis.org/). The mission of this organization is to "find co-ordinated and sustainable solutions to the payment difficulties experienced by debtor nations." The London Club is a similar organization made up of private donor banks.

In some instances it is difficult to decide under which type of risk a particular factor or indicator should be evaluated. This is especially the case with evaluations of the implications of nepotism, corruption, rackets, as well as nationalism for country risk. These factors can be classified as both political and economic. Economic crimes often are related to legal risk of FDI, which blurs the line between political and economic risk, and can be classified in either of them, depending on the angle of analysis. In this book, economic crimes are primarily analyzed as an aspect of economic risk of investment. Some factors of legal risk are manageable and have unsystematic characteristics, but most do not.

Raiding is an economic crime that poses a serious threat to businesses in many EMCs. Unlike in developed countries, in the GEM raiding is a practice associated with organized crime. In some EMCs it is not uncommon for organized crime to obtain official ownership documents of a legitimate company by bribing an employee. They then establish a new company, to which they transfer ownership of the legitimate company, using the official ownership documents. Almost immediately, the criminal organization then sells ownership of the legitimate company to another legitimate company. Following this transaction, the company formed by the criminal organization will legally disband and disappear, leaving the two legitimate companies in a very complicated and expensive legal dispute. In the majority of EMCs, the legal code does not yet protect against this type of raiding activity, making it very difficult to prosecute such acts. In many cases, when corruption does not totally inhibit prosecution, raiders are charged with minor civil offenses. Even the vague possibility of such raiding is a major deterrent for foreign investors, and it should be a major priority of governments in EMCs where this activity occurs to develop anti-raiding laws.

Economic, social, and industrial infrastructure issues are primarily a systematic risk. Regardless of the richness or abundance of a country's resources, foreign companies will not be able to utilize them without the existence of basic industrial infrastructure. For this reason, prior to deciding on the location of an investment project, an evaluation of the proximity of telecommunication, transportation, and social infrastructure should be done. The same concept applies to the existence of available labor resources, regarding the quality of education and expertise required by a particular project. The proximity of technological parks and special scientific technological zones is particularly important for knowledge-based companies. These types of companies can hire much fewer employees by contracting with technological and scientific companies, which are often concentrated around special scientific and technological zones. For companies involved in the development of industrial infrastructure, the risk of its activity can be both systematic and unsystematic. Even large multinational corporations can fall victim to the governmental bureaucracies of small countries. For example, bureaucratic inertia and a lack of leadership in Albania delayed national progress by threatening a multimillion-dollar investment project of GE. In 2006 partisan quarrels embarrassingly led to the suspension of the company's railway infrastructure project between the Durress Seaport and the Albanian capital, Tirana.[46]

Strategists always have to keep in mind when making conclusions about any political or economic risk factors of FDI that they may be generally systematic, but for a particular company in certain situations, they are not automatically unmanageable. Unsystematic economic risk is analyzed later in this chapter.

Commercial and Legal Risk: Corruption, Raiding, and Intellectual Property Rights

In the GEM, the most corrupt governmental agencies are those responsible for contracts, tax collection, privatization, real estate development, and law enforcement. The IMF has estimated that between 2 and 5 percent of GWP—between \$962 billion and \$2.4 trillion, based on 2006 GDP data—is laundered globally every year.[47] In EMCs, bribery plays an even larger role. In June 2008 the government of Ukraine published a study of the biggest bribes during the past 12 months. At the top of this list was a bribe of $53.1 million taken by a local authority in the Black Sea Crimea region for transactions related to landowner-ship.[48] It is estimated that companies in heavily corrupt business environments allocate 10 to 20 percent of profit to bribe bureaucrats and officials. These bureaucrats use their position in government not for the betterment of society, but for their own selfish interests. Corruption is, in effect, a regressive taxation mechanism, with the poorest people taxed the most and the wealthiest paying the smallest proportion of their income.

In 1955, Dr Simon Kuznets observed that "with increasing productivity of labor, inequality initially increases, but later decreases."[49] He illustrated this phenomenon with an upside-down symmetric U curve. For his empirical studies and analysis of the influence of economic growth on social dynamics, Dr Kuznets received the 1971 Nobel Prize in econom-ics. However, his observation is not fully applicable in EMCs, unless the influence of widespread corruption is factored into the equation (see Figure 8.7). A *corruption coefficient* makes the upside-down U asymmetric, substantially decreasing the rate at which inequality decreases. Corruption and nepotism inhibit the process of reducing income inequality. Corruption negatively influences entrepreneurship from the very beginning when indi-vidual investors or executives try to start or register a new business. In the GEM, the coefficient results in balancing of inequality during the continuous increase in the product-ivity of labor, but at a rate of two to four times slower than inequality increases.

From an analysis of data provided by Transparency International (www.transparency.org), a global organization dedicated to monitoring and fighting corruption, it is possible to conclude that the poorer the country and the lower the productivity of its labor, the higher the corruption, and the more obstacles there are for FDI. This organization conducted a survey of perceptions of corruption in 180 countries. In African countries, on average more than 55 percent of people surveyed admitted that they paid a bribe in the previous 12 months to the police (see Figure 8.8). High corruption exists in some countries belong-ing to regions that average lower levels of corruption than Africa. This is the case in countries including Myanmar, Azerbaijan, Russia, Thailand, and Mexico. A high concentra-tion of FDI has an accumulative effect; i.e. as FDI flows and stock increase in a country, corruption also tends to be reduced.

Some governments, such as China and Iran, use the legal system to fight corruption, going as far as to institute capital punishment. But even a deterrent as strong as death will not end widespread corruption. Ivan the Terrible and Peter the Great both punished bribe taking with death, and yet centuries later Russia is still one of the most corrupt countries in the world. The only way to substantially reduce corruption is through economic reform and the development of free-market institutions. The more restrictions, regulations,

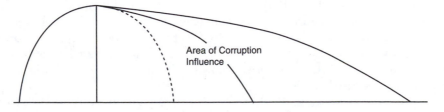

Dynamic of asymetric increasing and declining income distribution inequality

Figure 8.7 Changing Dynamics of the Kuznets Curve Under the Influence of Corruption in the GEM.

Source: © Dr Vladimir Kvint, 2006.

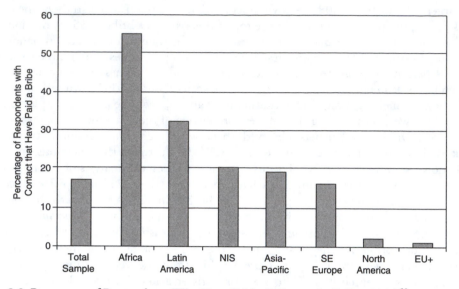

Figure 8.8 Percentage of Respondents Who Have Paid a Bribe to the Police, 2006.[50]

Source: Reprinted from *Global Corruption Report 2007.* Copyright 2007 Transparency International: the global coalition against corruption. Used with permission. For more information, visit http://www.transparency.org.

Note: NIS is newly independent states (relating to former Soviet Republics).

licenses, quotas, permits, etc., in an economy, the greater the need for a business mafia and the more opportunities there are for bureaucrats to exploit the system for their own personal gain. As free-market institutions develop and mature, corruption tends to decline. For example, boards of trade and stock exchanges tend to develop at a faster rate than custodians and trust institutions. As a result, the business mafia satisfies the demand for enforcement agents. As trust institutions and custodians develop and become part of stock transactions, the need for an illegal enforcer disappears.

Fighting corruption has become a very popular area of advocacy during elections in EMCs. However, usually nothing more than empty promises are made—and once the election is over, nothing is done. In some instances, newly elected politicians prosecute a few cases of bribery to make it seem as if fighting corruption is a priority, but they will do little to address the systemic causes. When Vladimir Putin was first elected president of Russia, he declared "war against kleptocrats." A few were exiled or sent to jail. In his second term, he went after a few police, federal security officers, federal accounting officials (Schetnaya Palata), mayors, deputy governors, and senators. This did have important implications for foreign investors and companies. Putin has effectively made it difficult for bureaucrats and officials to create artificial barriers to force foreigners to bribe them, i.e. the creation of a racket. However, even at the end of the first decade of the twenty-first century, corruption, which is usually initiated by a businessperson, is one of the highest barriers for FDI in Russia. This issue again became a priority following the 2008 election of Putin's successor, President Dmitry Medvedev.

There is a method of substantially decreasing corruption and at the same time increasing employment. This can be done through a declaration of fiscal or economic amnesty. Several countries, including Italy, Turkey, Germany, and even the US, achieved substantial success using this method. In EMCs, quite frequently, democratic reforms and the development of the free-market economy go at a faster pace than changes in the law. As a result, people who made money in the initial stages of development of a free market unintentionally find themselves on the wrong side of the law. In order to avoid punishment and confiscation, they send their money abroad to tax havens such as Luxembourg, Switzerland, Austria, the Cayman Islands, and Panama. Later, when the law is updated accordingly in their native countries, they are usually hesitant to bring their money back home, for fear of being prosecuted for their prior violations. At this point, EMC governments should declare amnesty on gray capital, i.e. capital that was accumulated in the underground economy but is not related to crimes such as narcotics or human and weapons trafficking. In most cases, entrepreneurs who return money have to pay very low taxes but must invest most of it for business development and the creation of new jobs. Successful amnesty programs usually last for up to six months. However, countries in which an amnesty is initiated with the aim of increasing tax revenue miss out on the opportunity to utilize this capital. This was the cause of failure of Russia's capital amnesty attempt in 2007–2008.

During the strategic consideration of the cross-border investment destination, it is important to evaluate the extent to which the legal system treats citizens and governmental officials equally. A country cannot be considered an emerging market if major disparities in legal treatment exist. EMCs are in the processes of transitioning from a society in which rulers are above the law to one in which the government is accountable to society and to the law in the same way as regular citizens. Currently, in most EMCs the legal system treats foreign-owned property and investment differently than domestic-owned property and investment. In most cases, as the domestic economy matures and foreign investment continues to flow, the legal distinctions erode and a unified legal framework on investment and property emerges. However, some EMCs are increasing restrictions on foreign investment as the result of a misguided and backward pursuit of national interests or effective lobbying by domestic executives or oligarchs. This is the case in Venezuela and Bolivia—which are no longer considered EMCs—and to a certain extent, Russia, where direct or indirect attempts to increase state control over companies with partial foreign ownership were made in 2007–2008. There is also a tendency in EMCs to illegally nationalize companies that were legally purchased by domestic entrepreneurs during the chaotic transitional period of economic liberalization. Whether a government attempts to nationalize domestic or foreign companies, the result is the same: investors lose faith in the government's willingness and ability to protect property rights, causing an outflow of foreign and domestic capital. It also causes domestic companies to register and declare their initial public offerings abroad, in places that they are confident will uphold the law and protect property rights, such as London, Frankfurt, Zurich, or New York. All facilities are located within their own national borders, however, furthering the outflow of capital. Ultimately, the government only undermines its own rule of law and economic freedom.

As investment continues to flow into the GEM and standards of living continue to rise, it is becoming an increasingly important market for luxury goods and services. For example, the Trump Organization (www.trump.com), a high-end real estate development company, is active in Mexico, Panama, the Dominican Republic, South Korea, and the United Arab Emirates. Donald Trump has registered trademarks of all of his companies in these countries. As of 2008 the Trump Organization has not invested in Russia, although it has considered doing so. However, the company registered trademarks there in areas of real estate development and construction. It has also registered the trademark of the Trump International Hotel & Tower, lengthening the rights of the trademark until 2016. This reflects the Trump Organization's growing faith in Russia's ability to protect intellectual property rights. In 2003 visitors to Albania would be surprised to find the presence of Burger King. However, a closer inspection would reveal that despite the similar interior design and marquee, they would actually be in a Burger Queen—likely a violation of intellectual property regulations in the developed world. It is not an uncommon occurrence in the GEM for well-known trademarks and brands to be slightly altered and used to promote goods and services below the quality of the original brands. This dilutes the reputation of the brand and misleads consumers.

Failure to enforce intellectual property rights has prevented a great deal of potential investment in the GEM. The WTO has a special branch that oversees and conducts investigations into this issue. In September 2007 the WTO opened a formal investigation into the role of the Chinese government in preventing piracy and counterfeiting. All EMCs should make decisive and forceful action against counterfeiting and piracy in order to illustrate their willingness and ability to protect intellectual property rights to the international business community. The WTO has the right to authorize trade sanctions against any country that does not sufficiently enforce intellectual property rights, trademarks, and copyrights. Unfortunately, red tape and bureaucracy often inhibit punishment for such infractions.

The governments of all developed countries and many EMCs, as well as their regional economic organizations, have developed different institutions and watchdogs to protect intellectual property rights. The US government uses the Office of the United States Trade Representative (USTR), which is similar to the ministries of foreign economic relations of many other countries. The office of the USTR annually publishes the "Special 301" Report, which reviews "the global state of intellectual property rights protection and enforcement."[51] This report includes the *Priority Foreign Countries* list, which was first developed in 1974. The first country on the 2008 list is China, followed by Russia, Argentina, Chile, India, Israel, Pakistan, Thailand, and Venezuela.[52] Placement on this list creates substantial restrictions for international trade and investment. As a result, most countries at least show some effort to obey intellectual property regulations set forth by the WTO. For example, Argentina, which, according to the USTR's list was once "the worst expropriator of the intellectual property of the research-based pharmaceutical industry in the Western Hemisphere, and one of the worst in the world,"[53] as of 2008 occupies the third position, due to its efforts to address these problems. Figure 8.9 shows the estimated US trade loss due to copyright piracy in 2006.

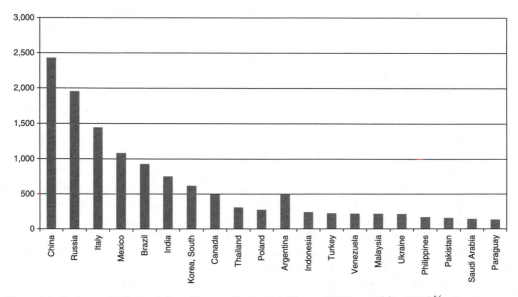

Figure 8.9 Estimated US Trade Loss Due to Copyright Piracy (Millions of $), 2006.[54]

In order to address legal risk, foreign investors often seek the services of internationally recognized law firms. An evaluation of the presence of such firms is crucial when deciding on the location of a potential FDI. Subsidiaries and partnerships with foreign law firms in EMCs are usually employed by investors to file the corporation registration and other key documents with the government. Ideally, these firms have a deep-rooted knowledge of the local law and enforcement regimes, which are crucial during the process of establishing IJVs or executing acquisitions. During the twenty-first century, legal fees for real estate transactions have tremendously increased. Registration costs and other legal fees are especially high in South Korea, Greece, Spain, Hungary, and the Czech Republic. In these countries legal expenses for property-transaction costs as a percentage of the total value of the real estate are higher than that of the United States, which is well known for its expensive legal costs.[55] Confidentiality of purchase and sale agreements, clean title, trade secrets, technology, and even operational information are all legal issues that should be addressed during the formation of the entry strategy.

Natural Disasters as a Risk of Investment

One of the least manageable but still somewhat predictable risk factors of investment is related to the natural environment on a regional, national, and global scale. Improvements and protection of environmental conditions can be achieved. But this requires not only a long-term vision from national, regional, and global leadership, but also a change in the mentality of the global population. Some environmental issues can be solved more efficiently on a regional level, such as water or air pollution, but others, such as the greenhouse effect, rising sea levels, or the development of a system of tsunami and earthquake monitoring and prediction, are beyond regional authorities, requiring global attention. There are some global challenges that cannot be solved with the technology of the early twenty-first century; however, they can at least be anticipated. For example, experts can forecast which parts of the world will be affected most adversely by rising sea levels. Such issues should be taken into strategic consideration by multinational corporations. If possible, companies should adjust their strategies to allocate production facilities and investments to areas that will experience less damage. This is especially related to the health care industries, the production of first-necessity goods, and the preservation of important artifacts and information.

The global workplace has been experiencing growing damage from natural disasters. According to the Johannesburg Declaration on Sustainable Development, "natural disasters are more frequent and more devastating."[56] Furthermore, "the Munich Re Foundation, part of one of the world's leading re-insurance companies, estimated that 2005 had witnessed the largest financial losses ever as a result of weather-related natural disasters, at more than $200 billion."[57] Managers and executives responsible for corporate operations have a tendency to ignore these issues. From a strategic point of view, the correct forecast or long-term strategic plan, which inevitably evaluates the influence of natural disasters, not only brings competitive advantages to a corporation, but also in some cases can lead to the protection of human life. This is why an evaluation of the systematic risk of natural disasters is of great importance. Some corporations can be established only for the purpose of operating in times of ecological catastrophes to provide people with assistance, including goods of first necessity, medical supplies, and shelter. Many corporations develop a *force majeure* strategy for such disasters only as part of the worst-case scenarios of the exit strategy.

Unsystematic Risk of Investment

Unsystematic Factors of Economic Risk

Some factors of economic risk of direct investment belong to the category of unsystematic, company-specific risk. These factors are mostly related to the scale and conditions of the economic factors of the external corporate environment. According to a study by Professor Michael R. Walls, of the Colorado School of Mines:

> [I]ntuitively one might argue that the degree of risk aversion decreases as wealth increases or, alternatively, the degree of risk tolerance increases with wealth. As we accumulate more and more wealth our willingness to take financial risk, on an absolute basis, increases. Similarly, as the firm grows and accumulates wealth its ability to take on larger, more risky projects also grows.[58]

This basic correlation is supported by studies of several other authors. At the same time, smaller companies, in order to maintain competitiveness, can pursue a more aggressive strategy and be successful, despite a higher ratio of risk to resources. The conclusion of Professor Walls' study does not contradict this idea. Companies that "reveal a relatively high risk propensity, compared to their competitors, generate significantly higher asset returns."[59] This is a simple example of an unsystematic factor of economic risk of investment.

Another factor of economic risk that can be partially unsystematic and somewhat manageable is the level of competition. In less-familiar EMCs, companies from the developed world experience specific difficulties in gaining and maintaining market share when confronted by both foreign and domestic competition. The smaller the scale of a region related to the influence of the company's competition, the more this factor is manageable. The lower the intensity of competition, the larger the territory in which competition risk can be adjusted by the company's risk-management system. When there are only a few competitors in a market, the economic risk of competition can be managed.

The use of basic economic factors within a corporation is also related to unsystematic economic risk. An obvious example of this is the use of labor resources. Multinational corporations from developed countries are under much less government regulation and oversight in EMCs than in their native countries. Many exploit this to underreport work-related accidents and deaths. In the case of IJVs, some corporations delegate responsibility to foreign investors to avoid reporting deaths and accidents. British Petroleum PLC did not report in corporate papers the deaths of about 14 people that occurred at the facilities of one of its Russian joint ventures in 2006, despite the fact that it owned 50 percent of the assets. This reflects a lack of respect for human life and projects a terrible image of the company to the public. In order to get an idea of a country's labor regulations, strategists should consult the Index of Economic Security developed by the International Labour Organization (www.ilo.org). This index is an evaluation of income and representation security, labor market, employment and job security, work and skill reproduction security.[60] These major categories are a summary of more specific indicators such as incidences of job-related deaths, accidents, sicknesses, etc., which present the characteristics of risk of the use of a country's labor resources. This risk is generally manageable and is another example an unsystematic factor of economic risk.

Industrial Infrastructure in Emerging-market Countries

Increased competition for FDI has led the governments of EMCs to realize the importance of industrial infrastructure, such as transportation, energy, and telecommunications networks in attracting foreign investors. The improvement of industrial infrastructure is particularly challenging in large EMCs. Beyond its importance for attracting FDI, the development of infrastructure is extremely beneficial to the hundreds of millions of people who do not live in capital or major regional cities. Poor infrastructure is one of the causes of both the disparities of economic development within EMCs and the tendency of certain regions to be more closely integrated with foreign economies than with other domestic regions within their own borders. In the GMP, international transportation traffic is growing at a faster rate than domestic transportation traffic. The dynamics of this trend indicate that it will continue to grow due to the higher level of integration of EMCs with developed countries in the GMP than among themselves in the GEM. In some European EMCs, certain regions will have closer ties with foreign developed countries than with other regions within their own national borders. Attempts to rectify this disparity create a substantial demand for companies that can develop infrastructure, especially high-tech and telecommunication. These companies are usually from the developed world. Most of the expected growth in demand will be for road transportation. By 2025 the world's motor vehicle fleet is expected to be well over one billion. The further development of the GEM will intensify this trend due to the poor air-transportation infrastructure in most EMCs. However, aircraft transportation of cargo and people will increase at a higher rate in the more developed EMCs.

The development of the transportation sector of the GEM can be seen as both a systematic as well an unsystematic risk factor. In general, companies are able to manage risks related to these factors. They can do so by the strategic allocation of production facilities near existing transportation infrastructure and the development of relationships—including acquisitions—with shipping and delivery companies. Companies from developed countries operating in the GEM have the option of using existing transportation networks or investing in their own private ones. Strategists also have to balance the tradeoffs between speed and cost. Air delivery is fastest and most expensive, while delivery by sea is the slowest and cheapest. This tradeoff is not only determined by how best to serve consumers and clients. Reducing inventory costs and getting operational capital back is often most important. Cargo stuck on a ship is money that a company cannot use as operational capital. Another advantage of air transportation is that it avoids many legal and logistical issues related to ground and sea delivery. For this reason, charter aircraft services have been growing at an exponential rate. Negotiating charter party contracts has become a key service offered by law firms to companies operating in the GEM. In the end, cost advantage is often the most important factor in determining what method of delivery to use.

Products are packaged very differently in the GEM than in developed countries. In developed countries, low cost and waste reduction are key. These issues are of very little importance in the GEM; the most relevant issue there is how well the product is protected. The delivery process is much rougher due to the extreme conditions of many EMCs and the carelessness of package handlers in the GEM. It is also important that instructions be written not only in the language of the country of origin of the product, but also in that of the destination country. Companies should not assume that package handlers in foreign countries will be fluent readers of the company's language, even if it is English. This is especially important for hazardous materials. The relatively common practice of putting advertising on cargo is not a good idea for products going to the GEM, as it will confuse the handlers.

Practically all telecom companies from developed countries are giving special attention to capturing market share in the GEM, as traditional domestic markets have much lower growth rates, especially in the mobile phone market. Telecommunication infrastructure should be analyzed first and foremost in terms of technological development of the environment for FDI (which is why it is evaluated later in this chapter in the section on technological risk of investment). When strategists analyze potential locations, the quality and availability of telecommunication and transportation infrastructure is a top priority.

In developing countries and P-EMCs, a weak national industrial strategy is a major obstacle for attracting FDI. National governments of these countries have not made the initial investment to make attractive infrastructural conditions for FDI. These issues should also be the focus of multilateral, regional international institutions such as the European Bank for Reconstruction and Development, Inter-American Bank, etc.

Business Risk of Investment

Business risk of FDI is the core of unsystematic risk of investment. This type of risk is typically related to corporate operational activity. Strategists have to analyze business risk in terms of the prevention and minimization of production risk as well as commercial and financial risk during entry-strategy implementation. Business risk is usually divided into two major categories: *product risk* and *financial risk*. A more accurate name for product risk is *production risk*, because it is related to processes of preparation of production, production itself, the results of these processes—products, goods, and services—and their commercialization through distribution, sales, and post-sales warranties. Among the major indicators of production risk are the availability of the necessary resources, product-design issues, and the possibility of injury during the production and usage of the product. Potential technological achievements that would make a company's product obsolete are also among the major dimensions of production risk. Production risk covers the availability and quality of supply (raw materials, parts, energy, etc.)—*raw-material/parts risk*—and the availability, quality, and motivation of labor resources—*human resource risk*. If the company that is analyzing production risk is in the financial services industry, its financial/credit risk is its production risk. The stability of production processes and the required efficiency and production cost control are aspects of *operational risk*. The quality of a company's products, the products' life after sales, and the competitiveness of products in the marketplace are usually covered by product risk. Factors in the product-risk subcategory also include regulatory and even legal risk. However, the logic behind such an inclusion is flawed, as these things are mostly systematic risks, due to the fact that changes in law and regulation are functions exclusively of national and regional authorities. Processes of sales of final products and post-sales services are usually covered by *commercial risk*. All of these types of risk are aspects of production risk. Some text- and source books use the umbrella term "product risk" to refer to all of these risks. In this case, product risk has two meanings—specifically related to products and to all processes of production and commercialization, which is why this book uses the term "production risk."

The other category of business risk—financial risk—is related to all facets of a company's borrowing, usage, and repayment of credit as well as the use of profit. Financial risk is usually divided into four basic categories: *financial instrument risk*, *credit risk*, *operational risk*, and *market risk*. Risk analysis of all of these categories is typically done by an evaluation of the following general indicators of financial risk:

- settlement risk;
- interest rate risk;
- contingent risk;
- direct risk;
- title risk;
- fraud risk;
- volatility risk;
- spread risk;
- currency risk;
- derivative risk;
- liquidity risk;
- transactions risk;

- relations with the London Club;
- equity risk;
- communications risk;
- commodity risk.

In financial institutions and even in industrial companies, strategists together with financial professionals develop strategies to reduce financial risk according to all or some of the above listed indicators, depending on the specific industry and practice of the firm or corporation. The development of a strategy according to these indicators makes it possible to strategically position a company on the market and/or avoid losses by monitoring the market. In other words, such indicators are useful for strategic risk management.

Risk is involved in every strategic decision. Losses related to risk are an inevitable possibility in the GEM, but a carefully crafted strategy brings success. In the words of Jack Welch, "if GE's strategy of investment in China is wrong, it represents a loss of a billion dollars, perhaps a couple of billion dollars. If it is right, it is the future of this company for the next century."

In order to minimize and monitor financial risk in international transactions, several multinational governmental and non-governmental institutions were established beginning in the 1970s. One of the first of these institutions was the Basel Committee on Banking Supervision, which is made up of representatives of developed countries and one formal participant from the GEM—Spain. The enlargement, speed, and frequency of FDI to the GEM require the same type of authorities to monitor FDI inflows and outflows specifically related to the GEM.

International Business Infrastructure in Emerging-market Countries

What does a company need to be successful or even to operate in a foreign country? From a practical point of view, first of all a company needs to be able to open an account in a reliable commercial bank. Typically, financial executives and entrepreneurs prefer to open accounts in the same banks with which they are accustomed to working in their country of origin. So the presence of subsidiaries and branches of international banks—or at the very least their joint ventures with domestic banks of EMC—is very important. The absence of such banks is an immediate red flag, and an indication of a potentially high business risk of investment. In order to obtain capital to finance an investment in a foreign country, companies work with investment banks. The company's relationship with the investment institution will be much better if this institution also has a presence in the country receiving FDI. As mentioned earlier in this chapter, investment institutions will usually insist that any project that they finance in the GEM be insured against political risk—the process of acquiring such insurance is much easier when insurance companies have a presence in the potential recipient country. The same applies to the presence of auditing and accounting firms, especially the Big Four. During strategy implementation, a company engaging in an FDI will be much more confident if it can get counsel from well-known international law firms that have an established branch in the FDI destination (see Table 4.13 for a global analysis of the presence of these institutions). From this perspective, an evaluation of business risk can be done through an analysis of the international business infrastructure of an EMC in the following order:

- commercial banks;
- investment banks;
- insurers;
- auditing and accounting firms;
- law firms.

For companies with a strategic approach related to public markets of EMCs, the presence of domestic and international capital market infrastructure is vitally important. These companies should evaluate business risk in terms of the existence of the following institutions:

- stock exchanges;
- currency exchanges;
- trust services;
- trading and brokerage houses;
- settlement organizations;
- custodians;
- clearinghouses.

The presence of these institutions not only attracts FDI, but it also brings a certain level of stability to capital markets of EMCs as well as to society in general.

Development of Banking Systems in the Financial Conditions of the Global Emerging Market

CORRELATION BETWEEN CURRENCY EMISSIONS, INFLATION, AND THE DEVELOPMENT OF CONSUMER MARKETS

The development of both business and capital market infrastructure requires and facilitates financial stability in EMCs. In order to be considered an emerging market, a country must have already established a single institution of currency emission, typically a central bank. It is extremely important for the establishment of financial stability and the improvement of a country's standard of living to have a reliable institution to manage the monetary supply and inflation. Figure 8.10 demonstrates that three of the four biggest EMCs—Brazil, Russia, India, and China—the so-called BRIC—have established reliable patterns in the emissions of national currencies. Russia has a less stable domestic monetary policy than India, China,

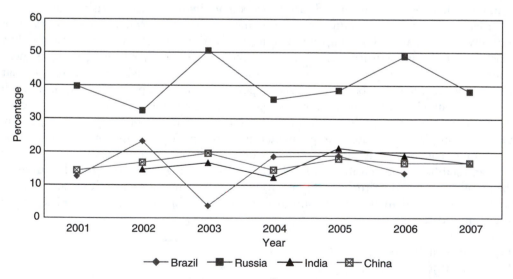

Figure 8.10 M2 Growth Rate in BRIC, 2001–2007.[61]

Note: M2 relates to the total amount of money in circulation and bank accounts, and is used as an indicator of possible inflation.

and Brazil. Unfortunately for Russia's people and investors, the high growth of currency emissions has had political motivations. During parliamentary or presidential-election years, Russian authorities increase currency emission by as much as 50 percent.

Several EMCs, mostly producers of natural resources in high demand—oil, natural gas, non-ferrous metals, etc.—have gained tremendous wealth. In order to prevent high inflation, the authorities of these countries created various wealth funds. By investing natural resource-generated revenue into these funds, it is removed from general circulation. However, on the other hand, the standards of living in these countries are typically far below that of the developed world. By not investing this revenue in service industries such as health care, education, and the development of social and industrial infrastructure, they are preventing the use of surplus capital for the improvement of the standards of living of their citizens. This is an inefficient money-management strategy. Among the fourteen largest of these funds in the world, eight were established in EMCs (Botswana, China, Russia, Chile, Korea, United Arab Emirates, and Singapore) and P-EMCs (Saudi Arabia).[62] Strategists should monitor the activity of these funds. Sooner rather than later, the money in these funds will be available to purchase foreign goods such as medical or technological equipment. Transactions such as these do not lead to inflation but do increase the standard of living.

A long-term strategy is crucial to successful investment abroad. It is also important to be able to react to the present financial and monetary situation, which can change very rapidly, especially in EMCs. Local financial and monetary conditions have an important impact on production costs of FDI-based projects. Inflation can severely increase production costs by reducing the purchasing power of the domestic currency. Inflation is essentially excess currency relative to the amount of goods and services produced domestically and imported from abroad. When a central bank emits too much currency, the purchasing power of the currency—and of the general population—is reduced. Extra currency creates an excess of demand over supply—a deficit—for certain goods or services, causing prices to rise. While this situation is clearly harmful to the economy as a whole, it can create opportunities for investors if their facilities produce, or are capable of producing the goods that are in deficit. However, investors that are not capable of producing these goods suffer as a result of rising labor costs. In some cases production may substantially decrease or freeze as a result of increased costs and a decline in purchasing power of the general population.

For generations of entrepreneurs, inflation concerns were focused on the specific location of their productive facilities. The integration of markets that were once separated by national borders and different historical and cultural traditions into a single GMP has multiplied the difficulty of anticipating events that trigger inflation. In the GMP, a shortage of goods caused by natural (a drought, for example) or technogenic (destruction of production facilities) catastrophes in a key country can affect prices throughout the world. Rapid economic growth, increasing standards of living, and expanding appetite for energy and other raw materials in the GEM, have the potential to become sources of global inflation. The uneven economic development in some of the emerging giants, such as India, China, Russia, Egypt, and Ukraine can actually be harmful to themselves, the GEM, and the GMP.

Unfortunately, governments, especially those of EMCs, do not always fully understand inflation. Many governments blame economic and financial instability on globalization and foreign speculators rather than taking responsibility for their own errors, inexperience, and lack of strategy. In fall 2007 increasing standards of living and unfettered emission of currency in several EMCs caused food prices to rise. A few EMCs that had well-thought-out strategies and national reserves were able to use the proper financial and economic mechanisms to prevent inflation within their borders. Many of the governments that lacked a strategy and the necessary reserves were incapable of doing so, and blamed globalization. Global inflation was 3.7 percent in 2007, which is not very high. In the US, it was even lower at 2.7 percent. However, in some EMCs, inflation was between 11 and 12 percent. Inflation was as much as six to seven times higher than the global rate in parts of the GEM. A well-crafted strategy would have anticipated and reduced the impact of global inflationary pressures.

The governments of many EMCs wrongly blamed their domestic financial problems on China and India despite the fact that the rate of inflation in these two countries was roughly 4 and 7.5 percent, respectively. The example of the government of the Russian Federation's lack of financial strategy is indicative of the situation in many EMCs. From 2000–2006, the Russian consumer price index (CPI), an indicator of inflation, increased by 119 percent, while that of the world, US, and EU increased by 21 percent, 17 percent, and 15 percent, respectively (see Figure 8.11). In the GMP all governments experience the same general financial trends. What differs substantially is the sophistication of the strategies that they use to deal with these trends, which is reflected in the CPI data. Very often, a rise in the prices of certain types of goods can trigger global inflationary pressures. For example, in 2007, the increasing purchasing power of consumers in the GEM led to rising prices for food, a significant inflationary pressure. In China the average price of eggs increased by 20 percent, vegetables by 23 percent, and all other food products by 18.5 percent. This caused increases in food prices in Japan, India, and even in countries as far away as Chile, which experienced a 15 percent increase in food prices.[63] However, the governments of many other EMCs found mechanisms to keep general inflation under control. It is important for investors to understand the financial strategies (or lack thereof) of national, regional, and local governments of the territories in which they make investments.

Many EMCs were unable to control inflation due to their reliance on imported food. For example, 35 percent of the Russian daily diet is imported despite the fact that 27 percent of its labor force is employed in the agricultural sector; yet Russia still cannot feed its population. By comparison, only a little over 3 percent of the labor forces of the US and EU are employed in the agricultural sector. Historically, a substantial amount of agricultural goods are imported from developed countries to EMCs despite the fact that far more people in EMCs are engaged in agricultural activity. This is the result of several factors. As previously discussed, private initiative still suffers from the legacy of command management systems, which did not offer normal economic incentives. This is especially the case in the agricultural sector, substantially reducing productivity. Another factor is the superior technology and know-how in developed countries, such as modern agricultural and food-processing machinery, fertilizers, and genetically enhanced livestock. As a result of the lack of advanced farming technology and techniques in much of the GEM, many farmers and entrepreneurs are beginning to take advantage of the very lucrative opportunities for FDI in agriculture in EMCs. Furthermore, many local, regional, and national governments in the GEM have set up incentives to reinvigorate rural areas, which can provide financial support for

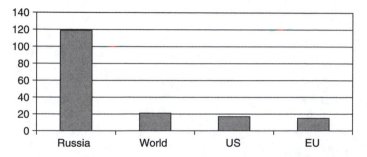

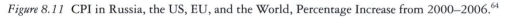

Figure 8.11 CPI in Russia, the US, EU, and the World, Percentage Increase from 2000–2006.[64]

entrepreneurs and investors from developed countries. FDI from developed countries is bringing sophisticated farming methods, technology, and badly needed capital, rebuilding many villages that were once abandoned. It is not uncommon for farmers to import cows or sheep from Australia, Holland, or the US to improve the productivity of their livestock. In addition, a lack of suitable transportation and telecommunication infrastructure further inhibits productivity. This makes it very difficult for farmers to deliver their goods to major urban markets; a lack of fuel for trucks and cars exacerbates the lack of infrastructure. This issue can be resolved by the production of ethanol and other biofuels from agricultural waste and timber byproducts. Unfortunately, the taxation systems of many EMCs essentially prevent the development of these industries. The situation is of course the complete opposite in developed countries, where ethanol production is heavily subsidized. The governments of some EMCs, such as China, India, Kazakhstan, and Spain have already established national programs to support domestic ethanol production and decrease the dependence of private agriculture and rural areas on the centralized fuel supply. The absolute world leader in ethanol production is Brazil. A substantial part of Brazil's agricultural sector is driven by government initiatives for the production and distribution of ethanol, which removed Brazil from the list of oil-importing countries.

Most EMC governments do not have a strategy to replace imported food with domestic agricultural production and have not been able to motivate domestic producers. Nonetheless, the role of the GEM in the agricultural sector is increasing in the world.[65] In some cases, food crises and inflation can be the result of excessive food exports to developed countries. This was the case with vegetable-oil products and fish products in 2007. Sometimes a local food crisis can be the result of improvements in standards of living. As people become more prosperous, they tend to become more health conscious. Many consumers in EMCs have become aware of the health risks related to trans- and saturated fats and have begun to use vegetable oil instead. Some EMC governments have even gone as far as to enact restrictions on transfat. As a result, the export of vegetable oils and high-quality butter has decreased from many EMCs due to rising domestic consumption.

Agricultural sectors of EMCs still need time to be ready to compete in terms of price and cost production with products from developed countries. This is a major issue of discussion of the Doha Development Agenda of the WTO. Underdeveloped countries, developing countries, and EMCs have to temporarily implement a certain amount of protectionist instruments to prevent foreign dominance of their agricultural markets. They need time for domestic agricultural and food-processing companies to stand on their own feet. In the Doha negotiations, Western countries, especially the US and member-states of the EU, push EMCs to lower import tariffs and quotas by as much as 90 percent in some cases. Leaders of developed countries are afraid to lose their customers, not only in big EMCs such as India, China or Russia, but even in small ones. For this reason, the Doha round of negotiations has been contentious.[66] In most EU countries, subsidies per one cow can reach about 2,000 euros annually, which is several times more than the GDP per head of some countries.

All of the above-mentioned challenges to domestic agricultural production in the GEM have the potential to be multiplied by an unsophisticated monetary strategy. Populist tendencies of national governments are a major cause of inflationary pressures and of financial and production risk for foreign investors. It is not uncommon in the GEM for governments to emit excess currency near parliamentary or presidential elections. Following up on promises to increase salaries and wages (with obvious implications for FDI), pension contributions, and military and student stipends can increase the amount of money in circulation at a much faster pace than the rate of food production and first-necessity goods. That is why food shortages are more likely to occur during or immediately following election years in many EMCs. The increase in government expenditures actually end up decreasing people's real purchasing power, as it increases the amount of currency in circulation without increasing the amount of goods and services available, inevitably causing prices to rise. The balance between these two factors is basically what determines the amount of inflation. Governments can prevent and reduce inflation by slowing the currency printing presses and reducing the rise of salaries and wages, significantly reducing the risks for foreign investors. This issue is definitely strategically important for foreign investors in EMCs.

Corporate strategists also have to be aware of the fact that in EMCs with more sophisticated financial systems, inflationary pressures can come from other sources. In order to attract FDI inflows and make their domestic currency more appealing to investors, EMC governments often attempt to make their currency freely convertible as soon as possible. The pursuit of a freely convertible currency often motivates governments with otherwise stable financial and monetary policies to print extra currency notes in order to make them available for foreign currency speculators. If more notes are printed than demanded by the foreign currency markets, the country will have a surplus of currency notes relative to the volume of domestic consumer goods. This causes a decrease in the purchasing power of the domestic currency—the opposite of the desired goal of making the currency freely convertible. This phenomenon played a role in the Asian financial crisis of 1997 and in inflation in Russia in the fall of 2007. In both cases, foreign investors saw their profits decrease as a result. This situation requires governmental intervention in order to create a balance between the money in circulation and the goods and services available. Many instruments used to achieve this balance are not restrictive. Subsidies can create incentives to increase production of certain items such as food and first-necessity goods. National governments can also increase reserves of these goods, which can be supplied to the poor during times of high inflation. Strategists of foreign companies operating in these markets should take into consideration the fact that depending on the specific situation, EMC governments may increase or decrease import quotas.

Usually, inflation in the GEM is most harmful to the middle class and poorest parts of society. The prices of first-necessity goods, food, and low-quality products tend to rise at a much higher rate—up to three times faster—than the prices of luxury and high-quality goods. If these prices increase by more than 1 percent per month over several months, the likelihood of galloping inflation is very high. Wise investors pay very close attention to these price levels in order to prevent skyrocketing prices and to be prepared to produce goods that are suddenly in higher demand, especially investors that produce agricultural and consumer goods.

Strategists, who often try to use their experience in developed countries when entering the GEM, should keep in mind that the dynamics of prices in developed countries are very different. During times of financial instability, the larger and much wealthier middle and upper classes in developed countries immediately invest in gold and luxury goods. As a result, the prices for these products rise at a much faster pace than the prices of first-necessity goods. This is a major difference between the economic and financial systems of developed countries and the GEM. Regardless, in all types of economies, the government shoulders the responsibility of preventing inflation. Everyone—domestic entrepreneurs, government officials, foreign investors, etc.—should be aware of changes in prices, as they are the most sensitive and painful receptor of an economy.

BANKS AND THE CASH ECONOMY

Without the presence of commercial and investment banks in a country, companies will be hesitant to make an investment. Beginning in the end of the 1980s, internationally recognized banking institutions such as Citigroup (www.citi.com/citigroup), Chase Manhattan (www.chase.com), HSBC (www.hsbc.com), Barings (acquired by ING in 1995 www.ing.com), Merrill Lynch (www.ml.com), and Credit Suisse First Boston (www.credit-suisse.com) established their presence throughout the GEM, initially by opening representative offices. Later operational subsidiaries and branches were established, which at first served only foreigners, though eventually obtained the necessary licenses to provide full service for locals as well. Demand from clients in developed countries to invest in EMCs, combined with EMCs' financial deregulation, growing stability, and increasing economic freedom were the main factors in the spread of internationally recognized banks in the GEM. *Global Finance* (www.gfmag.com) was one of the first publications to realize the importance of the banking sector in the GEM. Since 1994 it has published its annual list of "the Best Emerging Market Banks in the World." Citigroup has occupied the no. 1 spot on this list for many years, a result of its activity in Latin America, Central Europe, and more recently, Russia, where it is the leading bank. In central Moscow, Citigroup's branches are almost as prevalent as they are in New York City. However, Citigroup's branches abroad do not offer the same services in the GEM. Many branches will work only with businesses or foreigners, and there are often restrictions on transferring money from EMCs. In Moscow, for example, US citizens have different rights from Russian citizens when it comes to transferring money abroad. However, even for US citizens, transferring money abroad is difficult and highly restricted, requiring numerous official documents. ING Barings has been the leading bank in Europe and has also had tremendous success in Africa and the Middle East. *Global Finance* was also one of the first publications to rank the best domestic banks of EMCs.

Foreign companies that choose to work with domestic banks instead of internationally recognized banks, perhaps for cheaper services, should be very cautious. Even the leading domestic banks of the GEM are much more vulnerable to failure than internationally recognized banks and have much smaller amounts of governmentally protected money in the accounts of companies and individuals. Peregrine Bank, once considered the best domestic bank in Asia, impressed several leading international banks when its Hong Kong book of some 45 million shares set a record for oversubscription. Less than a year later, the Peregrine Bank collapsed from the aftermath of the Asian financial crisis in 1997. The strategies of foreign banks from developed countries tend to specialize in particular services in the GEM. The risk of specialization is that a crisis in the area of activity can lead to the loss of hundreds of millions of dollars. Focusing on bond trading in Russia caused Credit Suisse First Boston to lose hundreds of millions when the Russian ruble collapsed in 1998. Merrill Lynch and ING, which specialize in several different services in several different regions, profited from a safer strategy. Merrill Lynch equity research activity is concentrated mostly in the Middle East; its debt origination is mostly in Asia, and debt research mostly in Latin America. ING Barings is well known for its corporate finance in Europe, its equity research in Africa and Latin America, and equity sales and trading in Asia. Strategists of international investment banks from developed countries tend to shift banking activity from EMC to EMC, in search of potentially higher profits. Merrill Lynch's $4.5 billion Emerging Europe Fund, managed by Alain Bourrier, increased its profits by more than 79 percent by relocating from Poland and Hungary to Russia. It was ranked "no. 1 over the past 12 months [as of March 2006] among 1,000 funds that invest in European stocks and are tracked by Bloomberg with a growth rate over 300 percent from 2003 to 2006."[67]

The transition from command economies to free markets typically starts with the development of free-market institutions to serve growing private businesses and individual customers. During dictatorships, all banking institutions were not only under complete control of the government, but also were owned by the government. There were no privacy laws, and as a result, when private companies first began to appear and operate, they were forced to open accounts only in state-owned banks. At that time, it was one of the causes of the rapid development of gray economies in the GEM. Many companies preferred to operate under the state's radar and obviously did not open accounts in state-owned banks. As a result, in the initial stages of a private sector's development, it is typical in EMCs for a substantial part of the economy to be cash based. Companies are usually not officially registered yet, and officially do not have any registered employees. They pay their unofficial employees in cash, buy raw materials and parts with cash, and even pay the rent for their office and commercial space in cash. Because these companies are not registered and their employees are off the books, the overwhelming majority of their activity is not reported by governments and municipal offices. Subsequently, many companies and their employees do not pay taxes. The accelerating development of the cash economy results in EMCs with huge budget deficits and high unemployment statistics. A substantial part of this unemployment consists of people who work but do not pay taxes, do not even have taxpayer IDs, and are not included in official statistics.

In response to these issues, governments of EMCs began to motivate the development of private commercial banks. If governments of the GEM have a strategic vision for this process, typically, at the initial stages they try to protect local financial markets from immediate participation of foreign commercial banks and branches and subsidiaries of international banks, or they limit the licenses granted to a few foreign banks. Otherwise, the small and underdeveloped local banking sector, with a tiny level of capitalization in inexperienced domestic banks, will be totally overwhelmed by foreign banks. Strategists of foreign banks who are interested in cooperating with domestic EMC banks have to be aware of the fact that in most cases, it takes three to five years of preliminary activity of domestic commercial banks, bankers, executives and managers to be ready to cooperate with foreign banking institutions. Foreign strategists should also anticipate the fact that domestic banks will be ready to compete with foreign banks within 10 to 15 years. The development of banking regulations, establishment of oversight committees and commissions, the reorientation of the central bank from command economy to free-market system, and the development of all other banking institutions, such as collection and settlement agencies, brings the local financial market to the point at which private entrepreneurs and individuals start to transition from the gray sector to legitimacy. However, the dominance of the cash economy does not immediately end. During this period, EMCs lack a business culture that is accustomed to using checks to pay suppliers, employee wages, and acquire receivables. In most cases, prior to the widespread use of checks, countries develop interbank wire transactions, followed by the implementation of a debit card system. Companies open debit card accounts for their employees and transfer money through affiliated commercial banks to employees' individual accounts. Employees can then go to banks or cash machines and use their debit card to get cash or pay for goods or services. Lacking experience and faith in the protection of their money in banks, there are often long lines at cash machines, where people try to withdraw their entire wages. Slowly, as they realize that money is not disappearing from their accounts, people leave some of their wages in the bank, and commercial banks have more operational capital. Somewhere during this process, companies, commercial banking institutions, and local populations become ready to develop credit systems. In EMCs, where people have no credit history and the overwhelming majority of them do not have bank accounts, this system develops slowly. Strategists of banks that are planning or anticipating the implementation of a credit system should be aware that in many cases, more than half of the population has zero savings. At this stage of development, many people begin to prepare to buy durable goods, TV sets, refrigerators, cars, apartments, and homes. This is the beginning of the establishment of the middle class, which requires commercial banks to provide credit. The operational activity of several domestic and foreign commercial banks, and the competition between them for customers, finally creates the situation where banks are willing to issue credit. Executives of foreign banks responsible for credit policy have to be aware that, unfortunately, many inexperienced customers take out loans without fully comprehending the difficulty of making monthly payments. During these initial processes in EMCs, credit and mortgage-debt crises are not unusual. Civilian courts are often filled with cases of banks and mortgage institutions filing against their customers, leading to a huge growth in the demand for collection agencies. In most EMCs, the losing side pays all court expenses; the losing side is usually the customer. This is one of the major differences between people in debt in the developed world and in EMCs. In the US, with an average GDP per head of about $45,800, the average American has $3,020 of credit card debt. Unlike in developed countries, in the GEM, the most common form of payment is still cash. Nevertheless, the acceptance and use of major credit cards, which first appeared at the end of the 1980s, is spreading rapidly. Initially, they were accepted only in hotels, a few restaurants, and department stores catering to foreigners. Eventually, international commercial banks began issuing credit cards to their most reliable clients in EMCs. Later, IJVs between domestic and foreign commercial banks began issuing credit cards, and finally, domestic commercial banks started to issue debit cards (linked to customer's bank accounts), with their own brand names.

Strategists and international credit risk agencies should also analyze financial stability in terms of financial relationships among EMCs. The more international financial transactions that an EMC has with other EMCs and the less with developed countries, the more vulnerable it is to the spread of financial instability from other parts of the GEM. One of the first evaluations of external vulnerability was created by Fitch Ratings in 2007.[68] Rating agencies should explore other methods to measuring external vulnerability and international credit risk. Foreign investors would benefit tremendously from more comprehensive strategic evaluations of these issues.

EMERGING CAPITAL MARKETS AND THE GLOBAL MONETARY SYSTEM

The global and regional trends of currency integration, which began in the EU, are also underway in the GEM. However, unlike most EMCs, the countries that adopted the euro as an official currency in 2002 already had freely convertible currencies. There is a great deal of variation in the level of maturity and convertibility among currencies of the GEM. Some, such as the Czech koruna, are already convertible, while others, such as the Argentinean peso, used to be almost freely convertible and were pegged to the US dollar after successful economic restructuring. However, the financial crisis of 2001 ended the period of free convertibility in Argentina. Most EMCs have currencies of limited convertibility. In these countries the exchange rate between national and foreign currencies is established by central banks, not by the market; this is the case with the Russian ruble and the Chinese renminbi. Others are not convertible at all, such as the Tunisian domestic dinar. Some countries restrict the amount of currency that can be converted by individuals or companies in a given period of time (such as the Indian rupee); some restrict the type of currency for which it can be exchanged; and some use a combination of these factors. Many regional blocs of EMCs, such as Mercosur, are trying to increase convertibility among their various currencies. Russia has unsuccessfully tried several times to turn the CIS (a group of 10 countries) into a currency union based on the ruble. Russia and Belarus also made several attempts to establish the ruble as a shared currency. Some European countries that are not members of the EU unilaterally replaced their national currency with the euro. This was the path that Montenegro chose upon achieving its independence. In order to officially adopt the euro and join the Economic and Monetary Union of the EU, a country must give control of currency circulation and interest rates to the European Central Bank, which the Slovak Republic chose to do in 2008. Over time, national central banks gradually regain the right to set interest rates. Strategists should anticipate that the majority of EMCs will have limitedly convertible currencies for the first quarter of the twenty-first century.

The increasing role of the euro has destroyed the dollar's monopoly as the world's banking and reserve currency. As a result, a substantial portion of national reserves that were once in the form of US dollars in central and private banks in EMCs have been diversified into euros, sterling pounds, and Swiss francs. Typically, this substitution is done in proportion to the foreign trade balance of an EMC. Companies from EMCs make profits in their own national currencies. In order to realize their profit in dollars, they have to purchase dollars from banks. Later, when they buy any raw materials, parts, or equipment, or when distribution networks buy consumer-goods products from companies in the 16 countries of the Eurozone, for example, they have to exchange their dollars for euros. Through these currency transactions, companies lose a substantial part of their profits. For this reason, banks and multinational corporations started to diversify their foreign currency reserves, holding euros, sterling pounds—and for some companies that are active in the GEM—Chinese renminbi or Russian rubles, in addition to US dollars. Under the influence of this trend, during the first decade of the twenty-first century, the dollar slowly depreciated compared with the euro and especially the pound.

The health of the dollar is actually very important for the overwhelming majority of EMCs, and especially for those that rely heavily on the export of raw materials, such as oil, natural gas, precious metals, or iron ore, as global commodity markets typically operate in dollars. Furthermore, reserve funds of countries such as China, Russia, Korea, Saudi Arabia, etc., are primarily held—at least 30 to 60 percent—in dollars. The slow decline of the dollar is manageable for such funds, but the failure of the dollar altogether is not in the strategic interest of these countries. The relationship of natural-resource-exporting countries with the value of the dollar is quite complex. For example, rising oil, gold, and other precious metal prices, as well as all other commodities, increase their export revenues. In response, the national financial strategies of EMCs such as Saudi Arabia, Russia, South Africa, Brazil, etc., have become very sophisticated since the beginning of the twenty-first century.

In the same way that EMCs are calling for increased representation in the multilateral institutions of the global business order, they are also asserting themselves in the global monetary system. Decreasing foreign demand for US dollars will eventually reduce foreign interest in US fixed-income securities. Among foreign buyers of US treasury debt and US fixed-income securities, there are many EMCs, which was not the case in the twentieth century. While, in terms of political influence, new poles are appearing primarily in the GEM, in the global monetary system, new poles are coming from developed countries of Western Europe. The financial strategies of companies in the GEM have to be more sophisticated to deal with the increasing complexity of the global monetary system. Many companies lost tremendous amounts of money due to overinvestment in telecom and Internet sectors at the turn of the twenty-first century. As a result, capital retreated to the safer waters of its country of origin. However, increased liquidity, as well as an inverted yield curve, have resulted in many companies and banks reorienting themselves toward the riskier and more profitable markets of EMCs. From 2003 to 2004 there was a huge wave of FDI inflow into the GEM. Some of this was capital that fled the US after the tragedy of September 11, 2001. There are several similar strategic challenges of national capital markets in the GEM. As a first priority, national financial strategists of the GEM should consider the following seven steps:

- Development of a law of protection of minority shareholders' rights.

- Enforcement of legal rights of minority shareholders.
- Improved access of medium-size and small companies to capital market.
- Continuation of the increasing role of the public sector in the national capital markets.
- Prevention of central and regional governments from breaching contracts.
- Increasing level of convertibility of the national currency.
- WTO membership and improvement of capital control.

CURRENCY RATES AND EXCHANGES

Many governments attempt to strengthen their currencies, without a strategic analysis of the implications for the general population and domestic business. The stronger the domestic currency, the more expensive it is for foreigners to buy domestic goods, which obviously has a negative effect on people employed in export-oriented industries. Export-oriented companies' sales will decline, bringing less profit, eventually lowering the wages of their employees. This also reduces profits after they are converted from dollars or euros back to the national currency, causing a reduction in tax revenues from profit taxes and value-added taxes. This decreases funding for state pension funds, health funds, etc. However, there is a benefit to a strong currency; assuming the government does not emit more currency, inflation will decrease. International banks are more likely to invest in a strong currency and EMC governments, as mentioned earlier in this chapter, increase the money supply in an attempt to increase the convertibility of domestic currency. This makes it easier for foreign banks to buy the domestic currency, and ensures that there is enough currency in circulation to meet demand, preventing deflation. Strategists of foreign companies should anticipate that EMC governments usually increase the money supply by too much and cause inflation. It is important that a strong EMC currency has a strong backing, either in foreign currency or gold reserves. National strategists can also back a strong currency through a positive foreign trade balance. This ensures that there are more opportunities to develop domestic currency convertibility.

The positive impact of a strong currency on the general population is stability and reliability. People are more apt to invest and save domestic currencies, as opposed to hoarding dollars, pounds, euros, etc. Also, foreign goods are more affordable, which is great for consumers but may harm domestic producers. People living and traveling abroad enjoy benefits from a strong currency because it makes foreign currencies and services cheaper. Foreign and domestic investors in real estate profit from less expensive mortgages, which are a result of lower interest rates from the central bank for domestic commercial banks. Affordable mortgages are extremely important for the development of a property-owning middle class, which is what usually makes the transition from a centralized economy to a free-market economy irreversible. Property owners are typically very strong supporters and defenders of economic and political freedom.

The results of a strong currency are mixed in all countries. In the GEM, the positives outweigh the negatives, bringing increased stability, economic maturation, and eventually, a fully convertible currency. Convertibility creates many opportunities for domestic markets, which become very attractive to foreign businesses and investors. It makes it much easier for foreign companies to operate, to make and receive international payments, and to repatriate profits.

The growing involvement of the GEM in the GMP required the development of new ways and means of converting profit made in inconvertible currencies. In the majority of countries this was created through the establishment of national and international currency exchanges as a legal entity. In many cases, at the beginning of these entities' operational activities, the government would sell a certain amount of freely convertible currency.

Companies that bought seats at the currency exchange could buy the freely convertible currency through open biddings with currency of the country in which they made their profits. The need to have a standard means of evaluating different currencies led to the establishment of currency-risk ranking systems. One of these ranking systems is regularly published by the *Emerging Markets Monitor*, a publication of the Royal Bank of Canada (RBC) Financial Group (www.rbc.com/economics).

In order to increase demand for their currencies and make them more stable and attractive to currency speculators, EMC governments use a number of strategies. Some EMCs, such as Taiwan, Hong Kong, and Russia, choose to hold a tremendous amount of foreign currency and gold reserves. An alternative strategy used by Argentina, Brazil, Chile, Thailand, and the Czech Republic, among others, is to allow their currency to float freely, with varying limitations. Some of these countries, such as Taiwan and South Korea, also use a hybrid strategy. Countries such as China, India, Singapore, Hungary, Russia, Poland, and Turkey manage the float of their currency within a certain range. Countries such as Hong Kong and Malaysia peg their currency to a leading currency, such as the US dollar. Some countries replace their national currency completely with a leading foreign currency—El Salvador, Panama (mostly), and Ecuador with the US dollar, and Montenegro with the euro, as previously mentioned.

Portfolio Investment and Stock Exchanges

With the increasing presence of foreign and domestic investors in EMCs, in order to finance further development, they began to look to public markets to raise capital through portfolio investment. They became especially motivated to be listed on foreign and domestic exchanges. In turn, the establishment of stock exchanges in EMCs and the appearance of stocks of GEM companies on foreign exchanges increased the interest of portfolio investors from the developed world in these companies. Portfolio investment primarily falls under the category of systematic risk, which cannot be fully avoided through strategies such as diversification. For portfolio investors the world economy or a particular national economy represents the same unavoidable and unmanageable systematic risk. The economic and especially business nature of portfolio investment is different from that of direct investment. FDI always requires investors to make a choice of where to invest—which country, region, etc.—because direct investment, by definition, needs the investor to play an influential or executive role. Individual portfolio investors, on the other hand, generally do not play a managerial role. It is not necessary for the portfolio investor to make a choice about the particular location of the company's facilities that their money may be financing.

The nature of corporate portfolio investment is also different from FDI. Corporate investors diversify risk by buying shares mostly of corporations with lower profitability from stable markets, making significantly fewer investments in companies from high-risk countries, such as those of the GEM. However, this is beginning to change. A few portfolio investment funds specialize in the GEM and even in particular EMCs, such as the Vietnam Opportunity Fund Ltd and the Templeton Russia & Eastern European Fund. These funds represent a trend, which first gained momentum in the middle of the 1990s, whereby portfolio managers from developed countries began to invest in companies from the GEM— primarily in economies in bloom and emerging-market democracies. Dynamics of the GMP do not affect investments in the GEM in the same way that they affect those in developed countries. A slowing growth rate of the GMP could lead to more portfolio investment in the GEM from investors seeking higher returns. This can be a risky move for small portfolio investors. The "Asian" financial crisis (1997–2000) and the failure of the Russian ruble (1998) convinced many small investors to buy high-yielding Argentinean bonds.

This proved to be a disastrous investment following the Argentinean debt default in December 2001.

When domestic investors from EMCs observed the great interest of individual investors and portfolio investment funds from developed countries in corporate shares of their countries, they started to compete with them. This process initiated the impetus to create stock exchanges in the GEM. In some EMCs, several exchanges were created. By the mid-1990s in Argentina, there were 17 stock exchanges, although the majority of all transactions were done at the Buenos Aires Stock Exchange. As of 2008 several stock exchanges operate in each of the following EMCs: Brazil, India, China, among others. In countries of the Caribbean, such as Barbados, and in former communist states of Eastern Europe, stock exchanges appeared during the early stages of privatization. Newly privatized small and medium-size companies in these countries were in need of investment to renovate production facilities and equipment, and even for operational capital. The first private owners of these companies initiated the creation of stock exchanges with the hope of attracting investment from the public. Several of these new Eastern European stock exchanges were modeled after the Vienna Stock Exchange, which only operated half a day, two to three times a week. In many cases newly privatized GEM companies could not procure adequate capital to finance their development on domestic stock exchanges. At the end of the 1990s, but most heavily at the beginning of the twenty-first century, companies from the GEM attained widespread direct representation on the stock exchanges of developed countries. They enjoyed a great deal of interest from portfolio investors on the NYSE, the American Stock Exchange, NASDAQ, and even on the Over The Counter Bulletin Board (OTCBB) (all of which are in New York City), as well as on the London and Frankfurt stock exchanges. Companies from Asia-Pacific often preferred to be listed on the Hong Kong, Shanghai, or Singapore exchanges. These exchanges, despite the fact that they are located in the GEM, have a long and successful history. In some cases, GEM companies went to other emerging-market exchanges such as India's Bombay Stock Exchange, where the capitalization of companies is not large but there are a great deal of companies listed. As cross-border economic and financial activity continues to increase among EMCs, so too will occurrences of companies raising capital via stock exchanges in other foreign EMCs.

In order to be listed directly on any stock exchange, a company must prove that its accounting system is in compliance with international or US standards. The company must undergo evaluation by one of the Big Four auditing firms or one of their affiliates or subsidiaries for each of the three years prior to its IPO. The company must have no pending legal issues. Ideally, it should have an investment rating from all or several of the major rating agencies, such as S&P, Moody's, Fitch, etc. In most cases, in order to be listed on the NYSE, a company will have to issue at least one million shares and demonstrate dynamics of increasing capitalization and profit over a sustained period. In the US, exchanges such as the American Stock Exchange and regional trading floors such as the Boston and Philadelphia stock exchanges, among others, are more suited for smaller companies. In terms of minimum number of shares, profitability, and history of success, the requirements for being listed on emerging-market stock exchanges are generally much less strenuous than those of the developed world.

NASDAQ is well suited for companies from the GEM because it is capable of monitoring the GMP around the clock. When in 1997 a similar computer system was installed in the London Stock Exchange, NASDAQ, through a joint affiliation, became an international stock exchange. Its members can trade "over the counter" on both sides of the Atlantic. NASDAQ was the first stock exchange to move toward the technological globalization of capital. By listing their shares on NASDAQ, companies from the GEM gain access to US and even European capital. The OTCBB is pretty similar to NASDAQ and works under its supervision. However, companies listed on the OTCBB have not met NASDAQ require-ments in terms of size, capitalization, and profitability. The OTCBB is a good avenue for smaller companies from the GEM to access US capital, however, they cannot be listed on both the NASDAQ and the OTCBB at the same time. Companies from the GEM often experience difficulties when they temporarily transition from the NASDAQ, NYSE, or London Stock Exchange to the OTCBB while they improve their economic and financial indicators. If a company operating in any EMC declares bankruptcy, it cannot be listed on the OTCBB. Regardless of which stock exchange a company chooses, it has to be able to submit quarterly and annual reports to the US Securities and Exchange Commission or an equivalent organization of the country in which it is listed.

Prior to direct listings, GEM companies appeared on these exchanges via ADR and global depositary receipts (GDR). Through these instruments, companies were not directly listed; investment banks from developed countries took responsibility for the shareholding GEM companies. The Bank of New York has a great deal of experience in this practice on the NYSE and has represented several companies from the GEM. This allowed investors from the US and other developed countries to buy shares in GEM companies in a manner with which they were more comfortable and experienced.

Regardless, even when relatively big funds invest in a particular EMC by buying shares of companies, they generally do not participate in the management of these companies. Otherwise, their portfolio investment would qualify as a direct investment. There are several new global portfolio investors, such as global mutual and equity funds, that allow investors to buy shares from companies throughout the world. According Mike Thompson, a managing director of Thomson Reuters:

> What's changed is the idea that you need to treat US and foreign stocks as distinct assets. In a world where around 65 percent of McDonald's (MCD, Fortune 500) revenue comes from overseas and 35 percent of Toyota's (TM) sales are made in North America, what's the point?[69]

This attitude, however, does not apply to FDI, which always requires a country- and even region-specific analysis. For individuals who make a portfolio investment in McDonald's or Toyota, for example, the risk of investment is practically unchanged when one of these corporations expands its presence in the GEM. However, for the corporate leadership of Toyota or McDonald's, the development of their presence in a new country and even the opening of new facilities in a country in which they already have a presence via direct investment is a serious strategic decision. For this reason, portfolio investment is not a focus of this chapter or this book. Furthermore, the analysis of systematic risk in this book primarily applies to country/region-specific FDI risk.

The formation of capital markets and the increasing capitalization in EMCs, which occurred during the initial stages of the transition to free-market economies, required the development of domestic stock exchanges and the institutions that typically accompany them, such as trust companies, settlement organizations, as well as security and exchange commissions, and other governmental bodies.

During the initial stages of capital market development in the GEM, experienced foreign branches of investment banks and financial and trading companies were the dominant players. Eventually, domestic GEM companies learned from their foreign counterparts and became active participants. The subsequent stage of development will involve domestic companies of the GEM becoming important partners and competitors of foreign branches from the developed world. As domestic exchanges mature, governments of EMCs have allowed domestic companies to be listed on foreign stock exchanges and foreign companies to be listed on domestic stock exchanges. This is resulting in a huge increase in the capitalization of companies from the GEM, as they are listed in multiple stock exchanges. Traditionally, companies from the GEM prefer to be listed on the leading stock exchanges of developed countries, such as London, New York, Frankfurt, and even Toronto. In a very interesting development toward the end of the first decade of the twenty-first century, companies from EMCs are looking to other parts of the GEM, such as stock exchanges in Shanghai, Hong Kong, Singapore, Warsaw, and Moscow. This is greatly increasing the capitalization of GEM countries. Speculators, investment banks, and wealthy individuals are keenly interested in investing in GEM companies that have already demonstrated rapid, steady growth and are internationally recognized. This has led to a huge increase in financial activity in the capital markets of the GEM. A great deal of this activity is handled by leading financial institutions in their offices in London and New York, where emerging-market dealer communities are flourishing. In a study on IPOs in the US by GEM companies, professors Robert Burner, Susan Chaplinsky, and Latha Ramchand compared

> the issue costs of 299 companies from emerging and developed market countries making initial public offerings (IPOs) in the United States between 1991 and 2001. Our results indicate that IPOs from emerging markets experience the same costs on average as IPOs from developed market countries. Although there is a large gap between the country risk ratings of the emerging and developed market countries, IPO issuers from emerging markets appear to bridge that gap by being large issuers in their respective home countries, listing more frequently on the NYSE, and having a greater proportion of activity in manufacture and infrastructure segments, and a lower proportion in high-tech segments. These issues occur following periods of strong US and home market equity performance which helps to alleviate country risk. In comparison to their developed market peers, emerging market issuers are a select group of higher-quality firms.[70]

Emerging-market Securities, Derivatives, and Foreign Debt

The increasing importance of the GEM has led to an explosion in complexity and growth in the global capital market. According to the BIS, the daily turnover of currency trades is worth more than the annual income of economies such as Germany and China. Global strategists have to deal with new complications as a result of the increasing scale of international financial transactions under the influence of globalization of the world financial system, which allows risks and uncertainty to be dispersed and absorbed like never before. Bankers and investors from the GEM are becoming more skilled and can compete with their counterparts in developed countries via complex investment instruments such as financial derivatives linked to currencies. As a result, the daily trading of these derivatives is worth more than $2 trillion. In 2007, "emerging market currencies were involved in almost 20 percent of all transactions."[71] The number of branches and employees of international dealer firms has increased substantially in the GEM. A few EMCs account for most of the trade volume in the GEM, such as Brazil (35 percent), Mexico (15 percent), Russia (more than 14 percent), followed by Venezuela (a developing country), and Turkey. Among EMCs that account for more than 2 percent of GEM trade volume are Colombia, Ecuador, the Philippines, Peru, and Argentina. MarketAxess, a provider of a unified platform for credit dealers, evaluated the trade of 36 EMCs, and found that Brazil had the largest share, and Guatemala and Jamaica each had the lowest share at 0.01 percent.

Countries that once begged for money in the form of aid are now players in international financial markets. They have already become investors in non-developed countries in projects with a high probability of success. High commodity prices (especially those of oil and fertilizer) have filled the coffers of several P-EMCs and EMCs with excess cash. In general, if a country can get a higher return on an investment than the interest rate of its debt, then it should invest. Governments should have companies (international and domestic) compete to come up with projects that address national needs while yielding a high return. However, if the financial strategy of a country is not sophisticated enough to allow efficient investments, it is best to immediately repay the foreign and multilateral debt. The best-case scenario is to earn a large enough return on the investment to gradually repay the debt on the agreed schedule, as loans from multilateral institutions usually have below-market interest rates, but with many restrictions.

First issued in 1994 as a part of Brazil's debt restructuring, its C-bond with a maturity between 20 and 30 years has placed Brazil in the leading position in emerging-market securities. According to the Emerging Markets Traders Association (EMTA) as of 2003, Brazilian C-bonds made up 10 percent of all emerging-market debt traded.[72] Nigeria, which was once one of the most heavily indebted countries in the world, tapped the international Eurobond markets by launching a bond worth about $1.5 billion. The proceeds of the bond are being used to repay Nigeria's outstanding foreign debt.

In the 1990s, there were very few mutual or public (especially pension) funds in the GEM. Now there is not a single EMC without them. For example, as of January 2007, Russia had 259 non-governmental pension funds, with 6.2 million people related to these funds, plus 300,000 people who had invested in mutual funds. To the surprise of many foreign strategists, pension funds in EMCs grow at double-digit rates annually, unlike their 4 to 5 percent average growth rates in developed countries. According to the IMF, major Western pension, mutual, and hedge funds invested 16 percent of their assets in EMCs in 1994, compared with 0.5 percent in 1987.[73] At the beginning of the twenty-first century, all major mutual and pension funds diversified their portfolios with emerging-market debt and assets:

> The surge in cross-border capital flows from mature market institutional investors has helped broaden the investor base for emerging-market external sovereign debt, leading to the stability and lower volatility of this asset class over the past five years—as reflected in the global spreads of the JPMorgan Chase Emerging Markets Bond index (EMBI). Interest in emerging market assets has undergone a structural upward shift, with institutional investors such as US pension funds adding emerging market external debt to their benchmark portfolio allocation.[74]

All of these movements increased the necessity for strategists to consult with agencies such as Fitch Ratings, as well as specialized advisory firms. Strategists should take into consideration that with the dissemination of technology and the consolidation of financial assets in these funds, investing has become less speculative. Derivatives initially originated as instruments to hedge against currencies and interest rate fluctuations, but globalization made them a crucial instrument for strategic investors. Investors often use derivatives in countries with rapidly growing economies, which often comes along with current account deficits (though not the case for China and Russia) and relatively low inflation. Without the formation of the GEM, derivatives might never have become a globally accepted financial instrument.

Technological Risk of Foreign Direct Investment

Technological risk of FDI is a function of the correlation between the technology to be implemented in a cross-border investment project and natural, social, economic, and technological conditions of the country and particular region where the investment will occur. In order to evaluate this risk, strategists must have extensive knowledge of the level of technological advancement of a potential country or region recipient. In the GEM an evaluation of this risk is of great importance because of the substantial variations in techno-logical progress among EMCs. The GEM includes countries that are considered among the global technological leaders of some knowledge-based industries—Taiwan in semi-conductors and Russia in nuclear, space, and nanotechnology industries, as well as countries with little to no experience with modern technologies. For this reason, it is important for strategists to get the opinions of rating agencies specializing in evaluations of R&D capabil-ities. A.T. Kearny, one of the leading global management consultancies, regularly publishes its FDI Confidence Index, which is "constructed using primary data from a proprietary survey administered to senior executives of the world's 1,000 largest corporations."[75] The countries at the top of this list are considered to have a level of technological development sufficient to attract FDI in R&D. According the 2006 rating, Eastern Europe is "viewed positively as an R&D location, offering both low costs and strong scientific and engineering capabilities. Nearly one-third of global investors are planning R&D-oriented FDI in Eastern Europe over the next three years."[76] Among the leading EMCs in this evaluation are China, India, Poland, Russia, Brazil, Hong Kong, and Hungary.

When strategists have to decide about the location of an investment, one of the key aspects of technological risk to consider is the availability of specific natural resources and work power. For example, a large and steady source of water is necessary for chemical production, as it is a very water-intensive process. The production of aluminum is energy intensive, so obviously, a reliable source of energy is needed. As a result, quite frequently, aluminum production facilities are located not in the country in which the natural resources—bauxite and nefelin—are found, but where energy sources are cheaper and more widely available. Car or machinery assembly plants require a cheap low-skilled workforce, while software and high-tech industries require specifically trained, highly educated profes-sionals. Existing production facilities should also be strategically examined to see if they can be harmonized within the production process of the potential direct investment. If the production process requires highly enriched raw materials, the quality of the products of local enrichment facilities may not be acceptable for companies from developed countries. For example, an EMC may have mines that are much richer sources of metals than in any developed country, but the product of the local enrichment facilities creates raw materials with too much sulfur. This would require additional capital to build an agglomerated factory to remove the sulfur from the raw material, substantially increasing costs.

Indicators of technological development that influence technological risk include (among others): numbers of scientists and scholars per 1,000 people; government and private fund-ing of research and development; access to scientific and technological information; quality of research labs, facilities, and science and technological parks; commercial applications of scientific and technological advancements; and penetration of low and high technologies. Many technological risk indicators are directly related to the quality of the country's educa-tion system. Others derive from political risk, such as the interruption of education by civilian disobedience, issues of gender equality, vulnerability to cyber terrorism, fraud, hacking, etc. Many indicators are related to cultural norms and attitudes toward innovative technologies. There are several other factors that determine technological risk, such as regional climates. The climates of EMCs vary much more than those of developed countries in Western Europe and North America. In the GEM, production could occur above the Arctic Circle in Russia, in the tropical conditions of Latin America or Africa, or even extreme desert conditions, such as in Saudi Arabia or Mongolia. All of these climates require a regionalization of production processes specifically suited to the local environment.

Equipment that is not designed for extreme conditions will not operate efficiently, if at all. Certain metal products that function properly in the moderate conditions of Florida or France would be destroyed after only a few minutes of use in northern Siberia, Inner Mongolia of China, or the southernmost parts of Argentina in the winter. Cars that are suitable for New York or Moscow are not efficient or safe in desert areas and require substantial mechanical alterations. In order to exploit a huge, rich coal basin in Siberia, for example, special equipment is required, such as excavators or draglines that can move several thousand tons of coal per hour. In moderate areas of the US, Europe, and Asia, this extremely powerful equipment is inefficient. Strategists should be aware that the implementation of equipment of such capacity in any of these regions would nearly bankrupt a company: natural resources are not as large and rich as they are in the extreme climates of parts of the GEM. The process of modernizing equipment according to regional specific conditions is called technological regionalization (see Chapter 3). The most successful FDI in the GEM tailors cutting-edge global technology and management systems to exploit local conditions and opportunities.

Manual labor's share of the total labor force is rapidly decreasing in the GEM. This trend already occurred in developed countries, which are of course more technologically advanced. As the level of technological development continues to improve in the GEM, manual labor's share of the total workforce will continue to decrease, which also decreases technological risk. This is especially the case in EMCs outside of economies in bloom, which are already technologically advanced. Over the last century, manual labor's share of global work power has decreased by more than three times. Companies from technologically advanced EMCs are already competing with their counterparts in developed countries. Increased competition from the GEM forces companies based in developed countries to invest heavily to maintain or regain their technological edge.

In general, the GEM is far behind developed countries in terms of technological maturity, which is the cause of its higher levels of technological risk. There are a few exceptions in certain industries, such as Brazil's ethanol industry, nuclear and space industries in Russia, and IT services in India. However, the national economies of developed countries are much more technologically advanced than any EMC. The level of technological development of a national economy is a major determinant of a country's competitive advantage and technological risk. In order to reduce technological risk for FDI, it is important for EMCs that are not technologically advanced to develop national strategies to stimulate investment (domestic and foreign) in high-tech sectors and companies as well as the development of national educational programs. Foreigners investing in high-tech industries should receive special treatment, as should technologically advanced domestic companies. The development of domestic companies and universities specializing in high-tech industries requires preferential treatment by the national government. A certain level of protectionism is needed for countries to jumpstart their technological development.

Despite the fact that technology and other fixed assets in the GEM are nowhere near as modern as those in developed countries, EMCs have demonstrated a much higher speed in the implementation of technological achievements, which has important implications for technological risk. According to the 2008 World Bank Report *Technology Diffusion in the Developing World*, during the last decade of the twentieth century, Chile, Hungary, and Poland increased the level of technological achievement by more than 125 percent. In general, lower- and middle-income countries have a higher speed of technological development than high-income countries. Nonetheless, a wide gap in the use of modern technologies is still in place—higher-income countries are far ahead of middle- and lower-income countries. The greatest disparity is related to the use of patents, followed by the use of tractors and rural sanitation, and mobile ITs. There is also a significant gap between urban and rural areas in EMCs. According to the World Bank, "the IT-enabled services sector in urban India employs world-class technologies, but less than 10 percent of the country's rural households have telephone access as of 2007."[77] Among EMCs, disparity in the use of basic technologies from developed countries is being reduced at a substantially faster rate than disparities in the use of high-tech, cutting-edge technologies. This has important implications for technological risk of FDI related to high technologies. Access to industrial infrastructure is an important characteristic that determines the extent to which many basic technologies are implemented in the GEM. While transportation infrastructure in Russia and China is far behind countries of Latin America and the Indian subcontinent, Russia is ahead of the overwhelming majority of other EMCs in terms of access to electrical grids. In rural areas of sub-Saharan Africa and some Asian countries, such as Myanmar, less than 10 percent of the population has access to electricity. P-EMCs have much less access to the Internet and personal computers compared with economies in bloom and emerging-market democracies. The use of technology, both cutting-edge and basic, is largely correlated to the internationalization of an economy. According to the same World Bank report, "the high-tech business processes, products and services that flow into a country through foreign trade, foreign direct investment (FDI), and contact with migrant populations living abroad offer the critical exposure required to jumpstart technological diffusion."[78]

The World Bank uses the indicator *total factor productivity* to demonstrate the role of technological advancement. According to this indicator, since 1990 the most significant technological progress occurred in countries of Southeast Asia, followed by European and Central Asian EMCs. The least amount of technological progress during this period occurred in Latin American, the Caribbean, and sub-Saharan countries.[79] Among EMCs, the most attractive for technologically oriented FDI are those that are already technological leaders not only within the GEM, but also in the GMP, such as Taiwan, Israel, India, South Korea, and the Czech Republic. According to an evaluation of FDI projects dedicated to R&D as a share of total number of FDI projects by OCO Consulting Ltd (http://www.ococonsulting.com/), a leading provider of information on foreign investment, a few EMCs that are quite technologically advanced are not among the leaders. It is especially surprising that Russia, which is technologically advanced in many areas, is not one of the higher ranked EMCs. There are two explanations for this. Some EMCs, such as Russia, do not aggressively seek FDI in high technology and even restrict it in sectors of its economy that it considers to be of strategic national importance. Also, other sectors of the economy attract massive FDI inflows, making the share of FDI projects dedicated to R&D less significant. Both of these explanations are relevant to FDI in Brazil, Russia, and Kazakhstan. Brazil is the leading recipient of FDI related to R&D in Latin America. What may also be surprising for strategists evaluating the African market is that technologically intensive FDI projects in Morocco have surpassed those in South Africa. At the beginning of the twenty-first century, technology-related FDI started to play an important role in middle-income countries, where its average role in the GEM is more than 3 percent of GDP. Modern technology is a major vehicle for bringing non-developed countries out of poverty and is one of the most important factors in the process of improving standards of living and economic development.

Information Technology in the Global Emerging Market

An analysis of telecommunications is usually conducted during the development of the entry strategy. Some preliminary evaluations can be made as early as during the development of strategic scenarios. However, in EMCs, where telecommunication infrastructure is more of a vital issue due to delayed technological development, it is strategically appropriate to analyze telecommunications and IT during the study of technological risk. In response to a lack of fixed lines and low levels of personal-computer penetration, EMCs are implementing very sophisticated national IT strategies. The rate of growth of these new technologies is unprecedented. An evaluation of 16 EMCs by the Forrester Research Institute estimates that personal-computer penetration will grow by more than 30 percent annually until 2010 in the GEM.[80] The study cited China, India, Mexico, and Indonesia as the most promising personal-computer markets. Use of mobile phones in the GEM is growing at an even faster pace than that of personal computers. In India, the number of cell phones is projected to increase from 93 million (9 percent penetration) in 2006, to 278 million (a little more than 25 percent penetration) in 2010.[81] Technological risk is closely correlated to access to information and telecommunication technology. The consulting firm, Ops A La Carte suggests an efficient manner by which to analyze technological risk: "the identification, categorization and prioritization of hardware and software threats to achieving key reliability business objectives."[82] This approach can be used for strategic evaluation of FDI in this industry, but it has to be understood within the context of the specific international financial and economic transactions with the GEM. The changing nature of the use of mobile phones has important implications for technological risk. The conversion of GSM (Global System for Mobile communication) to Third Generation (3G) networks is facilitating the convergence of personal-computer and mobile phone functions, as is the increasing sophistication of mobile software applications. These developments provide broadband flexibility and increasing connectivity.

In absolute numbers, the GEM recently overcame developed countries in terms of fixed lines and mobile phone usage. China Mobile Communications Corporation is the largest provider of mobile phone services, with more than 350 million subscribers.[83] China also has the most fixed and mobile lines in the world. Initially, telecom companies targeted major capitals of EMCs, but as competition increases, they are beginning to expand into more remote regions. Nokia is expanding its activity from the Pacific Coast and southeastern region of China, to its least developed provinces. In 2005 it signed a deal worth $150 million with a subsidiary of China Mobile Communications Corporation to expand mobile telecommunication networks in the central province of Henan.[84] China is Nokia's largest market. It has partnered with Baidu.com, a Chinese-language search engine to improve the Internet capabilities of its phones. As of 2008, according to the International Telecommunications Union, there are more than three billion people with mobile phones in the world. During that year, mobile phone usage grew by approximately 80 percent in China, India, Southeast Asia, and Africa.[85] Nokia's focus on EMCs made it the leading mobile phone supplier in China, India, and the world.

The penetration of mobile telephones, as with all modern technologies, varies to a great extent throughout the GEM, which complicates strategic analyses of technological risk. According to an evaluation made by the OECD, there are four EMCs with a higher penetration of mobile phones than the United States: Portugal, Czech Republic, South Korea, and Poland.[86] The leading country by this indicator in Latin America is Mexico. All of these statistics are important not only for strategists from the telecom industry, but also for all businesses that are technology, service, trade, and tourism oriented. Between 2000 and 2005, five of the biggest EMCs (China, India, Brazil, Russia, and South Africa) annually increased spending on information and communication technologies by 19 percent—reaching $277 billion combined in 2005—compared to a 5.6 percent average for member countries of the OECD.[87]

For national strategists, in order expedite a country's technological and economic progress, Internet access for the general population and businesses should increase. This requires governments and government-related funds, especially in big EMCs, to allocate substantial capital to develop Internet and telecom infrastructure. Among EMCs, there is a great deal of variation in Internet penetration. Some, such as Hong Kong and Singapore, have a higher penetration rate than most developed countries (see Figure 8.12). Most, however, are far behind the developed world. In general, Internet usage is developing in the world proportionally to the scale of regional populations. This explains why Asia is the leading region in terms of total Internet users, and the Middle East and Australia have considerably fewer users. The only surprise is that Asia has already surpassed the most developed regions—Europe and North America—in terms of total Internet users.[88] In terms of penetration, Asia is actually behind the Middle East and Latin America, which is the leading emerging-market region by Internet penetration.[89] This was possible to predict as early as 1997–1998, when the Internet received tremendous attention in Argentinean and Brazilian universities and research centers. Among the emerging markets of Europe, the most rapid growth rate of Internet users was demonstrated by Russia, followed by Spain and Ireland, with a growth rate four times faster than the EU average as of September 2007.[90]

The most practical and important use of IT innovations is the development of e-commerce. The birth of this new business and economic phenomenon can be traced back to 1984, when the Electronic Data Interchange was standardized, allowing companies and consumers to utilize the Internet. But on a practical level, e-commerce began in 1995, when two major players in this market—Amazon and eBay—became active. Four years later, global e-commerce sales reached the $20 billion milestone. In 2003 Amazon.com turned an annual profit for the first time. The rapid development of e-commerce is also related to the moratorium by the majority of countries of an Internet sales tax. In EMCs, e-business is developing in all directions: business to business, business to consumer, business to government, and even consumer to consumer. The e-commerce market has expanded from $2.6 billion in 1996 to roughly $1 trillion at the beginning of 2008. In the GEM, e-commerce is still in the early stages of development due to problems related to technological infrastructure, cultural traditions, and high levels of criminal activity.

Strategists making a comparison between different countries through the lens of the

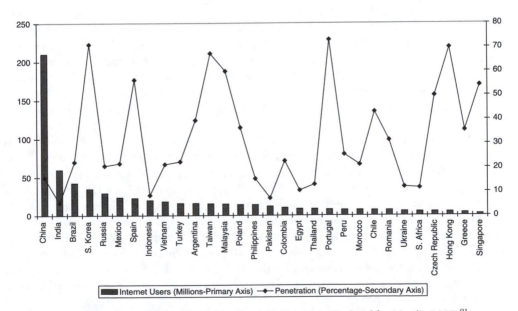

Figure 8.12 Internet Users in the GEM, Total and Penetration (Ordered by Total), 2007.[91]

expenses versus time ratio have to take into consideration the fact that in the GEM, the process of implementing modern technologies goes much faster. This can be explained by companies' ability to hire more qualified employees for much lower remuneration. For example, the average remuneration for IT managers in EMCs such as China, India, and Vietnam as of 2008 reached the median level of $26,000, compared with Switzerland, where the figure is $140,000, and about $105,000 in the United States.[92] The dynamics of technological development in the GEM, as well as increasing education levels and economic integration among EMCs and within the GMP, indicate that technological risk of FDI in the GEM will steadily decrease.

Foreign Direct Investment from the Global Emerging Market to Developed Countries

As the GEM continued to mature, at the beginning of the twenty-first century, an interesting trend appeared—an outflow of FDI from EMCs to developed countries. There are four economic reasons for this. The first is related to fluctuations and instability of FDI in the GEM. The second is the increasing power of domestic companies (with or without FDI) and industries in the GEM whose leaders feel that they are ready to play a more central role in the GMP. The third reason is primarily related to governmental and state-controlled semi-private companies that, for political reasons, are implementing strategies to invest in the developed world. Finally, there is a fourth reason—some EMCs have to deal with reversals of economic maturity, which causes private interests to relocate capital out of the country in order to protect it.

The outflow of FDI from the GEM to the US offers an illustration of these four reasons. In the first three quarters of 2007, Venezuela was the no. 1 Latin American source of FDI in the US. The reason for this was the reversal of progress in the country as a result of President Hugo Chavez' attempt to not only become the lifetime president, but also his initiation of the nationalization and expropriation of private domestic and foreign assets. This process in Venezuela has become a major concern not only for businesses from developed countries, but also for those from other EMCs, such as Brazil. The Venezuelan government nationalized the assets of several Brazilian companies without any internationally recognized legal basis. In order to protect themselves and their financial well-being, domestic private companies began to sell their assets and convert their profits to FDI in a stable and protected environment such as the US, EU, or other developed countries. However, government-related direct investment from Venezuela at the end of 2007 moved in the opposite direction. As a result, the annual balance of FDI from Venezuela for 2007 was actually negative.

A huge investment to the US economy from Bermuda and to Bermuda from the US is of a different economic nature. It is mostly a reinvestment of US money that left the country, for many reasons, including tax evasion. As of 2007 the United States had a negative balance of capital flows with Bermuda. Manufacturing facilities in the US based on FDI from the GEM are often more successful than their US rivals. A strategic analysis indicates that this increases the enthusiasm of other similar EMC companies to invest in the US. At the end of the twentieth century, while the Big Three car manufacturers of the US were struggling to keep their factories open, companies from South Korea and even China successfully opened car-manufacturing facilities in the US. Largely as a result, US market share of the Big Three decreased from 73 percent in 1980 to less than 50 percent in 2008. The main benefactors from this process have been consumers in developed countries. From 1990 to 2003, the overall consumer price index in the US increased by 53 percent, while the average price of a car grew by only 13.4 percent.[93]

Different strategic principles apply to Lukoil gas stations, which are prevalent throughout the East Coast of the United States, especially in New York and Pennsylvania. One may think that this is a result of increasing delivery of Russian oil to the US. This is not the case. Lukoil works primarily with oil from the same refinery plants as all other US gas stations. There are three possible reasons for Lukoil's expansion into the US market. One explanation is the desire of its owners to decrease risks to their fortune by investing it in one of the most protected and safe parts of the world, where private property ownership is one of the major priorities of the law. The second reason is related to a corporate strategy to position itself as an international player. As of 2008 Lukoil has penetrated the markets of 13 US states with ownership of about 2,000 facilities.[94] The third reason may be explained by the national interest of Russia to increase its role in the GMP and demonstrate its economic maturity around the world. For this reason, it gave special attention to the global hegemon. These motivations can be found behind the actions of other Russian companies, which are buying oil refineries and/or electrical distribution systems in Italy and other European countries. An obvious example of this is the state-controlled natural gas monopoly—Gazprom. Another interesting fact is that FDI from Russia to Canada is seven times higher than Canadian investment to Russia. An analysis of this investment indicates that it is the result of all of the four factors of FDI outflow from the GEM mentioned previously. Chinese companies adopted a similar strategy of purchasing oil facilities in the US; however, US government restrictions prevented them from coming to fruition. One better-documented case of the US blocking a strategic investment from a partially state-owned firm occurred when a company from Dubai with long-term experience of managing seaports unsuccessfully tried to acquire seaport facilities in the US. The reasons for the concerns of the US government were discomfort with the idea of a company from the Middle East—the region of the world from where most terrorist activity has originated—operating the sea gateway to America. For similar reasons, leaders of several developed countries, members of the G8, are opposed to sovereign wealth funds of EMCs being used as a major source of investment in strategically important companies. Not surprisingly, leaders from Russia, China, and some other EMCs do not see these as legitimate concerns. In the words of Russia's minister of finance, "the investment of sovereign wealth funds should be subject to the general rules of the free movement of capital."[95]

In other cases, this investment is dictated by pure economic factors, such as increasing vertical integration or the development of a distribution network. Other benign motivations exist. The Russian nuclear atomic state agency Rosatom is one of the largest buyers of uranium from Canada. In November 2007 the head of Rosatom, Sergey Kirienko (former prime minister of Russia under President Yeltsin), said:

> We have signed an agreement to establish two joint ventures. Diversification of uranium supplies is extremely important for Russia. We want not only to get uranium from Canada, but also we want to have an opportunity to invest in production of uranium in Canada.[96]

Strategists have to be cognizant of the fact that political and business leaders from EMCs eventually may succeed in their quest to establish equal treatment of FDI outflows in various forms from their countries to the developed world.

For developed countries, FDI from the GEM is often strategically important, especially for those countries with foreign trade and budget deficits. These deficits are partially financed by FDI inflows. Historically, these deficits were balanced by an increase in domestic investment. At the beginning of the twenty-first century, with the growing economic capability of the GEM, businesses from developed countries began to look abroad for financial solutions. The situation in the US is an obvious illustration of this point.

Foreign investment from the GEM plays a crucial role in the financing of the US current account and budget deficits.

As of 2008, FDI inflows to developed countries are still higher than inflows to the GEM. Despite subprime-mortgage issues and the slowdown in US real estate, the political and relative economic stability of the United States since 2003 has led investment strategists to recommend channeling FDI to the US. The $237.5 billion worth of FDI inflow to the US in 2007 was an increase of more than 35 percent from the previous year.[97] Since 2000, and especially after 9/11, FDI and domestic investment were fleeing the US market. The large inflow of FDI that began in 2003–2004 was definitely influenced by the absence of any major terrorist attack on US soil since the tragedy of 2001. The situation with FDI in the US signifies general trends in the twenty-first century: *investment goes to stable countries, with low terrorist activity, lack of breaches of contract by governments, freely or limitedly convertible currencies, and a high level of potential return under moderate risk.*

The importance of direct investment from foreign countries is usually underappreciated. For example, the role of FDI outflows from the United States can be better understood when strategists keep in mind that the return on US investments abroad is larger than all US foreign debt, which means that this investment is quite efficient. US investment abroad outpaces foreign investment in the US. Nonetheless, companies from EMCs are playing an increasingly key role as sources of foreign investment in the United States. Among the leading EMCs in terms of acquisition of US targets are Russia, United Arab Emirates, India, Saudi Arabia, Israel, and Brazil. Surprisingly, during some years (such as 2006), the small but wealthy United Arab Emirates invested more in the United States than Hong Kong, Singapore, Mexico, South Korea, or Brazil. However, out of the top 10 major acquisitions of US companies by foreign investors, three came from two EMCs: Singapore and Spain.[98] The role of China in terms of FDI in acquisitions to the United States was insignificant as of 2006. However, during 2007 this situation changed. This trend will continue due to the fact that in 2008 the US and Chinese governments agreed to develop an "an investment treaty that would guarantee access for the nations' companies to buy assets in the other country."[99] This agreement will prevent incidences such as what occurred in 2005, when China's biggest offshore state-controlled oil company, Cnooc, tried to buy the subsidiary of Unocal Corporation from California for $18.5 billion, but was prevented from doing so by US Congress.[100] The Chinese government has a long-term strategy to invest in key countries and key industries to gain access to oil and gas, non-ferrous metals, coal, freshwater, and major sea ports. Western Europe saw first hand the growing clout of Russia, as Gazprom so frightened the European leaders with its aggressive acquisition of several gas distribution and oil refinery plants that the EU began to develop regulations to prevent foreign providers of oil and gas from owning distribution infrastructure. When Tata Group, an Indian conglomerate, and CSN, a Brazilian company, competed for control of Corus, a British–Dutch steel producer, it was the first time that two companies from the GEM had fought over control of a Western European company. Figures 8.13, 8.14, and 8.15 represent the dynamics of GEM acquisitions of companies in the United States by investor country of origin from 2006 to the first half of 2008.

One of the most profound examples of a fund from the GEM investing in a banking institution of a developed country took place when the biggest bank in the US (in terms of assets) Citigroup Inc. received a $7.5 billion cash infusion from the Abu Dhabi Investment Authority, acquiring 4.9 percent of Citigroup stock, becoming its largest shareholder.[101]

The same incentives that lead strategic investors of companies from the GEM to the US have led them to target well-developed Western European markets. In 2006, out of $41.5 billion in acquisitions in Western Europe by companies from the GEM, 33.2 percent were from India, and almost 13 percent was from United Arab Emirates. Not far behind these

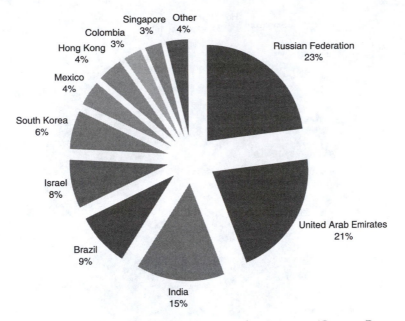

Figure 8.13 Acquisitions of US Targets by Emerging-market Investors (Country Percentage Share), 2006.

Source: © Dealogic (www.dealogic.com).

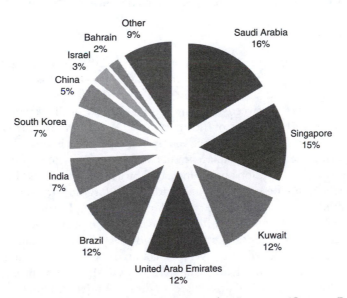

Figure 8.14 Acquisitions of US Targets by Emerging-market Investors (Country Percentage Share), 2007.

Source: © Dealogic (www.dealogic.com).

countries were Russia (12.6 percent), Singapore (11 percent), and South Africa (9.5 percent). China was not a leading country in terms of its acquisition of European targets, accounting for only 3.3 percent of Western European targets.[102] It is strategically possible to expect that Chinese investment in the EU will increase.

In 2004, EMC acquisitions abroad (not only in developed countries), were worth almost

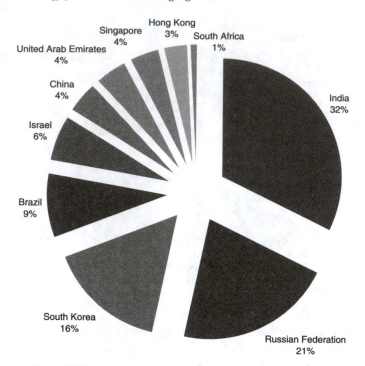

Figure 8.15 Acquisitions of US Targets by Emerging-market Investors (Country Percentage Share), 2008.

Source: © Dealogic (www.dealogic.com).

$55 billion, in 2005 almost $120 billion, and in 2006 (as of November), about $180 billion.[103] Strategists of companies from EMCs have crafted winning strategies for developed markets and have demonstrated that they can indeed compete with well-established investors. Between 1990 and 2005, outflow of FDI from EMCs to service sectors aboard increased by a factor of 72. In 1990, FDI outflow stock from the GEM was roughly $11.62 billion to overseas service industries. By 2005 this number reached about $831 billion. During the same period, accumulative foreign investment from EMCs to food, beverages, and tobacco production abroad increased by a factor of 5.7 and by a factor of 17 in overseas production of textiles, clothing, and leather. The largest growth in investment from the GEM is related to business services, which increased by a factor of 347 from 1990 to 2005.[104] This surge of FDI outflow is further proof of the maturation of businesses in the GEM. With increasing experience of strategists and executives, companies from EMCs are investing more and more heavily in developed countries. One unintended but significant side effect was a loss of potential investment in the GEM. Capital of entrepreneurs and companies from EMCs, which could be used to decrease unemployment and poverty and reduce migration from GEM countries, is itself migrating, which can also be understood as an indication of the maturation of strategic investors in the GEM. Figure 8.16 shows FDI outflow by category of country between 1991 and 2006.

Corporate and governmental strategists from EMCs found it very efficient to pursue soft targets in other EMCs and even in developing countries, the conditions of which they are much more accustomed to than their competitors from developed countries. For this reason, investment banks and large companies from the GEM are also acquiring entities in other EMCs and developing countries. The Abu Dhabi Investment Authority (ADIA) established an emerging-markets department and invests a significant amount of Abu Dhabi's petrodol-

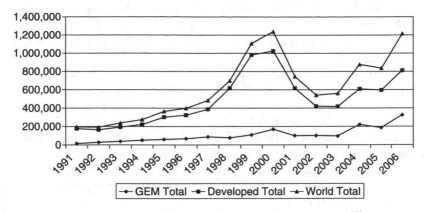

Figure 8.16 FDI Outflow by Category of Country (Millions, $), 1991–2006.[105]

Source: © Dr Vladimir Kvint, 2008.

lars into the GEM. The ADIA has been a strategic investor in privatization in Saudi Arabia, Kuwait, and Tunisia,[106] all Arab/Maghrib countries with moderate political regimes and stable economies. Executives of the ADIA clearly have a preference for business climates with which they are already well acquainted. The same applies to the Chinese cross-border investment strategy. Despite the heavy media coverage of the attempted Chinese acquisitions of US companies, the majority of Chinese investment is in the GEM. One of China's biggest investments was the 2005 purchase of PetroKazakhstan by China National Petroleum Corporation for $4.2 billion. Kazakhstan is a very attractive recipient of FDI from other EMCs as well. Several Middle Eastern countries have made significant investments in the banking and service sectors of this Central Asian country.

With the birth of the GEM, FDI became a global phenomenon. FDI does not only bring new technologies, modern managerial skills, employment, and increased development of markets for national products. Most important, FDI, through its various organizational vehicles, brings peace and stability to markets of new opportunities. According to professors Ceyla Pazarbaşıoğlu, Mangal Goswami, and Jack Ree:

> Aside from the institutional money and banking finance, foreign direct investment (FDI) originating from mature market countries has also partially recovered since the bursting of the dot-com bubble. FDI inflows to emerging markets have been increasing but remain largely concentrated, with China accounting for about 50 percent of emerging market flows since 2002. Among the emerging markets, Asia-Pacific and emerging Europe are the leading recipients of FDI, while inflows to Latin America, dominated by Brazil, have fallen since 2000.[107]

When foreign investments are made in volatile parts of the world, it plays two key functions: it provides proof that it is possible to cooperate with or within a territory, and it brings international and global cooperation to the people of this land. The success of FDI in the GMP has developed a better environment for multilateral institutions to address truly global issues, a function that they have yet to fulfill. Foreign investment builds bridges between nations.

Study Questions

1. Describe the major economic incentives that lead companies and entrepreneurs to go overseas.
2. Describe the major reasons for national and regional governments to encourage foreign companies to make direct investments.
3. What are the differences between FDI and foreign portfolio investment?
4. Describe the economic nature of FDI.
5. How do the inflow and outflow of FDI indicate the business and socioeconomic climate of a country?
6. Describe the major organizational forms of FDI.
7. Describe the economic correlation between domestic competition, investment overseas, and outsourcing.
8. Describe the cumulative economic and social effects of FDI on the recipient country.
9. Why are China and India among the leading recipients of FDI and outsourcing?
10. At what point does FDI become a significant economic factor for the recipient country?
11. How do currency exchange rates influence the dynamics of FDI?
12. Describe the major stages of a risk-management system.
13. Describe the differences between systematic and unsystematic risk.
14. Can systematic risk be managed?
15. What are the major rating agencies that should be consulted during the development of FDI strategy?
16. Why should outside sources be consulted? What should strategists do when confronted with conflicting opinions from ratings agencies?
17. How should strategists begin an investment risk analysis?
18. Describe the emerging-market risk system.
19. What is political risk? How is it related to the recipient countries of FDI?
20. What is a greenfield FDI project?
21. Where do investment banks and insurance companies fit in to decisions about FDI?
22. Describe the major integrated indicators of political risk of investment.
23. What agencies provide political risk insurance for FDI?
24. How do political risk insurance providers evaluate the level of risk of FDI?
25. How is political risk classified and evaluated?
26. How does the national currency of an EMC affect political risk?
27. What is a breach of contract?
28. How does international terrorism affect FDI flows?
29. What can cause a reversal in the progress of a country's level of political risk?
30. Describe what can draw FDI to countries in states of war.
31. What is economic risk of investment?
32. Describe the similarities and differences between economic and political risk of investment.
33. How is economic risk of investment related to democracy, freedom, and stability in a potential FDI destination?
34. Describe the major factors of economic risk of investment.
35. How is economic risk of investment related to the industrial infrastructure of a potential FDI destination?
36. What is the Paris Club? How is it related to economic risk of investment?

37. Describe the correlation between economic risk and economic crimes such as corruption and rackets.
38. How is economic risk related to social infrastructure and the educational system of a potential FDI recipient?
39. How does a country's membership in economic multilateral institutions influence economic risk of investment?
40. Describe the relationship between the dynamics of labor productivity and income inequality and the correlations with economic risk of investment.
41. How are intellectual property rights related to economic risk of investment?
42. How are natural disasters classified as a risk factor of FDI?
43. Describe the major characteristics of unsystematic risk of investment.
44. Describe the business risk of FDI.
45. Describe the major characteristics of production risk.
46. How are production risk, product risk, and financial risk related?
47. Describe the major indicators of financial risk.
48. For what type of company are product risk and financial risk the same risk?
49. Describe the major elements of the international business infrastructure of EMCs and how it influences foreign investor's strategic decision-making process?
50. What is the difference between international business infrastructure and capital market infrastructure in an EMC?
51. How does currency emission and inflation influence business risk?
52. Describe the BRIC and/or BRICS grouping and the relationship among these countries? Do they qualify as a regional economic organization?
53. How do the dynamics of M2 influence profit expectations of FDI-based companies?
54. What are the advantages and disadvantages of FDI in food production in the GEM?
55. Describe the specifics of banking activity in relation to cash in EMCs.
56. How does the cash economy influence business risk of investment?
57. Describe the specifics of the credit strategies of foreign banks in EMCs.
58. How do regional currency unions influence FDI dynamics?
59. What are the major challenges for capital markets in the GEM?
60. How does the development of capital market institutions affect corruption and other economic crimes in non-developed countries?
61. Describe the major means of foreign portfolio investors to acquire shares of GEM companies.
62. Describe the relationship between GEM companies and international stock exchanges.
63. Describe the relationship between ADR and the development of capital markets in the GEM.
64. How has the formation of the GEM influenced the development of derivatives of international instruments?
65. Describe the technological risk of FDI.
66. Describe the major indicators of technological risk of investment in an EMC and the approach of different agencies to its evaluation.
67. Describe the difference between country recipients of FDI and cross-border investors regarding technological risk.
68. Describe the dynamics and economic role of GEM FDI in developed countries.
69. Describe the four reasons that drive the FDI outflow from the GEM to developed countries.
70. Describe the major obstacles for FDI from the GEM into developed countries.

Notes

Epigraph

1. Aurelius Antoninus Augustus, Marcus. (2000). *Mediations*. Chestnut Hill, MA: Adamant Media Corporation. p. 106.

Introduction: A Path to Strategy

1. Kvint, Vladimir. (1990, October 28). Opportunities in Soviet Disintegration. *The New York Times*. Retrieved July 14, 2008 from http://query.nytimes.com/gst/fullpage.html?res=9C0CE1D91731F93BA15753C1A966958260.
2. Kvint, Vladimir. (1990, February 19). Russia Should Quit the Soviet Union: Rusia as Cinderalla. *Forbes*. pp. 103–108.

1   A Strategic Evaluation of the Global Marketplace

1. Rucker, Rudolf. (1977). *Geometry, Relativity and the Fourth Dimension*. Mineola, NY: Dover Publications. p. 118.
2. Saroyan, William. (1968). *I Used to Believe I Had Forever, Now I'm Not So Sure*. Spokane, WA: Cowles. p. 166.
3. Compiled on the base of data from Maddison, Angus. (2001). *The World Economy: A Millennial Perspective*. Paris: Organization for Economic Cooperation and Development. Retrieved December 27, 2007 from http://www.theworldeconomy.org/publications/worldeconomy/MaddisontableB-18.pdf.
4. Compiled on the base of data from The World Bank World Development Indicators. Retrieved January 3, 2008 from http://econ.worldbank.org/WBSITE/EXTERNAL/EXTDEC/0,,menuPK:476823~pagePK:64165236~piPK:64165141~theSitePK:469372,00.html.
5. Compiled on the base of data from The World Bank World Development Indicators. Retrieved January 3, 2008 from http://econ.worldbank.org/WBSITE/EXTERNAL/EXTDEC/0,,menuPK:476823~pagePK:64165236~piPK:64165141~theSitePK:469372,00.html.
6. Kalter, Eliot. (2008, January). Local Capital Markets: Emerging Market Investment Opportunities. Executive Summary. Medford, MA: Center for Emerging Market Enterprises.
7. Compiled on the base of data from The World Bank World Development Indicators. Retrieved February 1, 2008 from http://econ.worldbank.org/WBSITE/EXTERNAL/EXTDEC/0,,menuPK:476823~pagePK:64165236~piPK:64165141~theSitePK:469372,00.html.
8. Siebert, Horst. (2002). *The World Economy Second Edition*. London: Routledge. p. i.
9. The World Bank. (2008). *Global Economic Prospects 2008: Technology Diffusion in the Developing World*. Retrieved February 19, 2008 from http://econ.worldbank.org/WBSITE/EXTERNAL/EXTDEC/EXTDECPROSPECTS/GEPEXT/EXTGEP2008/0,,contentMDK:21603834~isCURL:Y~noSURL:Y~pagePK:64167689~piPK:64167673~theSitePK:4503324,00.html.
10. Maddison, Angus. (2001). *The World Economy: A Millennial Perspective*. Paris: Organization for Economic Cooperation and Development. p. 19.
11. Mandelson, Peter. (2008, February 8). Alcuin lecture. Retrieved February 19, 2008 from http://ec.europa.eu/commission_barroso/mandelson/.
12. EU NGOs. (2007, July). Indian helicopters for Myanmar. Amnesty International UK and

Saferworld. Retrieved January 12, 2008 from http://www.saferworld.org.uk/publications.php/270/indian_helicopters_for_myanmar_.

13. Mehta, Stephanie N. (2007, August 20). Carlos Slim, the Richest Man in the World. *Fortune*. Retrieved January 4, 2008 from http://money.cnn.com/2007/08/03/news/international/carlosslim.fortune/index.htm.

14. Compiled on the base of data from The World Bank World Development Indicators. Retrieved January 25, 2008 from http://econ.worldbank.org/WBSITE/EXTERNAL/EXTDEC/0,,menuPK:476823~pagePK:64165236~piPK:64165141~theSitePK:469372,00.html.

15. Compiled on the base of data from The World Bank World Development Indicators. Retrieved January 25, 2008 from http://econ.worldbank.org/WBSITE/EXTERNAL/EXTDEC/0,,menuPK:476823~pagePK:64165236~piPK:64165141~theSitePK:469372,00.html.

16. Compiled on the base of data from The World Bank World Development Indicators. Retrieved January 25, 2008 from http://econ.worldbank.org/WBSITE/EXTERNAL/EXTDEC/0,,menuPK:476823~pagePK:64165236~piPK:64165141~theSitePK:469372,00.html.

17. Calculations based on statistics from the World Bank World Development Indicators, 2007 retrieved July 15, 2008 from http://econ.worldbank.org/WBSITE/EXTERNAL/EXTDEC/0,,menuPK:476823~pagePK:64165236~piPK:64165141~theSitePK:469372,00.html.

18. Compiled on the base of data from The World Bank World Development Indicators. Retrieved January 15, 2008 from http://econ.worldbank.org/WBSITE/EXTERNAL/EXTDEC/0,,menuPK:476823~pagePK:64165236~piPK:64165141~theSitePK:469372,00.html.

19. Compiled on the base of data from The World Bank World Development Indicators. Retrieved January 15, 2008 from http://econ.worldbank.org/WBSITE/EXTERNAL/EXTDEC/0,,menuPK:476823~pagePK:64165236~piPK:64165141~theSitePK:469372,00.html.

20. Compiled on the base of data from The World Bank World Development Indicators. Retrieved January 15, 2008 from http://econ.worldbank.org/WBSITE/EXTERNAL/EXTDEC/0,,menuPK:476823~pagePK:64165236~piPK:64165141~theSitePK:469372,00.html.

21. The International Comparison Program. 2005 International Comparison Program Preliminary Results. Retrieved December 30, 2007 from http://siteresources.worldbank.org/ICPINT/Resources/backgrounderFAQ.pdf.

22. The International Comparison Program. 2005 International Comparison Program Preliminary Results. Retrieved December 30, 2007 from http://siteresources.worldbank.org/ICPINT/Resources/backgrounderFAQ.pdf.

23. Elekdag, Selim and Lall, Subir. (2008, January 8). Global Growth Estimates Trimmed After PPP. *IMF Survey Magazine*. Retrieved January 19, 2008 from http://www.imf.org/external/pubs/ft/survey/so/2008/RES018A.htm.

24. Elekdag, Selim and Lall, Subir. (2008, January 8). Global Growth Estimates Trimmed After PPP. *IMF Survey Magazine*. Retrieved January 19, 2008 from http://www.imf.org/external/pubs/ft/survey/so/2008/RES018A.htm.

25. Bell, Daniel. (1999). *The Coming of the Post-Industrial Society*. New York: Basic Books. p. xcvi.

26. Compiled on the base of data from The World Bank World Development Indicators. Retrieved January 28, 2008 from http://econ.worldbank.org/WBSITE/EXTERNAL/EXTDEC/0,,menuPK:476823~pagePK:64165236~piPK:64165141~theSitePK:469372,00.html.

27. Compiled on the base of data from The World Bank World Development Indicators. Retrieved January 28, 2008 from http://econ.worldbank.org/WBSITE/EXTERNAL/EXTDEC/0,,menuPK:476823~pagePK:64165236~piPK:64165141~theSitePK:469372,00.html.

28. Vaknin, Sam. (2000, January 17). The Blessings of the Informal Economy. *Central Europe Review*. Retrieved January 13, 2008 from http://www.ce-review.org/00/40/vaknin40.html.

29. Gettman, Jon B. of the US Department of Health and Human Services quoted in *Forbes* March 26, 2007. p. 81.

30. Leontief, Wassily. (1986). *Input-Output Economics*. Oxford: Oxford University Press. 436 pgs.

31. Fontela, Emilio. (2004). Leontief and the Future of the World Economy. In *Wassily Leontief and Input-Output Economics*. Dietzenbacher, Erik and Lahr, Michael (eds). Cambridge: Cambridge University Press. p. 31.

32. Döös, Bo R. (2002, December). Population Growth and Loss of Arable Land. *Global Environmental Change* Vol. 12, No. 4. pp. 303–311.

33. The CIA World Factbook. Country Rank Area. Retrieved November 15, 2007 from https://www.cia.gov/library/publications/the-world-factbook/rankorder/2147rank.html.

34. Bold, Audrey. (2007). 440,000 m/day—SWRO Desalination Plants in Spain Saving Energy with PX Technology. Retrieved May 15, 2008 from http://www.energyrecovery.com/news/documents/440K_Spainaward%20PR_FINAL101107.pdf.

35. Food and Agriculture Organization of the United Nations. Aquastat. Retrieved July 14, 2008 from http://www.fao.org/nr/water/aquastat/dbase/index.stm.

36. Compiled on the base of data from the Aquastat database of the Food and Agriculture Organization of the United Nations, Aquastat. Retrieved January 10, 2008 from http://www.fao.org/nr/water/aquastat/main/index.stm.

37. Compiled on the base of data from the Aquastat database of the Food and Agriculture Organization of the United Nations. Retrieved January 10, 2008 from http://www.fao.org/nr/water/aquastat/main/index.stm.

38. Nile Basin Initiative. Retrieved January 6, 2008 from http://www.nilebasin.org/.

39. Compiled on the base of data from the Aquastat database of the Food and Agriculture Organization of the United Nations. Retrieved January 10, 2008 from http://www.fao.org/nr/water/aquastat/main/index.stm.

40. Energy Information Administration. International Total Primary Energy Consumption and Energy Intensity. Retrieved January 17, 2008 from http://www.eia.doe.gov/emeu/international/energyconsumption.html.

41. Compiled on the base of data from the Aquastat database of the Food and Agriculture Organization of the United Nations. Retrieved January 10, 2008 from http://www.fao.org/nr/water/aquastat/main/index.stm.

42. Sampson, Roy J. and Calmus, Thomas W. (1974). *Economics: Concepts Applications Analysis.* Boston: Houghton Mifflin Company. p. 384.

43. Compiled on the base of data from the Aquastat database of the Food and Agriculture Organization of the United Nations. Retrieved January 10, 2008 from http://www.fao.org/nr/water/aquastat/main/index.stm.

44. The International Monetary Fund. (2005). The World Economic Outlook 2005. p. 162 of Chapter 4. Retrieved May 7, 2008 from http://www.imf.org/external/pubs/ft/weo/2005/01/pdf/chapter4.pdf.

45. Compiled from several sources by the Energy Information Administration. Retrieved January 17, 2008 from http://www.eia.doe.gov/emeu/international/contents.html. PennWell Corporation. (2006, December 18). *Oil & Gas Journal*, except United States. Oil includes crude oil and condensate. Data for the United States are from the Energy Information Administration, US Crude Oil, Natural Gas, and Natural Gas Liquids Reserves, 2005 Annual Report, DOE/EIA-0216(2005) (November 2006). *Oil & Gas Journal*'s oil reserve estimate for Canada includes 5.2 billion barrels of conventional crude oil and condensate reserves and 174 billion barrels of oil sands reserves.

46. PennWell Corporation. (2006, December 18). *Oil & Gas Journal*, except United States. Oil includes crude oil and condensate. Data for the United States are from the Energy Information Administration, US Crude Oil, Natural Gas, and Natural Gas Liquids Reserves, 2005 Annual Report, DOE/EIA-0216(2005) (November 2006). *Oil & Gas Journal*'s oil reserve estimate for Canada includes 5.2 billion barrels of conventional crude oil and condensate reserves and 174 billion barrels of oil sands reserves.

47. Energy Information Administration. (2007, January 9). World Proved Reserves of Oil and Natural Gas, Most Recent Estimates. Retrieved January 12, 2008 from http://www.eia.doe.gov/emeu/international/Notes%20for%20Most%20Recent%20Estimates%20of%20Proved%20Oil%20and%20Natural%20Gas%20Reserves.html.

48. PennWell Corporation. (2006, December 18). *Oil & Gas Journal*, except United States. Data for the United States are from the Energy Information Administration, US Crude Oil, Natural Gas, and Natural Gas Liquids Reserves, 2005 Annual Report (November 2006). Department of Energy/Energy Information Administration IA-0216.

49. United States: Energy Information Administration. Unpublished file data of the Coal Reserves Data Base (April 2007). All Other Countries: World Energy Council, Survey of Energy Resources 2004, December 13, 2004.

50. Energy Information Administration. Country Analysis Briefs: Iran. Retrieved December 27, 2007 from http://www.eia.doe.gov/emeu/cabs/Iran/Oil.html.

51. International Energy Agency. Map of World Energy Production. Retrieved December 27, 2007 from http://www.iea.org/Textbase/country/maps/world/prod.htm.

52. International Energy Agency. Map of World Energy Production. Retrieved December 27, 2007 from http://www.iea.org/Textbase/country/maps/world/prod.htm.

53. International Energy Agency. (2007). *Key World Energy Statistics 2007*. p. 6. Retrieved January 3, 2008 from http://www.iea.org/textbase/nppdf/free/2007/key_stats_2007.pdf.

54. The White House. 2007 State of the Union: Twenty in Ten: Strengthening America's Energy

Security. Retrieved January 1, 2008 from http://www.whitehouse.gov/stateoftheunion/2007/initiatives/energy.html.

55. Energy Information Administration. International Energy Outlook 2007. Retrieved January 1, 2008 from http://www.eia.doe.gov/oiaf/ieo/highlights.html.

56. Based on data from the International Energy Agency. Retrieved January 1, 2007 from http://www.eia.doe.gov/fuelelectric.html with changes by the author.

57. Yardley, Jim. (2007, November 18). China Banks on Hydropower to Cut Emissions, but at Huge Human Cost. *The International Herald Tribune—Asia Pacific.*

58. International Energy Agency. (2007). *Key World Energy Statistics 2007.* Retrieved January 3, 2008 from http://www.iea.org/textbase/nppdf/free/2007/key_stats_2007.pdf.

59. International Energy Agency. (2007). *Key World Energy Statistics 2007.* p. 19. Retrieved January 3, 2008 from http://www.iea.org/textbase/nppdf/free/2007/key_stats_2007.pdf.

60. World Nuclear Association. (2008, February). Nuclear Power in China. Retrieved February 15, 2008 from http://www.world-nuclear.org/info/inf63.html.

61. America's Vulnerable Economy. (2007, November 15). *The Economist.* Retrieved July 15, 2008 from http://www.economist.com/opinion/displaystory.cfm?story_id=10134118.

62. International Energy Agency. (2007). *Key World Energy Statistics 2007.* p. 16. Retrieved January 3, 2008 from http://www.iea.org/textbase/nppdf/free/2007/key_stats_2007.pdf.

63. International Energy Agency. (2007). *Key World Energy Statistics 2007.* p. 30. Retrieved January 3, 2008 from http://www.iea.org/textbase/nppdf/free/2007/key_stats_2007.pdf.

64. Energy Information Administration. International Total Primary Energy Consumption and Energy Intensity. Retrieved January 1, 2008 from http://www.eia.doe.gov/emeu/international/energyconsumption.html.

65. Energy Information Administration. International Total Primary Energy Consumption and Energy Intensity. Retrieved January 2, 2008 from http://www.eia.doe.gov/emeu/international/energyconsumption.html.

66. Compiled on the base of data from Energy Information Administration. International Total Primary Energy Consumption and Energy Intensity. Retrieved January 1, 2008 from http://www.eia.doe.gov/emeu/international/energyconsumption.html.

67. Compiled on the base of data from Energy Information Administration. International Total Primary Energy Consumption and Energy Intensity. Retrieved January 1, 2008 from http://www.eia.doe.gov/emeu/international/energyconsumption.html.

68. Compiled on the base of data from Energy Information Administration. International Total Primary Energy Consumption and Energy Intensity. Retrieved January 1, 2008 from http://www.eia.doe.gov/emeu/international/energyconsumption.html.

69. Compiled on the base of data from Energy Information Administration. International Total Primary Energy Consumption and Energy Intensity. Retrieved January 1, 2008 from http://www.eia.doe.gov/emeu/international/energyconsumption.html.

70. Compiled on the base of Energy Information Administration. International Total Primary Energy Consumption and Energy Intensity. Retrieved January 1, 2008 from http://www.eia.doe.gov/emeu/international/energyconsumption.html.

71. Wingless Migration. (2007, November 1). *The Economist.* Retrieved July 14, 2008 from http://www.economist.com/science/displaystory.cfm?story_id=10062451.

72. International Energy Agency. (2007). *Key World Energy Statistics 2007.* p. 45. Retrieved January 3, 2008 from http://www.iea.org/textbase/nppdf/free/2007/key_stats_2007.pdf.

73. United States Geological Survey. Aluminum. Retrieved January 15, 2008 from http://minerals.usgs.gov/minerals/pubs/commodity/aluminum/alumimcs07.pdf.

74. United States Geological Survey. Copper. Retrieved January, 15, 2008 from http://minerals.usgs.gov/minerals/pubs/commodity/copper/coppemcs07.pdf.

75. Hunt, Graeme, BHP Bilton. (2007, June 6). Growth Through Optionality. Retrieved January 15, 2007 from http://www.bhpbilliton.com/bbContentRepository/070531GhUbs2007ConfLondon.pdf.

76. United States Geological Survey. Nickel. Retrieved January 15, 2007 from http://minerals.usgs.gov/minerals/pubs/commodity/nickel/nickemcs07.pdf.

77. United States Geological Survey. Cobalt. Retrieved January 15, 2008 from http://minerals.usgs.gov/minerals/pubs/commodity/cobalt/cobalmcs07.pdf.

78. United States Geological Survey. Cobalt. Retrieved January 15, 2008 from http://minerals.usgs.gov/minerals/pubs/commodity/cobalt/cobalmcs07.pdf.

79. United States Geological Survey. Platinum-group Metals. Retrieved January 15, 2008 from http://minerals.usgs.gov/minerals/pubs/commodity/platinum/platimcs07.pdf.

80. United States Geological Survey. Platinum-group Metals. Retrieved January 15, 2007 from http://minerals.usgs.gov/minerals/pubs/commodity/platinum/platimcs07.pdf.
81. The International Monetary Fund. The United States: International Reserves and Foreign Currency Liquidity. Retrieved January 15, 2008 from http://www.imf.org/external/np/sta/ir/usa/eng/curusa.htm.
82. United States Geological Survey. Gold. Retreived January 15, 2008 from http://minerals.usgs.gov/minerals/pubs/commodity/gold/gold_mcs07.pdf.
83. Gold. (2008, January 26). *The Economist*. p. 94. Compiled on the base of data from GFMS, a precious metals consultancy.
84. Compiled on the base of data from The World Bank World Development Indicators. Retrieved January 15, 2008 from http://econ.worldbank.org/WBSITE/EXTERNAL/EXTDEC/0,,menuPK:476823~pagePK:64165236~piPK:64165141~theSitePK:469372,00.html.
85. Shaparev, Nikolay. (2007). Natural Resources of China. *Herald of the Russian Academy of Sciences* Vol. 77, No. 10. p. 928.
86. Jingrong, Li. (2003, October 28). China's Artificial Forest Area Ranks First in the World. *China Through a Lens*. Retrieved January 15, 2008 from http://japanese.china.org.cn/english/2003/Oct/78535.htm.
87. Compiled on the base of data from the FAOSTAT database of the Food and Agriculture Organization of the United Nations. Retrieved January 15, 2008 from http://faostat.fao.org/site/381/default.aspx.
88. The CIA World Factbook. Population Rank—Order. Retrieved October 29, 2007 from https://www.cia.gov/library/publications/the-world-factbook/rankorder/2119rank.html.
89. Compiled on the base of data from The World Bank World Development Indicators. Retrieved January 1, 2008 from http://econ.worldbank.org/WBSITE/EXTERNAL/EXTDEC/0,,menuPK:476823~pagePK:64165236~piPK:64165141~theSitePK:469372,00.html.
90. Compiled on the base of data from The World Bank World Development Indicators. Retrieved January 15, 2008 from http://econ.worldbank.org/WBSITE/EXTERNAL/EXTDEC/0,,menuPK:476823~pagePK:64165236~piPK:64165141~theSitePK:469372,00.html.
91. Compiled on the base of data from The World Bank World Development Indicators. Retrieved January 25, 2008 from http://econ.worldbank.org/WBSITE/EXTERNAL/EXTDEC/0,,menuPK:476823~pagePK:64165236~piPK:64165141~theSitePK:469372,00.html.
92. Compiled on the base of data from The World Bank World Development Indicators. Retrieved January 15, 2008 from http://econ.worldbank.org/WBSITE/EXTERNAL/EXTDEC/0,,menuPK:476823~pagePK:64165236~piPK:64165141~theSitePK:469372,00.html.
93. Compiled on the base of data from the US Census, International Database. Retrieved September 2, 2007 from http://www.census.gov/ipc/www/idb/idbprint.html.
94. CIA World Factbook. Literacy Rates. Retrieved October 19, 2007 from https://www.cia.gov/library/publications/the-world-factbook/fields/2103.html.
95. CIA World Factbook. Literacy Rates. Retrieved October 19, 2007 from https://www.cia.gov/library/publications/the-world-factbook/fields/2103.html.
96. Compiled on the base of data from the UNESCO Education Statistics. Retrieved January 26, 2008 from http://stats.uis.unesco.org/unesco/TableViewer/document.aspx?ReportId=136&IF_Language=eng&BR_Topic=0.
97. United Nations Development Program. (2007, November). The Human Development Report: Inequality in Income or Expenditure. Retrieved January 30, 2008 from http://hdrstats.undp.org/indicators/147.html.
98. The Human Development Report. (2007, November). Inequality in Income or Expenditure. Retrieved January 30, 2008 from http://hdrstats.undp.org/indicators/147.html.
99. Compiled on the base of statistics from the International Labour Organization. (2007, September). *Key Indicators of the Labour Market*. Retrieved February 1, 2008 from http://www.ilo.org/public/english/employment/strat/kilm/.
100. Compiled on the base of data from the OECD database. Retrieved January 13, 2008 from http://stats.oecd.org/WBOS/Default.aspx?DatasetCode=PDYGTH.
101. United Nations Development Program. (2007, November). Human Development Index Rankings. Retrieved January 13, 2007 from http://hdr.undp.org/hdr2006/statistics/.
102. August, Ray. (1993). *International Business Law: Text, Cases and Readings*. Englewood Cliffs, NJ: Prentice Hall. p. 369.
103. Bank for International Settlements. History of the Basel Committee and Its Membership. Retrieved February 23, 2008 from http://www.bis.org/bcbs/history.htm.

104. Bank for International Settlements. Fact Sheet Basel Committee on Banking Supervision. Retrieved February 23, 2008 from http://www.bis.org/about/factbcbs.htm.
105. Compiled on the base of data from the International Monetary Fund. Data Template on International Reserves and Foreign Currency Liquidity. Retrieved January 28, 2008 from http://www.imf.org/external/np/sta/ir/colist.htm except China, data for which is from the World Bank. (2006). Foreign Currency Reserves Minus Gold. Retrieved January 28, 2008 from http://siteresources.worldbank.org/INTEAPHALFYEARLYUPDATE/Resources/550192–1194982737018/Indicators-EAP-Update-Nov2007.pdf.
106. Compiled on the base of data from the International Monetary Fund. (2007, October). Global Financial Stability Report: Financial Market Turbulence: Causes, Consequences and Policies. Statistical Appendix. p. 139. Retrieved January 17, 2008 from http://www.imf.org/external/pubs/ft/gfsr/2007/02/pdf/statappx.pdf.
107. The International Monetary Fund. (2008, February). Gold in the IMF. Retrieved February 28, 2008 from http://www.imf.org/external/np/exr/facts/gold.htm.
108. Compiled from the International Monetary Fund International Financial Statistics. Retrieved February 12, 2008 from http://www.imf.org/external/data.htm#data.
109. The International Monetary Fund. (2006, October). Special Drawing Rights. Retrieved February 12, 2008 from http://www.imf.org/external/np/exr/facts/sdr.htm.
110. Bank for International Settlements. Banking Services for Central Banks. Retrieved January 28, 2008 from http://www.bis.org/banking/index.htm.
111. Bank for International Settlements. Banking Services for Central Banks. Retrieved January 28, 2008 from http://www.bis.org/banking/index.htm.
112. Compiled on the base of data from the International Monetary Fund. (2007, October). Global Financial Stability Report: Financial Market Turbulence: Causes, Consequences and Policies. Statistical Appendix. Retrieved January 17, 2008 from http://www.imf.org/external/pubs/ft/gfsr/2007/02/pdf/statappx.pdf.
113. Compiled on the base of data from the International Monetary Fund. (2007, October). Global Financial Stability Report: Financial Market Turbulence: Causes, Consequences and Policies. Statistical Appendix. Retrieved January 17, 2008 from http://www.imf.org/external/pubs/ft/gfsr/2007/02/pdf/statappx.pdf.
114. Compiled on the base of data from the International Monetary Fund. (2007, October). Global Financial Stability Report: Financial Market Turbulence: Causes, Consequences and Policies. Statistical Appendix. Retrieved January 17, 2008 from http://www.imf.org/external/pubs/ft/gfsr/2007/02/pdf/statappx.pdf.
115. Kalter, Eliot. (2008, January). Local Capital Markets: Emerging Market Investment Opportunities Executive Summary. Bretton Woods Committee Meeting.
116. Compiled on the base of data from the International Monetary Fund. (2007, October). Global Financial Stability Report: Financial Market Turbulence: Causes, Consequences and Policies. Statistical Appendix. Retrieved January 17, 2008 from http://www.imf.org/external/pubs/ft/gfsr/2007/02/pdf/statappx.pdf.
117. Compiled on the base of data from the International Monetary Fund. (2007, October). Global Financial Stability Report: Financial Market Turbulence: Causes, Consequences and Policies. Statistical Appendix. p. 136. Retrieved January 17, 2008 from http://www.imf.org/external/pubs/ft/gfsr/2007/02/pdf/statappx.pdf.
118. The International Monetary Fund. (2007, September). Global Financial Stability Report: Financial Market Turbulence: Causes, Consequences and Policies. Statistical Appendix. Retrieved January 17, 2008 from http://www.imf.org/external/pubs/ft/gfsr/2007/02/pdf/chap3.pdf.
119. Sy, Amadou. (2007, September 18). Malaysia: An Islamic Capital Market Hub. *Islamic Finance*. Retrieved January 28, 2008 from http://www.imf.org/external/pubs/ft/survey/so/2007/CAR0919A.htm.
120. J.D. Power Automotive Forecasting. (2008, January). North American Light Vehicle Production Update. Retrieved February 20, 2008 from http://128.121.187.28/publicData/prodEstimate_northamerica.htm.
121. J.D. Power Automotive. (2008, January). Estimated Pan-European Passenger Car Assembly by Model. Retrieved February 20, 2008 from http://128.121.187.28/publicData/prodEstimate_europe.htm.
122. J.D. Power Automotive. (2008, January). Estimated Pan-European Passenger Car Assembly by Model. Retrieved February 20, 2008 from http://128.121.187.28/publicData/prodEstimate_europe.htm.

123. Ben-David, Dan. (2008). Brain Drained: A Tale of Two Countries. *VOX*. Retrived April 29, 2008 from http://www.voxeu.org/index.php?q=node/984.
124. World Science Forum. (November 8–10, 2003). *Knowledge and Society*. Summaries. Knowledge-based Society. Budapest.
125. European Federation of National Academies of Sciences and Humanities. News. Retrieved April 10, 2008 from http://www.allea.org/cfdata/output/news_archive.cfm.
126. The World Bank. (2007). Knowledge Assessment Methodology. Retrieved February 3, 2008 from http://info.worldbank.org/etools/kam2/KAM_page5.asp.
127. The World Bank. (2008). *Global Economic Prospects 2008: Technology Diffusion in the Developing World*. Retrieved February 19, 2008 from http://econ.worldbank.org/WBSITE/EXTERNAL/EXTDEC/EXTDECPROSPECTS/GEPEXT/EXTGEP2008/0,,contentMDK:21603834~isCURL:Y~noSURL:Y~pagePK:64167689~piPK:64167673 ~theSitePK:4503324,00.html.
128. Merkel, Angela. (2006, July 14). German Science Policy 2006. *Science AAAS*. p. 147.
129. *Battelle-R&D Magazine*. (2008). Globalization Distributes More of the R&D Wealth. *Global R&D Report 2008*. Retrieved February 3, 2008 from http://www.rdmag.com/pdf/RD79GlobalReport.pdf.
130. *Battelle-R&D Magazine*. (2008). Globalization Distributes More of the R&D Wealth. *Global R&D Report 2008*. Retrieved February 3, 2008 from http://www.rdmag.com/pdf/RD79GlobalReport.pdf.
131. National Science Foundation, Division of Science Resources Statistics. (2007). *Asia's Rising Science and Technology Strength: Comparative Indicators for Asia, the European Union, and the United States*. NSF 07-319. Arlington, VA. Retrieved October 3, 2008 from http://www.nsf.gov/statistics/nsf07319/content.cfm?pub_id=1874&id=4.
132. The World Bank. (2008). *Global Economic Prospects 2008: Technology Diffusion in the Developing World*. Retrieved February 19, 2008 from http://econ.worldbank.org/WBSITE/EXTERNAL/EXTDEC/EXTDECPROSPECTS/GEPEXT/EXTGEP2008/0,,contentMDK:21603834~isCURL:Y~noSURL:Y~pagePK:64167689~piPK:64167673~ theSitePK:4503324,00.html.
133. The World Bank. (2008). *Global Economic Prospects 2008: Technology Diffusion in the Developing World*. Retrieved February 19, 2008 from http://econ.worldbank.org/WBSITE/EXTERNAL/EXTDEC/EXTDECPROSPECTS/GEPEXT/EXTGEP2008/0,,contentMDK:21603834~isCURL:Y~noSURL:Y~pagePK:64167689~piPK:64167673 ~theSitePK:4503324,00.html.
134. Speech of First Deputy Prime Minister S. Ivanov at the Ministry of Education and Science of the Russian Federation. February 19, 2008. From the Russian Information Agency Novosti.
135. The World Bank. (2008). *Global Economic Prospects 2008: Technology Diffusion in the Developing World*. Retrieved February 19, 2008 from http://econ.worldbank.org/WBSITE/EXTERNAL/EXTDEC/EXTDECPROSPECTS/GEPEXT/EXTGEP2008/0,,contentMDK:21603834~isCURL:Y~noSURL:Y~pagePK:64167689~piPK:64167673 ~theSitePK:4503324,00.html.
136. The World Bank. (2008). *Global Economic Prospects 2008: Technology Diffusion in the Developing World*. Retrieved February 19, 2008 from http://econ.worldbank.org/WBSITE/EXTERNAL/EXTDEC/EXTDECPROSPECTS/GEPEXT/EXTGEP2008/0,,contentMDK:21602245~isCURL:Y~noSURL:Y~pagePK:64167689~piPK:64167673 ~theSitePK:4503324,00.html.

2   The Global Emerging Market

1. Bacon, Francis. (2004). *Novum Organum: True Directions Concerning the Interpretation of Nature*. Whitefish, MT: Kessinger Publishing.
2. Kipling, Rudyard. (1927). We and They. *Rudyard Kipling's Verse*. Garden City, NY: Doubleday, Page & Company. p. 820.
3. Sartre, Jean-Paul. (1963). *Les Mouches Drame En Trois Actes*. King Aegistheus. Act 2.
4. Nekipelov, Alexander. (2004, October 15). Public Preferences and their Role in Shaping Russian Economic Development. *Distinguished Lecture Series N. 14*. Warsaw: Academy of Entrepreneurship and Management. p. 3.
5. Park, Keith K.H. and Van Agtmael, Antoine W. (eds). (1993). *The World's Emerging Stock Market: Structure, Developments, Regulations and Opportunities*. Chicago and Cambridge: Probus Publishing Company. 650 pgs.
6. International Finance Corporation Press Release (1994, November 11). Retrieved November 15, 2007 from http://www.ifc.org/ifcext/pressroom/ifcpressroom.nsf/PressRelease?openform&25C5388C0DB59B92852569680057A8D1.
7. World Bank. Country Classification. Retrieved November 12, 2007 from http://web.world

bank.org/WBSITE/EXTERNAL/DATASTATISTICS/0,,contentMDK:20420458~menuPK:
64133156~pagePK:64133150~piPK:64133175 ~theSitePK:239419,00.html.

8. Van Agtmael, Antoine W. (2007). *The Emerging Market Century: How a New Breed of World-Class Companies Is Overtaking the World*. New York: Free Press. p. 5.

9. Russell Investments. S&P/IFC Emerging Market Indexes. Retrieved November 2, 2007 from http://www.russell.com/us/glossary/indexes/s&p_ifc_emerging_markets_indexes.htm.

10. Kvint, Vladimir. (1995). A Different Perspective on Emerging Markets. *The Fourth Annual World Economic Development Congress, Addendum: A Special Summit Briefing of Some of the Speakers' Addresses*. pp. 50–54.

11. Survey of the World Economy. (2006, September 16). *The Economist*. p. 6.

12. World Economic Forum. Global Competitiveness Network. Retrieved November 19, 2007 http://www.weforum.org/en/initiatives/gcp/FAQs/index.htm#network1.

13. Moody's. National Scale Ratings. Retrieved November 6, 2007 http://www.moodys.com/cust/content/loadcontent.aspx?source=staticcontent/free%20pages/nsr/nsr.htm.

14. The *globalEDGE*. Market Potential Index. Retrieved July 16, 2008 from http://globaledge.msu.edu/resourceDesk/mpi.asp#MarketPotential.

15. Price, Margaret. (1994). *Emerging Stock Markets: A Complete Investment Guide to New Markets around the World*. Highstown, NJ: McGraw Hill, Inc. p. 11.

16. Dizzy in Boomtown. (2007, November 15). *The Economist*. Retrieved December 1, 2007 http://www.economist.com/opinion/displaystory.cfm?story_id=10136509.

17. Dizzy in Boomtown. (2007, November 15). *The Economist*. Retrieved December 1, 2007 from http://www.economist.com/opinion/displaystory.cfm?story_id=10136509.

18. The *globalEDGE*. Market Potential Index. Retrieved September 19, 2007 http://globaledge.msu.edu/resourceDesk/mpi.asp#MarketPotential.

19. Adapted from data from the European Bank Savings Banks Group. Retrieved September 16, 2007 from http://www.esbg.eu/uploadedFiles/Events/EBRD%20Final.pdf. With Dr Kvint's updates.

20. America's Vulnerable Economy. (2007, November 15). *The Economist*. Retrieved November 25, 2007 from http://www.economist.com/opinion/displaystory.cfm?story_id=10134118.

21. Dizzy in Boomtown. (2007, November 15). *The Economist*. Retrieved December 1, 2007 from http://www.economist.com/opinion/displaystory.cfm?story_id=10136509.

22. Arrow, Kenneth J. (1963). *Social Choice and Individual Values*. New Haven and London: Yale University Press. p. 61.

23. The CIA World Factbook. Retrieved October 16, 2007 from https://www.cia.gov/library/publications/the-world-factbook/.

24. Kazakh Ecology Ministry Drops Chevron Tengiz Probe. (2007, April 4). *Reuters*. Retrieved November 23, 2007 from http://www.reuters.com/article/companyNewsAndPR/idUSL0433100620070404.

25. Kazakh Ecology Ministry Drops Chevron Tengiz Probe. (2007, April 4). *Reuters*. Retrieved November 23, 2007 from http://www.reuters.com/article/companyNewsAndPR/idUSL0433100620070404.

26. Shah, Saeed. (2004, August 5). Shell Hit by $1.5bn Oil Pollution Claim from Nigerian Senate. *Energy Bulletin*. Retrieved December 9, 2007 from http://energybulletin.net/1739.html.

27. Krauss, Clifford. (2006, September 6). Major US oil discovery in Gulf of Mexico. *The International Herald Tribune*. Retrieved June 28, 2008 from http://www.iht.com/articles/2006/09/06/business/oil.php.

28. Brenton, Hal. (2007, November 13). Russians Arrest Crab Mogul. *The Seattle Times*. Retrieved November 29, 2007 from http://seattletimes.nwsource.com/html/localnews/2004010535_russiancrab13m.html.

29. Brenton, Hal. (2007, November 13). Russians Arrest Crab Mogul. *The Seattle Times*. Retrieved November 29, 2007 from http://seattletimes.nwsource.com/html/localnews/2004010535_russiancrab13m.html.

30. The CIA World Factbook. Retrieved October 4, 2007 from https://www.cia.gov/library/publications/the-world-factbook/.

31. Sidenko, V. (2007). Structural Shifts in Economic Relations of Ukraine and the Russian Federation. *World Changes* No. 3. Moscow, Russia. pp. 66–67.

32. Sidenko, V. (2007). Structural Shifts in Economic Relations of Ukraine and the Russian Federation. *World Changes* No. 3. Moscow, Russia, p. 64.

33. European Commission. Bilateral Trade Relations. Retrieved November 19, 2007 from http://ec.europa.eu/trade/issues/bilateral/countries/ukraine/index_en.htm.

34. Survey of the World Economy. (2006, September 16). *The Economist*. pp. 2–3.

35. Mercer LLC. 2008 Global Compensation Planning Report. Retrieved July 16, 2008 from http://www.imercer.com/default.aspx?page=surveydetail&surveyid=2851&menuId=344&new RegionId=3.
36. International Fund for Agricultural Development. (2007). Sending Money Home: Worldwide Remittance Flows to Developing Countries. Retrieved June 28, 2008 from www.ifad.org/events/remittances/maps/.
37. Compiled on the base of data from World Bank World Development Indicators www.worldbank.org, US Department of Labor www.dol.gov and Eurostat ec.europa.eu/eurostat. Retrieved September 19, 2007.
38. Special Report: Innovation. (2007, October 11). *The Economist*. Retrieved October 30, 2007 from http://www.economist.com/specialreports/displayStory.cfm?story_id=9928154.
39. The World Bank. (January 2008). Highly-skilled Migrant Populations Facilitate Technology Transfer. *Technology Diffusion in the Developing World*. Retrieved April 5, 2008 from http://siteresources.worldbank.org/INTGEP2008/Resources/4503313-1199473339970/Highly-skilled-migrant-(large).gif.
40. Compiled on the base of information from the International Fund for Agricultural Development. (2007). Sending Money Home: Worldwide Remittance Flows to Developing Countries. Retrieved November 29, 2007 from http://www.ifad.org/events/remittances/maps/index.htm.
41. Compiled on the base of information from the International Fund for Agricultural Development. (2007). Sending Money Home: Worldwide Remittance Flows to Developing Countries. Retrieved November 29, 2007 from http://www.ifad.org/events/remittances/maps/index.htm.
42. Abed, George T. and Gupta, Sanjeev. (eds). (2002). *Governance, Corruption and Economic Performance*. Washington, DC: IMF. 564 pgs. Treisman, Daniel. (2000). The Causes of Corruption: A Cross-national Study. *Journal of Public Economics* Vol. 76 No. 3. pp. 399–457.
43. Knight, Frank H. (1921). *Risk, Uncertainty, and Profit*. Boston and New York: The Riverside Press. 408 pgs.
44. Franklin D. Roosevelt, from a prepared speech for Jefferson Day on April 13, 1945.
45. Based on data from Standard & Poor's. (2005). Global Stock Markets Factbook.
46. Park, Keith K.H and Van Agtmael, Antoine W. (eds). (1993). *The World's Emerging Stock Market: Structure, Developments, Regulations and Opportunities*. Chicago and Cambridge: Probus Publishing Company. p. 9.
47. Walters, Greg and Mauldin, William. (2008, May 8). Gazprom Passes GE, China Mobile, Becomes World No. 3. *Bloomberg*. Retrieved May 9 from http://www.bloomberg.com/apps/news?pid=20601095&sid=aZomK8T5CtUs&refer=east_europe.
48. The CIA World Factbook. Retrieved October 19, 2007 from https://www.cia.gov/library/publications/the-world-factbook/.
49. Survey of the World Economy. (2006, September 16). *The Economist*. p. 4.
50. Compiled on the base of the World Bank World Development Indicators, CIA World Factbook and Department of Investment Services of "Invest in Taiwan". Note: data from 1980–1990 consists of developing countries that eventually became EMCs.
51. Compiled on the base of data from the World Bank World Development Indicators, and the International Monetary Fund
52. The United Nations Department of Economic and Social Affairs Population Division. (1999). World Urbanization Report: 1999 Revision Key Findings. Retrieved October 11, 2007 from http://157.150.195.10/esa/population/pubsarchive/urbanization/urbanization.pdf.
53. The United Nations Department of Economic and Social Affairs Population Division. (1999). World Urbanization Report: 1999 Revision Key Findings. Retrieved October 11, 2007 from http://157.150.195.10/esa/population/pubsarchive/urbanization/urbanization.pdf.
54. The CIA World Factbook. Retrieved October 11, 2007 from https://www.cia.gov/library/publications/the-world-factbook/.
55. Compiled on the base of data from the United Nations. (2007). The World Investment Report: Transnational Corporations, Extractive Industries and Development. United Nations Conference on Trade and Development.
56. The World Bank. (2001). *World Development Report 2000/2001*. New York: Oxford University Press. p. 51.
57. Initiated by the City of London, and managed by Z/Yen. Retrieved October 19, 2007 http://www.zyen.com/Activities/On-line%20surveys/GFCI.htm.
58. The Global Financial Centres Index of the City of London. (2007). Retrieved December 19, 2007 from http://213.86.34.248/NR/rdonlyres/0C0332C0-4CE5-4012-9AF7-2CF98A32E618/0/BC_RS_GFCI07_FR.pdf.

59. The Global Financial Centres Index of the City of London. (2007). Retrieved December 19, 2007 from http://213.86.34.248/NR/rdonlyres/0C0332C0-4CE5-4012-9AF7-2CF98A32E618/0/BC_RS_GFCI07_FR.pdf.

3   Ten Modern Global Political, Economic, and Technological Trends

1. Churchill, Winston. (1947, November 11). Speech at the House of Commons.
2. Wilde, Oscar. (1915). *The Soul of Man Under Socialism*. London.
3. Jessop, Bob. (1999). Reflections on Globalisation and its (il)logic(s). In Olds, Kris, Dicken, Peter, Kelly, Philip F., Kong, Lily, and Wai-chung Yeung, Henry (eds), *Globalisation and the Asia Pacific: Contested Territories*. London: Routledge. p. 37.
4. Thompson, Grahame. (2000). The Nature and Limits of Economic Globalization. In Held, David (ed.), *A Globalizing World? Culture, Economics, Politics*. London: Routledge. p. 94.
5. National Intelligence Council. (2000). *Global Trends 2015: A Dialogue About the Future With Nongovernment Experts*, Washington, DC. Retrieved February 20, 2007 from http://www.dni.gov/nic/NIC_globaltrend2015.html.
6. National Intelligence Council. (2000). *Global Trends 2015: A Dialogue About the Future With Nongovernment Experts*, Washington, DC. Retrieved February 20, 2007 from http://www.dni.gov/nic/NIC_globaltrend2015.html.
7. Ministry of General Affairs of the Netherlands. (2008, June 9). Countries Sign New Benelux Treaty. Retrieved June 19, 2008 from http://www.minaz.nl/english/News/Press_releases_and_news_items/2008/Juni/Countries_sign_new_Benelux_Treaty.
8. Tagliabue, John. (1996, September 25). North Italy's Separatist Leader Says He Is Willing to Negotiate. *New York Times*. Retrieved February 5, 2008 from http://query.nytimes.com/gst/fullpage.html?res=9F05E1D61E3DF936A1575AC0A960958260&scp=1&sq=North+Italy%92s+Separatist+Leader+Says+He+Is+Willing+to+Negotiate&st=nyt.
9. United Nations. Growth in United Nations Membership 1945–Present. Retrieved January 15, 2008 from http://www.un.org/members/growth.shtml.
10. Chia, Lin Sien. (2003). *Southeast Asia Transformed: A Geography of Change*. Singapore: Institute of Southeast Asian Studies. p. 303.
11. Breslin, Shaun, Higgot, Richard, and Rosamond, Ben. (2002). Regions in Comparative Perspective. In Breslin, Shaun, Hughes, Christopher W., Phillips, Nicola, and Rosamond, Ben. (eds), *New Regionalisms in the Global Political Economy*. London: Routledge. p. 2.
12. Manning, Tony. (2008). Emerging markets everywhere—the strategist's dream come true. *BA UpFront*. Retrieved April 10, 2008 from http://www.tonymanning.com/asp/downloads/articles/Tony%20Manning%20-%20Emerging%20markets%20everywhere%20-%20Sept%202005.pdf.
13. Loughlin, John and Mazey, Sonia. (eds). (1995) *The End of the French Unitary State? Ten Years of Regionalization in France (1982–1992)*. London: Routledge. p. 2.
14. Keating, Michael. (September 1983). Decentralization in Mitterrand's France. *Public Administration: An International Quarterly* Vol. 61, No. 3. pp. 237–252.
15. Stiglitz, Joseph. (2007). *Making Globalization Work*. New York, London: W.W. Norton and Company. p. 52.
16. Litvack, Jennie, Ahmad, Junaid, and Bird, Richard. (1998). *Rethinking Decentralization in Developing Countries*. Washington, DC: The World Bank. p. 4.
17. Index compiled by Professor Christine Kearney of Saint Anselm College. December 30, 1999. Retrieved February 19, 2008 from http://www.econ.brown.edu/faculty/henderson/decentralization.pdf.
18. United Nations Development Program. Local Governance and Decentralization in Europe and the CIS. Retrieved February 29, 2008 from http://europeandcis.undp.org/governance/lgdc/show/F8B06B55-F203-1EE9-B73274DA527AD025.
19. Matsui, Kazuhisa. (March 2005). Post-decentralization Regional Economies and Actors: Putting the Capacity of Local Governments to the Test. *The Developing Economies, XLII-1*. p. 171.
20. Asia-Pacific Economic Cooperation. About APEC. Retrieved February 27, 2008 from http://www.apec.org/content/apec/about_apec.html.
21. Asia-Pacific Economic Cooperation. About APEC. Retrieved February 27, 2008 from http://www.apec.org/content/apec/about_apec.html.
22. Asia-Pacific Economic Cooperation. About APEC. Retrieved February 27, 2008 from http://www.apec.org/content/apec/about_apec.html.

23. Mucchielli, Jean-Louis, Buckley, Peter J., Cordell, Victor V. (eds). (1996). *Globalization and Regionalization: Strategies, Policies and Economic Environments*. New York: International Business Press. p. xi.

24. Wallin, Bruce. Privatization of State Services in Massachusetts: Politics, Policy and an Experiment that Wasn't. Prepared for the Economic Policy Institute. pp. 3–4. Retrieved February 15, 2008 from http://archive.epinet.org/real_media/010111/materials/wallin.pdf.

25. See Pirie, Madsen. (1985). *Privatization in Theory and Practice*. London: The Adam Smith Institute.

26. Bulgartabac Holding AD. Homepage. Retrieved February 28, 2008 from http://www.bulgartabac.bg/?&LanguageCode=en.

27. Vatahov, Ivan. (2005, February 18). Another Bulgartabac Privatisation Attempt. *Sofia Echo*. Retrieved February 24, 2008 from http://www.sofiaecho.com/article/another-bulgartabac-privatisation-attempt/id_10793/catid_23.

28. Estrin, Saul and Stone, Robert. A Taxonomy of Mass Privatization. *Beyond Transition: The Newsletter About Reforming Economies*. Washington, DC: World Bank. Retrieved February 17, 2008 from http://www.worldbank.org/html/prddr/trans/novdec96/doc6.htm.

29. Fungacova, Zuzana. (April 2005). Building a Castle on Sand: Effects of Mass Privatization on Capital Market Creation in Transition Economies. *Working Paper Series, Center for Economic Research and Graduate Education Academy of Sciences of the Czech Republic Economics Institute*. Retrieved February 9, 2008 from http://www.cerge-ei.cz/pdf/wp/Wp256.pdf.

30. Kogut, Bruce and Spicer, Andrew. (2002). Capital Market Development and Mass Privatization are Logical Contradictions: Lessons from Russia and the Czech Republic. *Industrial and Corporate Change* Vol. 11, No. 1 (abstract).

31. Lesova, Polya. (2007, December 17). Emerging Markets Drive Record IPO Activity: Ernst & Young Study Documents China's 2007 Dominance. Emerging Markets Report. *MarketWatch From DowJones*. Retrieved February 20, 2008 from http://www.marketwatch.com/news/story/emerging-markets-drive-global-ipo/story.aspx?guid=%7B3D345195-EBA1-4A70-B837-AC31D8D14A64%7D.

32. Ernst & Young Press Release (2007, December 17). Retrieved February 20, 2008 from http://www.ey.com/global/Content.nsf/International/Media_-_Press_Release_Year_End_IPO_Activity.

33. Ernst & Young Press Release (2007, December 17). Retrieved February 20, 2008 from http://www.ey.com/global/Content.nsf/International/Media_-_Press_Release_Year_End_IPO_Activity.

34. Boutchkova, Maria K. and Megginson, William L. (2000). Privatization and the Rise of Global Capital Markets. *Financial Management* Vol. 29 No. 4. Retrieved February 19, 2008 from http://ideas.repec.org/a/fma/fmanag/maria00.html.

35. Compiled on the base of Annual Global IPO Activity from Ernst & Young. (2006). *Accelerating Growth Global IPO Trends 2006*. p. 2. Retrieved from http://www.altassets.com/pdfs/eyGlobal_IPO_Survey2006.pdf. BRIC IPO values from Ernst & Young Press Release (2007, December 17). Retrieved February 20, 2008 from http://www.ey.com/global/Content.nsf/International/Media_-_Press_Release_-Year_End_IPO_Activity. Except 2005 values, which are from Ernst & Young Press Release (2007, June 21). Retrieved February 20, 2008 from http://www2.eycom.ch/media/mediareleases/releases/20070621/en.aspx.

36. Ernst & Young. (2006). *Accelerating Growth Global IPO Trends 2006*. p. 2. Retrieved from July 16, 2008 from http://www.altassets.com/pdfs/eyGlobal_IPO_Survey2006.pdf.

37. Reed, Stanley. (2003, November 10). School Daze at British Universities. *BusinessWeek*. Retrieved June 13, 2008 from http://www.businessweek.com/magazine/content/03_45/b3857109_mz054.htm.

38. MacLeod., Donald. (September 2007). Education Worth More to British Exports than Banking. Education *Guardian* of the UK. Retrieved June 13, 2008 from http://education.guardian.co.uk/students/internationalstudents/story/0,,2171234,00.html.

39. Sports Direct International. Overview. Retrieved February 25, 2008 from http://www.sportsdirect-international.com/main.asp?pid=3.

40. Braithwaite, Tom. (2008, February 5). Sports Direct in China Alliance. *Financial Times*. Retrieved February 15, 2008 from http://www.ft.com/cms/s/0/a610697e-d413-11dc-a8c6-0000779fd2ac.html.

41. Braithwaite, Tom. (2008, February 5). Sports Direct in China Alliance. *Financial Times*. Retrieved February 15, 2008 from http://www.ft.com/cms/s/0/a610697e-d413-11dc-a8c6-0000779fd2ac.html.

42. UBS. History of UBS. Retrieved February 5, 2008 from http://www.ubs.com/1/e/about/history/2001_2006/2003.html.
43. Bream, Rebecca, Burgess, Kate, and Saigol, Lina. (2008, February 1). Dawn Raid for Rio Tinto Stuns BHP. *Financial Times*. Retrieved Februray 19, 2008 from http://www.ft.com/cms/s/0/a51f903e-d09f-11dc-953a-0000779fd2ac.html.
44. Politi, James. (2007, November 28). Hostile Takeovers Make a Comeback. *Financial Times*. Retrieved February 5, 2008 from http://www.ft.com/cms/s/0/a51f903e-d09f-11dc-953a-0000779fd2ac.html?nclick_check=1.
45. BenDaniel, David J. and Rosenbloom, Arthur H. (1999, June 4). *The Handbook of International Mergers & Acquisitions*. Englewood Cliffs, NJ: Prentice-Hall, Inc. pp. 12–13.
46. Business Wire. (1999, August 4). Metromedia International Group's Ningbo Ya Mei Joint Venture Receives Notice of Project Status. Retrieved March 6, 2008 from http://findarticles.com/p/articles/mi_m0EIN/is_1999_August_4/ai_55341682.
47. PaineWebber's New Role. (1999, June 4). *New York Times*. Retrieved February 9, 2008 from http://query.nytimes.com/gst/fullpage.html?res=9F04E5DF1639F937A35755C0A96F958260&scp=1&sq=Paine+Webber%27s+New+Role&st=nyt.
48. Claessens, Stijn and Schmukler, Sergio L. (June 2007). International Financial Integration Through Equity Markets: Which Firms from Which Countries Go Global? *International Monetary Fund Working Paper WP/01/138*. p. 24. Retrieved February 6, 2008 from http://www.imf.org/external/pubs/ft/wp/2007/wp07138.pdf.
49. Claessens, Stijn and Schmukler, Sergio L. (June 2007). International Financial Integration Through Equity Markets: Which Firms from Which Countries Go Global? *International Monetary Fund Working Paper WP/01/138*. p. 24. Retrieved February 6, 2008 from http://www.imf.org/external/pubs/ft/wp/2007/wp07138.pdf.
50. Claessens, Stijn and Schmukler, Sergio L. (June 2007). International Financial Integration Through Equity Markets: Which Firms from Which Countries Go Global? *International Monetary Fund Working Paper WP/01/138*. p. 24. Retrieved February 6, 2008 from http://www.imf.org/external/pubs/ft/wp/2007/wp07138.pdf.
51. Selected from United Nations Conference on Trade and Development. (2007). *The World Investment Report: Transnational Corporations, Extractive Industries and Development*. Annex Table A.I.13. p. 229. Retrieved December 20, 2007 from http://www.unctad.org/Templates/webflyer.asp?docid=9001&intItemID=4361&lang=1&mode=downloads.
52. Selected from United Nations Conference on Trade and Development. (2007). *The World Investment Report: Transnational Corporations, Extractive Industries and Development*. Annex Table A.I.15. p. 235. Retrieved December 20, 2007 from http://www.unctad.org/Templates/webflyer.asp?docid=9001&intItemID=4361&lang=1&mode=downloads.
53. The United Nations Conference on Trade and Development. (2007). *The World Investment Report: Transnational Corporations, Extractive Industries and Development*. p. 12. Retrieved December 20, 2007 from http://www.unctad.org/en/docs/wir2007_en.pdf.
54. FDI as a global trend and practice will be analyzed in detail in Chapter 8.
55. Khazindar, Abid. (2003, October 19). The Roots of Terrorism. *Arab News*. Retrieved February 21, 2008 from http://www.arabnews.com/?page=13&section=0&article=33849&d=19&m=10&y=2003.
56. UNICEF. At a Glance: Saudi Arabia. Retrieved February 15, 2008 from http://www.unicef.org/infobycountry/saudiarabia_statistics.html.
57. UNICEF. At a Glance: Iraq. Retrieved February 15, 2008 from http://www.unicef.org/infobycountry/iraq_statistics.html.
58. The United Nations Conference on Trade and Development. (2007). *The World Investment Report:*
59. Krueger, Alan B. (2007). *What Makes a Terrorist: Economics and the Roots of Terrorism*. Princeton, NJ: Princeton University Press. p. 3.
   Transnational Corporations, Extractive Industries and Development. p. 13. Retrieved December 20, 2007 from http://www.unctad.org/en/docs/wir2007_en.pdf.
60. World Intellectual Property Organization. (2007). WIPO Patent Report: Statistics on Worldwide Patent Activities. p. 14. Retrieved March 3, 2008 from http://www.wipo.int/export/sites/www/freepublications/en/patents/931/wipo_pub_931.pdf.
61. *The 9/11 Commission Report: Final Report of the National Commission on Terrorist Attacks Upon the United States*. (2004). New York: Norton & Company. p. 378.
62. Kephart, Janice L. (September 2005). Immigration and Terrorism: Moving Beyond the 9/11 Staff Report on Terrorist Travel. Executive Summary. Center for Immigration Studies. Retrieved March 1, 2008 from http://www.cis.org/articles/2005/kephart.html.

63. Federation for American Immigration Reform. Immigration and National Security. Retrieved February 25, 2008 from http://www.fairus.org/site/PageServer?pagename=iic_immigrationissuecentersb1c7.
64. US Code of Federal Regulations 28 C.F.R. Section 0.85.
65. US Customs and Border Protection. (November 2004). Securing the Global Supply Chain: Customs Trade Partnership Against Terrorism Security Plan. Retrieved February 21, 2008 from http://www.cbp.gov/linkhandler/cgov/import/commercial_enforcement/ctpat/what_ctpat/ctpat_strategicplan.ctt/ctpat_strategicplan.pdf.
66. Section 2656f(a) of Title 22 of the United States Code.
67. Section 2656f(d) of Title 22 of the United States Code.
68. US Department of Treasury. (2007). *National Money Laundering Strategy*. p. 105. Retrieved February 14, 2008 from http://www.treas.gov/press/releases/docs/nmls.pdf.
69. Jennings, Peter. (2004, February 16). Terrorism and Australian Business. *Strategic Insights Australian Strategic Policy Institute*. p. 1.
70. US Department of Treasury. (2007). *National Money Laundering Strategy*. p. 105. Retrieved February 14, 2008 from http://www.treas.gov/press/releases/docs/nmls.pdf.
71. Citation of the IMF in Jennings, Peter. (2004, February 16). Terrorism and Australian Business. *Strategic Insights Australian Strategic Policy Institute*. p. 3.
72. Foreign Direct Investment. (2008, July 3). *The Economist*. Retrieved July 15, 2008 from http://www.economist.com/markets/indicators/displaystory.cfm?story_id=11670637.
73. NYC Visit.com. NYC Statistics. Retrieved February 29, 2008 http://www.nycvisit.com/content/index.cfm?pagePkey=57.
74. Taylor, Francis. (2002, March 14). The Impact of Global Terrorism. Remarks to Executives Club of Chicago Leadership Symposium. Retrieved March 14, 2002 from http://www.state.gov/s/ct/rls/rm/8839.htm.
75. Jennings, Peter. (2004, February 16). Terrorism and Australian Business. *Strategic Insights Australian Strategic Policy Institute*. p. 3.
76. Taylor, Francis. (2002, March 14). The Impact of Global Terrorism. Remarks to Executives Club of Chicago Leadership Symposium. Retrieved March 14, 2002 from http://www.state.gov/s/ct/rls/rm/8839.htm.
77. Hoggins, Kenneth. A Look at Terrorism and its Effect on the Insurance Industry. William Gallagher Associates. Retrieved February 24, 2008 http://www.wgains.com/Assets/White Papers/Terror702.PDF.
78. Hoggins, Kenneth. A Look at Terrorism and its Effect on the Insurance Industry. William Gallagher Associates. Retrieved February 24, 2008 http://www.wgains.com/Assets/WhitePapers/Terror702.PDF.
79. Weidenbaum, Murray. (May 2002). *USA Today Magazine* Volume 130, No. 2684. p. 26.
80. Cohen, Ariel and O'Driscoll, Gerald P. Jr. (2003, January 22). Privatization and the Oil Industry: A Strategy for Postwar Iraqi Reconstruction. *In The National Interest*. Retrieved February 26, 2008 from http://www.inthenationalinterest.com/Articles/Vol2Issue3/Vol2Issue3CohenDriscoll.html.
81. OECD Secretariat. (March 2002). The Impact of the Terrorist Attacks of 11 September 2001 on International Trading and Transport Activities. p. 17. Retrieved February 16, 2008 from http://www.olis.oecd.org/olis/2002doc.nsf/LinkTo/td-tc-wp(2002)9-final.
82. OECD Secretariat. (March 2002). The Impact of the Terrorist Attacks of 11 September 2001 on International Trading and Transport Activities. p. 17. Retrieved February 16, 2008 from http://www.olis.oecd.org/olis/2002doc.nsf/LinkTo/td-tc-wp(2002)9-final.
83. Chen, Andrew H. and Siems, Thomas F. (June 2004). The Effects of Terrorism on Global Capital Markets. *European Journal of Political Economy* Vol. 20, No. 2. pp. 349–366.
84. CNN. (2006, July 11). At Least 174 Killed in Indian Train Blasts. Retrieved February 12, 2008 from http://www.cnn.com/2006/WORLD/asiapcf/07/11/mumbai.blasts/.
85. Ruggles-Brise, Olivia. (2005, July 8). World Travel and Tourism Council Crisis Committee Issues Estimate of London Bombing Impact. Hotel Online. Retrieved February 26, 2008 from http://www.hotel-online.com/News/PR2005_3rd/July05_LondonImpact.html.
86. *Taipei Times*. (2006, August 17). Business Counts Cost of Terrorism. p. 10. Retrieved February 17, 2008 from http://www.taipeitimes.com/News/worldbiz/archives/2006/08/17/2003323578.
87. CNN. (2006, February 22). Bush, Congress Clash Over Ports Sale. Retrieved February 19, 2008 from http://www.cnn.com/2006/POLITICS/02/21/port.security/.
88. Nigeria Militants Fight Military. (2006, March 9). *BBC News*. Retrieved February 19, 2008 from http://news.bbc.co.uk/2/hi/africa/4789274.stm.

89. Shell's Nigeria Output Cut by 20 percent. (2006, January 13). *BBC News*. Retrieved February 19, 2008 from http://news.bbc.co.uk/2/hi/africa/4789274.stm.
90. World Travel and Tourism Council. Home. Retrieved February 15, 2008 from http://www.wttc.travel/index.php?LANG=eng.
91. Based on statistics from the World Tourism Organization: International Tourist Arrivals by Country of Destination. Retrieved February 29, 2008 from http://www.photius.com/rankings/tourism_2001.pdf.
92. Drakos, Konstantinos, Drakos and Kutan, Ali. (2003). Regional Effects of Terrorism on Tourism in Three Mediterranean Countries. *Journal of Conflict Resolution* Vol. 47, No. 5.
93. Jennings, Peter. (2004, February 16). Terrorism and Australian Business. *Strategic Insights Australian Strategic Policy Institute*. p. 3.
94. UNCTAD Secretariat. (2007). Information Economy Report 2007–2008: Science and Technology for Development: the New Paradigm of ICT. p. 23. Retrieved February 19, 2007 from http://www.unctad.org/en/docs/sdteecb20071_en.pdf.
95. Based on data from UNCTAD Secretariat. (2007). Information Economy Report 2007–2008: Science and Technology for Development: the New Paradigm of ICT. p. 22. Retrieved February 19, 2007 from http://www.unctad.org/en/docs/sdteecb20071_en.pdf.
96. List of Country Groupings and Sub-groupings for the Analytical Studies of the United Nations World Economic Survey and other UN Reports. Retrieved March 3, 2008 from http://unpan1.un.org/intradoc/groups/public/documents/un/unpan008092.pdf.
97. Based on data from the UNCTAD Secretariat. (2007). Information Economy Report 2007–2008: Science and Technology for Development: the New Paradigm of ICT. p. 26. Retrieved February 19, 2007 from http://www.unctad.org/Templates/webflyer.asp?docid=9479&intItemID=1397&lang=1&mode=toc.
98. List of Country Groupings and Sub-groupings for the Analytical Studies of the United Nations World Economic Survey and other UN Reports. Retreived March 3, 2008 from http://unpan1.un.org/intradoc/groups/public/documents/un/unpan008092.pdf.
99. UNCTAD Secretariat. (2007). Information Economy Report 2007–2008: Science and Technology for Development: the New Paradigm of ICT. p. 23. Retrieved February 19, 2007 from http://www.unctad.org/en/docs/sdteecb20071_en.pdf.
100. Silberglitt, R.S., Anton, Philip S., Howell, David, Wong, Anny, Gassman, Natalie, Jackson, Brian A., Landree, Eric, Pfleeger, Shari Lawrence, Newton, Elaine M., Wu, Felicia. (2006). *The Global Technology Revolution 2020, In-depth Analysis:Bio/Nano/Materials/Information Trends, Drivers, Barriers and Social Implications*. Santa Monica, CA: RAND National Security Research Division. p. xviii.
101. UNCTAD Secretariat. (2007). Information Economy Report 2007–2008: Science and Technology for Development: the New Paradigm of ICT. p. 25. Retrieved February 19, 2007 from http://www.unctad.org/Templates/webflyer.asp?docid=9479&intItemID=1397&lang=1&mode=toc.
102. The 10 Emerging Technologies of 2008. (March/April 2008). *Technology Review*. Retrieved March 29, 2008 from http://www.technologyreview.com/Infotech/20249/.
103. World Intellectual Property Organization. (2007). WIPO Patent Report: Statistics on Worldwide Patent Activities. p. 20. Retrieved March 3, 2008 from http://www.wipo.int/export/sites/www/freepublications/en/patents/931/wipo_pub_931.pdf.
104. Anton, Philip S., Silberglitt, Richard, and Schneider, James. (2001). *The Global Technology Revolution: Bio/Nano/Materials Trends and Their Synergies with Information Technology by 2015*. Santa Monica, CA: RAND National Defense Research Institute. p. xi. Available online at http://www.rand.org/pubs/monograph_reports/MR1307/.
105. Gates, Bill. (1996). *The Road Ahead*. New York: Penguin Books.

4 Strategic Country Classification of the Global Marketplace

1. Quoted by Plato in *The Republic* (approximately 360 BC).
2. Engen, Darel. (1985). The Economy of Ancient Greece. *EH.Net Encyclopedia*, edited by Robert Whaples. Retrieved April 29, 2008 from http://eh.net/encyclopedia/article/engen.greece.
3. Finley, Moses I. (1985). *The Ancient Economy*. Berkeley: University of California Press. p. 28.
4. Boughton, James H. (October 2001). *The Silent Revolution: The International Monetary Fund 1979–1989*. Washington DC: The International Monetary Fund. p. 246 (footnote). Retrieved April 9, 2008 from http://www.imf.org/external/pubs/ft/history/2001/ch05.pdf.

5. World Bank. GNI per Capita Operational Guidelines & Analytical Classifications. Retrieved March 12, 2008 from http://siteresources.worldbank.org/DATASTATISTICS/Resources/OGHIST.xls.

6. World Bank. Country Classification. A Short History. Retrieved March 1, 2008 from http://web.worldbank.org/WBSITE/EXTERNAL/DATASTATISTICS/0,,contentMDK:20487070~menuPK:64133156~pagePK:64133150~piPK:64133175~theSitePK:239419,00.html.

7. World Bank. Country Classification. A Short History. Retrieved March 1, 2008 from http://web.worldbank.org/WBSITE/EXTERNAL/DATASTATISTICS/0,,contentMDK:20487070~menuPK:64133156~pagePK:64133150~piPK:64133175~ theSitePK:239419,00.html.

8. World Bank. Country Classification. Retrieved March 5, 2008 from http://web.worldbank.org/WBSITE/EXTERNAL/DATASTATISTICS/0,,contentMDK:20420458~menuPK:64133156~pagePK:64133150~piPK:64133175~theSitePK:239419,00.html.

9. Compiled on the base of the World Bank. GNI per Capita Operational Guidelines & Analytical Classifications. Retrieved March 12, 2008 from http://siteresources.worldbank.org/DATASTATISTICS/Resources/OGHIST.xls.

10. World Bank. GNI per Capita Operational Guidelines & Analytical Classifications. Retrieved March 12, 2008 from http://siteresources.worldbank.org/DATASTATISTICS/Resources/OGHIST.xls.

11. World Bank. GNI per Capita Operational Guidelines & Analytical Classifications. Retrieved March 12, 2008 from http://siteresources.worldbank.org/DATASTATISTICS/Resources/OGHIST.xls.

12. World Bank. Country Groups. Retrieved March 5, 2008 from http://web.worldbank.org/WBSITE/EXTERNAL/DATASTATISTICS/0,,contentMDK:20421402~pagePK:64133150~piPK:64133175~theSitePK:239419,00.html.

13. World Bank. Country Groups. Retrieved March 5, 2008 from http://web.worldbank.org/WBSITE/EXTERNAL/DATASTATISTICS/0,,contentMDK:20421402~pagePK:64133150~piPK:64133175~theSitePK:239419,00.html.

14. Boughton, James H. (October 2001). *The Silent Revolution: The International Monetary Fund 1979–1989*. Washington DC: The International Monetary Fund. p. 246 (footnote). Retrieved April 9, 2008 from http://www.imf.org/external/pubs/ft/history/2001/ch05.pdf.

15. Boughton, James H. (October 2001). *The Silent Revolution: The International Monetary Fund 1979–1989*. Washington DC: The International Monetary Fund. p. 246 (footnote). Retrieved April 9, 2008 from http://www.imf.org/external/pubs/ft/history/2001/ch05.pdf.

16. The International Monetary Fund. (May 1997). The World Economic Outlook. Washington, DC: The International Monetary Fund. Retrieved March 6, 2008 from http://www.imf.org/external/pubs/WEOMAY/02advan.htm.

17. The International Monetary Fund. (October 2007). *Global Financial Stability Report Financial Turbulence: Causes, Consequences, and Policies*. Washington DC: The International Monetary Fund. p. 139 of the statistical appendix. Retrieved March 12, 2008 from http://www.imf.org/external/pubs/ft/gfsr/2007/02/pdf/statappx.pdf.

18. The International Monetary Fund. (September 2003). *World Economic Outlook: Public Debt in Emerging Markets*. Washington, DC: The International Monetary Fund. p. 177 of the statistical appendix. Retrieved March 13, 2008 from http://www.imf.org/external/pubs/ft/weo/2003/02/index.htm.

19. The International Monetary Fund. Debt Relief Under the Heavily Indebted Poor Countries (HIPC) Initiative. Retrieved March 16, 2008 from http://www.imf.org/external/np/exr/facts/hipc.htm.

20. The International Monetary Fund. (2007). *World Economic Outlook: Globalization and Inequality*. Washington, DC: The International Monetary Fund. p. 209 of the statistical appendix. Retrieved March 16, 2008 from http://www.imf.org/external/pubs/ft/weo/2007/02/pdf/statapp.pdf.

21. The International Monetary Fund. (2007). *World Economic Outlook: Globalization and Inequality*. Washington, DC: The International Monetary Fund. p. 210 of the statistical appendix. Retrieved March 16, 2008 from http://www.imf.org/external/pubs/ft/weo/2007/02/pdf/statapp.pdf.

22. The International Monetary Fund. (2007) *World Economic Outlook: Globalization and Inequality*. Washington, DC: The International Monetary Fund. p. 211 of the statistical appendix. Retrieved March 16, 2008 from http://www.imf.org/external/pubs/ft/weo/2007/02/pdf/statapp.pdf.

23. The International Monetary Fund. (2007). *World Economic Outlook: Globalization and Inequality.* Washington, DC: The International Monetary Fund. pp. 212–213 of the statistical appendix. Retrieved March 16, 2008 from http://www.imf.org/external/pubs/ft/weo/2007/02/pdf/statapp.pdf.

24. The International Monetary Fund. (2007). *World Economic Outlook: Globalization and Inequality.* Washington, DC: The International Monetary Fund. p. 211 of the statistical appendix. Retrieved March 16, 2008 from http://www.imf.org/external/pubs/ft/weo/2007/02/pdf/statapp.pdf.

25. United Nations. Composition of Macro Geographical (Continental) Regions, Geographical Sub Regions, and Selected Economic and Other Groupings. Retrieved March 17, 2008 from http://unstats.un.org/unsd/methods/m49/m49regin.htm#developed.

26. United Nations. Composition of Macro Geographical (Continental) Regions, Geographical Sub Regions, and Selected Economic and Other Groupings. Retrieved March 17, 2008 from http://unstats.un.org/unsd/methods/m49/m49regin.htm#developed.

27. United Nations. Composition of Macro Geographical (Continental) Regions, Geographical Sub Regions, and Selected Economic and Other Groupings. Retrieved March 17, 2008 from http://unstats.un.org/unsd/methods/m49/m49regin.htm#developed.

28. United Nations. Composition of Macro Geographical (Continental) Regions, Geographical Sub Regions, and Selected Economic and Other Groupings. Retrieved March 17, 2008 from http://unstats.un.org/unsd/methods/m49/m49regin.htm#developed.

29. United Nations. Composition of Macro Geographical (Continental) Regions, Geographical Sub Regions, and Selected Economic and Other Groupings. Retrieved March 17, 2008 from http://unstats.un.org/unsd/methods/m49/m49regin.htm#developed.

30. United Nations. Composition of Macro Geographical (Continental) Regions, Geographical Sub Regions, and Selected Economic and Other Groupings. Retrieved March 17, 2008 from http://unstats.un.org/unsd/methods/m49/m49regin.htm#developed.

31. United Nations. Composition of Macro Geographical (Continental) Regions, Geographical Sub Regions, and Selected Economic and Other Groupings. Retrieved March 17, 2008 from http://unstats.un.org/unsd/methods/m49/m49regin.htm#developed.

32. United Nations. Composition of Macro Geographical (Continental) Regions, Geographical Sub Regions, and Selected Economic and Other Groupings. Retrieved March 17, 2008 from http://unstats.un.org/unsd/methods/m49/m49regin.htm#developed.

33. United Nations Conference on Trade and Development. UN recognition of the Least Developed Countries. Retrieved March 20, 2008 from http://www.unctad.org/Templates/Page.asp?intItemID=3618&lang=1.

34. United Nations. Composition of Macro Geographical (Continental) Regions, Geographical Sub Regions, and Selected Economic and Other Groupings. Retrieved March 17, 2008 from http://unstats.un.org/unsd/methods/m49/m49regin.htm#developed.

35. Standard & Poor's. (January 2008). *S&P/Citigroup Global Equity Index Methodology.* p. 7. Retrieved March 21, 2008 from http://www2.standardandpoors.com/spf/pdf/index/SP_Citigroup_Global_Equity_Indices_Methodology_Web.pdf.

36. Standard & Poor's. (January 2008). *S&P/Citigroup Global Equity Index Methodology.* pp. 7–8. Retrieved March 21, 2008 from http://www2.standardandpoors.com/spf/pdf/index/SP_Citigroup_Global_Equity_Indices_Methodology_Web.pdf.

37. Zelner, Arnold. (1998). Risk and the Economy Commentary. In Stone, Courtney C. (ed.). (1998). *Financial Risk: Theory, Evidence and Implications.* New York: Springer. p. 121.

38. Koopmans, Tjalling C. and Montias, John Michael. (March 1974). On the Description and Comparison of Economic Systems. *Political Science Quarterly* Vol. 89, No. 1. pp. 236–238.

39. Compiled on the base of data from The World Bank World Development Indicators. Retrieved March 21, 2008 from http://econ.worldbank.org/WBSITE/EXTERNAL/EXTDEC/0,,menuPK:476823~pagePK:64165236~piPK:64165141~theSitePK:469372,00.html.

40. Compiled on the base of data from the United Nations Industrial Development Organization. Retrieved March 16, 2008 from http://www.unido.org/doc/3474.

41. Sass, Magdolna. (2003). *The ICT Manufacturing Sector in Hungary.* Budapest: Institute of Economics of the Hungarian Academy of Sciences and ICEG European Center. Retrieved March 27, 2008 from http://www.ifri.org/files/Economie/Elargissement_Sass.pdf.

42. Sass, Magdolna. (2003). *The ICT Manufacturing Sector in Hungary.* Budapest: Institute of Economics of the Hungarian Academy of Sciences and ICEG European Center. Retrieved March 27, 2008 from http://www.ifri.org/files/Economie/Elargissement_Sass.pdf.

43. Sass, Magdolna. (2003). *The ICT Manufacturing Sector in Hungary.* Budapest: Institute of

Economics of the Hungarian Academy of Sciences and ICEG European Center. Retrieved March 27, 2008 from http://www.ifri.org/files/Economie/Elargissement_Sass.pdf.

44. Piribo. (2006). *The World Nanotechnology Market*. London: Piribo. From the Abstract. Retrieved March 22, 2008 from http://www.piribo.com/publications/technology/world_nanotechnology_market_2006.html.

45. Canton, James. (2001). *The Strategic Impact of Nanotechnology on the Future of Business and Economics. National Science Foundation*. Retrieved April 11, 2008 from http://www.futureguru.com/article17.php.

46. These two agencies jointly publish a list of Countries of Nuclear Strategic Concern that can be found at http://www.sipri.org/contents/expcon/cnscindex.html.

47. Esty, Daniel C., Levy, M.A., Kim, C.H., de Sherbinin, A., Srebotnjak, T., and Mara, V. (2008). 2008 Environmental Performance Measurement Project. New Haven: Yale Center for Environmental Law and Policy. Also available at http://www.yale.edu/esi/.

48. Organization for Economic Cooperation and Development/European Environment Agency. The OECD/EEA Database on Instruments Used for Environmental Policy and Natural Resources Management. Retrieved March 29, 2008 from http://www2.oecd.org/ecoinst/queries/index.htm.

49. Bennett, M.K. (September 1951). International Disparities in Consumption Levels. *American Economic Review* Vol. 41, No. 4. p. 632.

50. This algorithm was developed in unison with the help of Dr Veniamin N. Livchits and Dr Peter L. Vilenskiy.

51. Harper, Stephen. (2007, June 4) Speech. Berlin. Retreived from http://pm.gc.ca/eng/media.asp?id=1681.

52. World Bank. *Where is the Wealth of Nations? Measuring Capital for the 21st Century*. Washington, DC: The World Bank. p. 20.

53. Esty, Daniel C., Levy, M.A., Kim, C.H., de Sherbinin, A., Srebotnjak, T., and Mara, V. (2008). 2008 Environmental Performance Measurement Project. New Haven: Yale Center for Environmental Law and Policy. Also available at http://www.yale.edu/esi/.

54. Brown, Heidi. (April 2008). The World's Richest Government. *Forbes*. Retrieved April 9, 2008 from http://www.forbes.com/businessbillionaires/2008/03/28/russia-billionaires-duma-biz-cz_hb_0401russiapols.html.

55. Robinson, Richard and Hadiz, Vedi R. (2004). *Reorganizing Power in Indonesia: The Politics of Oligarchy in an Age of Markets*. Hong Kong: Routledge. p. xii.

56. Gills, Barry K. (2000). The Crisis of Postwar East Asian Capitalism: American Power, Democracy and the Vicissitudes of Globalization. *Review of International Studies*. Retrieved April 3, 2008 from http://journals.cambridge.org/action/displayAbstract?fromPage=online&aid=54159.

57. "Election Conditionalities." *Amandala Online*. Retrieved March 27, 2008 from http://www.amandala.com.bz/index.php?id=6592.

58. CIA World Factbook. Gabon: Government. Retrieved April 2, 2008 from https://www.cia.gov/library/publications/the-world-factbook/geos/gb.html.

59. IFC's Operational Evaluation Group. (June 2005). An Evaluation of IFC's Frontier Country Strategy. *OEG Evaluation Brief No. 4*. Retrieved April 3, 2008 from http://www.ifc.org/ifcext/ieg.nsf/AttachmentsByTitle/Frontier+Strategy+EvalBrief.pdf/$FILE/Frontier+Strategy+EvalBrief.pdf.

60. Stockholm International Peace Research Institute. International Arms Embargos. Retrieved July 16, 2008 from http://www.sipri.org/contents/armstrad/embargoes.html.

61. Stearns, Peter N. (2007). *The Industrial Revolution in World History*. Cambridge, MA: Westview Press. p. 248.

62. World Bank. *Where is the Wealth of Nations? Measuring Capital for the 21st Century*. Washington, DC: The World Bank. p. 20.

63. Prahalad, C.K. (2006). *The Fortune at the Bottom of the Pyramid: Eradicating Poverty through Profits*. Upper Saddle River, NJ: Wharton School Publishing, Pearson Education, Inc. p. 24.

5   The Emerging Global Business Order

1. Reagan, Ronald. (1981, January 20). Inaugural Address.

2. Fulbright, J. William, with Tillman, Seth P. (1989). *The Price of Empire*. New York: Pantheon Books. p. 148.

3. Miller, Lynn H. (1998). *Global Order: Values and Power in International Politics*. New York: Westview Press. p. xi.

4. US Department of Treasury. Frequently Asked Questions: Currency. Retrieved April 12, 2008 from http://www.treas.gov/education/faq/currency/portraits.shtml#q3.
5. Barry Brence, Steven. (2001). Multiculturalism: The Refusal and Reconstruction of Recognition. Disertation Presented to the Department of Philosophy Graduate School of the University of Oregan. p. v. Retrieved from April 15, 2008 from https://scholarsbank.uoregon.edu/dspace/bitstream/1794/2038/2/Multiculturalism_the_refusal_and_reconstruction.pdf.
6. Cohen, Raymond. (2001). Language and Negotiation: A Middle East Lexicon. In Kurbalija, Jovan and Slavik, Hannah (eds). *Language and Diplomacy*. Malta: Diplo Foundation. p. 177.
7. International Monetary Fund. Articles of Agreement of the International Monetary Fund. Retrieved on April 15, 2008 from http://www.imf.org/external/pubs/ft/aa/aa12.htm#2.
8. International Monetary Fund. By-Laws of the International Monetary Fund. Retrieved April 15, 2008 from http://www.imf.org/external/pubs/ft/bl/bl10.htm.
9. Braithwaite, John and Drahos, Peter. (2001). Bretton Woods: Birth and Breakdown. *Global Policy Forum*. Retrieved May 3, 2008 from http://www.globalpolicy.org/socecon/bwi-wto/2001/braithwa.htm.
10. Halper, Stefan and Clarke, Jonathan. (2004). *America Alone: The Neo-Conservative and the Global Order*. Cambridge: Cambridge University Press. p. 11.
11. Freyer, Tony A. (2006). *Antitrust and Global Capitalism, 1930–2004*. New York: Cambridge University Press. p. 144.
12. Gavin, Michael. (2000). Comments. In Fernandez-Arias, Eduardo and Hausmann, Ricardo (eds). *Wanted: World Financial Stability*. Washington, DC: Inter-American Development Bank. pp. 228–229.
13. Energy Information Administration. Non-OPEC Fact Sheet. Retrieved April 22, 2008 from www.eia.doe.gov/emeu/cabs/nonopec.html.
14. Organization of the Petroleum Exporting Countries. Organization of the Petroleum Exporting Countries Functions. Retrieved May 23, 2008 from http://www.opec.org/aboutus/functions/functions.htm.
15. Stell, Jeannie. (2007, November 1). Gas Cartel a Non-starter, Pace Reports. *Oil and Gas Investor This Week*. Retrieved April 22, 2008 from www.allbusiness.com/energy-utilities/oil-gas-industry-oil-processing-products/8918900-1.html.
16. Goodenough, Patrick. (2008, May 1). *Cybercast News Service*. Retrieved May 22, 2008 from www.cnsnews.com/ViewForeignBureaus.asp?Page=/ForeignBureaus/archive/200805/FOR20080501c.html.
17. Ahuja, Ambika. (2008, May 2). Thailand Pitches Cartel of Rice-producing Nations. *Associated Press*. Retrieved May 5, 2008 from http://abcnews.go.com/Business/wireStory?id=4770402.
18. Tabuchi, Kiroko. (2008, May 4). Japan Weighs Move to Open Rice Reserves. *The Wall Street Journal*. Retrieved May 12, 2008 from http://online.wsj.com/article/SB121130872443807657.html?mod=googlenews_wsj.
19. Dow Jones Indexes. DJ BRIC 50 Overview. Retrieved July 10, 2008 from http://www.djindexes.com/bric50/.
20. Bernstein, Steven. (2007). *Global Liberalism and Political Order: Toward a New Grand Compromise?* State University of Albany, NY: New York Press. pp. 3–4.
21. Held, David, McGrew, Anthony, and Goldblatt, David. (1999). *Global Transformations: Politics, Economics and Culture*. Palo Alto, CA: Stanford University Press. p. 50.
22. International Medical Corps. About IMC. Retrieved May 20, 2008 from http://www.imcworldwide.org/section/about/mission.
23. Academy for Educational Development. About AED. Retrieved May 20, 2008 from http://www.aed.org/About/index.cfm.
24. Médecins Sans Frontières/Doctors Without Borders. About US. Retrieved May 20, 2008 from http://www.doctorswithoutborders.org/aboutus/.
25. Oxfam International. Frequently Asked Questions. Received May 20, 2008 from http://www.oxfam.org/en/about/faq/.
26. NGO Committee on Migration. Homepage. Retrieved May 20, 2008 from http://ngocom.blogspot.com/.
27. Sayer, Peter. Google Search Share Up, Yahoo and Microsoft Down. *IDG News Service*. Retrieved April 22, 2008 from http://www.pcworld.com/businesscenter/article/143621/google_search_share_up_yahoo_and_microsoft_down.html.
28. Singh, Indu B. (1995). Global Network 2000: Emerging Concepts and Strategic Applications. In Hanson, Janice and Liebowitz, Jay (eds). *Advances in Telematics, Volume 3: Emerging Information Technologies*. Westport, CT: Greenwood Publishing Group. p. 196.

29. Drucker, Peter. (November 1994). The Age of Social Transformation. *The Atlantic Monthly* Vol. 274, No. 5. p. 80.
30. Pareto, Vilfredo. (1906). *Manual of Political Economy*. 1971 translation of 1927 edition, New York: Augustus M. Kelley.
31. Wicksell, K. (1959). *Selected Papers on Economic Theory*, E. Lindhahl (ed.), R.S. Stedman (trans.). London: Allen & Unwin.
32. Paquete, Luis F. (2006). *Stochastic Local Search Algorithms for Multiobjective Combinatorial Optimization: Methods and Análisis*. Amsterdam: IOS Press. pp. 31–32.
33. Williamson, John. (2002, November 6). Did the Washington Consensus Fail (Speech)? Washington DC: Center for Strategic & International Studies. Retrieved April 29, 2008 from http://petersoninstitute.org/publications/papers/paper.cfm?ResearchID=488.
34. Williamson, John. (2002, November 6). Did the Washington Consensus Fail (Speech)? Washington DC: Center for Strategic & International Studies. Retrieved April 29, 2008 from http://petersoninstitute.org/publications/papers/paper.cfm?ResearchID=488.
35. Ramo Cooper, Joshua. (2004). *The Washington Consensus: Notes on the New Physics of Chinese Power*. London: The Foreign Policy Center. p. 3. Retrieved April 26, 2008 from http://fpc.org.uk/fsblob/244.pdf.
36. Ramo Cooper, Joshua. (2004). *The Washington Consensus: Notes on the New Physics of Chinese Power*. London: The Foreign Policy Center. pp. 5–6. Retrieved April 26, 2008 from http://fpc.org.uk/fsblob/244.pdf.
37. Fukuyama, Francis. (2004). *State-Building: Governance and World Order in the 21st Century*. Ithaca, NY: Cornell University Press. p. 120.
38. Williett, Thomas D. and Banian, King. (1988). Explaining the Great Stagflation: Toward a Political Economy Framework. In Willett, Thomas D. (ed.). *Political Business Cycles: The Political Economy of Money, Inflation, and Unemployment*. Durham, NC: Duke University Press.
39. Selected from Annex Table A.I.16 from the United Nations. (2007). The World Investment Report: Transnational Corporations, Extractive Industries and Development. United Nations Conference on Trade and Development. p. 236. Retrieved April 30, 2008 from http://www.unctad.org/Templates/webflyer.asp?docid=9001&intItemID=4361&lang=1&mode=downloads.
40. Selected from Annex Table A.I.16 from the United Nations. (2007). The World Investment Report: Transnational Corporations, Extractive Industries and Development. United Nations Conference on Trade and Development. p. 236. Retrieved April 30, 2008 from http://www.unctad.org/Templates/webflyer.asp?docid=9001&intItemID=4361&lang=1&mode=downloads.
41. Bernstein, Steven. (2007). *Global Liberalism and Political Order: Toward a New Grand Compromise?* Albany, NY: State University of New York Press. p. 4.
42. University of Sydney Australia. New Global Economic Order. Retrieved April 29, 2008 from http://www.eng.usyd.edu.au/current-students/InnoManage/ENGG4005/lectures/globalisation.pdf.
43. Baliño, Tomas J.T., Enoch, Charles, et al. (1997). *Currency Board Arrangements Issues and Experiences*. Washington DC: International Monetary Fund
44. Currency Boards and Dollarization. Currency Boards. Retrieved December 15, 2008 from www.Dollarization.org.
45. International Monetary Fund. IMF Member' Quotas and Voting Power and IMF Board of Governors. Retreived April 22, 2008 from http://www.imf.org/external/np/sec/memdir/members.htm.
46. Mekay, Emad. (2003, May 6). Rich Nations Continue to Wield Power in Global Bodies. *Inter Press Service*. Retrieved April 30 from http://www.globalpolicy.org/ngos/int/bwi/2003/0506bodies.htm.
47. The International Monetary Fund. IMF's Financial Resources and Liquidity Position. Retrieved April 22, 2008 from http://www.imf.org/external/np/tre/liquid/2008/0208.htm.
48. World Bank. Interactive Lending Map. Retrieved May 5, 2008 from http://geo.worldbank.org/.
49. Hong Kong Monetary Authority. Economic and Financial Data for Hong Kong. Retrieved April 29, 2008 from http://www.info.gov.hk/hkma/eng/statistics/index_efdhk.htm.
50. The International Monetary Fund. World Economic Outlook Database. Retrieved April 23, 2008 from http://www.imf.org/external/pubs/ft/weo/2008/01/weodata/weorept.aspx?sy=2002&ey=2009&scsm=1&ssd=1&sort=country&ds=.&br=1&pr1.x=58&pr1.y=10&c=603&s=D&grp=1&a=1.
51. Cautious Welcome for G8 Debt Deal. (2005, June 12). *BBC News*. Retrieved April 22, 2008 from http://news.bbc.co.uk/1/hi/business/4084574.stm.

52. OECD. Net Official Development Assistance in 2007. Retrieved April 23, 2008 from http://www.oecd.org/dataoecd/27/55/40381862.pdf.
53. International Chamber of Commerce. How ICC Works. Retrieved April 22, 2008 from http://www.iccwbo.org/id96/index.html.
54. Inter-American Development Bank. About the IDB. Retrieved April 22, 2008 from http://www.iadb.org/aboutus/I/mission.cfm?language=English.
55. Dempsey, Mary A. (February 2002). The Andean Development Corp., A Regional Development Bank. *Latin Trade*. Retrieved April 29, 2008 from http://findarticles.com/p/articles/mi_m0BEK/is_2_10/ai_82801165.
56. BBC News. Profile: Mercosur—Common Market of the South. Retrieved April 30, 2008 from http://64.233.167.104/search?q=cache:xizubKeQP9oJ:news.bbc.co.uk/1/hi/world/americas/5195834.stm+mercosur+bank&hl=en&ct=clnk&cd=3&gl=us&client=firefox-a.
57. Caribbean Development Bank. About the Caribbean Development Bank. Retrieved May 1, 2008 from http://www.caribank.org/titanweb/cdb/webcms.nsf/AllDoc/A541525E64242BE7872572BF007AECAC?OpenDocument.
58. Zitner, Aaron. (1999, October 5). In New Hampshire, Forbes Calls for Eliminating IMF. *The Boston Globe*. p. A14.
59. Jacobson, Harold K. and Oksenberg, Michel. (1990). *China's Participation in the IMF, the World Bank, and GATT: Toward a Global Economic Order*. Ann Arbor: University of Michigan Press. p. 3.
60. Bailin, Alison. (2005). *From Traditional to Group Hegemony: The G7, the Liberal Economic Order and the Core–Periphery Gap (G8 and Global Governance)*. Aldershot: Ashgate Publishing Company. p. viii.
61. G8 Summit 2007 Heiligendamm. We Need Each Other. Retrieved May 2, 2008 from http://www.g-8.de/nn_92160/Content/EN/Artikel/__g8-summit/2007-06-08-g8-gipfel-abschluss__en.html.
62. Bretton Woods Committee. Mission Statement. Retrieved May 12, 2008 from http://www.brettonwoods.org/.
63. Club of Rome. About. Retrieved May 12, 2008 from http://www.clubofrome.org/about/index.php.
64. World Economic Forum. History and Achievements. Retrieved May 12, 2008 from http://www.weforum.org/en/about/History%20and%20Achievements/index.htm#history.
65. MMC. About. Retrieved May 12, 2008 from http://www.mmc.com/.
66. World Economic Forum. (2007). Annual Meeting 2007 Shaping the Global Agenda: The Shifting Power Equation. p. 25. Retrieved May 16, 2008 from http://www.weforum.org/pdf/summitreports/am2007/am2007.pdf.
67. MMC. MMC News. Retrieved May 16, 2008 from http://www.mmc.com/news/climateChange.php.
68. Council on Foreign Relations. Frequently Asked Questions. Retrieved May 16, 2008 from http://www.cfr.org/index.html.
69. Council on Foreign Relations. Mission. Retrieved May 16, 2008 from http://www.cfr.org/about/mission.html.
70. Illuminati Conspiracy Archive. The Council on Foreign Relations and the New World Order. Retrieved May 17, 2008 from http://www.conspiracyarchive.com/NWO/Council_Foreign_Relations.htm.
71. *The Charlie Rose Show*, April 11, 2006.
72. Trilateral Commission. Homepage. Retrieved April 14, 2008 from http://www.trilateral.org/.
73. Tinbergen, Jan, Dolman, Anthony J., and Ettinger, Jan van. (1976). *Reshaping the International Order: A Report to the Club of Rome*. New York: Dutton. p. 104.
74. Europa. Treaty of Lisbon. Retrieved May 16, 2008 from http://europa.eu/lisbon_treaty/glance/index_en.htm.
75. Peterkin, Tom. (2008, June 13). EU Referendum: Ireland Rejects Lisbon Treaty. *Telegraph*. Retrieved June 16, 2008 from http://www.telegraph.co.uk/news/worldnews/europe/2122654/EU-referendum-Ireland-rejects-Lisbon-Treaty.html.
76. Dutta, Manoranjan. (1999). *Economic Regionalization in the Asia-Pacific: Challenges to Economic Cooperation*. Northampton: Edward Elgar. p. 229.
77. Tinbergen, Jan. (1977). The Ambitious Need for an Innovation of the World Order. *Journal of International Affairs* Vol. 31. pp. 305–314.
78. Foreign Policy. (June 2008). Seven Questions: The New World Energy Order. Retrieved June 11, 2008 from http://www.foreignpolicy.com/story/cms.php?story_id=4326.
79. Calculated based on data from the World Bank World Development Indicators.

80. Calculated based on data from the World Bank World Development Indicators.
81. Drucker, Peter. (November 1994). The Age of Social Transformation. *The Atlantic*. Retrieved May 2, 2008 from http://www.theatlantic.com/politics/ecbig/soctrans.htm.
82. Kurdish Studies Program at Florida State University. Retrieved May 2, 2008 from http://www.xs4all.nl/~tank/kurdish/htdocs/announce/KSF.html.
83. Cohen, Jean L. (2008). From International Society to a Decentered World Order: Beyond Sovereignty? In Barry, Christian and Pogge, Thomas (eds). *Global Institutions and Responsibilities: Achieving Global Justice*. Danvers, MA: Blackwell Publishing. p. 167.

6   Global Economic Strategy

1. CNN Interactive. Knowledge Bank Profiles. Retrieved June 27, 2008 from http://www.cnn.com/SPECIALS/cold.war/kbank/profiles/adenauer/.
2. Kvint, Vladimir. (2005). *The Global Emerging Market in Transition: Articles, Forecasts, and Studies*. New York: Fordham University Press.
3. Hammond, G.T. (2001). *The Mind of War: John Boyd and American Security*. Washington DC: Smithsonian Institution Press. p. 161.
4. Yarger, Harry. (2006). *Strategic Theory for the 21st Century: The Little Book on Big Strategy*. Darby, PA: Diane Publishing Co. p. 73. Available online at http://www.au.af.mil/au/awc/awcgate/ssi/strat_theory_21c_yarger.pdf.
5. University of Rochester. Major in Economics and Business Strategies. Retrieved May 15, 2008 from http://www.econ.rochester.edu/UG/businesseconomics.html.
6. Ohmae, Kenichi. (1982). *The Mind of the Strategist: The Art of Japanese Business*. New York: McGraw-Hill. p. 13.
7. General Electric. What Is Six Sigma? Retrieved June 27, 2008 from http://www.ge.com/en/company/companyinfo/quality/whatis.htm.
8. Nobel Foundation. The Nobel Prize in Chemistry, 1977. Retrieved June 27, 2008 from http://nobelprize.org/nobel_prizes/chemistry/laureates/1977/.
9. Davenport, Thomas H., Leibold, Marius, and Voelpel, Sven. (2006). *Strategic Management in the Innovation Economy: Strategy Approaches and Tools for Dynamic Innovation Capabilities*. Berlin: Wiley-VCH. p. 121.
10. Rosenkranz, Zeev. (1998). *The Einstein Scrapbook*. Baltimore: The Johns Hopkins University Press. pp. 32–33.
11. Microsoft. PressPass Information for Journalists—Bill Gates. Retrieved May 4, 2008 from http://www.microsoft.com/presspass/exec/billg/bio.mspx.
12. Gates, Bill. (1995). *The Road Ahead*. New York: Viking Penguin. p. xii.
13. Reuters. (2007, April 18). Netflix Profit Up, Revenue at Low End of Estimates. Retrieved May 2, 2008 from http://www.reuters.com/article/companyNewsAndPR/idUSWEN65832007041.
14. Helft, Miguel. (December 28, 2007). Google's Market Share Grows and Grows and Grows. *New York Times*. Retrieved May 1, 2008 from http://bits.blogs.nytimes.com/2007/12/28/googles-market-share-grows-and-grows-and-grows/.
15. Quintilian, Marcus Fabius. (1805). *Quintillian's Institutes of Eloquence: or The Art of Speaking in Public, in Every Character and Capacity*. Volume I. London: Dewick and Clarke. p. 313.
16. Immorlica, Nicole and Mahdian, Mohammad. (January 2005). Marriage, Honesty, and Stability. In *Proceedings of the Sixteenth Annual ACM-SIAM Symposium on Discrete Algorithms*. Philadelphia: Society for Industrial and Applied Mathematics. p. 56.
17. Nekipelov, Alexander. (2004, October 15). Public Preferences and their Role in Shaping Russian Economic Development. *Distinguished Lecture Series n. 14*. Warsaw: Academy of Entrepreneurship and Management. p. 17.
18. Brown, Shona L. and Eisenhardt, Kathleen M. (1998). *Competing on the Edge: Strategy and Structure Chaos*. Watertown, MA: Harvard Business Press. pp. 11–12.
19. Mintzberg, Henry, Ahlstrand, Bruce, and Lampel, Joseph. (1998). *Strategy Safari: A Guided Tour Through the Wilds of Strategic Management*. New York: Simon and Schuster. p. 15.
20. Ramde, Dinesh. (2008, June 8). Companies Offering Free Gas to Attract Business. *Business Week*. Retrieved June 27, 2008 from http://www.businessweek.com/ap/financialnews/D91627380.htm.
21. Linux. What Is Linux? Retrieved June 15, 2008 from http://www.linux.com/whatislinux/119700.

22. Linux. Feature: Desktop Software. Retrieved June 27, 2008 from http://www.linux.com/feature/114560.
23. Zuckerman, Mortimer. (2008, January 14). What They Should Have Said. *US News and World Report.* p. 68.
24. Frolund, Svend. (1996). *Coordinating Distributed Objects: An Actor-Based Approach to Synchronization.* Cambridge, MA: MIT Press. p. 115.
25. Osborne, Steve R. (2002). *Winning Government Business: Gaining the Competitive Advantage.* Vienna, VA: Management Concepts. p. 100.
26. Johns Hopkins University. Strategic Studies. Retrieved June 27, 2008 from http://www.sais-jhu.edu/academics/functional-studies/strategic/.
27. Worldwide Team Action Network. Albert S. Humphrey. Retrieved July 15, 2008 from http://www.webbnet.ltd.uk/Humphsprofile.htm.
28. Man on a Mission. Dow Jones Mission Statement. Retrieved July 15, 2008 from http://manonamission.blogspot.com/2005/04/dow-jones-dj-mission-values-statements.html.
29. Dow Jones. Core Values. Retrieved July 15, 2008 from http://www.dowjones.com/TheCompany/CoreValues.htm.
30. Merrill Lynch Annual Report. (2006). Retrieved from http://www.ml.com/annualmeetingmaterials/2006/ar/pdfs/annual_report_2006_complete.pdf.
31. Merrill Lynch. Building a Culture of Excellence. Retrieved July 15, 2008 from http://www.ml.com/annualmeetingmaterials/annrep2001/ar/.
32. Valdmanis, Thor. (2002, October 10). Mighty Merrill Lynch Bogs Down in Legal Troubles. *USA Today.* Retrieved July 15, 2008 from http://securities.stanford.edu/news-archive/2002/20021010_Settlement03_Valdmanis.htm.
33. Gates, Bill. (1995). *The Road Ahead.* New York: Viking Penguin. p. 18.
34. Pietersen, Willie. (2002). *Reinventing Strategy: Using Strategic Learning to Create and Sustain Breakthrough Performance.* New York: J. Wiley and Sons. p. 76.
35. Specific Characteristics of Business Strategy in EMCs. Jose Apestgeguia (Department of Economics, Public University of Navarre. josej.apesteguia@unavarra.es), (Department of Economics and ELSE, University College London. s.huck@ucl.ac.uk), (Department of Economics, University of Heidelberg. oechssler@uni-hd.de).
36. Newell, Michael W. (2005). Preparing for the Project Management Professional (PMP) Certification. AMACOM/American Management Association. p. 3.
37. IBM. Boolean Variables. Retrieved July 15, 2008 from http://publib.boulder.ibm.com/infocenter/comphelp/v7v91/index.jsp?topic=/com.ibm.vacpp7a.doc/language/ref/clrc03boolean_variables.htm.
38. Van Den Bosh, F.A.J. (1997). Porter on Business Strategy. In Van Den Bosh, F.A.J and De Man, A.P. (eds). *Perspectives on Strategy: Contributions of Michael E. Porter.* New York: Springer. p. 9.
39. Reading, Clive. (2002). *Strategic Business Planning: A Dynamic System for Improving Performance and Competitive Advantage.* London: Kogan Page. p. 366.
40. Insurance Journal. General Electric Exits Insurance; Sells Insurance Solutions, Employers Re to Swiss Re. November 18, 2005.
41. Haynes, Williams. (1953). *Cellulose, the Chemical that Grows.* Garden City, NY: Doubleday. p. 303.
42. Drujinina, Angela. (2005, August 19). Starbucks Targets Russia after Trademark Win. CEE-Foodindustry.com. Retrieved July 15, 2008 from http://www.cee-foodindustry.com/news/ng.asp?id=62002-starbucks-russia-trademark.
43. Blomfield, Adrian. (2007, November 9). Starbucks Opens Quietly in Moscow. *Telegraph.* Retrieved July 15, 2008 from http://www.telegraph.co.uk/news/main.jhtml?xml=/news/2007/09/10/wrussia110.xml.
44. Quoted in Slater, Robert. (1998). *Jack Welch and the GE Way.* Columbus, OH: McGraw-Hill. p. 200.
45. Cohen, William. (2004). *The Art of the Strategist: 10 Essential Principles for Leading Your Company.* New York: AMACOM. p. ix.
46. Lass, Andrew and Quandt, Richard. (eds). (2000). *Library Automation in Transitional Societies: Lessons from Eastern Europe.* New York: Oxford University Press. p. 431.
47. Accenture. KSB: Reengineering. Retrieved July 13, 2006 from http://www.accenture.com/Global/Services/By_Industry/Industrial_Equipment/Client_Successes/KSBReengineering.htm.
48. Forbes, Steve. (1999). *A New Birth of Freedom.* Washington, DC: Regnery Publishing, Inc. p. 59.
49. Schneiderjans, Marc J., Schneiderjans, Ashlyn M., and Schniederjans, Dara G. (2005). *Outsourcing and Insourcing in an International Context.* Armonk, NY: M.E. Sharpe. p. 3.

50. MassMutual Financial Group. (2007, October 9). New Report: Women Entrepreneurs Should Plan Early on How to Sell their Businesses. Retrieved June 19, 2008 from http://www.massmutual.com/mmfg/about/pr_2007/10_09_07.html?print=true.
51. Oyez US Supreme Court Media. Arthur Andersen LLP v. United States. Retrieved June 25, 2008 from http://www.oyez.org/cases/2000–2009/2004/2004_04_368/.
52. Business.com. Metromedia Fiber Network—MFNXQ-Profile. Retrieved July 15, 2008 from http://www.business.com/directory/telecommunications/business_solutions/metromedia_fiber_network/profile/.
53. MassMutual Financial Group. (2006). Where There's a Plan, There's a Continued Business. Retrieved June 19, 2008 from http://www.massmutual.com/mmfg/prepare/articles/business.html.
54. Robbins, Stever. (June 2005). Exit Strategies for Your Business. Entrepreneur.com. Retrieved June 19, 2008 from http://www.entrepreneur.com/management/operations/article78512.html.
55. Wright, Peter, Pringle, Charles D., and Kroll, Mark J. (1992). *Strategic Management: Text and Cases*. Boston: Allyn and Bacon in partnership with Ginn Press. p. 27.

7 Strategic Management Systems

1. Welch, Jack and Welch, Suzy. (2007). *Winning the Answers: Confronting 74 of the Toughest Questions in Business Today*. New York: HarperCollins. p. 50.
2. Morita, Akio, Reingold, Edwin M., and Shimomura, Mitsuko. (1997). *Made in Japan: Akio Morita and Sony*. New York: Penguin Group. p. 164.
3. Davies, Brent and Davies, Barbara. (2005). Strategic Leadership. In Davies, Brent (ed.). *The Essentials of School Leadership*. Thousand Oaks, CA: Paul Chapman Educational Publishing. p. 12.
4. Kickson, D.J., Hinings, C.R., Lee, C.A., Schneck, R.R., and Pennings, J.M. (1971). A Strategic Contingencies Theory of Intra-organizational Power. *Administrative Science Quarterly* Vol. 16. pp. 216–229.
5. Friedman, Mike and Tregoe, Bejamin B. (2003). *The Art and Discipline of Strategic Leadership*. New York: McGraw-Hill. p. xv.
6. Davenport, Thomas H., Leibold, Marius, and Voelpel, Sven. (2005). *Strategic Management in the Knowledge Economy: New Approaches and Business Applications*. Erlangen: Publicis Corporate Publishing and Wiley-VCH-Verlag GmbH & KgaA. p. 136.
7. Friedman, Mike and Tregoe, Benjamin B. (2003). *The Art and Discipline of Strategic Leadership*. New York: McGraw-Hill. p. 3.
8. Mockler, Robert J. (2002). *Multinational Strategic Management: An Integrative Entrepreneurial Context-specific Process*. Binghampton, NY: The Haworth Press. p. 230.
9. Camillus, John C. (1998). *Strategic Planning and Management Control: Systems for Survival and Success*. Lanham, MD: Lexington Books. pp. 231–232.
10. Mockler, Robert J. (2002). *Multinational Strategic Management: An Integrative Entrepreneurial Context-specific Process*. Binghampton, NY: The Haworth Press. p. 281.
11. *The Essentials of Strategy*. (2006). Watertown, MA: Harvard Business School Press. p. 275.
12. Paquette, Laure. (2002). *Political Strategy and Tactics: A Practical Guide*. Hauppauge, NY: Nova Science Publishers Inc. p. 121.
13. World Bank. Force Majeure Definition. Retrieved June 14, 2008 from http://rru.worldbank.org/Documents/Toolkits/Highways/0_outils/glossary/f.htm.
14. Kicking Ass in an Unflat World. (2007, November 1). *The Economist*. Retrieved January 7, 2008 from http://www.economist.com/business/displaystory.cfm?story_id=10063865.
15. Cisco. Cisco TelePresence System 3200. Retrieved July 13, 2008 from http://www.cisco.com/en/US/products/ps9573/index.html.
16. COSO. About Us. Retrieved July 13, 2008 from http://www.coso.org/aboutus.htm.
17. Galliers, Robert D. and Leidner, Dorothy E. (eds). (2003). *Strategic Information Management: Challenges and Strategies in Managing Information Systems*. Boston: Butterworth-Heineman. p. xi.
18. Galliers, Robert D. and Leidner, Dorothy E. (eds). (2003). *Strategic Information Management: Challenges and Strategies in Managing Information Systems*. Boston: Butterworth-Heineman. p. 2.
19. Goodstein, Leonard, Nolan, Timothy, and Pfeiffer, J. William. (1992). *Applied Strategic Planning: A Comprehensive Guide*. Hoboken, NJ: Pfeiffer & Co. p. 3.
20. Goodstein, Leonard, Nolan, Timothy, and Pfeiffer, J. William. (1992). *Applied Strategic Planning: A Comprehensive Guide*. Hoboken, NJ: Pfeiffer & Co. p. 1.

21. The Fading Lustre of Clusters. (2007, October 11). *The Economist*. Retrieved July 13, 2008 from http://www.economist.com/surveys/displaystory.cfm?story_id=9928211.
22. Foff, C. Davis. (1994). *Team-based Strategic Planning: A Complete Guide to Structuring, Facilitating and Implementing the Process*. Boston: AMACOM. p. 3.
23. Ohmae, Kenichi. (1982). *The Mind of the Strategist: The Art of Japanese Business*. Columbus, OH: McGraw-Hill. p. 78.
24. McGrath, Michael E. (2001). *Product Strategy for High Technology Companies*. Columbus, OH: McGraw-Hill. p. 21.
25. Camillus, John C. (1998). *Strategic Planning and Management Control: Systems for Survival and Success*. Lanham, MD: Lexington Books. p. 4.
26. Reed, Michael. (2002). From the "Cage" to the "Gaze"? The Dynamics of Organizational Control in Late Modernity. In Morgan, Glenn and Engwall, Lars (eds). *Regulation and Organizations: International Perspectives*. London: Taylor and Francis Group. p. 24. Referenced in quote: Zuboff, Shoshana. (1988). *In the Age of the Smart Machine: The Future of Work and Power*. New York: Basic Books. p. 323.
27. Georgia Plans Free Economic Zone. (2006, December 27). *Civil Georgia*. Retrieved July 13, 2008 from http://www.civil.ge/eng/article.php?id=14382.
28. Kvint, Vladimir. (2005, May 23). The Scary Business of Russia. *Forbes Magazine*. Retrieved July 14, 2008 from http://www.forbes.com/business/forbes/2005/0523/042.html.

8 Investment Strategy for the Global Emerging Market

1. Maugham, W. Somerset. (1915). *Of Human Bondage*. New York: Garden City Publishing Company. p. 304.
2. UNCTAD. (2007). World Investment Report 2007: Transnational Corporations, Extractive Industries and Development. p. 11. Retrieved June 12, 2008 from http://www.unctad.org/en/docs/wir2007_en.pdf.
3. UNCTAD. (2007). World Investment Report 2007: Transnational Corporations, Extractive Industries and Development. p. 227. Retrieved June 12, 2008 from http://www.unctad.org/en/docs/wir2007_en.pdf.
4. Stiglitz, Joseph. (2006). *Stability with Growth: Macroeconomics, Liberalization and Development*. New York: Oxford Press. p. 206.
5. Adapted from "Employment Related to Inward and Outward FDI and Total Employment in Selected Economies, Most Recent Year" (Table I.5.) from the UNCTAD World Investment Report 2007: Transnational Corporations, Extractive Industries and Development. p. 10. Retrieved July 8, 2008 from http://www.unctad.org/en/docs/wir2007_en.pdf.
6. A.T. Kearny. (2007). Offshoring for Long-term Advantage: The 2007 A.T. Kearney Global Services Location Index. Retrieved July 7, 2008 from http://www.atkearney.com/main.taf?p=5,3,1,185.
7. Ramachandran, Vijaya and Cleetus, Rachel. (1999). *Export Processing Zones: The Chinese Experience and its Lessons for Tamil Nadu*. Retrieved July 8, 2008 from http://www.cid.harvard.edu/archive/india/pdfs/china_epz0899.pdf.
8. Compiled on the base of data from The World Bank World Development Indicators. Retrieved June 15, 2008 from http://econ.worldbank.org/WBSITE/EXTERNAL/EXTDEC/0,,menuPK:476823~pagePK:64165236~piPK:64165141~theSitePK:469372,00.html.
9. UNCTAD. (2002). World Investment Report: Part Three Promoting Export-Oriented FDI. p. 214. Retrieved July 8, 2008 from http://www.unctad.org/en/docs/wir2002p3ch7_en.pdf.
10. Hale, David. (November 2003). China Takes Off. *Foreign Affairs*. Retrieved July 8, 2008 from http://goliath.ecnext.com/coms2/summary_0199-1184886_ITM.
11. World Bank. World Development Indicators. Retrieved July 8, 2008 from http://econ.worldbank.org/WBSITE/EXTERNAL/EXTDEC/0,,menuPK:476823~pagePK:64165236~piPK:64165141~theSitePK:469372,00.html.
12. Compiled on the base of data from UNCTAD FDI Statistics. Retrieved July 1, 2008 from http://www.unctad.org/Templates/Page.asp?intItemID=3199&lang=1.
13. Michkin, Frederic. (2004). *Can Inflation Targeting Work in Emerging-market Countries?* Washington DC: International Monetary Fund. p. 4. Retrieved June 29, 2008 from http://www.imf.org/external/np/res/seminars/2004/calvo/pdf/mishki.pdf.
14. Standard & Poor's. S&P Raises Brazil to Investment Grade. Retrieved July 8, 2008 from http://

www2.standardandpoors.com/portal/site/sp/en/la/page.hottopic/BrazilUP_sp_viewpoint/
3,1,1,0,0,0,0,0,0,0,0,0,0,0,0,0,0.html.

15. Chamie, Nick and Biszko, Paul. (2007, September 18). A Brave New World: Asset Class Views:
    07Q4 Update. *Emerging Markets Research*, RBC Capital Markets. p. 3.
16. Chamie, Nick and Biszko, Paul. (2007, September 18). A Brave New World: Asset Class
    Views: 07Q4 Update. *Emerging Markets Research*. RBC Capital Markets. p. 3.
17. IMD. 2008 World Competitiveness Scoreboard. Retrieved June 19, 2008 from http://
    www.imd.ch/research/publications/wcy/upload/scoreboard.pdf.
18. World Bank. The Doing Business Project. Retrieved June 14, 2008 from http://
    www.doingbusiness.org/economyrankings/.
19. UNCTAD. (2007). World Investment Report 2007: Transnational Corporations, Extractive
    Industries and Development. Annex A. p. 211. Retrieved July 8, 2008 from http://
    www.unctad.org/en/docs/wir2007_en.pdf.
20. Compiled on the base of data from UNCTAD FDI Statistics. Retrieved July 1, 2008 from
    http://www.unctad.org/Templates/Page.asp?intItemID=3199&lang=1.
21. Compiled on the base of data from UNCTAD FDI Statistics. Retrieved July 1, 2008 from
    http://www.unctad.org/Templates/Page.asp?intItemID=3199&lang=1.
22. Segal, Julie. (July 2007). Fueling the Flow of Capital. *Institutional Investor*. p. 109.
23. Setser, Brad. (2007, February 7). Testimony before the US–China Economic and Security Review
    Commission. Retrieved July 5, 2008 from http://www.uscc.gov/hearings/2008hearings/written
    _testimonies/08_02_07_wrts/08_02_07_setset_statement.php.
24. Multilateral Investment Guarantee Agency. Guarantees Overview. Retrieved July 6, 2008 from
    http://www.miga.org/guarantees/index_sv.cfm?stid=1509.
25. Multilateral Investment Guarantee Agency. Terms and Conditions. Retrieved July 6, 2008
    from http://www.miga.org/guarantees/index_sv.cfm?stid=1550.
26. Multilateral Investment Guarantee Agency. Guarantees Projects. Retrieved July 8, 2008 from
    http://www.miga.org/guarantees/index_sv.cfm?stid=1546.
27. Overseas Private Investment Corporation. (2007). Annual Report 2007. p. 2. Retrieved June 29,
    2008 from http://www.opic.gov/pdf/annualreport_2007.pdf.
28. Overseas Private Investment Corporation. Insurance. Retrieved June 29, 2008 from http://
    www.opic.gov/insurance/index.asp.
29. Overseas Private Investment Corporation. (2007). Annual Report 2007. p. 12. Retrieved June
    29, 2008 from http://www.opic.gov/pdf/annualreport_2007.pdf.
30. Overseas Private Investment Corporation. Insurance. Retrieved June 29, 2008 from http://
    www.opic.gov/insurance/index.asp.
31. Overseas Private Investment Corporation. (2007). Annual Report 2007. p. 42. Retrieved June
    29, 2008 from http://www.opic.gov/pdf/annualreport_2007.pdf.
32. Multilateral Investment Guarantee Agency. Compania Espanola de Seguros de Credito a la
    Exportacion (Spain). Retrieved June 29, 2008 from http://www.fdi.net/documents/WorldBank/
    databases/pri-center_mockup/cesce.html.
33. AIG. About AIG. Retrieved July 8, 2008 from http://www.aig.com/About-aig_20_19308.
    html.
34. AIG. Political Risk Insurance. Retrieved July 8, 2008 from http://www.aig.com/Political-Risk-
    Insurance_20_27192.html.
35. Freedom House. Freedom in the World: Combined Average Ratings—Independent Countries.
    Retrieved June 30, 2008 from http://www.freedomhouse.org/template.cfm?page=366&year=
    2007.
36. Friedman, Milton. (2002). *Capitalism and Freedom*. Chicago: University of Chicago Press.
    p. 20.
37. Philippines Includes RMB, Won in List of Convertible Currencies. (2006, November 10).
    AsiaPulse News. Retrieved June 29, 2008 from http://www.accessmylibrary.com/coms2/
    summary_0286-25445640_ITM.
38. FATF GAFI. Home. Retrieved July 2, 2008 from http://www.fatf-gafi.org/pages/
    0,2987,en_32250379_32235720_1_1_1_1_1,00.html.
39. FATF GAFI. Members and Observers. Retrieved July 2, 2008 from http://www.fatf-gafi.org/
    pages/0,3417,en_32250379_32236869_1_1_1_1_1,00.html.
40. FATF GAFI. Non-cooperative Countries and Territories: Timeline. Retrieved July 2, 2008
    from http://www.fatf-gafi.org/document/54/0,3343,en_32250379_32236992_33919542_1_1
    _1_1,00.html.
41. Oxfam. (October 2007). Africa's Missing Billions: International Arms Flows and the Cost of

Conflict. Retrieved July 8, 2008 from http://www.oxfam.org.uk/resources/policy/conflict_ disasters/bp107_africasmissingbillions.html.

42. Ackerman, Alan R. (ed.). (2003). *Investing Under Fire: Winning Strategies from the Masters for Bulls, Bears, and the Bewildered*. Princeton, NJ: Bloomberg Press. 326 pgs.

43. Economist Intelligence Unit. Country Risk Service. Retrieved July 3, 2008 from http://store. eiu.com/product/60000206.html?ref=Products.

44. Country Risk Ratings: European Stability. (2008, May 27). *The Economist*. Retrieved July 2, 2008 from http://www.economist.com/markets/rankings/displaystory.cfm?story_id=11435378.

45. Gage, Jack and Bigman, Dan. (eds). (2008, June 26). Special Report: The Best Countries for Business. *Forbes*. Retrieved June 29, 2008 from http://www.forbes.com/2008/06/26/denmark-ireland-finland-biz-cx_db_jg_bizcountries08_0926bizcountries_lander.html.

46. SEEurope.net. Albania: General Electric Says Ready to Negotiate Contract with Albanian Government. Retrieved July 8, 2008 from http://www.seeurope.net/?q=node/152.

47. World Bank. (2007, October 11). Private Sector Development Blog: ATM the Latest in Money Laundering. Retrieved July 8, 2008 from http://psdblog.worldbank.org/psdblog/2007/10/atm-the-latest-.html.

48. Gazeta. (2008, June 28). Ministry of Internal Affairs of Ukraine Publishes Bribery Rating. Retrieved June 28, 2008 from http://www.gazeta.ru/news/lenta/index.shtml.

49. Kuznets, Simon. (March 1955). Economic Growth and Income Inequality. *American Economic Review* Vol. 46, No. 1. pp. 1–28.

50. Transparency International. (2007). *Global Corruption Report 2007: Corruption in Judicial Systems*. New York: Cambridge University Press. p. 316. Retrieved July 3, 2008 from http://www.transparency.org/publications/gcr/download_gcr/download_gcr_2007#book.

51. Office of the United States Trade Representative. (2008). "Special 301" Report. p. 1. Retrieved July 8, 2008 from http://www.ustr.gov/assets/Document_Library/Reports_Publications/2008/2008_Special_301_Report/asset_upload_file553_14869.pdf.

52. Office of the United States Trade Representative. (2008). Special 301 Report. p. 19. Retrieved July 8, 2008 from http://www.ustr.gov/assets/Document_Library/Reports_Publications/2008/2008_Special_301_Report/asset_upload_file553_14869.pdf.

53. Office of the United States Trade Representative. (2001). PhRMA Special 301 Submission. p. 4. Retrieved July 8, 2008 from http://www.cptech.org/ip/health/phrma/301-01/301-01.pdf.

54. International Intellectual Property Alliance. USTR 2007 Special 301 Decisions. Retrieved April 5, 2008 from http://www.iipa.com/pdf/IIPA2007TableofEstimatedTradeLossesand PiracyLevelsfor2006USTRDecisions060607.pdf.

55. Global Property Guide. Housing Transaction Costs in the OECD. Retrieved July 8, 2008 from http://www.globalpropertyguide.com/investment-analysis/Housing-transaction-costs-in-the-OECD.

56. UN Department of Economic and Social Affairs Division for Sustainable Development. Johannesburg Declaration on Sustainable Development. Retrieved June 24, 2008 from http://www.un.org/esa/sustdev/documents/WSSD_POI_PD/English/POI_PD.htm.

57. United Nations Environment Programme. (2006). *Global Environment Outlook Yearbook 2006: An Overview of Our Changing Environment*. p. 3. Retrieved June 24, 2008 from http://www.unep.org/geo/yearbook/yb2006/PDF/Complete_pdf_GYB_2006.pdf.

58. Walls, Michael R. (2005, September 15). Corporate Risk-taking and Performance: A 20-year Look at the Petroleum Industry. *Journal of Petroleum Science and Engineering* Vol. 48, Nos. 3–4. p. 135.

59. Walls, Michael R. (2005, September 15). Corporate Risk-taking and Performance: A 20-year Look at the Petroleum Industry. *Journal of Petroleum Science and Engineering* Vol. 48, Nos. 3–4. p. 139.

60. International Labor Organization. Socioeconomic Security Programme. Retrieved June 29, 2008 from http://www.ilo.org/public/english/protection/ses/download/docs/definition.pdf.

61. Compiled on the base of data from the Central Bank of the Russian Federation (http://www.cbr.ru/eng/), the People's Bank of China (http://www.pbc.gov.cn/english/), the Reserve Bank of India (http://www.rbi.org.in/home.aspx), the Central Bank of Brazil (http://www.bcb.gov.br/?english) and the International Monetary Fund (http://www.imf.org/external/np/sec/pn/2007/pn07114.htm), (http://www.imf.org/external/np/sec/pn/2007/pn0709.htm), and (http://www.imf.org/external/pubs/ft/wp/2007/wp0714.pdf)

62. International Monetary Fund. Global Financial Stability Report. Annex 1.2. Sovereign Wealth Funds. p. 48. Retrieved June 12, 2008 from http://www.imf.org/external/pubs/ft/gfsr/2007/02/pdf/annex12.pdf.

63. Kvint, Vladimir. (2007, November 28). Inflation Rising. *Forbes*. Retrieved July 11, 2008 from http://www.forbes.com/2007/11/27/russia-inflation-rising-oped-cx_vkv_1128kvint.html.

64. Compiled on the base of data from the World Bank World Development Indicators. Retrieved July 9, 2008 from http://econ.worldbank.org/WBSITE/EXTERNAL/EXTDEC/0,,menuPK:476823~pagePK:64165236~piPK:64165141~theSitePK:469372,00.html.

65. UN News Centre. (2006, July 5). Developing Countries to Play Growing Role in Agricultural Trade. Retrieved July 9, 2008 from http://www.un.org/apps/news/story.asp?NewsID=19102&Cr=agriculture&Cr1=&Kw1=developing&Kw2=countries&Kw3=argicultural.

66. New Economist. (2006, June 26). Doha Round: A Global Failure of Will? Retrieved July 9, 2008 from http://neweconomist.blogs.com/new_economist/2006/06/doha_again.html.

67. Clarke, David. (2006, March 28). Funds: Merrill Fund Beats Rivals by Going Further Afield. *The International Herald Tribune*. Retrieved April 15, 2008 from http://www.iht.com/articles/2006/03/27/bloomberg/bxfund.php.

68. Beadle, Sible. (2007, September 3). Banking in CEE/CIS Progress, EBRD Role and Involvement in Retail and SME. p. 5. Retrieved April 19, 2008 from http://www.esbg.eu/uploadedFiles/Events/EBRD%20Final.pdf.

69. Bigda, Carolyn. (2008, June 17). Global Investing: One World, One Fund. *Money Magazine*. Retrieved June 19, 2008 from http://money.cnn.com/2008/06/13/pf/funds/global_funds.moneymag/index.htm?postversion=2008061604.

70. Burner, Robert, Chaplinsky, Susan, and Ramchand, Latha. (September 2006). Coming to America: IPOs from Emerging Market Issuers. *Emerging Markets Review* Vol. 7, No. 3. pp. 191–212.

71. Ress, Mathew. (2006, September 26). A Global Game Explodes: Currencies. *The Wall Street Journal*. p. C5.

72. Guerrero, Antonio. *Global Finance*, October 2005, p. 1010.

73. Kvint, Vladimir. (October 1995). *The Kvint Newsletter* Vol. 3, No. 1.

74. Pazarbaşıoğlu, Ceyla, Goswami, Mangal, and Ree, Jack. (March 2007). The Changing Face of Investors. *Finance & Development* Vol. 44, No. 1. Retrieved July 10, 2008 from http://www.imf.org/external/pubs/ft/fandd/2007/03/pazar.htm.

75. A.T. Kearney. 2005 Foreign Direct Investment Confidence Index. Retrieved July 6, 2008 from http://www.atkearney.com/main.taf?p=5,3,1,140,14.

76. A.T. Kearney. 2005 Foreign Direct Investment Confidence Index. Retrieved July 6, 2008 from http://www.atkearney.com/main.taf?p=5,3,1,140,14.

77. World Bank. (2008). Global Economic Prospects: Technology Diffusion in the Developing World. p. 91. Washington DC: World Bank Publications. Retrieved June 14, 2008 from http://econ.worldbank.org/external/default/main?pagePK=64167689&theSitePK=4503324&contentMDK=21603882&noSURL=Y&piPK=6416767.

78. World Bank. Globalization & Technological Progress in Developing Countries. Retrieved June 25, 2008 from http://econ.worldbank.org/WBSITE/EXTERNAL/EXTDEC/EXTDECPROSPECTS/GEPEXT/EXTGEP2008/0,,contentMDK:21603860~isCURL:Y~noSURL:Y~pagePK:64167689~piPK:64167673~ theSitePK:4503324,00.html.

79. World Bank. Technological Progress and Development. Retrieved June 25, 2008 from http://siteresources.worldbank.org/INTGEP2008/Resources/complete-report.pdf.

80. Sharma, Dinesh C. (2004, December 14). Global PC Market to Double by 2010. Cnet News. Retrieved July 11, 2007 from http://news.cnet.com/Global-PC-market-to-double-by-2010/2100-1042_3-5490500.html?hhTest=1.

81. Reuters. (2006, May 27). "Made in India" Phones Set to Tap Global Markets. Zdnet.com. Retrieved July 11, 2007 from http://www.expressindia.com/news/fullstory.php?newsid=68370.

82. Ops A La Carte. Technology Risk Assessment. Retrieved July 5, 2008 from http://www.opsalacarte.com/Pages/reliability/reliability_con_techrisk.htm.

83. Jie, Liu. (2008, March 3). China Mobile Releases Responsibility Report. *China Daily*. Retrieved July 1, 2008 from http://www.chinadaily.net/bizchina/2008-03/03/content_6502654.htm.

84. Nokia Expands Henan MCC's GSM Network in $200 Million Deal. (2005, January 1). *European Telecom*. Retrieved July 2, 2008 from http://www.allbusiness.com/electronics/computer-electronics-manufacturing/8120299-1.html.

85. Nokia to Expand Phone Coverage in China. (2006, July 6). *The Associated Press*. Retrieved July 3, 2008 from http://newsofchina.com/cnews/china/ewire/article.php/37_428.

86. OECD. Information and Communications Technologies: OECD Communications Outlook 2007. Retrieved July 3, 2008 from http://www.oecd.org/dataoecd/3/50/38988835.pdf.

87. OECD. Information and Communications Technologies: OECD Communications Outlook 2007. p. 3. Retrieved July 3, 2008 from http://www.oecd.org/dataoecd/3/50/38988835.pdf.

88. Internet World States. World Internet Users March 2008. Retrieved July 2, 2008 from http://www.internetworldstats.com/stats.htm.

89. Internet World States. World Internet Penetration Rates March 2008. Retrieved July 2, 2008 from http://www.internetworldstats.com/stats.htm.

90. Comscore. European Internet Usage September 2007. Retrieved December 9, 2008 from http: //www.comscore.com/solutions/technology.asp.

91. Compiled on the base of data from Internet World Statistics. Internet Usage Statistics: The Internet Big Picture. Retrieved July 1, 2008 from http://www.internetworldstats.com/stats10.htm#spanish.

92. Calculations based on Mercer's 2007 IT Pay Around the World Survey. Retrieved July 1, 2008 from http://www.mercer.com/pressrelease/details.jhtml/dynamic/idContent/1285110.

93. Slaughter, Mathew J. (2007, September 26). Let's Have a Real Debate About Globalization. *The Wall Street Journal*. p. A21.

94. Lukoil. General Information. Retrieved July 1, 2008 from http://www.lukoilamericas.com/geninfo.htm.

95. Minister Alexei Kudrin quoted in Russia Opposes Limits on Sovereign Wealth Funds. (2007, October 21). *Daily Times* (Pakistan). Retrieved July 9, 2008 from http://www.dailytimes.com.pk/default.asp?page=2007%5C10%5C21%5Cstory_21–10–2007_pg5_14.

96. Russian PM Looks for More Trade with Canada. (2007, November 30). *Russia Today*. Retrieved July 9, 2008 from http://russiatoday.ru/business/news/17808.

97. Calculations based on data from US Department of Commerce Bureau of Economic Analysis. Retrieved July 3, 2008 from http://www.bea.gov/agency/uguide1.htm#_1_19.

98. Goodman, Peter S. and Story, Louise. (2008, January 20). Overseas Investors Buy Aggressively in US. *New York Times*. Retrieved July 8, 2008 from http://www.nytimes.com/2008/01/20/ business/20invest.html?_r=1&scp=2&sq=414&st=nyt&oref=slogin.

99. Delaney, Rob and Drajem, Mark. (2008, June 18). US China to Open Negotiations on Investment Treaty. *Bloomberg.com*. Retrieved July 9, 2008 from http://www.bloomberg.com/apps/news?pid=20601087&sid=a3EbVuiAoth0&refer=home.

100. China's CNOOC Drops Bid for Unocal. (2005, August 2). *Associated Press*. Retrieved June 19, 2008 from http://www.msnbc.msn.com/id/8795682.

101. Candappa, Dayan and Rao, Sujata. (2007, November 27). Abu Dhabi Blazes Trail with Citi Deal. *Reuters*. Retrieved July 9, 2008 from http://today.reuters.com/news/articlenews.aspx?type =businessNews&storyid=2007–11–27T171201Z_01_L27410094_RTRUKOC_0_US-CITI-ABUDHABI-FUNDS.xml.

102. Data provided by Dealogic, quoted in Thal Larsen, Peter. (2006, November 29). Emerging Markets Bite Back. *Financial Times*. Retrieved July 9, 2008 from http://www.ft.com/cms/s/0/1bade3d6–7f93–11db-a3be-0000779e2340,dwp_uuid=45d2327a-7f07–11db-b193–0000779e2340.html?nclick_check=1.

103. Khalaf, Roula. (2006, March 23). Abu Dhabi Focus on Investment in Emerging Areas. *Financial Times*. Retrieved July 9, 2008 from http://us.ft.com/ftgateway/superpage.ft?news_id=fto032220061913541832.

104. UNCTAD. (2007). World Investment Report 2007: Transnational Corporations, Extractive Industries and Development. p. 226. Retrieved June 12, 2008 from http://www.unctad.org/en/docs/wir2007_en.pdf.

105. Compiled on the base of data from UNCTAD FDI statistics. Retrieved July 9, 2008 from http://www.unctad.org/Templates/Page.asp?intItemID=3199&lang=1.

106. Khalaf, Roula. (2006, March 23). Abu Dhabi Focus on Investment in Emerging Areas. *Financial Times*. Retrieved July 9, 2008 from http://us.ft.com/ftgateway/superpage.ft?news_id=fto032220061913541832.

107. Pazarbaşıoğlu, Ceyla, Goswami, Mangal, and Ree, Jack. (March 2007). The Changing Face of Investors. *Finance & Development* Vol. 44, No. 1. Retrieved July 10, 2008 from http://www.imf.org/external/pubs/ft/fandd/2007/03/pazar.htm.

Bibliography for Reading on Strategy and Economics of the Global Emerging Market

Abed, George T. and Gupta, Sanjeev. (eds). (2002). *Governance, Corruption, & Economic Performance.* Washington, DC: International Monetary Fund. 564 pgs.

Ackerman, Alan R. (ed.). (2003). *Investing Under Fire: Winning Strategies from the Masters for Bulls, Bears, and the Bewildered.* Princeton, NJ: Bloomberg Press. 326 pgs.

Alexander, Dean. (2002). *Terrorism and Business: The Impact of September 11, 2001.* Ardsley, NY: Transnational Publishers, Inc. 265 pgs.

Almaney, A.J. (2001). *Strategic Management: A Framework for Decision Making and Problem Solving.* Salem, WI: Sheffield Publishing Company. 279 pgs.

Anderson, Terry L. (ed.). (2004). *You Have to Admit It's Getting Better: From Economic Prosperity to Environmental Quality.* Stanford, CA: Hoover Institution Press. 212 pgs.

August, Ray. (2003). *International Business Law.* Upper Saddle River, NJ: Prentice Hall. 832 pgs.

Bagwell, Kyle and Staiger, Robert W. (2002). *The Economics of the World Trading System.* Cambridge, MA and London: MIT Press. 244 pgs.

Barney, Jay B. (2006). *Gaining and Sustaining Competitive Advantage.* Upper Saddle River, NJ: Prentice Hall. 592 pgs.

BenDaniel, David J., Rosenbloom, Arthur H., and Hanks, James J. (eds). (2002). *International M&A, Joint Ventures & Beyond: Doing the Deal.* New York: John Wiley & Sons, Inc. 640 pgs.

Booth, Ken. (2002). *Worlds in Collision: Terror and the Future of Global Order.* New York: Palgrave Macmillan. 386 pgs.

Chia, Lin Sien. (2003). *Southeast Asia Transformed: A Geography of Change.* Singapore: Institute of Southeast Asian Studies. 450 pgs.

David, Fred R. (2002). *Strategic Management: Concepts and Cases.* Upper Saddle River, NJ: Prentice Hall. 832 pgs.

De Kluyver, Cornelis and Pearce, John. (2003). *Strategy A View from the Top: An Executive Perspective.* Upper Saddle River, NJ: Prentice Hall. 176 pgs.

Deresky, Helen. (2002) *Global Management: Strategic and Interpersonal.* Upper Saddle River, NJ: Prentice Hall. 398 pgs.

Emerging Market Investments. (1996). London: World Markets Research Centre, DRI/McGraw-Hill. 238 pgs.

Enderwick, Peter. (2007). *Understanding Emerging Markets: China and India.* New York: Routledge. 249 pgs.

Evens, P. and Wurster, T. (September/October 1997). Strategy and the New Economies of Information. *Harvard Business Review.* pp. 13–34.

Fatehi, Kamal. (1996). *International Management: A Cross-cultural and Functional Perspective.* Upper Saddle River, NJ: Prentice Hall. 643 pgs.

Forbes, Steve. (1999). *A New Birth of Freedom: Vision for America.* Washington, DC: Regnery Publishing, Inc. 204 pgs.

Forrester, Jay W. (1977). *World Dynamics.* Cambridge, MA: MIT Press. 142 pgs.

Friedman, Milton. (1962). *Capitalism & Freedom: A Leading Economist's View of the Proper Role of Competitive Capitalism.* Chicago: University of Chicago Press. 202 pgs.

Gates, Bill. (1999). *The Road Ahead.* New York: Viking Penguin. 286 pgs.

Gardels, Nathan. (ed.). (1997). *The Changing Global Order: World Leaders Reflect.* New York: Wiley-Blackwell. 240 pgs.

Ghemawat, Pankaj. (2007). *Redefining Global Strategy: Crossing Borders in a World Where Differences Still Matter.* Watertown, MA: Harvard Business School Press. 304 pgs.

Goodstein, Leonard, Nolan, Timothy, and Pfeiffer, J. William. (1993). *Applied Strategic Planning: How to Develop a Plan That Really Works.* New York: McGraw-Hill Inc. 379 pgs.

Granberg, Alexander. (2000). *Regional Development in Russia: Past Policies and Future.* Northampton, MA: Edward Elgar Publishing. 232 pgs.

Grant, Robert M. (2007). *Contemporary Strategy Analysis: Concepts, Techniques and Applications.* Oxford: Blackwell Business. 496 pgs.

Halibozek, Edward P., Kovacich, Gerald L., and Jones, Andrew. (2008). *The Corporate Security Professional's Handbook on Terrorism.* Burlington, MA: Butterworth-Heinemann. 288 pgs.

Hill, Charles W.L. (2000). *International Business: Competing in the Global Marketplace.* Columbus, OH: McGraw-Hill. 692 pgs.

Griset, Pamala L. and Mahan, Sue. (2003). *Terrorism in Perspective.* London: Sage Publications. 320 pgs.

Horvath, Gyula. (1993). *Regional Policy and Local Government.* Budapest: Akademiai Kiado. 215 pgs.

Janis, Irving L. (1989). *Crucial Decisions: Leadership in Policymaking and Crisis Management.* New York: The Free Press. 388 pgs.

Jayasuriya, Kanishka. (2005). *Asian Regional Governance: Crisis and Change.* London: Routledge. 284 pgs.

Johnson, Barry and Neledescu, Oan. (March 2005). Impact of Terrorism on Financial Markets. *IMF Working Paper WP/05/60.* Washington DC: International Monetary Fund.

Kierkegaard, Soren. (1985). *Philosophical Fragments/Johannes Climacus.* Princeton, NJ: Princeton University Press. 400 pgs.

Kopstein, Jeffrey and Lichbach, Mark Irving. (eds). (2005). *Comparative Politics: Interests, Identities, and Institutions in a Changing Global Order.* New York: Cambridge University Press. 512 pgs.

Kvint, Vladimir. (ed.). (1998). *Emerging Market of Russia: Sourcebook for Investment and Trade.* New York: John Wiley & Sons, Inc. 752 pgs.

Kvint, Vladimir. (2004). *The Global Emerging Market in Transition: Articles, Forecasts and Studies.* New York: Fordham University Press. 723 pgs.

Lumpkin, Dess. (2003). *Strategic Management: Creating Competitive Advantages.* New York: McGraw-Hill Irwin. 455 pgs.

McNamara, Kerry S. (2003). *Information and Communication Technologies, Poverty and Development: Learning from Experience.* Washington DC: World Bank. 90 pgs.

Mead, Richard. (2005). *International Management: Cross-cultural Dimensions.* Malden, MA: Blackwell Publishing. 454 pgs.

Mintzberg, Henry, Lampel, Joseph, Quinn, James Brian, and Ghoshal, Samantha. (2003). *The Strategy Process: Concepts, Context, Cases.* Upper Saddle River, NJ: Prentice Hall. 489 pgs.

Mishkin, Frederic S. (March 2004). *Can Inflation Targeting Work in Emerging Market Countries?* Washington DC: International Monetary Fund.

Mobius, Mark. (1996). *Mobius on Emerging Markets.* London: Financial Times/Prentice Hall. 364 pgs.

Mucchielli, Jean-Louis, Buckley, Peter J., and Cordell, Victor V. (eds). (1996). *Globalization and Regionalization: Strategies, Policies and Economic Environments.* London: Routledge. 347 pgs.

Obstfeld, Maurice and Taylor, Alan M. (2004). *Global Capital Markets: Integration, Crisis and Growth.* New York: Cambridge University Press. 354 pgs.

Ohmae, Kenichi. (1991). *The Mind of the Strategist: The Art of Japanese Business.* New York: McGraw-Hill, Inc. 283 pgs.

Oster, Sharon M. (1999). *Modern Competitive Analysis.* Oxford: Oxford University Press. 434 pgs.

Overholt, William H. (1993). *The Rise of China: How Economic Reform Is Creating a New Superpower.* New York: W.W. Norton & Company. 436 pgs.

Pareto, Vilfredo. (1984). *The Transformation of Democracy* (trans. Renata Girola). Piscataway, NJ: Transaction Publishers. 93 pgs.

Park, Keith K.H. and Van Agtmael, Antoine W. (eds). (1993). *The World's Emerging Stock Market:*

Structure, Developments, Regulations and Opportunities. Chicago, IL: Probus Publishing Company. 650 pgs.

Pearce, John A. and Robinson, Richard B. Jr. (2007). *Strategic Management: Formulation, Implementation and Control*. New York: McGraw-Hill Irwin. 436 pgs plus BusinessWeek Cases.

Pelle, Stefano. (2007). *Understanding Emerging Markets: Building Business BRIC by Brick*. London: Sage Publications. 248 pgs.

Peng, Mike W. (2006). *Global Strategy*. Mason, OH: Thompson South-Western. 582 pgs.

Pomeranz, Kenneth. (2000). *The Great Divergence: China, Europe and the Making of the Modern World Economy*. Princeton, NJ: Princeton University Press. 382 pgs.

Porter, Michael E. (1980). *Competitive Strategy: Techniques for Analyzing Industries and Competitors*. New York: Free Press. 397 pgs.

Porth, Stephen J. (2003). *Strategic Management: A Cross-functional Approach*. Upper Saddle River, NJ: Prentice Hall. 266 pgs.

Price, Margaret M. (1993). *Emerging Stock Markets: A Complete Investment Guide to New Markets Around the World*. New York: McGraw-Hill, Inc. 414 pgs.

Ramo, Joshua C. (2004). *The Beijing Consensus*. London: The Foreign Policy Center. 78 pgs.

Ree, Stig. (1995). *Strategy, Innovation and Politics: A Process Approach*. Copenhagen: Copenhagen Business School Press. 174 pgs.

Rochester, J. Martin. (2002). *Between Epochs: What's Ahead for America, the World, and Global Politics in the Twenty-first Century?* Upper Saddle River, NJ: Prentice Hall. 308 pgs.

Rosenbloom, Arthur H. (ed.). (2002). *Due Diligence for Global Deal Making: The Definitive Guide to Cross-border Mergers and Acquisitions, Joint Ventures, Financings, and Strategic Alliances*. Princeton, NJ: Bloomberg Press. 343 pgs.

Sabonis-helf, Theresa and Burghart, Daniel L. (eds). (2005). *In the Tracks of Tamerlane: Central Asia's Path to the 21st Century*. Honolulu, HI: University Press of the Pacific. 478 pgs.

Sharma, Kishor. (2003). *Trade Policy, Growth, and Poverty in Asian Developing Countries*. London: Taylor & Francis. 240 pgs.

State of the World 2008: Toward a Sustainable Global Economy. (2008). New York: W.W. Norton. 288 pgs.

Suter, Keith. (2003). *Global Order and Global Disorder: Globalization and the Nation-state*. Westport, CT: Praeger Publishers. 256 pgs.

Sweeney, Paul. (2000). *The Celtic Tiger: Ireland's Continuing Economic Miracle*. Dublin: Oak Tree Press. 270 pgs.

Van Agtmael, Antione. (2007). *The Emerging Markets Century: How a New Breed of World-class Companies is Overtaking the World*. New York: Free Press. 374 pgs.

Weaver, Samuel C. and Weston, Fred. (2008). *Strategic Financial Management: Applications of Corporate Finance*. Mason, OH: Thomson/South-Western College Pub. 672 pgs.

Wheelen, Thomas L. and Hunger, J. David. (2007). *Strategic Management and Business Policy*. Upper Saddle River, NJ: Prentice Hall. 1,064 pgs.

Whitehead, Laurence. (2002). *Emerging Market Democracies: East Asia and Latin America*. Baltimore, MD: The Johns Hopkins University Press. 240 pgs.

Wright, Peter, Kroll, Mark J., and Parnell, John. (1998). *Strategic Management: Concepts and Cases*. Upper Saddle River, NJ: Prentice Hall. 708 pgs.

Yergin, Daniel and Stanislaw, Joseph. (2002). *The Commanding Heights: The Battle for the World Economy*. New York: Free Press. 512 pgs.

Yukl, Gary. (2001). *Leadership in Organizations*. Englewood Cliffs, NJ: Prentice Hall. 508 pgs.

Yunas, Mohammad. (1999). *Banker to the Poor: Micro-lending and the Battle Against World Poverty*. New York: PublicAffairs. 258 pgs.

Specialized Periodicals on the Global Emerging Market and Business Strategy

Emerging Markets, MarketAxess Holdings Inc., www.marketaxess.com, New York.

Emerging Markets Analyst (monthly), BCA Publications, Ltd, Quebec, Canada.

Emerging Markets Bond Index Monitor, JP Morgan Securities Inc., New York.

Emerging Markets Monitor (weekly), Business Monitor International, Ltd, http://www.emerging marketsmonitor.com/, London.

Emerging Markets Monitor, RGE Monitor, www.rgemonitor.com/emergingmarkets-monitor, New York.

Emerging Markets Quarterly, Institutional Investor, www.investmentresearch.org, Plano, TX.

EmergingPortfolio.com Fund Research, Global Investor Publishing, Inc. www.EmergingPortfolio.com, Cambridge, MA.

GlobalEdge, Michigan State University, www.globaledge.msu.edu/, East Lansing, MI.

Strategic Analysis, Institute for Defense Studies and Analysis, http://www.idsa.in/index.htm, New Delhi, India.

Strategy+Business (quarterly), BoozAllen Hamilton Inc., www.strategy-business.com, New York.

The Euromoney Emerging Markets Handbook (annual), Euromoney Yearbooks, part of Euromoney Institutional Investors, PLC, www.euromoney-yearbooks.com/default.asp?page=5&pcID=9115, Colchester, Essex, UK.

The International Journal of Emerging Markets, Emerald Group Publishing Limited, www.emeraldinsight.com, Manchester, NH.

The Journal of Business Strategies (semi-annual), Gibson D. Lewis Center for Business and Economic Development, Sam Houston State University, http://www.shsu.edu/~coba/jbs/, Huntsville, TX.

Index

Note: Page references in **bold** refer to Tables; those in *italics* refer to Figures

A.T. Kearney Global Services Location Index 351
Abramovich, Roman 199
Abu Dhabi Investment Authority 406, 408–9
Academy for Educational Development 227
Academy of Sciences of Turkmenistan 117
Accenture 304
acquisitions 132, 133–4
African Development Bank 243
African Union 373
agricultural sector 15
Air Transport Association 243
Airbus 274
Albanian–American Enterprise Fund 205–6
Alcoa 134
algorithmic multiplication function 186
algorithmic summary 185
Alliance of Small Island States 254
Allias, Maurice 54
aluminum 39–40, 41, 399
Amazon 403
American Bank of Albania 205
American depositary receipts (ADR) 63, 343
American International Group (AIG) 206, 366
Americanization 305
anchor currency 241
Andean Community 373
Andean Development Corp. 244
Andersen Consulting 304
Andersen Worldwide 135
ArcelorMittal 305
Argentinean peso crisis 58, 391, 395
Arrow, Kenneth 89
Arthur Andersen International (AAI) 135
Arthur Andersen, LLP 308
ASEAN 113, 122–3, 222, 224

Asian financial crisis 58, 221, 235, 239, 240, 252, 255, 350, 389, 394
Asia-Pacific Economic Cooperation (APEC) 123
asymmetric strategic response 274–5
ATA Airlines 274
automobile production facilities 66–8, 67–8
averaging down 131
Avis Car Rental Company 129

Bailian 133
Bailin, Alison 246
Baker & McKenzie 206
bandwagon effects 274
Bank for International Settlements (BIS) 61; Investment Pool (BISIP) 61
Bank of New York 396
banking sector 61–2, 383, 384–94
Barings 389
Basel Committee 59
Basel Committee on Banking Supervision 383
Baturina, Mrs Yelena 199
bauxite 39–40, 399
Beijing Consensus 219, 234
BenDaniel, David J. 134
Benelux Customs Union 122
Benelux Economic Union 122
Bennett algorithm 185–6, 188
Berlin Wall, fall of 4, 7, 76
Better Life 133
Bilderberg group 250
Birol, Faith 253
BLC 133
Blockbuster 267
Bloomberg LP 133
Boeing 274
Booz Allen Hamilton Inc. 289
bottom of pyramid (BOP) 50, 205, 238–9, 301
brand loyalty 301
breach of contract 369

Bretton Woods 235, 237, 238;
    Committee 213, 246–7, 251;
    Conference 2, 215, 247; Formula 242;
    Institutions 162, 215–18, 244
BRIC countries 130, 384, *384*
BRIC 50 Index 223
BRIC IPOs 130, **130**
British Petroleum PLC 380
Bulgartabac Holding AD 126
Burger King 377
Business Council for International
    Understanding (BCIU) 367
business order 76, 211–57
business risk 359, 382–3

Callaway Golf Co. 274
capital 58–66
Capital Hospitality Index 371
capitalization 62–3, *63*
carbon dioxide emissions 39, *40*
Caribbean Community (CARICOM)
    123
Caribbean Community and Common
    Market 123
Caribbean Development Bank 244
Carrefour 133
cash economy 388–91
cash privatization 126, 127–30
Cassel, Gustav 12
Center for Immigration Studies 142
Central American Free Trade Agreement
    (CAFTA) 123
CESCR 365
Channel Club, Santa Barbara 250
chaos 273–4
Chase Manhattan 388
Chavez 108
Chevron 92
China Investment Corporation (CIC)
    363
China Mobile Communications
    Corporation 402
China Mobile Ltd 101
China National Petroleum Corporation
    409
China Resources Vanguard 133
China Unicom 134
Chinalco 134
Chongqing New Century 133
Churchill, Winston 2, 111, 216
Cisco Systems 325; networking
    Academies 109
Citigroup 98, 176, 388, 389, 406;
    environmental protection in entry
    strategy 91–3
Cleveland Council on World Affairs
    249
Clifford Chance 206
Club of Rome 248, 250
CNN 370

Cnooc 406
coal 27–8, *27*
cobalt 42–3, *43*, *44*
Coca-Cola 302
Cold War 2, 225; end of 5, 226, 253
command economies, failure of 76–8
commercial risk 374–9, 382
Committee of Sponsoring Organizations
    (COSO) 325, 330
commodity risk 383
Common Market for Eastern and
    Southern Africa (COMESA) 123
Commonwealth of Independent States
    (CIS) 123, 162
communications risk 383
company-specific forecast 282
consumer markets 384–8
consumer price index (CPI) 386, *386*
contingent risk 382
Convention for the Prevention and
    Punishment of Terrorism 143
Convention for the Suppression of
    Financing of Terrorism 143
copper 40–1, *41*, *44*
corporate entry strategy 301–3
corruption 99, 125–6, 374–9, *375*
corruption coefficient 375
Corus 406
Council on Foreign Relations 213,
    249–50, 251
Counter Terrorism Committee 143
Country Ceiling Ratings 81
country classification systems:
    alternative 175–7; developing
    countries category 202–3; economies
    in bloom category 196–7; emerging-
    market countries category 196;
    emerging-market democracies
    category 197–8; emerging-market
    dictatorships category 200–1; flawed,
    of major multilateral institutions
    161–77; glossary 209; industrial
    structure 178–82, **179–81**; oligarchic
    emerging markets category 198–200;
    pre-emerging markets category
    201–2; strategic approach 177–88;
    strategic comprehensive 188–208;
    strategic necessity 160–1; superpower
    category 193–4; technologically
    advanced economies category 194–5;
    underdeveloped countries category
    203–5; wealthy nations 195
country risk 361
credit risk 382
Credit Suisse First Boston 389
cross-border investment 346–54
cross-border merger 132
CSC 370
CSN 406
cultural convergence 305

culture as a strategic risk factor 306–7
currency board 240; characteristics 241
currency emissions 384–8
currency inconvertibility 368
currency rates and exchanges 393–4
currency risk 382
currency-risk ranking systems 394
current market value 341
Customs and Border Protection Agency (CBP) 144
Customs-Trade Partnership against Terrorism (C-TPAT) 143

debt relief 243
Decentralization Index 121
decision-making process 312
Deloitte Touche Tomatsu 206
democratization 78, 111–13
derivative risk 382
Deutsche Post AG 236
developing countries 3
dictatorships 76–8, 120, 198
direct risk 382
Direction of Trade Statistics 81
dishonesty 272–3
Disney, Walt, Co. 307
Disneyland Paris 307
dissipative structure 261
Doha Development Agenda 230, 387
dollar (US) bill, symbols on 213
Dow Jones & Company 286
Drucker, Peter 230, 254
Dubai Ports World (DP World) 147
Dun and Bradstreet 80, 81
DynCorp 370

eBay 403
Economic and Monetary Union 391
Economic Community of West African states (ECOWAS) 123
Economic Freedom of the World 81
economic risk 359, 370–4; systematic 355–79; unsystematic factors 380
economies of uncertainty 100
Economist Intelligence Unit 80, 176; Country Risk 361
education 52, **53**
Einstein, Albert 1, 264, 267, 269
electricity generation 29–31, *30*, **30**
Electronic Data Interchange 403
Eli Lilly 121
emerging economies, history of creation of 76
emerging-market countries (EMCs): classification 84–8, **86–7**; emergence 2–4; major characteristics 82–4; regional integration into global marketplace 93–100; size of territory 94–5
Emerging Market database 79

emerging-market economy, definition 75
emerging markets 78, 82
Emerging Markets Bond Index (EMBI) 398
Emerging Markets Monitor 394
emerging stock markets 78, 82
employment 55–8
energy 23–39; consumption 15–16, 32–3, *33*; consumption per capita 36–9, *37–8*; in global marketplace 28–9; intensity 33–5, *34–6*; pollution 39; production in the GMP 28–9, *28*; reserves 26; transportation 38
Enron Corporation 331
environmental pollution, energy-related 39
environmental protection 184–5
Environmental Sustainability Index 184
equity risk 383
Erdogan 108
Ernst & Young 206
Eurasia Group 361
euro 392
European Atomic Energy Community 122
European Bank for Reconstruction and Development 356, 382
European Central Bank 392
European Communities 122
European Constitution 251
European Economic and Monetary Union 240
European Economic Community 122
European Steel and Coal Community 122
European Union (EU) 8, 14, 122, 124, 222, 373
Eurostar 14
Evil Empire 115
executives, managers, and staff 318–21
exit strategy 303, 307–9
exports, changes in value 146
extremism *see* terrorism and extremism
ExxonMobile 92

fairness opinion 341
Financial Action Task Force (FATF) 368, 369
financial instrument risk 382
financial risk 382
first law of strategy 297
Fitch Ratings 80, 356, 391, 398
five competitive forces (Porter) 294
Forbes 199, 371; Billionaire List 128, 194, 195
force majeure 324–5
forecasting 258, 280–3
foreign currency reserves 59–60, *60*
foreign direct investment (FDI) 99, 124,

373, 404–9; definition 346; economic
nature 346–9; in EMCs 350–4, *352*,
353; employment 350, **350**; inflows
to EMCs 106–8; risk of 346,
354–404; systematic risk 356
Foreign Direct Investment Confidence
Index 399
forestry 46–8, *47*
fraud 341
fraud risk 382
Free Trade Area of the Americas 123
Freedom House International 366
freshwater 20–3, **21–5**
Friedman, Milton 234, 367
Fulton Speech (1946) 2

G6 (Group of Six) 245
G7 245
G8 245–6, 251
G14 245, 246
Gas Exporting Countries Forum (GECF)
221
Gates, Bill 157, 267
Gazprom 101, 405, 406
GE Insurance Solutions 296
GE Power Generation 296
General Electric 101, 135, 260, 296,
330, 383
General Motors 274
Geographical Spread Index 136
Gini coefficient 54
Gini index 54
glasnost 115
Global Business Coordinating Council
(GBCC) 239
global business order 219–23; definition
211; in dynamics of global order
219–23; global optimum 231–5;
global trends 230–1; major
characteristics 252–6; objective and
subjective factors influencing 229–35;
triggering events 235–9
global capital market 62–6
Global Competitiveness Report 81
Global Corruption Report 81
global depositary receipts (GDR) 396
global emerging market (GEM) 3–4;
birth of 76–82; business perspective
89–91; current role 100–4; definition
75; future in global marketplace
109–10; genesis 88–100; input in
world economy 88–9; as new
economic and political phenomenon
78–82
Global Emerging Market Database 84
Global Emerging Market Monitoring
and Coordinating Agency
(GEMMCA) 39, 251
Global Emerging Markets (company) 84
Global Finance 389

Global Financial Centres Index 108
global financial market 58–62
Global Fishing 93
global governance 255–6
Global Insight 372
global marketplace (GMP): defining 1,
6–8; economic integration into
8–10; genesis 1–5; world economy
5–10
global monetary system 391–3
global order 2; definition 211; dynamics
of 218–29; evolution of 224–5;
genesis 211–15; revolution 225–9
global risk management in strategic
decision-making process 323–5
global trends, ten 113–14
global workplace 5, 218, 220–2, 229,
252–253, 305, 333, 340, 346–7, 350,
370, 379
globalEDGE 81, 88
globalization 279; as objective trend
111–13
glocalization 120
goals setting 287–9
gold 44, 45–6, *45*
gold reserves 60, **60**
gold stocks 60
gold-dollar standard system 235
Google 228, 263, 265, 270
Great Depression 212
Great Seal 213
greenfield investments 361–2, *362*
gross domestic product (GDP) 11, 14,
18; GDP per capita 10–11, *11*, *13*,
14, 80; GDP PPP 12–13, *12–13*,
14–16, 18, **90–1**, 101, 204
gross national income (GNI) 16; GNI
per capita 79, 80, 163, **163**
gross national product (GNP) 16, 18
gross world product (GWP) 2, *2*, *3*, 18;
during formation of GMP 10, *10*;
trade as percentage of 2, *3*
GSM (Global System for Mobile
Communication) 402
GUAM group 123
Gulf Cooperation Council 369

Halliburton 370
Heritage Foundation 80, 81
Heritage Fund Index of Economic
Freedom 109
Hezbollah 148
history, learning from, strategist and
269–70
Hong Kong Center for Economic
Research 81
hostile takeover 132, 133–4
Hotels.com 274
HSBC 389
Hualien 133

Human Development Index (HDI) 56–7, **57**
human resource risk 382
human rights 231
hydrogen fuel cells 39, 44
hydropower generation 29–31, **30**

IBM 236, 325
illegal immigration 139
illiteracy 140
IMD 357–8, 259
Immigration and Customs Enforcement Agency (ICE) 144
implementation plan 304
imports, changes in value 147
improvement strategy 260, 261
income inequality, uncertainty, and risk 98–100
Index of Economic Freedom 81, 186, 200
Index of Economic Security 380
Index of International Business Infrastructure **206–8**, 208
indexation of national economies' technological maturity 183–4
industrial infrastructure 374, 380–2
inertia 271
inflation 384–8
information technology (IT) 6, 401–4
informatization 59
ING 389
initial public offerings (IPOs) 130–1, 320, 343, 397
innovation, strategic advantages 276–7
insourcing 305
Integrated Country Ratings 201
intellectual property 302, 374–9
Inter-American Development Bank 244, 356
interest rate risk 382
intergovernmental organizations (IGOs) 227
Internal Revenue Service (IRS) 144
International Atomic Energy Agency (IAEA) 184
International Bank for Reconstruction and Development (IBRD) 162–3, 216
international business infrastructure 205–8, 383–98
International Chamber of Commerce (ICC) 244
International Consortium for Cooperation on the Nile 22
International Credit Ratings 81
international depository receipts (IDR) 63, 343
International Energy Outlook, US Energy Information Administration 29

International Finance Corporation (IFC) 78, 79
International Financial Statistics 80–1
International Fund for Agricultural Development 97
international gold standard 216
International Institute for Management Development (IMD) 81
international joint venture (IJV) 132, 134–8, 332–44; agreement 336–7; decision-making process 340–2; economic genesis 333–6; failure 333–7, *334–7*; key factors 338–9; management system implementation 342–4; management systems 340–4; market-entry strategy 338
International Labor Organization 243, 380
International Medical Corps 227
International Monetary Fund (IMF) 9, 14, 59, 60, 80, 216, 217, 227, 237, 239–40, 242–3, 247, 251, 254, 256, 279, 373; country classification 161, 165–71, **168**, 175
international monetary system 59
International Olympic Committee 227
international order 211
International Telecommunications Union 243, 402
International Trade Administration 80
International Trade Organization 216
internationalization 114, 131–9; investment deficit as consequence of 139; strategic reasons 131–8
Internet 8, 69, 238, 326–7, 403, *403*; bandwidth 72; penetration 150, **152**, *154*; viruses 145
investment in GEM and EMCs, reasons to 349–54
investment risk analysis, system of 359
Iraq invasion by US 132
Iron Curtain 2
ITAT Group 133

Johannesburg Securities Exchange 147
Joint Annual Meeting of the World Bank and IMF 80, 247

Kantorovich, Leonid 294
KazMunayGas 92
Kearney, Christine 121
Kellogg Brown and Root 370
Keynes, John Maynard 217
KGB 115
Kipling, Rudyard 75
knowledge-based economy 8, 15, 68–9, 183, 230
Knowledge Economy Index 69, **70–1**
Koopmans, Tjalling 177–8
KPMG 206

KSB 304
Kuznets, Simon 54, 375
Kuznets Curve 375, *375*
Kvint algorithm 186, 188, **189–93**
Kvint's Integrated Country ratings
    189–93
Kvint's 15 rules for strategist 266–78
Kyoto Protocol 230

labor productivity 56, 97
labor resources 48–52; in global
    emerging market into the global
    marketplace 96–8
League of Nations 117, 143
legal risk 37, 374–9
Leontief, Wassily 17–18, 229
letter of intent (LOI) 336–7
liabilities 341
life expectancy 51–2, **52**
Limited Brands 268
Linux Corporation 274
liquidity risk 382
Lisbon Strategy 219
Lisbon Treaty 251, 256
literacy 52, **53**
London Club 373, 383
London Tourism Action Group 147
Lukarco 92
Lukoil 404–5
Luxembourg Income Study 54

majority, strategist and 267–8
managerial tools, aids, and strategic
    information technology 325–7
manual labor 400
market risk 382
Markowitz, Harry 100
Marriott Marquis Hotel 285
Marsh & McLennan Companies 248
Masonic movement 212
Masquerader program 122
mass privatization 126, 127–8, **128**
Massachusetts Miracle 294
matrix organizational systems 316
maturity of emerging-market countries,
    ratings and evaluations 80–2
McDonald's 302, 305–6, 396
Médicins Sans Frontières/Doctors
    Without Borders 227
memorandum of understanding (MU)
    336–7
Mercer 2008 Global Compensation
    Planning Report 97
Mercosur 102, 122, 123, 124, 222, 391
Mercosur Development Bank 244
merger 133
Merrill Lynch 389
metals 39–46
Metromedia International Group, Inc
    134

Metromedial Fiber Network Inc. 308
Microsoft Corporation 157, 265, 267,
    274, 286
Microsoft Vista 307
middle class, role in economic
    maturation of EMCs 108–9
mission statement 258, 284–6
mobile phone penetration 150, *150*,
    151, *153*, 402
Mockler, Robert 317, 318
Modern-tech Manufacturing Index 186
molybdenum 46
money laundering 148
Monroe Doctrine 1–2
Montias, John Michael 177–8
Moody's 80, 81, 356
Morales 108
Morgan Stanley Capital International
    Barra (MSCI Barra) 80, 112
multidomestic organizations 237
Multilateral Investment Guarantee
    Agency (MIGA) 363–4
multinational corporations **137**, *138*,
    236–7

narcotics, trafficking of 148
NASDAQ (National Association of
    Securities Dealers Automated
    Quotations) 63, 395–6
national agendas and benefits to society
    of emerging-market countries
    104–9
National Broadcast Corporation 296
National Commission on Terrorist
    Attacks Upon the United States 141
national credit risk 360
National Money Laundering Strategy
    144
*National Trade Estimate Report on Foreign
    Trade Barriers* 81
natural disasters as risk of investment
    379
natural gas 26–7
needs, client, strategist and 277–8
nefelin 399
Nekipelov, Alexander 78
nepotism 99
Nestle 236
Netflix 267
new dimensions strategy 260, 261
new world order 211
nickel 41–2, **42**, 44
Nile Basin Initiative 22
Nokia 402
non-governmental organization (NGO)
    227, 228, 272; Committee on
    Migration 227
Norilsk Nickel 42, 44, 45, 126
North American Free Trade Agreement
    (NAFTA) 122, 123

North Atlantic Treaty Organization (NATO) 115, 216
nuclear electricity 31–2, *31*, **32**
Nuclear Nonproliferation Treaty 184

OAO Gazprom 101, 405, 406
objectives 287–9
OCO Consulting Ltd 401
oil 24–6, *25–6*
oligomerization 224
operational risk 382
ophelimity 231–2
opportunities, threats, strengths and weaknesses (OTSW) analysis 283–4
Ops A La carte 402
optimistic strategy 275
Organization for Economic Cooperation and Development (OECD) 14
Organization of the Petroleum Exporting Countries (OPEC) 220–1, 225
organizational structure 311, 316–18
Osaka Action Agenda (OAA) 123
osmium 44
outsourcing 351
Over the Counter Bulletin Board (OTCBB) 395–6
overestimation of competitor 276
Overseas Private Investment Corporation (OPIC) 364–6
Oxfam International 227

PaineWebber Group, Inc. 133
PaineWebber International 135
palladium 43–4
paper and paperboard production **48**
Pareto Optimum 231, 232
Pareto's principle 255
Paris Club 373
patents 2, 72, *73*, 104, *142*, 156, *156*
Patriot Act (USA) 143–4
Peninsular & Oriental Steam Navigation 147
Peregrine Bank 389
perestroika 115
PERT 325
pessimistic strategy 275
PetroKazakhstan 409
Petronas–Petroliam Nasional Berhad 135
Philips Electronics 236
platinum-group metals 43–5, *44*
political disintegration 113, 114–18
political risk 359–69
political stability indices 361
pollution 39
population 49–50, *49–50*; age 50–1, **51**; of EMCs 105–6
Porter, Michael E. 294–5
portfolio investment 394–7

Potsdam Conference 216
poverty 139, 140
Prahalad, C. K. 205
pre-emerging-market country (P-EMC) 54, 254
Pricewaterhouse 361
PricewaterhouseCoopers 206, 330
Prigogine, Ilya 261
privatization 113, 124–31
product risk 382
product-sharing agreement 369
production facilities 66–8
production risk 382
Program Evaluation and Review Technique (PERT) 289
Protocol for Suppression of Unlawful Acts against the Safety of Fixed Platforms Located on the Continental Shelf 143
purchasing power parity (PPP) 12, 14

quality of life 77
Quantum Fund 239

raiding 374–9
rating agencies 356–9
raw-material/parts risk 382
RBC Capital Markets 357
regional decentralization 120
regional economic integration 113; trend of 121–4
regional economic organizations 222
regionalization 113, 118–21
regulatory risk 37
remittances, distribution of 98–9, *99*
Ren Ren Le 133
Repsol YPF SA 135
research and development (R&D) 69–73, *70*; spending as percentage of GDP 71
Reuters 133
Rio Tinto 134
risk of FDI 346, 354–404
risk-management systems 102, 354
Rosatom 405
Rosenbloom, Arthur H. 134
Royal Dutch Shell 92, 236
Russian ruble default 58, 394

Sartre, Jean-Paul 77
Schwab, Klaus 248
science, research, and technology 68–73, 114
Securities and Exchange Commission 285, 308, 396
securities, derivatives, and foreign debt 397–8
Sen, Amartya 54
September 11, 2001 55, 139, 143, 144, 145, 195, 219, 235, 392
service industries 178–81, **179–81**

settlement risk 382
Shanghai Cooperation Organization 373
Shell Oil Company 148
Shell Petroleum Development Corp
   (SPDC) 92
short executive summary 277
shortage of capital 114
siloed approach to strategy 295
Six Sigma 260, 261, 330–1
Skadden, Arps 206
Skyworth 131, 284–5
Société Générale 331
Society of Petroleum Engineers 46
South Asia Free Trade Agreement
   (SAFTA) 123
sovereign risk 360–1
Soviet Union, collapse of 4, 115
spacetime 264, 269, 277
special drawing right (SDR) 60, **60**
Special Theory of Relativity (Einstein)
   264, 269
Sports Direct 133
spread risk 382
Stalin, Joseph 215, 216
Standard and Poor's (S&P) 80, 356; S&P/
   Citigroup Global Equity index 176;
   S&P/IFC Global Index 79; S&P/IFC
   Investable Emerging Markets Index
   79
standard of living 57, 77, 102
Starbucks 302
Stiglitz, Joseph 120–1, 233, 349
Stillwater Mining Company 44
stock exchanges 394–7
strategic adjustment 331
strategic alliance 132, 133
Strategic Comprehensive Country
   Classification System 80, 357
strategic control 312
strategic decision-making process
   321–5
strategic development 280–96, 304–7;
   stages of 280–4
strategic factors and limitations 290–5;
   qualitative limitations 293–5;
   quantitative limitations 290–3
strategic leadership 312–16; in strategy
   formulation 312–14; in strategy
   implementation 315–16
strategic management system: concept of
   311–12, *312*; functions of 327–32
strategic mindset 258–65
strategic monitoring and control 330–2
strategic motivation 312, 328–30
strategic plan 258, 287–9, 312, 327–8
strategic reengineering 304
strategic scenario, tactic, and policy 290,
   290
strategic thought: characteristics 262–4;
   stages 262, *262*; three axes 264–5

strategist 265–6; 15 rules 266–78;
   definition 258; position of 269, *269*
strategy: correlation between tactic,
   policy and 279–80; definition 258;
   hierarchy of 279; system of 279–80,
   280
strategy assessment 331
strategy formation 289, *289*
strategy formulation 282, 284–9;
   strategic leadership in 312–14
strategy implementation 296–304, *297*,
   304–7, 331; strategy leadership in
   315–16
strategy of subordinate units 295–6
strengths, weaknesses, opportunities,
   and threats (SWOT) analysis 283
sudden stop 355
sukuk 64
Swiss Civil Code 139
Swiss Re 296
Synthesized Country Rating of
   Technological, Economic, and Social
   Advancement 185–8, 194, 195
systematic risk 355–79; evaluation 359,
   360; of FDI 356

tactic 303–4
Tata Group 406
techno-economic paradigm 238
technological achievements in GEM and
   EMCs 104
technological advancements 6–7
technological development 181, **182**
technological risk 359; of FDI 398–404
technological trends 149–57
Templeton Russia & Eastern European
   Fund 394
tender offer 131
Tengizchevroil (TCO) 92
territory 19–20, **19**
terrorism and extremism 114, 235, 368;
   defining 142–3; economic impact
   139–49; global emerging market and
   148–9; impact on global marketplace
   144–8; responses to 143–4; threat of
   145
Terrorist Risk Insurance Act (2002)
   145
Third Generation (3G) networks 402
Third World database 79
Thomson Corp 133
time, strategist and 277
time-sensitive resource analysis 296–301
Tinbergen, Jan 251, 252
titanium 46
title risk 382
Total 236
total factor productivity 401
Total Primary Energy Supply (TPES) *29*
tourism 147

Toyota 396
transactions risk 382
Transnationality Index for host
  economies *141*
Transparency International 81
transportation 38–9, 381
Trilateral Commission 250, 251
Trump Organization 377
Trust Mart 133
Tungsram 183
'Twenty in Ten' initiative 29

UBS PaineWebber, Inc 133
unemployment 55–6, *55, 97*
Union Bank of Switzerland 133
Union for the Mediterranean 222
United Nations (UN) 17–18, 227, 242,
  252; country classification 161,
  171–5; Development Program 121;
  General Assembly and Security
  Council 218; Millennium Project 230
United Nations Conference on Trade and
  Development (UNCTAD) 136, 171,
  175, 349
United Nations Environment
  Programme 243
United Nations Industrial Development
  Organization (UNIDO) 186
United Nations Security Council 217,
  254; Resolution 1373 143
United Nations System of Organizations
  243
United Nations World Investment
  Report 236
United States: Bureau of Alcohol,
  Tobacco, Firearms and Explosives
  (ARF) 144; Department of Commerce
  80
United States Secret Service (USSS) 144
United States–Taiwan Business Council
  367
United States Trade Representative 81,
  378
Unocal Corporation 406
unsystematic risk of investment 380–3
uranium 46
US-ASEAN Business Council 367

Velvet Divorce 115
Versailles Treaty 117
Videoton 183
Vietnam Opportunity Fund Ltd 394
vision 258, 286–7

Vodafone 98
volatility risk 382

Wall Street Journal 80, 81
Wal-Mart 133, 265
war, investment in countries in states of
  369–70
Warsaw Pact 216
Washington Consensus 219, 232–4
wealth distribution 52–4, **54–5**
White and Case 206
Williamson, John 232–3
working hours 56, *56*
World Affairs Council of Oregon 249
World Bank 9, 71, 79, 195, 203–4, 217,
  227, 239, 242, 243, **243**, 247, 251,
  252, 254, 256, 279, 357, 373; Doing
  Business Project 357; Ease of Doing
  Business 356, **357**
World Bank Governance Indicators 361
World Bank Group (WBG) 80, 242;
  country classification 161, 162–5,
  164; International Comparison
  Program 14
World Competitiveness Scoreboard 357
World Competitiveness Yearbook 81
World Development Indicators 80
World Economic Development Congress
  80
World Economic Forum 81, 247–9,
  250, 251
World Economic Outlook 80, 166–70,
  167–8, 169–70
world economy 1; basic economic factors
  18–19, *18*; global marketplace and
  5–10; global workplace 5, 218,
  220–2, 229, 252–253, 305, 333, 340,
  346–7. 350, 370, 379
World Health Organization (WHO)
  242, 243
world order 211
World Tourism Organization 148
World Trade Organization (WTO) 7, 9,
  124, 227, 242, 247, 251, 254, 256,
  279, 356; country classification 161,
  171, 175; Doha Development Agenda
  387; intellectual property rights and
  378
World Travel and Tourism Council's
  Crisis Committee 147

Yalta Conference 216
Yalta Declaration 216